A FLEA IN

HER REAR

(or ANTS IN
HER PANTS)

and

other

vintage

French

Farces!

To the fond memory of

Susan Featherston Frazer,

who loved a good laugh

ABOUT THE TRANSLATOR

Norman R. Shapiro, professor of Romance Languages and Literatures at Wesleyan University, is a leading translator of French theater, poetry, and fiction. Among his verse translations, medieval to modern, are *The Comedy of Eros: Medieval French Guides to the Art of Love*, *Négritude: Black Poetry from Africa and the Caribbean*, *Fables from Old French*, and *Fifty Fables of La Fontaine*. Most recently he is the author of *The Fabulists French: Verse Fables of Nine Centuries* (chosen by the American Literary Translators Association for its Outstanding Translation Award of 1992) and *La Fontaine's Bawdy: Of Libertines, Louts, and Lechers* (nominated for the P E N—Book-of-the-Month-Club translation prize). Among his previous theater translations are *Four Farces by Georges Feydeau* (National Book Award nominee), *Feydeau, First to Last: Eight One-Act Comedies*, and a series of comedies published by Applause Theatre Books: Meilhac and Halévy, *The Brazilian*, Labiche, *A Slap in the Farce* and *A Matter of Wife and Death*, and Feydeau, *The Pregnant Pause, or Love's Labor Lost*. His translations are widely performed throughout the United States and other English-speaking countries.

CONTENTS

Publication of this work has been aided
by a grant from the Thomas and Catharine
McMahon Fund, of Wesleyan University,
established through the generosity of
the late Joseph McMahon.

INTRODUCTION

Farce, that most challenging of theatrical forms—ask even the best directors if you don't believe it—has been a favorite French genre since the Middle Ages, when, according to one etymology of the term, the same word as that used for culinary stuffing, brief comic pieces were "stuffed" between long, usually ponderous works for much-needed relief. If, in more modern days, French farce felt the need to validate its existence by taking on the trappings of existential and absurdist angst, as in the case of the Ionescos, Adamovs, and Arrabals, to name a few of the prominent practitioners, the adepts of the genre during its more traditional heyday a century-plus earlier felt no such obligation.

To be sure, serious interpretations and considerations can be extracted from, or grafted onto, the farce of that period as well: one can evoke the prototypical Innocent Victim in almost any farcical context. (I myself plead guilty.) And, on a less philosophical plane, one can certainly find in many a farce, along with the usual situational disorder begging to be put right, ample food for reflection on social foibles, character flaws, personality quirks, and even physical imperfections, all served up with varying helpings of linguistic banter, sight gags, and other "superficial" provocation to laughter. Because the simple fact remains that Labiche, Meilhac, and company—and especially the incomparable Feydeau, who cooked up the genre to perfection—were concerned, precisely, with producing robust laughter, not profound philosophy.

After all, what more immediate and gratifying means, for a playwright, to appreciate the power he exerts—a subject worthy of a lengthy essay in itself, with analogies ranging from combat to sex—than to see, or at least visualize, his audience physically and vocally reacting to his efforts? (And that, by the way, not always or exclusively with the frantic slamming of doors, chases, dropping of pants, or other "business" that many take as farce's indispensable hallmark.) If laughter, as Bergson tells us, may betoken superiority in the laugher at the expense of the laughee—the terms are Carlyle's—it should not be forgotten that in the author/reader or playwright/spectator relationship it represents yet another exercise of power: the authorial. *Je fais rire, donc je suis,* "I make them laugh, therefore I am," might well be the comic playwright's Cartesian-inspired motto. And, if laughter is, as they say, the best sauce, then what the French dubbed "digestive comedy," referring to those postprandial romps that flourished in the Boulevard theaters, needed no other or more basically human justification. Not that all farce is of the unabashed, blatant stripe, however. Farce is not a monolith. Like all generic labels the term is fuzzy around the edges; a Procrustean bed serving a variety of comic pieces whose common denominator is, precisely, their *principal* goal: to provoke laughter without afterthought. Visceral laughter, otherwise known as "belly-laughs." Now, if afterthought and cerebral laughter come along with it as a bonus—in the form of psychological, social, or philosophical reflection, or, not negligibly, in an appreciation of the farceur's meticulous craftsmanship—so much the better. It's a question of priorities.

The plays in this collection embody that variety. Replete with mistaken identities, concealments and sudden revelations, jack-in-the-box irruptions, physical disorder, and assaults on logic, both situational and linguistic—in short, the expected panoply of the unexpected—they do, nonetheless, invite afterthought in varying degrees. For those devoted to categorization, some of them, with other emphasis, might well pass for less frivolous forms of comedy. Neither Courteline's gullible, almost pathetic Boubouroche nor the flamboyant protagonist of Meilhac and Halévy's *Signor Nicodemo,* for example, differently dosed, would be uncomfortable in a comedy of character. Nor would the couple in Sardou's *For Love or Monkey*—two young people obviously destined from the start to fall in love—be unreminiscent of a less word-conscious Marivaux or a less poetic Musset, were it not for the rather absurd intermediary of their amours: to wit, a willful pet monkey (or squirrel, in the original). As for the mismated couple in Feydeau's *Going to Pot,* it has often been pointed out by myself and others that the maritally doomed duo, the same one that, in different guises, grumbles and grapples its way through all his late one-acts, would not even be out of place in the somber-hued, naturalistic *pièces rosses* ("bitchy plays") peopled by their theatrical congeners and coevals, à la Ibsen and Strindberg. And, as for the pathetically droll antihero of Allais's lightly drawn sketch, *The Poor Beggar and the Fairy Godmother,* his plight, foreshadowing the tragic farce of our own day, is too serious, despite its farcical elements, not to evoke a sympathetic sigh or two amid the chuckles.

A couple of paragraphs are in order concerning my versions. Unlike translators of more serious plays, a translator of farce, I think, has a triple obligation: to the text, to his potential audiences, and to himself. Clearly, as with any work, he must not so distort or tinker with it that it becomes unrecognizable. For me, this principle extends to precluding the modernization or denationalization of the text: my versions never update or uproot their originals. Still, laughter being of the essence, the farce translator—perhaps "adapter" is a more accurate term—has not only the right, I feel, but the duty to take whatever liberties of language and "business" offer themselves to evoke and provoke it. An even not-too-close comparison of my versions with the French texts would show that I don't shrink from peppering the former with puns, sight gags, and other devices not always present in the latter. In so doing I am fulfilling the farce translator's third obligation: namely, to himself. Like the author, the translator too wants visible (or visualizable) evidence of his "authorial power." The work becomes partly his own creation, albeit a re-creation: a collaboration between himself and the text. He is not a self-effacing artisan, handmaiden in the artist's service, impersonally rendering his every jot and tittle, joke and titter, and his alone, for the benefit of the literary scholar and theatrical archivist. Such translators of farce no doubt exist, selflessly devoted to accuracy and scholarship, but I am not of their number. Dogged fidelity, while useful to the researcher, would ill serve the theatergoing spectator—for whom, in the final analysis, the play exists—as well as myself, depriving him of another belly-laugh or two and me of my own creative (or re-creative) satisfaction.

To be sure, some of the liberties I take are not nearly so self-serving. Besides altering obscure allusions whose transformation affects neither plot nor action, I often change characters' names for a variety of reasons. Some, simply because they are hard for Anglophone actors' tongues to negotiate; others, because their English equivalents connote the opposite gender. But most, in order to preserve characteristics implied to the French ear. ("Loche" and "Mousquetard", in *A Flea in Her Rear,* rebaptized from "Poche" and "Ferraillon", are good cases in point, suggesting respectively *pochard,* a drunkard, and *ferrailleur,* a swashbuckler.) I also see fit to include much more blocking than most of the playwrights themselves provide, with the exception of the almost compulsively scrupulous Feydeau (who, reputation for exactitude notwithstanding, even slips up himself on rare occasions). Needless to say, save for those cases where my, or the original, stage directions play an organic part in the action, directors will choose to observe, modify, or ignore them altogether.

Regarding my usually less-than-literal titles, I admit that I can seldom resist a bad pun, and the worse the better. A reading of Scribe's *The Castrata,* for instance, will clarify what might seem like both a grammatical liberty and an anatomical impossibility. On that score, let me explain, in conclusion, the title I have chosen for the centerpiece of this collection. Feydeau's *La Puce à l'oreille* has been rendered by several other translators, usually rather literally as *A Flea in Her Ear,* using an expression more in the British than the American lexicon, the latter generally substituting a bug for a flea. Comparative entomology and etymology aside, these translators have quite overlooked the fact that the French expression has long had a double meaning: one, equivalent to the English idiom; and another, in which the ear is, orificially speaking, a female sexual metaphor.[1] (This is clearly brought out in the last scene of the original.) My title, neither a misprint nor a gratuitously suggestive come-on, is an attempt to restore at least the overtones of Feydeau's outrageous wordplay.

Two of these plays, *Going to Pot* and *A Fitting Confusion,* have been previously published. I include them in this collection since they are no longer easily available in their previous incarnations. Both these plays and a third, *The Poor Beggar and the Fairy Godmother,* previously unpublished, have already enjoyed performances—*Going to Pot,* especially—most notably under the inspired directorship of H. Stuart Shifman. To him and his leading lady Grete Fries, my appreciation for their continued and always helpful involvement with my scripts.

Special thanks also to Glenn Young, of Applause Theatre Books, for his encouragement and patience; to M. D. Carnegie, for tirelessly letting his fingers do the talking; to Sylvia Kliman and Caldwell Titcomb, for many proofs of good judgment; to J. French Wall II, for bridging some technical gaps; to Annette Tetto, Barbara Croken, and Gareth Bannister, for editorial chores; to Lillian Bulwa, Seymour O. Simches, and Evelyn Simha, for much gentle urging; to the expert reference staff of Harvard's Widener Library; and to directors Dudley Knight and Michael Haney, for their valued interest.

---

[1] See Claude Duneton, *La Puce à l'oreille: anthologie des expressions populaires avec leur origine* (Paris: Stock, 1978), pp. 44-49.

THE CASTRATA

Adaptation of

Le Soprano

by

Eugène Scribe and Mélesville

(1831)

CHARACTERS

PIZZICATO, a musician, probably in his thirties, with an exaggerated opinion of his talent

CARDINAL DI GORGONZOLA, an elderly, ambitious Roman churchman

THE PRINCE, the cardinal's headstrong and romantic young nephew

FRANCESCO, a servant in the cardinal's palace

GIANNINA, a beautiful young soprano

VIOLA, the cardinal's matronly, middle-aging housekeeper

Several servants, *ad libitum*

A sumptuous salon in the palace of Cardinal di Gorgonzola, in late eighteenth-century Rome, decorated with ornate paintings, vases, statues, etc. ad libitum. *Down right, an open doorway, appropriately draped, leading onto an unseen corridor. Down left, a window, similarly draped. Up left, a door. Down center, two armchairs facing each other at an angle. Down left, a writing-table and chair, the latter with a cushion on it and facing the footlights. On the table, an elegantly bound Bible, and a large portfolio evidently bulging with papers.*

At rise, it is morning. The door, up left, is wide open. PIZZICATO, *alone, is impatiently pacing up and down between the doorway and the door.*

PIZZICATO [*looking at his pocket watch*]: Madonna mia! How long is he going to make me wait? Just because he's a cardinal... [*Peering into the corridor, down right.*] Isn't there a soul in this whole blessèd palace? [*Crossing up left, looking out the door.*] Doesn't he know it's impolite to keep a great artiste waiting?... [*Pacing.*] Impoliteness... One of the cardinal sins... And punctuality... One of the cardinal virtues... [*Stopping, realizing his unintentional bon mot.*] So to speak!... At least, they should be... [*Looking at his watch, shaking his head.*] Tsk tsk tsk! More than two hours already... Well, I've waited this long, I can't leave now... But how many times can I look at the same paintings! [*Walking about the room among the various art objects.*] Not that they aren't worth a second look, I'm sure... But a third?... A fourth? A fifth?... All in the same morning? [*After a pause, shaking his head in admiration.*] Pfff! Talk about money... Some people have it all... [*Reflecting.*] Or most of it... Not like me... Maestro Benito Pizzicato, virtuoso extraordinaire... I can chase it up the scale till doomsday, with arpeggios to boot, and still never catch it! Talent galore, but not a lira to my name... [*Coming down right.*] Well, at least I've got my pride. We geniuses always have that to fall back on! [*Suddenly his eye is caught by someone approaching in the corridor.*] Ah! Finally... Someone... [*Peering.*] Good! A woman... How better to strike a responsive chord! And con brio!... [*With a determined look, to himself.*] A tempo, Pizzicato!... [*Bowing exaggeratedly several times as* VIOLA *appears, a very mature and robust matron.*] Signora... Signora...

VIOLA [*entering, to herself*]: Who in the name of Saints Peter, Paul and Mary...?

PIZZICATO [*bowing and scraping*]: A pleasure, signora...

VIOLA: A what?

PIZZICATO: Indeed, a rare pleasure...

VIOLA [*aside*]: Odd chap!

PIZZICATO [*obsequiously*]: No doubt we're an important part of Cardinal di Gorgonzola's household!

VIOLA: We are?

PIZZICATO: You, that is... You, signora...

VIOLA: Important? I'm His Eminence's housekeeper. No more, no less.

PIZZICATO [affecting great interest and conviction]: Aha... Aha... That just proves what they say... That His Eminence has a keen eye for beauty, signora!... I find that reassuring.

VIOLA: Oh?

PIZZICATO: Good taste in beauty, good taste in the arts... They go hand in hand. A grand duo concertante... [Cajoling.] Clearly he has the first... [VIOLA makes a gesture of protest.] So he must have the second. Indeed, very reassuring...

VIOLA: Signore?

PIZZICATO [coming to the point]: That being the case, I venture to hope that the signora might take me—how shall I put it?—under her wing...

VIOLA: The signora? What signora?

PIZZICATO: You, that is.

VIOLA: My wing?

PIZZICATO: Yes. Artistically speaking...

VIOLA [aside]: Odd chap! [To PIZZICATO.] Just what was it you had in mind? To what do we owe the pleasure...?

PIZZICATO: An audience, signora... With His Eminence, the cardinal... [Risking a bit of levity.] After all, what's a musician without an audience, I ask you!

VIOLA [unimpressed]: Of course...

PIZZICATO: For weeks now... No, months... For months I've been taking the liberty of writing. Every day... Sometimes twice...

VIOLA: Your diary, signore?

PIZZICATO: My... No, letters... To His Eminence... For an audience... But he never answers. So today, since I happened to be in the neighborhood, just passing by... I thought I might as well try in person. Besides... [Holding up his writing hand.] I have a cramp.

VIOLA: Yes... [Aside.] Very odd... [Aloud.] And you've been waiting...

PIZZICATO: For two hours! [Looking at his watch.] And twenty minutes, to be exact... Mind you, rests are terribly important to a composer. A half-note rest here, a whole-note rest there... Even a couple of measures at a time... But this one strikes me as a trifle too long. One endless fermata...

VIOLA: Ah... Then I take it you're something of a musician, signore?

PIZZICATO: "Something"?... Indeed! [With a bow.] Maestro Benito Pizzicato... Organist, choirmaster, composer par excellence, and protégé of the great Pergolesi, signora...

VIOLA: Umberto Pergolesi? The watchmaker by the Coliseum?

PIZZICATO: The... Well hardly... Giovanni Pergolesi, the famous composer... You know... Stabat Mater, for example... Stabat Mater... [Aside.] Who hasn't heard of Pergolesi?

VIOLA: Oh... I see, signore.

PIZZICATO: Si, signora... I grew up in his house. My mother was his cook... I was four when he died, but still... The atmosphere, the inspiration... I used to spend hours, sitting in the kitchen, turning the spit... [Gesturing appropriately.] Turning the spit... In perfect rhythm, too...

VIOLA: I'm sure... [Aside.] Very, very odd...

PIZZICATO: Four quarter time... Perfect, even at four years old... And drinking in the music, steeping myself in his greatness...

VIOLA [aside]: And his gravy...

PIZZICATO: Inhaling his genius...

VIOLA [aside]: And the smell of his roast...

PIZZICATO [lyrically, apostrophizing]: Ah! Divine Pergolesi! [To VIOLA.] Yes, his spit was the source of my life as a musician. As a servant of the muse... The passion, the sacred fire, the fever... [Turning aside, again apostrophizing.] Ah! Blessèd spit! [To VIOLA, continuing.] Coursing through my veins... Pumping with every turn... [Turning an imaginary spit in rhythm.] One-two-three-four, one-two-three-four... I can still feel it! There!... [Grasping her hand.] His spit in my hand...

VIOLA [instinctively pulling her hand away]: Signore...

PIZZICATO: Don't worry, signora, the fever's not contagious! Neither is my poverty, lucky for you!... If it were, I could start my own epidemic! The way things are in my life... You can't imagine... A musician... [Holding out his hands.] A musician to the tips of my fingers... [VIOLA pulls back discreetly, out of reach.] Symphonies, songs, sonatas... Oh, the scores in my head... Scores... Scores by the score... And in my pocket, nothing... Zero... Not a lira!

VIOLA: Nothing?... You can't win much with a score like that, signore.

PIZZICATO: To say the least...

VIOLA: But why...?

PIZZICATO: Why?... What can I say? An unlucky star... Fate... Who knows? The evil eye...

VIOLA [crossing herself]: Oh!

PIZZICATO: All I know is, I've written ten magnificent masses... Two rousing Te Deums... [Stopping for a moment, reflecting on his grammatical accuracy.] "Te Dea"?... [With a nod, deciding.] Te Deums... [Continuing.] Cantatas, oratorios... A requiem in the Phrygian mode...

VIOLA [misunderstanding]: Brrr!

PIZZICATO [ignoring her gaffe]: And none of them, not one, has ever been performed! [Sighing.] Ah! "Vox clamantis in deserto," signora!

VIOLA: The title of one of the cantatas, signore?

PIZZICATO: No, no... Just a personal lamentation, alas! [Continuing his tale of woe.] Why, I even turned the requiem into an operetta. Sprightly... Lots of castanets and dancing-girls... Today's audiences, don't you know!...

VIOLA [shaking her head]: The masses have no taste.

PIZZICATO: At least not for masses... [Continuing.] But I still couldn't find a theater willing to produce it.

VIOLA: Tsk tsk tsk!

PIZZICATO: No taste, no taste... And so, in desperation, signora... [Crossing left, to the table, picking up the portfolio.] I gathered up all my opuses... [Stopping again, as before, in a grammatical quandary.] "Opuses"?... My opi?... [Remembering his Latin, pronouncing with proper classical accent.] My opera, I mean...

VIOLA [misunderstanding]: Opera?... I thought you said it was an operetta, signore.

PIZZICATO [returning right, with the portfolio under his arm]: No... That is, I assembled all my works... The plural of "opus"... All my compositions...

VIOLA: Aha...

PIZZICATO: And, learning that His Eminence, Cardinal di Gorgonzola, had just dismissed his chapel organist... For excessive use of the deceptive cadence,

I suspect, as well as various contrapuntal indiscretions...

VIOLA [*shocked*]: Indiscretions?... Oh no! Not Maestro Sforzando! He was as pious as the day is long, that one! He would never—

PIZZICATO [*interrupting*]: I'm sure... At any rate, I decided to offer my services. [*Cajoling.*] With your help and your precious intercession, bella donna... If I may be so bold...

VIOLA [*correcting him*]: "Viola," signore...

PIZZICATO: Ah! As in viola d'amore!

VIOLA: Please?

PIZZICATO: In fact, I have a fugue for four of them that I'd like to give you...

VIOLA [*aside*]: A few...?

PIZZICATO: ...and to dedicate to you, with your kind permission.

VIOLA: To me? [*Aside.*] A few what?

PIZZICATO: If only you would—how shall I put it?—use the power of your position... Your "good offices," in a word...

VIOLA [*very literal*]: Or two...

PIZZICATO: Yes... [*Reflecting.*] Your influence... [*Pointedly.*] In a word... To help me gain access to His Eminence's employ... Ah! My gratitude, signora... [*Correcting himself, suggestively.*] Viola... Violetta... My gratitude would know no bounds, and I should be eternally indebted and much obliged.

VIOLA: Oh?

PIZZICATO: Forever!... In a... [*Catching himself.*] In two words, "Pizzicato obbligato," if I may say...

VIOLA [*aside*]: Odd chap! [*To* PIZZICATO.] Well, really, signore...

PIZZICATO [*correcting her*]: "Benito"! Please... "Benito"...

VIOLA [*moving about the room as she speaks*]: I can try, but I don't know... I don't have the "influence" with His Eminence that I once had. Now that Prince Giorgio is living here, don't you know...

PIZZICATO [*following her with his eyes*]: Who?

VIOLA: Prince Giorgio, his nephew... And a typical Gorgonzola he is! [*Tilting her nose in the air with her forefinger.*] With that air about him, believe me!

PIZZICATO: Oh...

VIOLA: Still, I'll do my best. [*Aside.*] It's the least I can do for those few... whatevers of his.

PIZZICATO: Bless you... Bless you...

VIOLA [*by the table, left, with a note of resentment*]: Anyone would think that no one else mattered. It's "my nephew this... Prince Giorgio that..."

PIZZICATO: Shameful!... Especially when His Eminence has a majordomo... [*Stopping, questioning himself as before.*] "Majordoma"?...

VIOLA: A housekeeper, signore... Signor Caramello is His Eminence's majordomo.

PIZZICATO [*continuing*]: A housekeeper, then, of such... such impressive proportions and such eminent good sense. And one with such an appreciation of the finer things... Especially good music...

VIOLA [*with a note of connivance*]: And good musicians!

PIZZICATO [*approaching her, standing behind the chairs, down center*]: Who knows? Perhaps one day I can even return the favor. Surely it won't hurt to have someone in the household to sing your praises... To warble a lauda from time to time in His Eminence's ear...

VIOLA: Beg pardon... A...?

PIZZICATO: Lauda... Lauda...

VIOLA [*misunderstanding, raising her voice, almost shouting*]: I said: "Beg pardon..."

PIZZICATO [*confused*]: Not at all... I only meant... If music, as they say, "hath charms to soothe the savage breast..."

VIOLA [*putting her hand to her mouth with a shocked little gasp*]: Oh... Please, signore...

PIZZICATO [*quick to justify his liberty*]: No, no... [*Reiterating.*] They say... [*Emphasizing.*] They...

VIOLA: Ah...

PIZZICATO: Or "beast," if you prefer... Well, certainly I should be able to work its charms on our primate... Our prince of the Church... His Prince Giorgio notwithstanding...

VIOLA: If you think so, I'd certainly be most obliged... Benito!

PIZZICATO [*with a laugh*]: Yes... "Viola obbligata," right?... [*He comes right, around the chairs, enjoying his mot; then, stopping, seriously.*] So... I can count on you, then? You'll help me? You... [*Insinuating.*] You'll do me the honor of letting me help you...?

VIOLA: I'll try.

PIZZICATO: Ah!... [*Relieved, he sits down on the chair to the right, jumping up after a few seconds, realizing his faux pas, and indicating the other chair to* VIOLA.] Please... Please...

VIOLA [*sitting down*]: Of course, it depends...

PIZZICATO [*likewise*]: On...?

VIOLA: Your character...

PIZZICATO: Beyond reproach...

VIOLA: Your morals...

PIZZICATO: As perfect as a final cadence!

VIOLA: And whether or not you have the proper credentials...

PIZZICATO: But I told you... The great Pergolesi!...

VIOLA: Yes, but... He's dead, and... and you were only four. Besides, all you did was tend to his spit.

PIZZICATO: But the atmosphere... The inspiration...

VIOLA: Really, I don't think that will convince His Eminence. Surely you must have had a more responsible position... More artistic... And more recent, I should think...

PIZZICATO: Yes... Yes...

VIOLA: Ah? And where?

PIZZICATO: Why, in Pisa... Just last year... Organist and choirmaster...

VIOLA: Well, that's more interesting.

PIZZICATO: And on weekdays I gave lessons to the choirboys... And the delightful child who pumped my organ... I trained their ears...

[*He links the last two words rather too closely.*]

VIOLA [*with a start*]: Their what?

PIZZICATO: Their ears... Solfeggio... [*Illustrating, singing.*] Do re mi fa... [*Speaking.*] You know... The young ladies too...

VIOLA [*fanning her face with her hand*]: Ah... And what made you leave, if you don't mind my asking?

PIZZICATO: A personal problem... A... A dissonance that simply defied resolution... [*Standing up, gazing off, nostalgically.*] It was all because of a certain young Romeo. A loathsome young viper... Tall, dark and handsome...

VIOLA: Oh?

PIZZICATO: And madly in love with one of my pupils... A beautiful young lady from a penniless Pisa family... And talented? Ah! The voice of an angel!... Such a gift... Such natural inclination... One of those rare leanings...

VIOLA [*risking a bon mot*]: Like the tower...

PIZZICATO [*ignoring it*]: I knew that the wretch would never stop chasing her. Even after we were married...

VIOLA [*jumping up*]: Married?... Who?

PIZZICATO: My pupil and I...

VIOLA: But... That changes everything! Don't you know that no woman can set foot in the palace? His Eminence won't allow it!

PIZZICATO [*with a reassuring gesture*]: No danger, I assure you! Heaven knows where she is! I lost her the day of the wedding.

VIOLA: Oh! I'm sorry...

PIZZICATO: The very same day! Can you imagine?... Not even time to... to...

VIOLA [*comprehending*]: Yes... Tsk tsk tsk!

PIZZICATO [*reflecting, puzzled*]: But tell me... If no woman is allowed... You... I mean...

VIOLA: No woman... [*Hesitating.*] under a certain age, that is... Under fif... [*Catching herself, clearing her throat.*] forty... forty...

PIZZICATO [*hands on hips, pretending shocked surprise*]: And you have the cheek to ask me about *my* morals? You, who must have lied so shamelessly to His Eminence!...

VIOLA: What?

PIZZICATO: It's obvious!

VIOLA: It is?

PIZZICATO: It... It sticks out like a tritone in a Palestrina mass!

VIOLA [*torn between her vanity and her desire to defend herself*]: Well...

PIZZICATO: My dear lady, my eyes are as sharp as my ears. Clearly you cheated by a dozen years, at least!

VIOLA: I...

PIZZICATO: For shame!... [*Exaggeratedly.*] Oh! For shame!

VIOLA: Well, I... That is... [*Aside.*] Charming chap!

PIZZICATO [*aside*]: At last...

VIOLA [*aside*]: Odd, but charming...

PIZZICATO [*aside*]: The overture I've been praying for!

[DI GORGONZOLA *is heard offstage right, approaching.*]

VIOLA [*aloud, to* PIZZICATO]: Ah! His Eminence, signore...

PIZZICATO: Please! "Benito"...

VIOLA: He's coming...

PIZZICATO: "Benedictus qui venit..."

VIOLA: Quick! You'd better go. Let me talk to him. I'll let you know when it's time.

PIZZICATO [*about to exit, down right*]: Ah! How can I ever thank you...? [*With *affected tenderness.*] Viola...

VIOLA [*stopping him*]: Not that way! [*Pointing up left.*] There!

PIZZICATO [*dawdling, moving about the room, joyously*]: "Laudamus te!... Benedicimus te!..."

VIOLA [*uneasily, looking right*]: Yes, yes... [*Pointing up left.*] Please...

PIZZICATO [*at the door*]: Attacca subito, dear lady!... Don't quaver!... [*As he exits.*] Or even semi-quaver...

[*He disappears just as* DI GORGONZOLA *appears down right, with his servant* FRANCESCO *following behind.*]

DI GORGONZOLA [*entering, grumbling*]: Unthinkable!... Simply unthinkable!... Bah! [*To* FRANCESCO.] My carriage, Francesco!

FRANCESCO ⎫   ⎧ Yes, your Eminence!
            ⎬ [*together*]: ⎨
VIOLA [*aside*] ⎭   ⎩ Oh my!

[FRANCESCO *exits, up left.*]

DI GORGONZOLA [*noticing* VIOLA, *stopping*]: Ah! Signora Viola...

VIOLA [*approaching him*]: Your Eminence is leaving?

DI GORGONZOLA: For the Vatican... Immediately...

VIOLA: But... On an empty stomach?... No caffè latte? Nothing?

DI GORGONZOLA: I won't be long. Half an hour at the most... Dispensations, and other matters... Urgent business with His Holiness... You know, that bull...

VIOLA: Ah...

DI GORGONZOLA [*on edge*]: Besides, things are all at sixes and sevens. I haven't the slightest appetite. If I dared take a swallow it would all turn to gall.

VIOLA: But Your Eminence dined so well last evening...

DI GORGONZOLA: Yes, but that was last evening. This morning is this morning. Perhaps the fresh air... A little hustle and bustle... Perhaps I'll have more of an appetite for lunch. We'll see when I return.

VIOLA: Of course... If Your Eminence is sure... It's just that I'm concerned. He seems so out of sorts.

DI GORGONZOLA: Quite so, signora... "Out of sorts," to say the least!... Prince Giorgio... My nephew...

VIOLA [*aside, impatiently*]: Again?

DI GORGONZOLA: Oh! That rapscallion!... To do this to me, after all I've done for him!... My own flesh and blood... To put me in such an unthinkable position!...

VIOLA: Your Eminence?

DI GORGONZOLA: Just imagine... [*Sighing.*] I may as well tell you. I've got to tell someone, and I'm sure you'll find out anyway! [*Sighing.*] Just imagine... For years it's been my dream... my fondest desire... to arrange a magnificent marriage for that ungrateful scoundrel... Ah, what a nuptial mass that would be!

VIOLA: Oh?

DI GORGONZOLA: With Cardinal Manicotti's niece... A match made in heaven!... A Gorgonzola and a Manicotti!... You know, signora... The one in such good odor with the Holy See... With the College of Cardinals, especially... [*Quick to defend himself.*] Not that that has anything to do with it, mind you!... The prince's happiness is all that concerns me.

VIOLA: That's not very often.

DI GORGONZOLA: "Really, uncle," he told me, "as a cardinal it's your duty to be a patron of the arts. If you want to go down in history with the Medicis and... and..." [*Searching his own memory.*] "and all the others, you should invite this young artist to come live in your palace."

VIOLA: And...?

DI GORGONZOLA: And so I said yes. Why not? What's one more mouth? Another one, more or less...

VIOLA [*aside*]: Especially when it can sing for its supper...

DI GORGONZOLA: Besides, I thought it would humor him... Just another little bribe... [*Angrily.*] But no! [*Pointing into the corridor.*] Do you know what he said? [*She shakes her head.*] I'm ashamed to tell you!... Even you, signora... Ashamed to let it pass my lips... "Me? Marry that cow?... Never!"

VIOLA: Oh!

DI GORGONZOLA: Can you imagine? "That cow..."! A Manicotti!... [*Shaking his head in growing despair.*] Oh! He's a mule, that one! A mule!

VIOLA [*aside*]: Maybe if she were a horse...

DI GORGONZOLA [*losing control, pacing up and down*]: A stubborn, ungrateful, inconsiderate mule!

VIOLA: Please, Your Eminence...

DI GORGONZOLA [*beginning to blabber*]: My word... My honor... My... My career...

VIOLA [*echoing*]: My, my, my...

[*During her exclamation,* FRANCESCO *appears, down right.*]

FRANCESCO [*to* DI GORGONZOLA, *who has stopped up right in front of* VIOLA]: A young gentleman to see Your Eminence... A Signor Giannino...

DI GORGONZOLA: Ah! Our castrato!

FRANCECSCO: He says he received an invitation.

DI GORGONZOLA [*impatiently*]: Yes, yes... I know, I know!... Of all times... Well, I'm certainly in no mood to see anybody now!

FRANCESCO: No, Your Eminence!

DI GORGONZOLA [*to* VIOLA]: You... You take care of it, signora.

VIOLA: "It"...?

DI GORGONZOLA: Greeting him, I mean...

VIOLA [*uneasy*]: Me?... Must I, Your Eminence? I... [*With a little shudder.*] People like that... I...

DI GORGONZOLA: I know, but he's quite harmless.

VIOLA: I'm sure...

DI GORGONZOLA: Just ask him to stay for lunch, with the prince and myself.

VIOLA [*with another little shudder*]: Well...

DI GORGONZOLA [*to* FRANCESCO]: Are the horses ready?

FRANCESCO: Yes, Your Eminence.

DI GORGONZOLA: Good!... My crimson gloves... [FRANCESCO *crosses left and hands the gloves to* VIOLA, *who gives them in turn to* DI GORGONZOLA.] Very good... [*As he puts them on, to* VIOLA.] I'll be back before long. [*He moves toward the door, up left, as if to leave; then, stopping short, to* VIOLA.] Ah! I almost forgot... [*To* FRANCESCO.] It's a wonder I can think at all, he's got me in such a state! [*To* VIOLA.] Just a little light luncheon... Nothing too fancy... [*To* FRANCESCO.] They don't eat much, do they? [*To* VIOLA, *as*

VIOLA: Indeed...

DI GORGONZOLA: Still, I can't help thinking, after all... Manicotti did have me named secretary of state, and... and it's not impossible that, at the next conclave... That is, it's just barely possible, with all the votes he controls... And with mine too...

VIOLA [wide-eyed]: Does Your Eminence mean...

DI GORGONZOLA: I mean, God bless the Holy Father, and all that... And let him live forever... [Reconsidering.] Or almost... But still, he's old... Very old... And not well... Not well at all...

VIOLA: Tsk tsk tsk!

DI GORGONZOLA: They say that two doctors were just brought in to treat him. Only for a head-cold, but... At his age, even a cold... At any rate, there's hope...

VIOLA: Oh! Does Your Holiness... [Correcting herself.] Does Your Eminence really think so?

DI GORGONZOLA: Shhh!... Quiet, my child! We mustn't let venal thoughts raise their ugly heads, now must we!... Besides, it's unlucky... And anyway, now I have other things to think about!

VIOLA: Of course! The prince...

DI GORGONZOLA: Ah! Only last week he told me: "Do what you like, uncle. If she's good enough for you, she'll be good enough for me." So I did. I went ahead... Yesterday it was all arranged... Manicotti, his niece... Even His Holiness gave it his blessing. Everyone agreed... Everyone, that is, except one person... [Furious.] One! Only one!...

VIOLA: Oh?

DI GORGONZOLA [pointing right, into the corridor]: Prince Giorgio! Now he absolutely refuses... You should have heard him just now.

VIOLA: Why? What's his objection?

DI GORGONZOLA [with a dismissive little wave]: Bah! Last night he finally saw her. He says he thinks she's ugly as sin... As "all the sins rolled into one," he told me... As if that mattered!... "So what?" I said. "You don't have to love the woman! I'm only asking you to marry her, for heaven's sake!"

VIOLA: And for Your Eminence's sake!... Tsk tsk tsk!... [Happy to have an excuse to criticize.] I should think he could be more considerate!

DI GORGONZOLA: Of course he could! Just a moment of self-sacrifice... You would think he wasn't a Christian!

VIOLA: And there's no way to coax him?... Some little bribe or other?...

DI GORGONZOLA: With what, by all the saints? What is there left to bribe him with? I've already bought the blackguard every last thing he ever asked for!... A pack of hounds... A stable of horses... Anything he ever wanted!...

VIOLA [shaking her head in hypocritical agreement]: Tsk tsk tsk!

DI GORGONZOLA: His own villa... A magnificent estate in the country... Full of precious paintings... Everything! Everything!... [After a moment of reflection.] Of course, it was the Church that paid, but I picked it all out.

VIOLA: Your Eminence is too kind! Some people simply don't deserve such generosity!

DI GORGONZOLA: Why, only yesterday, at the Vatican, His Holiness had a new castrato... Singing for him, that is... And when my nephew heard him, he came back utterly ecstatic. "Magnificent!" he kept saying. "The voice of an angel!... A voice that comes along once in a lifetime!..."

FRANCESCO *shrugs his shoulders.*] And no eggs... No oysters... [*To* FRANCESCO.] Why bother, after all? [*To* VIOLA.] Perhaps just the rest of last evening's delicious trout...

VIOLA: Yes, Your Eminence.

DI GORGONZOLA [*to* VIOLA]: Superb fish!... [*To* FRANCESCO.] From Lake Geneva... [*Smacking his lips on his fingertips.*] Superb!... [*To himself, approaching the door, up left, with* FRANCESCO *close behind and* VIOLA *following them.*] What a shame to waste it on those Protestants! [*As he and* FRANCESCO *exit.*] Tsk tsk tsk! [*Suddenly returning, with* FRANCESCO *on his heels.*] Ah! I almost forgot again... [*Sighing, still obsessed by his problem.*] Is it any wonder? [*To* VIOLA.] And the Hollandaise sauce... Please... You'll be sure...

VIOLA [*center stage*]: Very good, Your Eminence.

DI GORGONZOLA [*to* FRANCESCO]: From Holland... [*Slapping his forehead with the heel of his hand, with a sudden realization.*] Ah!... [*To himself.*] More Protestants!... More...

[*He exits, still mumbling, with* FRANCESCO *close behind.*]

VIOLA [*center, watching him leave*]: That's all I need! To play nursemaid to his... his... [*With a little shudder, as before.*] Whatever... And another mouth to feed... [*Echoing* DI GORGONZOLA'*s recent observation.*] "What's one more mouth?"... Ha!... If he did the marketing, and the cooking, and the baking... And the cleaning, and... and everything!... [*Mimicking.*] "One more mouth" indeed!... One more body, he means... [*After a moment's reflection.*] Well, most of one, anyway... [*Coming down right.*] As if the prince isn't enough to put up with!... You can bet this new one will settle in and try to run things too! [*Grumbling under her breath.*] I've got half a mind not to bone his trout!

[*In the meantime,* GIANNINA, *disguised as a man, has appeared at the door, up left.*]

GIANNINA [*hanging back, timidly, noticing* VIOLA]: Pardon me, signora, but...

VIOLA [*aside*]: Speak of the devil!

GIANNINA: ...they tell me that His Eminence, Cardinal di Gorgonzola, has just gone out.

VIOLA [*brusquely*]: They're right, whoever told you... [*She tries, unsuccessfully, to repress another shudder.*] He asked me to tell you that he and his nephew want you to stay for lunch. [*Satisfied that her mission is accomplished.*] So, there!... [*Curtly.*] Arrivederci...

[*She turns as if to leave, down right.*]

GIANNINA [*still very timidly, moving toward her, center*]: Please... Don't go.

VIOLA [*surprised at the liberty*]: I beg your pardon?

GIANNINA: May... May I have just a word?

VIOLA: With me?

GIANNINA: Yes... Please! I'm so happy to find that there's a woman here, signora. I didn't think... I mean, I had heard—

VIOLA [*interrupting*]: Oh? [*Aside, with a laugh.*] Good luck! A lot of good it's going to do you. [*To* GIANNINA.] And why is that?

GIANNINA: Because... That is... I need someone to advise me. About something I've done... Something foolish... But I had to... [*As* VIOLA, *obviously misinterpreting, nods knowingly with a shudder or two.*] And only a woman can know how I feel.

VIOLA: Well, not quite... Maybe a little...

GIANNINA: Oh yes! I'm sure!

VIOLA: And anyway, what's the difference? It's too late now. What's done is done!

GIANNINA: Oh no! Not at all...

VIOLA [shocked]: No?... You mean, you can... They can... [Aside.] Dio mio!

GIANNINA: I just have to decide. It would solve all my problems.

VIOLA: Problems, signore? You?... [Bitterly.] With the prince for a patron... With His Eminence the cardinal for a host, I would say you've already become one of the family!

GIANNINA: Exactly! That's the problem! I don't want to be, signora!

VIOLA: You don't?

GIANNINA: But I don't know how to tell him.

VIOLA: You... [Approaching her, with a sudden change of heart, sympathetically.] Well, well... You poor thing... Tsk tsk tsk!... [Indicating the left chair, down center, affectionately.] Come, let's talk... [Aside.] What a sweet child after all! [Aloud.] Tell Viola all about it.

GIANNINA: Oh, thank you! If you're sure...

[She sits down in the chair.]

VIOLA [sitting in the other chair]: Now then, you were saying... Before I cut you off... [Quickly trying to cover her faux pas.] Interrupted you, I mean... "Tell him" what?...

GIANNINA: Yes... [Still very timidly.] That... That I'm here in Rome, all alone, signora... A stranger, with no one to turn to... Separated from things that I've always known and loved...

VIOLA [aside]: Indeed!

GIANNINA: And... And that, all of a sudden, he appears from out of nowhere... Cardinal di Gorgonzola, I mean... And he wants me to come live here... [With a sweeping gesture of admiration.] In this magnificent palace... But... That I'm terribly grateful, but that I simply cannot accept...

VIOLA: Aha... Aha... And why, just out of curiosity?

GIANNINA: I... You're sure I can tell you?

VIOLA: Of course, my child. Everyone tells Viola everything.

GIANNINA: And... And you won't give me away? You won't tell my secret?

VIOLA: My lips are sealed, signore.

GIANNINA: Because, if you did, I don't know what I would do! [VIOLA gives her a reassuring gesture.] The fact is... I'm sure you must think that I'm just another man... No more, no less...

VIOLA: Well... [Aside, again with a little shudder.] Almost... Certainly no more... [Aloud.] That is...

GIANNINA: But the fact is, I... I...

VIOLA: You...?

GIANNINA: I'm not...

VIOLA: No...

GIANNINA [standing up, taking the bull by the horns]: I'm a woman!

VIOLA [jumping up]: You're what? [Crossing herself in panic.] You... You... [Shrinking back, holding out her index and little fingers to ward off the evil eye.] Dio mio!... You... You...

GIANNINA: Please... Shhh! Please, signora...

VIOLA [*gradually calming down*]: But... But how... [*Suddenly realizing the implication of her revelation.*] Dio mio! Here... In the palace... You... You...

GIANNINA: Please! If you'll only let me explain... It's really very simple.

VIOLA: Yes! Indeed... I wish you would!

GIANNINA: You see, signora... I was just a poor orphan, all alone in my village... Not a lira in my purse, not a soul to turn to... No one's shoulder to cry on...

VIOLA: Tsk tsk tsk!

GIANNINA: With nothing in the world but the clothes on my back... [*Explaining.*] Other clothes... Not these... Woman's...

VIOLA: Of course...

GIANNINA: And a rather pleasing voice... Or at least so people tell me... [*Musing.*] Then, one day, all of a sudden, my music teacher asked me to marry him. For no reason at all... Me! Can you imagine?

VIOLA [*a little wryly*]: I'm sure he had a reason.

[*As* GIANNINA *continues recounting her adventures, growing more and more emotional, she moves left little by little, looking off into space, recollecting, and stopping from time to time to address* VIOLA *directly as the latter stands listening in rapt attention.*]

GIANNINA: But the day of the wedding... The very day, signora... Just hours after the priest had pronounced us man and wife, the most frightful thing happened. He had rented a little coach...

VIOLA: The priest?

GIANNINA: My husband... And we were riding along, not too far from the inn where we were going to spend the night. It was almost dark already, and my husband was in a hurry to get there.

VIOLA: No doubt... [*Aside.*] They're all alike.

GIANNINA: The coachman had told him that there were highwaymen on the roads. But he wanted to water the horse...

VIOLA: Your husband?

GIANNINA: The coachman... So we stopped, and my husband got down too...

VIOLA [*aside*]: To water the grass...

GIANNINA: Then, next thing I knew, two rifle shots rang out!

VIOLA: No!

GIANNINA: Yes! Two... One after the other... Right behind us...

VIOLA: Oh!

GIANNINA: And I saw the coachman running off in a panic. And my husband too... Not thinking for an instant that I was still there, quaking in my boots...

VIOLA [*taking her literally, aside*]: Boots?...

GIANNINA [*to* VIOLA]: Can you imagine?

VIOLA [*still aside*]: With a wedding-dress?

GIANNINA: Screaming at the top of my lungs... And the poor horse, terrified, rearing up and galloping off as fast as his hooves could carry him... [*To* VIOLA.] With me still inside, signora... Galloping... Galloping off into the darkness...

VIOLA: Dio mio!

GIANNINA: ...for half a league at least!

VIOLA: What a fright! I think I would have died on the spot!

GIANNINA: Me too!... [*Naively.*] But I didn't... [*Continuing.*] Then the worst thing was when I heard voices behind me. Men... Chasing the coach and... and catching the horse... Heaven only knows how!... Grabbing his bridle and making him stop...

VIOLA: Ah!

GIANNINA: Then I saw them, signora... Two men, on foot, with rifles...

VIOLA [*crossing herself*]: The highwaymen!

[*By now* GIANNINA *is standing down far left.*]

GIANNINA: The... Oh no! Not at all!... [*With a noticeable change of tone.*] They were young and... and as elegant as you've ever seen! Perfect gentlemen... One was even handsome!

VIOLA: Oh?

GIANNINA: Next minute another one came running up... Their groom, or something... And a whole pack of hounds...

VIOLA: Hounds?

GIANNINA: ...that they had been hunting with in the hills... That's why we had heard the shots... The ones that frightened off my horse...

VIOLA [*moving toward her and standing by the chairs, down center, with a little laugh*]: Not to mention your husband!

GIANNINA: Oh, that's all right, signora. You can mention him if you like... [*Continuing.*] Well, you can guess how surprised they were to see me. All alone... In that coach... At night... Dressed like a bride...

VIOLA [*aside*]: Why not? With a groom...

GIANNINA: When I told them what had happened they were terribly kind, and they did their best to help. They even lit torches and looked all over, high and low, trying to find him.

VIOLA: But...?

GIANNINA [*shaking her head*]: No... Not a trace...

VIOLA [*making a little joke*]: He must be all the way to Sicily by now!

GIANNINA [*taking her seriously*]: Do you suppose...? [*After a moment of reflection.*] I doubt it... Besides, I don't think he can swim.

VIOLA [*renouncing her attempt*]: Ah... Well...

GIANNINA: Anyway, signora, one of them said there was a villa nearby, and that they could take me to it. The handsome one... The one his friend and the groom called "Your Highness"...

VIOLA: My, my, my!

GIANNINA: I didn't think I should, but... What choice did I have? It was late, and dark, and... What else could I do? I was cold, and frightened... At my wit's end...

VIOLA: I'm sure...

GIANNINA: So I let them take me there. And when we arrived... [*Waxing lyrical.*] Oh, signora, I never imagined... [*Moving counterclockwise, upstage, with sweeping gestures of retrospective comparison.*] The most beautiful... The most exquisite... The absolutely most magnificent estate!... And what's more, it was his!

VIOLA: The handsome one's?

GIANNINA: Yes! And he told me I could stay in his sister's quarters... At least, he said they were...

VIOLA [*cynically*]: Of course! They always have a sister!

GIANNINA [*continuing her arc about the salon, appropriately indicating the art*] *objects in her path*]: Paintings... Statues... Tapestries... [*Coming down right, by the open doorway.*] Drapes... Never, signora... Never in my life had I seen a place like that! In my poor little village, not even in my dreams!... And women to serve me... To wait on me, hand and foot...

VIOLA: And "His Highness"?

GIANNINA: The prince?... Because that's what he was... Did I tell you?... A prince...

VIOLA: Of course. They're all princes. [*With a sneer, aside.*] We have one, too.

GIANNINA: He was simply as kind and generous as could be. And so considerate, so respectful... Why, I didn't even think of being frightened anymore. In fact, I didn't think of anything...

VIOLA [*sarcastically*]: Except your husband...

GIANNINA: Oh yes, signora... Every day... [*As if to prove her concern.*] For an hour, at least... And all the time the prince was growing more and more... more...

[*She pauses, embarrassed, groping for an appropriately innocent term.*]

VIOLA: Considerate...

GIANNINA: Yes... I kept telling him that I really couldn't stay... That I had to leave... But he simply wouldn't hear of it. And each day he begged me to stay till the next. On his knees, signora.

VIOLA: No!

GIANNINA: Oh!... The sight of a man at your feet... In tears... Especially a prince...

VIOLA: One's Highness brought low!...

GIANNINA: It's so terribly touching. So pathetic, don't you know?... But then, I'm sure you must...

VIOLA: Well... Yes... Not recently, but—

GIANNINA [*joining her at the chairs, interrupting*]: And so, one night... Since I knew it was useless to resist much longer... One night... I just knew I didn't have the strength, signora... I mean, he was so terribly insistent, and so charming...

[*She pauses.*]

VIOLA: Yes...

GIANNINA [*unwittingly whetting* VIOLA'*s appetite*]: And so, one night... [*She pauses again.*] Finally...

[*And again.*]

VIOLA [*losing patience*]: Yes, yes, yes... One night... "One night," what?

GIANNINA: One night I took the bull by the horns!

VIOLA: So to speak!... And...?

GIANNINA: And I made up my mind!

VIOLA: To...?

GIANNINA [*anticlimactically*]: To run away, signora... Without telling him...

VIOLA: Oh?

GIANNINA: Somehow I managed to make my way to Rome. But when I got here, here I was, all alone... Not a lira in my purse... Not a soul to turn to...

VIOLA [*nodding, forestalling her lament*]: No one's shoulder to cry on...

GIANNINA: No one's... Yes... And with nothing but the clothes on my back...

VIOLA [*with a sense of* déjà entendu]: But woman's clothes... [*Pointing.*] Not those...

GIANNINA: A kind innkeeper's wife let me sleep on her floor. Next morning she asked me what I was going to do... "I don't have a lira in my purse," I told her...

VIOLA [aside]: "And not a soul to turn to..."

GIANNINA: "But I do have a rather pleasing voice. Or at least so people tell me... Perhaps I could sing in the pope's chapel choir." Then she burst out laughing, and said: "You poor, silly goose! You'll sing in his choir when cows fly and hell freezes over, not before! Didn't anyone ever tell you?" [Continuing, naively.] "But cows can't fly at all," I told her, "and hell is too hot to freeze."

VIOLA [aside]: Simple child!

GIANNINA [imitating]: "And no woman will ever sing for the Holy Father! Or for his cardinals either... You can be sure of that!"

VIOLA: Exactly!

GIANNINA: That's when I began to cry.

VIOLA [aside]: On her shoulder?

GIANNINA: And she smiled at me, and said: "Of course, what they don't know can't hurt them, now can it? You could put on man's clothes and pretend you're a boy soprano... Make believe you're..." [Pondering.] "'gilded'," I think she said... Or something...

VIOLA [surprised, aside]: Gelded?

GIANNINA [continuing]: Probably because of my golden voice...

VIOLA [aside, punning]: Or a little hoarse one! [To GIANNINA, discreetly, under her breath.] She meant: "Make believe you're a castrato," I think. [She gives a shudder at the thought.]

GIANNINA: She did? [Ingenuously.] Why? What's that?

VIOLA: "What's..." [Dismissing the question with a wave.] Nothing... Less than nothing... [Aside.] Two times less... [Aloud, to GIANNINA.] And so?

GIANNINA [displaying her costume]: So I did. And you know what? Just last night I sang at the Vatican!

VIOLA: So I've heard.

GIANNINA: All of Rome was there! At least that's how it seemed. All the most important people... [Moving about, right, here and there, reveling in the recollection.] Oh! What an absolute triumph, signora! The cheers... The applause... Never, never in my dreams... In my wildest, wildest dreams... Why, I was so excited, I almost gave myself away.

VIOLA: Oh?

GIANNINA: Yes. I almost curtsied!

VIOLA: My! That would never do!

GIANNINA: But I didn't. And now everyone wants me to sing. And they're offering me a fortune... Ten thousand lira... And...

VIOLA [aside, agog]: Ten thousand... [Aloud, to GIANNINA.] A year?

GIANNINA: A year!... [Getting carried away.] And Cardinal di Gorgonzola says he wants to be my patron, and that I simply must come live here in his palace!... [Stopping, down right, and coming back to reality.] But how can I, signora? Now that you know, tell me. What should I do?

VIOLA [moving down right, approaching her]: Do?... Exactly what you're doing, dear child... She was right. What they don't know can't hurt them! [Aside.] Ten thousand lira...

GIANNINA: But...

VIOLA: But nothing... Your secret is safe with me... [*With a note of exaggerated complicity.*] young man!... Now then, you're the cardinal's protégé, understand? And you're staying for lunch, with His Eminence and his nephew.

GIANNINA: But...

VIOLA: Leave everything to me. I'll talk to his majordomo, Signor Caramello.

GIANNINA: Can you trust him?

VIOLA: Completely! He eats out of my hand. Between the two of us we'll convince His Eminence that you really shouldn't live here. [*Rather bitterly.*] Especially since it wasn't his idea in the first place...

[*Just then voices can be heard offstage, approaching up left.*]

GIANNINA [*to* VIOLA] ⎫ [*together*]: ⎰ Well, if you're sure...
DI GORGONZOLA'S VOICE ⎭ ⎱ But why, for goodness sake?

VIOLA [*to* GIANNINA] ⎫ [*together*]: ⎰ Shhh! Here they are...
DI GORGONZOLA'S VOICE ⎭ ⎱ A Manicotti and a Gorgonzola...

VIOLA [*to* GIANNINA]: Not a word!

[DI GORGONZOLA *and* THE PRINCE *enter, up left, arguing.*]

DI GORGONZOLA: It's a match made in heaven, I tell you!

THE PRINCE: Then I'll wait till I get there, uncle dear!

DI GORGONZOLA [*out of patience*] ⎫ [*together*]: ⎰ You...
GIANNINA [*recognizing* THE PRINCE, *startled*] ⎭ ⎱ Oh!

THE PRINCE [*to* DI GORGONZOLA]: But as long as I'm on this earth, I'll never marry that... that cow!

VIOLA [*to* GIANNINA, *whispering*]: What is it?

GIANNINA [*to* VIOLA, *likewise*]: It's... It's him!

[*They continue their whispered exchange, down right, as* DI GORGONZOLA *and* THE PRINCE, *coming center without noticing them, continue theirs.*]

DI GORGONZOLA [*to* THE PRINCE]: But... You must have a reason!

VIOLA [*to* GIANNINA]: Prince Giorgio?

THE PRINCE [*to* DI GORGONZOLA]: I told you. She's ugly!

GIANNINA [*to* VIOLA]: The one who took me to his villa...

DI GORGONZOLA [*to* THE PRINCE]: But she's Manicotti's niece. I promised...

VIOLA [*to* GIANNINA]: And fell in love with you...

GIANNINA [*to* VIOLA]: I suppose...

DI GORGONZOLA [*to* THE PRINCE]: It's all arranged. She said yes...

VIOLA [*to* GIANNINA]: Remember... Not a word!

DI GORGONZOLA [*to* THE PRINCE]: His Holiness thinks she'll make a perfect wife.

GIANNINA [*to* VIOLA]: I'll be careful...

THE PRINCE [*to* DI GORGONZOLA]: Good! I hope he'll be very happy with her!

DI GORGONZOLA [*scandalized*]: Oh! Bite your tongue! [*Aside.*] Impudent young—

THE PRINCE [*suddenly noticing* VIOLA *and* GIANNINA, *interrupting*]: Oh!

VIOLA [*to* DI GORGONZOLA]: Your Eminence... [*To* THE PRINCE.] Your Highness...

DI GORGONZOLA [*to* VIOLA]: Ah, signora...

VIOLA [*to* DI GORGONZOLA, *gesturing to* GIANNINA]: May I present the young cas... [*Catching herself.*] the young soprano Your Eminence was expecting...

DI GORGONZOLA: Indeed... Indeed...

THE PRINCE [*coming toward them, stopping center*]: Ah! Signor Giannino! What a pleasure!

VIOLA [*aside to* GIANNINA, *whispering*]: Not a word!

THE PRINCE [*to* GIANNINA, *stammering*]: It's... I... I... It's so good of you to join us, signore.

GIANNINA [*trying to conceal her obvious emotion*]: No, no... It's so good of Your Highness to insist.

THE PRINCE: No, no... [*Aside.*] His voice... It's... [*To* GIANNINA, *beginning to babble.*] That is, yes... I do, I... We, I mean... [*Pointing to* DI GORGONZOLA.] He... Both of us...

GIANNINA [*to* DI GORGONZOLA, *with a crisp little bow*]: Your Eminence...

THE PRINCE: We... I...

DI GORGONZOLA [*aside to* THE PRINCE, *joining him, center*]: What on earth is the matter with you?

THE PRINCE [*to* DI GORGONZOLA] ⎫
                                 ⎬ [*together*]: ⎧ With me?
VIOLA [*aside to* GIANNINA] ⎭   ⎩ Be careful! He suspects...

THE PRINCE [*to* GIANNINA, *mustering his aplomb*]: Your performance was a triumph, signore. Last night... I... I've never been so moved... So touched...

DI GORGONZOLA [*aside, tapping his forehead*]: Very... Very...

[*Two* SERVANTS *enter, down right, carrying in a table that they put down, midstage right. During the ensuing scene, they exit and reenter several times by the same door, bringing in three armchairs—placing them behind it and on each side—meticulously setting the table, and laying out an elegant meal.*]

GIANNINA [*to* THE PRINCE]: Ah? Your Highness was there?

THE PRINCE: I was indeed! All of Rome was there, signore! Or at least that's how it seemed.

[GIANNINA *and* VIOLA *exchange brief glances.*]

VIOLA [*to* THE PRINCE]: Yes... All the most important people...

THE PRINCE [*to* VIOLA] ⎫
                        ⎬ [*together*]: ⎧ Quite... Quite...
DI GORGONZOLA [*aside*] ⎭   ⎩ Well, all but one...

GIANNINA [*to* THE PRINCE]: Your Highness is too kind! I'm flattered.

THE PRINCE [*aside*]: It's uncanny... [*To* GIANNINA, *joining her, down right, as* VIOLA *steps discreetly aside, behind the chairs, down center.*] Perhaps you heard me when you stepped out to sing. A little sigh... A cry that I couldn't hold back...

GIANNINA: Ah? Was that Your Highness?

DI GORGONZOLA [*to* GIANNINA]: Even before you opened your mouth! [*To* VIOLA, *joining her, down center, wryly.*] Now that's a music-lover, signora!

THE PRINCE [*to* DI GORGONZOLA]: If only you could have heard him, uncle... The voice of an angel... [*Tongue-tied with emotion.*] Like the cheraphim and serubim... Like the hovenly heasts...

DI GORGONZOLA: Please?

THE PRINCE [*partially correcting himself*]: Hosts... Heavenly hosts... Utterly sublime... Why, I didn't sleep at all last night. I... Not a wink... That voice... [*To* GIANNINA.] I couldn't...

GIANNINA [*ingenuously*]: Oh! I'm sorry, Your Highness!

THE PRINCE: Sorry?

DI GORGONZOLA [*aside*]: He should have counted cows!

THE PRINCE [*to* GIANNINA, *continuing*]: Not at all, signore!... Please! Keep me from sleeping every night of the week! Believe me, you have in me an impassioned admirer... An indomitable, indefatigable... [*Stammering.*] in... in...

DI GORGONZOLA [*aside*]: ...somniac?

THE PRINCE: ...in...

VIOLA [*aside*]: ...sufferable?

THE PRINCE: ...inspired devotee!... And what's more, a... a friend! [*He takes her hand as if to shake it.*]

GIANNINA: Oh! Your Highness...

THE PRINCE: Why, signore, you're trembling.

VIOLA [*mumbling a warning under her breath, in* GIANNINA'*s direction*]: Careful...

GIANNINA [*to* THE PRINCE]: I am?

THE PRINCE [*to* GIANNINA]: But you needn't... [*Taking both her hands in his.*] When you know me better you'll understand my attraction... My affection... My... My...

DI GORGONZOLA [*aside, sarcastically*] ⎫
THE PRINCE [*as* GIANNINA *tries*   ⎬ [*together*]: ⎰ My, my, my!
          discreetly to pull away] ⎭   ⎱ My...

VIOLA [*aside*]: My foot!

GIANNINA [*finally disengaging, to* THE PRINCE]: Your Highness...

THE PRINCE [*continuing*]: My love of all the arts... And music, especially... The queen of them all!... My passion... Like yours... Ever since I can remember... Since... Since I was old enough to tell Palestrina from Pergolesi...

VIOLA [*aside*]: Another one with his Pergolesi...

THE PRINCE [*to* GIANNINA]: Now then, signore, consider this your home. [*He puts his right arm affectionately around her waist and brings her around counterclockwise.*] His Eminence insists... [*To* DI GORGONZOLA.] Don't you, uncle?

DI GORGONZOLA [*unenthusiastically*]: Of course... I insist.

VIOLA [*aside*]: We'll see about that!

THE PRINCE [*escorting* GIANNINA *past* VIOLA *and* DI GORGONZOLA, *moving up left with broad gestures, as if displaying the premises*]: Your home... For as long as you like...

GIANNINA [*trying feebly to protest*]: But...

THE PRINCE: As long as it suits your fancy... [*As they come near the door, up left, turning counterclockwise and continuing his leisurely amble with her, upstage, crossing right.*] Weeks... Months... Years...

VIOLA [*aside*]: Days, hours, minutes...

GIANNINA [*to* THE PRINCE, *hesitant*]: But... But Your Highness... I don't know how to—

THE PRINCE [*interrupting*]: No, no... You needn't thank me...

DI GORGONZOLA [*to* THE PRINCE]: You?... [*Emphasizing.*] Me!

THE PRINCE [*correcting, pointing downstage to* DI GORGONZOLA]: Him... [*After a brief reconsideration.*] Us... You needn't thank us...

GIANNINA: But...

THE PRINCE [*to* GIANNINA]: And all we ask in return is a song or two each day.

GIANNINA: But...

THE PRINCE: A recitativo and aria, perhaps...

DI GORGONZOLA [*aside to* VIOLA]: A wretched what?

THE PRINCE [*as* VIOLA *shrugs back in response*]: A nice little cavatina...

GIANNINA: But Your Highness, I—

THE PRINCE [*stopping as they arrive up right, interrupting*]: Ah! My friend, my friend... Your fortune is made! I'll spread your name and fame far and wide... Rome... Milan... Naples... [*After a brief pause.*] Poggibonzi...

VIOLA [*aside to* DI GORGONZOLA]: Poggibonzi?

DI GORGONZOLA [*aside to* VIOLA]: He was born there.

[*By this time the table, midstage right, is set, and the* SERVANTS, *satisfied with their handiwork, have made their final exit.*]

THE PRINCE [*to* GIANNINA]: In fact, I've already arranged a recital. Ten lira a head... People will kill for a ticket! You'll be swimming in money! Just leave it to me...

GIANNINA: Your Highness is terribly kind, but—

THE PRINCE [*remembering one last detail*]: Ah! And don't forget... Your rehearsal at noon for the *Stabat Mater*...

VIOLA [*To* THE PRINCE, *offhandedly authoritative*]: Oh? Pergolesi's?

THE PRINCE [*to* VIOLA, *surprised at her knowledge*]: Pergo... Why yes... How do you... [*To* GIANNINA.] If you have no objection, I'd love to come listen.

GIANNINA: I... Really, I don't know...

THE PRINCE: Please, signore... Just for a little while...

DI GORGONZOLA [*aside to* VIOLA, *in a whisper*]: What a passion he has for music! I never knew...

THE PRINCE [*to* GIANNINA, *continuing*]: Any excuse to hear that voice!

VIOLA [*aside to* DI GORGONZOLA, *replying in a whisper*]: So much the better!...

GIANNINA [*to* THE PRINCE, *relenting*]: If Your Highness insists...

VIOLA [*aside to* DI GORGONZOLA, *continuing* sotto voce]: We'll use this Giannino to talk him into the marriage.

THE PRINCE [*to* GIANNINA, *continuing*]: That golden voice...

DI GORGONZOLA [*aside to* VIOLA, *replying likewise*]: Oh? How?

VIOLA [*aside to* DI GORGONZOLA, *likewise*]: Leave everything to me!

[FRANCESCO *enters, down right, followed by a* SERVANT *who is carrying a small table with bottles of wine in a cooling-bucket.*]

FRANCESCO [*standing in the open doorway as the* SERVANT *places the table center stage, between the luncheon-table, right, and the writing-table, left, and exits, down right*]: Luncheon is served, Your Eminence.

DI GORGONZOLA: Ah!... Come... [*To* THE PRINCE *and* GIANNINA.] Come, nephew... Signore... [*He goes to the table, right, and is helped into the chair facing the footlights by* FRANCESCO.] Come... [*Pointing to the chair on his right, to* THE PRINCE.] You, here... [*Pointing left, as* THE PRINCE *holds the other chair for* GIANNINA.] And our young virtuoso here... [*Aside to* VIOLA, *in a whisper.*] "Virtuosa"?...

[*As* VIOLA *shrugs in reply,* GIANNINA *sits down, reluctantly, and* FRANCESCO *holds the other chair for* THE PRINCE, *who sits down as well.*]

GIANNINA [*nodding to* DI GORGONZOLA *and* THE PRINCE *in turn*]: Your Eminence... Your Highness...

[*As the three of them settle in,* FRANCESCO *exits, up left, and* VIOLA *goes over to the chair behind the writing-table, down left, removing its cushion.*]

VIOLA [*crossing back to the luncheon-table, to* DI GORGONZOLA]: Your Eminence doesn't have his cushion. [*She places it solicitously behind his back, then manages to whisper in* GIANNINA'*s ear, in passing.*] Careful...

DI GORGONZOLA: Ah...

VIOLA [*to* DI GORGONZOLA]: Or his foot-warmer...

DI GORGONZOLA: True...

VIOLA: I'll go fetch it.

DI GORGONZOLA: Thank you, signora. [*To* GIANNINA.] She thinks of everything, that one!

VIOLA [*to* DI GORGONZOLA, *overhearing*]: Not quite... I forgot to ask Your Eminence for a very special favor...

DI GORGONZOLA: Aha!... [*To* GIANNINA, *with a laugh.*] You see? She knows how to twist me around her little finger! Always when I'm eating!... [*To* VIOLA.] Yes? What is it?

VIOLA [*behind* GIANNINA'*s chair, to* DI GORGONZOLA]: Speaking of Pergolesi... I neglected to mention that a protégé of his would like an audience with Your Eminence. A poor devil who—

THE PRINCE [*interrupting*]: A protégé?... Of Pergolesi?... [*To* VIOLA.] But he's been dead for years!

VIOLA [*to* THE PRINCE]: A protégé while he was alive, Your Highness...

DI GORGONZOLA [*to* VIOLA]: And what does he want to talk about, this poor devil of yours?

VIOLA: Your Eminence's organ... And Maestro Sforzando's discharge...

DI GORGONZOLA: Aha... Aha...

VIOLA: He would like to replace him.

DI GORGONZOLA: Well! No need to let him interrupt our lunch!... I'll listen between mouthfuls! Show him in, signora. With our two experts here...

VIOLA: Very good, Your Eminence.

[*She exits, up left.*]

DI GORGONZOLA [*to* THE PRINCE, *who has been sitting, staring open-mouthed at* GIANNINA, *absentmindedly holding his fork in the air*]: Right, nephew?

THE PRINCE [*oblivious to the question, to himself*]: It's uncanny... The resemblance...

DI GORGONZOLA [*to* THE PRINCE, *repeating*]: Right?

THE PRINCE [*to* GIANNINA]: The more I look at you, signore, the more I—

DI GORGONZOLA [*to* THE PRINCE, *impatiently*]: Right? [*Aside, noticing the fork poised in the air.*] Is he going to conduct him? [*To* THE PRINCE.] Nephew?... Isn't that right?

THE PRINCE [*finally*]: Hmm?... Oh...

GIANNINA [*aside, apprehensively*]: God help me!

THE PRINCE [*to* DI GORGONZOLA]: Of course, uncle... Of course...

GIANNINA [*aside*]: Don't let him suspect...

[VIOLA *enters, up left, carrying a foot-warmer and followed by* PIZZICATO, *portfolio under his arm.*]

VIOLA [*to* PIZZICATO, *softly*]: Come... His Eminence is in a good mood. As long as he's eating...

PIZZICATO [*surveying the copious repast from a distance*]: Ah! Then I see I have time!

[*As he hangs back, respectfully,* VIOLA *approaches with the foot-warmer.*]

VIOLA [*passing beside* GIANNINA, *whispering in her ear*]: Careful!... I'm going to speak to Caramello. I'll be back... [*Placing the foot-warmer under the table, at* DI GORGONZOLA'*s feet, aloud.*] There!

DI GORGONZOLA: Thank you, signora. [*To* GIANNINA, *whose back remains turned to* PIZZICATO.] What would I do without her!

VIOLA [*to* DI GORGONZOLA, *introducing*]: Your Eminence, the organist... Maestro, His Eminence, Cardinal di Gorgonzola...

[*She exits, up left, as* PIZZICATO, *unsure what kind of obeisance befits a cardinal, stands awkwardly bowing and scraping.*]

DI GORGONZOLA [*to* PIZZICATO]: Come... Come, maestro... Come sit down...

PIZZICATO [*delighted, approaching the luncheon-table*]: Oh! Thank you, Your Eminence...

[*He looks around for a fourth chair.*]

DI GORGONZOLA [*pointing left, to the chair behind the writing-table*]: There... There...

PIZZICATO [*disillusioned*]: Ah...

DI GORGONZOLA: We'll be with you shortly.

[PIZZICATO *gives an awkward little bow, as* DI GORGONZOLA, THE PRINCE, *and* GIANNINA—*her back still turned to pizzicato—begin eating.*]

PIZZICATO [*sitting down*]: Hmm! I thought... [*Aside.*] Oh well... [*Watching* THE PRINCE *and* DI GORGONZOLA *attack their food, as* GIANNINA *picks timidly at hers, to himself.*] Lucky people! Not a care in the world... A table full of food, all the wine they can drink... [*Sighing.*] What works of genius I could compose at a table like that! [*Gazing at the wine bottles on the little table between himself and the others.*] Ah! What hosannahs I could pour from those bottles! What glorious glorias, magnificent magnificats!... A tonic for the soul!... Each delicious drop, a melody... a melisma... Diatonic, chromatic... A tonic... [*Getting carried away.*] A supertonic... [*Looking lovingly at the luncheon-table.*] And in that immense pâté... Each delectable morsel, a harmony... a counterpoint... A veritable symphony of delights... [*Sighing.*] Ah! But genius dries up on an empty stomach, alas! [*Watching the others, still aside.*] Madonna mia! Look at them eat! They've forgotten all about me.

[*He discreetly clears his throat to remind them of his presence.*]

DI GORGONZOLA [*holding up his glass, addressing no one in particular*]: Wine... Wine...

[PIZZICATO *jumps to his feet, as if the exclamation were meant for him, takes one of the bottles, and goes over to the luncheon-table.*]

PIZZICATO [*to* DI GORGONZOLA, *serving him*]: Certainly, Your Eminence...

DI GORGONZOLA [*surprised*]: Hmm?... You?... Too kind, maestro... [*He drinks.*] Too kind... [*Holding out his glass.*] "Maestro" what, by the way?...

PIZZICATO [*pouring again*]: Maestro Pizzicato... [*As* DI GORGONZOLA *waves him away.*] Benito Pizzicato...

GIANNINA [*with a start, almost choking, as* PIZZICATO *replaces the bottle on the little table*]: Pizzi... [*Stealing a look at him, aside.*] Good God! My husband!... Here!

DI GORGONZOLA [*reflecting*]: Pizzicato...

GIANNINA [*still aside*]: How—

THE PRINCE [*to* GIANNINA]: What is it, signore? Is something—

GIANNINA [*to* THE PRINCE]: Nothing... Nothing, Your Highness... Just a bone... [*She gives an unconvincing little cough.*]

DI GORGONZOLA ⎱ [*together*]: ⎰ Pizzicato... Pizzicato...
THE PRINCE [*to himself*] ⎰   ⎱ A bone?... In the pâté?

GIANNINA [*aside*]: He mustn't recognize me!

DI GORGONZOLA: Ah! Now I remember... Pizzicato... [*To* PIZZICATO.] Aren't you the one who wrote me a letter or two?

PIZZICATO [*center stage*]: Yes, Your Eminence... [*Aside.*] Or fifty, or sixty... [*Aloud, to* DI GORGONZOLA.] I took the liberty... Every day... Sometimes twice...

DI GORGONZOLA [*as he and* THE PRINCE *continue eating with gusto*]: You have a fine hand, I seem to recall. I admire good penmanship.

PIZZICATO: Fingering is one of my fortes, Your Eminence.

THE PRINCE [*aside to* GIANNINA, *quipping*]: Fortissimo, even!

[GIANNINA *manages a wan smile in response. She will sit picking at her food throughout the following exchange, trying to be as inconspicuous as possible.*]

DI GORGONZOLA [*to* PIZZICATO]: And you say you play the organ? And the pianoforte?...

THE PRINCE [*to* PIZZICATO]: And you have talent?

PIZZICATO [*to* DI GORGONZOLA]: Indeed, Your Eminence! [*To* THE PRINCE.] Talent, Your Highness?... [*Categorically.*] A portfolio full, Your Eminences!... [*Confused.*] Your Highnesses... If Your Graces don't mind my saying... [*Reaching into his portfolio and taking out sheaves of papers.*] Masses... Motets... Cantatas... Operas... Dozens by the score...

THE PRINCE: Beg pardon?

PIZZICATO [*correcting himself*]: I mean, scores by the dozen... [*To* THE PRINCE.] That speak for me, Your Eminence...

THE PRINCE [*pointing to* DI GORGONZOLA, *correcting him*]: Him... Him...

PIZZICATO [*continuing, to* DI GORGONZOLA]: That sing out my talent... That shout it for all to hear...

DI GORGONZOLA: Aha... Aha...

PIZZICATO: Unfortunately, no one listens. Our century is deaf to genius, I'm afraid.

THE PRINCE [*to* PIZZICATO]: And you come well recommended?

DI GORGONZOLA [*to* PIZZICATO]: You have references, I presume?

PIZZICATO [*to* THE PRINCE]: Indeed... [*To* DI GORGONZOLA.] Indeed, Your Highness...

DI GORGONZOLA [*pointing to* THE PRINCE, *correcting him*]: Him... Him...

PIZZICATO [*looking from one to the other*]: I was a protégé of Pergolesi, Your... Your...

THE PRINCE: Yes, so I've heard.

PIZZICATO: And I think I can say that the great Cimarosa owes some of his finest works to me.

THE PRINCE [*impressed*]: Really? How so, signore?

PIZZICATO: I tuned his pianoforte.

DI GORGONZOLA [*sarcastic*]: Impressive...

PIZZICATO: I would go to his house and say to him: "Well, old man..." [*To* DI GORGONZOLA.] No formalities... [*To* THE PRINCE.] Brothers in art, after all...

DI GORGONZOLA } [*together*]: { Of course...

THE PRINCE } { Indeed...

PIZZICATO: "Well, old man, how goes it today?" And one day he answered: "Not at all, old man..." [*Quick to explain.*] I was really very young, but he called me "old man"...

THE PRINCE [*nodding*]: Brothers in art...

PIZZICATO [*continuing*]: "Oh? And why is that?" I asked him. "No inspiration... Nothing... I can't find the notes..." And he held up a piece of music he was writing. "See? An aria from *Il Matrimonio segreto,* that I simply can't finish..." Well, I looked inside the pianoforte and, sure enough, there were three strings out of tune... [*Reflecting.*] Maybe four... I don't remember... So I rolled up my sleeves and went to work. [*Miming.*] La, la, la, la... Plink, plink, plink... No more than five minutes, and... "Presto, maestro! Try again!" I told him. [*Proudly.*] And he sat down at the keyboard, found his notes, and finished the aria!

DI GORGONZOLA [*still rather sarcastic*]: Amazing...

THE PRINCE: Quite...

PIZZICATO: There are ten or a dozen like that... That we composed together, I mean... But I also have others that I composed all by myself. [*To* DI GORGONZOLA.] If Your Eminence would like to hear one... A short one, perhaps...

DI GORGONZOLA [*none too enthusiastically*]: With pleasure, maestro...

PIZZICATO [*ecstatic*]: Really?... I mean, Your Eminence is sure? [*Rummaging through his papers, to himself.*] At last! Somebody who's willing to listen... I can't believe it!

THE PRINCE [*to* PIZZICATO, *taking out his pocket watch*]: A very short one, if you don't mind... We have a rehearsal at noon. Just show us your best.

PIZZICATO: But... But everything I have is my best, Your Highness. I don't compose anything *but* my best!

THE PRINCE: I'm sure...

PIZZICATO [*still rummaging*]: If it has to be short... [*Pulling out a sheet of music.*] Perhaps this one... [*Reconsidering.*] Oh... Except that it's a duet... [*To* DI GORGONZOLA.] For two voices, Your Eminence...

DI GORGONZOLA [*still eating*]: Yes... I assume...

PIZZICATO [*to* DI GORGONZOLA]: Soprano and tenor... Too bad... It's staggering, believe me! [*To* THE PRINCE.] The introduction alone would make Your Highness swoon! [*Shaking his head.*] But two voices... Tsk tsk tsk...

THE PRINCE: Well, if that's the only problem... [*To himself.*] I'm not sure I want to swoon, but... [*To* PIZZICATO, *pointing to* GIANNINA, *who has kept her back turned to* PIZZICATO *throughout.*] Our young friend here is an absolutely magnificent soprano!... The finest voice in all of Italy, maestro...

PIZZICATO: A soprano?... Ah, well! In that case... [*Addressing* GIANNINA, *who*

keeps looking away.] What an honor for me!... And for my music, signore!... [*To* THE PRINCE.] It's a duet from my opera, *Abu Ibn Hooha.*
THE PRINCE [*getting up*]: *Abu...?*
PIZZICATO: *...Ibn Hooha...*
DI GORGONZOLA [*to* THE PRINCE]: Yes, nephew... The famous Arab sheikh... Tenth century, anno Domini...
PIZZICATO [*to* DI GORGONZOLA]: Ah... Then Your Eminence knows the story... [*To* THE PRINCE.] A sheikh who marries his sister, Your Highness... [*To* DI GORGONZOLA.] If Your Eminence will pardon a biographical indiscretion...
DI GORGONZOLA [*dismissing the disclaimer with a wave*]: Pfff! I've heard worse.
PIZZICATO: Well now... I'll sing Ibn Hooha... [*Holding out another sheet toward* GIANNINA.] And this is the part for the soprano.
[THE PRINCE *goes over to him and takes the music.*]
THE PRINCE [*handing it to* GIANNINA]: Signore...
[GIANNINA *reluctantly takes it and stands up, trying to keep her head turned away from* PIZZICATO *as much as possible. At the same time* DI GORGONZOLA *begins to rise from his chair as well.*]
PIZZICATO [*rushing over to pull out* DI GORGONZOLA's *chair, portfolio and music notwithstanding, sycophantically*]: Your Eminence...
THE PRINCE [*to* DI GORGONZOLA, *gesturing toward the two chairs, down center*]: Come, uncle...
[*He turns the chairs around, back to the footlights, at an angle to each other. As he and* DI GORGONZOLA *are about to sit down, left and right respectively,* PIZZICATO *comes running down and holds the chairs for them, awkwardly caught between the two.*]
PIZZICATO [*as they finally sit down*]: There!... [*Moving center, to* GIANNINA, *who is still standing apprehensively by her chair, head turned.*] Ready, signore? [*To* DI GORGONZOLA *and* THE PRINCE.] I'm sorry I don't have an orchestra to play the ritornello... [*Explaining.*] The introduction...
DI GORGONZOLA [*to* THE PRINCE, *sarcastically*]: If only we had known...
PIZZICATO: Or even a pianoforte... But no matter... I can sing it.

| THE PRINCE | } [*together*]: | { Fine... |
| DI GORGONZOLA | | { Indeed... Indeed... |

[PIZZICATO *assumes a concertizing stance, center stage. But no sooner has he got out the first two or three notes than the* SERVANTS *enter, down right, and begin clearing the table, removing the wine, etc., with enough commotion to interrupt his repeated beginnings.*]
PIZZICATO [*singing, as the* SERVANTS, *removing the luncheon-table, the three chairs, and the little table, center, make their final exit, down right*]: La, la, la... La, la, la, la...[1]
[DI GORGONZOLA *and* THE PRINCE *exchange glances of obvious distaste as he continues his rendition.*]

---

[1] Unlike the other brief musical interludes in this comedy—omitted in the present adaptation—for which the author supplies melodies by the then common practice of indicating popular airs of the period, no musical suggestion is given for this passage, a lengthy ensemble in the original. Present-day directors can, of course, give PIZZICATO's ritornello and duet any music they see fit; though it should, for consistency, be in the style of the period, and, for the situation, especially inept and unattractive [Translator's note].

DI GORGONZOLA [*as he brings it to a conclusion, to* THE PRINCE, *sotto voce*]:
Vile...

THE PRINCE [*to* DI GORGONZOLA, *likewise*]: Utterly... He's right. I'm swooning...

PIZZICATO [*enthusiastically*]: Now the duet... [*Singing.*]

> Fair Zelma, object of my ardent quest,
> What burning passion now consumes my breast!
> To think—O passing strange, the ways of life!—
> That you, my sister, should become...

[*Looking up at* GIANNINA, *who faces him squarely for the first time, and, shocked to recognize her, shouting.*] My wife!

GIANNINA [*emitting a high-pitched scream that can easily be taken for a musical note*]: Aaaaah!

PIZZICATO [*in a dither, speaking, but in a manner that* DI GORGONZOLA *and* THE PRINCE *mistake for attempted singing*]:

> Good God in heaven! How can it be?...
> My wife... My wife... But I... But she...

GIANNINA [*aside, distraught*]: He knows!

THE PRINCE [*to* DI GORGONZOLA, *sotto voce, as before*]: Utterly vile!

DI GORGONZOLA [*to* THE PRINCE, *likewise*]: Disgusting!

[THE PRINCE *stands up and applauds politely.*]

GIANNINA [*aside*]: If only I could warn him...

PIZZICATO [*to* THE PRINCE]: If Your Highness will excuse me... [*To* DI GORGONZOLA.] And Your Eminence... I'm really not in voice, I'm afraid. It's too early in the day, and... And besides, it's the full moon.

THE PRINCE: Yes, well... [*Looking at his watch.*] I do wish we had time to wait for it to change... [*With a polite smile.*] The moon, that is... Not your voice... But, the rehearsal, maestro... It's time... [*To* GIANNINA.] Come, signore...

[*He strides purposefully up left, waiting for her near the open door.*]

GIANNINA: Of course... Just let me...

[*She approaches* PIZZICATO, *ostensibly to return her sheet of music. He takes it, gaping at her in disbelief and confusion, and backs up, down left, leaning against the writing-table, all the while never taking his eyes off her.*]

THE PRINCE [*to* GIANNINA]: Come... My carriage is waiting.

GIANNINA [*frustrated in her attempt to whisper a few words of explanation in* PIZZICATO's *ear, aside*]: Impossible...

[*During the following exchanges she tries to gesture surreptitiously to* PIZZICATO, *but to no avail.*]

THE PRINCE [*to* GIANNINA]: We mustn't be late.

PIZZICATO [*still perplexed, to himself*]: Madonna mia! Did I marry a castrato?

THE PRINCE [*to* GIANNINA, *continuing*]: Promptness is a virtue...

DI GORGONZOLA [*still seated, to* PIZZICATO, *quipping*]: Not always a cardinal virtue, I'm afraid...

PIZZICATO [*aside*]: How...?

THE PRINCE [*to* GIANNINA, *continuing*]: And we don't want the maestro to be angry, now do we!

PIZZICATO [*continuing, aside*]: No! It's some fiendish plot! It's got to be!... [*Approaching* DI GORGONZOLA, *aloud.*] Pardon me, Your Eminence, but... If Your Eminence has a moment... I wonder if he could accord me the briefest of audiences... [*Glaring at* GIANNINA.] In private... [*In a semi-whisper.*] To discuss a serious and most important affair...

GIANNINA [*overhearing, as she edges reluctantly up left, aside*]: God!... He mustn't...
[*She keeps trying to gesture to him.*]

DI GORGONZOLA [*to* PIZZICATO]: Of course, maestro...

GIANNINA [*growing more desperate*]: Oh!

DI GORGONZOLA [*aside, continuing*]: As long as he doesn't sing it!

THE PRINCE [*to* GIANNINA]: Come, Signor Giannino. I need some good music to calm my nerves. [*With a meaningful look at* PIZZICATO, *emphasizing.*] Good music...

PIZZICATO [*aside*]: Much obliged!

GIANNINA [*aside*]: I'll come back as soon as I can and tell him everything. If only it's not too late... [*To* THE PRINCE, *as he disappears out the door.*] Your Highness...
[*She follows him out after a few more fruitless gestures toward* PIZZICATO.]

PIZZICATO [*watching her leave, taking a few steps toward the door, his back to* DI GORGONZOLA, *aside*]: I'm sure of it!... He... She... [*Mortified, still aside.*] Oh! Married to a ... a castrato, am I? Well, we'll see about that!... She... He... I'll let them all know that he's my wife... That she's my... Whatever she... Whatever he is...

DI GORGONZOLA [*still seated*]: So, maestro? You had something to tell me?

PIZZICATO [*returning down center*]: I did indeed, Your Eminence! [*Cautiously.*] Are we alone?

DI GORGONZOLA [*with a sweeping gesture*]: It would seem...

PIZZICATO [*looking up left and down right, toward the exits*]: And no one can hear us?

DI GORGONZOLA: Goodness! Is it such a secret?

PIZZICATO: I'm afraid so. Your Eminence knows that one can't be too careful when delicate matters are being discussed.

DI GORGONZOLA: Aha... Aha...

PIZZICATO [*lowering his voice, pointing up left*]: How well does Your Eminence know that young soprano?

DI GORGONZOLA: Signor Giannino? Not at all, maestro...

PIZZICATO: Well, I do!

DI GORGONZOLA [*inviting him to sit down in the chair next to him*]: Please... That is, I know that he sang at the Vatican yesterday... [*As* PIZZICATO, *with a bow, is about to sit down.*] And that he must be very talented, because he was offered a salary of ten thousand lira...

PIZZICATO [*jumping up before his backside can touch the chair*]: What?... Ten thousand lira?... To sing?

DI GORGONZOLA: Of course to sing... [*With a little laugh.*] What else can a castrato do?

PIZZICATO: Ten thousand...

DI GORGONZOLA: I think he's signing the contract today.

PIZZICATO [*crossing himself, aside*]: Madonna mia! I almost lost a fortune!

DI GORGONZOLA: Now then, what was it you had to tell me, maestro?

PIZZICATO [*playing innocent*]: Me, Your Eminence?

DI GORGONZOLA: The deep, dark secret...

PIZZICATO: Oh... Nothing, really... Only that everything Your Eminence has heard about her... [*Coughing, to cover his faux pas.*] about him... is true. Completely true...

DI GORGONZOLA: Ah?

PIZZICATO: That he's an absolutely magnificent soprano... That no one is more worthy of Your Eminence's consideration and protection...

DI GORGONZOLA: That's what you had to tell me?... In private?

PIZZICATO: Perhaps the greatest in all of Italy today!

DI GORGONZOLA: You mean, you know him?

PIZZICATO: Of course! Who doesn't?

DI GORGONZOLA: And you've heard him? I didn't think—

PIZZICATO: Oh, hundreds of times, Your Eminence! In Pisa... Who hasn't!... [*Laughing at the obvious.*] Her?

DI GORGONZOLA [*with a start*]: "Her"?

PIZZICATO [*catching himself*]: "Heard..." Who hasn't heard him?... Your Eminence has my personal guarantee. As a protégé of Pergolesi and a collaborator of Cimarosa...

DI GORGONZOLA: Yes, yes... That's all well and good. But certainly that's not your "delicate matter"...

PIZZICATO [*embarrassed, looking for a suitable explanation*]: Well... Actually... Your Eminence must have noticed a little discomfort when he saw me...

DI GORGONZOLA: When I saw you?

PIZZICATO: No, no... When he saw me... The soprano...

DI GORGONZOLA: Perhaps... I thought he was just bashful.

PIZZICATO: No, it goes much deeper, I'm afraid. It... It began when she... [*Clearing his throat, catching himself again.*] when he was my bride...

DI GORGONZOLA: Your...?

PIZZICATO [*quickly recovering*]: My pride... and joy... [*Embroidering on the truth.*] The star of my opera...

DI GORGONZOLA: Oh?

PIZZICATO: Yes... *Il Matrimonio interrotto*... "The Interrupted Marriage"... I was counting on it to bring me fame and fortune. But he left me in the lurch, the very first night.

DI GORGONZOLA: Tsk tsk tsk...

PIZZICATO: Before the grand opening... The consummation of my desires...

DI GORGONZOLA: He left you? Just like that?

PIZZICATO: High and dry, as they say... Even before the first gun was fired...

DI GORGONZOLA: How unfortunate for you!

PIZZICATO: Yes... And frustrating, Your Eminence... So he probably thinks that I still hold it against him. But I don't, goodness knows! We artistes, after all... We have a right to be a little temperamental now and then. Why, I remember one time when I—

DI GORGONZOLA [*cutting him off, impatiently*]: Yes, yes... I'm sure... But you still haven't said what it is you have to tell me!

PIZZICATO: Ah?... What I have to tell Your Eminence...? What I... Yes... Well... It's just that I thought that Your Eminence might be good enough to patch things up between us... To bring us back together...

DI GORGONZOLA: Oh?

PIZZICATO: To tell him that I'm really not angry at all... On the contrary... That I'm delighted at his salary of ten thousand lira... Perfectly delighted for him... And that I would like nothing better than to renew our harmonious association.

DI GORGONZOLA [smiling]: And revive your opera, The... The...

PIZZICATO: The Interrupted Marriage... Quite... I have every intention... Especially if Your Eminence decides to take me into his household.

DI GORGONZOLA [hesitating]: Ah... Well... That's really another matter. I mean, we hardly heard enough to appreciate your talents.

[He turns aside, grimacing at the thought.]

PIZZICATO: But I assure Your Eminence... He only has to ask the soprano. I'm sure he'll be happy to vouch for me.

DI GORGONZOLA: Well... We'll see, maestro. I'll ask him. If he approves... And if my nephew and Signora Viola agree... I suppose... [Aside.] He has to play the organ better than he sings!

PIZZICATO [heaves a sigh; then, jubilant, aside]: Hallelujah, amen! [To DI GORGONZOLA.] Your Eminence won't regret his decision!

[As he begins humming Handel's Hallelujah Chorus to himself, voices can be heard offstage, approaching.]

THE PRINCE'S VOICE: No, no... I insist...

PIZZICATO [cocking an ear, aside]: Ah! His Highness, patron of the arts!

VIOLA'S VOICE: But Your Highness... I hardly think—

THE PRINCE [entering, up left, talking out the door, interrupting]: Please! It's all taken care of...

DI GORGONZOLA [rather surprised to see him back so soon]: Nephew?... [Pointing to the door.] Who...?

THE PRINCE [coming center, as PIZZICATO stands aside by the table, left]: Signora Viola, uncle... Making mountains out of moleskins, as usual...

PIZZICATO [aside]: "Mole..."?

THE PRINCE: I don't know why, but Caramello says that Signor Giannino's quarters won't be ready for a week. If I hadn't just happened to leave the rehearsal early, they were going to send the poor child back to his miserable inn.

PIZZICATO [who has been listening, casually butting in]: In a palace this size? There must be plenty of room!

DI GORGONZOLA [to THE PRINCE]: Nonsense! I won't hear of it.

THE PRINCE [after glaring in PIZZICATO's direction, to DI GORGONZOLA]: Exactly what I told her... So I've asked my valet to put him in my quarters, in the bedroom next to mine.

PIZZICATO [aside]: What?

DI GORGONZOLA [to THE PRINCE]: Won't he be in your way?

THE PRINCE: Not at all! That's where I want him.

PIZZICATO [aside]: But I don't, damn it!

THE PRINCE [to DI GORGONZOLA]: We'll make beautiful music from dawn to dusk.

DI GORGONZOLA: You?

PIZZICATO [*aside*]: And dusk to dawn!... With my wife? No thank you!

THE PRINCE [*to* DI GORGONZOLA]: And he'll give me lessons. He can teach me so much.

PIZZICATO [*aside*]: And vice versa, I'm afraid...

DI GORGONZOLA [*a little impatient, to* THE PRINCE]: Good heavens, nephew! What a passion for music!... I never knew... And what a sudden infatuation with our talented young friend!... [*To* PIZZICATO.] He won't let him out of his sight for an instant!

PIZZICATO [*anxious*]: Yes, I see...

DI GORGONZOLA [*to* THE PRINCE]: I must say, I find it a trifle surprising. [*Aside.*] Not to say disconcerting...

THE PRINCE: You would find it even more so, uncle, if you knew the reason why.

DI GORGONZOLA: I would?

THE PRINCE: If you knew that it's not our soprano himself that I'm so fond of...

DI GORGONZOLA: His talent, you mean?

THE PRINCE: Not even...

PIZZICATO [*to* THE PRINCE, *butting in again*]: His voice?

THE PRINCE [*after another glare at* PIZZICATO, *to* DI GORGONZOLA]: Perhaps I'm just a romantic young fool... But... [*As he slowly crosses right, reminiscing.*] What I love so much about him is... is a memory... A recollection... An uncanny resemblance...

DI GORGONZOLA: A what?

THE PRINCE: Yes, uncle... Believe it or not, he's the image of a beautiful young woman I once met.

PIZZICATO [*aside*]: Ayyy!

THE PRINCE: Feature for feature... The loveliest, the most charming... The most delightful...

DI GORGONZOLA: And you say you met this person...

THE PRINCE: Near my villa... One night, in the forest... All alone...

DI GORGONZOLA: You?

THE PRINCE: Her...

DI GORGONZOLA [*scandalized*]: Alone? A young woman...?

THE PRINCE [*up right*]: A newlywed, uncle... She had just lost her husband...

DI GORGONZOLA: Ah! A widow...

THE PRINCE: I hope so...

PIZZICATO [*aside, crossing himself*]: Miserere mei!

THE PRINCE [*to* DI GORGONZOLA]: And still in her wedding-dress... Crying her eyes out... So alone, so helpless...

DI GORGONZOLA: Tsk tsk tsk!

THE PRINCE: And in spite of it all, so beautiful... [*Coming down toward* DI GORGONZOLA.] Really, what else could I do? [*Dramatically, mixing metaphors.*] One doesn't just leave a rose among thorns, to wither on the vine!

PIZZICATO [*aside*]: Oh! Another viper!

THE PRINCE: I simply had to—

DI GORGONZOLA [*jumping to conclusions*]: What? You didn't!...

THE PRINCE: ...to come to her rescue, and... and offer her the hospitality of my villa.

DI GORGONZOLA ⎫   ⎧ Oh...
                 ⎬ [*together*]: ⎨
PIZZICATO [*aside*] ⎭   ⎩ Ayyy!

THE PRINCE [*to* DI GORGONZOLA]: She stayed for three days.

PIZZICATO [*aside*]: Madonna mia! And three nights...

THE PRINCE: Needless to say, I respected her like a sister.

PIZZICATO [*aloud, in spite of himself*]: Impossible!

THE PRINCE [*giving him a look*]: I beg your pardon?

PIZZICATO [*as agreeably as possible, to cover his faux pas*]: I mean... Your Highness is much too modest! It's... It's impossible for a prince as... as handsome as himself, not to... not to...

THE PRINCE: "Not to..."?

PIZZICATO: With a beautiful woman at his villa, that is... For three days... And all alone...

THE PRINCE: Signore!

PIZZICATO: Not to be led into temptation, Your Highness...

DI GORGONZOLA [*making the sign of the cross in* PIZZICATO's *direction*]: "But deliver us from evil..."

PIZZICATO [*justifying his observation, to* DI GORGONZOLA]: Just a little, Your Eminence...

THE PRINCE [*to* PIZZICATO]: Certainly not! Not for a moment... [*To* DI GORGONZOLA.] Though I have to admit, on the third day—

DI GORGONZOLA [*quipping, to* THE PRINCE]: You rose from the dead...

PIZZICATO [*to* THE PRINCE]: I knew it!

DI GORGONZOLA: "...secundum scripturas"!

THE PRINCE [*to* DI GORGONZOLA]: No, but I did begin to weaken.

DI GORGONZOLA: Please... [*Covering his ears.*] Spare me the details.

THE PRINCE: There are more, I'm afraid. On the third day she up and left... Ran away...

PIZZICATO [*relieved, aside*] ⎫   ⎧ Ah...
                                ⎬ [*together*]: ⎨
DI GORGONZOLA ⎭   ⎩ Oh?

THE PRINCE: Disappeared... And I couldn't find hide nor hair of her, no matter how I tried.

PIZZICATO [*with a sigh, raising
    his eyes to heaven, aside*] ⎫   ⎧ Gloria in excelsis Deo!
                                 ⎬ [*together*]: ⎨
DI GORGONZOLA [*nodding, aside*] ⎭   ⎩ So much the better!

THE PRINCE [*to* DI GORGONZOLA, *continuing*]: But imagine, uncle, how delighted I was when, there, in Signor Giannino, I found the living image of my beautiful stranger!

DI GORGONZOLA [*dismissing the thought*]: Pfff!

THE PRINCE: It's incredible! And not only her face... Her voice, especially... In that angel's voice of his!... Ah! [*Moving up center, fantasizing romantically.*] I'll make him sing for me all day long! I'll... I'll—

DI GORGONZOLA [*losing patience*]: Bah! [*Getting up, to* THE PRINCE.] And it's for a childish, foolish tale like that that Prince Giorgio, the nephew of Cardinal Di Gorgonzola, turns up his nose at a Manicotti...

PIZZICATO [*still down left*]: Tsk tsk tsk!

DI GORGONZOLA: ...with all the obvious advantages she represents... [*As* THE PRINCE *glares at* PIZZICATO.] for a woman he'll never see again! It's unheard of!

PIZZICATO [*to* THE PRINCE]: If Your Highness wants my opinion...

THE PRINCE [*glaring at him again; then, to* DI GORGONZOLA]: But I will, uncle! I know I will! My heart tells me I will!

DI GORGONZOLA: Your heart...

THE PRINCE: And when I do...

DI GORGONZOLA: My eye!

THE PRINCE: ...I'll never, never let her leave me. I swear it!

PIZZICATO [*risking an opinion, excited, to* THE PRINCE]: Perhaps Your Highness shouldn't swear. One never knows...

THE PRINCE: I beg your pardon!

PIZZICATO: Things happen... Obstacles...

DI GORGONZOLA: Exactly!

PIZZICATO: Perhaps her husband—

THE PRINCE: He's dead!

PIZZICATO: Maybe not... Who knows?

THE PRINCE: Then he will be!... If I find him, I'll kill him, and I'll marry her on the spot!

PIZZICATO [*aside*]: Ayyy!

[*He moves around the table and, during the following exchange, shuffles about, cowering by the window in an obvious quandary.*]

DI GORGONZOLA [*to* THE PRINCE]: Marry her? [*With a cynical laugh.*] And you think I'll permit...

[FRANCESCO *enters, up left.*]

FRANCESCO [*standing at the door, to* DI GORGONZOLA]: Your Eminence... His Eminence Cardinal Manicotti's notary has been waiting for some time.

DI GORGONZOLA: Ah! About the marriage contract... [*To* FRANCESCO, *waving him off.*] Yes... I'll be right there.

FRANCESCO: Very good, Your Eminence.

[*He leaves by the same door.*]

DI GORGONZOLA [*to* THE PRINCE]: I hope you didn't tell him...

THE PRINCE: Not a word... Why should I? It's your contract, uncle. It's none of my business!

DI GORGONZOLA: None of your... Oh! [*To himself.*] Did you ever... [*To* THE PRINCE, *moving up left.*] Now let's not be hasty. I'm sure something can be arranged. Let's consider the problem like mature human beings.

THE PRINCE: Fine... [*Moving down right.*] And while you're considering it, I'll go make sure that the young man's room is ready.

[*Both he and a disgruntled* DI GORGONZOLA *leave by their respective exits.*]

PIZZICATO [*to himself*]: Now what?... Would I rather be a cuckold... [*He gives his forehead a pair of horns with his index fingers.*] or a corpse? [*He draws his thumb across his throat.*] Either way I lose! [*Coming center.*] Ah! My head!... My poor head!... Whoever thought... So far, so good... [*Repeating the cuckold gesture.*] as far as these are concerned. Nothing has happened yet, to hear him tell it. But who knows, when she lives here! With her room next to his!... Woe is her!... [*Reflecting.*] Her?... Me! [*Clapping his hand to his forehead.*] Woe is me! Woe is me!... [*He begins pacing right and left.*] Ah! I should have guessed! I should have known that no prince could love music that much!... That... That he had to have an interior motive... [*He stops, briefly reflecting.*] "Exterior..."? [*Shrugging, continuing his pacing.*] Well, what does he think? That I'm just going to sit by, with my... my baton between my legs... pianissimo, tranquillo... while he... while she...? Me? A protégé of the great Pergolesi? [*Scornfully.*] Ha ha!... Fame and fortune are fine, but honor... [*Stopping in his tracks.*] Honor comes first!... [*Reflecting.*] Whenever possible... [*Pacing again.*] Does he think I'll hold still and not make any noise? [*Stopping and apostrophizing.*] Well, we'll see, Your Highness! I'll... I'll sing it from the rooftops!... Noise?... I'm not a musician for nothing, by Jes... [*Catching himself.*] By Gesualdo! [*Pacing again, angrily, then stopping.*] Besides, if she... if she... [*Emphasizing.*] performs with him, how many others will come and try to pluck her strings, as it were! [*Pacing, then stopping.*] No, no! No thank you! One Pizzicato per wife is quite enough! Marriage is a duet, not a... a concerto grosso! [*He begins pacing again.*] Of all the... [*Gradually calming down.*] Ah, well... [*To himself, stopping.*] Temper, maestro... Temper... Rallentando... Ritardando... [*Pacing.*] There has to be a way... Something... Something I can do to mute this young Romeo's passion... [*Reflecting.*] Something bold and daring... Heroic... [*Stopping short.*] Ah! I've got it!... A note to his uncle!... [*Going over to the writing-table, left.*] Anonymous, of course... [*Taking pen and paper, without sitting down.*] Something subtle but direct... [*Quickly, reading as he writes.*] "Your Eminence's castrato is a castrata..." [*Musing for a moment.*] Hmm... No... [*Taking another sheet of paper.*] "Your Eminence's castrato isn't. He's a woman. I can prove it." Signed "A friend"... There! Now we'll see how long she lives here! [*Folding the note and looking around for a place to put it.*] Hmm... How to get it to him...

VIOLA'S VOICE [*offstage, up left*]: His Eminence's Bible?

PIZZICATO [*continuing, to himself*]: That's the question...

VIOLA'S VOICE: In there, I think... On the table...

PIZZICATO [*pricking up his ears*]: His Bible?... Of course! [*He slips the note quickly into the Bible.*] Perfect!... [*As VIOLA enters, up left, obviously distraught, followed by a SERVANT.*] If he ever reads it...

VIOLA [*spying the Bible, to the SERVANT, pointing*]: Ah... See? [*She takes it and hands it to him.*] Quick! Take it to him!

[*The SERVANT bows and exits by the same door.*]

PIZZICATO [*to himself, watching him go*]: Clever of me, if I do say so myself! [*To VIOLA.*] Ah! Signora... [*Correcting himself.*] Viola... You seem upset.

VIOLA [*on the other side of the table from him*]: Oh! Benito...

PIZZICATO: Is something wrong?

VIOLA [*pointing up left*]: The soprano... Signor Giannino... [*Sighing, without thinking.*] She—

PIZZICATO [*pouncing on her gaffe*]: "She"?... You mean, you know...?

VIOLA: "Know"?

PIZZICATO: Her secret...

VIOLA [*protesting*]: No...

PIZZICATO: She told you?

VIOLA: No, no... She... [*Trying to recoup.*] He—

PIZZICATO: No... Please... I know! I know!

VIOLA [*surprised*]: You do? But—

PIZZICATO: Yes! I know!... She told me... He's a... She's a woman!... He's a she!

VIOLA [*frightened*]: Shhh! He... For God's sake, not so loud!... If His Eminence finds out... Or anyone else... If he ever suspected... [*Crossing herself.*] Dio mio! Heaven help us! [*Moving center, apostrophizing.*] Poor child!

PIZZICATO: So? The cardinal will lose a guest, and... and the prince will lose a neighbor... [*Aside.*] Thank goodness!

VIOLA: But... But that's not all, believe me! It's much worse! [*As* PIZZICATO *is about to question her.*] Just now... I was talking to Signor Caramello... His Eminence's majordomo...

PIZZICATO: I know...

VIOLA: To ask his advice... "Oh, signora!" he said. "If I were you, I'd be careful!" And then he told me about a soprano, years ago... Another one... A woman, who dressed up like a man and sang for the Holy Father and all his cardinals...

PIZZICATO: And...?

VIOLA: And when they found out, you can't imagine!... They threw her in the dungeon at Castelparadiso! With her husband too—

PIZZICATO: Her husband?

VIOLA: And they were never seen again!

PIZZICATO [*trembling*]: Castelparadiso?... With her husband...? But why...?

VIOLA: Because they said he was her accomplice... That it was all his idea...

PIZZICATO: But it wasn't!... I mean, it couldn't have been! It...

VIOLA [*ignoring his observation, looking off, up left, wringing her hands and apostrophizing*]: Poor child!

PIZZICATO		It didn't have to be...
	[*together*]:	
VIOLA		Tsk tsk tsk...

PIZZICATO: It... [*Babbling.*] It might have been, but... [*Aside.*] Ayyy!

VIOLA [*still apostrophizing*]: Poor child!

PIZZICATO [*looking off, up left, to himself*]: My note!... In his Bible!... [*Crossing himself.*] Kyrie eleison! The dungeon... God in heaven!

VIOLA [*to* PIZZICATO]: So you see, we have to be terribly careful! For her!...

PIZZICATO: Yes!... For her... For her... [*To himself.*] Lucky it's anonymous! No one knows about *me*, and there's no way they will!

[*Just then* GIANNINA *comes running in, up left, out of breath.*]

GIANNINA [*spying* PIZZICATO, *rushing down to him*]: Ah, signore! At last!... [*She gives him a hug and a kiss before a startled* VIOLA.] Now I can tell you...

PIZZICATO [*clearing his throat, objecting*]: But—

GIANNINA [*as he tries desperately to signal her subtly to keep quiet*]: Before, with the cardinal and the prince... You understand...

VIOLA: What?

GIANNINA [*to* PIZZICATO, *not noticing his attempts*]: I couldn't!... But now...

PIZZICATO [*trying to avoid her*]: Signore... I'm afraid...

GIANNINA: Since fate has brought you back to me...

VIOLA [*to* GIANNINA]: "Back"?...

PIZZICATO [*to* GIANNINA]: There must be some mistake...

[*He keeps trying to signal.*]

GIANNINA [*to* VIOLA, *ignoring him*]: Yes, signora! And he's my husband!

PIZZICATO [*aside*]: Ayyy!

GIANNINA [*to* VIOLA]: The one I lost... The one I thought I would never see again...

PIZZICATO ⎫   ⎧ Me?
         ⎬ [*together*]:   ⎨
VIOLA   ⎭   ⎩ Your husband?

PIZZICATO [*to* GIANNINA *starchily, for* VIOLA'*s benefit*]: Begging your pardon, signor... [*Hesitating.*] ...a... [*Correcting himself.*] ...e... But apparently you're mistaking me for somebody else. I'm afraid I don't know you.

GIANNINA: What? You—

PIZZICATO [*moving center, toward* VIOLA, *whispering to* GIANNINA *in passing*]: For God's sake! Don't say a word!

GIANNINA: But—

VIOLA [*to* PIZZICATO, *now standing on her left*]: You don't know him... her...? But you just told me... You knew that he—

PIZZICATO: I know, but—

VIOLA: That she...

PIZZICATO [*defensively*]: But I had nothing to do with it, believe me!

VIOLA: "To do..." Whoever said...?

GIANNINA [*to* PIZZICATO, *archly*]: So, signore! You're not my husband?

PIZZICATO [*approaching her*]: Me? [*Whispering.*] Please! Not a word!... Castelparadiso... [*Moving back to* VIOLA, *with a disclaiming shrug and shake of the head.*] Signora...

VIOLA [*still confused, to* PIZZICATO]: Signore...

GIANNINA [*on the verge of tears, uncomprehending*]: Oh!

[*She goes over to the window, down left.*]

PIZZICATO [*coming down center, toward the chairs, aside*]: Madonna mia! There must be an easier way to get married! [*To* VIOLA.] I think I'd better be going.

[*He moves toward the door, up left, as if to leave.*]

GIANNINA [*back turned to him, sobbing*]: Abandoning me again?... How could he! [*Turning, watching him.*] Just when I needed him most!... Just when His Highness... The prince... Not ten minutes ago...

PIZZICATO [*jumping to conclusions, stopping short at the threshold, to* GIANNINA]: The prince? What did he... [*Coming down and standing between her and* VIOLA.] What about the prince? What? What?

GIANNINA *and* VIOLA [*together*]: "What"?

PIZZICATO [*to* GIANNINA, *reiterating*]: What!... What, I asked you! What!

GIANNINA [*to* PIZZICATO]: What business could it possibly be of yours, signore? You're not my husband!

VIOLA [*to* PIZZICATO]: You're not her—

PIZZICATO [*moving back and forth between them, stammering*]: No, no... I... But... But I... I want to know! I... I have to... [*To* VIOLA, *pointing to* GIANNINA.] For her... To protect her... [*Aside to* GIANNINA, *whispering.*] Please! Be patient! I'll explain... [*Aloud, to* VIOLA, *beginning to babble.*] A selfless act of chastity... [*Correcting himself.*] Of charity... Charity, signora... That's how I am! My heart... My soul... [*To* GIANNINA.] My head... Castelparadiso... [*Clutching his throat.*] My neck... [*Moving back toward* VIOLA, *as* DI GORGONZOLA *can be heard offstage, aside.*] Madonna mia! What am I... I don't know what I'm saying!

[DI GORGONZOLA *enters, up left.*]

VIOLA: Ah! His Eminence...

DI GORGONZOLA: By Lucifer! Some people!... Cursèd disciples of Satan!

VIOLA [*as he approaches her, center*]: Your Eminence?

DI GORGONZOLA: Can you imagine? [*Brandishing* PIZZICATO'*s note.*] This... This...

VIOLA   ⎫   ⎰ What is it?
                         ⎬ [*together*]:   ⎱
PIZZICATO [*aside*]   ⎭   Ayyy!

DI GORGONZOLA: An anonymous letter! In this day and age!

PIZZICATO [*aside*]: At least he'll never guess...

[*He begins casually crossing right, as if intending to leave.*]

DI GORGONZOLA: Just listen! [*Reading.*] "Your Eminence's castrato isn't. He's a woman. I can prove it."

VIOLA   ⎫   ⎰ Outrageous!
                                  ⎬ [*together*]:   ⎱
GIANNINA [*still at the window, aside*] ⎭   God in heaven!

DI GORGONZOLA [*to* VIOLA]: Oh, don't worry! I don't believe it for a moment. I have eyes to see with, thank goodness! [*Looking at* GIANNINA, *moving toward her.*] Eyes to see with!... [*Pointedly, as* GIANNINA *gives him a wan little smile.*] And ears to hear why the scoundrel wrote it!

VIOLA: "The..." Then Your Eminence knows who...?

DI GORGONZOLA [*standing between the two women, menacingly*]: I do indeed! [*To* GIANNINA, *as* PIZZICATO *stops, down right, facing the footlights, agape.*] A wretch, signora!... [*To* VIOLA.] An ungrateful blackguard, welcomed into my household with your blessing...

VIOLA: Me?

DI GORGONZOLA [*pulling another sheet of paper from a pocket*]: Fortunately I still have one of his letters... [*Glaring at* PIZZICATO.] His many, many letters... And I could compare the handwriting... [*Waving both letters, to a mortified* PIZZICATO.] Maestro Pizzicato!

PIZZICATO [*innocently*]   ⎫   ⎰ Me?
VIOLA   ⎬ [*together*]:   ⎨ What?
GIANNINA   ⎭   ⎱ Him?

VIOLA [*approaching* PIZZICATO]: You, Beni... [*Catching herself.*] You, signore?

GIANNINA [*aside, trying to remain*
inconspicuous]   ⎫   ⎰ Oh my...
                                    ⎬ [*together*]:   ⎱
DI GORGONZOLA [*approaching him,*
waving the letters]   ⎭   Well?

PIZZICATO [*to* DI GORGONZOLA]: Your Eminence, I... I...

DI GORGONZOLA: You... You... "You, you" what? [PIZZICATO *opens his mouth to reply but nothing comes out.*] Well?... Why did you write it?... Why? Why?

PIZZICATO [*inadvertently echoing*]: I... I... [*As casually as he can.*] No reason, Your Eminence... I... I wanted to try a new quill I'd just sharpened...

DI GORGONZOLA and VIOLA [*together*]: What?

PIZZICATO: I... I...

DI GORGONZOLA [*to* PIZZICATO]: Come now! Surely you must have had one!

PIZZICATO [*with feigned good nature*]: A quill, Your Eminence?

DI GORGONZOLA [*sharply*]: A reason, by all the saints!

PIZZICATO: No...

DI GORGONZOLA: Then you're nothing but a vicious scandalmonger!

PIZZICATO: More... Much more... A protégé of—

DI GORGONZOLA [*cutting him off*]: Then prove your accusation, my friend! [*With a sarcastic smile, pointing to* GIANNINA, *still cowering by the window.*] Prove to me that Signor Giannino is a woman!

PIZZICATO		
VIOLA	[*together*]:	Prove...?
GIANNINA [*aside*]		Your Eminence...
		Oh!

DI GORGONZOLA [*to* PIZZICATO]: If not, I'll have you taken away in chains and thrown into prison!

PIZZICATO [*terrified*]: But—

DI GORGONZOLA: And let you rot!

PIZZICATO: But...

GIANNINA: But...

VIOLA: But...

DI GORGONZOLA: The honor of my household demands it! [*To* VIOLA.] Prison, unless he talks!

PIZZICATO [*aside*]: And Castelparadiso if I do!... Madonna mia!

[FRANCESCO *enters, up left.*]

FRANCESCO [*standing at the door*]: Your Eminence...

DI GORGONZOLA: Yes, Francesco? What is it?

FRANCESCO [*moving toward him, holding out a paper*]: The marriage contract, Your Eminence... Cardinal Manicotti's notary has brought it back.

DI GORGONZOLA: Indeed!

FRANCESCO: He says everything is in order, according to Your Eminence's wishes, and that it only requires Your Eminence's signature and that of His Highness.

DI GORGONZOLA [*angrily*]: And would he like me to move the Rock of Gibraltar?

FRANCESCO: He didn't say, Your Eminence.

DI GORGONZOLA [*grabbing the contract from him, crumpling it up*]: Ha! Just what I need!... [*Storming up right.*] Already?... He couldn't give me a few more days to convince the prince?... Make him listen to reason... He couldn't let me wait...?

VIOLA [*aside*]: Until the cow comes home!

FRANCESCO [*to* DI GORGONZOLA]: He said something about striking while the iron is hot, Your Eminence.

DI GORGONZOLA: Ha!... Hot?... [*To* FRANCESCO.] But it's cold, Francesco!... [*Pacing back and forth, up right.*] Cold! Cold! Cold!

FRANCESCO: Yes, Your Eminence.

VIOLA [*to* DI GORGONZOLA, *moving toward him*]: Please! Your Eminence mustn't excite himself. It's not good for his liver.

DI GORGONZOLA: I don't care! [*Sputtering.*] I'm... He... I'll fix him!... [*Looking at* GIANNINA.] I'll cut him off!

VIOLA [*to* DI GORGONZOLA, *misunderstanding, pointing at* GIANNINA]: Him? The castra—

DI GORGONZOLA [*ignoring her*]: I'll disinherit the rapscallion!... But first I'll

get my revenge... [*Pointing to* PIZZICATO, *still down right.*] On that one!...
[*To* FRANCESCO.] Get the hangman, Francesco!

FRANCESCO: Yes, Your Eminence.

[*He exits, up left, as* DI GORGONZOLA *comes stalking toward center stage.*]

PIZZICATO [*to* DI GORGONZOLA]: Really... I'd rather rot, if it's all the same...

GIANNINA [*moving to intercept*
    DI GORGONZOLA*]*
VIOLA [*to* DI GORGONZOLA,
    following him]   } [*together*]: { Wait... Wait...

    Please, Your Eminence...

GIANNINA [*continuing*]: There's something Your Eminence still doesn't know.

DI GORGONZOLA [*stopping, center*]: More treachery of his, signore?

GIANNINA: Well...

DI GORGONZOLA: Tell me...

PIZZICATO [*aside*]: "Hell hath no fury..."

DI GORGONZOLA [*to* GIANNINA]: I'm listening!

GIANNINA: I... I would, Your Eminence, but... but only if Your Eminence can find it in his heart to show mercy...

DI GORGONZOLA [*pointing at* PIZZICATO]: To him? That... That...

PIZZICATO [*aside*]: Ah...

GIANNINA: No, not him...

PIZZICATO [*aside*]: Oh...

GIANNINA: Someone else...

DI GORGONZOLA [*pacing up and down, angrily*]: No one, signore! No one!

VIOLA [*to* DI GORGONZOLA]: Please! Your Eminence's liver...

DI GORGONZOLA [*to* VIOLA]: No one! I'm in no mood for mercy!

VIOLA: His gall bladder... His spleen...

GIANNINA: Even if I promise to convince his nephew?... To persuade him to sign that contract...?

DI GORGONZOLA [*holding up the crumpled contract*]: This?... Ha! If you can, you're not a musician. You're a magician!

GIANNINA: I can!

DI GORGONZOLA [*down center, by the chairs*]: Do that, and anything you name is yours! Anything!

GIANNINA: I have Your Eminence's word?

DI GORGONZOLA: More than my word... [*Crossing himself.*] My solemn promise!... [GIANNINA *takes the contract from him.*] But how the devil—

VIOLA [*putting her hand to her mouth, shocked*]: Your Eminence!

DI GORGONZOLA [*to* GIANNINA]: How on earth do you think you can do that?

GIANNINA: If Your Eminence would leave the details to me... That's my affair.

[THE PRINCE *can be heard offstage, humming a tune, approaching.*]

PIZZICATO [*edging gradually upstage and toward the left, as if intent on escape, aside*]: And mine too, I'm afraid!

GIANNINA [*crossing right, joining* VIOLA]: Ah! The prince... [*To* DI GORGONZOLA.] If Your Eminence would be good enough to leave me alone with him...

VIOLA [*aside to* GIANNINA,
    softly]
PIZZICATO [*stopping up
    right, to himself*]   } [*together*]: { Are you sure?

    Alone?... With *him*?...

GIANNINA [*aside to* VIOLA, *softly*]: Trust me, signora.

DI GORGONZOLA [*to* GIANNINA]: Well, if you think... [*Going up left, calling.*] Francesco! [*Returning down center, to* GIANNINA.] Believe me, it will be a miracle!

[*As* PIZZICATO *continues edging left, toward the door,* FRANCESCO *and* THE PRINCE *enter simultaneously; the former, up left, and the latter, down right, humming.*]

FRANCESCO: Your Eminence?

DI GORGONZOLA [*to* FRANCESCO, *pointing at* PIZZICATO, *now up left*]: Him!... Take him away!

FRANCESCO [*seizing* PIZZICATO]: Very good, Your Eminence.

PIZZICATO   }   { But... But...
                                                     } [*together*]:   {
THE PRINCE [*down right, to* DI GORGONZOLA]   }   { Uncle?

DI GORGONZOLA [*to* THE PRINCE]: And, as for you, nephew... You stay here with him. [*He points to* GIANNINA, *who is still standing center with* VIOLA.] And do what he tells you! Or else, never bother to darken my door again!

THE PRINCE: What?

DI GORGONZOLA [*gesturing to* FRANCESCO *to remove the recalcitrant* PIZZICATO; *then, to* THE PRINCE]: You heard me!

PIZZICATO: But... I'm a protégé of Pergolesi...

DI GORGONZOLA [*to* VIOLA]: Come, signora...

PIZZICATO: A... A collaborator of Cimarosa...

[*He continues voicing appropriate objections as* FRANCESCO *hauls him off, down right, followed out by* VIOLA *and* DI GORGONZOLA.]

THE PRINCE [*after a brief silence, joining* GIANNINA, *center*]: You have something to tell me, signore?

GIANNINA [*timidly*]: I do, Your Highness... About... [*Uncrumpling the contract and holding it up.*] About Your Highness's marriage...

THE PRINCE: Oh?

GIANNINA [*moving slowly left, back turned to him*]: Yesterday he was willing, and today he refuses.

THE PRINCE [*following her*]: But that was yesterday, signore. I told you... Since last night... Since I laid eyes on you, and... and remembered...

GIANNINA [*at the window, still with her back turned, completing his sentence*]: ...a woman that Your Highness hardly saw... and that he'll never see again...

THE PRINCE [*moving toward her and standing by the writing-table, as she gazes nostalgically out the window*]: Please! It breaks my heart to hear you say that!... Besides, who knows? Perhaps some day...

GIANNINA [*with an involuntary little cry*]: Ah...

THE PRINCE: But for now, I only want to remember... [*Sighing.*] To relive those illusions that I cherished by her side... The fantasies... [*Passionately.*] Memories... Like that moment when I pressed her sweet hand to my lips... The hand that she held out to me—

GIANNINA [*quickly turning to face him, forgetting protocol, correcting*]: That you took!... [*Catching herself.*] That your Highness took, Your Highness!...

THE PRINCE [*surprised*]: Ah?

GIANNINA [*emphasizing*]: That he *took*!...

THE PRINCE: Who... How did you... Who told you, signore? I never told a soul!

GIANNINA [*embarrassed*]: I... Who... Who else does Your Highness think could have told me, if... if not the lady herself?

THE PRINCE: Herself?... You mean, you... You've seen her?... [*Approaching her, excited.*] You know her?

GIANNINA [*avoiding him, moving right, around behind him*]: Know her? [*Stopping, center stage, stalling for time.*] I should hope I would know her!... I... [*Sighing.*] Ah... Since I can't hide the truth any longer...

THE PRINCE: Yes? Yes?

GIANNINA: The resemblance that Your Highness noticed...

THE PRINCE: Yes?

GIANNINA: I should think he might have guessed that... that it's because... because I... I...

THE PRINCE [*more and more excited*]: Yes? You...

GIANNINA: I have a sister!

THE PRINCE: A... You mean, she... My beautiful stranger...

GIANNINA: Yes, Your Highness... She's my sister...

THE PRINCE: Ah! Your... Your sister!... [*Pacing right and left, in front of her.*] You're right! I should have guessed! No two strangers could possibly... [*Stopping, center, and embracing her, elated.*] Ah! Signore!... Giannino! Then... That means that... Tell me about her...

GIANNINA [*breaking free, trying to interrupt*]: Your Highness—

THE PRINCE: Where is she? What is she doing?... When—

GIANNINA: Your Highness—

THE PRINCE: When can I see her?... Does she know that I think of her, day and night? That I can't put her out of my mind?... That I can't forget her...

GIANNINA: But Your Highness will have to... He must!

THE PRINCE [*pacing again*]: Forget her? Me?... Impossible! Tell Orpheus to forget Eurydice!... Tell... Tell Abélard to forget Eloise!...

GIANNINA: Well, under the circumstances...

THE PRINCE: Tell Paris to forget Helen!

GIANNINA: But she wants him to...

THE PRINCE [*stopping, right*]: No! She can't mean it!

GIANNINA: She begs him... [*Imitating.*] "Tell him he has to forget me! Please!..." That's what she said... [*Imitating, but not without difficulty.*] "For me... For me... For my sake! He must!"

THE PRINCE: Ah...

GIANNINA: And she's right... If Your Highness will pardon the liberty... What hope does he have? I... I... [*Catching herself.*] I mean, she... she has a husband. [*A little wistfully.*] A husband that she loves...

THE PRINCE: You don't know what you're saying! She doesn't!

GIANNINA: But I do... [*Catching herself again.*] I do know what I'm saying! She does, Your Highness... She loves him. [*Aside.*] At least, she should...

THE PRINCE [*reproachfully*]: Ah! Giannino, Giannino!... He means more to you than I do, this brother-in-law of yours!

GIANNINA [*in spite of herself*]: Oh no! He... I—

THE PRINCE: Then tell me where she is...

GIANNINA: But... I can't! She made me swear—

THE PRINCE: Please! I'm begging you! See?... [*Getting down his knees.*] If... If you have any affection at all for me...

GIANNINA [*tenderly*]: Your Highness...

THE PRINCE: Please! I wouldn't do anything to hurt her... I... When she knows how much I love her, and...

GIANNINA: But—

THE PRINCE: ...and how much I've suffered since she left me, Giannino... She can't be so heartless!

GIANNINA: But Your Highness—

THE PRINCE: If I have to give her up... If... If she orders me to, I will. But at least... at least let me hear it from her lips. Let me see her... Just one more time, Giannino...

GIANNINA: But...

THE PRINCE: I beg you. Just one more time...

GIANNINA: What? To see her just once—

THE PRINCE: I would give my fortune!... My villa, my hounds, my... Everything! My... My life!

GIANNINA: That much?

THE PRINCE: And more!

GIANNINA: Really, Your Highness doesn't have to... If only he obeys his uncle... [*Holding up the contract.*] If only he signs this... I can promise him, he'll see her!

THE PRINCE [*standing up*]: I will? I'll see her? You... You're sure?... You promise?

GIANNINA: I swear, Your Highness.

THE PRINCE: When? When?... How soon?

GIANNINA: Tomorrow...

THE PRINCE: Tomor... [*Seizing the contract from her.*] Here! Let me have it! [*He takes it over to the writing-table.*]

GIANNINA [*with very mixed emotions*]: Ah...

THE PRINCE [*preparing to sign*]: You see? For one day of happiness... [*He goes to sign, then stops.*] You'll tell her, Giannino, won't you? You'll tell her that, for one day... one moment of happiness... [*About to sign, but stopping again.*] You'll tell her what a sacrifice I'm making, just to see her... [*He heaves a resigned sigh, signs the contract, and leaves it on the table.*]

GIANNINA [*sadly*]: I will, Your Highness.

THE PRINCE [*looking at the contract, as* GIANNINA *brushes away a tear or two, to himself*]: Good God! [*Shaking his head.*] Mine, for life... That cow!... [*Aloud, to* GIANNINA, *noticing her tears.*] Why... What is it, my friend? What's the trouble? Why are you—

GIANNINA [*recovering her aplomb*]: No, no... Nothing... I was thinking how much Your Highness deserves the love of a woman like mys... [*Catching herself.*] my sister, and how touched she's going to be. [*Moving right, looking off into space, sadly.*] He must love her very much...

THE PRINCE: Ah...

GIANNINA [*facing him*]: Well, such noble, selfless love should be rewarded! And it will be!... Your Highness will see her today! [*Holding out her hand to him.*] This very day...

THE PRINCE [*rushing to her side, ecstatic*]: Today? [*He throws his arms around her neck and covers her with kisses.*] Ah! My friend... My dear, dear friend!

GIANNINA: Please...

THE PRINCE: Today?

[PIZZICATO *is heard offstage, quickly approaching.*]

PIZZICATO'S VOICE: But I tell you... Pergolesi... Cimarosa, for heaven's sake!...

GIANNINA [*struggling to break free, to* THE PRINCE]: Please, Your Highness...

PIZZICATO [*running in down right, looking back over his shoulder*]: Ayyy!... Dies irae!...

GIANNINA [*as he crosses up left, aside*]: Him!

THE PRINCE [*to* GIANNINA, *still embracing her*]: You've made me the happiest man alive!

PIZZICATO [*overhearing, stopping short*]: What?

FRANCESCO [*entering, down right, in pursuit, to* PIZZICATO]: Signore!

THE PRINCE [*to* GIANNINA, *continuing*]: What more could you give me?

GIANNINA [*to* THE PRINCE, *breaking free*]
PIZZICATO [*avoiding* FRANCESCO, *to himself*]
} [*together*]: { Please... Please...
"What more..." [*Slapping his forehead.*] She didn't!

FRANCESCO [*to* PIZZICATO]: Come, you!

GIANNINA [*in tears, running off, down right*]: Oh...

PIZZICATO [*to* THE PRINCE, *approaching him, menacingly*]: That's quite enough, Your Highness!

THE PRINCE [*to* PIZZICATO, *startled, finally noticing him*]: You? [*Waving off* FRANCESCO, *who has been trying to apprehend* PIZZICATO, *to the latter.*] How dare you...

[FRANCESCO *gives a little shrug and exits, down right.*]

PIZZICATO [*center stage*]: No one manhandles my wife!

THE PRINCE [*agape*]: Your...

PIZZICATO [*to himself*]: "Womanhandles"?...

THE PRINCE: Your... Your...

PIZZICATO [*to* THE PRINCE]: Not even a prince!

THE PRINCE: Your wife? [*Pointing down right.*] How... [*Pointing to* PIZZICATO.] You?

PIZZICATO: Me! [*Pointing down right.*] Him... Her... The soprano!

THE PRINCE: What?... But his sister... [*With a sudden realization.*] My beautiful stranger... [*To* PIZZICATO.] You mean, he's a woman?

PIZZICATO [*snidely*]: Oh yes! As if Your Highness didn't know!

THE PRINCE: But... But I didn't! I... I swear! I—

PIZZICATO [*surprised*]: Oh?... But just now... She and Your Highness... [*He mimes hugs and kisses.*]

THE PRINCE [*ignoring him*]: How can he... How can she... [*To* PIZZICATO.] Are you sure?

PIZZICATO [*reflecting briefly*]: Well, almost... I never had time to... But I'm sure he's my wife!

THE PRINCE: Why didn't you tell me before? Why didn't you—

PIZZICATO: Of course! And let Your Highness kill her husband? Much obliged!

THE PRINCE [*pacing back and forth between him and the writing-table*]: But... But she... I... Just a word... Just a hint... [*At the table, pointing to the contract, shaking his head.*] Before... Before this... Before I ruined my life forever! [*Picking it up, determined.*] Well, we'll see about that!

[*As he is about to rip up the contract,* DI GORGONZOLA *comes rushing in, down right, quickly crossing left to him.*]

DI GORGONZOLA [*jubilant*]: Ah! Nephew, nephew... [*Snatching the contract from his hands.*] Signor Giannino just told me the splendid news! Congratulations! What a match! [*To* PIZZICATO.] What a match! [*To* THE PRINCE.] A match made in heaven!

THE PRINCE [*under his breath*]: In hell, you mean!

DI GORGONZOLA: Manicotti has been consumed... [*To* PIZZICATO.] Devoured with doubt... [*To* THE PRINCE.] I can't wait to tell him!... [*To* PIZZICATO.] You'll play at the wedding, maestro! [*Aside.*] Just not *Abu Ibn Hooha!*... [*To* THE PRINCE.] I'll celebrate the nuptial mass myself... [*As an afterthought.*] Unless the Holy Father, that is...

THE PRINCE: And Giannino?

DI GORGONZOLA [*absorbed in his thought*]: Ah! What an opportunity! The whole College of Cardinals...

THE PRINCE: And Giannino?

DI GORGONZOLA [*finally hearing him*]: Why, he'll sing, of course!

THE PRINCE [*impatient*]: Where is he, uncle?

DI GORGONZOLA: Where?... [*Looking around.*] Why, I thought I would find him here... When he saw how delighted I was, the dear child, he couldn't hold back the tears... I gave him a great big hug and a kiss!

PIZZICATO [*aside*]: Him too?

THE PRINCE [*to* DI GORGONZOLA]: But where is he?

DI GORGONZOLA: Then he ran off... Something about "keeping my promise to His Highness," I thought he said... I was sure he would be here.

[*Just then* VIOLA *enters, down right.*]

VIOLA [*to* DI GORGONZOLA, *overhearing*]: He is, Your Eminence!

DI GORGONZOLA [*looking around*]: Where?

VIOLA [*as* GIANNINA, *dressed as a woman, follows her in*]: Right behind me...

THE PRINCE	} [*together*]: {	Ah!... Her!
DI GORGONZOLA [*horrified*]		A woman!

PIZZICATO: Thank heaven!

GIANNINA [*to* DI GORGONZOLA, *pointing to* PIZZICATO]: His wife, Your Eminence!

PIZZICATO: My... [*To* DI GORGONZOLA.] Yes... But don't blame me!

DI GORGONZOLA	} [*together*]: {	A... A woman!
PIZZICATO		I had nothing to do with it!

GIANNINA [*to* DI GORGONZOLA]: Besides, there's no harm. We're leaving at once for Naples.

THE PRINCE: Naples?

GIANNINA [*to* THE PRINCE]: They've made me an offer there of twenty thousand lira, Your Highness...

PIZZICATO: Twenty thousand?...

GIANNINA [*to* THE PRINCE]: I really can't refuse.

PIZZICATO: Refuse?... [*To* GIANNINA.] Ah! Giannina... Giannina mia... At last I've found you! After so many lonely days...

VIOLA [*aside*]: And nights...

DI GORGONZOLA [*still aghast*]: He's a woman!... [*With a sudden realization, gasping.*] And... Oh! I... I... [*Crossing himself furiously.*] Santa Maria, madre di Dio! I... I kissed her!

GIANNINA [*joining* PIZZICATO, *center, and timidly addressing* DI GORGONZOLA]: Can Your Eminence forgive me?

DI GORGONZOLA [*gazing heavenward*]: A woman!

GIANNINA: I'm afraid I've violated one of his strictest rules...

DI GORGONZOLA [*hardly listening*]: And here!... In my palace!

GIANNINA: ...and that I've caused him much more trouble than I'd imagined.

DI GORGONZOLA [*to* GIANNINA]: You're a woman, signore! Do you realize that?

GIANNINA [*with a timid smile*]: I think so...

DI GORGONZOLA: At least, if you were a castrato...

PIZZICATO [*aside, as* VIOLA *gives a little shudder*]: Thank you!

DI GORGONZOLA: ...I wouldn't have lost my honor!

VIOLA		No, but she would have lost her... [*Confused.*]
	[*together*]:	He... She... That is...
THE PRINCE		No, but he would have lost his... [*Confused.*]
		She... He... That is...

[*They look at each other and shrug.*]

GIANNINA [*to* DI GORGONZOLA]: I hope that, since I did help Your Eminence realize his fondest dream...

VIOLA [*aside*]		Well, almost his fondest...
THE PRINCE [*with a gesture of disgusted resignation*]	[*together*]:	Ugh!

GIANNINA [*to* DI GORGONZOLA]: I hope that he won't let anyone know my secret.

DI GORGONZOLA: Ha! You needn't worry! I have no intention of being the laughingstock of the College! [*Aside.*] If they ever found out... [*To* VIOLA, *approaching her, right.*] You hear, signora? Not a word!... Not one syllable!

VIOLA: My lips are sealed!

GIANNINA [*to* DI GORGONZOLA]: Your Eminence is too kind. Nothing will ever make me forget... [*Continuing, but looking at* THE PRINCE, *tenderly.*] his consideration and affection... I'll always remember him, wherever I go.

PIZZICATO [*to* DI GORGONZOLA, *pro forma*]: Likewise... Even Naples...

DI GORGONZOLA [*to* GIANNINA, *unconvincingly*]: Yes... Thank you... [*To* PIZZICATO.] Thank you...

THE PRINCE [*to* PIZZICATO]: And rest asssured, we'll always remember your music, maestro...

PIZZICATO [*surprised*]: Oh? I didn't think—

THE PRINCE: That memorable duet from... from *Aba Ibn Hoohoo*...

PIZZICATO [*deferentially*]: *Abu Ibn Hooha*, Your Highness...

THE PRINCE: Yes... [*Continuing, but looking at* GIANNINA, *nostalgically.*] And all the duets that might have been... [*With a sly smile.*] And others yet to come... [*Looking at* PIZZICATO *again.*] From the talented pen of Maestro Pizzicato... Protégé of Pergolesi...

PIZZICATO: Ah! [*Delighted.*] Your Highness...

VIOLA: And collaborator of Cimarosa...

THE PRINCE [*to* PIZZICATO]: Please... [*Joining him and* GIANNINA, *center, standing behind them, arms outstretched in a gesture of embrace, to* PIZZICATO.] Think of me as your friend... Your protector... [*Turning subtly to* GIANNINA, *with a look full of innuendo.*] Your... Your... [*Turning back to*

PIZZICATO.] patron... Ready to spread your fame far and wide...

PIZZICATO: Ah...

THE PRINCE: The world has waited too long for *Abu Ibn Hahoo,* my friends.

PIZZICATO, GIANNINA, VIOLA *and* DI GORGONZOLA [*together*]: Hooha...

THE PRINCE: *Hooha... Hooha...*

PIZZICATO [*to* THE PRINCE, *ecstatic*]: And my masses?... My cantatas?... My oratorios?... My—

THE PRINCE: Everything! Every note you ever wrote, or write...

DI GORGONZOLA [*to* PIZZICATO, *good-humored*]: Except the anonymous ones, that is!

PIZZICATO [*to* DI GORGONZOLA, *as the others laugh obligingly*]: Never again, Your Eminence!

THE PRINCE [*leaving* GIANNINA *and* PIZZICATO, *striding up left, to* DI GORGONZOLA]: Now then, uncle dear... If I recall correctly, you did say that, once I promised to marry that... that...

VIOLA [*aside*]: Cow...

THE PRINCE: ...that charming creature, you would have no objection if I went traveling a little?

DI GORGONZOLA [*joining him*]: None at all!...

THE PRINCE [*aside*]: To the ends of the earth!

DI GORGONZOLA: None at all!...

THE PRINCE: Good! Then I leave tomorrow...

DI GORGONZOLA: Tomorrow? But—

THE PRINCE: At dawn... [DI GORGONZOLA *gives a shrug.*] And my first stop is Naples.

DI GORGONZOLA, VIOLA, GIANNINA, *and* PIZZICATO [*together*]: Naples?

THE PRINCE: To attend the debut of a certain young soprano!...

GIANNINA [*aside*]   ⎫   ⎧ Ah...
                                           ⎬ [*together*]: ⎨
DI GORGONZOLA [*going up left, calling*] ⎭   ⎩ Francesco!

PIZZICATO [*to* THE PRINCE]: And to applaud her husband's triumphs, Your Highness!

THE PRINCE: Her... [*Coming over to* PIZZICATO, *with exaggerated enthusiasm.*] Of course, my friend! Her husband...

FRANCESCO [*entering*]: Your Eminence?

PIZZICATO [*to* GIANNINA]: Just think of the duets!

DI GORGONZOLA [*to* FRANCESCO]: Go send for His Eminence, Cardinal Manicotti.

THE PRINCE [*aside*]: Just think of the trios!

FRANCESCO [*to* DI GORGONZOLA]: Yes, Your Eminence.

[*He leaves, as* THE PRINCE *stands shaking* PIZZICATO's *hand and looking tenderly at* GIANNINA.]

DI GORGONZOLA [*crossing down right, behind them*]: We have a wedding to plan, he and I... [*To* VIOLA.] A banquet, signora... Every Gorgonzola and Manicotti for miles around...

VIOLA [*nodding*]: Your Eminence...

DI GORGONZOLA [*joining her*]: With His Holiness... And the College of Cardinals... All of them... [*Confidentially.*] After all, you never know... Some day... Some day...

CURTAIN

IT'S ALL RELATIVE

Adaptation of

Les Suites d'un premier lit

by

Eugène Labiche and Marc-Michel

(1852)

CHARACTERS

TREBUCHARD, a bachelor in his late thirties or early forties, well-off and eager to get married

PRUDENVAL, the father of Trébuchard's latest fiancée, something of a hypochondriac

PIQUOISEAU, a military man, dashing but none too bright

CLAUDINE, Prudenval's beautiful young daughter, Trébuchard's fiancée

MATHILDE, Trébuchard's middle-aged and quite unattractive stepdaughter by a previous marriage

DELPHINE, his maid

Trébuchard's well-furnished salon. A door, up left, set diagonally into the corner, leads to the outside; another door, similarly set up right, leads to other rooms of the apartment. In the upstage wall, two open French doors looking out on a small balcony, whose railing, above the street, is visible. Two other doors, down left and down right, lead, respectively, to Mathilde's and Trébuchard's rooms. Near the upstage wall, to the left of the balcony, a coatrack with Mathilde's hat and shawl, and Trébuchard's hat and coat. On the upstage wall, to the right of the balcony, a cuckoo clock. Down right, a little serving-cart or table, with bottles, glasses, a carafe of wine, an ashtray, etc. Behind it, on the wall down right, a mirror. Midstage left, two armchairs facing the audience and at a slight angle to each other. Down left, a table. Other furniture—lamps, chairs, loveseat, pictures, etc.—ad libitum.

At rise, DELPHINE *is out on the balcony with dustpan and broom.*

DELPHINE: Damnation! Not again!... Butts, butts, butts!... Every day... *[Pointing and counting, half under her breath.]* One, two... Five, six, seven... Eleven, twelve... Fourteen! *[With a sigh of disgust.]* Fourteen of his damn cigar butts! *[She gives a look up at the window of the floor above, hands on hips, shaking her head.]* Oh! *[Carefully sweeping up the butts into the dustpan.]* Some people!... They just don't care where they throw their trash!... Tsk tsk tsk!... I never... *[She proceeds to empty the dustpan over the railing, into the street, still shaking her head, as* TREBUCHARD *enters, down right, overhearing her complaint.]*

TREBUCHARD: You never what, Delphine? What's the matter this time?

DELPHINE *[at the threshold]*: The matter, monsieur? *[Pointing to the balcony.]* That! That's the matter! *[*TREBUCHARD *gives a quizzical look outside.]* Fourteen this morning!... Fourteen more cigar butts...

TREBUCHARD *[suddenly comprehending]*: Oh...

DELPHINE: Fourteen, monsieur!

[She puts the dustpan and broom aside, against the rear wall, and indicates "fourteen" with the fingers of both hands: ten, ten, and four.]

TREBUCHARD: Yes, I heard you.

DELPHINE: It's a disgrace, that's what it is!

TREBUCHARD: I must say he's improving! Yesterday it was only a dozen.

DELPHINE *[grumbling to herself]*: If he thinks all I have to do...

TREBUCHARD: Who the devil does he think he is? Officer or not... Since when is my balcony that idiot's private ashtray! I mean, some of my best friends are soldiers, but still...

DELPHINE: At this rate, monsieur, by the end of the year... Well, monsieur can just imagine...

TREBUCHARD: Quite!... Perhaps I should have a word with him.

DELPHINE *[to herself]*: High time, if you ask me!

TREBUCHARD [*going out onto the balcony*]: Yes, I think a brief tête-à-tête would be in order. [*Looking up to the floor above.*] You, up there... Monsieur... Mon capitaine...

DELPHINE [*to herself, reacting to his remark*]: You can say that again!

TREBUCHARD [*after a brief pause, repeating*]: Monsieur... Mon capitaine...

DELPHINE [*misunderstanding, to* TREBUCHARD, *excusing herself*]: Oh no, monsieur... I didn't mean...

PIQUOISEAU'S VOICE: Who's calling?... What is it?

TREBUCHARD: Down here, monsieur... Your neighbor, Trébuchard...

PIQUOISEAU'S VOICE: So? What do you want?

TREBUCHARD: Well, it's just that... I thought I'd suggest, if it's not too much to ask... Nothing against the military, mind you... I'm in the reserves myself... But I thought, perhaps... If you could manage to stop flicking your cigar butts down here...

PIQUOISEAU'S VOICE: Oh? And why's that?

TREBUCHARD: Why? [*Aside.*] Why indeed! [*To* PIQUOISEAU.] Because they're filthy, that's why! It's disgusting! Throw them somewhere else, why don't you!...

PIQUOISEAU'S VOICE: Like where, for example?

TREBUCHARD: I don't care. Anywhere... The street...

PIQUOISEAU'S VOICE: What? And hit somebody? Some officer maybe?

TREBUCHARD [*losing patience*]: Oh...

[*He comes inside and moves downstage.*]

PIQUOISEAU'S VOICE: Where the blazes were you brought up?

DELPHINE [*stepping out onto the balcony, to* TREBUCHARD]: Fifteen, monsieur!

[*She comes back in and stands at the threshold.*]

TREBUCHARD [*turning*]: What?

DELPHINE: One more. [*Pointing.*] Just now...

TREBUCHARD: That does it! [*Stalking outside.*] All right... [*Calling up to* PIQUOISEAU.] You leave me no choice, my friend. I'm going to report you to your commanding officer!... Tomorrow... First thing...

[*He comes back inside.*]

PIQUOISEAU'S VOICE: Go fry an egg! I *am* my commanding officer!

TREBUCHARD [*to* DELPHINE]: What did he say?

DELPHINE: I think he told monsieur to go fry an egg.

TREBUCHARD [*furious*]: He... Oh!... Is he still up there?

[DELPHINE *goes out and looks.*]

DELPHINE [*returning*]: No, monsieur. He's gone back in.

TREBUCHARD: Lucky for him! Of all the... Oh!... [*Calming down.*] As if I didn't have other things on my mind...

DELPHINE: Yes, monsieur.

TREBUCHARD: More important than that... that... [*He sighs.*] Tell me, Delphine...

DELPHINE: Monsieur?

TREBUCHARD [*downstage, looking around almost surreptitiously, in a whisper*]: Did you do what I told you? Did you pack my bag?

DELPHINE: Yes, monsieur. It's all packed and ready to go. [*Pointing down right.*] Right inside monsieur's door.

TREBUCHARD: Shhh! Not so loud!... [*Nodding toward* MATHILDE's *door, down left.*] She's not supposed to know.

DELPHINE: No, monsieur.

TREBUCHARD: Not a word, you understand?

DELPHINE: Yes, monsieur. Not a word...

TREBUCHARD [*forefinger to lips*]: Please... [*He takes a few steps, moving left.*] Is she still in bed?

DELPHINE: Oh no, monsieur. She's already slapped me twice this morning... And called me a "crouton" or something... Four times, I think...

TREBUCHARD: Oh?

DELPHINE: On account of her corset... But it's not my fault if it won't lace up, monsieur. I pulled it as tight as I could, but...

[*She shrugs.*]

TREBUCHARD: I know... I know...

DELPHINE [*after a brief pause, as if struck by a new thought*]: Does monsieur want me to tell her that he's going to Lyon?

TREBUCHARD [*with a start*]: Do I... No, no! For goodness' sake! What did I just say? Not a word, you understand?

DELPHINE: Yes, monsieur. Not a word.

TREBUCHARD: I'll write to her when I get there. No long, drawn-out good-byes, thank you!

DELPHINE: Then monsieur won't be taking her with him?

TREBUCHARD: Taking her... Certainly not! How many times do I... That's all I need!

DELPHINE: And he expects me to stay here with her? The whole time? Just me and her?

TREBUCHARD: Of course.

DELPHINE: But monsieur knows how afraid she gets when she's alone.

TREBUCHARD: Well, she won't be alone. You'll be with her.

DELPHINE: Maybe so... But she's afraid when the two of us are alone together...

TREBUCHARD: Bah! Just because she's my daughter... I can't wrap her up like a... a papoose, and drag her everywhere I go. No, I'm better off leaving her here, Delphine... Before she even knows I'm gone.

DELPHINE: But she'll hit me, monsieur, like she always does.

TREBUCHARD: Then hit her back. You're old enough to take care of yourself, I daresay!

DELPHINE: Yes, monsieur. [*Aside.*] And so is she!

[*As she goes about her business tidying up the room, the door, down left, opens and* MATHILDE *appears, pulling on her gloves. She is a portly, middle-aged woman.*]

TREBUCHARD [*aside*]: Damn! Speak of the devil...

MATHILDE [*coming in, to* TREBUCHARD]: Good morning, papa!

TREBUCHARD [*aside*]: "Papa!" God in heaven! [*To* MATHILDE.] Good morning, mademoiselle...

MATHILDE [*drawing back, a little piqued*]: "Mademoiselle," papa?... Is something wrong?... I hope you're not angry with your little Mathilde...

TREBUCHARD [*aside*]: My little... [*Aloud.*] Angry?... Why should I be... Not at all... [*Forcing himself.*] daughter dear. [*Aside.*] Ugh!

MATHILDE: Good! Because... [*Hesitating.*] I have something to ask you.

TREBUCHARD: Oh?

MATHILDE: Yes... If I may.

TREBUCHARD: Of course you may! What is it?

MATHILDE: It's just that I would like to go out this morning...

TREBUCHARD [*impatient*]: So? Who's stopping you? Go...

MATHILDE: Well, if you're sure... If I have your permission, papa...

TREBUCHARD: My per... By all means, mademoi... [*Correcting himself.*] daughter dear... Please!... Anywhere you like! [*Aside.*] For as long as you like!

MATHILDE: Aren't you going to ask me where? Don't you even want to know?

TREBUCHARD [*beginning to lose his composure*]: Who gives a... [*Taking a deep breath, very properly.*] Why yes, my child... [*He turns aside with a grimace, then continues.*] Do tell papa where you're going this morning.

MATHILDE: To the florist's...

TREBUCHARD: I see...

MATHILDE: To buy some flowers...

TREBUCHARD [*aside*]: How quaint!

MATHILDE: Tulips, I think...

TREBUCHARD: An excellent choice... Yes, do go buy some tulips... [*Looking at his pocket watch.*] And take as long as you like. Four hours... Five, six, seven...

MATHILDE: Oh? Aren't you coming with me, papa?

TREBUCHARD: With you?... No... Sorry! I'm busy... Very busy...

MATHILDE: Too busy for me?

TREBUCHARD: It's... I... It's important! [*Looking for an excuse.*] I'm... I... I'm expecting my tailor...

MATHILDE: Oh yes! Very important! [*Pouting.*] Never mind. I know. You don't have to make excuses.

TREBUCHARD: Excuses?

MATHILDE: You think I'm a nuisance, don't you?

TREBUCHARD: I never said—

MATHILDE: And you'd like to get rid of me, papa! Go on, admit it!

TREBUCHARD: But —

MATHILDE: Well, you can, you know. There's a very easy way.

TREBUCHARD [*suddenly interested, drawing closer*]: There is?

MATHILDE: Yes. [*Matter-of-fact.*] Find me a husband.

TREBUCHARD [*let down*]: Oh yes, of course... [*Aside.*] Just like that! Move the Rock of Gibraltar! [*To* MATHILDE.] Yes, well... We'll see... I'll look...

MATHILDE: Thank you, papa.

TREBUCHARD [*aside*]: Don't ask me where! [*To* MATHILDE.] Only not today. I'm busy.

MATHILDE: I know... With your tailor...

TREBUCHARD: So... You go buy your tulips. Delphine will go with you.

DELPHINE [*down right, pricking up her ears*]: I will?

MATHILDE: But papa, do you think it's safe? Entrusting me to a domestic?... I mean, with all those men out there, ready to take advantage of a poor, defenseless woman...

DELPHINE [*under her breath*]: Defenseless? Ha!

TREBUCHARD: Really, I wouldn't worry. At night you might have a problem, but not in broad daylight.

MATHILDE: Are you sure?

TREBUCHARD: Trust me... I assure you... [*Aside.*] As long as they can see you...

MATHILDE: Well...

TREBUCHARD [*going over to the coatrack, up left, and handing her her shawl, but leaving her hat*]: Here! [*Urging her toward the door, up left.*] Now hurry, or I'll be... [*Catching himself.*] Or you'll be late.

MATHILDE [*putting on the shawl*]: Late? Late for what?

TREBUCHARD: For the tulips... The best ones always get sold before noon. It's common knowledge... [*Motioning to* DELPHINE *to accompany her.*] Delphine...

MATHILDE: Oh, I didn't know...

[DELPHINE *moves reluctantly toward the door, up left.*]

DELPHINE: Well, if I have to...

MATHILDE [*giving her a push in passing*]: Come on, cretin! Come on!...

DELPHINE: I'm coming! [*Aside, to* TREBUCHARD.] See, monsieur?

TREBUCHARD [*aside, to* DELPHINE]: Well, hit her back, I told you. You have my permission.

MATHILDE [*at the door*]: Bye-bye, papa.

TREBUCHARD [*turning his back on her, very offhand*]: Bye-bye... Bye-bye...

MATHILDE: Don't I even get a kiss?

TREBUCHARD [*approaching her, reluctantly*]: Of course. What was I thinking! [*He gives her a grudging peck, then turns his head aside.*] Ptui! [*Aside.*] Like kissing my grandmother!

MATHILDE: Bye-bye... [*To* DELPHINE, *giving her another poke.*] Go on! Go on!

DELPHINE: Damnation!

[TREBUCHARD *watches them disappear out the door, then goes to the coatrack and puts on his coat.*]

TREBUCHARD [*coming downstage, to the audience*]: Well, now you've seen her... Oh yes, I know what you're thinking. [*Affecting another voice.*] "Your daughter, monsieur?... You expect me to believe that that rather... mature individual..." [*In his own voice.*] I know... I know... She's fifty if she's a day! [*In the other voice.*] "Whereas you, monsieur..." [*In his own voice.*] Me? A mere twenty-nine... Give or take... [*Sighing.*] Yes, it's absolutely absurd... Absurd, but true... And all because... [*He shakes his head.*] Ah! When I think of it... All because... [*Looking at his watch.*] I still have five minutes. Let me tell you the story... The whole ugly story, from the beginning. [*Crossing right.*] I was born... [*Reconsidering.*] No... No need to go back that far. Everyone gets born sooner or later, I suppose... Anyway, my parents were rich, but... Well, stingy, to put it mildly... [*Ambling upstage.*] Which didn't help me much with my studies, I can tell you!... Five long years of medicine... [*Taking the broom and using it as a billiard queue, miming.*] And billiards!... Yes, billiards and medicine... [*Laying the broom aside and coming downstage.*] Two very expensive fields of academic endeavor! Especially when you haven't a sou to your name! [*He looks at his watch.*] Well, to make a long story short, one morning I got up... "Time to take stock of the situation," I told myself... And not very pretty! Nothing but debts, debts, debts! Nine thousand eight hundred thirty francs and seventy-five centimes, to be precise... On the credit side, not much... Two clay pipes and a pack of cigarette papers... And no tobacco, I might add... Well, just as I'm getting ready to go back to bed, there's a little knock at the door... "Come in, come in..." [*Moving up left, toward the coatrack.*] And in comes old widow Dufour, of all people... The one who runs my favorite bistro in the Latin Quarter... For months I'd been paying my tabs with nothing but lustful and provocative glances... [*He demonstrates, gazing soulfully at the coatrack, still topped with* MATHILDE'*s hat.*] Not exactly coin of the realm, you understand, but since she didn't object... She even tried to give me change in kind! Which was something to see, believe me!... Anyway, there she is. In the flesh... Such as it was... "Monsieur Trébuchard..." And she's all trembling and out of breath... From climbing up to my seventh-storey garret, I imagined... But no, not quite... "Monsieur Trébuchard," she tells me, "I've come to inform you that I have assumed all of your financial obligations. Now all of your debts are mine..." "Well, that's a nice arrangement," I answered. "Very considerate, I must say. How can I ever thank you?" "I'm afraid you misunderstand," she went on. "I've bought them, monsieur. Now it's me you owe... And at twenty percent per annum." [*Addressing the coatrack.*] "But madame, I'm afraid..." "No buts, monsieur..." "But..." [*Imitating her displeasure.*] "For years you've been toying with my affection..." "I have?" "...and now I'm offering you my hand." [*With a grimace, to the audience.*] Good God! Not her hand, or anything else! No thank you! [*To the coatrack.*] "Ah, madame, what a pleasure... If only I could accept... But I've taken a vow of chastity, and I'm about to become a monk..." [*To the audience.*] I don't think she believed me... "My hand, monsieur, or prison. It's up to you. Take your choice..." Well, all things considered... [*He comes down center.*] So I wound up in prison... With my two clay pipes and my cigarette papers... And still no tobacco!... The first month, no problem... I passed the time training a couple of spiders and writing vicious quatrains about old widow Dufour. But the second month... [*He looks at his watch.*] Let me tell you... Tobacco or not tobacco, that is the question!... Frankly, I couldn't stand it. "After all," I asked myself, "can she really be so bad?... Old, ugly, yes... And dried up like a prune... But maybe, if I keep her buttoned up to the chin..." So I sent her a note. "My love, come save me from this craving deep within me: this longing to fill my lungs..." [*Correcting himself.*] "...my heart... This longing to fill my heart with warm billows of joy!" Not terribly original... But, of course, it worked... A week later we were man and wife. More or less, that is... Because, actually, that night—our wedding-night, so to speak—I bribed my reserve commander to put me on active duty. Then and there... No deferment... For as long as he liked... [*He goes over to the bottles, down right, and pours himself a drink from the carafe.*] Two years later... Tsk tsk tsk!... I was a widower... [*He raises his glass heavenward in an unspoken toast and takes a sip.*] Just one minor complication: the dear departed left me her amazon of a daughter... [*With a nod toward the door, up left.*] From a previous marriage, thank you!... And fifty in the shade!... And who keeps calling me "papa"... In front of my ladyfriends, damn it!... And whines all day that I should take her out for a walk!... A walk? Along the boulevard, with that... that mammoth on my arm? Can't you just see it? [*He lays down his glass and moves left, laboriously, as if dragging a heavy weight, tipping an imaginary hat to imaginary passers-by.*] "Monsieur... Madame..." If only I could get rid of her!... But how in heaven?... I would if I could. It's not that I haven't tried!... But she clings... And clings... Like a vine!... Poison ivy... [*He mimes trying to disentangle himself.*] Damn!... [*Sitting on the arm of one of the chairs, left.*] I even tried marrying her off to a friend... Gaston Billetdoux... Well, he used to be a friend... Before the duel, that is... He claimed I insulted him by just suggesting it... Not that I blame him... [*Getting up, pacing left and right.*] I wouldn't mind so much if she kept her bad luck to herself... If she stayed an old maid for the rest of her life... But no! [*Stopping down center.*] Let me tell you... Me... Hector Trébuchard... Seven engagements, and all of them up in smoke!... That's right, seven... Nipped in the bud, thanks to her. Would you believe it?... It's not that I don't make an excellent impression... Au contraire, I assure you... The minute they see me, if I do say so myself... It's always the same tune... [*Imitating several voices.*] "What a charming young man!..." "Did you see his lovely teeth?..." "And so witty, so clever..." "And he's still got all his hair!..." Fine!... But then I introduce my daughter, bless her heart! And... [*With a wave.*] Pfft! The kiss of death! That's that! No more! Fini!... [*Moving right.*] Well, that's why, this time, I'm not taking any chances, understand? Tell me I'm a bounder, and a cad, and a sneak... Tell me I'm not a good father. I don't care!... I'm off to change my luck with the beautiful number eight! Far off! All the way to Lyon this time... Where no one knows a thing about the bane of my existence... And where they'll never find out!... That I'm a widower, yes... No harm in that. But nothing about my daughter!... By this time next Saturday I'll be the proud and happy husband of Mademoiselle Claudine Prudenval... Ravishing creature... Innocent, young... Only eighteen years old... [*Picking up his drink and toasting.*] "To your health and long life, Madame Trébuchard!..." At last! [*He drinks.*] And no children by a previous marriage, thank you!.. [*Raising the glass again.*] "And to Monsieur Prudenval, my new father-in-law!..." A pleasant enough chap, all things considered... [*He finishes the drink and puts down the glass.*] He wanted to make the wedding here in Paris, heaven help us! Lucky for me I was able to talk him out of it. Seven is enough! This is one wife my sweet little cherub won't frighten off!... When it's over I'll send her a wedding announcement, and invite her to vacate the premises. On the spot!... Oh, no need to feel sorry... With old widow Dufour's millions... [*Reconsidering.*] Well, some of them, that is... [*He looks at his watch.*] Damn! Look at the time!... My bag... I'll miss my train...

[*He runs off, down right, and returns a moment later with his valise.*]

PRUDENVAL'S VOICE [*offstage*]: Thank you, my good man... We'll just go right in.

TREBUCHARD: What? That voice... Don't tell me... It can't be... [*Running to the balcony and peering over the railing.*] Good God in... It is!... [*Running back in, still carrying the valise, not knowing which way to turn.*] Prudenval and his daughter!... The two of them! Here!... But... Oh! I should have known better than to trust that... that...

[*The door, up left, opens and* PRUDENVAL *enters, followed by* CLAUDINE. *He has an umbrella dangling from his arm and is carrying several valises and an assortment of packages. She is wearing a hat and carrying a parasol.*]

PRUDENVAL [*taking* TREBUCHARD *for a domestic*]: Good morning, monsieur. Please announce us to your... [*Realizing his error.*] Oh! I say!... You are your... [*With a silly little laugh.*] I mean...

TREBUCHARD: Monsieur...

PRUDENVAL: It's you... Trébuchard...

TREBUCHARD [*backing into the room as the pair advance*]: Quite...

PRUDENVAL: Because for a minute I thought...

TREBUCHARD [*babbling*]: Yes... No...

PRUDENVAL: But it's you...

TREBUCHARD: Yes... Yes... So it seems...

PRUDENVAL [*trying to hold out his arms, but obviously encumbered*]: Son!

TREBUCHARD: Monsieur!

PRUDENVAL: No, no!... Please!... "Father!"

TREBUCHARD [*down center, putting down his valise but making no move to relieve* PRUDENVAL *of his*]: Yes... Of course... [*Under his breath.*] Whatever...

PRUDENVAL: And... [*Turning, trying unsuccessfully to point to* CLAUDINE]: And my daughter...

TREBUCHARD: Yes... Your... My...

CLAUDINE [*with a little curtsy*]: Monsieur!

TREBUCHARD [*aside*]: Damn! Five minutes sooner, and...

CLAUDINE [*to* TREBUCHARD]: You must be surprised to see us!

PRUDENVAL [*aside*]: I wish he would tell me to put these things down!

TREBUCHARD [*to* CLAUDINE]: Well...

PRUDENVAL [*to* TREBUCHARD]: We've come from Lyon.

TREBUCHARD: No! What a coincidence! I was just on my way there! [*Picking up his valise.*] Come! We'll all go back together!

[*He moves hurriedly up left.*]

PRUDENVAL [*following him*]: Go back?

CLAUDINE: Back? Why on earth...?

PRUDENVAL [*to* TREBUCHARD]: Don't be silly! Why go back? [*Trying to gesture.*] Now that we're here... [*Aside.*] I do wish he would tell me...

CLAUDINE [*to* TREBUCHARD]: You didn't expect us, did you?

PRUDENVAL [*to* TREBUCHARD]: But I hope you're not angry...

TREBUCHARD [*to* CLAUDINE]: Expect you...? [*To* PRUDENVAL.] Angry? [*To* CLAUDINE.] Well, I... [*To* PRUDENVAL.] Why should I be angry? It's just that I thought—

PRUDENVAL [*coming down center, interrupting*]: I know... I know...

TREBUCHARD: I mean, the wedding... I thought it was all agreed... Lyon...

PRUDENVAL: And it was, son. You're right. Only... [*To* CLAUDINE, *up left.*] You tell him, ma petite...

CLAUDINE: No, no, papa. You!...

PRUDENVAL: But since it was your idea...

TREBUCHARD [*suddenly noticing* MATHILDE'*s hat on the coatrack, aside*]: Good God! She forgot her hat...

CLAUDINE [*coming down left, to* PRUDENVAL *as* TREBUCHARD *stuffs the hat under his arm*]: I know, but you can explain it much better.

PRUDENVAL: Well...

TREBUCHARD [*aside*]: What if she comes back for it?

[*He goes over to the balcony and peers out.*]

PRUDENVAL [*to* CLAUDINE]: If you think so... [*To* TREBUCHARD.] You see, son, it's my condition...

TREBUCHARD [*pacing uneasily between the balcony and the door, up left*]:

Yes... I see... Your... [*Stopping.*] What condition?

PRUDENVAL: Why, the same one as before. You remember...

TREBUCHARD: I do?

PRUDENVAL: The one I told you about in Lyon. Each time you came to visit.

CLAUDINE [*to* TREBUCHARD]: You remember, monsieur. Each time...

TREBUCHARD [*at the balcony, offhand*]: Aha... Yes... That...

PRUDENVAL: Because... Well frankly, son, it's getting worse.

TREBUCHARD [*peering out, preoccupied*]: Yes... That's nice...

PRUDENVAL ⎫   ⎧ What?
          ⎬ [*together*]: ⎨
CLAUDINE ⎭   ⎩ Monsieur?

TREBUCHARD [*realizing his gaffe*]: Oh... "Worse... Getting worse..." I thought you said...

PRUDENVAL: Yes, much worse...

TREBUCHARD: Tsk tsk tsk!

PRUDENVAL: You see, every time I eat... It's like a dull ache... Or maybe more like an itch... But inside... [*Trying in vain to indicate the location.*] Inside... [*As an afterthought.*] In fact, even when I don't eat...

TREBUCHARD [*stealing an anxious glance over the balcony*]: Tsk tsk tsk!

PRUDENVAL [*shrugging*]: Who knows what it is? Do I? [*Shaking his head, then with a nod in* CLAUDINE'*s direction.*] Does she? [*Shaking his head.*] And my doctor?... No idea!

TREBUCHARD: Tsk tsk tsk! Tsk tsk tsk!

CLAUDINE [*to* TREBUCHARD]: So I told him, monsieur...

PRUDENVAL: That's right. It was her idea. She said: "You really should go see a doctor in Paris!"

CLAUDINE [*to* TREBUCHARD]: I was right, monsieur, wasn't I?

TREBUCHARD: Of course, mademoiselle! No question! [*Aside.*] Much obliged!

PRUDENVAL: Anyway, since we're here... Well, we may as well kill two birds with one stone, as they say.

TREBUCHARD: Yes. As they say...

CLAUDINE [*crossing right, to* TREBUCHARD]: Besides, I've always wanted to be married in Paris. It's so much more chic...

[TREBUCHARD, *still very preoccupied, continues to steal glances out the balcony.*]

PRUDENVAL: And even if it does cost much more than in Lyon... [*With a nod toward* CLAUDINE.] She's worth it, don't you think?

TREBUCHARD [*hardly listening*]: I'm sure... If you say so...

PRUDENVAL: If *I* say so, son?

TREBUCHARD [*catching himself*]: Oh, her!... [*Pointing to* CLAUDINE.] You mean her!... Certainly she's worth it! Every sou! Every centime, monsieur!

PRUDENVAL [*correcting*]: Please!... "Father..."

TREBUCHARD: Yes... Of course...

PRUDENVAL: And we'll spare no expense, believe me. The best food, the best wine... Champagne... Pâté, caviar... All that sort of thing... And oysters... Lots of oysters...

TREBUCHARD: Oh?

PRUDENVAL: Yes. The doctor thinks they may be good for my condition.

TREBUCHARD: Aha... [*Under his breath.*] Good for your itch, I'm sure!

PRUDENVAL [*approaching* TREBUCHARD, *up center*]: Well son, now that that's settled... I say... Would you mind if I put these things down?

TREBUCHARD: Why bother? We're leaving!... Come, I'll take you to the hotel. [*Hurrying toward the door, up left, beckoning.*] There's a lovely one only a half-day's walk from here.

PRUDENVAL: Hotel?... Don't be silly! We don't need a hotel! We'll just stay here with you.

TREBUCHARD [*freezing*]: You will?

PRUDENVAL [*coming down left*]: Of course! We don't mind...

CLAUDINE [*still down right, with a little pout, to* TREBUCHARD]: Unless you think we would be in the way, monsieur.

TREBUCHARD: In the way? Not at all... My pleasure, mademoiselle! I was going to suggest... [*Stealing a look at* MATHILDE's *hat under his arm, aside.*] Oh my!... [*Coming down center, between the two, to* CLAUDINE.] It's just that I thought you might be more comfortable...

CLAUDINE: Because, if you don't have the room... With the baby and all, that is...

[PRUDENVAL *gives a knowing little chuckle.*]

TREBUCHARD [*to* PRUDENVAL]: Baby? [*To* CLAUDINE.] What baby?

PRUDENVAL: Oh, you're a sly one, you are, son!

TREBUCHARD: I am?

PRUDENVAL: Not telling us about your daughter...

CLAUDINE: That's right...

TREBUCHARD [*thunderstruck, to* PRUDENVAL]: Daughter... [*To* CLAUDINE.] Baby... [*Aside.*] God in heaven! [*Beginning to babble.*] My... My...

PRUDENVAL [*good-naturedly*]: Because, I have my sources, you know!

TREBUCHARD: My... My...

CLAUDINE: Besides, I think it's charming!

TREBUCHARD [*to* PRUDENVAL, *innocently*]: You mean... I didn't tell you?

CLAUDINE: I simply adore babies!

TREBUCHARD [*to* CLAUDINE]: Oh?

CLAUDINE: And so does papa!

PRUDENVAL: Yes, as long as they don't grow up! [*With a little laugh.*] After five, they're insufferable!

TREBUCHARD [*aside*]: And after fifty?

PRUDENVAL [*to* TREBUCHARD]: Where is she, son?

TREBUCHARD: She... She's... [*With a vague gesture, down left.*] still asleep.

PRUDENVAL: So late?

CLAUDINE [*to* TREBUCHARD]: Is she weaned yet, monsieur?

TREBUCHARD: Is she... Almost... We're trying...

PRUDENVAL: And teeth?... Does she have any?

TREBUCHARD: Oh, a mouthful... Forty... Fifty...

CLAUDINE		What?
	[*together*]:	
PRUDENVAL		How many?

TREBUCHARD: I mean, four or five...

CLAUDINE: Oh, she must be simply precious! I can't wait to give her a big hug and kiss! I'll dress her up and play with her... And teach her to blow kisses!... She'll be my little doll...

TREBUCHARD: Yes... [*Aside.*] I can just see it!

CLAUDINE [*pointing to* PRUDENVAL's *packages*]: You see, monsieur? We've brought her some presents. I even knitted her a darling little bonnet, all by myself. All pink and white...

PRUDENVAL [*to* TREBUCHARD, *trying to indicate one of them*]: And guess what I brought her.

TREBUCHARD: Don't tell me... You knitted her some booties.

PRUDENVAL [*on whom the sarcasm is lost*]: No... I got her a giant gingerbread man.

TREBUCHARD: How thoughtful!

PRUDENVAL: And that's not all...

TREBUCHARD: You shouldn't have, monsieur.

PRUDENVAL: Please!... "Father!"

TREBUCHARD: Yes... Of course...

PRUDENVAL: After all, I'll be her grandfather... In a manner of speaking...

TREBUCHARD: In a manner...

CLAUDINE: Oh, I do hope she gets up soon!

TREBUCHARD: Yes... Well... In the meantime I'll show you to your rooms. [*To* PRUDENVAL, *gesturing.*] Please... This way...

CLAUDINE: I simply can't wait!

[TREBUCHARD *retrieves his valise and shows* CLAUDINE *out the door, up right.* PRUDENVAL *hangs back, midstage.*]

PRUDENVAL [*watching* CLAUDINE *and* TREBUCHARD *exit, shuffling his packages*]: I say, son... Oh well, no harm... [*He puts the valises and umbrella down on the floor, and the packages, on the table, down left.*] There!... [*Heaving a sigh and stretching.*] Well now, off to my room...

[*He picks up the packages, valises, and umbrella again, and begins crossing up right to go out. As he reaches the door,* MATHILDE *enters, up left, followed by* DELPHINE, *who is carrying three pots of flowers.*]

MATHILDE [*to* DELPHINE]: Careful, clumsy! [*Menacingly.*] If you dare drop them...

DELPHINE: Don't worry! [*Under her breath.*] Blasted crouton!

PRUDENVAL [*noticing* MATHILDE, *aside*]: Hmm! Now who's that, I wonder?

[MATHILDE *takes off her shawl and drapes it over the coatrack.*]

MATHILDE } [*noticing* PRUDENVAL, *aside, together*]: { Oh... A man!

DELPHINE } { Who the devil...?

PRUDENVAL [*coming center, to* MATHILDE]: I say... I take it you're looking for Monsieur Trébuchard?

MATHILDE: And to whom do I have the pleasure...?

PRUDENVAL [*managing a little bow*]: No, no... Please!... The pleasure is all mine!

MATHILDE: Too kind...

PRUDENVAL: Not at all...

MATHILDE [*joining him, center*]: Now then... Monsieur...?

PRUDENVAL: But really, I'm not... Not me...

MATHILDE: Not you?... I beg your pardon?

PRUDENVAL: No, I'm not... I'm Prudenval... From Lyon... I've just arrived.

MATHILDE [*still confused, with an inquisitive cock of the head*]: Monsieur?

PRUDENVAL: But I'll be happy to call him... [*With a nod toward the armchairs, left.*] If you would like to take a seat... [*Going up right, calling.*] Trébuchard!... Trébuchard!...

MATHILDE [*to* DELPHINE, *who has been watching, up left*]: Delphine! Don't stand there gaping! Take these flowers to my room!

PRUDENVAL [*overhearing, aside*]: Her room?

MATHILDE [*to* DELPHINE]: Well, you heard me!

PRUDENVAL [*aside*]: One of the family, no doubt! [*Calling.*] Trébuchard!

DELPHINE [*grumbling*]: I'm going...

MATHILDE [*to* DELPHINE]: Go on! [*Giving her a push out the door, down left.*] And be careful!

[DELPHINE *exits.*]

PRUDENVAL [*who has been scrutinizing* MATHILDE, *suddenly struck by a thought, aside*]: Of course!... His mother!... Same nose, same chin... The other one must be the wet nurse. [*The door, down right, opens, and* TREBUCHARD *enters. He has removed his coat.*] Ah! There you—

TREBUCHARD: What do you— [*Noticing* MATHILDE, *aside.*] Good God! Mathilde! [*Aloud, stammering.*] Ma... Ma... You're back!

PRUDENVAL [*aside*]: "Mamma!"... I guessed it!

MATHILDE [*still at the door, down left, to* TREBUCHARD]: Yes. And you were right. The tulips were all gone.

TREBUCHARD [*distraught, hardly listening*]: Aha...

MATHILDE: I never realized that by noon... Well, I had to settle for geraniums. Three pots...

TREBUCHARD [*as* PRUDENVAL *comes down right, standing to his right*]: Yes... Fine... Geraniums... [*Aside.*] Has she told him?

PRUDENVAL [*to* TREBUCHARD, *softly*]: Your mother is quite a woman... For her age...

TREBUCHARD [*confused, aside*]: She is? [*To* PRUDENVAL.]: Who told you?

[*The following exchanges are delivered* sotto voce *until otherwise indicated.*]

PRUDENVAL: No, no... [*With a nod toward* MATHILDE.] Madame... Your mother...

TREBUCHARD: My who?

PRUDENVAL: I guessed right away... You're the spit and image!

[MATHILDE *comes right and stands beside* TREBUCHARD, *to his left.*]

TREBUCHARD [*to* PRUDENVAL]: Aha... My... Yes... [*To* MATHILDE.] Please! Go to your room!

MATHILDE [*to* TREBUCHARD]: Who is that gentleman?

TREBUCHARD: A... A... A dear friend... [*Desperately.*] My tailor!

PRUDENVAL [*to* TREBUCHARD]: Introduce me, son, won't you?

TREBUCHARD: Who? Me?... To... To...

MATHILDE [*trying in vain to attract* PRUDENVAL'S *attention, aloud*]: Monsieur...

PRUDENVAL [*to* TREBUCHARD, sotto voce]: Your mother...

MATHILDE [*to* PRUDENVAL, *archly*]: Monsieur... I hate to complain, but those buttons on monsieur's last vest...

PRUDENVAL: Please?

MATHILDE: Well, they really leave something to be desired, don't you think?

TREBUCHARD [*to* PRUDENVAL, *still in a whisper*]: It's nothing... Ignore her...

PRUDENVAL [*to* TREBUCHARD, *whispering*]: Aren't you going to introduce me?

TREBUCHARD [*whispering*]: Of course! Give me a chance! [*Aside.*] Good God in heaven! [*To* MATHILDE, *aloud.*] I'd like you to meet Monsieur Prudenval... [*Whispering.*] Now please! Go to your room!

PRUDENVAL [*to* MATHILDE]: Delighted, madame!

MATHILDE [*under her breath*]: "Madame?"

PRUDENVAL: I brought a giant gingerbread man, you know... All the way from Lyon...

MATHILDE: You what?

PRUDENVAL: And toys for the baby...

TREBUCHARD } [*aside, together*]: { Ayyy!

MATHILDE }   { Baby?

PRUDENVAL: Anyway... [*To* MATHILDE, *managing to extend his right hand in front of* TREBUCHARD.] Grandpapas and grandmammas should always be friends, don't you—

[TREBUCHARD *quickly seizes his hand and shakes it vigorously.*]

MATHILDE [*to* PRUDENVAL]: I beg your pardon?

PRUDENVAL [*to* TREBUCHARD]: What are you—

TREBUCHARD [*to* MATHILDE]: It's a proverb! You know...

PRUDENVAL [*overhearing, aside*]: It is? [*To* MATHILDE, *clumsily trying to hold out his snuffbox.*] I say... May I give you a pinch, madame?

MATHILDE [*not noticing his offer*]: Monsieur!

TREBUCHARD [*to* MATHILDE, sotto voce]: Please! Go to your room!

PRUDENVAL [*to* MATHILDE]: Sorry... [*Aside, with a shrug.*] I thought maybe she sniffed...

MATHILDE [*to* TREBUCHARD, sotto voce]: Really, papa! Your tailor—

TREBUCHARD [*to* MATHILDE, *clapping his hand over her mouth*]: Shhh! Shhh! [*Pushing her toward the door, down left, whispering.*] Not now!... Please! Not now!...

MATHILDE [*at the door, to* PRUDENVAL, *with a very proper nod*]: Monsieur... [*She turns to leave.*]

PRUDENVAL: Madame... [*As she disappears out the door.*] Delighted to...

TREBUCHARD [*with a sigh, aside*]: My God, what a nightmare! [*He sits down in one of the armchairs, left, fanning his brow.*]

PRUDENVAL [*to himself*]: Yes, quite a woman... Well seasoned, but still... [*Moving left, to* TREBUCHARD, *trying to match the gesture to the word, good-naturedly.*] Naughty, naughty, son!

TREBUCHARD: Hmm?

PRUDENVAL [*with a nod toward the door through which she has just left*]: Madame... Mamma... You never told me you had a mother...

TREBUCHARD: Oh? It must have slipped my mind.

PRUDENVAL: That makes two little secrets...

TREBUCHARD: Two? [*With a tinge of irony.*] Mamma, and...?

PRUDENVAL: And the baby...

TREBUCHARD: Yes... Of course... The baby...

PRUDENVAL: I say... Does she play whist?

TREBUCHARD: The baby?

PRUDENVAL: No, no... Mamma...

TREBUCHARD: Oh, like a trooper!

PRUDENVAL: Delightful woman!... [Aside.] Do troopers play whist?

TREBUCHARD: Yes, delightful... Quite...

PRUDENVAL: Well, son... If you don't mind, I'm going to freshen up... Before I go see the doctor...

[He takes a few steps up right.]

TREBUCHARD [getting up]: Yes... Don't let me keep you...

PRUDENVAL [stopping]: About my condition... A specialist from the university... [TREBUCHARD nods.] You see, every time I eat... In fact, even when I don't eat...

TREBUCHARD [subtly urging him toward the door, up right]: Yes, by all means, go see him. It sounds very serious.

PRUDENVAL: I'm afraid so too. Oh well... [Nodding toward the door.] This way, right?

TREBUCHARD: Yes, all the way down... [Opening the door for him.] As far as you can go... [Aside.] Only not far enough!

PRUDENVAL [halfway out the door, returning]: Oh, and be sure to tell mamma what a pleasure it was to make her acquaintance! We'll play a spirited game of whist tonight and I'll tell her about my condition.

TREBUCHARD: Yes... I know she'll be delighted, monsieur.

PRUDENVAL [again halfway out and returning]: No, no... Please—

TREBUCHARD [cutting him off]: Father!

PRUDENVAL: "Papa!"... Please... "Papa!"

[He exits.]

TREBUCHARD [unnerved, gesturing alternately toward the doors, up right and down left]: Papa!... Mamma!... Mamma!... Papa!... Damn his whist! And damn his "condition"... God in heaven, what's next? [Coming down center.] They're sure to want to see her! And when they do... When the "baby" turns out to be a... a fifty-year-old colossus!... Pffft! Good-bye number eight!... [He begins pacing right and left.] If there were only some way... [With a glance toward MATHILDE's room, down left.] She's right... If only I could find her a husband... Maybe marry her off to some traveling salesman... One who would haul her halfway around the world... The farther the better... Like, say, Tibet!... Anywhere, just to get her out of my hair... Before I tear it all out by the roots! At the rate I'm going, I'll be bald before I'm... [Stopping, down right, with a noncommittal shrug.] thirty... Give or take...

[At that moment there is a noise of something falling on the balcony and breaking.]

PIQUOISEAU'S VOICE: Goddammit!

TREBUCHARD: What the devil...?

PIQUOISEAU'S VOICE: My favorite pipe!

TREBUCHARD [looking up at the ceiling]: Again? [Going to the balcony.] That... That... [Stepping out, surveying the damage.] His cigars aren't enough? Now he's got to throw his pipe?... I never... [Calling up.] Monsieur!

PIQUOISEAU'S VOICE [ignoring him]: Just when I had it all nice and broken in...

TREBUCHARD: "Broken in," my foot!... Just plain broken, monsieur! And all over my balcony! [After a pause, getting no reaction, calling.] Well?

PIQUOISEAU'S VOICE [finally replying]: You again? What is it this time?

TREBUCHARD: "What is..." Monsieur! It's your pipe...

PIQUOISEAU'S VOICE: It was, you mean... A damn good one, too... Goddamn sonofabitch!

TREBUCHARD: Monsieur! Hold your tongue! [*As an afterthought.*] I have a daughter...

PIQUOISEAU'S VOICE [*sarcastically*]: Oh, pardonnez-moi! [*Repeating the oath, but this time ostensibly holding his tongue between his fingers.*] Gaw-gang thung-a-the-thith!... [*With mock solicitude.*] Is that better?

TREBUCHARD: Oh!... [*At a loss for words.*] Go fry an egg! [*Coming back inside, under his breath.*] Barbarian!... I wish I could teach him a lesson!... [*Coming down left.*] Something really awful... Like some medieval torture!... Something ancient and disgusting... Something... [*Looking at* MATHILDE's *door, suddenly inspired.*] Eureka!... [*Pointing to the door, then to the ceiling, then clasping his hands together.*] Of course! Why not?... Kill two birds with one stone... [*Glancing toward the door, up right.*] As they say... [*Running out onto the balcony, calling up.*] Monsieur!... Monsieur!... Mon capitaine...

PIQUOISEAU'S VOICE: Now what?

TREBUCHARD [*in the most gracious of tones*]: Monsieur... I wonder... Would you do me the honor of coming down a moment?

PIQUOISEAU'S VOICE: Should I bring my sabre, or would you rather duel with pistols?

TREBUCHARD [*with affected good humor*]: Ha ha!... No... Nothing like that, monsieur. I have something terribly important to tell you.

PIQUOISEAU'S VOICE [*still rather snidely*]: Well, my egg isn't done yet... But if you insist...

TREBUCHARD [*coming back inside, down right, rubbing his hands*]: What a perfectly, absolutely brilliant idea! Why didn't I think of it sooner?... An army man, after all... Here today, and who knows where tomorrow? They get sent all over... One day to the next... Who can say where he'll take her? Africa, if I'm lucky... Or India even...

[PIQUOISEAU *appears at the balcony, feet first, ostensibly climbing down from the floor above. He is in uniform, with a handsome mustache and goatee, but rather disheveled and smoking a pipe.*]

PIQUOISEAU [*stepping inside*]: So?

TREBUCHARD: What...? Oh... You could have used the door, monsieur.

PIQUOISEAU: This was faster. I didn't want to keep you waiting... So, what is it?

TREBUCHARD [*terribly polite, approaching him*]: Please... Make yourself comfortable... [*Gesturing toward the armchairs, left, as* PIQUOISEAU *comes down center.*] Won't you have a seat, mon capitaine...? [PIQUOISEAU *remains standing and blows a puff of smoke in his face.*] Yes, well... [*With a cough.*] As I was saying... I just wanted to let you know how sorry I am about our... our little disagreement...

PIQUOISEAU [*curtly*]: Apologies accepted!

TREBUCHARD [*aside*]: Not a promising beginning!... [*As* PIQUOISEAU *turns to leave, holding him back, aloud.*] And... And I wanted to tell you how often I've thought to myself... With you up there in the window... Smoking cigar after cigar, and pipe after pipe... [PIQUOISEAU *blows another puff.*] Day after day... How often I've thought: "Now there's a fine young officer... A fine young French officer... Pride of the cavalry..."

PIQUOISEAU: Infantry...

TREBUCHARD: Infantry...

PIQUOISEAU [*blowing another puff, apparently unimpressed*]: So?

TREBUCHARD [*continuing*]: "There he is, sitting up there, all by himself...
Alone... All alone..."

PIQUOISEAU: I'm waiting for La Destinée...

TREBUCHARD: Aha!... Of course! I knew you had the soul of a poet, monsieur!

PIQUOISEAU: What, "poet"?... That's her name. Désirée La Destinée... She's a
dancer at the Alhambra.

TREBUCHARD: Oh...

PIQUOISEAU: Dances naked... Without a stitch...

[*He blows another puff in* TREBUCHARD's *face, and will continue to smoke
intermittently throughout the rest of the scene.*]

TREBUCHARD [*with affected jocularity*]: Sly devil, you!

PIQUOISEAU: Well, if that's all you had to say...

[*He turns upstage to leave.*]

TREBUCHARD: Wait!

PIQUOISEAU [*stopping, brusquely*]: Now what?

TREBUCHARD: I was wondering... I wanted to ask you... I take it you're not
married?

PIQUOISEAU: You take it right!

TREBUCHARD [*aside*]: Good!... [*Aloud.*] And tell me... Your regiment... Is it
staying in Paris long?

PIQUOISEAU: Two more weeks... Then Algeria...

TREBUCHARD [*aside*]: Even better!

PIQUOISEAU: Why? Who wants to know?

TREBUCHARD: Oh... No reason... Just making conversation... [*Aside.*] It's not
Tibet, but still... [*Putting his arm around* PIQUOISEAU's *shoulders and
gesturing toward the bottles, down right.*] May I offer you a drink?... A
glass of beer, perhaps?

PIQUOISEAU: Beer?... Never touch it...

TREBUCHARD: Oh?

PIQUOISEAU: Bad for the liver!... I only drink rum.

TREBUCHARD [*going over to the serving-cart, very accommodating*]: Then rum
it is! I just happen to have a bottle of the best! Straight from Jamaica...
[*Pouring two glasses.*] And I can't think of anyone I'd rather drink it with...
[*He returns to* PIQUOISEAU *and gives him a glass.*]

PIQUOISEAU: Much obliged...

TREBUCHARD [*indicating the armchair, left*]: Please... Make yourself at home.
[PIQUOISEAU *sits down as* TREBUCHARD *raises his glass in a toast.*] To your
health, monsieur!

[*They clink glasses and drink.* TREBUCHARD *sits in the other chair, to*
PIQUOISEAU's *right.*]

PIQUOISEAU: Hmm! Not bad!

[*He drinks again.*]

TREBUCHARD: Nothing but the best for the artillery, mon capitaine!

PIQUOISEAU: Infantry...

TREBUCHARD: Infantry...

PIQUOISEAU [*raising his glass*]: To La Destinée!

TREBUCHARD: To La... Yes, well... [*Clinking.*] Monsieur!

[PIQUOISEAU *drinks.*]

PIQUOISEAU [*raising his glass*]: And to all the lovely young ladies!

TREBUCHARD: Yes... [*Aside.*] And one of the others!

[PIQUOISEAU *finishes his glass.*]

PIQUOISEAU: Not bad at all...

TREBUCHARD [*getting up and taking the empty glass*]: Please, let me...

PIQUOISEAU: If you insist...

TREBUCHARD [*going over to the bottle and refilling it*]: I do... I do... [*Returning to* PIQUOISEAU, *with another toast.*] To marriage!

PIQUOISEAU [*raising his glass*]: To... [*Stopping.*] Well, I wouldn't go that far!

[*He drinks anyway.*]

TREBUCHARD [*still standing by his chair*]: Why not, monsieur? A man of your age... In the prime of life... dashing... debonair... distinguished...

PIQUOISEAU [*toasting*]: To me!

[*He drinks.*]

TREBUCHARD: And handsome...

PIQUOISEAU [*falsely modest*]: Well...

TREBUCHARD: Yes indeed!... I like your face!

PIQUOISEAU: And I like your rum. That makes us even.

[*He finishes his glass.*]

TREBUCHARD [*going over to the serving-cart and putting down his own glass*]: In fact, now that I think of it... [*As if struck by a sudden inspiration.*] You know... I have just the perfect woman for you, monsieur!

PIQUOISEAU: For me?... Not bloody likely, thank you!

[*He holds out his empty glass.*]

TREBUCHARD [*not noticing, aside*]: Hmm! It's not going to be easy! [*Aloud, ambling upstage as he speaks.*] Mature... Solid...

PIQUOISEAU [*waving his glass*]: Monsieur...

TREBUCHARD: Dynamic...

PIQUOISEAU: Pssst!

TREBUCHARD: Talented...

PIQUOISEAU [*aside*]: Goddamn!

[*He gets up, crosses right, and refills the glass himself.*]

TREBUCHARD [*at the balcony*]: And when I say "talented," my friend...

PIQUOISEAU: Does she dance naked at the Alhambra?

TREBUCHARD: No... [*Aside.*] Good God! The very thought... [*Aloud.*] She draws...

PIQUOISEAU [*crossing back to his chair, under his breath*]: What? Flies?

TREBUCHARD: And plays the piano... [*Continuing, very matter-of-fact, as* PIQUOISEAU *sits down and drinks.*] And she comes with a dowry of a hundred thousand francs.

PIQUOISEAU [*choking and spitting, jumping up*]: Sonofabitch! A hundred thousand...?

TREBUCHARD: In round figures...

PIQUOISEAU: Did you say...?

TREBUCHARD: A hundred thousand... Yes...

[PIQUOISEAU *finishes his glass in one gulp.*]

PIQUOISEAU: You know, it's not nice to try to fool the army!

TREBUCHARD: Word of honor, monsieur!

PIQUOISEAU: You mean, I could be marrying a hundred thousand francs?
TREBUCHARD: Quite...
PIQUOISEAU [*sitting down, nonplussed*]: But... But...
TREBUCHARD: Please, monsieur. No more "buts"... [*Glancing at the balcony.*] So to speak...
PIQUOISEAU: Goddamn! For that kind of woman... [*Raising his glass.*] To hell with La Destinée!
[*He goes to drink but sees that the glass is empty.*]
TREBUCHARD [*coming downstage, joining him*]: I assume, monsieur, that a gentleman of your discernment doesn't insist on a—how shall I say?—on a ravishing beauty...
PIQUOISEAU [*with a gesture*]: Pfff!... Not ravishing... No... [*Aside.*] For a hundred thousand!
TREBUCHARD: Or on a mere callow child...
PIQUOISEAU: No... No...
TREBUCHARD [*sitting down in his chair*]: Good... Because...
PIQUOISEAU [*jumping up, suspicious*]: Wait a bloody minute!... You're not trying to marry me off to just any old hag, are you?
TREBUCHARD [*affecting injured innocence*]: Certainly not, monsieur! [*Aside.*] Not just *any*... [*Aloud.*] Certainly not!
PIQUOISEAU [*sitting down*]: Well...
TREBUCHARD [*getting up and crossing right, to get the rum*]: Believe me, my friend... [*Returning and refilling* PIQUOISEAU's *glass.*] She's not just one of your everyday beauties...
PIQUOISEAU: No...
TREBUCHARD: Just another pretty face...
[*He crosses right, picks up his glass, and pours himself a drink.*]
PIQUOISEAU: I'll drink to that!
[*He drinks.*]
TREBUCHARD [*drinking, aside*]: So will I! [*Aloud.*] More in the classic mould, you might say... Stately... Strong features... Bold... Aggressive, if you know what I mean...
PIQUOISEAU: Aha...
TREBUCHARD: Especially her profile... Classic, monsieur... Classic... [*Under his breath.*] Like the Trojan Horse!... [*Aloud.*] Mind you, she's no Venus de Milo... [*Searching for another apt comparison.*] No "Winged Victory"...
PIQUOISEAU: Oh? You mean she's got arms and a head?... Well that's a start...
TREBUCHARD [*putting down his glass and crossing left*]: "Arms and a..." [*With an embarrassed little chuckle.*] Very good!... Yes, she has arms, and a head, and...
PIQUOISEAU [*having second thoughts*]: Well, still... I don't think...
TREBUCHARD [*approaching him, very matter-of-fact*]: And a hundred thousand francs...
PIQUOISEAU [*convinced*]: So? Where is the little lady?
TREBUCHARD: "The little..." Oh, I don't know if I would exactly call her "little"...
PIQUOISEAU: That's all right. I like them nice and tall.
TREBUCHARD: Well, let's say "substantial"...
PIQUOISEAU: And you wouldn't be trying to fool me, now... You did say a

hundred thousand...

TREBUCHARD: Right...

PIQUOISEAU: And a new wife to boot...

TREBUCHARD: Quite... [*Aside.*] At least, never used...

PIQUOISEAU: Well... It sounds good to me. If you're sure... A whole hundred thousand...?

TREBUCHARD: Not one centime less!... Now you stay right here. Don't move... I'll go get her... [*He goes toward* MATHILDE'*s door, down left, but stops at the threshold and turns.*] Oh, wait... [*He returns to* PIQUOISEAU, *takes his empty glass, and goes over to the serving-cart and puts it down.*] There!... [*He crosses back to* MATHILDE'*s door but stops again.*] Monsieur... Your pipe...

PIQUOISEAU: So? What about it?

TREBUCHARD: I think, perhaps, you should put it out. Don't you?

PIQUOISEAU: Out? Out where?... [*Pointing to the balcony.*] Out there?... I thought you didn't like—

TREBUCHARD [*cutting him off*]: No, no... Out... Just out... Stop smoking it, I mean. First impressions, you know...

PIQUOISEAU: Oh... Out... Well, if you think so...

TREBUCHARD [*turning to leave*]: I'll just be a minute.

[*He exits.* PIQUOISEAU *blows one more hearty puff.*]

PIQUOISEAU: Goddamn! Who ever would have thought...? A hundred thousand francs!... And my pay besides... If I invest it right... I can even afford a son... Maybe two... Why not? One for the cavalry and one for the infantry... Or the other way round... Unless one of them is a girl... [*Reflecting.*] Or the other... [*Getting up and crossing right.*] Or both of them, goddammit!... [*He pours himself another drink.*] No, they wouldn't dare!... [*He gulps it down.*] Well... [*He taps his pipe in the ashtray by the bottles and puts it in his pocket, then suddenly catches sight of his reflection in the mirror.*] Attention! [*He gives a smart salute.*] Like he said... "Dashing... debonair... distinguished..." It's the uniform! Whoever she is, the poor thing probably saw me on my balcony one day and just couldn't resist... [*Practicing his greeting, striking a variety of poses, with different tones of voice, nods, gestures, etc.*] Mademoiselle... Mademoiselle...

[TREBUCHARD *enters, down left, holding* MATHILDE *by the hand, as* PIQUOISEAU *continues.*]

TREBUCHARD [*to* MATHILDE, sotto voce]: Come, come... Up straight... Head up, head up...

PIQUOISEAU [*still facing the mirror, posing*]: Mademoiselle...

TREBUCHARD [*to* MATHILDE, *still whispering, pushing her head to one side*]: And show him your classic profile!

PIQUOISEAU [*continuing*]: Mademoiselle...

TREBUCHARD [*aside*]: Half as much is twice as good!

PIQUOISEAU [*twirling his mustache, seductively*]: Mademoiselle... [*Turning.*] Mademoi... [*Catching sight of* MATHILDE, *who is about to turn her face to him.*] Ouf!... [*Aside.*] Sonofabitch! That's her?

[TREBUCHARD *turns* MATHILDE's *head aside and brings her toward* PIQUOISEAU.]

TREBUCHARD [*as diffidently as possible, introducing*]: Monsieur... Mon capitaine... Mademoiselle Mathilde Trébuchard, my... [*Clearing his throat.*]

my daughter...

PIQUOISEAU [aside]: His daughter?... [Joining them down center, to TREBUCHARD, sotto voce.] You must have got a goddamn early start!

MATHILDE [to PIQUOISEAU, about to face him]: Monsieur...

TREBUCHARD [turning her head aside, then to PIQUOISEAU, in a whisper]: A hundred thousand francs, remember?

MATHILDE [to PIQUOISEAU, about to face him again]: Delighted to make your... [TREBUCHARD turns her head aside.] acquaintance, I'm sure...

TREBUCHARD [to MATHILDE, in a whisper]: Please! Profile, I said... [To PIQUOISEAU, in a whisper.] Say something, for heaven's sake!

PIQUOISEAU [to MATHILDE]: I... I... I... [Aside.] Ayayay! [To TREBUCHARD, sotto voce.] She's no chicken, that's for sure!

MATHILDE [to PIQUOISEAU, about to face him again]: Monsieur?

TREBUCHARD [turning her head aside again, this time holding it with his hand, to PIQUOISEAU, in a whisper]: Well?

[He will keep MATHILDE's head turned aside throughout the rest of the scene until otherwise indicated, reacting quickly to any attempt on her part to look squarely at PIQUOISEAU.]

PIQUOISEAU [to MATHILDE]: I... I... [To TREBUCHARD, sotto voce.] I can't... I... I...

TREBUCHARD [to MATHILDE]: You see how overcome he is with emotion? [To PIQUOISEAU.] Aren't you, monsieur?

PIQUOISEAU: I... I...

TREBUCHARD [to PIQUOISEAU, saluting with his free hand]: Aye aye, mon capitaine!... Aye aye! [To MATHILDE.] You see?... [To PIQUOISEAU.] Very touching! [To MATHILDE.] Very touching, indeed!...

PIQUOISEAU [about to protest]: That is...

MATHILDE [to TREBUCHARD]: I should say!

TREBUCHARD [to PIQUOISEAU, in a whisper]: A hundred thousand! [Aloud.] But the time has come... [To MATHILDE, grandiloquently.] Yes, the time has come, daughter dear... [Aside.] God help me!... [Aloud, to MATHILDE.] The time has come to let you try your wings... To let you fly from the paternal nest...

MATHILDE [to TREBUCHARD, moved]: Yes, papa...

PIQUOISEAU [under his breath]: Fly? She'll fall like a bloody rock!

TREBUCHARD [continuing]: ...and into the arms of a fine, upstanding soldier... [Gesturing.] Our distinguished Captain...

PIQUOISEAU [aside]: And dashing... And debonair...

TREBUCHARD [hesitating]: Captain... [To PIQUOISEAU, in a whisper.] Quick! What's your name?

PIQUOISEAU [whispering in reply]: Piquoiseau!

TREBUCHARD: Captain Piquoiseau...

MATHILDE [aside]: What a lovely name!

TREBUCHARD [continuing]: ...whose heart is utterly filled to overflowing...

MATHILDE [aside, musing]: "Madame Piquoiseau..."

TREBUCHARD [waxing eloquent]: A young man devoted to the service of his country... To the values of hearth, and home, and family... Always sitting on his balcony, deep in thoughtful meditation...

PIQUOISEAU [aside]: Me?

TREBUCHARD: Peacefully watching the passing parade...

MATHILDE [to PIQUOISEAU]: Oh, monsieur! I love parades!

TREBUCHARD: Kind, considerate, good-natured... A twinkle on his lips and a cigar in his eye... [Correcting.] That is... A twinkle in his eye and a cigar... [Correcting again.] I mean, a twinkle in his eye and a smile on his lips...

PIQUOISEAU [aside]: Bla-bla-bla!

TREBUCHARD [turning, to MATHILDE]: A smile of hope and a heart full of passion...

PIQUOISEAU [to TREBUCHARD, in a whisper]: Now wait just one minute!

TREBUCHARD [ignoring him, to MATHILDE, still keeping her head turned]: Look at him! See how he trembles with desire... How he quivers with expectation!...

MATHILDE [trying unsuccessfully to face PIQUOISEAU]: I can't...

PIQUOISEAU [to TREBUCHARD, sotto voce, objecting]: I said—

TREBUCHARD [to PIQUOISEAU, sotto voce, insisting]: A hundred thousand, damn it! [To MATHILDE.] How he waits for your answer...

PIQUOISEAU [aside]: What in blazes was the question?

TREBUCHARD [to MATHILDE, continuing]: The answer that he yearns for, that will fill his life with joy!

MATHILDE [sighing]: Oh... [To PIQUOISEAU, emotionally.] Papa's word is my command, monsieur. I accept!

TREBUCHARD [disguising his voice]: O ecstasy!... O rapture!... [To MATHILDE.] Did you hear? He said: "O rapture!"

MATHILDE ⎱   ⎰ He did?
          ⎰ [together]: ⎱
PIQUOISEAU [aside] ⎰   ⎱ I did?

TREBUCHARD [to PIQUOISEAU, whispering again]: Go on!... The iron's hot!... Strike!... Strike, for heaven's sake...

PIQUOISEAU: But... [To TREBUCHARD, whispering back.] And you're sure it's a hundred thousand?

TREBUCHARD [replying, still in a whisper]: Yes!... Now go ahead! Quick! Before she changes her mind...

PIQUOISEAU: Well... [To MATHILDE.] Mademoiselle, I have the honor...

TREBUCHARD [with a sigh of relief, letting MATHILDE's face go and clasping his hands in a gesture of victory, aside]: At last!

MATHILDE [to PIQUOISEAU, finally turning toward him, full face, quickly]: Yes, yes!... I accept, I told you...

PIQUOISEAU [getting a good look, aside]: Ouf!... [To MATHILDE.] I... I... That is... [Moving right, toward the bottles, as if tempted to pour himself a drink.] I think I should sleep on it...

MATHILDE: Sleep?... But it's only noon!

TREBUCHARD [following PIQUOISEAU, turning, to MATHILDE]: It's an expression!

PIQUOISEAU [resisting the rum, but seizing the excuse]: What? Noon?... Already? [Looking at his watch.] Five minutes to twelve?... I'll be late for my billiards...

MATHILDE [moving right, to PIQUOISEAU]: Monsieur...

PIQUOISEAU: With the major...

TREBUCHARD [to PIQUOISEAU]: But monsieur...

PIQUOISEAU [crossing up left]: The general...

TREBUCHARD [*following him*]: Mon capitaine... [*To* MATHILDE.] See how excited he is?

PIQUOISEAU [*at the door*]: The field marshal... Mustn't keep him waiting!

TREBUCHARD [*to* PIQUOISEAU, *sotto voce*]: Two hundred thousand! [*Turning, to* MATHILDE.] The ecstasy... The rapture...

MATHILDE [*calling to* PIQUOISEAU]: I accept, monsieur! I accept... [*She begins to follow as* PIQUOISEAU *disappears out the door.*]

TREBUCHARD [*stopping her*]: No, no! You stay here!... I mean, go to your room! And stay there, for God's sake!... Leave your fiancé to me! [*He exits, running, on* PIQUOISEAU's *heels.*]

MATHILDE [*to herself*]: My fiancé!... [*She sits in the armchair, far left.*] Handsome devil! [*Twirling an imaginary mustache and stroking an imaginary goatee.*] Papa was right. He certainly is distinguished!... [*As if hitting on the adjectives out of the blue.*] And dashing... And debonair... [*Musing.*] "Madame Piquoiseau..." Yes, monsieur... I accept...

[PRUDENVAL *and* CLAUDINE *enter, up right. He is still wearing his coat, and is carrying several children's toys and a giant gingerbread man. She is holding a pink and white knitted baby bonnet.*]

PRUDENVAL: Come... She must be awake by now.

CLAUDINE: I certainly hope so! I simply can't wait...

PRUDENVAL: Even an infant doesn't sleep all day!

MATHILDE [*noticing them, aside*]: Oh... That awful tailor again...

PRUDENVAL [*noticing her*]: Ah... [*To* CLAUDINE, *whispering.*] Her grandmother... Plays an excellent game of whist, I hear... I'll introduce you... [*Approaching* MATHILDE, *left, as* CLAUDINE *comes down right, with a little bow.*] Madame...

MATHILDE [*still seated, replying coldly*]: Monsieur... [*Aside.*] "Madame" indeed!

PRUDENVAL: [*unobtrusively taking out his snuffbox*]: I say... May I give you a pinch?

MATHILDE [*aside*]: Again? [*Aloud, to* PRUDENVAL.] Certainly not, monsieur! [*Aside.*] The man is some kind of pervert!

[CLAUDINE *clears her throat to remind* PRUDENVAL *of her presence.*]

PRUDENVAL: Ah, yes... [*To* MATHILDE, *indicating* CLAUDINE.] Madame, my daughter...

MATHILDE [*coldly*]: Yes... I see... [*Nodding toward* CLAUDINE, *emphasizing the salutation.*] Mademoiselle...

[CLAUDINE, *down right, gives a little curtsy.*]

PRUDENVAL [*continuing*]: Mademoiselle Prudenval... From Lyon... The intended...

MATHILDE: I beg your pardon?

PRUDENVAL: His intended...

MATHILDE: "Intended"?... "His"?... Whose?

PRUDENVAL: Why, monsieur's... Your son...

MATHILDE [*offended*]: My son?... My... What son? I have no son!

CLAUDINE [*joining* PRUDENVAL, *center*]: What?

PRUDENVAL [*to* MATHILDE]: Of course you do! [*To* CLAUDINE.] She does!

CLAUDINE: Of course!

PRUDENVAL [*to* MATHILDE]: The vest... The buttons... You know...

[*Emphasizing.*] Your son!

MATHILDE: Monsieur! I'll have you know I'm not married!

CLAUDINE: Oh!...

PRUDENVAL [*to* MATHILDE]: Not... [*Confused.*] But... Then...

MATHILDE: Not quite, that is... Almost...

PRUDENVAL: Oh... [*Apologetically.*] Please, madame... Mademoiselle... Really... I thought... [*Gesturing toward* CLAUDINE.] That is, we... I mean, we just assumed...

MATHILDE: Monsieur?

PRUDENVAL: That you must be the grandmother...

MATHILDE [*jumping to her feet*]: Grandmother? Me?

CLAUDINE [*to* MATHILDE]: Please excuse us, madame...

PRUDENVAL [*to* MATHILDE]: It was a natural mistake...

MATHILDE [*to* PRUDENVAL]: Oh? And just why, may I—

PRUDENVAL [*interrupting, eager to change the subject*]: I say... Is the tot awake yet?

CLAUDINE [*to* MATHILDE]: Yes, madame... Can we see her?

MATHILDE: Tot? Tot?... Awake?... What tot?

PRUDENVAL [*aside*]: Not very bright, whoever she is! [*To* MATHILDE.] His daughter, madame!

CLAUDINE: The baby!

MATHILDE [*to* CLAUDINE]: What baby? [*To* PRUDENVAL.] Whose daughter?

PRUDENVAL: Why, Monsieur Trébuchard's... My son-in-law...

MATHILDE [*to* PRUDENVAL]: "Monsieur..." Your... His... But monsieur, *I'm* his daughter!

[PRUDENVAL *drops everything but the gingerbread man.*]

PRUDENVAL   ⎫   ⎧ You?
                   ⎬   [*together*]:   ⎨
CLAUDINE [*backing away, down right*] ⎭ ⎩ What?

MATHILDE [*with a little bow, emphasizing*]: Mademoiselle... Mathilde Trébuchard...

CLAUDINE: You? [*Aside.*] What kind of baby...

PRUDENVAL [*picking up the toys*]: But... But... How can that...? Oh my!... [*Holding out the toys and the gingerbread man.*] And here I brought you all these... Brought her, I mean... That is... [*He lays the toys down on the table, down left, still holding the gingerbread man.*]

CLAUDINE: Indeed!

PRUDENVAL: Oh well... [*He takes a healthy bite, joining* CLAUDINE, *right.*] And my daughter, who knitted her... Who knitted you... Her...

MATHILDE: What?

CLAUDINE [*moving up right and quickly stuffing the bonnet into a pocket*]: Oh... Nothing! I assure you...

PRUDENVAL [*returning to* MATHILDE]: But really, madame... Mademoiselle... It's just that... You do seem a good deal... well... older than your father. [*Attempting a gallantry.*] That is, not quite as young...

MATHILDE [*sitting down, left, coyly*]: Yes... Well, perhaps a little...

PRUDENVAL [*sitting down in the other armchair*]: But... I mean, even a little... You have to admit, it is rather unusual...

CLAUDINE [*aside*]: Rather!

PRUDENVAL: ...to say the least!

MATHILDE [*to* PRUDENVAL]: Papa was mamma's second husband, monsieur.

PRUDENVAL: Her second... [*Suddenly comprehending.*] Oh, then... you mean...

MATHILDE [*still eager to justify herself*]: I was younger than the first.

PRUDENVAL: Monsieur... "Papa"... [*Nodding.*] Aha... [*To* CLAUDINE.] That explains it! Understand?... Monsieur Trébuchard...

CLAUDINE [*stiffly*]: Yes, papa. I understand!

PRUDENVAL [*standing up, suddenly struck by a novel thought*]: I say... That means... [*Approaching* CLAUDINE, *with a little chuckle, turning, to* MATHILDE.] That means you're going to be my daughter's daughter, aren't you!

MATHILDE [*standing up*]: Me?

CLAUDINE: Oh no she isn't!

PRUDENVAL [*center, to* CLAUDINE]: But of course she is, Claudine!... You're marrying her father, aren't you? It's only logical... [*With a little laugh.*] Mamma!

CLAUDINE: "Mamma" indeed!

PRUDENVAL: Of all things! [*To* MATHILDE.] It will make quite a story for the newspapers when we get home!

[*The cuckoo begins to strike twelve.*]

CLAUDINE: Oh, will it? [*Under her breath.*] Well, we'll see about that!

PRUDENVAL: Ah! Noon!... It's time I left... [*To* CLAUDINE.] The doctor's hours are from twelve to two. [*Moving up left, as if to leave, but returning center, to* MATHILDE.] My condition, you know... Every time I eat... [*Going to leave again, but returning, to* MATHILDE.] Or even when I don't...

MATHILDE: I see...

CLAUDINE [*to* PRUDENVAL]: I'll come with you, papa...

[*She begins to cross left, toward the door.*]

PRUDENVAL: No, no... Please... You just stay here and chat with your new daughter.

CLAUDINE [*furious*]: Papa!

PRUDENVAL [*moving again toward the door, to* CLAUDINE]: After all, you should get to know her...

CLAUDINE: Really! I hardly think...

PRUDENVAL [*returning, to* MATHILDE, *offering her what is left of the gingerbread man*]: Oh, here... You may as well...

MATHILDE: Thank you just the same...

PRUDENVAL [*placing it on the table, down left, and pointing to the toys, to* MATHILDE]: And if there's anything here you would like...

MATHILDE: You're too kind!

PRUDENVAL: Well, I'll be on my way. [*He moves again toward the door; then, reaching for his snuffbox, returning, to* MATHILDE]: And you're sure I can't give you a little pinch, mademoiselle...?

MATHILDE: Monsieur! Please!...

[*She turns in a huff and exits to her room, down left.*]

PRUDENVAL [*with a shrug*]: I say... [*To* CLAUDINE.] Well... Bye-bye, ma petite... Au revoir...

[*He exits, up left.*]

CLAUDINE [*fuming, going down left, glaring at* MATHILDE's *door*]: Oh! Of all the... [*Crossing right.*] Did you ever...? My daughter indeed! That... That... I'll be the laughingstock... I can hear my friends now: "Can we help you change her diapers?..." Oh! Monsieur Trébuchard!... That liar! [*She stamps her foot.*] Not weaned yet, my foot!... Why, he never would have told me! Not until it was too late! [*Glowering at the door, up left.*] And papa, who thinks that it's simply too funny! And that I should be delighted!... [*Crossing back, left.*] Well, it isn't, and I'm not! [*Hands on hips.*] And I won't have it! So there!... [*Turning on her heel and crossing up right, toward the door.*] The wedding is off! The minute papa comes back...

[TREBUCHARD *enters, up left, without noticing* CLAUDINE.]

TREBUCHARD [*coming down left, aside*]: Damn!... More time to decide, he tells me!... How much time does a man need?

CLAUDINE [*turning, noticing him*]: Well! There you are, Monsieur Trébuchard!

TREBUCHARD [*surprised, turning*]: What...? Ah! Mademoiselle... Claudine... [*Somewhat at a loss for conversation.*] Are you settled?

CLAUDINE: Yes, but not for long, thank you!

TREBUCHARD: Oh? [*Gesturing toward the door, up right*]: It's not too small, I hope?

CLAUDINE: Hardly, monsieur!... [*Emphasizing.*] It is too big!... And too old, if I may say so!

TREBUCHARD: What? Your room?

CLAUDINE: No, monsieur! Your baby!... The one you're still trying to wean, if I remember... We've just met...

TREBUCHARD: You... [*Aside.*] Good God! She told them!

CLAUDINE [*coming center*]: I'm sure you understand, monsieur, that under the circumstances our marriage is quite out of the question!

TREBUCHARD: What?... But...

CLAUDINE: I have no desire to hear a grown woman...

TREBUCHARD: But—

CLAUDINE: ...a very grown woman, monsieur, I might add...

TREBUCHARD: But—

CLAUDINE: ...call me her "mamma!"

TREBUCHARD: But... But...

CLAUDINE [*coming down center*]: And I don't think you can blame me! If I had known before...

TREBUCHARD: But... You don't have to worry! I'm having her sent off to Algeria... You'll never see her!...

CLAUDINE: You're what?

TREBUCHARD: Yes... I've found her a husband... It's all arranged... Well, almost...

CLAUDINE: Oh? So that I can become a grandmother? Thank you! You're much too kind!

TREBUCHARD [*with a little laugh, despite his dismay*]: Well, I don't think there's very much danger of that! Considering...

CLAUDINE: No, but it's possible! And as long as there's a chance...

TREBUCHARD: But—

CLAUDINE: I'm sorry, monsieur. My mind is made up! The wedding is off! [*She turns and moves toward the door, up right.*]

TREBUCHARD [*following her*]: Don't say that! Please!... What do you want me to do? I can't very well strangle her!

CLAUDINE [*stopping at the door, sarcastically*]: In her cradle? Hardly!... Or give her up for adoption either, I imagine!

TREBUCHARD: Quite... So you see...

CLAUDINE: But that's none of my concern. I only know I will never marry the man who turns me into that woman's mother! Of all things...

TREBUCHARD: But—

CLAUDINE [*opening the door*]: Never, monsieur!... Never, never, never!
[*She exits and slams the door.*]

TREBUCHARD [*watching her leave, distraught, then coming down left*]: "Never, never, never!"... Of course! Just like all the rest!... One through seven... No matter what I do... No matter how hard I try... This time, I thought... But no! I should have known... [*Pacing left and right.*] Oh for the good old days... When they still had human sacrifice!... Before we went and made laws about such things... Before we got civilized... [*Stopping.*] And had fifty-year-old daughters! [*Pacing again.*] My cross to bear... Damn rope around my neck... Thorn in my side... Pain in my... [*Stopping, down center.*] But... [*With a shrug.*] Who can blame her? A daughter old enough to be her mother...? It's humiliating! It's revolting! It's... It's grotesque!... [*Echoing* CLAUDINE.] "Never, never, never!..." [*Pacing again.*] Well, damn, damn, damn! What am I supposed to do? I can't make them change places! I can't just wave a magic wand and make Mathilde the mother and Claudine the daughter! I can't just... [*Stopping in his tracks, down center, struck by a sudden inspiration.*] Wait a minute! Why not?... Why can't I?... Of course I can! [*Pointing up right.*] Prudenval!... Of course! They're made for each other!... Like Philemon and Baucis... [*Searching.*] Jason and Medea... Scylla and Charybdis... He's a widower, isn't he? He must be looking for some sweet young thing... [*Reconsidering.*] Some mature, devoted creature... Someone to mend his meals and cook his stockings... I mean... [*With a gesture.*] Whatever... Well, anyway, I suppose even Mathilde could learn... And to play whist too... [*Moving up right.*] Besides, why shouldn't he suffer a little? Am I the only one...? [*At the door, determined.*] That's it! That's the answer!... Piquoiseau can go hang! Who needs him?... My father-in-law... That's the son-in-law I need!... Now if only I can convince him... [*Noticing* PRUDENVAL *entering, up left.*] Speak of the devil...

PRUDENVAL [*at the door, obviously disgruntled, aside*]: Bother! Some people...

TREBUCHARD: Ah! There you are, son...

PRUDENVAL [*aloud*]: Please?

TREBUCHARD [*correcting himself*]: Father... Papa!...

PRUDENVAL [*crossing down right*]: Did you ever see...?

TREBUCHARD [*coming down center, very solicitously*]: You seem upset, papa. Is something wrong? Did the doctor—

PRUDENVAL [*interrupting*]: Wrong? I'll say there's something wrong!... Can you imagine...? A doctor, of all people... Did you ever...?

TREBUCHARD: What did he say?

PRUDENVAL: Nothing! Not a blessed word!

TREBUCHARD [*with hypocritical interest*]: Oh? Really?... The doctor...?

PRUDENVAL: He wasn't there! Can you believe it? A doctor who tells you:

"Office hours from twelve to two..." And when you get there...

TREBUCHARD [*contemplating him, aside*]: How do I begin?

PRUDENVAL: When you ring the bell, some flunky opens the door and tells you: "I'm sorry. The doctor is in Dijon. He's been there since Sunday and there's no telling when he'll be back."

TREBUCHARD [*aside*]: I can't just say: "Father, I want you to marry my daughter!"

PRUDENVAL: It's a scandal!... Now I'll have to wait until tomorrow and go look for another doctor. Did you ever...?

[*He moves left, behind* TREBUCHARD, *toward the armchairs.*]

TREBUCHARD [*with mock compassion*]: Tsk tsk tsk! You're right... I never...

PRUDENVAL: And in the meantime, it's getting worse... My condition, that is... The ache...

TREBUCHARD: Yes, the itch... Tsk tsk tsk!

PRUDENVAL: I say... I don't suppose you would know a good specialist... One who doesn't go running off to Dijon when he has office hours in Paris?

TREBUCHARD: A specialist? [*Aside.*] Hmm! Maybe... [*Aloud.*] Not a specialist exactly... But... [*With false modesty.*] Well, actually, I have had some experience along those lines myself... If you like...

PRUDENVAL: You? A doctor?

TREBUCHARD: No, not quite... Though I did study medicine, mind you... Five years... [*Aside.*] Between billiard games... [*Aloud.*] Besides, my father was a veterinarian. You can't imagine how much I learned.

PRUDENVAL [*impressed*]: Aha!

TREBUCHARD: Once I helped him give birth to a litter of pigs...

PRUDENVAL: I say!

TREBUCHARD: Cows... Goats... Horses... I always had my hand in it...

PRUDENVAL: Yes, I should think...

TREBUCHARD: So, of course, if I can be of any help, monsieur...

PRUDENVAL: No, no... Please!...

TREBUCHARD [*quickly correcting himself*]: Papa... Papa... [*Continuing.*] If my modest talents can be of some use...

PRUDENVAL: Indeed!... I didn't realize... Shall we sit down? [*He sits in the armchair, left.*] You see, it's very strange, but every time I eat...

TREBUCHARD [*sitting in the other chair, facing him*]: Yes... And even when you don't...

PRUDENVAL: Oh? You can tell?

TREBUCHARD [*nodding*]: Quite...

PRUDENVAL: Do you want to see my tongue? [*He sticks out his tongue.*] Aaaah!

TREBUCHARD: Not especially, thank you... Do you want to see mine?
[*He sticks his out too.*]

PRUDENVAL: Oh... It's just that my doctor in Lyon always begins that way.

TREBUCHARD: Yes... [*Nodding, very professorial.*] They do that in Lyon... But in Paris... [*Taking out his pocket watch.*] Here... Let me take your pulse. [*Reaching across.*] Hmm!

PRUDENVAL: Well?

TREBUCHARD: Very interesting... It seems to be beating... Not too well, but at least—

PRUDENVAL [*alarmed, interrupting*]: It's my liver, isn't it!

TREBUCHARD: No...

[*He stands up and percusses* PRUDENVAL'*s chest and back several times in a very doctoral manner.*]

PRUDENVAL: What is it, then?

TREBUCHARD: Tsk tsk tsk!

PRUDENVAL: Well?

TREBUCHARD [*sitting down again*]: Do you mind if I ask you a few personal questions?

PRUDENVAL: No... Please... [*Anxiously.*] But—

TREBUCHARD: Tell me, when you see a pretty woman, what's the first thing you want to do?

PRUDENVAL: Well... Like anybody else... Play a hand of whist... But—

TREBUCHARD: Aha... Bid or no-bid?

PRUDENVAL: Bid, of course... But—

TREBUCHARD: Yes, just as I suspected...

PRUDENVAL: But—

TREBUCHARD: A classic case... I'm afraid what you've got, my friend, is a severe case of "widower's peritoneum." I've seen a lot of them.

PRUDENVAL: In cows and goats?

TREBUCHARD [*solemnly*]: A peritoneum is a peritoneum, monsieur!

PRUDENVAL: I didn't even know I had one! Where is it?

TREBUCHARD: Oh... [*With a vague gesture.*] Here and there...

PRUDENVAL: But—

TREBUCHARD: Tell me... Exactly how old were you when you got married, if I may ask?

PRUDENVAL: Why... Twenty-nine...

TREBUCHARD: Exactly?

PRUDENVAL: Well.. Twenty-nine years and nine months...

TREBUCHARD: Aha...

PRUDENVAL: And a few days, I think...

TREBUCHARD: Bad... Bad... Much too young...

PRUDENVAL: You're right. Marriage doesn't agree with me.

TREBUCHARD [*quickly*]: Don't say that! Of course it does! [*Aside.*] It has to!

PRUDENVAL: My wife was a fine woman, and all that. But enough is enough! Never again!

TREBUCHARD: "Never..." [*Standing up.*] You don't know what you're saying! [*He proceeds to percuss him again, more energetically.*] Just as I thought. It's getting worse!

PRUDENVAL: I say... This "widower's peritoneum"... Is it serious?

TREBUCHARD [*turning around and moving right, dramatically*]: Fatal... Very...

PRUDENVAL [*sinking into the chair*]: Oh...

TREBUCHARD: Worse than fatal... [*Turning back, quickly.*] But only if you don't follow my instructions to the letter...

PRUDENVAL: What? Anything!

TREBUCHARD: No... You won't want to... Never mind...

PRUDENVAL: I will! I will!

TREBUCHARD: What's the use? You won't do it...

PRUDENVAL: But I will, I tell you!

TREBUCHARD: My friend, the only cure is to get married again... And soon!

PRUDENVAL: Oh my!
[*He jumps up and begins running up left.*]
TREBUCHARD: Wait a minute! Where are you going?
PRUDENVAL: Back to Lyon... To find someone...
TREBUCHARD: But—
PRUDENVAL [*at the door, up left*]: I don't know a soul here in Paris!
TREBUCHARD: Yes you do! Yes you do!
PRUDENVAL: I do?
[*The door, down left, opens and* MATHILDE *appears at the threshold.*]
TREBUCHARD [*pointing to her*]: Her! [*Running to join her.*] Mathilde!
PRUDENVAL [*crossing down right, aside*]: His daughter?
TREBUCHARD [*to* MATHILDE, *whispering*]: Stand up straight and turn your head!
[*Aloud, solemnly.*] My child, the time has come to give your hand in marriage!
MATHILDE [*standing in profile, delighted*]: It has? Oh...
[*She begins to turn her head to face him.*]
TREBUCHARD [*pushing her head back to the side, whispering*]: Please!...
[*Aloud.*] And here, my sweet, is the happy bridegroom!
[*He takes a few steps back and the two look at each other.*]

MATHILDE } [*together*]: { His tailor?
PRUDENVAL } { Oh!...

TREBUCHARD [*between them, approving, aside*]: Voilà!
MATHILDE [*to* TREBUCHARD, *whispering*]: Isn't he a little old?
PRUDENVAL [*to* TREBUCHARD, *whispering*]: Really son, I don't think...
TREBUCHARD: Like Scylla and Charybdis!
MATHILDE [*objecting*]: But... [*To* PRUDENVAL.] I'm sorry, monsieur. But as flattered as I am at your gallant proposal, I'm afraid I simply cannot accept...
TREBUCHARD: What?
PRUDENVAL [*with an indifferent shrug*]: Aha... Well...
TREBUCHARD: Mathilde! What are you saying?
MATHILDE [*to* PRUDENVAL, *dramatically*]: You see, monsieur, I've been promised to another...
TREBUCHARD [*to* MATHILDE]: Piquoiseau?... Don't be silly!
PRUDENVAL [*to* MATHILDE]: Fine... Fine... I understand...
TREBUCHARD [*to* PRUDENVAL]: No you don't. [*Whispering.*] What do you mean: "Fine... Fine..."? It's not fine at all! What about your peritoneum?
PRUDENVAL [*to* TREBUCHARD]: Oh my! You're right! I wasn't thinking...
[*The following exchanges, until* PIQUOISEAU's *entrance, are delivered* sotto voce.]
TREBUCHARD [*to* MATHILDE]: Your Piquoiseau is a cad and a bounder! He's having an affair with Désirée La Destinée!... She dances naked!
MATHILDE [*to* TREBUCHARD]: That's not true!
PRUDENVAL [*looking askance at* MATHILDE, *aside*]: If I have to, I have to!
TREBUCHARD [*to* MATHILDE]: And he's a soldier, Mathilde! Who knows where they'll send him off to? He'll take you away from me!... [*With mock emotion.*] I couldn't bear it, ma petite!
MATHILDE [*to* TREBUCHARD]: Don't worry, papa. I'll write...

PRUDENVAL [*aside*]: My health, after all...

TREBUCHARD [*to* MATHILDE]: Besides, he doesn't love you! You'll see, he won't come back!

MATHILDE [*to* TREBUCHARD]: Yes he will! My heart tells me...

TREBUCHARD [*to* MATHILDE]: Your heart!

PRUDENVAL [*aside*]: My peritoneum...

[PIQUOISEAU *is heard approaching in the wings.*]

PIQUOISEAU'S VOICE [*singing*]:

> *Wine, wine,*
> *Fruit of the vine,*
> *Nectar divine,*
> *O won't you be mine...*

TREBUCHARD [*aside*]: Damn!

MATHILDE [*to* TREBUCHARD]: There! You see, papa? I told you!

[PIQUOISEAU *enters, up left.*]

TREBUCHARD [*moving up left to greet him*]: Mon capitaine...

PIQUOISEAU: I'm back, and I've made up my mind...

TREBUCHARD: And you refuse!

PIQUOISEAU: Says who? [*Whispering into* TREBUCHARD'*s ear.*]: For a hundred thousand francs?... Or two hundred thousand, wasn't it? [*Coming down left, to* MATHILDE, *still in profile, standing to her right.*] Mademoiselle... I have the honor...

MATHILDE [*as demurely as possible*]: Monsieur...

TREBUCHARD [*moving behind* MATHILDE *and forcibly turning her face toward* PIQUOISEAU, *holding it, aside*]: Oh no you don't...

PIQUOISEAU [*getting a good long look*]: Ouf! [*Aside.*] Sonofabitch! It's worse than I remembered! [*Aloud.*] On second thought... [*To* TREBUCHARD.] You're right! I refuse!

MATHILDE [*angrily*]: Oh!

PIQUOISEAU [*aside*]: Even two hundred thousand! [*Moving right and pouring himself a glass of rum.*] I'd never live it down! [*Drinking, with a shudder.*] Brrr!

[*He moves toward the door, up left.*]

MATHILDE: The cad!

TREBUCHARD [*rubbing his hands, aside*]: The bounder!

PRUDENVAL [*still down right, looking toward* PIQUOISEAU]: What did he say?

MATHILDE: Nothing! [*Moving right, extending her hand to* PRUDENVAL, *graciously.*] Monsieur Prudenval... My hand... I accept...

PRUDENVAL [*unenthusiastic*]: Ah... Well, I suppose... [*Looking for something to say.*] I say, mademoiselle... May I give you a little pinch?

[*He reaches for his snuffbox.*]

MATHILDE [*misunderstanding, coyly*]: Well, if you really think you should...

PRUDENVAL [*offering*]: Help yourself.

MATHILDE: Oh!... A pinch... You mean...

[*She takes a pinch with a little laugh, and sniffs.* PRUDENVAL *does likewise.*]

TREBUCHARD [*down left, sighing, aside*]: Free at last! [*He joins his hands together in mock reverence and looks heavenward.*] Thank you...

[*As he blows a kiss toward the ceiling, the door, up right, opens and* CLAUDINE *enters, with hat and parasol, followed by* DELPHINE, *who is carrying all the valises.*]

CLAUDINE [*to* PRUDENVAL]: Come, papa! We're ready to leave...

[*She stops, center, as* DELPHINE *gives the valises to* PRUDENVAL, *down right, and retreats up left beside* PIQUOISEAU.]

TREBUCHARD: Leave? [*To* CLAUDINE.] Don't be absurd! Everything is all arranged...

MATHILDE [*with a clumsy little curtsy, to* CLAUDINE]: That's right, mamma!

CLAUDINE [*furious*]: Again?

TREBUCHARD [*far left, to* MATHILDE]: No, no, no, Mathilde! Not "mamma!"... Now it's "daughter dear"... "Daughter..."

MATHILDE [*grudgingly, to* CLAUDINE]: Daughter dear...

CLAUDINE: What?... "Daughter..."? Who?

TREBUCHARD [*to* CLAUDINE, *gesturing toward* MATHILDE]: May I present the new Madame Prudenval-to-be... [*Whispering.*] You didn't want her for a daughter, so you've got her for a mother!

CLAUDINE [*turning to* PRUDENVAL]: But... Papa?...

PRUDENVAL: Say hello to your new mamma, Claudine... [*Whispering.*] I have to... For my condition... For my peritoneum...

CLAUDINE: Your...

TREBUCHARD [*overhearing, to* PRUDENVAL]: Tsk tsk! No secrets, son!

PRUDENVAL [*aside*]: "Son"? Me?... [*Reflecting for a moment.*] I say... He's right!

TREBUCHARD [*to* CLAUDINE, sotto voce, *pointing to* MATHILDE]: You see? Now she's the one who'll be the grandmother!... As often as you like!

CLAUDINE [*coyly*]: Why, Hector, whatever do you mean?

TREBUCHARD: Well, we have time to discuss such things...

[*He gives a broad wink to the audience. Then, crossing right, he fills three glasses with rum, gives one to* PRUDENVAL, *goes up left and gives one to* PIQUOISEAU, *and returns down left to* CLAUDINE.]

PIQUOISEAU [*during the preceding, to* DELPHINE]: Say, haven't I seen you before? Don't you dance naked at the Alhambra?

DELPHINE: No, monsieur... [*Tweaking his mustache.*] But I can learn...

PIQUOISEAU: I'll drink to that!

[*He drinks.*]

TREBUCHARD [*toasting*]: To the bride and groom... [*To* PRUDENVAL.] Papa!... [*To* MATHILDE.] Mamma!

MATHILDE: "Mamma"? Me?... Oh my...

PRUDENVAL [*correcting* TREBUCHARD, *toasting in turn*]: Don't you mean "the brides and grooms," monsieur?

TREBUCHARD [*quickly, to* PRUDENVAL]: No, no... Please! Not "monsieur!" Just call me "father," son!

PRUDENVAL: Well, now that you mention it...

[*He and* TREBUCHARD *drink.*]

PIQUOISEAU [*scratching his head*]: "Father... Son... Papa... Mamma..." What the blazes...?

PRUDENVAL [*pointing toward* TREBUCHARD]: He's marrying my daughter and I'm marrying his!

TREBUCHARD [*pointing toward* PRUDENVAL]: So my father-in-law is going to be my son-in-law, monsieur!

CLAUDINE [*pointing toward* TREBUCHARD]: You see, papa is marrying his daughter, so she's going to be my mother!

MATHILDE [*pointing toward* TREBUCHARD]: And I'm going to be my papa's mother-in-law, monsieur!

DELPHINE [*to* PIQUOISEAU]: Understand?

PIQUOISEAU: Not a goddamn word!

DELPHINE: Stupid crouton!

PRUDENVAL: I say...

[*The couples begin to explain once again, all talking at once, as the curtain falls on their explanations.*]

CURTAIN

FOR LOVE OR MONKEY

Adaptation of

L'Ecureuil

by

Victorien Sardou

(1861)

CHARACTERS

BONIFACE, a bachelor in his late twenties

PISTACHE, his concierge

VON GELTSACK, a wealthy, eccentric German

BABETTE, Boniface's beautiful young neighbor

BRÜNNHILDE, Von Geltsack's insufferable little daughter, very young and very spoiled

*A bachelor's modest bedroom, in utter disarray: clothes, papers, books, etc.
strewn here and there. Down left, a door leading out onto the corridor of a mid-
nineteenth-century Parisian pension. In the rear wall, up left, a curtained
double-paneled window looking out on a courtyard. When it is open one can see
a corner of the building, its wall at an angle to the rear wall of the set. In that
offstage wall, a corresponding window, ostensibly that of the next-door
neighbor. with window box and flowers. Against the stage right wall, midstage,
a bed. Close to it, downstage, a night table with a candle-holder and candle, a
pipe, and a tobacco pouch. Center stage, a table with two facing chairs, left and
right, all covered with miscellaneous articles. Midstage left, an armchair. Up
center, against the rear wall, a dresser cluttered with disparate objects. On a
small chair by the dresser, a monkey-cage, covered with a cloth, placed so that
it can be clearly seen from the neighboring window when both windows are
open. There is a monkey in the cage.[1] On the floor in front of the window, amid
a pile of clothes, a pair of trousers.*

At rise it is early morning. The window is closed. BONIFACE *is in bed, invisible
under a pile of covers. After a few moments there are several raps at the door,
then silence.*

PISTACHE'S VOICE [*after several more raps*]: Monsieur!... Monsieur Boniface!
BONIFACE [*his head appearing from under the bedclothes, groaning*]: Hmm?
PISTACHE'S VOICE: It's me, monsieur... Pistache...
BONIFACE [*grunting*]: Come in... Come in...
PISTACHE [*entering, carrying a feather duster, dustpan, and broom*]: I've come
   to make up the room.
BONIFACE [*without getting up*]: What day is it, Pistache?
PISTACHE [*at the threshold*]: Sunday, monsieur.
BONIFACE: And what time does my clock say?
PISTACHE [*looking around*]: What clock?... You have no—
BONIFACE [*still supine, cutting him off*]: Yes... Well, I'm not getting up until
   my clock says noon.
PISTACHE [*aside*]: Good luck! [*To* BONIFACE.] No matter... I'm going to make
   up your room anyway. [*He comes center and begins half-heartedly dusting
   off the table and chairs; then, sitting down on the chair to the stage left
   side, to himself.*] All alike, these traveling salesmen... [*Leaning the broom
   against the table and putting the dustpan and duster down on it.*] You can
   never get 'em out of bed on a Sunday! [*Taking a pinch of tobacco from his
   pocket, sniffing.*] Ah! That would have been the job for me!... House to
   house... Woman to woman... [*Sniffing.*] Selling 'em things... Telling 'em
   things...
BONIFACE: Pistache...

[1] In the event that a trained animal is not readily available, the technical director should have little
trouble rigging an articulated puppet to be controlled by strings from backstage [Translator's note].

PISTACHE [*continuing his musings*]: Sweet nothings... In one ear and... and in the other too...

BONIFACE [*raising his head*]: Pssst...

PISTACHE: A little hug here... A little kiss there...

BONIFACE [*more insistent*]: Pssst!

PISTACHE [*with a start*]: Oh... Yes, monsieur? Sorry... I was just—

BONIFACE: Be a good fellow and open the window, Pistache.

PISTACHE [*as* BONIFACE *hesitantly sits up*]: Of course... [*He stands up and goes to the window.*]

BONIFACE: I think I'll sit up and... [*Yawning, as* PISTACHE *opens the window, flooding the room with light.*] and have myself a smoke. [*He takes his pipe and tobacco pouch from the night table.*]

PISTACHE [*at the window*]: Ah! [*After several deep breaths.*] What a lovely summer day! [*As* BONIFACE *fills his pipe.*] I hope you're not planning to waste all that sun! Really, monsieur, you should get out of bed and go outside. Perhaps to the country...

BONIFACE [*puffing*]: Exactly what I intend to do, Pistache... This afternoon... When my clock says two...

PISTACHE [*with a shrug*]: Ha!... [*After a few more deep breaths, noticing something across the courtyard.*] Oh look! There's that German gentleman, monsieur... On his balcony... With the little girl...

BONIFACE: German?

PISTACHE [*coming center, to the table, and giving it a perfunctory dusting*]: Yes... The new tenant... A real millionaire... Has the whole of the second floor to himself... Him and his little daughter...

BONIFACE: Oh?

PISTACHE [*continuing*]: Four years old, and thinks she's a princess... A holy terror, monsieur... A holy terror... Why, just day before yesterday, I was outside, giving the courtyard a good sweep...

BONIFACE [*to himself*]: I'm sure...

PISTACHE: ...and they were up there... On the balcony, just like today... And she was nibbling on a slice of bread and jam...

BONIFACE [*puffing, sarcastically*]: Amazing!

PISTACHE: Well, he called me... "Herr concierge! Herr concierge!... Up, up!... Now!..." So I went running up and went inside. [*Shaking his hand up and down from the wrist in a gesture of wonderment.*] Phew! You can't imagine what it's like in there! All silk and satin... And gold all over...

BONIFACE: Yes... [*Puffing.*] Just like here, I imagine...

PISTACHE [*giving a little dusting here and there around the table*]: And he tells me: "Herr Pistatch..." [*Imitating the German accent and speech as best he can.*] "Goot friend... My Brünnhilde vants to giff to you taste of nice yam..."

BONIFACE: Yam?

PISTACHE: Well, I thought it was a little funny, but I couldn't say no. So I said: "That's nice of her." And then she comes over to me, monsieur, with her slice of bread... And as soon as I bend down to take a taste... You won't believe it... As soon as I bend down, she shoves it in my face and smears me with jam, and bursts out laughing!

BONIFACE [*pipe in mouth, grunting through his lips*]: Hmm!

PISTACHE: Him too... [*Imitating.*] "Ha ha! Ha ha!... Iss to laugh, no?..." And he takes her on his lap, and he gives her a great big hug and a kiss... "Ha ha!

Ha ha!..." Well, I don't have to tell you how I felt...

BONIFACE: And looked!

PISTACHE: Like a fool, monsieur... But the best part of it was that, as soon as he's done laughing, he shakes my hand and gives me a hundred francs! Then he points to the door and tells me: "Goot, Herr Pistatch! Now out... Now out..."

BONIFACE [*grunting*]: Hmm!

PISTACHE: A whole hundred francs, monsieur!... So yesterday I went outside again, at exactly the same time, and looked up at their balcony. Just in case she wanted me to taste her butter too... But no such luck...

[*He goes up toward the window.*]

BONIFACE: Tsk tsk tsk!

PISTACHE: Maybe tomorrow...

BONIFACE [*reflecting*]: By the way... [*Mock-seriously.*] Was that the jam on yesterday's toast, Pistache?

PISTACHE [*taking him seriously*]: Oh, monsieur!...

BONIFACE: Just asking...

PISTACHE [*giving the chair by the window a little dusting, as perfunctorily as everything else*]: I'd never... [*Lifting off the cloth covering the monkey-cage.*] Ah! You have one too, I see.

BONIFACE: "One"?... "Too"?...

PISTACHE [*jovially*]: Button my shoe! [*Laughing at his witticism.*] Ha ha!... [*Pointing to the cage.*] This, I mean... Like her... Your next-door neighbor... Mademoiselle Babette... She's got one just like it. [*Looking out the window.*] Hmm! That's funny... Her window's still closed. She's usually up long before this...

BONIFACE [*puffing, unconcerned*]: Oh?

PISTACHE [*continuing*]: Chirping away, monsieur... Even before my canaries!

BONIFACE [*yawning*]: Fascinating...

PISTACHE [*with a sidelong glance at the cage*]: Pretty little devil!

BONIFACE: Who? The neighbor?

PISTACHE: No, no... [*Coming over to the dresser, dusting as before.*] Your little pet, monsieur... The squirrel...

BONIFACE: Aha... The monkey, you mean...

PISTACHE: Squirrel, monkey... Whatever... Mademoiselle Babette isn't either one, believe me.

BONIFACE: No, I don't suppose...

PISTACHE: You should see what she does with her hands... The lace she makes with those pretty little fingers... And good? As the day is long, monsieur!... And a lady besides...

BONIFACE [*blowing a puff of smoke, dubiously*]: Pfff!

PISTACHE [*emphasizing*]: A lady...

BONIFACE: Pfff!

PISTACHE [*facing him squarely*]: A real lady, monsieur... Never meets me on the stairs without saying hello...

BONIFACE [*with a touch of irony*]: Yes! That's what I call a real lady, Pistache!

PISTACHE [*coming down to the armchair, giving it a half-hearted touch with the duster*]: You can say that again!... And pure as the driven snow!... And the proof... [*Crossing his arms.*] The proof is she's never flirted with you, monsieur. Right next door, and you've never even seen her!...

BONIFACE: You're right, Pistache. Never...

PISTACHE [*moving right and stopping behind the table, center*]: Not like the kind that... Well, it's none of my business, but... Not like the kind that lives across the courtyard and... and sits at her window making eyes at you, monsieur!

BONIFACE: Pistache!

PISTACHE: Like that cheeky Mademoiselle Claudine!

BONIFACE: "That..." Really, my friend! I'll have you know I'm particularly fond of Mademoiselle Claudine! In fact, I intend to marry her!

PISTACHE [*rather coldly*]: So I've heard, monsieur...

BONIFACE: Yes, well... Now you're hearing it again.

PISTACHE: But if you'd like my opinion...

BONIFACE: Thanks just the same! I wouldn't!

PISTACHE: Well, you can have it anyway. Free of charge...

BONIFACE [*beginning to lose patience*]: Pistache...

PISTACHE: A concierge knows his tenants!

BONIFACE: I'm warning you...

PISTACHE [*continuing, very matter-of-fact*]: And I know your Mademoiselle Claudine... And the letters she gets... And the young men who come to see her...

BONIFACE: Pistache...

PISTACHE: Every day, monsieur... [*Repeating, for emphasis.*] Who come to see her...

BONIFACE: Pis—

PISTACHE [*cutting him off, sarcastically*]: To *see* her...

BONIFACE: Pis—

PISTACHE [*again interrupting*]: Day in, day out!...

BONIFACE: [*throwing one of his pillows at him*]: That's enough, Pistache!

PISTACHE: Day out, day in!...

BONIFACE [*throwing the other pillow*]: Enough, I said, damn you!

PISTACHE: Night in, night out, I mean!

BONIFACE [*reaching for the candle-holder on the night table, about to heave it*]: Oh! [*Furious.*] Will you—

PISTACHE [*with one hand protecting himself with the pillows, and, with the other, gesturing to him to hold his fire*]: Never mind! Never mind!... That's all... [*Dropping the pillows.*] See? [*Kicking them aside.*] You can marry your Mademoiselle Claudine any time you like. See if I care!

BONIFACE [*menacing*]: Pistache...

PISTACHE: You can marry her to your heart's content! I wash my hands... I wash my hands of her...

BONIFACE: Pis—

PISTACHE [*cutting him off, as before*]: I wash my hands of the whole affair, monsieur!

BONIFACE: Pistache!...

PISTACHE: Just don't expect me to be your best man!

BONIFACE: Thank you! I'll remember!

PISTACHE [*giving the table one last casual touch with the duster*]: There... [*Starchily.*] Good afternoon, Monsieur Boniface. I'll make the bed later.

BONIFACE: Yes... When my clock says six!... Or sometime next month!

PISTACHE [*taking umbrage*]: Well really... [*Gathering up the dustpan and broom, which have remained in place, unused, and moving left, as if to *leave.*] It's not my fault if you... [*Stopping at the door, pointedly*] At ten in the morning...

BONIFACE [*waving him off*]: Out!

PISTACHE [*coming back center*]: And besides, if you think it's easy... If you think you can find anyone else to do the room so fast... Or so quiet that you hardly notice...

[*He moves left again, as if to leave.*]

BONIFACE: "Hardly notice" is right! I wonder why!

PISTACHE [*returning center again*]: I'm just doing my job, monsieur.

BONIFACE: Well, go do it somewhere else!

PISTACHE: Sorry, but I don't know where else I could go to clean your room...

BONIFACE [*pointing to the door*]: Out!

PISTACHE [*opening the door*]: And as far as your Mademoiselle Claudine is concerned... Her and all her young... Well...

BONIFACE [*losing his temper*]: Pistache!

PISTACHE [*with a shrug*]: Pfff, monsieur!... Double "Pfff"!

[*He exits.*]

BONIFACE [*jumping up and standing on the bed in his underpants, calling after him*]: You...

PISTACHE [*reentering*]: It's a scandal, monsieur! [*Standing at the threshold, noticing* BONIFACE'*s state of undress.*] Like the way you dress when there's company... Tsk tsk tsk!... And on a Sunday, too!

[*He exits, shaking his head, leaving the door open.*]

BONIFACE [*jumping down from the bed, furious*]: "When there's"... You... [*Crossing left, with fire in his eyes.*] Out, I said!... [*As he reaches the door, about to follow* PISTACHE.] Before I strangle you with my bare hands, damn it!... [*Stopping short at the threshold, quickly reconsidering, to himself.*] Oops! Better not!... With my luck I'll run into my neighbor. Then it *would* be a scandal!... Pure little Mademoiselle Innocence Herself!... [*Crossing back right.*] Bah! [*He jumps back onto the bed; then, after a moment of indecision.*] No... Instead, I think I'll do something unheard of for a Sunday... I'll get up, that's what I'll do!... [*As if to himself.*] Ready? One... Two... [*Jumping up.*] Three!... There! I've done it!... [*Going around the room, examining the varied clutter, muttering.*] Now, where are my pants? [*Looking here and there, finally arriving by the pile of clothes in front of the open window.*] Aha!

[*He bends over to rummage through them, backside toward the window, just as* BABETTE'*s window is seen opening.*]

BABETTE [*appearing at her window, watering-can in hand, stretching her arms*]: Ah... [*As she waters her flowers, singing.*]

> *Sweet heav'n, I love to see your moon*
> *When summer's day is done...*

BONIFACE [*taken aback, clapping his hands to his backside*]: My... [*Straightening up, embarrassed.*] My, my...

[*He steps quickly aside, mumbling under his breath, snatching up his pants and putting them on, as* BABETTE, *still unaware of his presence, continues her ditty.*]

BABETTE [*singing*]:

But even more, 'twixt dawn and noon,
I love your morning sun.

BONIFACE [as he puts on his shirt and arranges his suspenders]: There...
[BABETTE turns aside and puts down her watering-can, then stands in the
window for a moment, back to the audience, apparently looking about her
room for something or someone.]
BABETTE: Oh!... Now where do you suppose... [Calling, endearingly, but with a
note of alarm.] Bobo... Bobo...
BONIFACE [at his window, aside]: "Bobo"?
BABETTE: Bobo, love... Where are you hiding, you naughty boy, you?
BONIFACE [aside]: Ha! [Apostrophizing.] "Pure as the driven snow," Pistache?
BABETTE [noticing him at his window]: Ah! Monsieur...
BONIFACE [with a fatuous little nod]: Mademoiselle...
BABETTE [suddenly, pointing in his direction]: Bobo!... What are you doing
there?
BONIFACE [surprised]: "Boniface," mademoiselle... And I live here.
BABETTE [to BONIFACE]: My monkey, monsieur!...
BONIFACE: Your—
BABETTE [continuing, pointing to the cage]: You've got my monkey! My
Bobo!... You've stolen my—
BONIFACE [putting on his vest, protesting]: I beg your pardon! I've done
nothing of the kind! [Pointing.] This is my monkey, mademoiselle! My
Baba...
BABETTE: He's mine!
BONIFACE: He's a "she," mademoiselle! [To himself.] Even she should know
the difference! [To BABETTE.] And she's mine! My very own!...
BABETTE [insisting]: She's mine, monsieur! [Confused.] He... She... It's still
wearing the bow I tied around its neck! And the little bell...
BONIFACE: Oh? When was that, may I ask?
BABETTE: Why, just day before yesterday!
BONIFACE: Bah!
BABETTE: I can tell from here... I can hear it tinkling...
BONIFACE [aside]: Damn good ears!... [Knotting his flowing cravat, to
BABETTE.] Yes, well... I'll be hanged if she's yours! [Miming hanging
himself with the cravat, as if it were a noose.] See? I have a bow too!...
Perhaps you're just confused. Or hearing things... [Derisively.] Ding-a-ling!
Ding-a-ling!...
BABETTE: But he is, I tell you! She... It is! It is!
BONIFACE [putting on his frock coat]: My Baba is not an "it," mademoiselle!
[Rather stiffly.] And I'll be happy to take the matter up with the courts.
BABETTE [giving him tit for tat]: If you don't mind, monsieur, first you'll take it
up with me!
BONIFACE [with exaggerated civility]: Mind?... My pleasure, I assure you...
BABETTE: Good! Then kindly open your door. I'm coming in.
BONIFACE [with a flourish]: For you, mademoiselle, my door is always open.
BABETTE [very proper]: Thank you.
[She disappears from her window.]
BONIFACE [coming down left and opening the door, to himself]: Under different
circumstances... Who knows?

[*He stands at the door, adjusting his cravat, smoothing down his hair, dusting his coat, etc., and striking a pose. A moment later* BABETTE *enters, pert and pretty despite her obvious displeasure.*]

BABETTE: Monsieur!

BONIFACE [*with a little bow*]: Mademoiselle!... [*He crosses center, to the table, and, after clearing off the chair on the stage left side, holds it out to her.*] Please... Won't you make yourself comfortable?

BABETTE [*ignoring his offer, leaving him dangling, premptorily*]: Well? Are you going to give him back to me, or aren't you?

BONIFACE: "Her," mademoiselle... And no, I'm not. [*Finally putting back the chair, dramatically.*] Threaten me with all the tortures of the damned... The answer is still "no."

BABETTE [*striding right, in evident frustration, stopping on the other side of the table and facing him, hands on hips*]: I hope you're proud of yourself, monsieur!

BONIFACE: Very!... [*With an even more gallant little bow.*] Considering the beauty of the torturer, mademoiselle, my devotion to principle is truly heroic!

BABETTE: Monsieur has quite the wit!

BONIFACE [*nodding*]: And quite good taste, if I say so myself!

BABETTE: Yes... [*Twisting his observation*]: Too good for a cad who kidnaps a poor, defenseless monkey!...

BONIFACE: From a poor, defenseless, but utterly charming neighbor!

[*He continues eyeing her with growing interest.*]

BABETTE: Thank you, monsieur. You're much too kind. [*Cajoling.*] I'm sure that you're really a very reasonable young man... [*Catching herself, as an afterthought.*] Appearances notwithstanding... [BONIFACE *gives a little bow.*] I'm sure... [*Sitting down on the chair to the right of the table.*] I'm sure that, if we continued our little chat...

BONIFACE [*who hasn't taken his eyes off her*]: Please, feel free... As long as you like... [*Sitting down across from her.*] Nothing would please me more.

[*They sit eyeing each other, a little uncomfortably, for a long moment.*]

BABETTE [*finally breaking the silence*]: Tell me, monsieur... Just between you and me...

BONIFACE [*pointing to the cage*]: And Baba, mademoiselle...

BABETTE: Yes... And Bobo, monsieur... Tell me, how long have you had him?

BONIFACE: Her?... Since the day before yesterday... I left my window open, and when I came home that night I found the delightful little creature sitting on my dresser, delving—or should I say "digging"—into this important modern novel.

[*He picks up a book from the table, ostensibly chewed and ripped to shreds by the monkey, and holds it up to her.*]

BABETTE [*suddenly comprehending*]: Oh! Now I... [*Apologetically.*] Oh, monsieur... I'm so sorry!... Now I understand. Really, I'll be happy to pay for any damage... I hope you'll forgive him.

BONIFACE: Forgive her? Don't be silly!... She did me a favor. Now I don't have to read the rest of the foolish thing!

[*He chucks the book on the floor, onto one of the many piles of clutter.*]

BABETTE: But... I don't understand, monsieur. You admit that he's a runaway... You don't want me to pay... And you say you want to keep him.

BONIFACE: Exactly! I want to keep her.

BABETTE: But why on earth...?

BONIFACE: Quite simple... Because she's mine.

BABETTE: Yours? How can you say that?

BONIFACE: How? Because I owned her first, that's how.

BABETTE: "First"?

BONIFACE: I raised her from the cradle, mademoiselle. [*After a brief reflection on the absurdity of his statement.*] So to speak...

BABETTE [*standing up, quizzically*]: You... But I... I just told you...

BONIFACE [*standing up as well*]: I bought her one day, when she was no bigger than my fist. [*He holds up his fist to illustrate.*] For forty sou, at the Saint-Germain market... [*Calculating.*] Five sou per centimeter... Six months ago, mademoiselle...

BABETTE: Six months...?

BONIFACE [*with exaggerated theatricality*]: And three months later the little ingrate abandoned my bed and board...

BABETTE: So to speak!

BONIFACE [*continuing his little number*]: ...enticed, no doubt, by the seductive blandishments of a beautiful stranger... A ravishing temptress who mistook her for a him, and thought that *she* was a *he*!

BABETTE: Monsieur! Really...

BONIFACE [*going up left, standing by the cage, pointing dramatically*]: No need to plumb the mystery any further!... It's only too clear. One doesn't flee the paternal hearth unless one is provoked by some unprincipled schemer...

BABETTE [*looking around*]: "Hearth"...?

BONIFACE [*continuing, wagging an admonishing finger*]: Unconscionable, mademoiselle! Unconscionable...

BABETTE [*crossing left, to the armchair*]: But I didn't, monsieur! I wouldn't!

BONIFACE [*sarcastically*]: Oh no!

BABETTE: We'd never even met!... I didn't say a word to him! Not a word!... If he ran away from you, to take refuge with me, the decision was his, believe me...

BONIFACE [*shrugging*]: Humph!

BABETTE: A decision that hardly does you credit, I might add!

BONIFACE [*moving to join her, giving her tit for tat*]: No less than her escapade two days ago does you!

BABETTE [*moving up to the right of the dresser, to avoid him*]: Ah, but that's not the same, monsieur! With you it was an escape...

BONIFACE [*coming center, by the table, and facing her, back to the audience*]: Oh?

BABETTE [*continuing her train of thought*]: Whereas with me it was what you yourself just said: an escapade... an adventure... He wanted to see the world... Meet new people... Make new friends...

BONIFACE: Ha!

BABETTE: He only came back to pay you a friendly visit... [*With an almost imperceptible note of coyness in her voice.*] Like any neighbor, monsieur... And instead, you trapped him!

BONIFACE: I what?

BABETTE [*pointing to the cage*]: Imprisoned him... Held him against his will...

BONIFACE: Nothing of the kind! He... [*Correcting himself.*] She was perfectly willing...

BABETTE: Oh? Well, we'll see about that!

[*She goes up to the cage as* BONIFACE *does likewise.*]

BONIFACE [*picking it up and carrying it center*]: We certainly will! [*Behind the table, to the right, making a space amid the clutter and putting the cage down on it.*] There! Now...

BABETTE [*joining him, standing behind the table, to the left, addressing the monkey, wheedling*]: See? Mamma's right here, precious!

BONIFACE [*addressing it in turn, but looking past it at* BABETTE]: Pretty baby...

BABETTE [*momentarily taken aback; then, to the monkey, continuing*]: And she's not going to let the big nasty man keep you.

BONIFACE [*to the monkey*]: You want to stay here with papa, now don't you?

[*There is a brief pause as each of them tries to attract the animal's attention with appropriate grimaces and sounds.*]

BABETTE ⎫
          ⎬ [*after a moment, together, pointing*]: ⎰ See? He's looking at me...
BONIFACE ⎭   ⎱ See? She's looking at me...

[*They look at each other, then again at the monkey.*]

BABETTE ⎫
          ⎬ [*together*]: ⎰ He's smiling!...
BONIFACE ⎭   ⎱ She's smiling!...

BABETTE: At me!

BONIFACE: At me!

BABETTE [*to the monkey*]: Poor little darling... Snatched from under his Mamma Babette's nose!

BONIFACE: That's not true! [*To the monkey.*] You know it's not!

BABETTE [*continuing*]: Nice little Babette... [*Taking a cookie from her pocket and holding it out to the monkey.*] who always gave her nice little Bobo a nice little cookie...

BONIFACE: My nice little foot!... [*To* BABETTE, *categorically.*] Don't you know sugar is bad for monkeys?

BABETTE: Oh?

BONIFACE: Everyone knows that!... [*Taking a peanut from his pocket and holding it out.*] Besides, she'd rather have a peanut!... [*To the monkey.*] Wouldn't you, Baba! [*To* BABETTE.] Real food! Not dessert!

[*He gives it to the monkey.*]

BABETTE: Careful! You're frightening him!

BONIFACE: Nothing of the kind! You're trying to bribe her!

BABETTE: "Bribe" him?... Me?... I... [*Suddenly pointing to the monkey.*] Oh, look! He's holding out his little paws to me!

BONIFACE: Nonsense! She wants your cookie. [*To the monkey.*] Isn't that so, Baba?

BABETTE: And his name isn't Baba! It's Bobo, monsieur! How many times do I have to tell you?

BONIFACE: Her name—

BABETTE [*cutting him off*]: Good heavens! You make him sound like a pastry!

BONIFACE: Her name is—

BABETTE: Or some nasty old Turk!

BONIFACE: Baba!

BABETTE: Bobo!

BONIFACE: Baba!

BABETTE [*stamping her foot*]: Bobo!

BONIFACE [*about to lose his temper*]: Ba— [*Stopping short, composing himself.*] Bah! You can call her what you like, mademoiselle. It doesn't change the facts. Her name is Baba no matter what you call her. It's like calling a spoon a fork.

BABETTE [*indignant*]: Oh!

BONIFACE [*rather patronizingly*]: We call a spoon a spoon because that's what it is! And I call my Baba "Baba" because "Baba" is her name!

BABETTE: Monsieur, that's absurd!

BONIFACE [*categorically*]: She's Baba... [*Picking up the cage.*] She's mine... [*Returning up left.*] And that's all there is to it!

[*He replaces the cage on the chair.*]

BABETTE: Well, we'll just see about that! I'll... I'll sue you!

BONIFACE: Please do! My pleasure...

BABETTE: And I'll tell the judge everything I've ever done for him!

BONIFACE: For the judge?

BABETTE [*pointing to the monkey*]: For him!

BONIFACE [*correcting*]: For her!... Me too!

BABETTE [*misunderstanding*]: For you? What have I ever done—

BONIFACE: No, no... [*Pointing to the monkey.*] For her... Everything I've done for her...

BABETTE: You? [*Approaching him.*] What, for example?

BONIFACE: What?... "What"?

BABETTE: Yes... "What"?

BONIFACE [*as if it were obvious*]: Who do you think guided her first little steps?... Who taught her the principles of... [*A little embarrassed.*] of personal hygiene, and... and good manners? Who brought her up to get along in the world?

BABETTE: Oh yes! [*Sarcastically.*] And a fine job you did, I must say!

BONIFACE [*intentionally misinterpreting, with a little bow*]: Thank you!

BABETTE: A simply lovely job!... Why, when the poor darling came to me he was no little model gentleman!

BONIFACE: I should hope she wasn't!

BABETTE [*cataloguing her recriminations*]: Gluttonous, untidy...

BONIFACE: Oh?

BABETTE: ...ill-tempered, ill-mannered, and terribly ill-bred, monsieur!

BONIFACE [*trying to object*]: I really don't—

BABETTE [*interrupting*]: And as if that weren't enough, he was simply reeking of tobacco!

BONIFACE: Yes, but... Mine, mademoiselle... Not hers...

BABETTE [*ignoring his attempted witticism*]: Why, I'm sure if he could talk he would have cursed like a sailor!

BONIFACE: Well, I admit she's something of a tomboy...

BABETTE [*moving counterclockwise around the room, inspecting and gesturing as she goes*]: Besides, monsieur, now I understand why. Just look at this... this... [*Shaking her head, at a loss for words.*] Oh! To force my poor Bobo to live in such... [*Shaking her head.*] Especially after living in a nice clean room like mine!...

BONIFACE: No doubt...

BABETTE [*pointing to one of the pillows on the floor and gesturing toward the general disorder*]: Just look at this... this... this...

BONIFACE [*picking up the pillow*]: "Pillow," mademoiselle... We call this a—

BABETTE [*cutting him off, ignoring his patronizing bon mot*]: Shame on you, monsieur! [*As* BONIFACE *comes right and tosses the pillow onto the bed.*] Doesn't anyone ever clean up your room?... Or make your bed?...

BONIFACE [*picking up the other pillow and throwing it to join the first*]: Of course!... Old Pistache... Every morning... [*Standing center, by the table, surveying the room.*] More or less...

BABETTE [*by the armchair, left*]: Yes! So I see! But rather less than more!...

BONIFACE: Well...

BABETTE: Perhaps now you can understand why I simply cannot stand by... [*She sits down in the chair.*] and let my Bobo live in such... in such... [*Still unwilling to call a spade a spade.*] such...

BONIFACE: Pardon me, mademoiselle... But my Baba lives in "such... such... such..." quite nicely. [*Sitting down on the chair to the right of the table.*] And, for that matter, so do I!

BABETTE: At least if... if there were a female, monsieur... If there were a... a woman here to take care of... [*Looking at him, then catching herself.*] him... I wouldn't be so concerned.

BONIFACE: Ah? Well, if that's all that's bothering you... You can put your mind at ease, mademoiselle. I'm getting married in two weeks.

BABETTE [*getting up*]: Married?... Oh? [*Ambling casually downstage, affecting unconcern.*] And who, may I ask...?

BONIFACE [*getting up also*]: Please! Is that any business of yours?

BABETTE: Of course it is, monsieur!... [*Pointing to the monkey.*] For his sake!... For my Bobo!

BONIFACE [*in front of the table*]: Well, you needn't be concerned. I'm sure that your... my... I'm sure that our monkey will be pleased with my choice!

BABETTE [*approaching him, insisting*]: Who, monsieur?... Who?

BONIFACE [*recoiling against the table*]: Really, mademoiselle! It's none of your business!

BABETTE: But it is, I told you! For Bobo, monsieur... Our Bobo...

BONIFACE: Our... [*Exasperated.*] If you must know, damn it!...

BABETTE [*shocked, putting her hand to her mouth*]: Monsieur!

BONIFACE: Sorry!... If you must know, it's Mademoiselle Claudine... [*Pointing.*] Across the courtyard...

BABETTE: What?... Mademoiselle Clau... [*Aghast.*] Oh, monsieur! [*Retreating toward the armchair.*] Not that big skinny prune!... Not that—

BONIFACE: I beg your—

BABETTE: That... That...

BONIFACE [*turning his back, trying to end the discussion*]: Yes! "That... That..." Now you know!

BABETTE: "Know"?... [*Putting her foot down, categorically.*] No, no, no!

BONIFACE [*facing her, unable to believe his ears*]: "No"? "No"?

BABETTE: Yes, "no!" monsieur... [*Striding up left, to the window, looking out across the courtyard.*] I'm sorry, but she's quite unacceptable! I simply can't have it!

BONIFACE [*echoing, incredulously*]: You "simply can't have it"...

BABETTE: Certainly not!... My goodness! A person who lives on heaven-only-knows-what!... This one, that one... The first one who comes along... [*As* BONIFACE *stands agape.*] And the last one too, monsieur... Morning, noon, and... [*Turning aside, hesitating coyly*] and night...

BONIFACE [*moving toward her, by the armchair, finding his tongue*]: Mademoiselle!

BABETTE [*continuing unabated*]: Always gadding about... Theatres, dinners, balls, monsieur... And a terrible gossip... Talks about everybody...

BONIFACE: Really, mademoiselle! I hardly think—

BABETTE: No! [*Joining him by the armchair.*] I simply won't have it!

BONIFACE: But—

BABETTE: I won't! I won't!... [*With a pitiful glance toward the cage.*] The poor little thing would never get the proper care!

BONIFACE: Ha!... So! Now I have to pick a wife for your precious little pet!

BABETTE [*intentionally misunderstanding*]: He'll pick one for himself, monsieur! When he's old enough...

BONIFACE: That's not what I meant! You know what I... [*Sputtering.*] My wife!... Me!... I have to get married... [*Pointing to the cage.*] just for your... for your...

BABETTE [*emphasizing*]: *Our*, monsieur!...

BONIFACE: Our... My... Your... [*Flustered.*] Whatever...

BABETTE [*turning aside*]: Marry anyone you like! I'm sure—

BONIFACE: Oh? Thank you! You're sure I may?

BABETTE: Just as long as our Bobo is happy, monsieur...

BONIFACE: "Our Bobo... Our Bobo..." [*Losing patience.*] "Our Bobo," my... [*Controlling himself, euphemistically.*] bum-bum!

BABETTE: Oh! [*To the monkey.*] Did you hear that, precious!... [*To* BONIFACE.] Fine, monsieur!... Then I'll just take him home! [*Making a move toward the cage.*] If that's how much you care—

BONIFACE [*standing in her way*]: Oh no you won't! You'll leave her right where she is!

BABETTE [*hands on hips*]: Only if you promise not to marry that... that...

BONIFACE [*crossing right, mumbling to himself*]: Did you ever... [*By the bed, to* BABETTE.] Now look...

BABETTE [*going up to the cage and taking out the monkey, holding it in her arms, to* BONIFACE]: Don't you realize, monsieur?... Little creatures like this... [*Giving it a kiss.*] They need terribly to be loved... To be cuddled, and coddled, and... See how frightened he is, poor baby!... How he's looking at me... Just the thought of a nasty old stepmother...

BONIFACE: "Old"...?

BABETTE [*to the monkey*]: And you're absolutely right!... I know that one, believe me! You'll be lucky if she doesn't let you starve!... She'll beat you... And all you'll be able to do is cry... Like a helpless little child!

BONIFACE [*moving toward her, suddenly serious*]: Do you think so?

BABETTE: I know so!... [*Struck by his pensive air.*] Why monsieur... What ever is the matter?

BONIFACE [*behind the table, as she puts the monkey back in the cage, leaving the door open*]: Nothing... Nothing... It's just that... Something you said just now... A simple word...

BABETTE: Which one? [*Joining him, center.*] I said so many.

BONIFACE: The last one, mademoiselle... "Child"...

BABETTE: Ah?

BONIFACE: Yes... [*Turning aside.*] If you only knew... [*Hesitating.*] Tell me... Do you really think a child would be terribly unhappy with her?

BABETTE: With Mademoiselle Claudine? [*Shrugging.*] I suppose, if she had her own...

BONIFACE: Yes, but... What if she had someone else's? Do you think it could be happy?

BABETTE [*surprised*]: Someone else's? [*Naively.*] Is that possible? Can they—

BONIFACE: No, no... I mean a stepchild...

BABETTE: Oh? Whose, monsieur?

BONIFACE: Nobody's yet... [*Compounding the confusion.*] Mine, that is...

BABETTE: Your stepchild?

BONIFACE: Yes... No... I mean... [*Coming down right, with a sigh.*] I may as well tell you now that I've begun. Besides, you're good... You have a kind heart, I can tell. I know you'll understand...

BABETTE [*coyly*]: Thank you, monsieur.

BONIFACE: And maybe it was fate. Maybe heaven sent you here to give me your advice.

BABETTE [*drawing a little closer, reluctantly*]: Advice?

BONIFACE: Yes. And I need it desperately, mademoiselle! [*As she gives him an inquisitive look.*] You see, it... It's not just for myself that I'm getting married. It's... It's for...

BABETTE: For Mademoiselle Claudine... [*A little wryly.*] To make her happy...

BONIFACE [*shaking his head, continuing his thought*]: ...for a dear little thing I love more than anything in the world!

BABETTE [*pointing to the cage*]: Bobo?

BONIFACE: No... Not Bobo, not Baba!...

BABETTE: Another monkey, monsieur?

BONIFACE [*crossing left, announcing point-blank*]: Mademoiselle, I'm a father!

BABETTE [*naively, to herself*]: Of a monkey?

BONIFACE [*not listening to her, musing*]: Yes... I'm a father... [*Pacing left, and stopping intermittently to continue his confession.*] A couple of years ago... A youthful folly... Really, that's all it was!... She was a sweet young slip of a girl, and I... I was two years younger... [*Quick to explain.*] Not younger than her... I mean, younger than I am now...

BABETTE: Yes... I should think...

BONIFACE: But I wanted to do the right thing, believe me! I wanted to marry her and make her an honest woman! And I would have, if... if only she hadn't run off with a band of Gypsies... The day after he was born... My little Pupu...

BABETTE [*curious*]: "Pupu," monsieur?

BONIFACE: My son... It's short for "Paul"...

BABETTE: Oh? [*Aside.*] Not really... [*To herself, comparing.*] "Paul... Pupu..."

BONIFACE: My darling little Pupu... And if I told you, mademoiselle, that even now, after two whole years, I can't think of my Pupu without... without... [*He brushes a furtive tear from his eye, sighing.*] Ah...

BABETTE [*sympathetically*]: Oh...

BONIFACE: Oh...

BABETTE [*approaching him, down left*]: Ah...

BONIFACE: Because, whatever you might think of me... However gruff I may look, and talk, and act...

BABETTE: Oh no, monsieur... I don't... You don't...

BONIFACE [*continuing*]: ...down deep I'm not that way at all, mademoiselle... [*A *little timidly.*] Babette...

BABETTE [*turning aside, blushing*]: I'm sure...

BONIFACE: And... And especially when I love something... Or someone... I... [*Babbling.*] It's... I...

BABETTE: Monsieur?

BONIFACE: I do! I really do!... Real love, I mean... Deep... Sincere...

BABETTE: Yes!...

BONIFACE: Overpowering...

BABETTE: Oh yes! Yes, monsieur! I can tell...

BONIFACE [*pensively*]: And... That's why my Pupu... Why I feel so... so very... so much, so... such...

BABETTE: Yes, yes! Of course! I understand, monsieur... I do...

BONIFACE: He... [*Moving up to the armchair, looking off into space.*] He's so much like her... Happy... Young... [*As an afterthought.*] Only younger, naturally...

BABETTE: Naturally...

BONIFACE: Really, you should see him. You should see for yourself. You'll see why everyone loves my little Pupu...

BABETTE: Oh! [*Clapping her hands.*] Can I, monsieur?... Where is he? I'd love to...

BONIFACE: He's off in the country. I had to leave him with a nursemaid... To bring him up... After all... [*Moving about the room, pointing to the disorder.*] I couldn't very well keep him here... In this... [*By the foot of the bed, echoing her recent observation.*] "such... such... such...", as you put it...

BABETTE [*approaching him*]: Oh no, monsieur... I didn't mean—

BONIFACE: No, no... You're right! It's a hovel, a sty... A pigpen, Mademoiselle Babette...

BABETTE: Not at all monsieur...

BONIFACE: Please... "Boniface"...

BABETTE [*visibly moved, but ignoring his invitation, without conviction*] It's... It's quaint.

BONIFACE: I'm afraid it needs a woman's touch. [*Moving up left.*] Like me... Like my Pupu...

BABETTE [*trying to sound noncommittal*]: Ah?

BONIFACE [*at the window*]: That's why I thought that she... Mademoiselle Claudine... That's why I thought... I mean, even if she is a... [*Rather pointedly.*] a big skinny prune...

BABETTE [*standing in front of the table, retrenching*]: I'm sure she has her good points, monsieur.

BONIFACE: Please... "Boniface"...

BABETTE [*coyly*]: Monsieur Boniface...

BONIFACE [*continuing his train of thought*]: I kept telling myself that, with a husband like me, and my little Pupu on her lap... Well, she just couldn't help being a good mother, could she?

BABETTE [*with a marked lack of enthusiasm*]: I suppose... And you've told her, have you?

BONIFACE [*joining her by the table*]: Well, no... I... Somehow I've never dared. I... In fact, I was even thinking that today... With the lovely weather and all... I thought it would be a perfect excuse to take her out to the country and let her see him. You know... [*Moving back up to the window, looking across the courtyard.*] Just to see how she would feel about it...

BABETTE [*rather disillusioned*]: Oh... Please, you mustn't let me keep you.

[*She begins to move left, toward the door, as if to leave.*]

BONIFACE [*stopping her with a gesture*]: No, no... Not at all... I said: "I thought..." I was thinking, but... but I'm not anymore.

BABETTE: Oh? And why not, Monsieur... Boniface?

BONIFACE: Because... [*Coming down, standing behind the armchair.*] Because... Well, frankly, Mademoiselle Babette, I wouldn't dream of trusting someone with my Pupu that... that you wouldn't trust with your Bobo. [*Quickly correcting.*] With my Baba...

BABETTE [*concealing her joy*]: Oh!... But... [*With a hypocritical little shrug, moving up to the cage.*] I'm sure I could be wrong. I—

BONIFACE [*joining her, interrupting*]: No! You're not! You're right!... Besides, you're not the only one to think so. Old Pistache was saying the very same thing, not a half-hour ago.

BABETTE: Ah? [*Feigning half-hearted conviction.*] Then I must be right, mustn't I...

BONIFACE: About all the letters she gets... All the men who come to see her... Night in, night out... [BABETTE *puts her hand to her mouth in pretended shock.*] Why, you yourself just said so... "Always gadding about... Theatres, dinners, balls..."

BABETTE [*hypocritically*]: I did?

BONIFACE [*shaking his head, continuing*]: No... That's not for my son... That's not what he needs. [*Turning aside, after a pregnant pause, very subdued.*] Or me either...

BABETTE [*softly*]: Oh?

BONIFACE [*still looking away*]: What he needs... What I... What we need is a... [*Gradually turning to face her.*] a kind, sweet, sensible young woman. Someone who loves her home... Who wouldn't mind mothering another woman's child...

BABETTE [*trying to conceal her joy at the obvious implication*]: Why, of course!

BONIFACE [*continuing*]: Who... Who would take my little Pupu to her bosom... [*Apologizing quickly.*] If you'll pardon the expression... And think of him as her own...

BABETTE: And you mean... [*Glancing out the window, with a note of disdain.*] And you mean she wouldn't? [*Shaking her head.*] Tsk tsk tsk!... I should think any woman would jump for joy at the opportunity! A baby, after all!... And all... ready-made, so to speak... What could be better? All the pleasure and none of the pain...

BONIFACE: Exactly!

BABETTE: And who can already say "Mamma"...

BONIFACE: And "Papa"...

BABETTE: And besides, they're so precious at that age, aren't they!

BONIFACE [*growing more and more enthusiastic*]: Oh yes! They are!... They are!

BABETTE: I'm sure your son... your Pupu... is a perfect doll!

BONIFACE: Oh, he is, believe me!... [*As if struck by a sudden inspiration.*] In fact, why don't you come with me? Wouldn't you like to see him?

BABETTE: Me?

BONIFACE: Today... This afternoon... In the country...

BABETTE [*coming center, toward the table*]: Oh, I would love to, but...

[*Demurring demurely.*] I couldn't... I... Really, I simply couldn't.

BONIFACE: Please... [*Moving down, standing behind the armchair, insistent.*] It's such a lovely day. We can picnic on the grass.

BABETTE: Really, monsieur...

BONIFACE: "Boniface"...

BABETTE: Monsieur Boniface...

BONIFACE: But why not?

BABETTE [*coming down center, very proper*]: I mean... My goodness! Think of what the other tenants would say if they saw us leave together!

BONIFACE: So? Let them say what they like! Who cares?... I don't care. Why should you?

BABETTE: I'm afraid you're not a single young lady! You don't have a reputation to protect.

BONIFACE: True... [*Aside, to himself.*] At least, not a good one...

[*During the following dialogue the monkey is seen to grow more and more restless in the cage, finally taking advantage of the open door and jumping out the window.*]

BABETTE: It's not enough just to *be* virtuous, Monsieur Boniface. You have to let people *see* that you are. You see?

BONIFACE: I see... I see... [*A little disheartened.*] You mean... Are you telling me there's somebody important in your life?... A sweetheart? A... A fiancé?...

BABETTE: Heavens no! Who on earth would have me? I haven't a blessed sou to my name!

BONIFACE [*moving down towards her, enthusiastically*]: Is that all?

[*By this time, more or less, the monkey has made its escape out the open window.*]

BABETTE: "All"?... Isn't that enough? [*Cynically.*] You think I should share my poverty with a husband? [*Without giving him a chance to respond.*] No! I'll keep it to myself, thank you!

BONIFACE: But... But what if the husband didn't care? What if he wanted—

BABETTE [*interrupting*]: Oh! Care or not!... *I* care, and that's enough! I have my principles. No dowry, no husband...

BONIFACE [*approaching her*]: But Mademoiselle Babette...

BABETTE [*crossing far right, avoiding him*]: Please! I... I don't want to discuss it!

[*Just then the voices of a number of men and women, interspersed with children's laughter and exclamations of delight, can be heard coming from outside, shouting a variety of things like: "Oh, look!", "Quick, get him!", "A monkey!", "Up there!", "Catch him!", "Don't let him get away!", etc.*]

BONIFACE ⎫

             [*stopping short, turning
             toward the window, together*]:

BABETTE ⎭

⎧ What in the name—

⎩ What?

PISTACHE'S VOICE [*from the courtyard, calling*]: Monsieur Boniface!... Monsieur!... Mademoiselle Babette!...

BABETTE: Me?

PISTACHE'S VOICE: Your monkey... Your... One of your...

BABETTE [*noticing the open cage, rushing up to it, appalled*]: Ah! The cage...

PISTACHE'S VOICE: Somebody's monkey... Down here... Mademoiselle!... Monsieur!...

BABETTE: Good heavens! He's escaped!

BONIFACE [*following her*]: She what?... Again?

[*As he looks into the cage to confirm the disappearance,* BABETTE *goes over and looks down into the courtyard. As soon as she appears in the window the voices down below gasp a simultaneous "Ah!" of shocked disbelief.*]

BABETTE [*drawing back quickly*]: Good God! What have I done! They... They've seen me! Here!... [*To* BONIFACE.] In your room!... Oh! My honor!...

BONIFACE: Good!

BABETTE: My... [*Unable to believe her ears.*] "Good"?

BONIFACE [*reiterating*]: Good!

BABETTE: Good?

BONIFACE: Now you can come with me! You've got nothing to lose!

BABETTE [*not knowing which way to turn*]: Oh!...

[*Just as she throws her hands up in despair, the voices are heard outside once again, this time with cries of alarm at impending disaster: "That way!", "Stop him, Monsieur Pistache!", "He's got my cat!", "Bite him, Fifi!", etc. After several moments their cries and screams are interrupted by the crashing noise of breaking dishes and glasses, accompanied by a long simultaneous "Oh!" from the onlookers.*]

BONIFACE [*as the crowd continues to mutter its appropriate reaction, to* BABETTE, *timidly, fearing the worst*]: Did you hear something?

BABETTE [*nodding, no less aghast*]: I think so...

BONIFACE: A noise like broken dishes?...

BABETTE: Yes, rather...

BONIFACE: Do you suppose...

BABETTE: Do you think...

BONIFACE		
	[*together, sighing*]:	Your Bobo...
BABETTE		Your Baba...
BONIFACE		My Baba?... Your Bobo, you mean!
	[*together, objecting*]:	
BABETTE		My Bobo?... Your Baba, you mean!
BONIFACE		He'll cost you a fortune!
	[*together*]:	
BABETTE		She'll cost you a fortune!

BONIFACE: Every last sou you have!

BABETTE: Every sou to your name!

[*At that moment* PISTACHE *comes bursting in, carrying the monkey wrapped up in a towel.*]

PISTACHE [*panting, making for the bed, assuming that* BONIFACE *is still in it, not noticing him and* BABETTE *following quickly on his heels*]: Monsieur!... Monsieur!... [*He continues around to the desk, stopping as he sees them behind him, and holds out his bundle.*] Ah!... The monkey...

BONIFACE		
	[*pointing to each other, together*]:	Hers!
BABETTE		His!

PISTACHE [*up center, as* BABETTE *comes down right, and* BONIFACE, *down left, to each in turn*]: Yours... Yours... Whoever's!... [*Coming down right, to* BONIFACE.] If you think it was easy catching the little bugger!... [*Moving left, to* BABETTE.] He gave me quite a run for my money!

BABETTE [*quickly correcting him*]: She! She!...

BONIFACE: No! He!...

PISTACHE [*between them*] He, she! She, he!... Whichever... All I know is, I was out there, sweeping, like I always do, when all of a sudden I take one look, and there he is... [*Pointing to the window.*] There she is... sitting in the gutter and eating a cookie or something... Next thing I know he's sliding down the spout and chasing poor Madame Toudeloux's cat...

BABETTE: She!

BONIFACE: He!

PISTACHE [*continuing*]: ..."plop" in the middle of her crème Chantilly! The cook screamed bloody murder! Damn near cut off its tail with a carving-knife!

BONIFACE ⎫ [*instinctively, looking toward*   ⎧ My poor Baba!
      ⎬ *the window, together*]:   ⎨
BABETTE ⎭   ⎩ My poor Bobo!

PISTACHE: But it jumped out the window, across the courtyard, and up the spout... Then, one two three, down Mademoiselle Claudine's chimney!

BONIFACE ⎫   ⎧ Claudine!
      ⎬ [*together*]: ⎨
BABETTE ⎭   ⎩ Oh!

PISTACHE [*to* BONIFACE]: When I got upstairs she was having herself a nervous breakdown... Mademoiselle, I mean... [*To* BABETTE.] Imagine! [*With a chuckle.*] A monkey! Smeared with whipped cream and soot! [*As* BABETTE *represses a laugh, to* BONIFACE.] And in some young man's arms... Mademoiselle, that is... Moaning: "Help! Help me, treasure!... Help me, Pelléas"... I think I'm going to faint!" [*To* BONIFACE, *wryly.*] "Pelléas"... Is that you?

BONIFACE: Not quite...

PISTACHE: Hmm! Then I was right after all. "Day in, day out" too... Not only at night...

BONIFACE: Please, spare me...

PISTACHE [*returning to the subject at hand*]: Anyway, there we were... Them, me, and Bubu...

BABETTE: Bobo!

BONIFACE: Baba!

PISTACHE [*with a shrug*]: Whatever... And all of a damn sudden he's... [*Correcting himself.*] it's jumping out again... Lands on old man Le Bouzeur's head...

BONIFACE [*appalled*]: The landlord?

PISTACHE [*continuing*]: ...messes on his hat...

BONIFACE and BABETTE [*together*]: Oh!

PISTACHE [*continuing*]: ...and bounces up to the second-floor balcony, just while Von Geltsack is having his lunch...

BONIFACE: "Von" who?

PISTACHE: The German...

BONIFACE: Oh...

PISTACHE [*resuming his report*]: Hops up on the table, and smashes everything it can get its paws on...

BONIFACE and BABETTE [*together*]: Oh!

PISTACHE: Damn expensive stuff, too!... When I get there the German is cursing like a sonofa... [*Stopping short, in deference to* BABETTE.] like a trooper. At least I think he was... And his little girl is clapping her hands and laughing her head off!

BONIFACE and BABETTE [*together*]: Oh!

PISTACHE: Well, I push 'em out of the way, take a flying leap, and miss the little bugger!... The monkey, that is... But when I finally grab it and start to leave, the little imp stands there screeching... The little girl, that is... [*Imitating.*] "I vant! I vant!... No take! No take!"

BONIFACE and BABETTE [*together*]: Oh!

PISTACHE: I'm halfway out the door, when her father comes running after me, yelling: "Giff to me! Giff to me!" "But I can't," I tell him. "It's not mine. I can't..." And she's rolling around on the floor, and crying... [*Imitating the daughter.*] "I vant! I vant!" [*Imitating the father.*] "So! I buy! How much?... Vat price? Vat price?" And he follows me all the way over here.

BONIFACE ⎱
          [*pointing to the door, together*]: ⎰   { Out there?
BABETTE ⎰   You mean...

PISTACHE: Yes!... So! [*Going up to the cage and putting the monkey back inside, to* BONIFACE.] Name your price, monsieur! [*To* BABETTE.] Or mademoiselle... [*Shrugging.*] Whoever... Just don't expect me to go chasing it again!

[*He makes sure that the cage is shut. Throughout the ensuing exchanges,* BRÜNNHILDE *can be heard offstage, crying and screaming things like:* "Monkey, monkey!... Papa! I vant monkey!... I vant! I vant!"]

VON GELTSACK'S VOICE [*offstage, behind the door, in a thick German accent*]: Ach! Gott in Himmel!... Herr concierge! Herr concierge!... So? Vat price, you tell me!

PISTACHE [*to* BONIFACE *and* BABETTE] See?

VON GELTSACK'S VOICE: Now giffs meine Brünnhilde mit convulsions already!

PISTACHE [*to* BONIFACE, *coming down toward him*]: You hear that? Convulsions!...

VON GELTSACK'S VOICE: Und de shtamping mit de feet!...

PISTACHE [*to* BONIFACE]: So! Name your price!

BONIFACE [*to* PISTACHE]: But... Not me!... [*Pointing to* BABETTE, *moving toward her.*] Ask her!

BABETTE [*to* PISTACHE]: Not me... [*Pointing to* BONIFACE, *moving toward him.*] Ask him!

VON GELTSACK'S VOICE: Tausend... Tausend franc I pay!

PISTACHE [*echoing*]: A thousand francs!... [*To* BONIFACE.] Monsieur Boniface!

BONIFACE [*pointing to* BABETTE, *insistent*]: She's hers, I tell you!

BABETTE [*pointing to* BONIFACE, *likewise*]: He's his!

VON GELTSACK'S VOICE: Zwei tausend!

PISTACHE: Two thousand!

VON GELTSACK'S VOICE [*growing more desperate*]: Vier tausend!

PISTACHE: Four...

BONIFACE [*to* BABETTE]: But you're the one who raised her...

BABETTE [*to* BONIFACE]: Yes, but you bought him, remember? For forty sou...

VON GELTSACK'S VOICE: Acht!

PISTACHE [*trying to keep up*]: Eight!... Eight thousand!

BONIFACE [*to* BABETTE]: I know... But you're the one who taught her all she knows...

VON GELTSACK'S VOICE [*growing frantic, yelling over* BRÜNNHILDE'*s continuing cries*]: Zehn!... Zwölf!...

BABETTE [*to* BONIFACE]: Say yes, monsieur!

PISTACHE: Good God! Twelve thousand!

BONIFACE [*to* BABETTE]: Please... "Boniface"!... Say yes yourself!

VON GELTSACK [*bursting in*]: Ach! Gott! Fünfzehn tausend already!...

BABETTE: But...

VON GELTSACK: Herr Pistatch! She giffs now mit de blue in de face all over!

PISTACHE [*to* BONIFACE]: Please, Monsieur Boniface!

BONIFACE: All right!... I accept!

PISTACHE [*shaking* VON GELTSACK'*s hand*]: He accepts, monsieur!

BONIFACE [*to* BABETTE, *continuing*]: But not for me! For you!

BABETTE [*to* BONIFACE, *as* PISTACHE *goes up to the window*]: For me?

PISTACHE [*at the window, leaning out and calling down to the courtyard*]: He accepts!... He accepts!

[*He comes back down toward* BONIFACE *as the onlookers offstage break into applause, cheers, and appropriate exclamations of approval: "Bravo!", "Here, here!", "Hurrah!", etc.* VON GELTSACK, *meanwhile, peels off a number of oversized banknotes from a huge wad and comes over to* BONIFACE.]

VON GELTSACK [*handing him the money*]: For you, mein Herr...

BONIFACE [*taking it, as* VON GELTSACK *bows his way back toward the door*]: No, no... [*Pointing to* BABETTE.] For her! [*To* BABETTE, *giving it to her.*] For you, mademoiselle!

BABETTE [*to* BONIFACE, *coyly*]: Please... "Babette"...

BONIFACE [*to* BABETTE]: Your dowry!

BABETTE: My... [*Taking the money with one hand and holding out her other to him.*] Well, if you're sure...

BONIFACE: You mean, you... [*Taking her hand.*] You accept?

BABETTE [*turning aside, embarrassed*]: Now that I've lost my honor... [*Turning back to him.*] but found a dowry...

BONIFACE [*ecstatic, to* PISTACHE]: Did you hear that, Pistache? She accepts! She accepts!... I love her! She loves me! We're in love, Pistache! [*Giving him a big hug.*] In love!

PISTACHE [*disengaging*]: I know, Monsieur Boniface! I know! So does everyone else in the building!

BONIFACE: They do?... Well then, tell them... Tell them we're getting married! And good and loud! I want someone across the courtyard to hear it!

PISTACHE: I wonder who! [*Going up to the window and leaning out, calling down.*] She accepts! They're getting married!... Mademoiselle Babette and Monsieur Boniface are getting married!

[*As the crowd, once again, applauds and shouts its approval, one voice pierces the hubbub above the others, crying: "Damnation! That... That swine!"*]

PISTACHE [*at the window, turning to* BONIFACE]: Mademoiselle Claudine!

BABETTE [*to* BONIFACE]: Claudine?

BONIFACE [*nodding, very satisfied*]: Claudine!... [*Taking her hand.*] Well now, off to the country!

PISTACHE [*to* BONIFACE, *with good-natured sarcasm*]: Oh? Does your clock say two?

[*He picks up the cage and begins moving down toward* VON GELTSACK, *who has been standing by the door, uncomprehendingly watching the preceding exchanges.*]

BONIFACE [*laughing, to* BABETTE]: I don't think we have to worry what the neighbors will say!

BABETTE: No!

BONIFACE [*to* PISTACHE, *noticing what he is doing*]: What are you doing with that?

PISTACHE [*to* BONIFACE]: For fifteen thousand, Monsieur Boniface, I think we can throw in the cage, don't you?

[*He gives it to a delighted* VON GELTSACK.]

VON GELTSACK: So! [*To* PISTACHE.] Danke schön, mein Herr!... [*Clicking his heels, to* BONIFACE.] Monsieur... [*To* BABETTE.] Mademoiselle...

BONIFACE [*looking at the cage a little ruefully, addressing the monkey*]: Poor baby!... We're going to miss you...

BABETTE: But with our Pupu we wouldn't have much time for our Bobo...

BONIFACE [*quickly correcting*]: Our Baba...

BABETTE [*likewise*]: Our Bobo...

BONIFACE [*just as little* BRÜNNHILDE *appears at the open door*]: Baba...

BABETTE: Bobo...

VON GELTSACK [*holding out the cage to* BRÜNNHILDE]: So! For you, Bubu... Here, meine Bubu... For you...

PISTACHE [*to himself, throwing up his hands*]: Baba, Bobo, Pupu, Bubu...

BRÜNNHILDE [*jumping up and down, clapping her hands in glee*]: Oh!...

[*She opens the cage as* VON GELTSACK *holds it out, and lovingly takes out the monkey, caressing it.*]

VON GELTSACK [*to* BRÜNNHILDE]: So! Vat you call it den already?

BRÜNNHILDE [*after a moment's reflection*]: Boniface!

BONIFACE [*laughing, to* BRÜNNHILDE]: I'm flattered, but I think "Babette" would be better!

BABETTE [*laughing, to* BRÜNNHILDE]: No! "Boniface!"

BONIFACE [*looking tenderly at* BABETTE, *with a sigh*]: Babette...

BABETTE [*reciprocating*]: Boniface...

BONIFACE [*taking her in his arms*]: Babette...

[*He gives her a discreet kiss as* BRÜNNHILDE *plays with the monkey, quite uninterested in their emotion, while* PISTACHE *looks on approvingly and a puzzled* VON GELTSACK *stands scratching his head.*]

CURTAIN

SIGNOR NICODEMO

Adaptation of

Tout pour les dames!

by

Henri Meilhac and Ludovic Halévy

(1867)

CHARACTERS

MONTGISCARD, a bachelor in his early thirties, always one step ahead of his many creditors

NICODEMO, a middle-aged Italian, very rich and very romantic, chivalrous beyond belief

PETITFOUR, an elegant roué, friend of Montgiscard

OCTAVE, Montgiscard's butler-cum-confidant

BOUQUET, one of Montgiscard's many creditors

MATHILDE, Petitfour's wife, in love with Montgiscard

EMMA, the lovely young object of Montgiscard's affection

The drawing room in Marcel de Montgiscard's apartment. Up left, an angled wall with a double door leading to a vestibule and the rest of the apartment. In the corresponding angled wall, up right, a window flanked by two long drapes reaching to about one foot from the floor. Down right, a door opening inward. In the upstage wall, center, a fireplace with the usual appurtenances. Over the mantelpiece, a painting of a nude. Right, facing the wall between the door and window, a small desk and chair. On the desk, papers, pen and ink, a book, etc. Downstage, right of center, a loveseat. Up left, not far from the door, an armchair. On it, a man's hat and coat. Midstage left, a small table with two chairs. On the table, a newspaper. Other appropriate furniture—lamps, pictures, occasional chairs, etc.—ad libitum.

At rise, BOUQUET *enters, up left, obviously impatient, followed by* OCTAVE.

BOUQUET [*crossing down right, sitting on the loveseat*]: It's a scandal, my friend! An absolute scandal!
OCTAVE: Monsieur Bouquet...
BOUQUET: And I won't have it!
OCTAVE: Monsieur...
BOUQUET: I won't have it! You hear?
OCTAVE: But...
BOUQUET [*getting up*]: He's in Paris! I know he is! I don't care what you tell me...
OCTAVE: But monsieur, I never said—
BOUQUET [*interrupting*]: And he's been here all day! Since last night...
OCTAVE: But...
BOUQUET: You see? I know, my friend... I know...
[*He crosses left and begins pacing.*]
OCTAVE: Quite right... Monsieur is quite right... Last night...
BOUQUET: Damn right, last night!... Damn right I'm quite right!
OCTAVE [*aside*]: Indeed! [*Aloud.*] Begging monsieur's pardon... Monsieur de Montgiscard did arrive last evening, but...
BOUQUET: But...?
OCTAVE: But he's out at the moment. That's what I was trying to tell monsieur.
BOUQUET: Oh? [*Pointing to the hat and coat on the armchair, up left.*] And what's that?
OCTAVE [*walking over confidently and putting on the hat, which is much too large for him*]: Mine, monsieur...
BOUQUET: Yes, I'm sure!
OCTAVE [*replacing the hat on the armchair*]: The minute he returns I'll tell him monsieur called. I know he'll be terribly disappointed to have missed him!... Terribly... Terribly...

BOUQUET: "Disappointed" my—

OCTAVE: Terribly, monsieur...

BOUQUET: All right, I'll leave! But not for long, my friend! I'll be back in half an hour!

OCTAVE: Aha... Then we'll have the pleasure of seeing monsieur again shortly.

BOUQUET: And I'll have the pleasure of seeing my money!

OCTAVE [*nodding, accompanying him to the door, left*]: Monsieur...

BOUQUET: Or he'll have the pleasure of hearing from me, damn it!

OCTAVE: Indeed, monsieur... With good news, let's hope... [BOUQUET *turns on his heel and leaves.*] No bad news, or I know he'll be terribly upset... [*Calling after him.*] Terribly... Terribly... [*He closes the door.*] And with that one, no news is good news, as they say... [*Returning downstage, with a sigh.*] A little too close for comfort this time!

[MONTGISCARD *enters right, cautiously.*]

MONTGISCARD: Is he gone?

OCTAVE: Yes, monsieur.

MONTGISCARD [*sighing*]: Well...

OCTAVE: Really, I don't know how much longer...

MONTGISCARD: Good work, Octave! Which one was it this time?

OCTAVE: Which one, monsieur?... Bouquet, as usual... Isn't it always?

MONTGISCARD: Ah yes... Dear Bouquet...

OCTAVE: In full flower, if I may say... Monsieur should have heard him! "It's a scandal, my friend! An absolute scandal!..." Why, he even tried to take the clock! [*Pointing up left, toward the door.*] The one in the hall...

MONTGISCARD [*pointing, incredulous*]: The grandfather clock?

OCTAVE: Yes, monsieur... But I didn't let him.

MONTGISCARD: I should hope not!

OCTAVE: No, I stopped him just as he was trying to lift it up on his back.

MONTGISCARD [*crossing right, to the desk*]: The nerve of some people!

[*He sits down, begins shuffling papers, writing, etc.*]

OCTAVE: Because, after all... Monsieur owes me a little something too, and... That is, if I let them all start carting off the furniture each time... Well, soon he wouldn't have anything left... As collateral, I mean... In case he can't pay me...

MONTGISCARD: Aha... [*Aside.*] His devotion overwhelms me!

[*There is a brief pause as* MONTGISCARD *continues to write.*]

OCTAVE: I'm sure monsieur remembers...

MONTGISCARD [*impatiently*]: Remembers?... Remembers what?

OCTAVE: The little something he owes me...

MONTGISCARD: Yes, yes! I remember!... How the devil could I forget?

OCTAVE: Perhaps he would like to discuss the matter now... While the subject is at hand...

MONTGISCARD: Please, Octave! This is hardly the time... If you think that's all I have on my mind...

[*There is another pause.*]

OCTAVE: If monsieur doesn't mind my saying... He's in rather a nasty mood.

MONTGISCARD: Oh? And whatever gave you that idea?

OCTAVE: Perhaps his trip to Deauville wasn't all that he expected...

MONTGISCARD: To say the least!

OCTAVE: In other words, monsieur, I take it we're not marrying the young lady... The one who was going to solve all our problems...

MONTGISCARD [*getting up*]: You take it correctly! We're not!

OCTAVE: Tsk tsk tsk! I'm sorry... [*He pauses again, as if waiting for* MONTGISCARD *to continue.*] Well, monsieur?

MONTGISCARD: "Well"?

OCTAVE: Details... Details... Monsieur shouldn't keep them to himself!

MONTGISCARD [*wryly*]: I shouldn't?

OCTAVE: It's not good to keep one's emotions bottled up! It's much better to... to uncork them, so to speak.

MONTGISCARD: Oh?

OCTAVE: Monsieur knows what they say... [*Declaiming.*]

> *The grieving heart should share its woe,*
> *Else it must yet more grievous grow.*

MONTGISCARD: They say that, do they?

OCTAVE: It's a poem, monsieur.

MONTGISCARD: Yes, I gathered...

OCTAVE: Really, monsieur should get it off his chest, as they say. He'll feel much better!... Details... Details...

MONTGISCARD [*putting down his papers and pen, and standing up, pacing*]: But there are no details, Octave! It's all perfectly simple!... I went to Deauville, I spoke with her guardian...

OCTAVE: That's right, monsieur... Go on, go on...

MONTGISCARD: And he told me that Emma... [*Correcting.*] that Mademoiselle Dufour had a dowry of ten thousand francs... There! Those are the details!

OCTAVE: Ten thousand, monsieur?

MONTGISCARD: Not one centime, more!

OCTAVE: Rather slim, if monsieur doesn't mind my saying! Especially for a lady who's supposed to solve all our problems...

MONTGISCARD: My sentiments exactly!... So I thanked him, bowed, turned around, and came home.

OCTAVE: Very wise... Monsieur did the right thing, I'm sure.

MONTGISCARD: No need to drag it out... That wouldn't have been proper.

OCTAVE: No, no! Certainly not! [MONTGISCARD *sighs.*] Well, I'm glad monsieur got the details off his chest. He must feel much better.

MONTGISCARD: Not a bit, thank you!

OCTAVE [*almost offended*]: Oh?

MONTGISCARD: Believe me, it wasn't easy, leaving like that. Without even saying goodbye... Without even seeing her...

OCTAVE: Is monsieur trying to say that he's fond of the young lady?

MONTGISCARD: Fond?... In a way... She's really very sweet.

OCTAVE [*nodding*]: Aha... I understand! Love... Love, monsieur... It makes the world go round, as they say.

MONTGISCARD: Yes, they do indeed... Well, love is all very well and good, but...

OCTAVE: But money talks!

MONTGISCARD: So to speak!

OCTAVE: And a mere ten thousand francs doesn't say very much!

MONTGISCARD: Please, Octave... Let's not discuss it!

OCTAVE: No, no... Let's not... I'm sure monsieur would prefer to discuss the other matter.

MONTGISCARD: Other...? What other matter?

OCTAVE: The little something he owes me...

MONTGISCARD: Again?

[*He moves left, sits down at the table, and picks up the newspaper.*]

OCTAVE: Monsieur will forgive me if I keep bringing it up. It's just that... Well, as monsieur's employee I've swept the apartment, shined his shoes, gotten rid of Monsieur Bouquet...

MONTGISCARD [*reading the paper, nodding*]: Yes, yes...

OCTAVE: All in a day's work, as they say... Whereas as monsieur's creditor...

[*He sits down on the other side of the table and takes a notebook from his pocket.*]

MONTGISCARD: I beg your pardon?

OCTAVE [*holding it out*]: Here... Monsieur can check my account book for himself. I always have it handy!

MONTGISCARD: I'm sure!

OCTAVE: See? Two hundred forty-two francs...

MONTGISCARD [*mechanically*]: Two hundred...

OCTAVE: For six weeks' wages... Monsieur remembers how much he agreed to pay me...

MONTGISCARD: Yes, yes...

OCTAVE: Plus two seats at the Comédie Française for monsieur's tailor... To make him stop coming round for his money, the way he used to...

MONTGISCARD: Yes... Right...

OCTAVE: Plus seven box seats at the Folies-Alcazar for monsieur himself... Plus seven long-stem roses... Plus...

MONTGISCARD [*getting up, throwing the newspaper down on the table and crossing right, impatiently*]: I know!... I know your book by heart!

OCTAVE: Monsieur is too kind!

MONTGISCARD: But you, of all people... You know I have no money! You can't squeeze blood out of a stone... [*Ironically.*] As they say...

OCTAVE: Well... [*Getting up.*] I hope monsieur will squeeze as best he can. Without money, after all, he can hardly expect...

MONTGISCARD: Believe me, I'm trying! If you'd just stop hounding me and... and let me squeeze in peace! The more you hound me, the harder you make it!... And the longer you'll have to wait!

OCTAVE: Begging monsieur's pardon, but... We've heard that song before, as they say!

MONTGISCARD: Oh?

OCTAVE: Monsieur understands... It's the creditor speaking, not the employee.

MONTGISCARD: Employee... Creditor... What's the difference? I can't pay you...

OCTAVE: I've used the same reasoning myself, more than once... On monsieur's behalf, of course... To Monsieur Bouquet, not to mention the others...

MONTGISCARD: I know... Much obliged...

OCTAVE: And he always reacts with a cynical smile and a choice of exclamations... Not in the best of taste, I might add...

MONTGISCARD: Really, Octave... I don't want to discuss it! Add another twenty francs to whatever I owe you, and leave me alone!

OCTAVE: Twenty francs, monsieur?... [*Writing in his notebook.*] Well, if monsieur insists... That makes two hundred sixty-two francs he owes me.

MONTGISCARD [*with a wave of the hand*]: Right... Right...

OCTAVE: Unless he prefers round figures, that is... Say, two hundred seventy...

MONTGISCARD [*losing patience*]: Fine! Two hundred seventy! I'm mad about round figures!

OCTAVE: Monsieur is too kind!

MONTGISCARD: Please, think nothing of it!... Now, if you don't mind...
[*He points up left, toward the door.*]

OCTAVE: If monsieur would allow me to show my appreciation by offering him one last word of advice...

MONTGISCARD: Octave...

OCTAVE: Not as an employee or a creditor, monsieur... As a friend... Just a friend...

MONTGISCARD: I'm touched!... What is it?

OCTAVE [*moving toward the door, left*]: I just want to say that monsieur should do his best to pay his debts, because there's no time like the present.

MONTGISCARD: But I just got through telling you...

OCTAVE: He should pay Monsieur Bouquet, and his tailor, and the others... And especially all the faithful help.

MONTGISCARD: What? What "faithful help?" You are the "faithful help!" You're all that's left!

OCTAVE: Thank you, monsieur! That's all the more reason...
[*He exits.*]

MONTGISCARD [*shaking his head*]: "Pay Bouquet... Pay the tailor..." You wonder if he heard a single word I said! In one ear and out the other... [*Mimicking.*] "As they say... As they say..." [*The doorbell rings.*] Now what? [*Calling.*] Octave!...
[OCTAVE *enters, up left.*]

OCTAVE: Monsieur?

MONTGISCARD: The bell... Someone rang...

OCTAVE: I know, monsieur. But there's really no hurry... It's only Monsieur Bouquet. He said he would be back.

MONTGISCARD: Bouquet?... Damn! You talk to him... Tell him I'm out... I just left...
[*He moves to the armchair, up left, and picks up his hat and coat, as if to leave.*]

OCTAVE: Please, monsieur! Not again!... I simply can't face him! Always the same story...

MONTGISCARD: But it's true... I'm leaving... I'm going to pay a call on the baroness...

OCTAVE: The baroness, monsieur? Madame de Petitfour? The one who keeps chasing monsieur, if I may say so?

MONTGISCARD: Of course... How many baronesses do I know?

OCTAVE: Just curious...

MONTGISCARD [*aside*]: The one who keeps throwing herself at my feet and threatening to leave her husband...

[*The bell rings again.* MONTGISCARD *moves up left, toward the door.*]

OCTAVE: Not that way, monsieur!... Bouquet... Monsieur Bouquet...

MONTGISCARD [*stopping in his tracks*]: Ah!... [*Pointing down right.*] Through the kitchen?

OCTAVE [*shocked*]: The backstairs, monsieur?... Heavens! Not like a... a domestic!

MONTGISCARD [*running up right, to the window, looking out*]: Well, there's always...

OCTAVE: Three stories, monsieur... I really don't think...

MONTGISCARD: Then the backstairs it is!

OCTAVE: But monsieur... It's not right! I'm an employee, and even I would never use the backstairs!

[*The bell rings again, more insistently.*]

MONTGISCARD: No, my friend, but I would!

OCTAVE [*crossing to the door, left*]: Coming... Coming...

[*He exits.*]

MONTGISCARD: Ah! Emma... Emma... Why couldn't you have at least fifty thousand?

[*He exits, right.*]

OCTAVE'S VOICE [*offstage*]: I'm sorry... Monsieur is out... He'll be terribly disappointed... Oh my! It's not...

NICODEMO'S VOICE [*offstage*]: Signore...

[NICODEMO *enters, followed by* OCTAVE.]

OCTAVE: But monsieur...

NICODEMO [*with an Italian accent*]: Signor Marcello de Montgiscard, eh?

OCTAVE: No... That is, yes... No... "Marcel," monsieur... "Marcel"...

NICODEMO: Si, si! Marcello!... And ees you, signore?

OCTAVE: I... No, monsieur... I'm afraid Monsieur de Montgiscard is out.

NICODEMO: Out? Ees out?

OCTAVE: I know he'll be terribly disappointed to have missed monsieur...

NICODEMO: So?

OCTAVE: Terribly... Terribly...

[NICODEMO *begins moving around the room, inspecting everything.*]

NICODEMO: Ees out... I am glad... Ees better so! Better...

OCTAVE: Better, monsieur?

NICODEMO: Si... Si...

OCTAVE [*aside*]: Who on earth... He can't be a creditor. He doesn't even know him!

NICODEMO [*examining*]: Bene... Bene... Very nice... Very nice...

OCTAVE: Excuse me, monsieur...

NICODEMO [*ignoring him*]: Good taste... Very seemple, but... Si, si... Good taste, good taste...

OCTAVE [*aside*]: Good heavens! He must be... He's worse than a creditor! He must be from the court... [*To* NICODEMO.] Excuse me, monsieur...

NICODEMO: Why? What you do?

OCTAVE: Do?... Nothing... I...

NICODEMO: So why I esscuse?... [*Picking up a book from the desk, right.*] Ah! Thees book... What ees, eh?

OCTAVE [*aside*]: Oh my! He's come to take away monsieur's things!

NICODEMO [*looking the book over*]: Ho, ho!... No, no, no!... Thees book, no!...
[*He puts the book in his pocket.*]

OCTAVE: Excuse me, monsieur, but... Monsieur de Montgiscard owes me a little
something too, and... and I really mustn't let you...

NICODEMO [*ignoring him*]: Bene... Bene...

OCTAVE: Besides, this isn't the proper way to go about it!

NICODEMO: Eh?... You say?

OCTAVE: A warrant, monsieur... You have to... Before you can seize any
property...

NICODEMO: Bene... Bene...

OCTAVE: Like that book, monsieur... You can't just take it and put it in your
pocket!

NICODEMO [*taking out the book and showing it to him*]: Si, si! I put een my
pocket, thees book!

OCTAVE: But...

NICODEMO: *Il Decamerone*, signore... Boccaccio... No nice, no nice... Ees better
for her she no see such theeng!
[*He pockets it again.*]

OCTAVE: "Her"?... Who?

NICODEMO [*ignoring his question, and examining the painting of the nude
above the fireplace*]: And thees!... Ho, ho! Mamma mia!... No, no, no!
[*He takes it off the wall.*]

OCTAVE [*rushing upstage*]: Just one minute, monsieur! What do you think
you're... I didn't let Bouquet take the clock, and I certainly won't let you
take that painting!

NICODEMO: Take?... No, no... I turn only!... I turn...
[*He turns the painting toward the wall and puts it on the mantelpiece.*]

OCTAVE: But...

NICODEMO: Ees better she no see... Si, si! Better no see... No see...

OCTAVE: "She"?... "See"?...

NICODEMO: Si, si! She... She... [*Pointing.*] Downstairs, signore...

OCTAVE [*aside*]: Who?... [*Aloud.*] You mean, you're not from the court,
monsieur?

NICODEMO: Court? Court?... But no! Why from court?

OCTAVE: Well, I thought...

NICODEMO: Now you tell me... [*Moving down right, toward the door.*] Thees
room, signore... What ees?... What ees, eh?
[*He opens the door.*]

OCTAVE: A sitting room, monsieur... But... If you're not from the court...

NICODEMO [*poking his head inside*]: Bene... Bene... Very nice... She wait een
comfort! Si, si!... Een comfort...

OCTAVE: But...

NICODEMO: I go now... Downstairs... I go breeng...

OCTAVE [*closing the door, right, mimicking*]: "Si, si!... Bene... Bene..."

NICODEMO [*at the door, left, giving the room another look, nodding*]: Very
nice... Very nice...
[*He exits.*]

OCTAVE: Amusing chap... [*Shrugging.*] Whoever he is... [*Opening the door,

left, looking out.] Gone!... And with monsieur's book, no less!... Strange, the people you meet in this city! They come into your apartment, pick up a book or something, put it in their pocket, and say they'll be right back!... Five minutes later, they're selling it in a second-hand shop, and that's the last you ever see of them! So good-bye book!... [*The doorbell rings.*] Now who in the name of... That must be Bouquet!... [*Preparing his greeting.*] "I'm sorry, but monsieur is out... He'll be terribly disappointed..."
[*He exits, left.*]

NICODEMO'S VOICE: Grazie, signore...

OCTAVE'S VOICE: You... Again?

NICODEMO'S VOICE: Si, si! I return!

OCTAVE'S VOICE: Ah... I thought...

[NICODEMO *enters, left. He is followed by* EMMA, *heavily veiled, whom he is holding by the hand, and by* OCTAVE.]

NICODEMO: And I breeng... I breeng... [*To* EMMA, *obviously hesitant.*] Come, come, signorina...

EMMA [*trembling*]: Oh... [*Looking around.*] His... His apartment...

NICODEMO: But why you shake, eh? Ees cold?

EMMA [*to* NICODEMO]: I never should have let you talk me into this, monsieur! Here... In his apartment...

NICODEMO [*with a broad gesture, nodding*]: Very nice... Very nice...

EMMA: With you, and... [*Pointing to* OCTAVE.] and a total stranger!

NICODEMO: Stranger?... No, no! No ees stranger, signorina... Ees domesteec of Marcello!

OCTAVE: I beg your—

NICODEMO [*to* EMMA]: And soon ees yours too!

OCTAVE [*aside*]: The man is a raving lunatic!

NICODEMO [*to* OCTAVE]: You... Please go downstairs and pay driver!

OCTAVE: Monsieur?

NICODEMO: Per piacere... Downstairs... Een front of door...

OCTAVE: Just like that, you tell me—

NICODEMO [*giving him a handful of coins*]: Here... Twenty franc... You keep change!... Si, si! You keep!

OCTAVE [*gaping at his coins*]: Twenty... [*Aside.*] Well, he may be mad, but his money looks healthy!
[*He pockets the money and exits, left.*]

EMMA [*sitting on the loveseat*]: I'm sorry if I seem upset, monsieur! It's not that I don't appreciate all you've done...

NICODEMO: And all I weell do, signorina! Weell do!... Nicodemo he just begeen!

EMMA: But I've never done anything quite like this before! I'm sure you understand...

NICODEMO: Oh, si!... Si, si!... Capisco... But ees no need! No worry... No be upset... Ees so seemple what I do!

EMMA: Perhaps for you, monsieur!

NICODEMO: Si, si! What ees more seemple?... I see you on beach, een Deauville... You cry, cry, cry... And I ask you: "Bella donna, why you cry? You tell me, eh? Why you cry, signorina?" And you say: "Ah, signore, I am so sad... so sad..."

EMMA [*sighing*]: Yes...

NICODEMO [*continuing*]: "The man of my dreams he want me to marry heem, but... but..." And more you cry... And more... And more...

EMMA: Oh, monsieur...

NICODEMO: So I ask you who ees thees man, and you say: "Marcello de Montgiscard, signore..."

EMMA [*sighing*]: Marcel...

NICODEMO: And I say: "Signorina, you love thees Marcello, eh?" And you tell me: "Oh, si! But... But..." And more you cry...

EMMA: I know, monsieur... If only my guardian... Oh, if only things were different! If... If only... [*She begins to weep softly.*] One day he was there, and... and the next day he was gone...

NICODEMO: Ah! No, no!... Per piacere! You no cry, signorina!... Finito! No more, eh?

EMMA: And when I asked Monsieur Billetdoux... When I asked my guardian why, all he would say was: "He's not for you, my child!... He's not for you!..." Oh, monsieur...

[*She begins to weep again.*]

NICODEMO: No, no! You no cry!... Bella donna she cry, and my heart she break een two!

EMMA: I'm sorry... Please forgive me...

NICODEMO [*taking a card from his pocket and showing it to her*]: My card, signorina... You no see my card?

EMMA [*wiping her eyes, reading*]: "Signor Nicodemo, Tutto Per Le Donne!" [*Not understanding.*] Monsieur?

NICODEMO: Si, si!... Eet mean... Nicodemo... [*With a little bow.*] Nicodemo he leeve and breathe for woman!... Si, si! For woman I do anytheeng!... Tutto, signorina!... Any woman... All woman...

EMMA [*returning the card*]: You have a heart, monsieur!

NICODEMO: Ees my life, ees my life! Ees reason for why I leeve! For woman... All woman!... Le donne, Dio mio!... Ees never too much I can do per le donne! I geeve everytheeng I have!... [*Growing more impassioned.*] Oh! Eef only I be keeng!... Si, si, signorina!... Keeng!... I geeve my crown! I geeve my thorn! I geeve my palace! Everytheeng! And I say: "Here, here... Ecco! Ees for you! Ees all for you!... Si, si! Tutto, tutto, tutto!" [*Getting carried away.*] Ah, ah! Woman!... Come, woman!... Hundred... Thousand... No, no! Ten thousand... Ten thousand woman! All woman who need Nicodemo... Come, come! I do for you anytheeng!... Everytheeng!... Tutto per le donne!... I geeve to you my money... my body... my heart... my soul... I geeve to you my life! Si, si! Ten thousand woman... Ten thousand...

EMMA [*timidly*]: Monsieur...

NICODEMO [*suddenly coming back down to earth, rather prosaically*]: But for now ees only one I have... Only you, signorina... And I feex! Nicodemo he take care... Si, si! Good care...

EMMA: But how, monsieur? Now that we're here... in his apartment... What are we going to do?

NICODEMO: What we do?... Dio mio! I tell you what we do!... Marcello he love you, eh? And you love Marcello?...

EMMA: Oh, yes!

NICODEMO: So! You marry, signorina!... Si, si!... That ees what we do!

EMMA: But...

NICODEMO: Why you theenk I keednap you last night, een Deauville? Why you theenk, eh?... Why I breeng you here?... Why, why, signorina?... Ees only for one reason!... Nicodemo he take care... You marry Marcello! And no more you cry, cry, cry!

[*The doorbell rings.*]

EMMA [*with a start*]: Oh please... If that's Marcel... Please, you talk to him... I couldn't!

NICODEMO: Si, si! I talk... [*He moves down right, to the door, and opens it.*]: Here... You go een, eh?... You wait een comfort...

EMMA [*at the door*]: And please, monsieur... Whatever you do, please tell him this was all your idea. I don't want him to think...

NICODEMO: Si, si, bella donna! I tell... You no worry...

[*EMMA exits. A moment later* BOUQUET *enters, up left, followed closely by* OCTAVE.]

OCTAVE: I'm sorry, but monsieur has just left. He'll be terribly disappointed...

BOUQUET: I'm sure!

OCTAVE: Terribly... Terribly...

BOUQUET: Did he leave you my money?

OCTAVE: I'm afraid he neglected that detail, monsieur. One can't think of everything, as they say...

BOUQUET [*furious*]: Oh!

NICODEMO [*at the door, overhearing, to* BOUQUET]: Money, signore?... Ees what you say, no?

BOUQUET [*aside to* OCTAVE]: Who the devil is that?

OCTAVE [*aside to* BOUQUET]: Some lunatic, monsieur. But harmless... And quite amusing! If monsieur would like to be entertained...

BOUQUET [*to* OCTAVE]: Thank you just the same! If I want to see a lunatic I can look in the mirror!... I must have been mad to lend Montgiscard those four hundred francs!

[*He sits down at the table, left.*]

NICODEMO [*overhearing, to* BOUQUET]: What you say, signore? [*To* OCTAVE.] What he say? [*To* BOUQUET.] What you say, eh?... You tell me...

BOUQUET [*aside to* OCTAVE]: What damn business is it of his?

NICODEMO [*to* BOUQUET]: You say sometheeng about you lend money, no?... To Marcello...

BOUQUET: "Marcello"?

OCTAVE [*aside to* BOUQUET]: I'm sure he'll say something that will give monsieur a laugh!

BOUQUET [*aside to* OCTAVE]: I doubt it, my good man! I'm not in any mood...

OCTAVE [*to* NICODEMO]: That's right, monsieur... That's what the gentleman was saying... A modest sum... Hardly worth mentioning...

BOUQUET [*to* OCTAVE]: My foot!

NICODEMO [*to* BOUQUET]: So! How much, eh?

BOUQUET: How much?

OCTAVE [*to* NICODEMO]: A mere four hundred francs, monsieur... A pittance...

NICODEMO: Si, si! A peetance!... [*To* BOUQUET.] And ees for thees peetance you make so much noise, signore?

BOUQUET: I... I beg your—

NICODEMO [*derisively*]: Four hundred franc?

BOUQUET: I... Just who do you think—

NICODEMO [*to* BOUQUET, *taking out his billfold*]: Ecco, signore!... Here! [*He pulls out a wad of bills.*] You take! You take!...
[*He offers them to* BOUQUET.]

BOUQUET: What?

NICODEMO: Ees peetance!... Peetance!... For thees you no more come bother Marcello...

BOUQUET [*flabbergasted*]: Monsieur?

NICODEMO: No more make noise!... No more, eh?... You hear?

BOUQUET [*counting the bills, unable to believe his eyes*]: He... He paid me... He...
[*He gets up.*]

OCTAVE [*aside*]: Good heavens! He paid Bouquet!

BOUQUET [*showing the bills to* OCTAVE]: Look! He paid me...

OCTAVE [*to* BOUQUET]: Come, come... I'll see monsieur out...
[*He motions him up left, toward the door.*]

BOUQUET [*at the door, still gaping at the bills in disbelief*]: He paid me... He paid me...

OCTAVE [*leading him off*]: Come, come... [*Aside.*] There is life after debt, after all! [*To* NICODEMO.] Monsieur... Signore...
[OCTAVE *and* BOUQUET *exit.*]

NICODEMO [*alone*]: So, Marcello he owe money, eh?... Maybe molto, molto!... Lots and lots of money... Maybe ees why... Si, si! Ees why Signor Billetdoux he no want Emma she marry... Ah si!... Si, si! Capisco... Ees why he say: "Ees no for you... Ees no for you..."
[OCTAVE *reenters, left.*]

OCTAVE [*aside*]: If he paid him... I wonder...

NICODEMO: Ah, signore... You come back...

OCTAVE [*almost obsequiously*]: Why yes... Yes, monsieur...

NICODEMO: Ees gone, thees man, eh? Thees man who make so much noise for... for peetance! Ees gone?

OCTAVE: Gone, monsieur?... Bouquet?... Why... [*Struck by a sudden inspiration.*] Why no... That is... I'm afraid he's still lurking in the shadows, monsieur...

NICODEMO [*not comprehending*]: Per piacere?... You say?

OCTAVE: Still lying in wait for Monsieur de Montgiscard...

NICODEMO: But I pay heem! I pay!... Why he wait, eh?... Why he lurk?

OCTAVE: Well, monsieur... It's really quite simple. Actually, Monsieur de Montgiscard owes him a little more.

NICODEMO: Oh?

OCTAVE: Yes, monsieur... A little more than the four hundred... Not much... Just a little... But he didn't want to say so.

NICODEMO: No?

OCTAVE: No... He thought it would seem rather gauche, monsieur.

NICODEMO: Bene... How much, eh? How much more he owe?

OCTAVE: Oh, less than a pittance... Only two hundred seventy... Well, three hundred francs in round figures, monsieur.

NICODEMO [*taking another handful of bills from his billfold*]: Si, si! Less than peetance!... Here, you geeve heem, per piacere!

OCTAVE [*taking them*]: Indeed, monsieur!... Of course!

NICODEMO: And you tell heem please he go! He no bother Marcello!... He go, and no come back, eh?

OCTAVE: Yes, yes, monsieur!... Si, si! Right away!... Bene... Bene... [*Moving upstage, pocketing the bills, aside.*] Good heavens! He paid me... He really did! He paid me!

NICODEMO [*at the door, down right, to himself*]: Ah! I hope she no hear, bella donna... So much noise for... for peetance!...
[*He exits. A moment later,* MONTGISCARD *enters, left.*]

OCTAVE [*seeing him*]: Ah! Monsieur will never guess what happened while he was gone...

MONTGISCARD: No, I probably never will!... [*Handing him his hat and coat, impatiently.*] Here... Take these... [*Aside.*] Damned waste of time!

OCTAVE: I've really been enjoying myself, monsieur!

MONTGISCARD [*to himself*]: The baron, not at home... Mathilde. not at home... I could have saved myself the trip!

OCTAVE: I don't think monsieur heard me... I said: "I've been enjoying myself..."

MONTGISCARD: Good! I'm delighted!

OCTAVE: A lunatic, monsieur... [*Pointing down right.*] In there... With a lady... Terribly entertaining...

MONTGISCARD: What?

OCTAVE: Terribly... Terribly...

MONTGISCARD: What are you babbling about, Octave?

OCTAVE: In there, monsieur... Wearing a veil... [*Covering his face with his free hand.*] All covered up...

MONTGISCARD: Who?

OCTAVE: The lady... The one he brought with him...

MONTGISCARD [*pointing down right*]: There's a lady in there?... With a veil?...

OCTAVE: That's what I've been trying to tell monsieur...

MONTGISCARD [*to himself*]: Oh my! The baroness... She's finally gone and done it! She's left Petitfour... [*Louder, but still not intended for* OCTAVE'*s ears.*] It's Mathilde.

OCTAVE [*overhearing*]: I don't know the lady's name, monsieur. I only know she came with the lunatic.

MONTGISCARD: What lunatic?

OCTAVE: If monsieur would only listen... I just told him... Some stranger... Utterly out of his mind...

MONTGISCARD: What?

OCTAVE: But perfectly harmless... All he seems to want to do is borrow monsieur's books, turn his paintings to the wall, and...

MONTGISCARD [*looking with surprise at the painting on the mantelpiece*]: What the devil...

OCTAVE: ...and pay monsieur's debts.

MONTGISCARD [*at the fireplace, turning the painting back and hanging it properly*]: Pay my... He what?

OCTAVE: Yes, monsieur... That's what I said.

MONTGISCARD: My debts?

OCTAVE: Monsieur Bouquet, for instance... He paid Monsieur Bouquet.

MONTGISCARD [*speechless*]: He...

OCTAVE: And myself!... I'm happy to say I'm no longer among the ranks of monsieur's esteemed creditors!

MONTGISCARD: You mean, some absolute stranger...

OCTAVE: Quite, monsieur! He paid me!... Down to the last centime, I might add... [*Aside.*] And then some!

MONTGISCARD: But...

OCTAVE: I have to admit, it wasn't exactly his own idea... But nevertheless...

MONTGISCARD [*crossing left*]: Damned if I understand...

[*The door, right, opens and* NICODEMO *appears.*]

NICODEMO [*striding in, noticing* MONTGISCARD]: Ah! Signore... Ees Marcello, no?

MONTGISCARD [*bowing*]: Monsieur...

NICODEMO [*to* OCTAVE]: You!... Domesteec!

OCTAVE [*obsequiously*]: Si?... Si?...

NICODEMO [*pointing up left, to the door*]: Please... You leave!

OCTAVE [*backing toward the door*]: Oh, indeed, monsieur... My pleasure... Whatever monsieur wishes... [*Aside to* MONTGISCARD, *in passing.*] Terribly amusing... Terribly... Terribly...

[*He exits, left.*]

MONTGISCARD [*looking* NICODEMO *up and down, aside*]: Why the devil should Mathilde drag some stranger along with her? [*Nodding politely and motioning* NICODEMO *toward the loveseat.*] Monsieur...

NICODEMO [*ceremoniously*]: Signore...

MONTGISCARD [*inviting him to be seated*]: Please...

NICODEMO: Grazie... Grazie...

[*He sits down.* MONTGISCARD *sits down by the table, left.*]

MONTGISCARD [*after a polite silence*]: So, monsieur... I take it you know Mathilde... [*Correcting himself.*] Madame de Petitfour...

NICODEMO [*not understanding*]: Per piacere?... What you say?

MONTGISCARD: Poor child!... We mustn't blame her! It's really not her fault... When a lady suffers the way she does... So young... So sensitive...

NICODEMO [*pricking up his ears*]: Suffer?... You say "suffer"?

MONTGISCARD: Her husband, after all... A rake if ever there was one! Charming fellow, but... Well...

NICODEMO [*taking a notepad and pencil from his pocket*]: Si... Si...

MONTGISCARD: But I don't have to tell you... The baron is a friend, and all that. But still... Right is right...

NICODEMO [*taking notes*]: "Signora de Petitfour..."

MONTGISCARD: And wrong is wrong, to coin a phrase...

NICODEMO [*ignoring his bon mot*]: "Petitfour"... How you spell?

MONTGISCARD: How... I beg your pardon?

NICODEMO: "Petitfour"... Her name... How you spell, eh?

MONTGISCARD: What are you... You know as well as I do. What kind of joke...

NICODEMO [*getting up*]: Mamma mia! No ees joke! No joke at all!... Ees sad, thees lady!... She suffer, you tell me... Ees enough! Si, si! I feex!...

MONTGISCARD: What?

NICODEMO: Nicodemo he take care!... But no now!... Later... Later... [*Pointing down right, toward the door.*] After thees one...

MONTGISCARD: Monsieur?

NICODEMO: So, where she leeve, per piacere? Where she leeve, thees... thees Signora de Petitfour?

MONTGISCARD: Where...

NICODEMO [*crossing to* MONTGISCARD]: Eef I no can find bella donna, how I help, eh?... Si, si, signore... How I help? How I help?

MONTGISCARD [*confused, getting up*]: You... You mean you don't know her?... You don't know Mathilde... the baroness... You don't know Madame de Petitfour?

NICODEMO: No, no... But no make deeference! She suffer?... Bene, bene... I help...

[*He hands* MONTGISCARD *his card.*]

MONTGISCARD [*reading*]: "Tutto..." What in heaven's name...

NICODEMO: "...Per Le Donne," signore... "Signor Nicodemo, Tutto Per Le Donne!"

MONTGISCARD [*still at a loss, giving back the card*]: Yes... I'm sure... [*Shrugging.*] "Tutto..." [*Suddenly struck by a thought.*] But... If you don't know Mathilde, monsieur... What the devil are you doing here?... And... [*Looking down right, toward the door.*] And who is that lady?

NICODEMO: Ah, signore... You heart she no tell you?

MONTGISCARD: My heart?... What are you...

[*He makes a move to go over to the door.*]

NICODEMO [*stopping him*]: No, no, no!... No yet! No yet!... Please, signore! I essplain...

MONTGISCARD: Yes, I certainly wish you would!

NICODEMO: Ees very seemple... Yesterday, signore, I am een Deauville...

MONTGISCARD: Deauville?

NICODEMO: Si, si... [*Pointing down right, toward the door.*] And I see signorina... Beautiful... Bella donna... And she cry, cry, cry... She so sad, signore...

MONTGISCARD [*aside*]: What the devil...

NICODEMO: And I ask her: "Why you cry, signorina?" And she say: "Ah, signore, I am so sad... so sad... The man of my dreams he want me to marry heem, but... but..." And more she cry... And more... And more...

MONTGISCARD: Please, monsieur! Get to the point!

NICODEMO: So I ask who ees thees man, and she say: "Marcello de Montgiscard, signore..."

MONTGISCARD: What?

NICODEMO: "Marcello..."

MONTGISCARD: Me?

NICODEMO: Si, signore... Youself!

MONTGISCARD [*startled*]: You mean... [*Pointing right.*] Emma...

NICODEMO: Si... Si...

MONTGISCARD: Here?... But how?

NICODEMO: I feex, signore... Bella donna she sad, eh?... Marcello he love her, and she love Marcello?... Bene, bene... I take care...

MONTGISCARD: You what?

NICODEMO: Si, si! Nicodemo he take care!... "Tutto Per Le Donne!"

MONTGISCARD: But...

NICODEMO: I keednap her last night...

MONTGISCARD [*agape*]: You...

NICODEMO: Een Deauville, eh?... And I breeng here... Now she marry Marcello, and she no more cry, cry, cry!

MONTGISCARD: But... But...

NICODEMO [*about to open the door, right*]: Bella donna, you come out—

MONTGISCARD [*holding him back*]: No, no, no! Not yet... Please, monsieur! Let me explain...

NICODEMO: Signor Billetdoux he forgeeve her when he know...

[*He goes to open the door again. At that moment the doorbell rings.*]

MONTGISCARD [*stopping him*]: Billetdoux... [*Looking up left, toward the door.*] Oh my! Who... [*To* NICODEMO.] But her guardian has nothing to do with it!

NICODEMO [*not understanding*]: Si... Si...

[*He tries again.*]

MONTGISCARD [*standing with his back against the door*]: That's not it at all, I'm telling you! There's a reason... A problem...

NICODEMO [*trying to push him out of the way*]: You come out, bella donna...

MONTGISCARD: No, no! Don't you understand?... I can't marry her... As much as I'd like to...

NICODEMO [*shocked*]: Oh!... But why? But why ees so, Marcello?

[*The door, left, opens and* OCTAVE *appears.*]

OCTAVE [*in the doorway, to* MONTGISCARD]: There's a lady, monsieur... With a veil... Another one...

MONTGISCARD [*aside*]: Good God! This time it must be Mathilde! [*To* NICODEMO.] Monsieur...

NICODEMO: Si, si! Capisco!... I understand!

MONTGISCARD: You do?

NICODEMO: But of course!... Other woman ees problem, eh? Ees why you theenk you no can marry signorina...

MONTGISCARD [*shaking his head*]: But...

NICODEMO [*categorically*]: So! I geeve you cinque minuti, Marcello!

MONTGISCARD [*quizzically*]: Please?

NICODEMO: Cinque minuti... Five minoot, you understand?

MONTGISCARD: What for?

NICODEMO: To get reed! To get reed of other woman, ees what for!... [*Pointing down right.*] Now I go een... I tell bella donna: "You wait, signorina..." Bene! Five minoot, I come out... You get reed!

MONTGISCARD: I beg your—

NICODEMO: Finito!... You tell other woman: "Finito!"

MONTGISCARD: I tell her—

NICODEMO: I know... She cry, cry, cry... Si, si! She suffer, other woman!... Ees too bad! But I feex! You tell me where she leeve... Nicodemo he take care...

MONTGISCARD: Monsieur...

NICODEMO: But later... Si, si! No now... Later, later...

MONTGISCARD: I...

NICODEMO [*to* OCTAVE]: You!... Domesteec!

OCTAVE [*still at the door, left*]: Monsieur?

NICODEMO: You breeng een other woman!

OCTAVE [*obsequiously*]: Of course, monsieur! My pleasure...
[*He exits.*]

NICODEMO [*to* MONTGISCARD]: Cinque minuti, Marcello!... [*He goes to the door, right.*] Five minoot!
[*He exits.*]

MONTGISCARD [*alone*]: My goodness! Now what?... [*Looking right.*] Emma... [*Looking left.*] Mathilde...
[*He leans against the loveseat. A moment later* OCTAVE *shows in* MATHILDE, *and exits immediately on a gesture from* MONTGISCARD.]

MATHILDE [*wearing gloves, carrying her hat and coat*]: Ah! Marcel... You're here!... I was so afraid you might not... [*Sighing.*] But you're here!
[*She places her hat and coat on the chair, up left.*]

MONTGISCARD [*troubled*]: Yes... So are you...

MATHILDE: I know this is a mad, impetuous thing to do! But I simply had to come! He's driven me to it! That... That beast!

MONTGISCARD: I never expected...

MATHILDE: The man is a monster! [*Beginning to raise her voice.*] It's too much! I can't bear it, Marcel! I can't bear it, you hear me?

MONTGISCARD: I hear you!... [*Casting anxious glances down right.*] Please... Please...

MATHILDE [*letting herself collapse onto one of the chairs by the table*]: It's too much! [*She throws her gloves down on the table.*] Oh! If you only knew...

MONTGISCARD: Please... Mathilde...

MATHILDE: Mistresses, mistresses!... Every day a new one!... The man is a cad! An unprincipled cad!

MONTGISCARD: Please...

MATHILDE [*getting up*]: And then, when I ask him a simple little favor... To take me to Deauville... [*Coyly.*] So I could be with you, dearest...

MONTGISCARD: Please...

MATHILDE: What does he tell me?... "I'm sorry!... Impossible..."

MONTGISCARD: Yes... Please, Mathilde...

MATHILDE [*pacing back and forth*]: And you know why, Marcel?... I'll tell you why! "Business!..." That's what he has the nerve to tell me... "Business!..."

MONTGISCARD: Really... I must ask you...

MATHILDE: Oh, I know what kind of "business" he has!... He can't pull the wool over my eyes, that... that beast!... [*Handing him a letter.*] See? Look what I found...

MONTGISCARD: What...

MATHILDE: I was going through his papers this morning... As usual... And there it was, plain as day!

MONTGISCARD [*reading*]: Oh my... I see...

MATHILDE: Now tell me he's not an unprincipled cad!

MONTGISCARD: "Fifi"?

MATHILDE [*taking back the letter*]: Fifi Laflamme!

MONTGISCARD [*aside*]: Lucky dog! [*Aloud.*] Yes, I must say...

MATHILDE: Tell me I shouldn't leave that monster!... That beast!...

MONTGISCARD: Well...

MATHILDE: No, don't try to talk me out of it, Marcel! My mind is made up! I'm leaving, and that's final! I'm going home to mother!

MONTGISCARD [*trying to coax her toward the door, left*]: Yes... Sorry you can't stay...

MATHILDE [*resisting*]: I left him a note... He's seen the last of me!

MONTGISCARD: Yes... Yes...

MATHILDE: I wrote: "You beast! You've seen the last of me! I'm going home to mother!"

MONTGISCARD [*aside*]: Direct and to the point!

MATHILDE: Then I left for the railroad station.

MONTGISCARD: You did?

MATHILDE: Yes... At first I didn't dare dream of coming here, Marcel. After all, I never have... I said to myself: "Heavens! What would he think?... No, no... I mustn't..."

MONTGISCARD [*aside*]: So I see!

MATHILDE: But I'm so superstitious... I decided I simply had to! [MONTGISCARD *gives her a quizzical look.*] I said: "If I miss my train, it's a sign that I should visit him before I leave..."

MONTGISCARD [*aside*]: Quaint...

MATHILDE: And I got to the station five minutes ahead of time.

MONTGISCARD [*after an expectant pause*]: Well?

MATHILDE: Well, I couldn't let five whole minutes go to waste. So here I am...

MONTGISCARD: But... Your train...

MATHILDE: Oh, I'm sure I must have missed it!... You see? I was right to come!

MONTGISCARD [*nodding*]: Aha... A sign...

MATHILDE [*nodding*]: A sign... Oh, it's mad, Marcel... I know... Coming here this way, I mean...

MONTGISCARD [*still trying to coax her toward the door*]: Yes...

MATHILDE: But you have to understand... It's so comforting to be with someone who cares... Someone who... who understands... You do understand, don't you?

MONTGISCARD: Oh yes... I understand...

[*He shrugs.*]

MATHILDE: Besides, I wanted to ask you... [*Pondering.*] Now what was it?... I know it was dreadfully important...

MONTGISCARD: Please... Your train...

MATHILDE: Ah! I remember... You will come visit me, won't you? While I'm at my mother's...

[*The doorbell rings.*]

MONTGISCARD [*unconvincingly*]: Of course... [*Aside.*] If she ever gets there! [*Aloud.*] Really, Mathilde... You'll miss the next one too...

MATHILDE [*enthusiastically*]: Oh, Marcel! Do you think so?

MONTGISCARD [*aside*]: I know... It's a sign...

[*The door, left, opens and* OCTAVE *appears.*]

MATHILDE [*quickly moving downstage*]: Oh...

OCTAVE [*entering, leaving the door ajar, to* MONTGISCARD]: Monsieur... It's the baron... Monsieur de Petitfour...

MONTGISCARD ⎱
⎰ [*with a start, together*]: ⎰ Petitfour?
MATHILDE ⎱ ⎱ My husband?

OCTAVE [*aside*]: Oh my!

MATHILDE: It can't be!

[*She begins looking around the room for a place to hide.*]

MONTGISCARD [*to* OCTAVE]: And you told him I was in? You—

OCTAVE: But... Monsieur doesn't owe him any money! He's not a creditor...

MATHILDE [*to* MONTGISCARD]: Please! Where can I hide?

MONTGISCARD [*following* MATHILDE *around the room, to* OCTAVE]: But... It's her husband, you fool! Her husband!

[MATHILDE *opens the door, right, and quickly retreats with a scream.*]

MATHILDE: Oh! There's... Marcel! [*Pointing.*] There's a woman...

MONTGISCARD: I know! I'll explain...

[*The door, right, opens and* NICODEMO *steps out.*]

NICODEMO [*to* MONTGISCARD]: Well, Marcello?... Ees done, eh?... You tell her?

MONTGISCARD: What?... I...

MATHILDE: Who in the name of—

NICODEMO: Si, si! Ees time!... I spend all day een thees room already!

OCTAVE [*up left, peeking out the door, to* MATHILDE]: I think madame should hurry! Monsieur is taking off his coat...

MATHILDE: But...

MONTGISCARD [*looking around the room, frantically*]: Good God! Where can I put her?

MATHILDE: That woman, Marcel...

NICODEMO [*to* MONTGISCARD]: You tell her, eh?... You tell her?

MONTGISCARD [*looking toward the window, up right, suddenly inspired*]: Ah!

[*He pushes* MATHILDE *in that direction.*]

MATHILDE [*still pointing down right*]: In there... That woman...

MONTGISCARD: Yes, yes... Later... Not now...

MATHILDE: But...

NICODEMO [*to* MONTGISCARD]: Cinque minuti I tell you, Marcello!

[MONTGISCARD *hides* MATHILDE *behind the left drape, with her shoes protruding.*]

OCTAVE [*still peeking out the door*]: He's taken it off, madame... [*Looking around for* MATHILDE, *not seeing her.*] Madame?...

MONTGISCARD [*to* OCTAVE]: Shhh! Shhh!... [*Pointing to the window.*] Over there...

OCTAVE [*peeking out again*]: And he's coming this way...

NICODEMO [*still at the door, right, protesting*]: Five minoot! Five minoot!

MONTGISCARD [*suddenly noticing* MATHILDE'S *hat and coat on the chair, up left*]: Oh God!

[*He picks them up, at a loss what to do with them.*]

NICODEMO [*moving up to the window, addressing the unseen* MATHILDE]: Cinque minuti I tell heem, signora! [*Crossing left, to* OCTAVE.]: Cinque minuti...

MONTGISCARD [*thrusting the hat and coat into* NICODEMO'S *arms.*]: Here, you...

NICODEMO: But Marcello...

MONTGISCARD [*pushing him down right*]: Later... Not now...

[He pushes him bodily out the door and slams it, heaving a sigh of relief.]

NICODEMO *[opening the door]*: But Marcello! I tell you cinque—

MONTGISCARD: Not now, damn it! *[He slams the door again, leaning against it as casually as possible.]* Heaven help us!

OCTAVE *[up left, announcing]*: Her husb... I mean, Monsieur de Petitfour!

*[*PETITFOUR, *overhearing, appears at the door, carrying his hat, cane and gloves.]*

PETITFOUR *[entering, to* OCTAVE, *archly]*: "Baron," my good man! "Baron de Petitfour..." *[Aside.]* Imbecile!

*[*OCTAVE *exits.]*

MONTGISCARD *[aside]*: Oh my! He must have found her note! He suspects... He knows she's here!

[Several raps are heard at the door, right.]

PETITFOUR: Well, my friend...

[He extends his hand as if waiting for MONTGISCARD *to join him halfway.]*

MONTGISCARD *[still with his back against the door, extending his hand]*: What a nice surprise!

[More rapping is heard, continuing sporadically throughout the scene.]

PETITFOUR *[moving closer]*: I hope you're well...

[He continues crossing right, hand extended.]

MONTGISCARD *[raising his voice to cover the noise]*: Oh... Couldn't be better!... And you?

PETITFOUR: Fine... Fine...

MONTGISCARD: Fine!

*[*PETITFOUR *finally reaches him and the two men shake hands.]*

PETITFOUR: Monsieur...

MONTGISCARD: Monsieur...

PETITFOUR: So good to see you looking so well!

MONTGISCARD: And you, monsieur... My pleasure!

PETITFOUR: Tell me, when did you return?

MONTGISCARD: Return?

PETITFOUR: From Deauville... I seem to recall...

MONTGISCARD: Oh... Oh yes... Why, last night...

PETITFOUR: And you had a pleasant trip, I hope?

MONTGISCARD: Very!... Very pleasant!

PETITFOUR: It was good of you to come pay me a visit... So soon, I mean...

MONTGISCARD: Monsieur?

PETITFOUR: Just now... I understand you stopped by to say hello.

MONTGISCARD: Why, yes... Sorry you weren't in...

PETITFOUR: But I found your card.

MONTGISCARD: Aha...

[The rapping becomes more and more insistent.]

PETITFOUR: I say, is someone knocking?

MONTGISCARD *[still against the door]*: Upstairs, monsieur... Upstairs...

PETITFOUR: Oh, I thought...

MONTGISCARD: You were saying?

PETITFOUR: Yes... I found your card... And a note from the baroness...

MONTGISCARD: A note?

PETITFOUR: From Madame de Petitfour...

MONTGISCARD: Of course... [*Aside.*] Oh my!

PETITFOUR: Because she was out too...

MONTGISCARD: Yes...

PETITFOUR: So she left me a note... To let me know when she'll be back, I imagine.

MONTGISCARD: When she'll be...

[*The rapping becomes still louder.*]

PETITFOUR: I didn't even... [*Changing his tone.*] Excuse me, but are you sure?

MONTGISCARD: Sure, monsieur?

PETITFOUR: That no one is at the door... It sounds so close.

MONTGISCARD: Upstairs... Upstairs...

PETITFOUR: Curious!... Well, as I was saying... I didn't even bother to read it...

MONTGISCARD: Her note?... You didn't? You mean you—

PETITFOUR: Since I know where she is!

MONTGISCARD [*with a start*]: You do?

[*Without leaving the door, he glances anxiously back and forth from* PETITFOUR *to the window.*]

PETITFOUR: Of course! What does she take me for?... What do you think I am?

MONTGISCARD: Me, monsieur?

PETITFOUR: She can't fool me! Though heaven knows she's trying!... I know, I know...

MONTGISCARD [*more and more distraught*]: But... Don't jump to conclusions! Don't—

PETITFOUR: She's gone to arrange the menu!

MONTGISCARD: She...

PETITFOUR: For my birthday, old boy... A little surprise she has up her sleeve... I do hope you can join us...

MONTGISCARD [*sighing*]: Your birthday?

PETITFOUR: I'll see that you're invited... [*Noticing* MONTGISCARD*'s upset state.*] Excuse me, are you ill? You look rather pale...

MONTGISCARD: No, no... Really... It's nothing...

PETITFOUR [*laughing*]: A little too much of that Deauville salt air?

MONTGISCARD: Yes... That must be...

PETITFOUR [*slyly*]: Or too many of those beautiful Deauville ladies!

[*The left drape quivers noticeably.*]

MONTGISCARD: Too many...

PETITFOUR: After all, there's more to the seashore than sand and water!

[*The drape quivers again.*]

MONTGISCARD [*noticing it, aside*]: Oh!... [*Aloud.*] Yes... Yes, so they tell me...

PETITFOUR [*laughing*]: But of course, you wouldn't know!

MONTGISCARD: I... No... That is...

PETITFOUR [*moving upstage*]: Come, come now! You can tell me!... I'm a grown-up! [*With a wink.*] How many?

MONTGISCARD [*still against the door*]: I beg your...

[*More rapping is heard.*]

PETITFOUR: I say, are you quite sure...

MONTGISCARD: Upstairs, monsieur... Upstairs...

[PETITFOUR *shrugs, turns his back, and sets his hat and cane down on the armchair, up left.* MONTGISCARD *takes a few anxious steps toward the window. Just then, the door, right, flies open and* NICODEMO *bursts out.*]

NICODEMO: Cinque minuti, Marcello! I tell you—

MONTGISCARD [*pouncing on him, clapping his hand over his mouth, whispering*]: Shhh!... Later! Later!... And stop that knocking!

[*He pushes him back out the door and shuts it.*]

PETITFOUR [*turning around*]: Beg pardon? I didn't hear what you said...

[*He moves back downstage.*]

MONTGISCARD [*clearing his throat*]: Upstairs, I told you...

PETITFOUR: Oh, I thought...

MONTGISCARD [*tentatively moving away from the door*]: You were saying?

PETITFOUR: Yes... Deauville, old boy... Did you enjoy it?

MONTGISCARD: Oh, immensely! The beach is a delight!

PETITFOUR [*with a knowing laugh*]: Yes! "Beach" indeed!... [*Aside.*] Sly devil! [*Aloud.*] My wife... The baroness was terribly eager to go up there... Kept insisting that I take her...

MONTGISCARD [*nodding, innocently*]: Aha...

PETITFOUR: I must say, we even had words...

MONTGISCARD: Tsk tsk tsk!

PETITFOUR: When she gets an idea into her head, you can't imagine... Temper, temper, temper! [*There is another noticeable quiver of the drape.*] But I managed to stand my ground! After all, a trip with your wife... Especially Deauville... Well, that's not much fun, now is it!

MONTGISCARD: No... I shouldn't think...

PETITFOUR: I mean, what's the point?... And besides, I couldn't just pick up and leave! I can't spare the time... Business, you know...

MONTGISCARD: Yes... Business is business...

PETITFOUR: One has to make a living!

MONTGISCARD: Yes... [*Aside.*] Even a baron!

PETITFOUR: Money doesn't grow on trees... Especially when you spend it the way some of us do...

MONTGISCARD: I'm sure... Business before pleasure!

PETITFOUR [*laughing*]: Well, I wouldn't go that far, old boy!... Let's say: "Business *for* pleasure!" That's much closer to the truth!

MONTGISCARD [*forcing a laugh*]: Of course...

PETITFOUR: You see... [*Sitting down at the table, left, confidentially.*] You see, there's a certain young lady of my acquaintance... [*Reconsidering.*] Lady?... Well... One Fifi Laflamme...

[*Another quiver of the drape.*]

MONTGISCARD: I know...

PETITFOUR: You know her?

MONTGISCARD: No, no... Only by reputation...

PETITFOUR: Well, one of these days I'll introduce you... In the flesh, so to speak!... [*Laughing.*] The flesh...

MONTGISCARD: Yes... Delighted...

PETITFOUR: You'll love her! She's terribly amusing!

MONTGISCARD: So I've heard...

PETITFOUR: And beautiful!... [*Sighing.*] That face... Those dainty feet... Those soft little hands... [*Suddenly he catches sight of* MATHILDE'*s gloves on the table, and bursts out laughing.*] Ho, ho!... I say...

MONTGISCARD: Monsieur?

PETITFOUR: Talk about her hands!

[*He picks up the gloves and lays his own on the table.*]

MONTGISCARD [*aside*]: Good God! Mathilde's gloves!

[*He positions himself between* PETITFOUR *and the window, trying to mask his view.*]

PETITFOUR [*getting up*]: You devil, you! Hardly back from Deauville, and already a little... [*Emphasizing.*] escapade!

MONTGISCARD: No!... That's not true!

PETITFOUR: Some sweet young thing... [*Brandishing the gloves.*] With adorable little hands...

MONTGISCARD: No, no! Those are mine!

PETITFOUR [*laughing*]: Of course they are! Of course! [*Examining the gloves.*] Congratulations, old boy! If the rest of her is anything like her hands...

MONTGISCARD: But I'm telling you...

PETITFOUR: Like my Fifi Laflamme!

MONTGISCARD: They're mine!... Those are my gloves...

PETITFOUR [*laughing*]: I know... I know... [*He takes a few steps toward the window, notices* MATHILDE'*s shoes, and bursts out laughing even louder.*] Like your shoes!

MONTGISCARD [*verging on panic*]: My what?

PETITFOUR [*pointing, doubled up with laughter*]: Those must be yours too! Right?... For your adorable little feet!

MONTGISCARD [*aside*]: Oh...

PETITFOUR: See? They're even moving!... By themselves!... [*Addressing the drape, with an exaggerated little bow.*] Mademoiselle...

[MONTGISCARD *rushes over to the window to ward him off.*]

MONTGISCARD: Please, monsieur!

PETITFOUR [*slapping him on the back and moving him down right*]: Come, come now! You should have told me!... Too much salt air, my foot!... [*Glancing at* MATHILDE'*s shoes, chuckling.*] If you don't mind my saying...

MONTGISCARD: But...

PETITFOUR: Now I see why you've been acting so strangely!

MONTGISCARD: But...

PETITFOUR: Really, why didn't you tell me?... All you had to say was... "Petitfour, I wish you'd leave!"

MONTGISCARD [*pushing him up left, toward the door*]: Petitfour, I wish you'd leave!... There! I've said it!... Now please...

PETITFOUR [*laughing*]: Right away... Just let me take one more look!

[*He crosses toward the window.*]

MONTGISCARD [*pulling him back*]: Don't you dare!

PETITFOUR: From here!... Don't worry! From here!... I'm the soul of discretion... [*Addressing the drape.*] Mademoiselle, let me tell you...

MONTGISCARD: Please...

PETITFOUR: ...that you have two utterly exquisite little feet! Two... Two feet of distinction... Two perfect works of art...

MONTGISCARD: Monsieur...

PETITFOUR: And when it comes to ladies' feet, I'm an expert, mademoiselle...

[*The drape quivers.*]

MONTGISCARD: Please, monsieur...

PETITFOUR [*addressing the shoes*]: Tsk tsk tsk! Don't be angry! No offense, you lovely creatures... You adorable, precious, divine little—
[*He begins moving closer.*]

MONTGISCARD [*trying to hold him back*]: No, no, no!

PETITFOUR [*to* MONTGISCARD]: Don't worry! The soul of discretion...
[*He keeps trying to move closer, as* MONTGISCARD *keeps trying to hold him.*]

MONTGISCARD: I told you...

PETITFOUR: Ah! Those elegant little feet!... Like my Fifi Laflamme...
[*The drape quivers even more energetically.*]

MONTGISCARD: That's enough! Will you please...

PETITFOUR [*suddenly suspecting*]: Oh, no!... [*Slapping himself on the forehead.*] You don't mean... Of course! Why didn't you say so?

MONTGISCARD: What?

PETITFOUR [*taking him aside, down left*]: She's a married woman, right? That's it, old boy, isn't it?

MONTGISCARD: No, no! What makes you think...

PETITFOUR: Are you sure?

MONTGISCARD: Of course I'm sure!

PETITFOUR: Well, I didn't see how she could be!... I mean, with feet like that...

MONTGISCARD [*confused*]: Yes... No...

PETITFOUR [*slapping him on the back*]: Then why all the secrecy? Why not let me see her? That's not very friendly!

MONTGISCARD: Oh? I...

PETITFOUR: What are friends for?... Come, come! Share and share alike!

MONTGISCARD: Share...

PETITFOUR: After all, I promised to introduce you to my Fifi! And you didn't even have to ask me!... We'll all go have dinner some night... Just the four of us...

MONTGISCARD: No, no!... Impossible!

PETITFOUR: You mean she's that ugly?
[*The drape quivers furiously.*]

MONTGISCARD: Please, monsieur! I must ask you... I really wish you'd leave!
[*He hands him his hat and cane, and pushes him up left, toward the door.*]

PETITFOUR [*returning with another sudden insight*]: You don't mean... [*Slapping himself on the forehead.*] Oh no!... I should have guessed!... That's it, isn't it?

MONTGISCARD: "It," monsieur?

PETITFOUR: It's obvious! If you don't want me to see her, I must know her! Right?... I know her...
[*He tries to move toward the window again.*]

MONTGISCARD [*holding him back*]: Know her? Know her?... No, no!... No!

PETITFOUR [*addressing the drape*]: Do I know you, mademoiselle? Have I ever had the pleasure—

MONTGISCARD [*still tugging*]: I just told you, damn it! You don't know her!... You don't!... [*Trying to push him up left, toward the door.*] Now will you please—

PETITFOUR [*still addressing the drape*]: Well, if I don't know you, I'm sure you must know me!... Petitfour, mademoiselle... All you ladies know me!

MONTGISCARD [*pushing*]: Will you please—

PETITFOUR: Fifi's friend, Petitfour!

MONTGISCARD: She doesn't! She doesn't!

PETITFOUR: You know... Fifi Laflamme...

MONTGISCARD [*at the end of his rope*]: For God's sake, will you leave!

PETITFOUR [*taking a few steps toward the window, in spite of* MONTGISCARD, *jovially*]: Just one last word, you charming thing, you!... If you take my advice, you'll watch out for this Montgiscard!... Oh, I know... You're probably wildly in love with him...

MONTGISCARD [*clinging to his arm*]: Monsieur!...

PETITFOUR [*continuing*]: And I don't blame you! He's a delightful chap!... Perfectly delightful!... But he doesn't have a faithful bone in his body!

MONTGISCARD: I...

PETITFOUR [*laughing*]: Why, the man is a cad! An unprincipled cad! He'll chase anything in skirts! You'll see, he'll break your heart!... He's a monster!... A beast!...

MONTGISCARD [*tugging at his arm*]: Will you please...

PETITFOUR [*laughing*]: But revenge is sweet, my child!... And I'm always available... Whenever you need me! Just send me a note... Petitfour... You won't forget... Fifi's friend, Petitfour... [*Emphasizing.*] Baron de Petitfour... [*To* MONTGISCARD.] Well, I really must be going! Au revoir, old boy!... Bye-bye...

[*He exits, up left, laughing heartily.*]

MONTGISCARD [*watching him leave, sighing*]: Finally!... [*Running to the window.*] He's gone!... You can come out now!

MATHILDE [*stepping out from behind the drape, furious*]: Oh! That... That... "Fifi's friend, Petitfour!..." Oh! That beast!... That monster!...

MONTGISCARD: Please...

MATHILDE: The nerve!... "We'll all go have dinner some night... Just the four of us..." I heard him!... Oh! Me and his Fifi!

MONTGISCARD: Mathilde... He didn't know...

MATHILDE: And you... you... "He'll chase anything in skirts!..." You heard what he said!

MONTGISCARD: It's not true!

MATHILDE: Oh? It's not?... And what about that woman? [*Pointing down right, toward the door.*] What about her? I suppose she's your mother!

MONTGISCARD: Mathilde...

MATHILDE: Well, we'll see about that! [*She runs over to the door and flings it open.*] Come, come, madame! Don't be bashful!

[NICODEMO *appears at the door.*]

NICODEMO [*with a bow, to* MATHILDE]: Buon giorno, signora!

MONTGISCARD: Oh my!

MATHILDE: What?... Who in the name of...

NICODEMO [*to the unseen* EMMA]: You come out now, signorina!... You no be afraid, eh? Nicodemo he take care...

[EMMA *appears timidly at the threshold.*]

EMMA [*reluctantly*]: But I... [*Noticing* MONTGISCARD.] Oh, monsieur... [*Noticing* MATHILDE, *mechanically.*] Madame... [*After a moment of reflection, puzzled.*] Madame...?

[*She slams the door shut.*]

MONTGISCARD [*aside*]: Ayyy!

EMMA [*to* MONTGISCARD, *pointing at* MATHILDE]: Who...

MATHILDE [*to* MONTGISCARD, *pointing at* EMMA]: Well?

NICODEMO [*striding up to* MONTGISCARD]: I tell you cinque minuti, Marcello! I geeve you five minoot, you tell other woman "finito!"

MONTGISCARD: You... But...

NICODEMO: So why you no do, eh? Why you no tell?

MATHILDE [*to* MONTGISCARD]: "Finito"?... What "other woman"?

EMMA [*to* NICODEMO]: You see, monsieur? [*Pointing to* MATHILDE.] He has a mistress!

MATHILDE } [*to* EMMA, *together*]: { I beg your pardon!

MONTGISCARD } { I what?

EMMA [*to* NICODEMO]: That's why he left Deauville in such a hurry!

MATHILDE: Deauville?

EMMA [*to* NICODEMO]: Without... Without even... [*On the verge of tears.*] saying good-bye!

MONTGISCARD: But...

MATHILDE [*to* MONTGISCARD]: So! That was the attraction!... Deauville, indeed!... To chase this little hussy...

EMMA [*to* MATHILDE, *scandalized*]: Oh! You... You...

MONTGISCARD [*to* EMMA]: Please, mademoiselle...

MATHILDE [*to* MONTGISCARD]: Oh yes!... "Anything in skirts..."

EMMA [*to* NICODEMO]: Did you hear...

NICODEMO [*to* MATHILDE, *wagging a finger*]: Tsk tsk tsk! Signorina...

MONTGISCARD [*not knowing which way to turn*]: Please... All of you...

MATHILDE [*to* NICODEMO]: Who the devil... Don't wag your finger at me, monsieur!

MONTGISCARD [*to* MATHILDE]: Madame de Petitfour... Please... [*To* EMMA.] Mademoiselle...

NICODEMO [*overhearing, with a start, to* MATHILDE]: Petitfour?... Ho! Ees you, Signora de Petitfour? Ees you?... [*To* MONTGISCARD.] Ees thees one, Marcello? Ees her, eh?... Ees her?

[*He moves closer to* MATHILDE.]

MATHILDE [*to* NICODEMO]: Of course it's me! So what?

NICODEMO [*to* MATHILDE, *kissing her hand*]: Ah! Signora... Signora...

[*During the following exchange,* MONTGISCARD *takes* EMMA *aside, whispering, and whisks her upstage, obviously trying to explain the situation.*]

MATHILDE [*trying to get* MONTGISCARD's *attention*]: Marcel! Who on earth...

NICODEMO [*to* MATHILDE]: Nicodemo he know everytheeng about you, signora. Marcello he tell me everytheeng!

MATHILDE [*shocked*]: He what?

NICODEMO: Si, si! Everytheeng!... [*Waving his notepad.*] I write down! I no forget!

MATHILDE [*to* MONTGISCARD, *who by now is up left*]: Marcel! Will you please—

NICODEMO: He tell me you suffer... He tell me Signor de Petitfour, how you say?... But Nicodemo he feex! He take care, signora!

MATHILDE: Who?

NICODEMO: Si, si!... [*Waving his card.*] "Tutto Per Le Donne!" I feex...

MATHILDE: But...

NICODEMO: So! You tell me where you leeve!

MATHILDE: Where I—

NICODEMO: And I feex!... Si, si!... But later! No now!... When I feeneesh... [*Pointing to* EMMA.] Weeth thees one... First she marry Marcello, signora... Then I feex...

MATHILDE: Marry...? Did you say...

NICODEMO: Si, si! [*Very matter-of-fact.*] He love her!

MATHILDE [*to* MONTGISCARD]: You do?

MONTGISCARD: Do?... Do what?

MATHILDE: Love her?

MONTGISCARD [*innocently*]: Who?

MATHILDE: Who? Who?... [*Pointing to* EMMA.] Her!

MONTGISCARD: Me?... No... I mean, that is... I...

EMMA [*rushing over to* NICODEMO]: You see, monsieur? You heard him! He doesn't love me! He never did!

MONTGISCARD: That's not what I said! I... I...

EMMA [*to* MONTGISCARD]: Oh? I suppose we didn't all hear you?

MONTGISCARD [*bumbling*]: I... Mademoiselle...

EMMA [*pointing at* MATHILDE]: And why is she still here? You promised to get rid of her...

MATHILDE: He what? [*To* MONTGISCARD.] Marcel, you didn't!

MONTGISCARD [*to* MATHILDE]: No!... Of course not! I... I...

[*The doorbell rings.*]

NICODEMO [*to* MONTGISCARD, *wagging his finger*]: Oh, Marcello! For shame!... You promeese Nicodemo you tell her "finito!"... I tell you five minoot, eh?... Already ees one hour, and steell you no tell!

[OCTAVE *appears at the door, left.*]

OCTAVE [*at the threshold, with great aplomb, savoring the effect he is about to make*]: Baron de Petitfour, monsieur!

[*He exits.*]

MONTGISCARD   ⎫   ⎧ What? It can't be!
                     ⎬ [*with a start, together*]: ⎨
MATHILDE   ⎭   ⎩ My husband! Not again?

[MATHILDE *runs behind the left drape.*]

EMMA [*terrified*]: Oh no! If anyone sees me here... [*She runs to the door, right, and tries unsuccessfully to open it.*] It's stuck, Marcel!... Quick! Where can I hide?

MONTGISCARD: I don't know! I don't...

[EMMA *makes a dash for the window and hides behind the right drape, as* MONTGISCARD, *down right, gives the door a sharp tug and opens it.*]

NICODEMO [*to* MONTGISCARD, *peremptorily*]: Ees time! I tell you cinque minuti...

MONTGISCARD [*fed up*]: You... Cinque... I've had your "cinque" up to here, goddammit!

NICODEMO [*offended*]: Oh! Marcello!

MONTGISCARD [*almost lifting him bodily and pushing him into the room, down right*]: Now get in there before you ruin everything!

[*He slams the door just as* PETITFOUR *enters.*]

PETITFOUR: I say...

MONTGISCARD [*aside*]: He must have read her note!

PETITFOUR [*jovially*]: Excuse me for barging in this way...

MONTGISCARD [*offhand*]: Oh?

PETITFOUR: But I had to come back... The gloves, old boy...

MONTGISCARD [*stammering*]: The... The... The gloves?

PETITFOUR: I took the wrong ones... I no sooner got to my door than I realized... [*Holding up* MATHILDE'*s gloves.*] See?... Your... [*Emphasizing, with a smile.*] young friend's...

[*He throws them down on the table, next to his own.*]

MONTGISCARD: My... My...

PETITFOUR: Oh, you mean... [*With a wink.*] She's not still here, is she? You don't mean... [*He goes over to the window, sees two pairs of shoes.*] Oh là là!... Look!... They've doubled!

[*He bursts into gales of laughter.*]

MONTGISCARD [*quickly picking up* PETITFOUR'*s gloves, almost throwing them at him*]: Monsieur! Your gloves...

PETITFOUR: Aha! The plot thickens!... [*Sitting down on the loveseat.*] This time I'll be staying, old boy!... One for you, one for me!

MONTGISCARD: Please...

[*Several sharp raps are heard at the door, right.* MONTGISCARD *leaps over and stands against it, as before. The rapping continues until* NICODEMO'*s entrance.*]

PETITFOUR: I say—

MONTGISCARD: Upstairs! Upstairs!

PETITFOUR [*laughing*]: "Upstairs," indeed!... Another one? [*Pointing to the door.*] Don't tell me you've got a third one in there!

[*He roars with laughter.*]

MONTGISCARD [*furious, pointing up left*]: Please! I'm asking you—

PETITFOUR: All right, you lucky dog, you! [*He gets up and moves to leave.*] I'm going!... [*Bowing in turn to each drape.*] Mademoiselle... Mademoiselle... Or Madame, as the case may be... [*Bowing toward the door, right.*] And to you, my dear... [*Admiring the two pairs of feet.*] Lovely!... Simply lovely!... [*Laughing.*] I'll have to tell Fifi!

MONTGISCARD [*impatiently*]: Yes...

PETITFOUR: Not my wife, though... The baroness... She'd never let me set foot in this house again! You... You rake, you!

[*Just at that moment the door, right, flies open, nearly knocking* MONTGISCARD *over, and* NICODEMO *appears.*]

NICODEMO: Ees time, Marcello! I no have all day!

PETITFOUR: Who in the name of... That's not...

MONTGISCARD: For God's sake, Petitfour! Help me throw this madman out of here!

NICODEMO [*to* MONTGISCARD, *pointing*]: "Petitfour," you say? Ees Signor Petitfour?... [*To* PETITFOUR.] Ees you? Ees you?

PETITFOUR: Of course!... That is, "baron..."

NICODEMO [*approaching him*]: You husband, eh?

PETITFOUR: Whose husband?

NICODEMO: Ees you make Signora Petitfour so sad?... Make her suffer, like she say? [*Brandishing his notepad.*] You see? I write. I no forget.

PETITFOUR [*to* MONTGISCARD]: Will you kindly tell me—

MONTGISCARD: I wish I knew!

NICODEMO [*to* PETITFOUR]: And when husband he make wife sad, you know what happen?

PETITFOUR [*puzzled*]: "What happen"?

[MATHILDE *suddenly steps out from behind the drape.*]

MATHILDE [*to* PETITFOUR, *confronting him, hands on hips, as* MONTGISCARD *looks on, aghast*]: "What happen"?... I'll tell you "what happen"! You... You...

PETITFOUR [*recoiling*]: Mathilde!

MATHILDE: His wife knows what he's up to! She knows when she's had enough! And she runs to his friend... The only one she can turn to...

PETITFOUR: You... What are you—

MATHILDE: And she asks him to tell her about Fifi Laflamme! [*Archly.*] That, monsieur, is "what happen"!

PETITFOUR: Fifi... Leave Fifi out of this! I'll thank you to explain what you're doing here, madame!

NICODEMO [*trying to interject a word, to* PETITFOUR]: Signore...

PETITFOUR [*to* MATHILDE, *pointing at* MONTGISCARD]: In his house!

MONTGISCARD: But...

MATHILDE [*to* PETITFOUR]: I just told you!

NICODEMO [*to* PETITFOUR]: Per piacere, signore... Signor Petitfour...

PETITFOUR [*to* NICODEMO, *impatiently*]: You... "Baron," damn it!

NICODEMO: Si, si!... You no worry, barone! No worry!... Ees no what you theenk!

PETITFOUR: Oh? I find my wife here... [*Pointing to* MONTGISCARD.] In his house!... Behind a curtain, of all things! And you tell me—

NICODEMO: No worry! No worry!... What Marcello he want weeth you wife, eh? What he want?... You wife! Ha ha ha!

MATHILDE: Oh!

NICODEMO [*to* PETITFOUR]: What he want weeth you wife when he marry hees bella donna?

PETITFOUR [*to* NICODEMO]				When he what?
MONTGISCARD	}	[*together*]:	{	When I what?
MATHILDE				What?

NICODEMO: When he marry... [*He goes over to the window and pulls aside the other drape.*] la signorina!

[EMMA *stands revealed, not sure which way to turn.*]

EMMA: Monsieur...

NICODEMO: Come, come!... Ees time! Ees time!

[*She moves downstage, obviously abashed, between* MONTGISCARD *and* NICODEMO.]

PETITFOUR [*to* MONTGISCARD]: Is that true?

MONTGISCARD: Damned if I know!

[OCTAVE *appears at the door, left, waving a telegram.*]

OCTAVE [*to* MONTGISCARD]: A wire, monsieur!... A telegram... From

Deauville...

MONTGISCARD and **EMMA** [*together*]: Deauville?

MONTGISCARD [*to* OCTAVE, *grabbing the telegram*]: Give me that...

EMMA: Oh my!... From my guardian...

MONTGISCARD [*opening it and reading*]: Billetdoux...

EMMA: He must be furious!

NICODEMO [*to* EMMA]: No worry! No worry, signorina! I feex! Nicodemo he take care...

MONTGISCARD [*reading to himself*]: I don't believe... Listen! [*Reading aloud.*] "Chivalry not dead... Stop... Faith in humanity restored... Stop... Abducting ward act of selfless devotion..."

EMMA: What?

MONTGISCARD: Abducting... Oh my, he thinks I... [*Continuing to read.*] "In spite of modest dowry of ten thousand francs... Stop... Overcome with emotion... Stop..."

[*He stops to catch his breath.*]

NICODEMO [*to* MONTGISCARD]: No, no, Marcello! No stop! No stop!

MONTGISCARD [*continuing*]: "Adding ninety thousand of my own, with my blessings..."

EMMA [*clapping her hands*]: Oh!

MONTGISCARD [*agape*]: A hundred thousand...

OCTAVE [*aside*]: A nice round figure!

EMMA [*throwing her arms around* NICODEMO's *neck*]: Oh, monsieur...

NICODEMO [*to* EMMA]: Ah! Bella donna! I tell you Nicodemo he take care! Now you believe, eh? [*To* PETITFOUR.] And you, signore... [*Correcting.*] Barone... You see? You no worry! Marcello he marry la signorina...

PETITFOUR: I say...

MONTGISCARD [*to* NICODEMO, *enthusiastically*]: Monsieur... Whoever you are... How can I ever thank you?

NICODEMO: No thank! No ees need!... Nicodemo he happy when everybody happy!... Si, si! Everybody happy!... [*To* PETITFOUR.] No? You no happy, barone?

PETITFOUR [*unconvincingly*]: Oh yes... Yes... [*Exchanging glances with* MATHILDE.] Delighted...

NICODEMO [*to* MATHILDE]: And you, signora?

MATHILDE [*sarcastically*]: Oh! Utterly ecstatic!

[*She storms off, left.*]

PETITFOUR [*following her*]: Mathilde...

[*He exits on her heels.*]

NICODEMO [*rubbing his hands*]: Bene! Bene!... Now I go!... Ees feeneesh my work here... And ees so many woman who need Nicodemo... [*Waving his notepad.*] So many who sad... So many who suffer...

OCTAVE [*approaching him*]: Excuse me, but... If monsieur would like another name... There's a certain young lady of my acquaintance... Jacqueline...

NICODEMO [*pricking up his ears*]: Ah?

[*He begins to write.*]

OCTAVE: Yes... And terribly sad, monsieur... Terribly... Terribly...

NICODEMO [*writing*]: Tsk tsk tsk...

OCTAVE: Because she loves me...

NICODEMO: Bene...

OCTAVE: Madly, I might add...

NICODEMO [*still writing*]: Si... Si...

OCTAVE: But Monsieur Albert has put his foot down! He won't hear of it!

NICODEMO: Alberto?... No ees problem! I feex!... [*Almost as an afterthought.*] Who ees, thees Alberto?

OCTAVE: Her husband, monsieur.

[EMMA *and* MONTGISCARD *burst out laughing.*]

NICODEMO: Mamma mia! You make joke, eh?

[*He joins the laughter.*]

MONTGISCARD [*slapping* OCTAVE *on the back and leading him up left, toward the door*]: Don't worry, Octavio! He feex!... He feex!...

EMMA [*laughing*]: He take care!

NICODEMO: Si, si! Nicodemo he take care!

[*He makes a flourish and a deep bow, as the curtain falls on their laughter.*]

CURTAIN

MARDI GRAS

Adaptation of

La Mi-carême

by

Henri Meilhac and Ludovic Halévy

(1874)

CHARACTERS

BOISLAMBERT, a thirtyish bachelor, something of a romantic, Jacqueline Lamberthier's spurned lover

BAGATELLE, the concierge in Jacqueline's fashionable building

BARON DE MORANCHARD, a society gent, one of Jacqueline's army of present admirers

ALBERT PAPONNET, an awkward adolescent, just awakened to the joys of puberty

GASTON
EDOUARD   } pretenders to Jacqueline's affection
COUNT RAOUL

A YOUNG MAN

A GENDARME

A DELIVERY BOY

JACQUELINE LAMBERTHIER, beautiful, youngish, confident of her charms, and merciless toward her admirers

MARCELLE DE NANTOULAS, Boislambert's former fiancée, the picture of refinement

YVETTE, Jacqueline's maid, the typical soubrette

MADAME PAPONNET, an elderly prude, Albert's domineering aunt

A YOUNG LADY

*The set is divided into two halves by a partition perpendicular to the footlights.
The stage right half represents the lobby of a fashionable apartment building.
Facing the public, in the upstage wall, the front door of the building, a double
door looking out onto a darkened street. Down right, the first few steps of the
staircase leading upstairs. In front of the steps, a mat. Other appropriate
furnishings—carpet, potted plant, benches, pictures, etc.—ad* libitum. *The stage
left half represents the concierge's quarters. In the partition, midstage, a door
opening in; and downstage, a small window through which the concierge talks
to those in the lobby. Next to this window, a long cord hanging from the ceiling,
which he pulls to open the front door. Close by, a shelf with various articles,
including a number of candles in holders, pen and ink, paper, etc. Upstage, far
left, a small flight of stairs leading up to a curtained doorway opening onto a
back room. Down left, an armchair. In the stage left wall, midstage, a fireplace.
Above it, a hunting horn. In the middle of the room, a small table with two
chairs, one left, the other right. On the floor by the table, all the elements of a
musketeer's costume—boots, French hose, cape, plumed hat, rapier—neatly
piled. On top of the pile, a false nose. Other furnishings—pictures, etc.— ad*
libitum.

At rise, YVETTE *and* BAGATELLE *are sitting at the table, playing cards. Outside,
one can hear the general sounds of merriment—horns, laughter, noisemakers,
etc.*

YVETTE [*after a few moments of deliberation, throwing down a card*]: There!
My game!
BAGATELLE [*throwing down his hand, in good-natured disgust*]: Not again!
Just when I had such a beautiful hand...
YVETTE [*scooping up the cards, with a laugh*]: How many is that now,
Monsieur Bagatelle?
BAGATELLE [*shaking his head*]: Luck! That's all it is... Beginner's luck!
YVETTE [*shaking her finger at him*]: Now, now... That's what madame says too,
every time I beat her!
BAGATELLE: See?
YVETTE: Year after year!
[*A loud horn sounds outside.* YVETTE *covers her ears. At the same time, a*
YOUNG MAN *dressed as a hussar, and a* YOUNG WOMAN *dressed as a
ballerina, appear, coming down the stairs, down right. The* YOUNG MAN *is
carrying a candle-holder with a lighted candle.*]
YOUNG MAN [*blowing out the candle as they reach the lobby, calling to*
BAGATELLE]: Door, please!
BAGATELLE [*getting up and going over to the window, to* YVETTE]: My two
little lovebirds from the top floor, rear... [*To the* YOUNG MAN *and* YOUNG
WOMAN.] Good evening!

YOUNG MAN: Good evening, Monsieur Bagatelle!

BAGATELLE [to the YOUNG WOMAN]: My, my! Don't we look pretty tonight!

YOUNG WOMAN: Thank you, monsieur.

[The YOUNG MAN hands his candle to BAGATELLE through the window.]

BAGATELLE: And where would we be going?

YOUNG MAN: Around the corner, monsieur... To Valentino's...

BAGATELLE: Oh! Fancy, fancy... Well, you're only young once! Have a good time, you two!

[He pulls the cord to open the front door.]

YOUNG WOMAN: Thank you, monsieur.

[She and the YOUNG MAN leave.]

BAGATELLE [to YVETTE]: Yes... You're only young once!

YVETTE: I can't argue with that, Monsieur Bagatelle!

BAGATELLE [sitting down at the table]: Besides, Mardi Gras only comes once a year...

YVETTE: Or with that either!

BAGATELLE: And anyone who doesn't enjoy it is a mean old grouch!

[Suddenly there are several more blasts from a horn outside.]

YVETTE [covering her ears]: Oh!

[BAGATELLE gets up and takes the hunting horn down from the fireplace.]

BAGATELLE: And that goes for me too!

[He blows several long, loud blasts, to YVETTE's obvious displeasure. After a few moments, the doorbell rings. BAGATELLE and YVETTE fail to hear it at first. It rings several more times.]

YVETTE [finally hearing the bell]: Monsieur... Monsieur... Someone's ringing the bell.

BAGATELLE: What?

YVETTE: The bell, monsieur...

BAGATELLE: Oh, thank you...

[He pulls the cord. JACQUELINE LAMBERTHIER enters, dressed with excessive affectation. She is followed by GASTON, an aristocratic gentleman, smoking a cigar.]

GASTON [pleading]: But really, Jacqueline—

JACQUELINE [cutting him off, angrily]: Please... Leave me alone!

GASTON: But I only thought—

JACQUELINE: Not now! Not now!

GASTON: But... But...

JACQUELINE: No "buts," Gaston! I said, "Leave me alone!" [At the window, to BAGATELLE.] Monsieur Bagatelle! Is my maid upstairs?

YVETTE [going out into the lobby]: Here I am, madame.

JACQUELINE: Ah! Yvette... Be a dear... Run upstairs and get me my dark gloves...

YVETTE: Yes, madame.

JACQUELINE: And my mink... [YVETTE begins to leave.] No, no... My sable...

YVETTE: Very good, madame.

[She leaves, up the stairs, down right.]

GASTON [still whining]: Jacqueline, please...

JACQUELINE: Not now, for heaven's sake!

[She strides into the concierge's quarters and slams the door in GASTON's *face.*]

GASTON: But...

[JACQUELINE, *grumbling, goes over to the armchair, down left, and sits down, obviously in a fit of pique. In the meantime,* GASTON *begins pacing the lobby, up and down, puffing on his cigar.*]

BAGATELLE: Madame seems upset, if she doesn't mind my saying...

JACQUELINE: Upset? I'm furious! Absolutely furious! The very idea... Just who does he think he is?... Give me a pen and ink, Monsieur Bagatelle... And a sheet of paper... And an envelope... Oh! The very idea...

BAGATELLE: Of course, madame.

[*He puts the horn under his arm and takes a sheet of paper, an envelope, and pen and ink from their shelf near his window, and hands them to* JACQUELINE, *as she continues grumbling under her breath.*]

JACQUELINE [*as she begins writing*]: No, I never... Never!... Can you believe such a thing, Monsieur Bagatelle? To do a thing like that... To me...

BAGATELLE [*respectfully quizzical*]: Excuse me, madame...?

JACQUELINE [*hardly listening to his replies*]: To me... Me! Jacqueline Lamberthier!... And who? Can you believe it, monsieur?

BAGATELLE: Madame?

JACQUELINE: A man like the baron...

BAGATELLE: Baron de Moranchard, madame? The one who... [*Discreetly.*] who visits madame every night?

JACQUELINE: Yes! That baron! That... Do you know what I just found out, Monsieur Bagatelle? Not one hour ago... At the theatre, of all places...

BAGATELLE: Why no. I can't say—

JACQUELINE: He's getting married! Next week! What do you think of that?

BAGATELLE: The baron? Married?

JACQUELINE [*furiously, writing*]: Just who does he think... Oh! I never...

BAGATELLE: Why, that's disgusting, madame!

JACQUELINE [*wryly*]: Yes, isn't it!

BAGATELLE: I mean... Every night, for how many months now...? And... And he's getting married? The baron?

JACQUELINE: Very married, monsieur! To some young widow... Madame de Nantoulas...

BAGATELLE: Disgusting!

JACQUELINE: Well, I've taken just about all I'm going to take from him! [*As she finishes writing.*] This letter should tell him a thing or two! We're finished, and that's that! Good riddance! That's all I have to say...

BAGATELLE: "Good riddance," madame?

[*He crosses left, to the fireplace.*]

JACQUELINE [*waving the letter to dry*]: Heavens, yes! I've been trying to get rid of him for months! That bore! Now he's given me the perfect excuse... He's getting married!

BAGATELLE: "Bore," madame? The baron?

JACQUELINE: Yes... That crashing, crashing bore!

BAGATELLE: Well... Not everyone can be like Monsieur de Boislambert!

JACQUELINE [*smiling*]: Ah yes... Poor Boislambert...

BAGATELLE: Madame could never call *him* a "crashing bore"!

JACQUELINE: No... Not Boislambert... Dear boy... You were fond of him, were you?

BAGATELLE: Oh yes, madame!

JACQUELINE: So was I, Monsieur Bagatelle...

BAGATELLE: Why, he used to come in and make himself at home... Sit right down... Right where madame is sitting... And he'd talk and talk... And laugh... My, my, didn't he laugh!... And never with his nose in the air... Not like some of them... Yes, a nice man, Monsieur de Boislambert... A nice man... *[Pausing, confidentially.]* He still owes me twenty-seven francs, madame...

JACQUELINE: He does?

BAGATELLE: And fifty centimes...

JACQUELINE: What on earth for?

BAGATELLE: For making sure he got home safe and sound... All those late nights... Back in the good old days, I mean... When he and madame...

JACQUELINE: Aha... Well, you can kiss your twenty-seven francs goodbye, monsieur. There's not much chance you'll ever see them again... Or even the fifty centimes, for that matter! The poor chap doesn't have a sou to his name!

BAGATELLE: Oh?

JACQUELINE *[casually]*: No, Monsieur Bagatelle... I'm afraid I ruined him.

BAGATELLE: Really, madame?

JACQUELINE: Utterly!

BAGATELLE: Tsk tsk tsk!

JACQUELINE: Yes... *[Sighing.]* Poor Boislambert! And now... Who knows where he is, I wonder? Who knows what's become of him... *[Folding her letter and putting it in the envelope.]* There! Even the baron should understand that!

[YVETTE *appears, coming down the stairs, with* JACQUELINE's *sable and dark gloves. She enters the concierge's quarters.*]

YVETTE [*to* JACQUELINE]: Madame's coat and gloves...

JACQUELINE: Thank you, Yvette. *[She gets up and changes her coat and gloves, giving* YVETTE *the ones she has been wearing.]* There...

YVETTE: Will there be anything else, madame?

JACQUELINE: Yes... The baron is going to be coming by shortly...

YVETTE: Baron de Moranchard, madame?

JACQUELINE: Quite. *[Snidely.]* Moranchard!... And I want you to give him this letter, understand? The minute he gets here...

YVETTE *[taking the letter and putting it in her pocket]*: Very good, madame.

JACQUELINE: And please, don't forget! It's terribly important!

YVETTE: Oh no, madame.

JACQUELINE: Good!... Now I'm going to run off and have dinner, Yvette. I'll be back before long. Please be sure you're here when I return.

YVETTE: Oh yes, madame... [JACQUELINE *moves to leave.*] Just one thing, if madame doesn't mind my asking...

JACQUELINE *[stopping at the concierge's door]*: Yes?

YVETTE: Well... I was hoping... That is, I was wondering if, maybe... When madame gets back, I mean... If maybe she would let me... Well, go to the ball, madame...

JACQUELINE: Yes, yes... Of course... Just wait until I return.

YVETTE: Oh, thank you, madame!

JACQUELINE [to BAGATELLE]: Good night, Monsieur Bagatelle.

BAGATELLE: Good night, madame.

[He pulls the cord to open the front door, as JACQUELINE goes out into the lobby.]

JACQUELINE [to GASTON, who is still pacing and puffing]: All right, you! Come along!

GASTON [pleading]: But really, Jacqueline—

JACQUELINE: No, no, no! Please! Don't start that again!

GASTON: But... But I only thought—

JACQUELINE: You thought! You thought! That's enough, for heaven's sake!... Who asked you to think...

[They go out the front door. As it opens, the sounds of merriment—horn blasts, etc.—can be heard outside. BAGATELLE blows another blast on his horn, as YVETTE goes over and lays JACQUELINE's coat and gloves on the armchair.]

YVETTE [jumping]: Monsieur!

BAGATELLE: Where's your spirit, Yvette? You're only young once!

YVETTE: I know... But my ears...

BAGATELLE [putting the horn back over the fireplace]: And Mardi Gras only comes—

YVETTE [interrupting]: Once a year! I know...

BAGATELLE [sitting down at the table]: Well, aren't you going to celebrate?

YVETTE [joining him, sitting down]: Of course I am! You heard madame tell me... As soon as she gets back, I'm putting on my costume and going to the ball. [She hands him the cards.] Your deal, monsieur...

BAGATELLE: Right...

[He deals the cards and they begin playing again, continuing throughout the following dialogue.]

YVETTE: Me and my young man, that is...

BAGATELLE: Your what?

YVETTE: My young man.

BAGATELLE: Oh? Anyone I know?

YVETTE: I should say you do! [Slyly.] He lives right upstairs!

BAGATELLE: Upstairs? In this building? You must be joking!

YVETTE: No, no, monsieur... No joke! In fact, he should be here any minute. And the first thing he's going to do when he comes in is look for a note I left him... [Pointing toward the staircase in the lobby, confidentially.] Under the mat...

BAGATELLE: No!

YVETTE: Yes!

BAGATELLE: A young man?

YVETTE: A young man!

BAGATELLE: In this building?

YVETTE: In this building!

BAGATELLE: Give me a hint!

YVETTE: No hints... You'll have to guess...

BAGATELLE [slyly]: A concierge?

YVETTE: Well, hardly!

BAGATELLE: Hmm! I can't imagine who...

[*The doorbell rings.* BAGATELLE *gets up and pulls the cord.* MADAME PAPONNET *comes in the front door, followed by* ALBERT, *an awkard young man in his teens.*]

MADAME PAPONNET: Come, come, Albert... No dawdling, now... [*To* BAGATELLE, *at the window.*] Good evening, Monsieur Bagatelle.

BAGATELLE [*nodding*]: Madame Paponnet...

[ALBERT *has gone over to the staircase and, quickly and cautiously, removes a note from under the mat.*]

MADAME PAPONNET [*to* BAGATELLE]: My candle, please...

BAGATELLE [*striking a match and getting ready to light the candle*]: Madame is coming in late tonight. Much later than usual...

MADAME PAPONNET: Yes... [*She turns toward* ALBERT, *who quickly hides the note behind his back.*] I thought my nephew deserved a little change. Mardi Gras, after all...

BAGATELLE: Yes indeed, madame... You're only young once...

[YVETTE *nods, and silently mouths "You're only young once!" along with him.*]

MADAME PAPONNET: And besides, you know how young people are today! [ALBERT *begins reading the note surreptitiously.*] If I didn't let him get out and enjoy himself now and then, heaven only knows what trouble he might get into!

BAGATELLE [*lighting the candle through the window*]: That's right...

MADAME PAPONNET: Wild women, Monsieur Bagatelle... Paris is simply full of them!

BAGATELLE: I know...

MADAME PAPONNET: And that would never do!

BAGATELLE: Certainly not!

MADAME PAPONNET: Believe me, I know women!... I was one, after all... [*Turning to* ALBERT, *who hurriedly stuffs the note into his pocket.*] Come here, Albert...

ALBERT: Yes, auntie dear...

[*He joins her at the window.*]

MADAME PAPONNET [*to* BAGATELLE]: Yes... He worked very hard yesterday... [*To* ALBERT.] Didn't you, Albert?

ALBERT: Yes, auntie dear...

MADAME PAPONNET [*to* BAGATELLE]: And I thought he deserved a nice little change. So we went to a lecture... On the life of the bee... And we had a simply splendid time. Didn't we, Albert?

ALBERT: Yes, auntie dear...

MADAME PAPONNET: And now he's going upstairs to bed. [*To* ALBERT.] Aren't you, Albert?

ALBERT: Yes, auntie dear...

MADAME PAPONNET: And tomorrow it's back to your schoolwork!

ALBERT: Yes, auntie dear...

MADAME PAPONNET [*to* BAGATELLE]: Good night, monsieur.

BAGATELLE: Good night, madame.

MADAME PAPONNET [*to* ALBERT]: Take the candle, Albert!

ALBERT [*taking it from her*]: Yes, auntie dear...

MADAME PAPONNET [*going to the staircase, to* BAGATELLE]: Good night, monsieur. [*To* ALBERT.] Say "good night" to Monsieur Bagatelle.
ALBERT [*to* BAGATELLE, *at the window*]: Good night, Monsieur Bagatelle.
MADAME PAPONNET [*on the staircase, to* ALBERT]: Come along! Come along!
ALBERT: Coming, auntie...
[*They disappear up the stairs.*]
YVETTE [*getting up, to* BAGATELLE]: Well, monsieur... There he is!
BAGATELLE: Him? Your young Romeo? Madame Paponnet's—
YVETTE: In the flesh!
BAGATELLE: I don't believe it!
YVETTE: Well, it's true! That's him!
BAGATELLE: "Young" is right! Why, he's still in diapers!
YVETTE: Oh, don't let his looks fool you! I thought so too, monsieur. Then yesterday I passed him on the stairs... His aunt was with him, and he didn't dare open his mouth, poor thing... But as soon as her back was turned... Well, you can't imagine! He threw his arms around me and he kissed me...
BAGATELLE: He didn't!
YVETTE: Oh, but he did! And not just once either!
BAGATELLE: I never would have thought...
YVETTE: Believe me, Monsieur Bagatelle... You could have knocked me up with a feather, like they say! I just knew he was trying to tell me something!
BAGATELLE: Yes... I imagine...
YVETTE: And sure enough, when I took him aside later, he said he was dying to go to the ball... And get all dressed up like one of the Three Musketeers... With a mask, and everything, so no one would know...
BAGATELLE: Of all things!
YVETTE: So I went out and got a costume...
[*She points to the pile of clothes etc., on the floor, by the table.*]
BAGATELLE: Oh! That's what all that is... I was wondering...
YVETTE: And I wrote him a note...
BAGATELLE [*pointing down right*]: Under the mat!
YVETTE: Right! And I told him to wait until his aunt was asleep, and then to sneak out and come down here and get dressed.
BAGATELLE: In here?
YVETTE: I knew you wouldn't mind...
BAGATELLE: Mind? Not at all! Like I always say, Yvette, you're only—
YVETTE: I know, Monsieur! I know! And Mardi Gras only comes once a year!
BAGATELLE: Exactly! And anyone who doesn't enjoy it—
YVETTE: Is a mean old grouch! I'm glad you understand...
BAGATELLE [*getting up and taking the costume up left, toward the curtained doorway*]: I'll just put all this in back... Tell young Romeo to make himself at home... Anytime...
[*He begins climbing the steps leading up to the doorway, when the bell rings.*]
YVETTE: Shall I get that, monsieur?
BAGATELLE: If you don't mind, Yvette...
[*He disappears into the back room as* YVETTE *gets up and pulls the cord. A moment later,* BOISLAMBERT *comes hurrying in the front door.*]

BOISLAMBERT [*stopping, standing in the lobby, sighing*]: Ah! At last! I... I can hardly believe it! Me... Here... It's... [*Emotionally.*] It's almost too much!... Jacqueline... Jacqueline... [*Looking around, reverently, pointing.*] Jacqueline's door!... Jacqueline's hall!... Jacqueline's stairs!... [*He goes over to the concierge's door, strikes a pose, then strides in, dramatically.*] Look! I'm back!

YVETTE [*startled*]: Oh!... My goodness! It's... No, it can't be... Monsieur...

BOISLAMBERT: Yvette!

YVETTE [*calling*]: Monsieur Bagatelle!... Monsieur Bagatelle!...

BAGATELLE [*reappearing*]: Yes, yes... What's the matter?

YVETTE: Look, monsieur... Look! It's... It's madame's ex—

BAGATELLE [*squinting, as if in disbelief*]: Monsieur...

YVETTE: Monsieur de Boislambert!

BAGATELLE [*running down to join them*]: Monsieur... Is it really—

BOISLAMBERT: Of course! Of course! I'm back... Back home, where I belong! After all these months... A year... A whole year... Exiled, banished... To the wilds of America...

YVETTE: The wilds, monsieur?

BOISLAMBERT: Well... Chicago...

YVETTE: No!

BOISLAMBERT [*continuing his rapturous outpouring*]: And now, back home! At last! Just as I left it... Jacqueline's house... [*Pointing to* BAGATELLE.]: Jacqueline's doorman...

BAGATELLE: "Concierge," monsieur...

BOISLAMBERT [*pointing to* YVETTE]: Jacqueline's maid... [*To* YVETTE.] Madame still loves me, doesn't she, Yvette?

YVETTE [*without much conviction*]: Oh yes, monsieur... [*Aside.*] Why should I be the one...

BAGATELLE [*to* BOISLAMBERT]: I should say... Why, she was just talking to me about monsieur... Not ten minutes ago...

BOISLAMBERT: She was?

BAGATELLE: Absolutely!... [*Mimicking* JACQUELINE, *exaggerating.*] "Poor Boislambert!..." That's what she said... "Poor Boislambert!..."

BOISLAMBERT: Ah! Jacqueline...

BAGATELLE: She almost had me in tears, monsieur... "Poor Boislambert!... I'm afraid I ruined him!..."

BOISLAMBERT [*almost proudly*]: That's true! She did!

BAGATELLE: And... "Who knows where he is, I wonder? Who knows what's become of him?"

BOISLAMBERT: "Who knows where... Who knows..." [*Sighing.*] Ah! And to think, there I was, at that very moment... Running to her side! Ah! Jacqueline... Jacqueline... [*To* YVETTE, *pointing upstairs, excitedly.*] Is she... Is she...

YVETTE: No, monsieur. I'm afraid madame is out. But if monsieur would like to wait, she should be back in an hour.

BOISLAMBERT: In an hour?

YVETTE: Yes, monsieur.

BOISLAMBERT [*emotionally*]: You mean... You mean, in an hour, I... I'm going to see her?

YVETTE: Yes, monsieur.

BOISLAMBERT [*ecstatic*]: Jacqueline... Jacqueline... [*Sighing.*] Ah! It's too much! I can't bear it...

[*He falls into* BAGATELLE's *arms.*]

BAGATELLE: Please, monsieur...

BOISLAMBERT: I'll try... I'll try...

YVETTE [*to* BOISLAMBERT]: Is monsieur all right?

BOISLAMBERT [*straightening up, to* YVETTE]: Yes, yes... Take me upstairs...

YVETTE: Monsieur?

BOISLAMBERT: To... To madame's apartment... [*Ready to swoon at the thought.*] Ah! Jacqueline's apartment...

[*He begins to fall into* BAGATELLE's *arms again.*]

BAGATELLE: Monsieur... Monsieur...

BOISLAMBERT [*catching himself, gazing at the ceiling, pointing upstairs, to* YVETTE]: Come... I'll wait for her there...

YVETTE [*embarrassed*]: In madame's apartment?

BOISLAMBERT: Yes, yes... If I can bear it...

YVETTE: I'm sorry, monsieur, but... I mean, I'm afraid that won't be possible...

BOISLAMBERT: It won't?

YVETTE: I'm afraid not, monsieur.

BOISLAMBERT: I can't wait in her apartment?

YVETTE: No, monsieur... That is...

[*She pauses. There is an embarrassed silence.*]

BOISLAMBERT: That is...?

YVETTE: That is...

BOISLAMBERT: She still loves me, Yvette... You said so yourself!

YVETTE: Yes, monsieur... It's just that... I mean...

BOISLAMBERT [*with a sudden realization*]: There's someone else, isn't there! That's what you're trying to tell me!

YVETTE: Well, monsieur... In a word...

BOISLAMBERT [*sighing*]: Ahhh...

[*He lets himself fall into* BAGATELLE's *arms again.*]

BAGATELLE: Monsieur... Please...

YVETTE: Monsieur...

BOISLAMBERT [*straightening up*]: Yes, yes... I'll try... I'll try... [*After a pause, to* BAGATELLE, *composing himself.*] Well now, what is he like?

BAGATELLE: Monsieur?

BOISLAMBERT: Some handsome devil? Dashing? Charming?

BAGATELLE [*with a deprecatory wave of the hand*]: Pfff!

BOISLAMBERT: No?

BAGATELLE: Not really...

BOISLAMBERT: No Boislambert, you mean!

BAGATELLE: Hardly, monsieur!

YVETTE: But he *is* a baron...

BOISLAMBERT [*to* YVETTE]: And you say he's upstairs?

YVETTE: No, monsieur... Not yet... But he'll be here any minute.

BOISLAMBERT: Aha! And he'll come through the front door?

YVETTE: Yes, monsieur...

BOISLAMBERT: And go up the stairs?

YVETTE: Of course...

BOISLAMBERT [*bringing a chair from the table over to the window*]: Fine! [*He sits down.*]

BAGATELLE: Monsieur is staying?

BOISLAMBERT: I wouldn't miss him for the world! And anyway, as long as I'm waiting for madame... [*Settling in.*] I say, Bagatelle, could you do me a favor?

BAGATELLE: A favor, monsieur?

BOISLAMBERT: I just realized I haven't eaten a thing all day. The excitement, don't you know...

BAGATELLE: Tsk tsk tsk!

BOISLAMBERT: I'd really be much obliged if you could run out and have someone send me over some dinner...

BAGATELLE: Certainly, monsieur... Just down the street...

BOISLAMBERT [*reaching for his billfold*]: Here, let me—

BAGATELLE: No, no, monsieur. That's quite all right. I'll just add it to the twenty-seven francs, monsieur...

BOISLAMBERT: The twenty-seven francs?

BAGATELLE: And fifty centimes...

BOISLAMBERT: What twenty-seven francs, Bagatelle?

BAGATELLE: Never mind, monsieur... We can talk about it later... Some other time... About all those late nights when I made sure monsieur got home safe and sound... Back in the good old days, when monsieur and madame...

BOISLAMBERT [*sighing*]: Ahhh...

BAGATELLE : No, no... Some other time, monsieur... Let's not talk about it now... Maybe later, after dinner... When monsieur feels more like himself, I mean... [*He pulls the cord.*] If anyone rings the bell while I'm gone, if monsieur would be good enough to pull the cord...

BOISLAMBERT: Of course... Of course... Ah! Jacqueline's bell...

[*Just as* BAGATELLE *is about to go out into the lobby, he hears several horn blasts outside, amid the general merriment. He goes over to the fireplace and takes down his horn.*]

BAGATELLE [*going out, to* BOISLAMBERT]: Mardi Gras, monsieur... Mardi Gras...

[BAGATELLE *exits, blowing the horn as loudly as he can, as* YVETTE *covers her ears.*]

BOISLAMBERT [*still sitting in the chair by the window*]: Well now, Yvette... Let's have a little chat.

YVETTE: Monsieur?

BOISLAMBERT: Yes, yes... Come sit down and talk to me. Tell me everything she's done since the first day I left. Everything. Yvette... Where she goes, what she says... [*Rapturously.*] Just... Just talk to me about her!

YVETTE [*bringing the other chair from the table and sitting down near him*]: My, my! Monsieur really still loves madame, I'd say!

BOISLAMBERT: Love her, Yvette? Love her...? A woman I gave the best months of my life to...? Not to mention my four hundred thousand francs!

YVETTE [*impressed*]: Four hundred thousand... Monsieur! That's love!

BOISLAMBERT: A woman I fought with my family over...? Because I do have a family, Yvette... You might not think so to look at me, but I do have a family... And they watch me like a hawk.

YVETTE [*aside*]: I can understand why!

BOISLAMBERT: Of course, when I say that I fought with them over madame... Well, there was really more to it than that... Actually, they were trying to marry me off. That's what started all the trouble...

YVETTE: Marry monsieur off?

BOISLAMBERT: To a perfectly charming lady, Yvette... A widow... Madame de Nantoulas... Marcelle de Nantoulas... Well, frankly, I didn't care one way or the other. At first, I mean... But then I began thinking, and I realized what a shock it would be to Jacqueline... [*Correcting himself.*] To madame... And I knew that I didn't have the right to break her heart...

YVETTE [*with a note of sarcasm*]: Of course not, monsieur.

BOISLAMBERT: So I called the whole thing off.

YVETTE: No!

BOISLAMBERT: Yes!... But that's not all. It's the way I did it that got everyone so upset.

YVETTE: How was that, monsieur?

BOISLAMBERT: The day before the wedding!

YVETTE: No!

BOISLAMBERT: Yes! The day before... Well, you can picture my family! They were furious! They told me this time I'd gone too far... That they'd had enough, or words to that effect... And they packed me off to America... To Chicago...

YVETTE: To the wilds...

BOISLAMBERT: Well, practically... And I stayed there a whole year. In a bank, Yvette... At a paltry two hundred fifty francs a month...

[*He stands up.*]

YVETTE [*standing up*]: "Poultry" is hardly the word, monsieur...

BOISLAMBERT: Hardly! [*Beginning to pace back and forth.*] Well, you can just imagine how long that lasted! I'd no sooner get my money than I'd gamble it away...

YVETTE: No!

BOISLAMBERT: Yes, I'm afraid so... And when I say "gambled"... In one hand and out the other... Lose, lose, lose... Every month, the same old story...

YVETTE: Tsk tsk tsk!

BOISLAMBERT: Then, all of a sudden, this month my luck changed! With my two hundred fifty I won myself eight thousand...

YVETTE: Eight thousand!

BOISLAMBERT: That's right, Yvette... Eight thousand francs! And I said to myself, "Look, this time, instead of gambling it all away, why not invest it?" And the more I thought, the better it sounded.

YVETTE: Of course, monsieur... And then?

BOISLAMBERT: Then I said to myself, "That's a good idea! Invest!"

YVETTE: Monsieur did a lot of talking to himself...

BOISLAMBERT: Who else, Yvette? [*With a shrug.*] In Chicago...

YVETTE: Aha... [*She pauses, waiting for him to continue.*] And then?

BOISLAMBERT: Then I did. I invested.

YVETTE [*nodding, pausing, waiting for the rest*]: In what, if monsieur doesn't mind my asking?

BOISLAMBERT: Not at all... In trained parrots.

YVETTE: Monsieur?

BOISLAMBERT: Trained parrots... I heard about a concert that was going to be given by a group of trained parrots...

YVETTE: No! What a country!

BOISLAMBERT: So I bought up every ticket the week before, and I sold them all for ten times what they cost. When I counted up the profits I had forty thousand francs!

YVETTE: Oh, monsieur...

BOISLAMBERT: And with forty thousand francs in my pocket, Yvette... Well, you can guess what I did first!

YVETTE: Monsieur talked to himself about madame!

BOISLAMBERT: Exactly!... And the second thing I did was to go to New York, and get on a boat. That was two weeks ago... Yesterday we landed... And tonight... Tonight I'm here... [*Waxing ecstatic again.*] Here... Here... [*Apostrophizing, ignoring* YVETTE.] Ah, Jacqueline... Jacqueline... [*To* YVETTE.] Madame still loves me, Yvette... You're sure?

[*During the preceding,* ALBERT *has appeared, coming down the stairs, down right. He is wearing a long, gaudy, floral robe and a tassled nightcap, and carrying a lighted candle. He is slightly tipsy.*]

ALBERT [*opening the concierge's door and going in, before* YVETTE *has a chance to answer* BOISLAMBERT's *question*]: Where is it? Where's my costume?

BOISLAMBERT: What on earth... Who's that?

YVETTE: My young man, monsieur... Monsieur Albert...

BOISLAMBERT: Interesting, I must say...

ALBERT [*handing* BOISLAMBERT *his candle*]: Here, you... Whoever you are... If you don't mind... [*As soon as a startled* BOISLAMBERT *has taken it,* ALBERT *flings his arms around* YVETTE's *neck and kisses her several times.*] There!... [*Taking back the candle.*] Thank you... That's all...

BOISLAMBERT: Really, young man...

YVETTE [*to* BOISLAMBERT]: Monsieur will have to excuse him. He's so young...

ALBERT: I'm so young!

BOISLAMBERT [*sarcastically*]: Charming, I'm sure...

YVETTE: Yes, isn't he, monsieur!

ALBERT [*to* YVETTE]: I did just what you told me... In your note, I mean... I waited until my aunt was asleep... And... And then, as soon as I heard her snoring, I sneaked out and came down... Well, almost...

YVETTE: Almost?

ALBERT: I mean, not right away... At first, I didn't dare. Then I found a bottle of rum... In her closet... And I drank it.

YVETTE: No!

ALBERT: Well, half of it... After that, it was easy... Now where is it? Where's my costume?

YVETTE [*pointing up left*]: It's all in there... In back... Quick! Go put it on...

ALBERT: You're sure it's all there? The boots, the cape...

YVETTE: Yes! Now hurry... [*To* BOISLAMBERT.] He's so young!

ALBERT [*crossing up left*]: I'm so young!

[*He climbs the stairs to the curtained doorway, almost stumbling several times, and disappears inside.*]

YVETTE [*watching him leave*]: And so sweet!

BOISLAMBERT: Yes, isn't he! Too bad it can't last!

YVETTE: Monsieur?

BOISLAMBERT: You're only young once, Yvette!

YVETTE: I know... [*Philosophically.*] And Mardi Gras only comes once a year, monsieur... [BOISLAMBERT *gives her a quizzical look.*] Well, I have to be going, if monsieur will excuse me...
[*She moves toward the door.*]

BOISLAMBERT: You're leaving?

YVETTE: Yes, monsieur. I've got to get into my costume. Monsieur Albert and I are going to the ball... As soon as madame gets back, that is... [*Moving up toward the curtained doorway, calling.*] Wait for me here, Albert. I won't be long...
[*She goes out into the lobby and runs up the stairs. A moment later,* ALBERT *reappears from behind the curtain, holding up one of the musketeer's boots.*]

ALBERT: I found it!
[*He disappears back inside.* BOISLAMBERT *looks around and realizes that he is alone.*]

BOISLAMBERT [*with a sigh*]: Well now... Back to the business at hand... He'll be here any minute, this baron of hers... So! We sit down and wait! [*He sits down on one of the chairs by the window.*] He comes in... He goes upstairs... He goes into her apartment... [*Emotionally.*] Jacqueline's apartment... [*Controlling himself.*] He waits for Jacqueline... So far, so good!... Then she comes back... Now what? [*He gets up and begins pacing, deep in thought.*] I suppose I could tell her... [*Pausing.*] No, no... [*Pacing.*] Or else... [*Pausing.*] No... [*Pacing.*] Or perhaps... [*Pausing.*] No, no, no... [*Pacing, after a few moments.*] Aha! I've got it!... She comes in... I throw my arms around her... I sweep her off her feet... I say, "Jacqueline, darling! I'm back, and I've got forty thousand francs in my pocket! Now we're going to Monte Carlo, just the two of us! This minute! And I won't take no for answer!..." She says yes, and we're off...
[ALBERT *pokes his head through the curtain.*]

ALBERT: I say... Monsieur...

BOISLAMBERT [*looking up*]: What?... Yes, what is it?

ALBERT: You know, at first I didn't dare... On account of my aunt, I mean... Then I drank half a bottle of rum. After that it was easy...

BOISLAMBERT [*uninterested*]: Very good... Very good...

ALBERT: "Very good"? You can say that again! It was delicious!
[*He disappears quickly behind the curtain.*]

BOISLAMBERT: Now then... [*He sits down again by the window.*] We get to Monte Carlo... We head straight for the Casino... I put six thousand francs on red, three times in a row... Red comes up each time... That's eighteen thousand... Then six thousand on black, and black comes up... Six thousand more... Three more times on red... Red wins, all three... Another eighteen thousand... Black again, and black wins... Red again, and red wins... That's twelve thousand more... Such luck! It's incredible!... That makes... [*Calculating on his fingers.*] That makes fifty-four... Fifty-four thousand francs, just like that! [*Satisfied with himself.*] Then I quit for the night... The next day...

[ALBERT *pokes his head out again.*]

ALBERT: Monsieur...

BOISLAMBERT [*looking up*]: Hmm?

ALBERT: How does a musketeer get his boots on, monsieur?

BOISLAMBERT: I beg your pardon?

ALBERT: His boots, monsieur... How does he get them on?

BOISLAMBERT [*wryly*]: First one, then the other!

ALBERT: Aha... Thank you, monsieur!

[*He disappears behind the curtain.*]

BOISLAMBERT [*back to his calculations*]: Next day, perhaps I'm not quite so lucky... Let's say thirty-six thousand... That makes... Thirty-six and fifty-four... That makes ninety thousand francs... Plus the forty thousand I've got already...

[ALBERT *reappears.*]

ALBERT: Monsieur...

BOISLAMBERT [*beginning to lose patience*]: What now?

ALBERT: I can't get them on!

BOISLAMBERT: Well, keep trying!

ALBERT: Yes, monsieur... Good idea...

[*He disappears, but his grunts and groans can be heard offstage from time to time, softly, as he tries—obviously unsuccessfully—to put on his boots.*]

BOISLAMBERT [*glaring toward the curtain*]: For heaven's sake! How can I think... Now where was I? [*He returns to his calculations.*] Ninety thousand francs, plus the other forty thousand... That makes a hundred thirty thousand... [*He nods, in evident satisfaction.*] Good! Then I ask Jacqueline, "What do you think? Should we keep going, or stop while we're ahead?" And she says, "First give me the hundred thirty thousand, then we'll decide..." [*The doorbell rings.*] And I tell her, "Don't be silly! If I give you the hundred thirty thousand, I won't have anything left to bet with! To bet you need money! If you didn't, everyone would bet!... [*The bell rings again.*] Really, Jacqueline..."

[ALBERT *reappears.*]

ALBERT: Monsieur...

BOISLAMBERT [*still musing*]: "If not, they might as well just give their money away..."

ALBERT: Monsieur... Monsieur...

BOISLAMBERT [*looking up, impatiently*]: Again?

ALBERT: The bell, monsieur... Someone's ringing the bell... What's the point of sitting there if you're not going to open the door?

[*He disappears. The bell rings again, more insistently.*]

BOISLAMBERT: Hmm! He's right...

[*He stands up and pulls the cord.* MARCELLE DE NANTOULAS *enters, elegantly dressed and heavily veiled. After making sure that there is no one in the lobby, she heads straight for the concierge's quarters and strides in.*]

MARCELLE [*to* BOISLAMBERT, *averting her glance*]: Monsieur...

BOISLAMBERT: Madame...

MARCELLE: First let me assure you that money is no object!

BOISLAMBERT: It isn't?

MARCELLE: I'm a wealthy woman, monsieur... Very wealthy...

BOISLAMBERT: Oh?

MARCELLE [*reaching into her purse*]: Here... This is for you... [*She gives him a handful of bills.*]

BOISLAMBERT [*objecting*]: But, madame—

MARCELLE [*with a wave of the hand, still looking aside*]: No, no! That's quite all right! I told you... Money is no object...

BOISLAMBERT [*looking at the money*]: So I see!... But madame, I'm afraid—

MARCELLE: Of course, I do want something in return...

BOISLAMBERT: You do?

MARCELLE: Certainly, my good man! You don't think I'm giving you a small fortune for nothing! [*She goes to the door and pokes her head out, looking up and down the lobby to see if anyone is coming.*]

BOISLAMBERT: No... No... [*Aside, putting the money on the shelf above the window.*] Giving it to Bagatelle, she means... I wouldn't feel right... [*To* MARCELLE, *as she returns.*] Now then, madame... What was it you had in mind?

MARCELLE: I just want you to let me sit here, monsieur. By the window... [*She sits on the other chair, the one vacated by* YVETTE.]

BOISLAMBERT: Sit here...? That's all? You're sure?

MARCELLE: Quite! [*She looks him squarely in the face for the first time, jumping up.*] Oh, my God! It's... It's not...

BOISLAMBERT: Madame?

MARCELLE: Monsieur de Boislambert!

BOISLAMBERT: You... You know me?

MARCELLE: Of course I do, monsieur... Why, I knew that you didn't have a sou to your name... But I never... Tsk tsk tsk!

BOISLAMBERT: Madame?

MARCELLE: How pathetic, monsieur! A gentleman of your birth... Your breeding... Obliged to work as a... a vulgar doorman...

BOISLAMBERT [*summoning up all his dignity*]: "Doorman..." I beg your pardon, madame! I'm nothing of the kind!

MARCELLE: Well... Concierge, if you prefer...

BOISLAMBERT: That's not what I—

MARCELLE [*reaching into her purse again, offering him another handful of bills*]: Here... Please... Let me give you—

BOISLAMBERT: Certainly not, madame!

MARCELLE: Come, come now, monsieur... Let's not be proud!

BOISLAMBERT: I am not a concierge!

[*All of a sudden,* ALBERT, *offstage, lets out several loud grunts.* BOISLAMBERT *glowers toward the curtained doorway.*]

MARCELLE [*with a quizzical tilt of the head at* BOISLAMBERT]: Monsieur... Are you all right?

BOISLAMBERT [*ignoring her question*]: I assure you, madame... I'm not "obliged," as you put it... The concierge merely stepped out for a moment, and I'm doing him a favor. I'm afraid it would take rather long to explain...

MARCELLE: Aha... Well then... [*Putting the money back in her purse.*] Please, monsieur, don't try... Really, I don't have a moment to lose...

[*She goes to the door, looks out again, up and down the lobby.*]

BOISLAMBERT [*aside*]: "Concierge," indeed!

MARCELLE [*returning*]: You see... I'm not what you're probably thinking, monsieur...

BOISLAMBERT: "Thinking," madame? I'm not thinking at all. You seem to know me, but I'm afraid I haven't the slightest idea—

MARCELLE: Coming here this way... I mean...

BOISLAMBERT: Really, madame...

MARCELLE: Monsieur, I'm a woman of impeccable character!

BOISLAMBERT [*trying to peek under her veil, jovially*]: My misfortune, I daresay!

MARCELLE: Please, monsieur! This is no time to be witty!... [*Continuing.*] Impeccable, you understand? Utterly impeccable...

BOISLAMBERT: Yes, I'm sure... I'm sure...

MARCELLE: Now, you're probably wondering what I'm doing here...

BOISLAMBERT [*with a shrug*]: Well...

MARCELLE: So I'll tell you, monsieur. Next week I'm getting married.

BOISLAMBERT [*unconcerned*]: Aha...

MARCELLE: Yes... To Baron de Moranchard...

BOISLAMBERT: I see... Congratulations!

MARCELLE: Thank you, monsieur. But I'm afraid congratulations are not quite in order.

BOISLAMBERT: Oh?

MARCELLE: Not after what I just found out, monsieur... At the theatre... Can you imagine?

BOISLAMBERT: I'm afraid I can't...

MARCELLE: To find out something like that, monsieur... About a man you're supposed to be marrying in a week?

BOISLAMBERT: Like "that," madame?

MARCELLE: It's scandalous! Simply scandalous!

BOISLAMBERT: If you say so...

MARCELLE: If I say so? Of course I say so! You don't think it's scandalous that the baron has a... [*Emphasizing, rather pompously.*] a paramour? That he comes running here every night, to the arms of some shameless tart... some brazen hussy...

BOISLAMBERT [*pricking up his ears, suddenly interested*]: "Here"? Did you say "here"?

MARCELLE: Here! In this very building!

BOISLAMBERT [*passionately*]: Jacqueline!

MARCELLE: Yes, that's her name... Jacqueline... Jacqueline Lamberthier!

BOISLAMBERT [*aside*]: So... *That* baron!

[*Suddenly* ALBERT's *grunts can be heard offstage, louder and more unpleasant than before.* BOISLAMBERT *gives another impatient look toward the curtain.*]

MARCELLE [*with a start*]: Excuse me, monsieur... Are you sure you're quite all right?

BOISLAMBERT [*feigning not to have heard the noise or the question*]: Hmm?

MARCELLE: That noise...

BOISLAMBERT: Noise, madame?

MARCELLE: Yes, I distinctly heard...

BOISLAMBERT: Perhaps something outside, madame... Mardi Gras, you know...

MARCELLE: Aha... Well, it only comes once a year...

[*She pauses.*]

BOISLAMBERT [*waiting for her to continue*]: Madame?

MARCELLE: Monsieur?

BOISLAMBERT: You were saying...? About the baron... The brazen hussy...

MARCELLE: Yes! I certainly was!

[*She pauses again.*]

BOISLAMBERT: Well?

MARCELLE: It's scandalous, monsieur!

BOISLAMBERT: I know. You said that.

MARCELLE: You can just imagine how I felt when I heard...

BOISLAMBERT: Of course...

MARCELLE: So I went to his club, and I stood outside the door... Waiting... Hiding in the shadows, like some common... [*She shudders at the thought.*] When he came out, monsieur, he gave this address. But my driver knew a short cut, and he got me here first.

BOISLAMBERT: Aha...

MARCELLE: I simply had to come here and see for myself. [*Pointing toward the front door.*] I just wanted to see that beast walk through the door... With my own two eyes...

BOISLAMBERT [*nodding sympathetically*]: Yes... Yes...

MARCELLE: The baron... Here... To see that... That tart! And a week before the wedding! Oh! It's scandalous!

BOISLAMBERT: Simply scandalous!

[*The doorbell rings.*]

MARCELLE: Ah! There he is!

BOISLAMBERT: Well, we'll see soon enough... [*He arranges the two chairs in front of the window.*] There! One for you, one for me... That way we'll both get a good look... How's that?

MARCELLE: Fine!

BOISLAMBERT: Can you see?

MARCELLE [*sitting down*]: Perfectly, monsieur! Just perfectly, thank you!

BOISLAMBERT: Then let's let him in!

[*He pulls the cord and sits down on the other chair.* MORANCHARD *enters, the picture of aristocracy.*]

MARCELLE [*looking through the window*]: There he is! I knew it!

BOISLAMBERT [*hypocritically*]: My compliments on your taste, madame! [*Aside, grimacing.*] Ugly, ugly, ugly!

MORANCHARD [*downstage, looking at his pocket watch, to himself*]: Right on time!... Well, at least they can't say I'm not a punctual lover! [*Stopping at the staircase.*] Heaven only knows, they're saying everything else! "Here he is, getting married in a week, the cad! And still... Tsk tsk tsk! You'd think he didn't love the poor woman he's marrying!..." But I do! I do!... Why, just tonight I sent her a magnificent bouquet... And a diamond that cost me an arm and a leg!

MARCELLE [*softly, to* BOISLAMBERT]: What is he saying?

BOISLAMBERT [*softly, to* MARCELLE]: I don't know. I can't hear him.

MORANCHARD: "Well, if that's the case," they'll say... "If you love her so much, how come you go running every night to your mistress?" [*Nodding, professorially.*] Excellent question... But it's really so simple... The fact is, when Jacqueline and I first... began, you might say... I promised I'd give her a thousand francs a month if I ever called it quits... Well, all things considered, I'm better off keeping her! And my wife will be better off too! After all, a thousand francs a month is twelve thousand a year... Not a fortune, but still... In twenty years that adds up to two hundred forty thousand... And two hundred forty thousand francs can make a dent in a couple's budget! It may not be right to keep a mistress, I'll admit. But it's worse to lose two hundred forty thousand francs!

[*He begins to climb the stairs, stops, returns to the lobby.*]

MARCELLE [*softly*]: What did he say?

BOISLAMBERT [*softly*]: I still couldn't hear him.

MORANCHARD [*at the foot of the stairs*]: Besides, when I say two hundred forty thousand... Actually it would be more. I'd have to sell off all kinds of stock... And since all my stocks are going down right now...

[*He begins pacing up and down.*]

MARCELLE [*softly*]: Is he leaving?

BOISLAMBERT [*softly*]: I think... [MORANCHARD *stops at the front door, turns, and comes back downstage.*] No, no... He's coming back...

[MORANCHARD *stops at the concierge's door.*]

MARCELLE [*frightened*]: Good heavens! I think he's going to come in here... Please, monsieur... He can't... I'll die if he sees me!

[*She runs to the fireplace and turns her back.*]

BOISLAMBERT: Don't worry, madame! I won't let him in!

[MORANCHARD *tries several times to open the door, but each time* BOISLAMBERT *slams it shut.*]

MORANCHARD: Hmm! It must be stuck!

[*Finally,* BOISLAMBERT *pulls the door open and strides out into the lobby, pulling the door shut behind him.*]

BOISLAMBERT [*face to face with* MORANCHARD, *aggressively*]: I should think you could take a hint, monsieur! The door is closed!

MORANCHARD [*looking him up and down*]: But... You're not the concierge!

BOISLAMBERT: I daresay!

MORANCHARD [*rather haughtily*]: Who are you?

BOISLAMBERT: I'm taking his place, monsieur... Expertly, I might add...

MORANCHARD: Well, in that case... Tell me, is Mademoiselle Lamberthier at home?

BOISLAMBERT: No, monsieur. She's not.

MORANCHARD: And her maid?

BOISLAMBERT: Yes... Her maid is at home, monsieur.

MORANCHARD: Thank you, my good man. Here... This is for you...

[*He gives him a coin.*]

BOISLAMBERT [*looking at the coin, as* MORANCHARD *disappears up the stairs*]: Five francs... Well, that much I may as well keep myself...

[*He pockets the coin. All of a sudden,* ALBERT *appears at the curtained doorway. He is wearing his boots, musketeer's cape, plumed hat, and grotesque false nose, but no trousers. He is brandishing the French hose in one hand, the rapier in the other.*]

ALBERT: I got the boots on, but now I can't get into the pants!

MARCELLE [*screaming at the apparition, running for the door*]: Good God!... Help! Help!

BOISLAMBERT [*rushing in, almost bumping into her*]: What is it? What's the matter?

MARCELLE [*pointing*]: That... That...

BOISLAMBERT [*hands on hips, to* ALBERT]: You... [*Waving him back.*] Out, out, out!

[*Just as* ALBERT *disappears behind the curtain,* MADAME PAPONNET *can be heard offstage, shouting.*]

MADAME PAPONNET'S VOICE: Albert!... Albert!...

BOISLAMBERT: Now what?

[MADAME PAPONNET *comes running down from the stairs in a long night gown, her face covered with white cream and her hair done up in a mass of curling papers. She lunges for the window and pokes her head through.*]

MADAME PAPONNET [*at the top of her lungs*]: Where is he, monsieur?

MARCELLE [*agape, screaming*]: Ayyy!

[*She falls into* BOISLAMBERT*'s arms, in a dead faint.*]

BOISLAMBERT [*to* MARCELLE]: Madame... [*Not knowing which way to turn, to* MADAME PAPONNET.] Madame?

MADAME PAPONNET: Albert!... My nephew!...

BOISLAMBERT [*torn between the two women, to* MADAME PAPONNET]: Your nephew?

MADAME PAPONNET: My Albert!... I woke up... I called him... He wasn't in bed... But look what I found! [*She waves* YVETTE*'s note.*] A letter! Look!... A letter!...

BOISLAMBERT: Yes, madame... I see, but... Really, I can't...

[*He tries to show her that he has his hands full.*]

MADAME PAPONNET [*not listening to a word he says*]: A letter!... From a woman!... And she's waiting for him at Valentino's... Well, we'll see about that! Door, please! [*Impatiently, as* BOISLAMBERT *is slow to react.*] Door! Door!

BOISLAMBERT [*dragging* MARCELLE *over to the cord, which he pulls with his free hand*]: With pleasure, madame! With pleasure!

[MADAME PAPONNET *runs out the front door, ranting and raving, leaving it open. Just as she disappears,* MARCELLE, *moaning, begins to come to. But, at the same moment, a terrified* ALBERT, *still semi-costumed as before—but this time without his false nose—comes dashing out from the back room, rapier in one hand and French hose in the other.*]

ALBERT: No! That's enough!...

[MARCELLE, *aghast, takes one look, groans, and faints again.*]

BOISLAMBERT [*to* MARCELLE]: Madame... Madame...

ALBERT [*rushing out into the lobby, in panic*]: I'm going back to bed...

[*At the foot of the stairs he bumps into* YVETTE, *dressed in a milkmaid's costume, coming down.*]

YVETTE: Albert... What's the matter?

ALBERT: No!... I'm going back to bed...

[*He runs up the stairs.*]

YVETTE [*shouting*]: Albert!... Albert!...

[*She runs up after him and disappears, still shouting. In the meantime,* BOISLAMBERT *has dragged* MARCELLE *over to the armchair, down left, and manages to get her seated.*]

BOISLAMBERT [*rubbing* MARCELLE'*s hands in an effort to bring her to*]: Madame... Please... [*He begins fanning her face with his hand, realizes that she is too heavily veiled to feel the effects, lifts her veil, and jumps back in surprise.*] Madame... No, it can't be!... Madame de Nantoulas!

MARCELLE [*coming to, feebly*]: Monsieur... Monsieur...

BOISLAMBERT: Madame de... The one my family wanted me to... No, it can't be... I don't believe it!

MARCELLE [*sitting up*]: Yes, monsieur. It is...

BOISLAMBERT [*embarrassed*]: Well, Madame... This is a pleasure... I mean, what a coincidence...

MARCELLE: Yes... Quite...

BOISLAMBERT: You, here... Like this... And me....

MARCELLE: Indeed, monsieur...

BOISLAMBERT: Well, as long as we're both here madame... Like this, I mean... Face to face... [*Clearing his throat, with a touch of pomposity.*] Perhaps I should take this opportunity to explain—

MARCELLE [*interrupting*]: Please, monsieur... No explanations... Just see me to the door and let me out of this... this madhouse!

[BOISLAMBERT *offers her his arm and they go into the lobby. At the same moment,* BAGATELLE *comes in the open door, followed by a* DELIVERY BOY *carrying a cloth-covered tray on his head.*]

BAGATELLE [*still carrying his horn, to* BOISLAMBERT]: Your dinner, monsieur!

BOISLAMBERT: Very good... I'll be right back...

BAGATELLE [*beckoning, to the* DELIVERY BOY]: This way, young man...

DELIVERY BOY: Yes, monsieur.

[*They go into the concierge's quarters.*]

BOISLAMBERT [*to* MARCELLE, *as they go out the front door*]: You see, it was all my family's idea... But I was in love, madame... Madly in love... So you really mustn't blame me...

[*They exit. In the meantime,* BAGATELLE *has replaced his horn above the fireplace. He and the* DELIVERY BOY *begin setting the table and laying out* BOISLAMBERT'*s meal. While they are doing so,* YVETTE *appears, coming down the stairs, dragging* ALBERT *bodily behind her.*]

ALBERT: No, no! It's too dangerous!... I want to go back to bed!

YVETTE [*tugging at his hand*]: Albert! You should be ashamed! Are you a man or a mouse?

ALBERT: I'm a man... A man... But—

YVETTE: Then prove it, for goodness' sake! Start acting like one...

[BAGATELLE *brings one of the chairs by the window over to the table.*]

BAGATELLE: There! [*to the* DELIVERY BOY.] I guess that's that... Come back in a little while and pick up the dishes.

DELIVERY BOY: Yes, monsieur.

[*He goes out into the lobby.* BAGATELLE *stands at the threshold.*]

ALBERT [*to* YVETTE]: I'm a man, I told you! And if you don't believe me... [*He pounces on the* DELIVERY BOY, *before a starled* BAGATELLE, *and gives him a sharp kick in the behind.*] There! You see?

YVETTE: Albert!

[*The* DELIVERY BOY *wheels around, gives* ALBERT *an innocuous shove that sends him to the floor, scratches his head, shrugs, and exits, closing the door behind him.*]

ALBERT [*on the floor, proudly, to* YVETTE]: See! I told you I'm a man... But it's still too dangerous! I want to go back to bed! If my aunt ever finds me... [*The doorbell rings.*] Good God! There she is!

[*He scrambles to his feet, and disappears up the stairs, as* BAGATELLE *goes in and pulls the cord.*]

YVETTE [*shouting*]: Albert!... Albert!...

[*She disappears in hot pursuit, continuing to shout. A moment later,* JACQUELINE *comes in the front door, still followed by* GASTON. *They leave the door open.*]

BAGATELLE [*stepping into the lobby, noticing the pair who have just entered, shouting*]: Monsieur Albert!... [*Going over to the staircase.*] Monsieur Albert! It's not your aunt!... Come back, Yvette! It's madame!... It's madame!...

[*He goes upstairs.*]

GASTON [*pleading, to* JACQUELINE]: But really, Jacqueline—

JACQUELINE: No, no, no! And that's final!

GASTON: But... But...

JACQUELINE: How many times do I have to tell you...

[YVETTE *comes running down the stairs, out of breath.*]

GASTON: But... But...

JACQUELINE [*ignoring him, to* YVETTE]: Ah! Yvette...

YVETTE: Madame...

JACQUELINE: Tell me... Did the baron—

YVETTE: Yes madame, he did. And I gave him madame's letter.

JACQUELINE: Very good... And he left?

YVETTE: No, madame. He's still...

[*She gives a nod toward the ceiling, as if to say "He's upstairs!"*]

JACQUELINE [*shaking her head*]: Some men never learn... Tsk tsk tsk!... [*Sighing.*] Well... Be a dear, Yvette... Run up and get me my cape and my mask...

YVETTE: Of course, madame.

[*She exits up the stairs, as* BOISLAMBERT *comes running in through the open front door.*]

BOISLAMBERT [*stopping short in the doorway, transfixed, gazing at* JACQUELINE, *finally finding his tongue*]: It... It's... It's Jacqueline!... I knew... I knew I saw her... [*Going up to her emotionally.*] Jacqueline... Jacqueline...

JACQUELINE [*very matter-of-fact*]: Why, Monsieur de Boislambert! What a nice surprise! What brings you here?

BOISLAMBERT [*impetuously, throwing all dignity to the wind*]: Tell me you still love me, Jacqueline... Tell me... Tell me...

GASTON [*clearing his throat*]: Hem, hem!

JACQUELINE [*to* BOISLAMBERT]: Monsieur?

BOISLAMBERT [*looking at* GASTON, *nodding*]: Aha! Of course... [*To* JACQUELINE, *very formally.*] Would madame do me the honor of stepping in here a moment? [*He motions toward the concierge's quarters.*] I'd like to have a word with her...

JACQUELINE: If you insist...

GASTON [*whining*]: But Jacqueline...

JACQUELINE [*to* GASTON]: You... Wait out here... I'll only be a minute.

[*She goes inside, as* BOISLAMBERT *and* GASTON *exchange frigid glances.* GASTON *begins pacing.*]

BOISLAMBERT [*following her in and closing the door, passionately*]: Jacqueline... At last! You're here, and... And I'm with you... The moment I've been waiting for... For a year... In Chicago... Ah! Jacqueline... Jacqueline...

JACQUELINE [*taking a compact out of her pocket and proceeding to powder her nose, unemotionally*]: Well?

BOISLAMBERT: "Well?" What do you mean... "Well?"

JACQUELINE [*still primping*]: What do you want to say?

BOISLAMBERT: What do I... What... Jacqueline, darling! Tell me you still love me! That's what I want to say!

JACQUELINE [*very offhand*]: Love you? Me? Heavens, don't be absurd! What ever gave you that idea?

BOISLAMBERT [*wiggling his little finger in his ear, as if he's not sure he has heard correctly*]: I beg your pardon?

JACQUELINE: You asked me if I love you, and I told you I don't. It's as simple as that...

BOISLAMBERT [*to himself*]: Hmm! She seems a little cold...

JACQUELINE: But please don't misunderstand, monsieur... I'm not being nasty... It's for your own good...

BOISLAMBERT: My own good?

JACQUELINE: Of course... I'm really being terribly considerate, you know. After all, it would be the easiest thing in the world to tell you I love you, even though I don't...

BOISLAMBERT: Jacqueline... Jacqueline...

JACQUELINE: Really, monsieur... Don't you think I know what's happened? Somehow, you've managed to get your hands on some money... Heaven only knows how... And what's the first thing you do? You come running back to throw it at my feet! Isn't that so?

BOISLAMBERT [*bumbling*]: Well... Yes... As a matter of fact...

JACQUELINE: I know! And I simply won't have it! Understand? I won't have it, monsieur! It's all well and good to ruin a man once... That's all in a day's work... But twice? No, no, no! That's going too far! You have to admit, monsieur... That would be just too perverse!

BOISLAMBERT: I know, but...

JACQUELINE: No, no, no! I'm not that kind of woman! I told you... I'm too considerate...

BOISLAMBERT: But...

JACQUELINE [*putting away her compact*]: Tsk tsk tsk!... Poor, dear Boislambert...

BOISLAMBERT [*dejected*]: Dear, sweet Jacqueline...

JACQUELINE: Now, promise me you'll come and visit some time...

BOISLAMBERT: You wouldn't mind?

JACQUELINE: Mind? Of course not... In fact...

[*She pauses.*]

BOISLAMBERT: Yes?

JACQUELINE: We must make it soon... You can take me to dinner...

BOISLAMBERT: When? When?

JACQUELINE [*reflecting*]: Well... I'm busy the rest of this month... And next... But perhaps sometime in April... [*Reconsidering.*] No... May, I think... Yes, May would be better... Toward the end of the month... Or early in June...

BOISLAMBERT [*in a passionate outburst*]: Jacqueline... Jacqueline...

JACQUELINE: Monsieur?

BOISLAMBERT: I love you! I love you!... Don't you understand? [*Emphasizing.*] I love you!

JACQUELINE [*casually*]: Yes, I know, monsieur. What of it?

BOISLAMBERT: What of it?... What... What... Come away with me, that's what! Just the two of us, Jacqueline... You and me... Now... This minute...

JACQUELINE [*with an incredulous smile*]: Just like that?

BOISLAMBERT: Yes, yes... Just like that! To Monte Carlo... We head straight for the Casino... I put six thousand francs on red, three times in a row... Red comes up each time...

JACQUELINE [*tapping her head with her forefinger*]: Tsk tsk tsk!

BOISLAMBERT: Jacqueline...

JACQUELINE: Really, monsieur... I think you need a rest...

[YVETTE *appears, coming down the stairs. She is carrying a hooded black cape and a black eye-mask on a stick.*]

YVETTE [*entering the concierge's quarters, to* JACQUELINE]: Madame's cape and mask...

JACQUELINE: Thank you, Yvette... [*Taking off her sable, which she gives to* YVETTE, *and putting on the cape.*] Is the baron still waiting?

YVETTE: Yes, madame.

JACQUELINE: Well, as soon as I'm gone, go up and show him out! And you needn't be polite!

YVETTE: Very good, madame.

BOISLAMBERT [*trying to help* JACQUELINE *adjust her cape*]: Jacqueline... Please, Jacqueline...

JACQUELINE [*tapping her head, to* BOISLAMBERT]: Really... A nice, long rest... Now you'll have to excuse me. I've got to be going...

BOISLAMBERT [*to himself*]: No two ways about it... She does seem rather cold... [*The doorbell rings.* YVETTE *pulls the cord, and* EDOUARD *enters. He is an aristocratic gentleman, no less elegant than* GASTON.]

EDOUARD [*rushing up to* JACQUELINE]: Jacqueline...

JACQUELINE: Edouard...

EDOUARD: I was just on my way up to see you! Are you going to the ball at the Hotel Royal?

JACQUELINE: Of course... I was just leaving...

EDOUARD: Well, lucky I stopped by! We can go together...

[*He offers her his arm.*]

GASTON [*who has been pacing all the while, stopping, archly, to* EDOUARD]: Monsieur! If you don't mind...

EDOUARD [*to* GASTON]: If I don't mind what, monsieur?

GASTON: Madame is with me!

EDOUARD [*waving him off, disdainfully*]: Come, come now... Really...

GASTON: Monsieur!

EDOUARD: Yes... What is it?

GASTON: Just this, monsieur!

[*He gives him a resounding slap across the face.*]

EDOUARD: I see, monsieur!

[*He counters in kind.*]

GASTON: Indeed?

[*He gives* EDOUARD *another slap.*]

EDOUARD: Indeed!

[*He reciprocates. After their exchange,* GASTON *and* EDOUARD *stand confronting one another, in perfect dignity, drawn up to their full height.*]

GASTON [*with the utmost courtesy*]: And now, monsieur, I think we should find our seconds...

EDOUARD: An excellent idea, monsieur...

GASTON: Perhaps at the club...

EDOUARD: No doubt...

GASTON: Shall we go?

EDOUARD: By all means... [*With a gesture.*] After you...

GASTON: No, no... After you, monsieur...

EDOUARD: No, please... I insist...

GASTON [*nodding*]: Monsieur...

[*He turns and begins to leave.*]

EDOUARD [*to* JACQUELINE]: Au revoir, Jacqueline... I trust you'll forgive us...

GASTON [*at the front door*]: Au revoir, Jacqueline...

[*They both give a little bow, and exit.*]

JACQUELINE [*watching them leave*]: Well! Really...

BOISLAMBERT [*poking his head through the window, timidly, to* JACQUELINE]: I say... Jacqueline...

JACQUELINE: Monsieur?

BOISLAMBERT: Now that they're both gone... I don't suppose... Perhaps you and I...

JACQUELINE [*laughing*]: Poor Boislambert! You never give up, do you!

BOISLAMBERT: Well, I only thought...

JACQUELINE: No, no, monsieur... Impossible... Now please, tell Yvette I'd like to see her, would you?

BOISLAMBERT [*dejectedly, to* YVETTE]: Madame would like to see you...

YVETTE: Thank you, monsieur.

[*She goes out into the lobby.*]

JACQUELINE [*to* YVETTE]: Ah!... Be a dear, Yvette... Count Raoul is outside... Just around the corner... Go tell him I'm waiting.

BOISLAMBERT [*still at the window, to himself*]: Raoul?

YVETTE [*to* JACQUELINE]: Yes, madame.

BOISLAMBERT [*aside*]: Another one?

YVETTE [*going to the front door, stopping, calling out*]: Door, please!... Door, please!

BOISLAMBERT [*pulling his head in, hands on hips, insensed*]: Oh!

JACQUELINE [*outside the window, imperiously, to* BOISLAMBERT]: Well?

[BOISLAMBERT *meekly turns and pulls the cord.* YVETTE *exits, leaving the door open.* JACQUELINE *takes out her compact and begins primping. After a few moments,* BOISLAMBERT *summons up his courage and pokes his head out the window again.*]

BOISLAMBERT: Jacqueline...

JACQUELINE [*without stopping*]: Yes, monsieur?

BOISLAMBERT: May I... Do you mind if I ask you a question?

JACQUELINE: Please... Go right ahead...

BOISLAMBERT: Have there always been... Were there always so many?... Even before, I mean... Even when you and I...

JACQUELINE [*laughing*]: Of course, you poor dear! Of course there were!

[*She puts away her compact as* YVETTE *enters, followed by* COUNT RAOUL. *He is even more elegant than the other two suitors.*]

COUNT RAOUL: Jacqueline, darling!

[*He kisses her hand.*]

JACQUELINE [*taking* COUNT RAOUL'*s arm, to* YVETTE]: Don't forget our friend... [*She gives a meaningful glance toward the ceiling.*] You know what to tell him...

YVETTE: Yes, madame.

JACQUELINE [*to* BOISLAMBERT, *still at the window*]: Au revoir, monsieur... [*With a wave.*] Ta ta... Now you will come and visit... First thing in July...

BOISLAMBERT [*resigned, nodding*]: July...

COUNT RAOUL [*to* JACQUELINE]: I've spoken to the notary, Jacqueline... About the house... They're only asking five hundred thousand...

JACQUELINE [*with a grand gesture*]: Pfff!

[*They exit.*]

BOISLAMBERT [*sitting down at the table*]: It's women like her that turn families gray!

[*He begins picking unenthusiastically at his dinner, as* BAGATELLE *appears, coming down the stairs.*]

YVETTE [*to* BAGATELLE]: Monsieur... Where's Albert? Can't you make him come down?

BAGATELLE [*laughing*]: Don't worry, Yvette! He's on his way. He finished off the rum...

YVETTE: He didn't!

BAGATELLE: And now he's putting on an evening gown!... At least, he's trying!

YVETTE [*joining in the laughter*]; An evening gown?

BAGATELLE: He says it looks funnier than the musketeer's costume!

YVETTE: No!

BAGATELLE: You'll have to see it!

YVETTE: I can't wait! As soon as I take care of the baron...

[*She runs up the stairs as* BAGATELLE *enters the concierge's quarters.*]

BOISLAMBERT: Ah! Bagatelle...

BAGATELLE: Monsieur...

BOISLAMBERT [*pouring a glass of wine, offering it to him*]: Won't you join me?

BAGATELLE: Why, thank you, monsieur!

BOISLAMBERT: Please...

[BAGATELLE *brings the other chair over from the window to the table and sits down across from* BOISLAMBERT, *who continues picking at his food for a few moments in uncomfortable silence.*]

BAGATELLE [*finally breaking the silence*]: I hope monsieur is enjoying his dinner.

BOISLAMBERT: As much as I can, Bagatelle... Under the circumstances...

BAGATELLE: "Circumstances," monsieur?

BOISLAMBERT [*shaking his head*]: Madame...

BAGATELLE [*nodding*]: Aha... Aha...

[*There is another uncomfortable silence.*]

BOISLAMBERT: You know, Bagatelle...

BAGATELLE: Yes, monsieur?

BOISLAMBERT [*with an air of profundity*]: Life can be funny...

BAGATELLE: Isn't it the truth, monsieur!

BOISLAMBERT: After all these years... I've learned more in the last five minutes, as her doorman, than in two years as her lover! How do you explain it?

BAGATELLE: Just imagine if monsieur had been her lover for five minutes and her doorman for two years!

[BOISLAMBERT *nods philosophically. There is another pregnant pause.*]

BOISLAMBERT: Tell me, Bagatelle...

BAGATELLE: Yes, monsieur?

BOISLAMBERT: Before... Back then... There were others, weren't there?

BAGATELLE [*reluctantly*]: Well...

BOISLAMBERT: It's all right... I know...

BAGATELLE: I suppose, monsieur...

BOISLAMBERT: And she used to make a fool of me... Didn't she, Bagatelle?

BAGATELLE [*objecting*]: Oh, monsieur! A fool...?

BOISLAMBERT: You know what I mean... Little lies, little tricks... Behind my back...

BAGATELLE: Well... Once in a while...

BOISLAMBERT [*nodding, ironically*]: Yes... Once in a while... [*He pauses.*] For example?

BAGATELLE: Monsieur?

BOISLAMBERT: For example... Tell me some of the things she did, Bagatelle.

BAGATELLE: Oh no! Monsieur wouldn't want me to do that!

BOISLAMBERT: Come, come...

BAGATELLE: No... Really... I'm afraid it would make monsieur angry!

BOISLAMBERT: With madame?

BAGATELLE: With me, monsieur... With me...

BOISLAMBERT: Not at all, Bagatelle! Why, I'll thank you for it...

BAGATELLE: No, no, monsieur! That's what they always say... Before... Then afterwards...

[*He draws his thumb across his throat in a significant gesture.*]

BOISLAMBERT: Really, Bagatelle... You know you can trust me!

BAGATELLE: Well...

BOISLAMBERT: Come, come... Have some more wine...

[*He refills* BAGATELLE'*s glass.*]

BAGATELLE [*drinking*]: If monsieur is sure...

BOISLAMBERT: Of course I'm sure!

BAGATELLE [*reluctantly*]: Well... It's not something I'd do for just anyone, monsieur... But... Well, monsieur... It's like I was telling madame... I never had any complaints with monsieur... Not like some of the others...

BOISLAMBERT [*nodding*]: Aha...

BAGATELLE: No... Monsieur was always very good to me, and I appreciate it.

BOISLAMBERT: Thank you, Bagatelle...

BAGATELLE: Anyway, if monsieur is sure, I suppose I can tell him...

[*He holds out his glass for more wine.* BOISLAMBERT *refills it.* BAGATELLE *sips, taking his good time.*]

BOISLAMBERT: Well...?

BAGATELLE: Let me think, monsieur... There were so many... [*He pauses, drinks.*] Like that time, monsieur...

[*He chuckles.*]

BOISLAMBERT: Yes...?

BAGATELLE: That night when monsieur came to see madame... And I kept him down here, and I wouldn't let him go up...

BOISLAMBERT: You mean that time you were so drunk?

BAGATELLE [*with a wry smile*]: Drunk, monsieur?

BOISLAMBERT [*standing up*]: Absolutely out of your mind, Bagatelle! Why, you could hardly stand up! [*Imitating a drunkard's gait.*] You staggered around, and kept bumping into me, and grabbing me, and pulling me away from the stairs...

BAGATELLE [*laughing*]: I remember...

[*He refills his own glass.*]

BOISLAMBERT: And all you kept saying was... [*Imitating a drunkard's speech.*] "No beggars allowed! No beggars allowed!..." You were so drunk, you didn't even know me! That's why I didn't mind...

[BAGATELLE *drains the glass and replaces it on the table.*]

BAGATELLE [*standing up, confidentially*]: I wasn't drunk, monsieur...

BOISLAMBERT [*laughing*]: Oh no! Not at all!

BAGATELLE: Really, monsieur... I wasn't...

BOISLAMBERT: Then you're an awfully good actor!

BAGATELLE: Thank you, monsieur!

BOISLAMBERT: What?

BAGATELLE: That's right, monsieur. It was all an act. Madame told me she didn't care how I did it, as long as I kept monsieur downstairs. So I did...

BOISLAMBERT [*shocked*]: Oh!

BAGATELLE [*mimicking* JACQUELINE's *voice*]: "Whatever you do, Bagatelle..." That's what she said... "Whatever you do, tonight of all nights, don't let him come up!"

BOISLAMBERT: Of all the...

BAGATELLE: Five minutes later, monsieur came in, and... Well, monsieur knows the rest.

BOISLAMBERT [*angrily*]: And the broom, Bagatelle? Remember? Did you have to hit me with your broom?

BAGATELLE: I know, monsieur... I was sorry about that... But if monsieur hadn't tried to make a dash for the stairs... Besides, it was just a tap...

BOISLAMBERT: Oh, really?

BAGATELLE: See? I knew I was going to make monsieur angry! I knew it! Monsieur asked me to tell him, and now he's angry!

BOISLAMBERT [*trying to control himself*]: I am not angry!

BAGATELLE: Not even a little?

BOISLAMBERT [*gritting his teeth*]: Not even a little!

BAGATELLE: I'm glad, monsieur, because... Like I was telling madame... I've always been very fond of monsieur. He wasn't like all the others...
[*He pours himself another drink.*]

BOISLAMBERT: I know! I know!... [*To himself.*] The idea...! [*To* BAGATELLE.] Tell me, who was he, anyway?

BAGATELLE [*drinking*]: That night, monsieur?... Some prince or other...

BOISLAMBERT [*impressed*]: A prince?

BAGATELLE: Some foreigner... And rich?... Pfff!
[*He gestures, with a shake of the hand, as if to say: "Unbelievable!"*]

BOISLAMBERT: A prince? A real one?

BAGATELLE: Of course! Monsieur doesn't think I would have taken the liberty... I mean, not just for one of madame's ordinary lovers...

BOISLAMBERT [*ironically*]: Hmm! Thank you, Bagatelle!

BAGATELLE: Not at all, monsieur... [*Beginning to get a little tipsy.*] It's like I was telling madame...

BOISLAMBERT: Yes, yes... I know... [*Reflecting bitterly.*] One of madame's small army of admirers... [*He shakes his head in resignation, sighing, as* BAGATELLE *continues to drink.*] You know, Bagatelle...

BAGATELLE: Monsieur?

BOISLAMBERT: If I'd had any sense, you know what I would have done?

BAGATELLE: What's that, monsieur?

BOISLAMBERT: I'd have listened to my family and married Madame de Nantoulas. She was pleasant... She was pretty... She was worth two million...
[*The doorbell rings.* BOISLAMBERT, *without thinking, goes to pull the cord.*]

BAGATELLE [*stopping him*]: Oh no, monsieur... Please... Not now... I wouldn't dream of it...
[*He pulls the cord. A* GENDARME *enters.*]

THE GENDARME [*at the window, to* BAGATELLE]: Does a woman named Madame Paponnet live here?

BAGATELLE: Yes, monsieur.

THE GENDARME: Well, somebody better come down and identify her.

BAGATELLE: Down where? What's the trouble?

THE GENDARME: To the station! We had to lock her up!

BAGATELLE: Madame Paponnet? What for?

THE GENDARME: What for? You name it... Disturbing the peace, disorderly conduct, public nuisance, indecent exposure, assault and battery on an officer of the law, resisting arrest...

BAGATELLE: Madame Paponnet?

THE GENDARME: That's the name she gave, monsieur!

BAGATELLE: All right... I'm coming... [*To himself, shaking his head.*] Madame Paponnet...

BOISLAMBERT [*offering* BAGATELLE *his hand, as if about to leave*]: Bagatelle... Nice seeing you... Perhaps we'll meet again...

BAGATELLE: Monsieur isn't leaving?

BOISLAMBERT: I may as well... [*Sighing.*] There's no point in my staying...

BAGATELLE: No, no, monsieur... Not yet... I'll just be a few minutes. If monsieur would mind the door until I come back...

BOISLAMBERT: Again?

BAGATELLE: Please! Monsieur can't say no... Just this one last time... [*Without waiting for* BOISLAMBERT'*s reply, to* THE GENDARME.] After you, monsieur! [*He takes another quick drink, goes out into the lobby, and exits with* THE GENDARME.]

BOISLAMBERT [*alone, hands on hips, watching him leave*]: Can't say no, can't I? [*He begins pacing back and forth.*] You mean I spent four hundred thousand francs on the... the daughter of the regiment... just to get smashed in the behind with a broom, of all things! And by a... a concierge, no less! And then he has the gall to tell me, "Monsieur can't say no!" Well, we'll see what I can say and what I can't say, my friend!... Door, please! Door, please! [*He pulls the cord.*] Much obliged, I'm sure! [*He goes out into the lobby and storms out the front door, leaving it open.*]

MORANCHARD'S VOICE [*offstage*]: Yes, yes... I'm going! And you can tell her I won't be back!

YVETTE'S VOICE [*offstage*]: Yes, monsieur.

[MORANCHARD *appears, coming down the stairs.*]

MORANCHARD [*in the lobby*]: Door, please! [*He turns and goes back up the first few steps, calling up.*] And tell her she can just forget the thousand francs a month! It's her fault, not mine! A bargain's a bargain!... [*Back out in the lobby.*] Door, please! [*He strides upstage as if to go out the front door, then stops dead in his tracks.*] Oh no!... Marcelle!... What is she doing here?... [*He beats a hasty retreat into the concierge's quarters.*] Excuse me, monsieur, but... [*He looks around, sees that he is alone.*] Monsieur?... Monsieur?... Now where do you suppose... [*He goes over to the window, as* MARCELLE *and* BOISLAMBERT *enter and come downstage, the former carrying an immense bouquet.*] There he is!... With Marcelle... What on earth is she doing with the concierge, of all people?

BOISLAMBERT [*to* MARCELLE]: What a pleasant surprise, madame! I was just on my way to see you...

MARCELLE: It's scandalous, monsieur! Simply scandalous...

BOISLAMBERT: Madame?

MARCELLE [*holding out her free hand, showing him a ring with a huge stone the size of a doorknob*]: This, monsieur!

BOISLAMBERT [*agape*]: Good God! It's... It's the Kohinur diamond!

MARCELLE: Well, not quite... [*Seething.*] That cad! That vile... That loathsome... Oh! He thinks he can buy me with his flowers and his... [*Holding up her fist with the ring.*] his trinkets!

BOISLAMBERT [*aside*]: Trinkets!... [*To* MARCELLE.] The baron, madame?

MARCELLE: Of course! The baron!... He comes here every night to that hussy of his, and he thinks all he has to do is send me a diamond!

BOISLAMBERT: You're absolutely right!

MARCELLE: Well, he can keep it! I'm not for sale! The minute I got it, I knew what I had to do... Come here... To the scene of his crime...

BOISLAMBERT [*correcting*]: Crimes, madame... His crimes...

MARCELLE: Yes... And throw it in his face!

BOISLAMBERT: Poetic justice!

MARCELLE: Exactly, monsieur!

[*She pauses, fuming.*]

BOISLAMBERT [*timidly*]: Do I take it, madame, that... that...

MARCELLE: That what, monsieur?

BOISLAMBERT: That since you're not keeping the ring, madame, you're not keeping the husband either?

MARCELLE: Him? Never!

BOISLAMBERT: Then... Then... [*Falling to his knees, in front of her.*] Marcelle... Marcelle..

MARCELLE: Monsieur! What are you doing?

BOISLAMBERT: I'm... I'm getting on my knees... Throwing myself at your feet, madame... Kissing the ground you walk on...

[*He begins joining the deed to the word.*]

MARCELLE: Here? In public?

BOISLAMBERT [*standing up*]: You're right... Of course... [*Taking her hand, pulling her toward the concierge's quarters.*] Come... In here... We'll be alone...

[*He tries, several times, to open the door, but each time* MORANCHARD, *in panic, slams it shut. Finally, as* BOISLAMBERT *backs up and prepares for one last assault,* MORANCHARD *runs to the back of the room and takes refuge behind the curtain.* BOISLAMBERT *rushes headlong against the door, and goes flying into the room, falling on all fours.* MORANCHARD *peeks out unnoticed, from behind the curtain.*]

MARCELLE [*running in after* BOISLAMBERT]: Monsieur... Are you all right?

BOISLAMBERT: Of course! Of course!... Where was I?

MARCELLE [*standing in front of him, still holding the bouquet*]: I believe you were kissing the ground I walk on...

BOISLAMBERT: Yes, yes... Now that we're alone... Marcelle...

MARCELLE: Monsieur?

BOISLAMBERT [*passionately*]: I love you!

MORANCHARD [*surprised, aside*]: "I love you!"

[*The doorbell rings.*]

BOISLAMBERT: I love you!

MORANCHARD [*aside*]: Of all things!

[*He disappears behind the curtain.*]

MARCELLE: The bell, monsieur...

BOISLAMBERT: I beg your pardon?

MARCELLE: The bell... Someone's ringing...

BOISLAMBERT: Are you sure?

[*The bell rings again.*]

MARCELLE: You see?

[BOISLAMBERT *stands up and pulls the cord.* GASTON *enters, closing the front door behind him, as* BOISLAMBERT *returns to his position on his knees at* MARCELLE'*s feet.*]

BOISLAMBERT: I love you, Marcelle!

MARCELLE: After all these years... After you ran off and left me in the lurch, monsieur...

GASTON [*poking his head in the window*]: Mademoiselle Jacqueline Lamberthier?

BOISLAMBERT [*still on his knees, looking up*]: I'm sorry, monsieur... She's out...

GASTON: Aha... Well, I'll wait... That is, if you don't mind...

BOISLAMBERT: Mind? Why should I mind?

GASTON [condescendingly]: I'll make it worth your while, my good man... Twenty francs...

BOISLAMBERT [uninterested]: Wait as long as you like...

GASTON [putting a coin on the sill]: There you are!

[He begins pacing up and down the lobby.]

BOISLAMBERT [to MARCELLE]: I love you, Marcelle!

[The doorbell rings.]

MARCELLE: The bell, monsieur...

BOISLAMBERT: Again?

MARCELLE: Again!

[BOISLAMBERT stands up and pulls the cord. EDOUARD enters. He and GASTON exchange haughty glances, as BOISLAMBERT returns to his position.]

BOISLAMBERT [on his knees]: I love you! I love you, Marcelle! I love you!

MARCELLE: Really, monsieur... This is hardly the time or place...

EDOUARD [poking his head in the window]: Mademoiselle Jacqueline Lamberthier?

BOISLAMBERT [losing patience]: She's out, damn it! Out!... Leave your twenty francs on the sill, and wait as long as you like...

EDOUARD [quizzically]: Twenty francs... [He shrugs.] My word!

[He reaches into his pocket, pulls out a coin, and puts it on the sill. Then he begins pacing up and down, in the opposite direction to GASTON. The two pause each time they pass, and glower at one another.]

BOISLAMBERT [during the preceding, to MARCELLE]: Time or place be damned, Marcelle! I love you... And I want you to marry me!

MARCELLE: You want me to what?

BOISLAMBERT: To marry me! Understand?

MARCELLE: That's easy to say, monsieur! I remember the last time...

BOISLAMBERT: Yes, but this time I mean it!

MARCELLE: I do believe you're serious!

BOISLAMBERT: Of course I am, Marcelle! I want you to marry me! You'll see, you won't regret it! I'll make you the happiest woman in the world! [Aside.] With her millions...

MARCELLE [weakening]: Well now... How can a woman refuse an offer like that?

BOISLAMBERT: Don't! Don't!

MARCELLE [smiling, tenderly]: I won't!

BOISLAMBERT: You won't?... [Jumping to his feet.] You mean... You... [Romantically.] You will?

MARCELLE: I mean... I have to admit, monsieur... I was only going to marry the baron out of spite... I really never stopped loving... [Coyly.] someone else...

BOISLAMBERT: Someone else?

MARCELLE [throwing herself into his arms]: Octave!

BOISLAMBERT: Marcelle!

[They embrace. After a moment, MORANCHARD appears from behind the curtain. He is wearing ALBERT's gaudy robe, nightcap, and false nose, and *is carrying his lighted candle. He begins tiptoeing out.*]

MARCELLE [*suddenly noticing him, throwing the bouquet of flowers up in the air, screaming*]: Ayyy!

BOISLAMBERT: What's the matter?

MARCELLE [*pointing*]: There... That... Ahhh!...

[*She faints dead away in* BOISLAMBERT'*s arms.*]

MORANCHARD [*trying to be as matter-of-fact as possible*]: Door, please!

BOISLAMBERT: Who the devil are you?

MORANCHARD [*in a whisper, making sure that* MARCELLE *can't hear him*]: Shhh! Shhh!... I'm Baron de Moranchard, monsieur... Madame's fiancé...

BOISLAMBERT: You?

MORANCHARD: Shhh! Shhh!... [*Indicating his disguise.*] I thought I could spare us all a nasty scene, monsieur... Accusations... Recriminations...

BOISLAMBERT: So instead you frighten her half to death!

MORANCHARD: Sorry, my good man... Accidents will happen...

BOISLAMBERT: Indeed!

MORANCHARD: Anyway, she's all yours... Though I must admit, I don't know what she sees in a concierge, if you don't mind my saying... When she could have had a baron...

BOISLAMBERT [*raising his voice*]: "Concierge," my foot! I'm just minding the door! My name is Octave de Boislambert, monsieur!

MORANCHARD: Shhh! Shhh!... [*Surprised.*] Boislambert?

BOISLAMBERT: Yes, yes...

MORANCHARD: Aha... [*Pausing to reflect.*] In that case, monsieur... Perhaps you can do me a favor...

BOISLAMBERT: I can?

MORANCHARD: Since you're marrying her, that is... I thought... Perhaps... [*Pointing.*] The ring...

BOISLAMBERT: You want me to buy the ring?

MORANCHARD: It's really very lovely... And you have to admit, she's worth it... Besides, it would save me the trouble of taking it back...

BOISLAMBERT: How much?

MORANCHARD: Forty thousand...

BOISLAMBERT [*raising his voice*]: Forty thousand?

[MARCELLE *groans, as if about to come to.*]

MORANCHARD: Shhh! Shhh!... [*Whispering.*] It's a bargain!

BOISLAMBERT [*whispering*]: I know... [*Joking.*] At half the price... Well, by a lucky coincidence, I just happen to have... [*He manages to reach into his pocket, and gives* MORANCHARD *a bundle of bills.*] Forty thousand, monsieur!

MORANCHARD [*counting them, whispering*]: Monsieur de Boislambert... How can I ever thank you?... [*Pocketing the bills.*] Well now... Door, please!

BOISLAMBERT [*about to object*]: Monsieur... I thought I told you—

MORANCHARD: Tsk tsk tsk... Not as a concierge, my friend... As a rival... And a gentleman!

[*He offers to shake hands, and* BOISLAMBERT *does so, not without difficulty.*]

BOISLAMBERT: Of course...

[*He awkwardly pulls the cord.*]

MORANCHARD [*bowing*]: Monsieur...

BOISLAMBERT: Monsieur...

[MORANCHARD *goes out into the lobby just as* MARCELLE *begins to come to. A moment later, the* DELIVERY BOY, *followed by the* YOUNG MAN *and the* YOUNG WOMAN, *still in their hussar's and ballerina's costumes, come in the front door, leaving it open. All three stop short in their tracks—as do* GASTON *and* EDOUARD, *who have been pacing throughout the preceding scene—as* MADAME PAPONNET *bursts in behind them. She is still dressed as she was when she left, her hair in curling papers and her face smeared with cream.*]

MADAME PAPONNET [*at the top of her lungs*]: Albert!... Albert!... [*Catching sight of* MORANCHARD, *wearing* ALBERT's *robe, nightcap, and false nose.*] Aha!... There you are... You monster! You... You...

[*She lunges at a nonplussed* MORANCHARD *and begins pummeling him.*]

MORANCHARD [*defending himself as best he can*]: Madame... Madame...

[MADAME PAPONNET *pulls off his false nose, stares in shocked disbelief for a few seconds, and screams. At the same moment,* YVETTE *and* ALBERT *come down the stairs, singing.* ALBERT *is dressed in an evening gown, obviously very drunk.*]

MADAME PAPONNET [*agape*]: Oh! My best dress... [*Shouting.*] Albert!... You beast!... My best dress!... [*Pointing at* YVETTE.] You!... You tramp!... Oh! Just let me get my hands on you two...

[*She begins chasing* ALBERT *and* YVETTE *around the lobby, still shouting, and out the open front door. A moment later,* JACQUELINE *and* COUNT RAOUL *hurriedly enter.*]

JACQUELINE [*to* COUNT RAOUL]: Of course I'm sure we'll be alone. Raoul... [*Noticing* GASTON, EDOUARD *and* MORANCHARD.] Well, almost... Hurry... Hurry...

[*She and* COUNT RAOUL *go running up the stairs, as the other three follow in hot pursuit.*]

GASTON: Jacqueline...

EDOUARD: Jacqueline...

MORANCHARD [*following with his lighted candle*]: Jacqueline...

[*All three disappear, one after the other. In the meantime* ALBERT *and* YVETTE *have come running back in the front door and around the lobby, pursued by* MADAME PAPONNET, *shouting. A moment later,* THE GENDARME *comes bursting in the open front door, and catches sight of her.*]

THE GENDARME [*pointing to* MADAME PAPONNET]: There she is!... Stop her!... Stop her!...

MARCELLE [*finally coming to*]: Where... Where am I?...

BOISLAMBERT: Marcelle...

[THE GENDARME *joins in the chase. After a few more rounds in and out of the lobby, accompanied by appropriate shouts,* ALBERT *and* YVETTE *go dashing into the concierge's quarters, followed closely by* MADAME PAPONNET *and* THE GENDARME.]

MARCELLE [*screaming, as they all burst in*]: Ayyy!

[*She faints again in* BOISLAMBERT's *arms.*]

BOISLAMBERT: Oh no! Not again!

[*He stands there, trying to revive her, as* BAGATELLE, *obviously drunk, comes staggering in the open front door and into the concierge's quarters, oblivious to everything.*]

BAGATELLE [*to* BOISLAMBERT]: I'm back, monsieur... I'm back...
[*He finishes off the bottle of wine, in the midst of the continuing chaos, makes his way to the fireplace as best he can, and takes down the horn, which he begins blowing stridently. The frantic chase continues, in and out, through the lobby and the concierge's quarters, upsetting the table, the food, etc., before the wide-eyed gaze of the* DELIVERY BOY, *the* YOUNG MAN, *the* YOUNG WOMAN, *and a helpless* BOISLAMBERT, *still trying his best to revive* MARCELLE. *From time to time she begins to come to, only to scream and faint again at each new irruption. Eventually,* BAGATELLE *catches* YVETTE *on the run, embracing her with his free hand and planting boisterous kisses on her lips between blasts on his horn, despite her vigorous protests. The curtain falls slowly on a scene of wild confusion.*]

CURTAIN

BOUBOUROCHE
or, She Dupes to Conquer

Adaptation of

Boubouroche

by

Georges Courteline

(1893)

CHARACTERS

BOUBOUROCHE, a portly forty, good-natured and credulous to a fault

ANDRE, young and handsome, the limber-tongued lover of Boubouroche's mistress

THE GENTLEMAN, elderly, dignified, and very well-spoken

POTASSE
FOUETTARD } Boubouroche's bridge-playing friends and drinking companions
ROTH

AMEDEE, a café waiter

ADELE, Boubouroche's beautiful but unfaithful mistress of many years

The cashier, a male visitor, a female visitor, three or four café customers

Act One

A little neighborhood bistro, lit by several gaslamps. Up center, the door, on each side of which extend the windows, with the name of the establishment seen from behind along with the backs of several signs. Along the stage left wall, the counter, appropriately equipped, with the cashier's cage up left. Close by it, a coatrack with the hats and coats of the assembled customers, as well as a cane. Right and left, a number of tables and chairs coming down to the footlights. Center stage, a table, separated from the others and covered with newspapers.

At rise, THE CASHIER, *a portly female, is at her post, where she will remain throughout the act, silently attending to her affairs. Three or four customers, likewise silent, will get up from their respective tables, retrieve their coats and hats, and leave, intermittently, during the first few moments of the act. Down left, at one of the tables,* THE GENTLEMAN, *elderly and very nattily dressed, is seated before a cup of coffee, engrossed in his newspaper. At another table, down right,* BOUBOUROCHE, ROTH, POTASSE, *and* FOUETTARD *are engaged in the final hands of a game of bridge. They are seated clockwise, in the order indicated, with* BOUBOUROCHE *on the stage right side of the table and his partner,* POTASSE, *across from him. On the table, in front of each of those two, are a glass of beer and several coasters, piled one on the other, that indicate that these are not their first.* ROTH *and* FOUETTARD, *each also behind a pile of coasters, sit sipping the remains of their last glasses of absinth, as the latter, leading the hand, throws down a card.*

BOUBOUROCHE [*puffing on his pipe and absentmindedly humming the Toreador Song from* Carmen, *after a moment of indecision, following with a card*]: There!

[*As* FOUETTARD *plays a card from* ROTH's *dummy hand,* BOUBOUROCHE *looks at* POTASSE *expectantly.*]

POTASSE [*to* BOUBOUROCHE]: What do you want me to do?

BOUBOUROCHE: Trump it! What do you think?

POTASSE: Trump it?

BOUBOUROCHE [*reiterating*]: Trump it!

FOUETTARD [*jocularly imitating a trumpet and blaring out a typical fanfare*]: Ba-ba-ba bá ba-bá!

POTASSE [*to* BOUBOUROCHE]: What with?

BOUBOUROCHE [*to* POTASSE, *as* ROTH *represses a laugh*]: Don't you have a trump?

POTASSE: No. I wasn't dealt any.

BOUBOUROCHE [*turning aside*]: Now he tells me... [*To* POTASSE.] And you couldn't let me know before?

POTASSE: What? And let them know too?

BOUBOUROCHE: Ha! [*Good-naturedly.*] The way you play, do you think it would matter?

POTASSE: But I—

BOUBOUROCHE [*to* ROTH *and* FOUETTARD]: Is that any way to play bridge, I ask you?

POTASSE [*somewhat piqued, hesitating over his hand, defensively*]: These English games!... I'm much better at whist.

BOUBOUROCHE [*laughing*]: I hope so!... [*To* POTASSE.] Never mind, just play... It's not your fault if all you know about bridge is what you learned at the dentist's. [*As* FOUETTARD *and* ROTH *both chuckle.*] Look at them. They're laughing at you...

POTASSE [*still hesitating*]: No. They're laughing at your joke!

BOUBOUROCHE: Well, you could cost us the hand. And that's no joke, Potasse.

POTASSE: All right then... What do I do?

BOUBOUROCHE [*studying the table and puffing, pointing to* FOUETTARD'*s last card, replying*]: If you can't trump it, duck it. [POTASSE *gives him a questioning look.*] Duck it, understand?... Duck...

FOUETTARD [*jokingly*]: Quack quack! Quack quack!

ROTH [*trying to go along with his joke*]: Gobble gobble!

BOUBOUROCHE [*to* ROTH, *with a good-humored nudge*]: That's a turkey, you idiot! [*To* POTASSE, *who is still trying to decide.*] So?

POTASSE [*finally throwing down a card*]: There!... How's that?

BOUBOUROCHE [*surprised*]: What? I... [*Laughing.*] I thought you said you didn't have any trumps?

POTASSE: Trumps?... But that's a spade... I thought...

ROTH: Good grief!

BOUBOUROCHE [*as* ROTH *and* FOUETTARD *resignedly shake their heads*]: Yes! And spades are trump, for goodness' sake!... Well, no harm done at least... [*To* ROTH *and* FOUETTARD.] Our trick, gentlemen!... [*Relishing the moment.*] And our hand, my friends! [*Laying down the rest of his hand, face up.*] All the rest are ours! See?

ROTH ⎫
⎬ [*together*]: ⎰ How on earth...
FOUETTARD ⎭ ⎱ Blast!

BOUBOUROCHE [*calculating, as he picks up the tricks*]: Book plus one... two... three... four... And doubled, makes... Four hundred. [*To* POTASSE.] Mark it down, Potasse.

POTASSE [*jotting down the score*]: Four hundred for the good side!

ROTH [*not a little miffed*]: Whose deal?

BOUBOUROCHE [*feeling his pockets*]: Fouettard's, I think... [*Looking around on the table.*] Where the devil is my tobacco?

FOUETTARD [*taking a pouch from his pocket, giving it to him*]: Ah... Beg your pardon! I wasn't thinking...
[*He gathers up the cards, shuffles them, and lays them down in front of* BOUBOUROCHE, *who, after cutting them, proceeds to refill his pipe and light it.*]

ROTH [*to* FOUETTARD]: Some good ones this time, eh?

FOUETTARD [*dealing, as* BOUBOUROCHE, *puffing, begins humming the Toreador Song again, replying*]: I'll do my best!... [*To* BOUBOUROCHE, *interrupting the deal, somewhat on edge.*] Really! Do you have to...? Is that the only tune you know?

BOUBOUROCHE: Hmm?

FOUETTARD: It's beginning to get on our nerves.

ROTH [*to* BOUBOUROCHE]: I say, it really is, old man... Can't you hum something else?

BOUBOUROCHE: Sorry... I don't know any others.

FOUETTARD [*completing the deal, to* BOUBOUROCHE]: I must say, you have an impressive repertoire! [*The players pick up their hands and study them for a few moments.*] Pass...

BOUBOUROCHE [*after a pregnant pause*]: Pass...

ROTH: Pass...

POTASSE [*confidently*]: Two spades...

BOUBOUROCHE [*reacting, a little surprised, to* POTASSE]: Two... [*To* POTASSE.] Are you sure?

POTASSE: Of course!

FOUETTARD [*to* POTASSE, *sarcastically*]: They're the black ones, Potasse... With the pointy top...

[POTASSE *gives him a sidelong look, as* ROTH *sits laughing.*]

BOUBOUROCHE [*to* POTASSE]: If you say so...

FOUETTARD [*shrugging*]: Just trying to help... [*Returning to the bid.*] Pass...

BOUBOUROCHE: Pass...

ROTH: Double...

[*They all look expectantly at* POTASSE.]

POTASSE [*after a pause, very matter-of-fact*]: Four diamonds...

BOUBOUROCHE, ROTH, *and* FOUETTARD [*agape, together*]: What?

ROTH: I say...

BOUBOUROCHE [*to* POTASSE, *as* ROTH *and* FOUETTARD *hold their sides, laughing*]: Four... You've got to be joking! You opened with two spades, for God's sake! Spades! How in the name of—

POTASSE: I know, I know!... I changed my mind.

BOUBOUROCHE: But that's not how it's done! You don't just "change your mind"...

FOUETTARD *and* ROTH [*to* POTASSE, *laughing, together*]: Like your trousers!

[*They look at each other, surprised at their identical comparison, laughing all the harder.*]

BOUBOUROCHE [*continuing, to* POTASSE]: It's like changing horses in midstream. It isn't done...

ROTH [*still laughing*]: Unless you're a woman!... [*To* POTASSE.] You aren't, old man, are you?

[*He and* FOUETTARD *continue chortling at* POTASSE'*s expense, as the latter grows visibly more and more offended.*]

BOUBOUROCHE [*to* POTASSE]: Who taught you to play?

FOUETTARD [*to* POTASSE]: "Who didn't?" he means.

BOUBOUROCHE: Damnation! It's not so complicated! You only have to be able to count!... If the English can play it I should think that any proper Frenchman—

POTASSE [*out of patience, interrupting*]: That's quite enough, thank you! [*He throws down his cards, then snaps his fingers in the air, calling.*] Amédée! [*He gets up.*]

AMEDEE [*behind the counter, where he has been polishing the glassware and the like during the preceding*]: Monsieur?

POTASSE [*testily*]: My hat and coat, please!

BOUBOUROCHE [*taken aback*]: What?... Potasse...

ROTH [*half standing up, to* POTASSE]: I say, old man—

POTASSE [*to* ROTH]: Go to blazes!

BOUBOUROCHE [*to* POTASSE]: But my friend...

ROTH [*to himself*]   ⎱ [*together*]: ⎰ What did I do?

FOUETTARD [*trying to calm things down*]   ⎰ ⎱ Potasse... Potasse...

POTASSE [*to* FOUETTARD]: You too!

[*The following three exclamations are delivered rapid-fire, almost on top of one another.*]

FOUETTARD: But—

ROTH: But—

BOUBOUROCHE: But—

POTASSE [*putting on his coat*]: Enough is enough!

BOUBOUROCHE [*to* POTASSE]: Please, Potasse! What's the matter?

POTASSE [*bringing his hand, palm down, up to his chin*]: To here!... Up to here with your... your bloody bridge!

[*Again, the following three exclamations are delivered in rapid succession, and in the most contrite of tones.*]

FOUETTARD: Potasse...

ROTH: Potasse...

BOUBOUROCHE: Potasse...

ROTH   ⎱ [*to* POTASSE, *together*]: ⎰ Really, old man, I didn't...

FOUETTARD ⎰ ⎱ We didn't mean...

BOUBOUROCHE [*to* POTASSE]: Please... If I said anything to hurt you... I... You know how I am when it comes to bridge.

FOUETTARD: Me too...

ROTH: And me...

POTASSE [*softening, to* BOUBOUROCHE]: Still...

BOUBOUROCHE [*cajoling*]: Come now... We're all friends... Let's let by-gones be by-gones...

ROTH: By all means...

POTASSE [*disarmed, taking off his coat*]: Well...

[*He hands his coat and hat back to* AMEDEE, *who replaces them on the coatrack and returns to his occupations.*]

BOUBOUROCHE: There!... Good! [*To* POTASSE.] Now pick up your cards and let's go on...

POTASSE [*sitting down*]: I can't. [*Pointing to his face-up hand.*] They've seen them...

BOUBOUROCHE: Ah... Well... [*As conciliatorily as possible.*] Misdeal then... Misdeal!... [*To* FOUETTARD.] Deal again, Fouettard.

[FOUETTARD *picks up everyone's hand, shuffles the cards, gives them to*

BOUBOUROCHE *to cut. As he deals them out, the latter begins humming the Toreador Song again.*]

FOUETTARD [*completing the deal, to* BOUBOUROCHE]: Must you, Boubouroche?

BOUBOUROCHE [*as he and the others pick up their hands*]: Sorry... Sorry...

FOUETTARD: Pass...

BOUBOUROCHE [*after studying his cards for a moment*]: One club...

ROTH: Pass...

POTASSE [*after a lengthy pause, during which the others look at him anxiously, trying not to offend him by their obvious uneasiness*]: Pass...

FOUETTARD [*shaking his head in disgust*]: One diamond...

BOUBOUROCHE: Two clubs...

ROTH [*shaking his head*]: Pass...

POTASSE [*pausing again, as again the others watch and wait, trying to appear unconcerned*]: Pass...

FOUETTARD [*looking at his hand, shaking his head again*]: Good God! Who dealt me these cards!

BOUBOUROCHE: Ha!

FOUETTARD [*finally, resigned*]: Pass...

ROTH [*to* FOUETTARD]: That's the best you can do?

BOUBOUROCHE [*exulting*]: You mean, we get it for two clubs?

ROTH [*still to* FOUETTARD, *joking*]: You couldn't deal yourself anything better?

BOUBOUROCHE [*reaching across the table, to* POTASSE, *shaking his hand*]: Ha ha! Cheap enough, partner!

ROTH [*still to* FOUETTARD, *continuing*]: Or me either!

FOUETTARD [*to* ROTH]: Sorry! I did my best!

BOUBOUROCHE [*laying out* POTASSE'*s hand, face up*]: So much for the dummy... [*To* POTASSE, *quickly, to avoid any misunderstanding.*] So to speak... So to... [*Suddenly noticing, to his chagrin, that* POTASSE'*s hand has a number of clubs.*] Oh!... But... [*Exaggeratedly.*] You have a dozen clubs, Potasse!

POTASSE ⎫
ROTH [*under his breath*] ⎬ [*together*]: ⎰ I know, but—
FOUETTARD [*likewise*] ⎭   ⎰ Good grief!
     ⎱ My God!

BOUBOUROCHE [*to* POTASSE, *on the verge of frustration again*]: Why didn't you bid... [*Stopping, controlling himself, eager not to ruffle his feathers.*] Well... No matter...

POTASSE [*sheepishly*]: I thought...

BOUBOUROCHE: One trick more, one trick less... They're all ours anyway...

[*The hand begins with* ROTH, *disgruntled, throwing down a card. It proceeds for half a dozen tricks, all taken by a jubilant* BOUBOUROCHE, *in a silence broken only by occasional interjections of obvious delight, on the one hand, and disgust, on the other. After another trick or two, also taken by* BOUBOUROCHE, *the latter, puffing contentedly on his pipe, unconsciously begins humming the Toreador Song again.*]

ROTH [*continuing the hand, to* BOUBOUROCHE]: Really, old man...

FOUETTARD [*likewise*]: Please, Boubouroche! How many times... How do you expect us to concentrate?

BOUBOUROCHE [*with a wry smirk, taking the trick*]: On what? On losing?... Why bother? [*To* POTASSE.] Right, Potasse? [*To* FOUETTARD *and* ROTH, *alternately.*] You're going to lose perfectly well without it! [*Laying down the rest of his cards, face up.*] See?... My king... And Potasse's ace and queen!

FOUETTARD ⎱
    ⎰ [*throwing down their cards, together*]: ⎰ Blast!
ROTH ⎰   ⎱ Did you ever?

BOUBOUROCHE: Another hand for the good side! [*To* POTASSE, *as he picks up the cards and begins shuffling.*] Mark it down, Potasse...

POTASSE [*hesitating*]: How?

BOUBOUROCHE [*still very indulgent*]: Never mind... [*Taking the score sheet and pencil.*] Here... Let me...

ROTH [*as* BOUBOUROCHE *calculates, to* FOUETTARD]: Did you ever see a hand like that?

FOUETTARD [*laughing*]: Yes! My own!

ROTH [*continuing*]: Are you sure you shuffled them?

BOUBOUROCHE [*passing the deck to* ROTH *for cutting, to* FOUETTARD]: Another?

FOUETTARD: No...

BOUBOUROCHE: [*insistent*]: Just one?

FOUETTARD: No... Really... You've had your dinner already... [*With a sly look at his girth.*] Obviously...

BOUBOUROCHE [*with a good-humored little chuckle*]: Oh?

FOUETTARD: Besides, it's getting late. [*To the waiter.*] What time is it, Amédée?

AMEDEE: A quarter to nine, monsieur.

ROTH ⎱
    ⎰ [*together, with a start*]: ⎰ What?
FOUETTARD ⎰   ⎱ That late?

ROTH: Good grief! I thought it was only seven thirty! [*He makes a dash for his hat and coat.*] And here I promised my wife I would take her to that new "cinema" thing!

FOUETTARD: And me, with company coming to dinner... [*Retrieving his hat and coat also.*] They must be looking for me at the morgue by now!

ROTH: She'll have my scalp!

FOUETTARD: And mine!

ROTH: Who? My wife?

FOUETTARD: No, mine! [*Calling.*] Amédée!

AMEDEE: Monsieur?

FOUETTARD [*pointing to the pile of coasters before* ROTH *and himself*]: How much?

AMEDEE [*counting the coasters and calculating*]: Four francs, twenty centimes, monsieur...

FOUETTARD [*to* ROTH]: Two and ten each...

ROTH: Right... Two and ten... [*Taking out his purse and digging around in it, as* FOUETTARD *does likewise; then, suddenly, to* BOUBOUROCHE.] I say, Boubouroche... Don't I owe you eight francs?

BOUBOUROCHE: Perhaps...

ROTH [*categorically*]: No "perhaps" about it... I do... I remember.

BOUBOUROCHE [*good-naturedly*]: Well... Any time...

ROTH: Oh? Are you sure?

BOUBOUROCHE: No hurry...

ROTH: Well, as long as you don't mind... Perhaps you could pay this, and we'll settle up at the end of the month.

BOUBOUROCHE: Why not?

ROTH: Thanks, old man...

BOUBOUROCHE [*with a wave of the hand*]: Please... [*As* ROTH *gets up to leave.*] Tomorrow night, then?

ROTH: Right... Tomorrow...

FOUETTARD [*to* BOUBOUROCHE]: Actually... If you could take care of mine too... Would you believe that I left the house without a sou?

BOUBOUROCHE: Ah...

FOUETTARD [*getting up*]: I'll pay you back tomorrow.

BOUBOUROCHE: Of course... No problem...

FOUETTARD: If you're sure you don't mind...

BOUBOUROCHE [*with a smile and a shrug*]: Pfff!

FOUETTARD: Well... Anyway...

[*The four turn alternately to one another and shake hands all around.*]

BOUBOUROCHE			Fouettard... Roth...
FOUETTARD	}	[*together*]: {	Boubouroche... Potasse...
POTASSE			Roth... Fouettard...
ROTH			Potasse... Boubouroche...

BOUBOUROCHE [*as* POTASSE *looks on*]: Au revoir... See you tomorrow...

[ROTH *and* FOUETTARD *exit, up center.*]

POTASSE [*after a moment, shaking his head*]: Boubouroche...

BOUBOUROCHE: Hmm?

POTASSE: Buy me another and I'll tell you your fortune.

BOUBOUROCHE [*laughing*]: And I'll tell you yours... You play a pitiful game of bridge, Potasse!

POTASSE: No, seriously...

BOUBOUROCHE: Seriously... I'll buy you one even without the fortune! [*Calling.*] Amédée!... Two more!... And careful... Not all head this time, you hear?

AMEDEE [*drawing the beers*]: Very good, monsieur. Two headless lagers, coming right up! [*Coming to the table, putting them down, jovially.*] Voilà! Two decapitated drafts for the gentlemen...

[*He returns to his occupations.*]

BOUBOUROCHE [*lifting his glass, to* POTASSE]: To your health!

POTASSE [*likewise, to* BOUBOUROCHE]: And yours!

BOUBOUROCHE *and* POTASSE [*together*]: To ours!

[*They clink glasses and drink.*]

BOUBOUROCHE [*after a brief silence*]: Well now... What's my fortune?

POTASSE [*with a sigh*]: Boubouroche, you're a dupe!

BOUBOUROCHE: A what?

POTASSE: A pigeon... A sucker...

BOUBOUROCHE: Since when?

POTASSE: Since the day your mother had you!... Much to the delight of every leech for miles around, I might add. [*Affectionately.*] That's "since when," you big oaf!

BOUBOUROCHE [*about to protest*]: But...

POTASSE: To let those two spongers make you pay for their drinks...

BOUBOUROCHE [*with a casual wave*]: Oh...

POTASSE: ...when they should have paid for ours! You should be ashamed!

BOUBOUROCHE: Me?

POTASSE: We won, remember?

BOUBOUROCHE [*a little pointedly*]: "We"?

[*He laughs.*]

POTASSE: Well, anyway, they lost.

BOUBOUROCHE: So?... You know me. I don't play to win...

POTASSE: A pigeon!

BOUBOUROCHE: I play for the game. You know how I love it... Besides, what's a couple of francs more or less?

POTASSE [*shaking his head*]: Just what I said... A pigeon!

BOUBOUROCHE [*with a little laugh*]: You're repeating yourself, Potasse.

POTASSE: A very nice pigeon, I'm sure... For those who like to dine on squab... Tasty and tender... But a pigeon all the same!

BOUBOUROCHE: Not really... I might seem like one to you, but—

POTASSE: Bah!

BOUBOUROCHE: Believe me, my friend, I know life inside and out... Top to bottom...

POTASSE [*with a tinge of sarcasm, nodding*]: Backwards and forwards...

BOUBOUROCHE: Right...

POTASSE: Almost as well as I know bridge!

BOUBOUROCHE: And if I want to keep on good terms with it... Well, why shouldn't I make a little... a little...

POTASSE [*completing his thought for him*]: ...compromise now and then?

BOUBOUROCHE: Exactly! I admit it.

POTASSE: Ha!

BOUBOUROCHE: But you see, Potasse, I do what I want to do, and I think what I want to think. I might look like a lamb, but I'm stubborn as a mule.

POTASSE: My friend, I don't care if you're tough as an elephant and fierce as a boar. The fact is, you can barely muster enough energy to step aside and let the hordes of barbarians lay waste to your wallet.

BOUBOUROCHE: Me?

POTASSE [*continuing*]: And barely enough... You hear me, Boubouroche?... [*Growing serious.*] Barely enough to cover your eyes and jump through a hoop when your mistress wants you to...

BOUBOUROCHE: Me?... My Adèle?...

POTASSE: You... Your Adèle...

BOUBOUROCHE [*growing serious too*]: Why do you say that? What do you know?

POTASSE: Know? Nothing... But I'm sure...

BOUBOUROCHE: So? If you don't know, don't talk. I admit that Adèle may have her little faults... And that I close my eyes now and then, just to keep peace...

POTASSE [*nodding*]: Aha...

BOUBOUROCHE: And tell her that she's right...

POTASSE: Yes. Even when she's wrong...

BOUBOUROCHE [*agreeing*]: Right... Sometimes... But jump through hoops? Hardly, Potasse!... Don't worry, I know what I'm doing. You don't live with a woman for eight years without knowing what she's about.

POTASSE: Eight years?

BOUBOUROCHE: Yes, my friend. Eight!

POTASSE: Good God, that's what I call an affair!

BOUBOUROCHE [*with a romantic sigh*]: Ah yes! My last...

POTASSE: Oh?

BOUBOUROCHE: And my first!...

POTASSE [*surprised*]: Your... [*Laughing.*] Well, you certainly didn't start in the cradle, now did you!

BOUBOUROCHE [*with a laugh*]: Not quite!... I was thirty. [*Noticing* POTASSE's *jaw drop in a look of amazed disbelief.*] What's the matter?

POTASSE: You were... You mean, you're thirty-eight?

BOUBOUROCHE: Just last month...

POTASSE: My goodness, I would have said forty-eight at least!

BOUBOUROCHE: Really?

POTASSE [*realizing his gaffe*]: No offense... I mean—

BOUBOUROCHE [*naively*]: Most people take me for much younger, actually. [*Patting his pot belly.*] If not for this, I'm sure you would too.

POTASSE: I'm sure.

BOUBOUROCHE [*stroking his face*]: After all, not a wrinkle... See?

POTASSE [*aside, rather touched, as* BOUBOUROCHE *leans forward, inviting inspection*]: Simple soul...

BOUBOUROCHE: None!... Not a one!...

POTASSE: And what made you wait till you were thirty, Boubouroche?... To treat yourself to a mistress, I mean...

BOUBOUROCHE: Oh, a lot of things, my friend... Shyness, for one... Deep down I've always been a little... Well... [*He takes a puff or two on his pipe, reflectively.*] And besides, I suppose I'm really a romantic at heart. Always looking, searching... waiting for just the perfect one... A soulmate, don't you know? A heart... [*Waxing lyrical.*] that could beat in time with my own... That could understand me... [POTASSE *laughs in spite of himself.*] Did I say something funny?

POTASSE: No, no... Don't mind me. Go on... You're a delight! [*Still laughing.*] I could hug you!

BOUBOUROCHE: Oh?... [*Continuing.*] Well, at any rate... I met Adèle at a friend's one night. She used to come every Sunday for tea and conversation.

POTASSE: Ah...

BOUBOUROCHE [*reminiscing*]: Twenty-four years old... Blonde... *Very* blonde... With that special, charming *je ne sais quoi* that mourning does for blondes...

POTASSE [*misunderstanding*]: Morning? You said "one night"...

BOUBOUROCHE: No, no... Mourning... Dressed in black...

POTASSE: Oh... Was she a widow?

BOUBOUROCHE; Six months before... [*Taking a long puff, nostalgically.*] Ah! One look, Potasse, and there I was, in love! Smitten, my friend!... Smitten!

POTASSE: Aha...

BOUBOUROCHE: It was something about her... Her elegance, her... her bearing...
That "proper lady" look, my friend, that any man can tell on the spot...

POTASSE: I'm sure.

BOUBOUROCHE: You know what I mean?

POTASSE [*repressing the urge to guffaw, diplomatically*]: Oh, quite... You're a
shrewd judge of character.

BOUBOUROCHE: And I thought to myself—a little sadly, you can imagine:
"Careful, Boubouroche! Don't go losing your heart! That delectable morsel
isn't for you..." [POTASSE *nods knowingly.*] But, then, one evening, just as
we were both about to leave, she took my arm and asked if I would mind
terribly seeing her home. [*Recollecting with a smile.*] "Mind?" Ha!... And
so we left together... I don't know what it was... [*Puffing.*] The quiet streets,
the moonlight... But something, Potasse... something came over me. All of
a sudden I felt myself full of courage, ready to risk everything...

POTASSE: Aha...

BOUBOUROCHE: There we were at the door... In the shadows... And... And...

POTASSE: And?...

BOUBOUROCHE: And, as we stood there saying our good-byes, I took her sweet
little hands in mine, like this... [*He takes* POTASSE'*s hands in his.*] I looked
into her eyes... [*He stares deeply and lovingly into* POTASSE'*s eyes.*] And in
a voice quivering with emotion, I said to her: "Madame, I love you. You
are the perfume of my life... You are a jewel, a flower, a bird..."

POTASSE: Indeed! [*Unintentionally prosaic.*] And a week later you were setting
her up in an apartment, and keeping her.

BOUBOUROCHE: A week later Adèle and I were sharing our lives together. It's
not quite the same.

POTASSE: Bah! Call it what you want. You give her money, don't you?

BOUBOUROCHE: Of course I do. Would you rather she gave it to me? What kind
of gentleman... I give her three hundred francs a month and I pay her rent.
That's all. [*Naively.*] It's not as if I were "keeping her," heaven knows!

POTASSE: Oh... [*Smiling.*] Sorry!

BOUBOUROCHE: You don't "keep" a woman just because you do what any
gentleman should do... Just because you try to make her life a little easier...
A little less complicated... [POTASSE *laughs.*] In fact, Potasse, I... I "keep"
her so much, as you put it, that... that we don't even live together! [POTASSE
laughs even harder, in spite of himself.] And if that's not enough...
[*Offering the definitive proof.*] I don't even have the key to her apartment!

POTASSE: What? Why not, good God?

BOUBOUROCHE: Because a proper lady shouldn't have a lover, that's why.
And... And you're not a "lover" if you don't have the key.

POTASSE: You're... [*Agog at his logic.*] What are you then?

BOUBOUROCHE: I'm a... a... [*Angling for an appropriate word, to no avail.*]
Damnation! I don't know...

POTASSE: Well, I do! You're a pigeon!

BOUBOUROCHE: You and your "pigeon"!... [*Wagging his pipe stem at him in
good-natured reprimand.*] You're repeating yourself again!... [*After a brief
pause.*] No... Adèle is no... no... [*Hesitating to call a spade a spade.*] Well,
you know what she isn't!... She's a well-bred young lady. A young lady
with a family, with friends... She doesn't want to compromise herself. And
I don't blame her. I think that's perfectly reasonable, don't you?

POTASSE: In other words, she's another one of those "what-I-know-she-isn't"s, who wants to do you-know-what, like all the rest...

BOUBOUROCHE: Really...

POTASSE: ...as long as no one else is any the wiser. Right?

BOUBOUROCHE: Really, Potasse...

POTASSE: No... "Really, Boubouroche..." [*None too delicately.*] The sidewalks of Paris are full of those "what-I-know-she-isn't"s!

BOUBOUROCHE: But why all the fuss? Where is it written that a woman should bare her life and let every Pierre, Paul, and Marie see how she lives it?

POTASSE [*eager to end the argument*]: You're right... Absolutely...

BOUBOUROCHE: I know I am.

POTASSE: Besides, I could never convince you!... [*Getting up.*] As long as you're happy...

BOUBOUROCHE: Happy as a lark!... And why not? I have everything I need. I do anything I want... Get up when I like, go to bed when I please... I'm well enough off, thank heaven, to fill my belly...

POTASSE [*with a meaningful chuckle*]: I daresay...

BOUBOUROCHE [*continuing*]: ...to quench my thirst, to smoke my pipe when and where I choose... [*He blows a big puff of smoke as if to illustrate.*] And even enough to lend a hundred sou, if need be, to some poor, unfortunate friend.

POTASSE [*pointedly*]: Or two...

BOUBOUROCHE: And, as if that weren't enough, I've got just the perfect mistress for a solid citizen like myself... A sensible little woman, economical to a fault, who loves me as much as I love her, and who never gives me a moment's concern... Faithful as a puppy...

POTASSE: Aha...

BOUBOUROCHE [*as* POTASSE *goes up to the coatrack*]: So of course I'm happy! As happy as a man can be... You see, Potasse, that's why I can afford to be a little generous now and then with a couple of poor bounders who can't stand the thought of losing a game of bridge, and who like my tobacco better than their own because it doesn't cost them anything.

POTASSE [*taking his hat, coat, and cane, and shaking his head*]: The soul of kindness!

BOUBOUROCHE: You're not leaving...?

POTASSE: I'm afraid so. See you tomorrow...

BOUBOUROCHE [*reluctant to see everyone leave*]: You won't have another beer?

POTASSE [*putting on his coat*]: No... It's getting late. I'm not as lucky as some people, my friend. I've got to be up at eight in the morning!

BOUBOUROCHE: Poor Potasse! [*They shake hands.*] Tomorrow, then?

POTASSE: Tomorrow... [*Nodding good-bye to* AMEDEE *and* THE CASHIER, *in turn.*] Amédée... Madame...

[*He leaves.* BOUBOUROCHE *sits back, puffing on his pipe for a few moments, then takes out his watch and consults it.*]

BOUBOUROCHE: Only ten past nine? My, my... The night is young. [*Musing.*] Perhaps I should go pay Adèle a little visit... [*Contemplating his still half-full glass.*] But first things first... No sense wasting a good draft... [*Looking toward* AMEDEE.] Decapitated or otherwise...

[*He drinks down his beer. In the meantime, as he has been musing,* THE

GENTLEMAN, *who has been sitting all the while at the table, down left, reading his newspaper, has stood up quietly, placed several coins on the table for his coffee, and now, hat in hand, crosses right, to* BOUBOUROCHE*'s table.*]

THE GENTLEMAN [*very distinguished and well-spoken, to* BOUBOUROCHE, *as the latter sits filling his pipe once again*]: I beg your pardon. Monsieur Boubouroche, if I'm not mistaken?

BOUBOUROCHE [*looking up, surprised*]: Hmm?... Why, yes...

THE GENTLEMAN: Ernest Boubouroche?

BOUBOUROCHE: Yes... Quite... And may I ask—

THE GENTLEMAN: The same Ernest Boubouroche whose mistress lives on Boulevard Magenta, number 111 B, fifth floor front?... A woman who goes by the name of Adèle?

BOUBOUROCHE [*growing more and more surprised*]: Yes, but—

THE GENTLEMAN: Please... A simple yes or no, monsieur... I'll explain in a moment.

BOUBOUROCHE [*vaguely disconcerted*]: Why I... The fact is... The young lady does happen to be a... a friend of mine, monsieur.

THE GENTLEMAN: Yes. I just wanted to be sure.

BOUBOUROCHE: Oh?

THE GENTLEMAN [*pleasantly, matter-of-fact*]: She's cheating on you, monsieur.

BOUBOUROCHE [*with a start*]: She's... Did you say...

THE GENTLEMAN: I did.

BOUBOUROCHE [*indicating the chair vacated by* POTASSE]: Please, monsieur... Have a seat. [*As* THE GENTLEMAN, *very calmly, complies.*] Can I offer you a drink? [THE GENTLEMAN *mimes his refusal with a discreet little gesture.*] Please! I insist!... [*Calling.*] Amédée!

AMEDEE [*approaching, to* BOUBOUROCHE]: Monsieur?

BOUBOUROCHE: Two drafts...

AMEDEE [*attempting a bit of humor*]: Decapitated, monsieur?

BOUBOUROCHE [*in no mood for banter, a little sharply*]: Whatever... [*As* AMEDEE *returns to the counter, drawing the beers, to* THE GENTLEMAN.] Now then, if you would be good enough to explain...

THE GENTLEMAN [*maintaining his dignified air, as* BOUBOUROCHE *grows more and more anxious*]: Of course... I would say "with pleasure," monsieur. But the fact of the matter is that what I have to tell you is anything but pleasant.

BOUBOUROCHE [*with a questioning tilt of the head*]: Monsieur?

AMEDEE [*arriving at the table and putting down the two beers along with their coasters, jovially*]: Two beheaded brews for the gentlemen...

BOUBOUROCHE [*waving him away, impatiently*]: Yes, yes... [*To* THE GENTLEMAN, *as* AMEDEE *returns to his duties at the counter.*] You were saying?

THE GENTLEMAN [*rather starchily, despite his obvious good nature*]: I was saying, monsieur, that I find it particularly unpleasant to have to shatter, as completely as I am about to do, your fondest illusions.

BOUBOUROCHE: My... You...

THE GENTLEMAN: You are, to all appearances, an extremely likeable individual... Which makes the mission on which I have embarked—if I may call it such—all the more distasteful.

BOUBOUROCHE: "Mission"...? What mission?

THE GENTLEMAN: A singularly difficult one, monsieur... Rather nasty, on the face of it, but actually quite selfless and generous, I think you'll find... Indeed, you might even say "philanthropic." But then, that's just how I am. It would be criminal, monsieur, to sit back and watch the dignity of an honest and upstanding gentleman fall prey to the wiles of a scheming little wench...

BOUBOUROCHE: "Wench"...?

THE GENTLEMAN: ...who fleeces him to a fare-thee-well, poisons what little is left of his youth in constant bicker and brawl, and who doesn't give two bloody raps for him to boot, if you'll pardon the expression!

BOUBOUROCHE: Your story...

THE GENTLEMAN: Not mine, monsieur!... Many others', alas! Not *my* story... Yours! [*Point blank, very dryly.*] Monsieur, you're a cuckold. [*Holding up his glass.*] To your health...

BOUBOUROCHE [*raising his glass, mechanically, almost babbling*]: To my... To your...

[*They clink glasses and drink.*]

THE GENTLEMAN [*smacking his lips*]: Mmm!... Rather good, actually...

BOUBOUROCHE [*trying to remain calm*]: Monsieur... I can tell just by looking at you and listening to the way you talk that it's not some common impostor sitting across the table. [THE GENTLEMAN *passes off the implied suggestion with a shake of the head and a wave of the hand.*] But... But I hope you understand, monsieur, that you have just made a rather serious accusation against a woman for whom I have the utmost affection...

THE GENTLEMAN [*drinking discreetly*]: No doubt.

BOUBOUROCHE [*attempting to equal his eloquence*]: And that it... it behooves you, monsieur, to support your assertion with some semblance of proof.

THE GENTLEMAN: Of course... [*Smiling.*] "Some semblance..." [*Sitting back on his chair.*] Monsieur, let me remind you that we no longer live in the Middle Ages... [*Pausing, as* BOUBOUROCHE, *drinking, ponders the assertion.*] when thick castle walls silenced cries and muted groans. Time has marched on. [*A little ironically.*] Mankind has made great strides. Today we live in buildings made of plaster and cardboard... [BOUBOUROCHE *gives him a puzzled look.*] The echoes of life's little scandals, monsieur, come seeping through the walls. Its pleasures as well as its pains... From upstairs and down, from right and left...

BOUBOUROCHE: Oh?

THE GENTLEMAN [*continuing*]: ...with all the resistance of a flannel undergarment, if you'll pardon the comparison!

BOUBOUROCHE [*as* THE GENTLEMAN *pauses briefly to drink*]: But why—

THE GENTLEMAN [*ignoring his incipient objection, interrupting*]: For eight years, I have had as my next-door neighbor that same individual whom you have no compunction—rather naively, I regret to say—to call your "friend."

BOUBOUROCHE: You...

THE GENTLEMAN: For eight years, through the paper-thin partition that separates our two abodes, I have been an unwilling, invisible witness to the vagaries of your romantic fortune...

BOUBOUROCHE: You...

THE GENTLEMAN: Your amorous ups and downs, as it were...

BOUBOUROCHE: You mean...

THE GENTLEMAN [*unstoppable*]: For eight years, I've heard you coming and going, laughing, chatting, humming the Toreador Song from *Carmen* in that pleasant falsetto that bespeaks a clear conscience, waxing the floor, winding up the clock, and complaining—a litle bitterly, I might add—about the high price of fish... Because I shouldn't forget to mention that it's you who keep house, and you who gladly do all the marketing yourself. [*He drinks.*] Am I right, monsieur?

BOUBOUROCHE: Quite...

THE GENTLEMAN: For eight years I've taken part in all your joys and tribulations, applauding the ones and commiserating with the others... Admiring your aplomb in fortune good or ill, and that infinite magnanimity of soul... [*Reflecting for an instant.*] if you'll pardon the redundancy... [BOUBOUROCHE *gestures his unconcern.*] that generosity of spirit that dissuades you from giving your "friend" a box on the ears each time she deserves one!

BOUBOUROCHE [*as* THE GENTLEMAN *pauses to drink*]: But I—

THE GENTLEMAN [*continuing*]: Now then, monsieur... And here I ask you to pay especial attention... Not once in those eight years, monsieur... Not one single, solitary day would dawn but what your "friend" would commit some new, vile little treachery... [*Delighting more and more in his own rhetoric.*] Not one night, but what you would retire to your bed, properly hoodwinked and cuckolded...

BOUBOUROCHE [*attempting to protest*]: I... I...

THE GENTLEMAN: Not once, monsieur... Not once, but what, when you crossed the threshold of the modest little dwelling paid for by your hard-earned coin of the realm, and home of your most cherished desires... Not once, but what a gentleman... [*Reconsidering.*] well, a man, at least... was secreted therein.

BOUBOUROCHE: A man?

THE GENTLEMAN: Yes, a man.

BOUBOUROCHE: Who?... What man?

THE GENTLEMAN: A man whose chatter I hear before your arrival, and whose laughter I hear, monsieur, after your departure... [*After contemplating a stunned* BOUBOUROCHE *for a moment.*] Rather trumps your ace, what?

[*He takes a long sip of his beer and sits back in his chair, clearly satisfied with a mission well acomplished, as* BOUBOUROCHE *sits staring blankly into space.*]

BOUBOUROCHE [*suddenly gulping down the rest of his beer and slamming the glass down on the table*]: No, no, no! That's rubbish!

THE GENTLEMAN [*questioning*]		"No, no, no"?
AMEDEE [*at the counter, misunderstanding, aside*] } [*together*]:		My beer?
BOUBOUROCHE [*affirmatively, to* THE GENTLEMAN]		Yes! "No"!
AMEDEE [*still aside*] } [*together*]:		"Rubbish"?

BOUBOUROCHE [*continuing*]: You don't know what you're talking about! I know Adèle better than you, my friend! [*Emphatically.*] She couldn't!... She wouldn't!...

THE GENTLEMAN: She can! [*Holding up his glass, as if to toast him.*] And she does! [*He drinks down the rest of his beer.*] Not meaning to be presumptuous, monsieur, but in this matter I daresay I'm better informed than you. As you yourself admitted—and I couldn't help overhearing—you don't even have a key to her apartment!

BOUBOUROCHE: So? What does that prove? I've come by unexpectedly hundreds of times, I assure you. Any hour of the day or night... And not once... Not once, damn it!, has she taken more than a couple of seconds to open the door and let me in!...

THE GENTLEMAN: Oh?

BOUBOUROCHE: You're mistaken, monsieur!... You're a dupe, a... [*Recalling* POTASSE's *recent epithet.*] a pigeon!...

THE GENTLEMAN: Me?

BOUBOUROCHE: Adèle may have her faults... A... A little peccadillo now and then...

THE GENTLEMAN [*nodding, to himself*]: If I'll pardon the redundancy...

BOUBOUROCHE: But nothing... [*Emphasizing.*] nothing will convince me that she's anything less than a woman of virtue...

THE GENTLEMAN [*nodding*]: Easy!...

BOUBOUROCHE [*ignoring his interjection*]: ...and decency, monsieur, utterly beyond the shadow of a doubt!

THE GENTLEMAN [*after a brief pause, with a wry smile, categorically*]: Monsieur, she's a little tramp.

BOUBOUROCHE [*almost choking with rage, trying to control himself, stammering*]: She... She... A... A little... [*Finally, catching his breath, calling out in a booming voice.*] Amédée! Two drafts!

AMEDEE [*behind the counter*]: Yes, monsieur... [*Aside, sarcastically.*] More rubbish?

[*During the ensuing dialogue he draws the beers, brings them to the table, removes the two empty glasses, and returns to his labors.*]

BOUBOUROCHE [*after a pause*]: Unfaithful?... Adèle?... Oh là là!... Why, I'd like to know? For money?... Ha! She doesn't care a thing for money. Not a thing!... She eats like a pigeon...

THE GENTLEMAN: So to speak!

BOUBOUROCHE: She wears everything ready-made... Why, she even uses elastic bands for garters!

THE GENTLEMAN: Most economical...

BOUBOUROCHE: For pleasure?... [*Ironically.*] Ha! She's not clever enough! No sense, monsieur... Hardly enough to fill a thimble, poor child!...

THE GENTLEMAN [*raising his eyes heavenward, declaiming poetically*]: "O Man!, thou blind and much bedeafened being!"... No sense, you say?... But my dear friend, it's you yourself who have little of that commodity! You remind me of those individuals, all congested with a head-cold, who confidently assert that the rose has no fragrance, simply because they fail to smell it... No sense?... Look here, monsieur, I know that we're speaking man to man. But still, there are certain ticklish questions that, even man to man, are too delicate to raise directly. I trust you won't mind if I don't call a spade a spade... [*Indicating the table, with an obvious ironic reference.*] In these precincts, especially...

BOUBOUROCHE: I don't under—

THE GENTLEMAN [*interrupting*]: A moment ago, I recalled that we no longer live in an age when walls smother cries—be they shrieks of pain or, indeed, squeals of delight. Permit me to repeat the observation. Enough said... "A word to the wise," as they say...

BOUBOUROCHE: But...

THE GENTLEMAN [*reluctant to cut short his tirade*]: And furthermore, even were she to have a mere thimbleful of sense, as you profess—or less... even a hundred times less—she would still be unfaithful.

BOUBOUROCHE: But... Why...?

THE GENTLEMAN: Why? Because "unfaithful", my friend, is synonymous with "woman"! Take the word of an elderly philosopher... One who knows only too well whereof he speaks, and who has, alas!, suffered the harsh realities of the apophthegms he proffers...

BOUBOUROCHE: "Apo..."?

THE GENTLEMAN: "...phthegms"... [*As* BOUBOUROCHE *continues to look a little puzzled, explaining.*] Axioms... Adages... [*Continuing.*] Men, monsieur, are unfaithful to women in the proportion of one out of two.

BOUBOUROCHE: Ah?

THE GENTLEMAN: Or fifty out of one hundred... While women, on the other hand, according to the best statistics, are unfaithful to men in the staggering proportion of ninety-seven percent.

BOUBOUROCHE [*open-mouthed*]: Ninety—

THE GENTLEMAN: Precisely! Ninety-seven out of one hundred!... And that, my friend, is no idle speculation. The figure, as I say, is arrived at according to mathematical statistics, and confirmed by the most elementary of observations.

BOUBOUROCHE: Ninety-seven...

THE GENTLEMAN: In short, for one reason or another—or, perhaps, for utterly no reason at all—at this very moment, as I speak, an interloper is under your roof. Sitting in your favorite chair... Warming the soles of his boots by the hearth grown used to toasting the soles of yours... Whistling through his teeth the Toreador Song from *Carmen,* that he's learned from years of listening to you...

BOUBOUROCHE [*shaking his head, weakly*]: No... I don't—

THE GENTLEMAN [*anticipating his objection*]: Believe it or not, that's your prerogative, monsieur. As for me, my conscience is clear. My mission is accomplished. I've performed my duty... Staunchly and unflinchingly, with neither fear nor rancor... [BOUBOUROCHE *is about to speak, but sits for a moment, open-mouthed and silent.*] Ah! If we men could bring to our lives that spirit of solidarity that women are able, so expertly, to bring to theirs... If only we did for one another what I have just done for you... Well, I daresay there would be no fewer cuckolds, to be sure. But at least—and this was my objective, my friend—at least it would simplify those complex and grueling separations that must, perforce, inevitably ensue. [*Getting up, with a nod to* BOUBOUROCHE.] Au revoir, monsieur. I thank you for the refreshment. [*He gets his coat from the coatrack, dons it; then, nodding to* THE CASHIER *and* AMEDEE.] Madame... Monsieur...

[*He exits.*]

BOUBOUROCHE [*after a long moment of bemused silence, finally erupting, pounding the table with his fist*]: Damnation!

AMEDEE [*running over*]: Monsieur? Was there something—

BOUBOUROCHE: No! Nothing!... [*He waves him off with a peremptory gesture; then, reconsidering.*] Wait!... [*Pointing to the coasters on the table.*] How much?

AMEDEE [*calculating*]: Nine francs twenty, monsieur.

BOUBOUROCHE [*throwing ten francs onto the table, gruffly*]: Keep the change!

AMEDEE: Thank you, Monsieur Boubouroche! [*As* BOUBOUROCHE *gets up, stalks up to the coatrack, and takes his coat and hat.*] Thank you... [*Following behind him.*] Thank you... [*Softly, to* THE CASHIER.] What's eating him, I wonder?

BOUBOUROCHE [*putting on his coat, as* THE CASHIER *shrugs uninterestedly*]: Damnation!

[*He exits.* AMEDEE, *scratching his head, watches him leave.*]

CURTAIN

Act Two

A modestly furnished living room. In the upstage wall, somewhat left of center, a double door leading onto a little vestibule. When the door is open one can see the front door of the apartment. Against the upstage wall, at a corresponding distance to the right, a large, double-doored, wooden cupboard. Down left, a door; down right, a window draped with a thin muslin curtain. Midstage right, a small table and chair; on the former, a sewing-basket and an oil lamp topped with a large shade. Midstage left, a chaise longue set at an angle, foot toward the footlights. Next to it, another small table. Other appropriate turn-of-the-century furnishings and decorations, ad libitum.

At rise, ANDRE *is sitting on the chaise longue meticulously polishing a brass bicycle horn with a chamois cloth.* ADELE *is sitting on the chair by the table, right, cutting materials, apparently for a dress. For a long moment the silence of the intimate domestic atmosphere is broken only by the snipping of her scissors. Suddenly* ANDRE *begins unconsciously humming the Toreador Song, without interrupting his efforts.*

ADELE [*looking up, mildly reproachful*]: Please!
ANDRE: Sorry...
   [*After another long moment of silence, the doorbell rings.* ANDRE *leaps to his feet and, without a word, dashes into the cupboard—inside of which can be seen a chair and a small table with a lighted candle—pulling the doors shut.* ADELE, *in the meantime, has got up, stepped out into the vestibule, leaving the double door open, and opens the front door.*]
THE MALE VISITOR [*standing at the threshold*]: Madame Castagnette?
ADELE: One flight up, monsieur..
THE MALE VISITOR: I beg your pardon.
ADELE: Not at all... [*She comes back in and closes the double door; then, opening the cupboard, to* ANDRE.] Wrong floor...
   [*Without a word,* ANDRE *returns to the chaise longue and continues his polishing, as* ADELE, *likewise, returns to her chair and scissors. The scene is exactly the same as at the beginning of the act. After another long silence* ANDRE *begins humming the Toreador Song again.* ADELE *puts down her work and casts an exasperated look in his direction.*]
ANDRE: Sorry...
ADELE: Thank you.
   [ANDRE *falls silent, and he and* ADELE *continue with their labors, to the click-clack of the latter's scissors and the rustle of her fabrics. After a moment, as before, the doorbell rings.*]
ANDRE [*jumping up*]: Damn!

[*The previous scene is repeated as he disappears into the cupboard, while* ADELE *once again exits into the vestibule and opens the front door.*]

THE FEMALE VISITOR [*at the threshold*]: Monsieur Fink?

ADELE: One flight down, madame...

THE FEMALE VISITOR: I beg your pardon.

ADELE: Not at all... [*She comes back in and closes the double door, as before; then, opening the cupboard, to* ANDRE.] Wrong floor...

ANDRE: Again? How many times...

ADELE: Of course! It's my fault, I suppose!

ANDRE [*coming back downstage*]: I didn't say that.

ADELE [*sitting down at her table*]: No, but you were thinking it. Like every other time someone picks the wrong door... I don't know what it is, but for weeks now you seem to be blaming me for their mistakes.

ANDRE: Really?

ADELE: Really!

ANDRE: Not at all... It's just that... Listen... It's just that I'm beginning to get a little fed up with that... that... [*Pointing to the cupboard.*] That sideboard of yours is getting on my nerves, if you must know.

ADELE [*a little petulantly*]: It's a cupboard, not a sideboard.

ANDRE [*curtly*]: You're right. Excuse me.

ADELE: Besides, now *you* listen... I think you're being terribly unfair. You know how I absolutely bend over backwards to let you out as soon as I can.

ANDRE: Ha!

ADELE [*pointing to the cupboard*]: And anyway, it's not as if you don't have all the comforts of home!... Light... A chair to sit on... A table to read at...

ANDRE: Oh yes! "All the comforts..."

ADELE: Well, almost... [*No less sarcastically.*] I suppose monsieur would like a bathroom too! [*As if to herself.*] Men can be so demanding sometimes.

ANDRE: And women can exaggerate!... Who said anything about a bathroom?... It's just that my parents didn't bring me into the world to spend my life in a sideboard!

ADELE: A cupboard.

ANDRE: A cupboard... [*Continuing.*] Be reasonable, for goodness' sake!

ADELE: Me?

ANDRE: And that's not all... [*Pointing to the cupboard.*] As impossible as that... that thing is for comfort, it's absolutely superb for acoustics! I can hear a pin drop out here when I'm in there!

ADELE: Oh?... So?

ANDRE: "So"?... So there are times, my sweet, when the silence of my solitude is troubled by... by certain embarrassing sounds that, between you and me, I'd rather not listen to... [*Reflecting for a moment.*] That is... Between you and me, yes... But not between you and him!... After all Adèle... [*Tenderly.*] I love you.

ADELE: Poor kitten!... [*After a pause.*] The sideboard in the dining room didn't have that problem, did it?

ANDRE: No, but it had another one. Every time I came out the smell of cheese and salami would come out with me—among other delicacies—and cling to my clothes with a... [*Ironically.*] an admirable persistence. [ADELE *gives a little chuckle.*] It got so bad that whenever I ran into someone I knew they would stand there sniffing me like an hors-d'oeuvre tray, and finally say:

"How come you smell like a ripe gorgonzola lately?" [ADELE *begins laughing heartily.*] I'm glad you think it's amusing!

ADELE: Not "it," love... You!

ANDRE: Thank you!

ADELE: Now, now...

ANDRE: Well, I don't. It's just that I'm beginning to get a little fed up—

ADELE [*interrupting*]: You said that.

ANDRE: ...with living like a frightened rabbit... With my ears always twitching at the slightest sound... Coming up out of my hole for air, only to scurry back again at the first sign of danger... It's... It's humiliating, Adèle. My self-esteem can't take it. [*Pausing, rather subdued.*] Or my confidence, either...

ADELE: Confidence?... [*Growing a little concerned.*] In...?

ANDRE: In you.

ADELE: In me?... [*Going on the offensive, archly.*] My! How flattering, monsieur!

ANDRE: Well, it's only logical, Adèle. Think about it. It's just that...

ADELE [*mimicking*]: "It's just that... It's just that..." That what? Tell me... What?

ANDRE: Look... [*Impatiently, moving down between the table and the window.*] For eight years now you've played this little game, pulling the wool over that poor fool's eyes...

ADELE [*joining him near the window*]: For you, if you hadn't noticed!

ANDRE: A decent sort, who didn't force you, I'm sure... Who didn't grab you by the hair and pull you into bed...

ADELE: Well, hardly!

ANDRE: And you've done it so cleverly, my love, with such finesse, that... that, frankly, if you must know, it rather appalls me!

ADELE: What? I hope you're not going to blame me for making a fool of that idiot Boubouroche! For us, after all... For our love...

ANDRE: No, no. It's not that. It's... It's—

ADELE [*interrupting, anticipating his declaration, mockingly*]: It's just that...?

ANDRE [*coming down center*]: When I think how calmly and coolly you trick him... Sly, cheeky little devil...

ADELE [*following him*]: Me?

ANDRE: ...and what talent you've had to waste doing something so bad so well... [*He pauses, reflecting.*]

ADELE: Well?

ANDRE: Well... It's just that... [*Stopping short, catching himself.*] I can't help wondering if... if perhaps I'm not somebody else's Boubouroche... And if a woman who's clever enough to hide a second lover from a first, by sticking him away in a sideboard... [*Correcting himself quickly.*] a cupboard... couldn't be hiding a third one from the second by stuffing him into a chest of drawers, or something!

ADELE: André! Really!

ANDRE: I'm sorry, but... [*A little sentimentally.*] You can't keep a man in love from being jealous.

ADELE: I know, but... You?... Of me?...

ANDRE: I'm not accusing you, Adèle.

ADELE: No, but you suspect me.

ANDRE [*sincerely*]: Not much... Really, just a little...

ADELE: I don't care! Even a little!... What have I done? What's my crime?... I prefer you to him. What's so awful about that?

ANDRE: It's just—

ADELE [*cutting him off*]: Besides, I know what he's capable of. I know him.

ANDRE: Oh?

ADELE: He would make mincemeat of you, believe me!

ANDRE: Him?... If you think I'm afraid... [*With an air of bravado.*] Not of him, or anyone!...

ADELE: Oh? Just let him catch us!...

ANDRE: Fine! He'll catch us.

ADELE: Good God! Don't say that!

ANDRE: Because he will, you know... Sooner or later... It's only a matter of time.

ADELE: Bite your tongue!

ANDRE: You'll see... [*Taking out his pocket watch.*] But not today, at least... Talking about time... Nine thirty already... He won't come tonight, I'm sure. [*Pointing to the door, down left.*] So, shall we?

ADELE: Well... He's never this late... But still, I think we'd better... Let's wait ten more minutes.

ANDRE: If you say so, my love...

[*He returns to the chaise longue and continues polishing his horn, as* ADELE *goes to her table and likewise resumes her work. For a long moment the scene is again as it was at the beginning of the act. Suddenly the doorbell rings, long and insistently.*]

ADELE [*jumping up*] ⎫ ⎧ Oh!
                    ⎬ [*together*]: ⎨
ANDRE [*likewise*] ⎭ ⎩ Damn! It's him!

[ANDRE *dashes up to the cupboard with his horn and cloth, and shuts himself in as* ADELE *exits into the vestibule and opens the front door.* BOUBOUROCHE *storms in, dressed as he was at the end of Act One, slamming both doors behind him.*]

ADELE: Ah, treasure...

BOUBOUROCHE [*obviously furious, flinging his hat on the table by the chaise longue*]: Don't "Ah, treasure!" me!...

[*He makes a beeline for the door, down left, pulls it open and pokes his head into the darkness. Surprised to find no lover, he comes right, to the window, and pulls the curtains violently apart.*]

ADELE [*who has been watching in growing consternation, following him*]: What are you... What's the matter?... Please..

BOUBOUROCHE [*point blank*]: You're cheating on me! That's what's the matter!

ADELE [*the picture of innocence*]: Cheating?... Me?... What ever do you mean?

BOUBOUROCHE [*mimicking*]: "What ever do you mean?... What ever..." I mean that you're making a fool of me!... That you're a liar and a cheat... [*Pacing back and forth.*] and that there's a man in here! That's what I mean!

ADELE: A man?

BOUBOUROCHE: Yes, a man!

ADELE: Who, for heaven's sake?

BOUBOUROCHE: A man, that's who!

ADELE [*after a tense pause, bursting into sardonic laughter*]: Now that's a good one!

BOUBOUROCHE [*shaking his fist, menacing*]: Don't laugh, woman!... And don't try to deny it! It's no use! I know!

ADELE [*with a shrug*]: Really!

BOUBOUROCHE: That's right... Try to make me think it's just gossip, and I'm foolish to believe what people tell me.

ADELE: People?... Who?

BOUBOUROCHE: What's the difference? Just people... [*With a sweeping gesture.*] As heaven is my witness, I thought so too at first. And I stood out there for ten minutes, on the sidewalk... [*Pointing down right.*] staring up at the window, telling myself I was crazy to believe it, and that I was a... an ungrateful wretch!

ADELE [*trying to sound offhand*]: To say the least!

BOUBOUROCHE: I was going to turn and leave... And I would have, I swear... But all of a sudden there you were! Your shadow, on the window... And then another one!... A man's...

ADELE [*pretending shocked disbelief, with a sarcastic little laugh*]: What?

BOUBOUROCHE: You heard me! A man!... [*Trying to control himself, with an air of affected calm.*] So!... Just hand him over. He's in here somewhere... I know... And we have some talking to do, the two of us. Important matters to discuss, and that are none of your affair...

ADELE: But Ernest...

BOUBOUROCHE [*raising his voice and shaking his fist again*]: Go get him, I said!... [*Subdued but no less emotional.*] Then perhaps... just perhaps, I may find it in my heart to forgive you, Adèle. [*Sincerely, despite a touch of theatricality.*] A heart filled with love... A love that knew no bounds, more than for anything else in life... A love that may let me forget, some day, the unspeakable pain of a desolate existence!

ADELE [*standing momentarily transfixed at his eloquence, at a loss for words, finally finding her tongue, anticlimactically*]: Silly!

BOUBOUROCHE: Not "silly," madame... Stupid!... Yes, stupid for eight years... A dupe, a... a pigeon! A stupid, blind fool who—God only knows why— refused to see the signs, the... the proof all around him!

ADELE: Ernest!...

BOUBOUROCHE [*ignoring her*]: Proof that only an idiot could miss!...

ADELE   ⎫   ⎧ Please...
                                              ⎬ [*together*]: ⎨
BOUBOUROCHE [*beating his breast*] ⎭   ⎩ An idiot, Adèle!...

ADELE: Don't be—

BOUBOUROCHE: An idiot!... Well, believe me, no more!... That's over! All over!... The rabble can win the battle, but they won't win the war!

ADELE [*taken aback, appalled at the epithet*]: "Rabble"?

BOUBOUROCHE: The good Lord's a decent sort! Sooner or later he sides with the righteous!

ADELE: Really! That's quite enough!

BOUBOUROCHE: Oh? You want me to keep quiet, I suppose?

ADELE: You "suppose" correctly! What kind of a lunatic... [*As if to herself.*] He comes bursting in here, goes off like a bomb... Slams the doors, rips the curtains... [*Continuing over* BOUBOUROCHE's *attempt to object to her exaggeration.*] Screams his lungs out all over the place... Treats me like the lowest of the low, like some... some common slut!

BOUBOUROCHE: Adèle...

ADELE: Even tries to strike me...

BOUBOUROCHE: I never—

ADELE: And all because he thinks he saw two shadows on the window!

BOUBOUROCHE: "Thinks"?...

ADELE: In the first place, monsieur, you're drunk!

BOUBOUROCHE: Not at all!

ADELE: Then you're lying.

BOUBOUROCHE: I'm not!

ADELE: Then you've *got* to be drunk. There's no other explanation. [*As he is about to protest, cutting him off.*] You either saw double, or you just want to pick a fight. One or the other...

BOUBOUROCHE: But... But... Neither one, Adèle... [*Beginning to lose his aplomb.*] It's just that... It's just that... [ADELE *turns aside with a look, as if to say: "Him too?"*] Someone told me... things... Terrible things...

ADELE: And, naturally, monsieur took them for gospel! [*Hands on hips.*] Of course!

BOUBOUROCHE: I—

ADELE: It never occurred to you to wonder if they were true!... To ask yourself how they could be!... We've only been together eight years, after all!

BOUBOUROCHE [*with a mortified little shrug*]: I... I thought...

[*He falls silent, chastised, hanging his head.*]

ADELE [*still pressing her advantage*]: Lovely!... Simply lovely!... So! Now I'm at the mercy of any derelict in the street!

BOUBOUROCHE [*softly*]: But it wasn't—

ADELE: Some lowlife comes along and says: "Your mistress is unfaithful..."

BOUBOUROCHE: But—

ADELE: ...and, of course, you believe him! He sings some wild tune, and I have to pay the piper! Is that how it is?

BOUBOUROCHE: Adèle...

ADELE: Well, open your eyes, monsieur!

BOUBOUROCHE [*aside*] ⎫   ⎧ God! What have I done?
                    ⎬ [*together*]: ⎨
ADELE   ⎭   ⎩ Shame on you!... Shame!

BOUBOUROCHE [*trying to recoup*]: But... But—

ADELE: You'd think you were born yesterday! Believing such things...

BOUBOUROCHE: Adèle...

ADELE [*taking the lamp from the table, right, and holding it out to him*]: Here! Take the lamp...

BOUBOUROCHE: What for?

ADELE: Go look for yourself!... Go see how I'm cheating!... [BOUBOUROCHE *waves off the lamp with a humbled expression.*] Don't just stand there gaping... Here!

BOUBOUROCHE [*justifying himself, with an air of contrition*]: You can't keep a man in love from being jealous, Adèle.

ADELE [*archly*]: I know. You already said that.

BOUBOUROCHE: I did? [*Confused.*] When?

ADELE: Just now, when you... [*Stopping short, realizing that she is confusing him with* ANDRE, *aside.*] Damn! [*Aloud.*] Never mind!... [*Holding out the lamp.*] Just take it and go look! [*Sarcastically, as he reluctantly takes the lamp.*] I think you know your way around the apartment!

BOUBOUROCHE: Adèle...

ADELE: Or would you rather I came with you?

BOUBOUROCHE [*utterly subdued*]: Please... Don't be cruel. Is it my fault if somebody wanted to have his little joke? Just say you forgive me and... and let's forget it ever happened.

ADELE: Forgive you?... *Me*, forgive *you?* You mean...? [*Sarcastically.*] I must have misunderstood. I thought *I* was supposed to beg *your* forgiveness! And repent, monsieur... And promise to be good...

BOUBOUROCHE: Please...

ADELE [*softening, changing her tone*]: Well, we'll see... I know that down deep you didn't mean any harm. You're right, it's not your fault if you're just a little too gullible... [*Echoing* BOUBOUROCHE'*s earlier tirade, ironically.*] And so, perhaps—just perhaps—I may find it in my heart to forgive you, Ernest... [BOUBOUROCHE, *rather pathetic, hangs his head.*] And I may even forget, some day, what an unspeakable, hateful insult—

BOUBOUROCHE [*cutting her off*]: Please, Adèle! You know I didn't mean it...

ADELE: Yes... But first I insist... I absolutely insist that you search every room from top to bottom! Scour every inch!... You're not going to leave until you do, do you hear?

BOUBOUROCHE: But...

ADELE: No "buts," Ernest... There's a man in here! I admit it!

BOUBOUROCHE [*embarrassed, pooh-poohing the blatant absurdity*]: No...

ADELE: Oh yes! I swear... On my word of honor!... In fact... [*Pointing to the cupboard, as if suddenly inspired, with exaggerated candor.*] There!... He's in there! [BOUBOUROCHE *gives a little laugh.*] Come see...

BOUBOUROCHE [*waving off the suggestion, delighted at her obvious vindication*]: Adèle...

ADELE: No, no... Come...

BOUBOUROCHE: What? And let you think I'm a fool?... A... A pigeon?...

ADELE [*changing her tack, offering him a key*]: Here... Here's the key to the cellar. Now you're going to go down and have a good look!

BOUBOUROCHE [*shaking his head*]: Cruel... Cruel...

ADELE: And especially behind the wine casks! That's where I hide all my lovers, Ernest!... [*Pointing to the door, down left.*] And in there too, don't forget!... In the closet... Under the bed... Behind the curtains... Go look! Go find as many as you can!

BOUBOUROCHE [*with a hangdog look, to himself*] } [*together*]: { It serves me right!

ADELE [*continuing*]   Go on... Go on...

[BOUBOUROCHE, *holding out the lamp, shuffles reluctantly toward the door, down left, turning around from time to time to cast rather piteous looks at a silent, haughty* ADELE, *who stands watching as he reaches the door. Just as he pulls it open, a gust of wind from inside the room blows out the lamp, plunging the room into darkness.*]

BOUBOUROCHE } [together]: { Oh my...

ADELE } [together]: { What the...

[*Suddenly the light from* ANDRE's *candle can be clearly seen under the cupboard door.*]

BOUBOUROCHE [*feeling his way, still facing left*] } [together]: { Now what...?

ADELE [*noticing the light, aside,* sotto voce] } [together]: { Damn!

BOUBOUROCHE [*turning in* ADELE's *direction*]: Do you have any matches? I'll just... [*Stopping short as he too notices the light.*] What on earth...? What's that?

[*He makes a beeline for the cupboard and pulls the doors wide, revealing* ANDRE *sitting at his table, the lighted candle and an open book before him.*]

ANDRE } [together]: { Oh...

BOUBOUROCHE [*with a shocked roar*] } [together]: { Aaaah!

[ANDRE, *quite unruffled, calmly steps out and places the candle on the table by the chaise longue, illuminating the scene.*]

ANDRE [*with a sardonic smile, to* ADELE, *who stands rooted to the spot*]: See? I told you... Sooner or later... [*Taking a calling card from his pocket and presenting it to a stunned* BOUBOUROCHE, *very matter-of-fact.*] I'll expect a visit from your seconds, monsieur. [BOUBOUROCHE *stands gazing blankly for a long moment.*] My card... [*Still holding it out.*] Please do me the honor...

BOUBOUROCHE [*mechanically*]: Your card... [*Taking it finally, then folding it in two and putting it in his pocket.*] You'll be hearing from me, monsieur. [*Pointing to the door, upstage, in a subdued but determined tone.*] Now get out...

ANDRE [*very much the proper gentleman, cool and collected*]: Pardon me, monsieur, but... I'm anxious to know your intentions once I leave. Not that I presume to demand a reply... I would hardly take the liberty, especially under the circumstances. It's just that... In a word, I'm concerned. You tend to be rather violent, and... and I'm afraid it might be less than judicious to leave you alone with a woman... a woman... whom...

BOUBOUROCHE [*growing less and less benumbed, and more and more outraged*]: Enough! You... You... [*Threatening.*] One more word... One more... Just one, goddammit!... [*Pointing to the window.*] and I'll throw you out, head first! Understand?

ANDRE [*very calmly*]: I beg your pardon, but—

BOUBOUROCHE [*shouting*]: Shut up, I said! One word... One syllable... One sound... [*Controlling his rage.*] If you had the slightest idea what I'm going through... What's going on inside me... If you knew how I'm trying to... [*Fuming.*] to keep from strangling you, monsieur... If you knew... [*Beginning to sputter.*] If... If... [*Taking a deep breath.*] Believe me, you won't even open your mouth if you know what's good for you!... It's lucky for you I know my strength!... Lucky for both of us, because, believe me... [*About to grow violent again.*] Now get out! That's all I have to say, monsieur. I'm a very unhappy man. I advise you not to make matters worse. [*Pointing up left.*] There's the door!... Now get out!... [*Beginning to lose control.*] Get out, you hear me?... Out! Out! Out!

ANDRE [*standing pat, still terribly proper*]: I beg your pardon again, monsieur. It's just that... A gentleman is always a gentleman, even when he's obliged by certain circumstances in his life to hide in a sideboard from time to time... [*With a glance toward the still mortified* ADELE, *correcting.*] Or a cupboard... You may threaten me all you like. [*Determined.*] I'm not moving from this spot until I have your absolute assurance that the person in question... [*Pointing to* ADELE.] madame... is in no danger...

BOUBOUROCHE [*chafing, beginning to huff and puff*]: You... You...

ANDRE [*continuing*]: ...and that you won't harm a single hair of her head! It's my duty as a gentleman to insist, monsieur. And yours, to give me your solemn word... I trust I have it.

BOUBOUROCHE: You... [*Exasperated.*] My... My...

ANDRE: Besides, I must say—if I may take the liberty—that I find you not a little impertinent, monsieur, presuming to throw me out of a home that is not your own.

BOUBOUROCHE [*growing more and more annoyed*]: You find me—

ANDRE [*interrupting*]: And if, in the light of your rather excited state, I'm willing to abide by your demands, it's only right, I'm sure you will agree, that you comply with mine.

BOUBOUROCHE [*slamming the lamp, which he has been holding, down on the table, left, exploding*]: I'll kill him! I will, goddammit! I will!...

ANDRE [*standing his ground, calmly*]: You're free to try, monsieur.

[*The two men stand for a long moment staring fixedly at each other, as* BOUBOUROCHE, *silently, attempts to quell his rage and frustration.*]

BOUBOUROCHE [*finally, pointing to the door, upstage, in as soft and civil a voice as possible*]: Please leave.

ANDRE: Do I have your word, monsieur?

BOUBOUROCHE: You do.

ANDRE: Thank you. So noted...

BOUBOUROCHE [*under his breath*]: Indeed...

[*There follows a long scene in which* ANDRE, *in no hurry, prepares to depart. First he goes up to the cupboard, opens it, and retrieves his possessions: bicycle horn, cloth, and book, as well as a newspaper or two and several magazines lying in a corner.*]

ANDRE [*about to leave the cupboard, spying a box of matches on the table inside*]: Ah... [*Placing the other objects on the chair, right, and holding up the matches, to* ADELE, *who has been watching in silence.*] The matches, madame... [*To* BOUBOUROCHE.] Monsieur was asking... [*Taking advantage of his find, he relights the lamp—on the table, left—puts the matches down next to it, returns to the cupboard and looks about inside for a moment; then, finding his comb and brush, he proceeds in leisurely fashion to use them to his satisfaction, after which, sticking the comb between the bristles of the brush, he tucks them both under one arm, picks up the other objects, nodding respectfully to* ADELE *and* BOUBOUROCHE, *in turn.*] Madame... Monsieur...

[*He gives an unobtrusive little click of the heels and exits, upstage.*]

BOUBOUROCHE [*after a weighty pause, softly, controlling his fury, to* ADELE]: Who is he?

ADELE [*with a shameless shrug*]: How on earth should I know?

BOUBOUROCHE [*stunned by her cynical pretense*]: "How on earth..." "How on earth..." Do you dare to stand there, woman, and tell me... [*Almost shrieking, obviously losing control.*] You lying, scheming, cheating... I'll kill you! I'll... I'll...
[*He leaps at her, out of his mind, lunging for her throat.*]

ADELE: Aaaah!

[BOUBOUROCHE, *livid with rage, has pushed her onto the chaise longue, for a moment seemingly ready to make good his threat. But just as his fingers are about to tighten around her neck, he lets go, unable to carry it out, leaving her sitting, flustered, trying to compose herself.*]

BOUBOUROCHE [*taking his head in his hands and breaking out in tears*]: I can't... I can't do it! Good God!... I can't!... I can't... [*Falling to his knees, burying his head in her skirts, sobbing pathetically.*] You're part of me, Adèle... Part of my flesh and blood... My life... [*Coming up momentarily for air, his face covered with tears.*] I can't!... I... I want to kill you for what you've done! I should! But I... I'm afraid I might hurt you... [*Sobbing.*] I should kill you, like a man, instead of crying like a baby! But I can't!... I can't... [*Sobbing uncontrolledly.*] Adèle, Adèle, Adèle!... Why?... Why did you do it?

ADELE [*gradually regaining her composure, innocently*]: Do what, Ernest?

BOUBOUROCHE [*ignoring her implicit disclaimer, continuing, pitifully*]: I know I'm not much... I'm not handsome, I'm not rich... But I tried so hard, Adèle. I tried to make you forget those little faults... I thought you were so happy... Nestled in my heart, like a bird in its nest... I was putty in your hands... [*Taking her hands in his.*] Your sweet little hands... Everything seemed so... You seemed so... [*Speechless, with a gasp.*] You seemed... [*Shaking his head.*] Why?... Tell me! Why?... Why?

ADELE [*grown quite calm, with a look of utter amazement*]: You mean, you... You're serious?

BOUBOUROCHE [*still at her feet*]: "Serious?"

ADELE: You're not joking, Ernest? [*Affecting grave concern.*] Please! What's the matter?... You worry me, treasure... Really, what's got into you?

BOUBOUROCHE: Me?

ADELE: What is it? What have I done?

BOUBOUROCHE: "What..."? Do I have to tell you, woman?... [*Pointing to the cupboard.*] Ask him!... Ask him what you've done!

ADELE [*innocently*]: Who?

BOUBOUROCHE: Him!... Your lover!

ADELE: My lover?... [*Pointing.*] Him?... [*With a cynical little laugh.*] What lover?... I have no lover...

BOUBOUROCHE: No?

ADELE: Of course not!

BOUBOUROCHE: Then who is he, liar? Who is that man, if he's not... if he's not...

ADELE [*a little mysteriously*]: I'm sorry. I can't tell you.

BOUBOUROCHE: Oh? And why?

ADELE: It's a family secret. I can't possibly tell you.

BOUBOUROCHE [*appalled, obviously unconvinced*]: What kind of story...

ADELE [*with an air of pretended resignation*]: You don't believe me? [*With a sigh.*] You're right... I can't blame you. I'm sure I'd think the same thing if

I were you... [*Standing up.*] Good-bye.

[*She turns to leave.*]

BOUBOUROCHE [*suddenly alarmed, getting to his feet*]: Where are you going?

ADELE: Nowhere... I just know we can't stay together, that's all.

BOUBOUROCHE: We... What do you mean?

ADELE [*in an accusing tone*]: No... It's finished between us. You've made that clear, Ernest.

BOUBOUROCHE: Me?... I... But you can't expect me to believe... Just because you say so... You can't expect me—

ADELE [*interrupting*]: You're right. Of course... Why should you believe a woman who has given you eight years of her life?... The best eight years... And who never... never... gave you the slightest reason to suspect her, or doubt her word!... Who... Who... [*Sighing, as if sadly resigned to her unjust fate.*] No... I *look* guilty... That's all that matters.

BOUBOUROCHE [*beginning to soften*]: Adèle...

ADELE: I can't blame you for being weak... For not having the... the strength of character to see through appearances... For accepting them blindly...

BOUBOUROCHE [*softly*] ⎫   ⎧ But Adèle...
                            ⎬ [*together*]: ⎨
ADELE   ⎭   ⎩ No, no... I can't blame you.

BOUBOUROCHE: Adèle...

ADELE: You're a man, Ernest. [*As if proving a theorem.*] You're weak.

BOUBOUROCHE [*with a note of desperation in his voice*]: But... But what do you expect, good God? Are you telling me it's right? What decent woman hides a man in... [*Pointing up right.*] in... in—

ADELE: "Decent"?... If I weren't a decent woman would I be doing what I'm doing? Would I sacrifice my life... [*On the verge of crocodile tears.*] my love?... Would I give up my happiness just to keep my solemn word? Just to keep a secret, and... and save another woman's honor?... Would I, Ernest? Would I?... [*As BOUBOUROCHE opens his mouth to speak, cutting him off.*] No... It's no use discussing it. We'll never agree. You... You're not a woman. [*Taking out her handkerchief.*] You can't possibly understand. There are some things that a man will simply never...

[*She sits back down on the chaise longue, sniffing into her handkerchief, convincingly.*]

BOUBOUROCHE [*tenderly*]: Adèle... Adèle...

ADELE [*with a sob in her voice*]: It's over... It has to be, Ernest. There's no other way. [*Turning her head aside.*] I won't ask you to kiss me... Just... [*Holding out her hand to him.*] Just give me your hand... This one last time...

BOUBOUROCHE [*standing beside the chaise longue, taking it*]: Adèle...

ADELE [*with mock solicitude*]: I hope you'll be happy. That's the worst I could ever wish you... In spite of what you've done...

BOUBOUROCHE [*still softly, without the outrage that her observation should normally provoke*]: What I...?

ADELE [*continuing, simply*]: I forgive you, Ernest. Only... Tell me you forgive me too, for the pain you've made me cause you.

BOUBOUROCHE: For...

ADELE: You know I didn't mean to. You know I never would.

BOUBOUROCHE: Please, Adèle... I know, I know... You're not a bad person. Of course I know...

ADELE: We could have been so happy, you and I!... Ah! Just tell me... Just let me believe that... [*Pointing up left.*] that when you cross that threshold, you'll never forget... [*Sniffling, and punctuating her dramatic pronouncement with little sobs.*] That... That sometime, somewhere... later, some day... when all this fades into a dim, distant past... That at least you'll remember with... with a touch of tenderness... the old friend you're leaving in this empty apartment... alone... So, so alone... [*She bursts into tears.*] Ah! Life, life, Ernest!... It really knows how to be cruel when it wants to!

BOUBOUROCHE [*sitting down beside her, sobbing quietly*]: Adèle... Adèle...

ADELE: No, no... Don't cry. Please, don't... I couldn't stand it! [*Patting her eyes with her handkerchief.*] Oh! I... I had no illusions. I knew that... that... [*With a gesture.*] that this... you and I... couldn't last forever. I knew that, one day... [*Sobbing.*] Still, I hoped... I thought we could share at least a few more years of happiness!

BOUBOUROCHE [*between his sobs*]: Just... Just promise you'll never do it again. I... I said I could find it in my heart to forgive you...

ADELE: I know how good you are, Ernest. But... [*With incontrovertible logic.*] But how can I promise never to do again what I didn't do before? How can I let you forgive me for a fault I didn't commit?

BOUBOUROCHE: Ah...

ADELE: And besides, what's the good? In spite of your love, you'll never trust me again. And a love without trust... No, no... I could never accept it.

BOUBOUROCHE: Adèle...

ADELE: Your love means everything in the world to me, Ernest. Everything... [*Blithely unaware of the absurdity.*] But your respect means even more. [*With affected pathos.*] The worm is in the apple... It's best we threw it out.

BOUBOUROCHE: I can't, Adèle!... [*Beginning to babble.*] The apple... I can't leave you. I... The worm... I can't! It's bigger than I am...

ADELE: You have to... Come, come... [*Maternally, as* BOUBOUROCHE *bursts into tears.*] There, there now... Big baby!... [*Gently patting his eyes with her handkerchief.*] Here... Let me dry your tears... Be strong... Be brave...

BOUBOUROCHE [*sobbing*]: I can't... I...

ADELE: Please...

BOUBOUROCHE: I...

ADELE: Try... That's life, Ernest... [*Committing an unintentional pun.*] Just one long "veil" of tears... One long mourning veil...

[*There is a long, silent pause, broken only by* BOUBOUROCHE's *gasps and sobs.*]

BOUBOUROCHE [*finally breaking the silence, his tail between his legs, softly and pitifully*]: Please... Let me stay.

ADELE: You know that's not possible.

BOUBOUROCHE: But I love you, Adèle. I love you too much to... to...

ADELE [*with pretended cynicism*]: Oh, I know...

BOUBOUROCHE: I can't live without you!

ADELE: Those are things we say, but... [*Sighing.*] After all, if I were dead, you would have to, now wouldn't you...

BOUBOUROCHE [*bursting into tears*]: Please, Adèle... Don't... Don't even say that! [*He continues sobbing, covering her hands with tearful kisses.*] Adèle... Oh, my Adèle...

ADELE [*trying to pull her hands away, feigning reluctant determination*]: Really, Ernest...

BOUBOUROCHE [*resisting*]: My Adèle...

ADELE ⎫
BOUBOUROCHE ⎭ [*together*]: { I... I can't... We must... I...
{ Adèle... Adèle...

ADELE [*pulling free*]: For the last time... Please... Good-bye.

BOUBOUROCHE: "Good-bye"?... "Good-bye"?... No! Never!...

ADELE ⎫
BOUBOUROCHE ⎭ [*together*]: { Please... Ernest...
{ I won't go, Adèle! I won't!...

ADELE: Be reasonable... Try to understand!

BOUBOUROCHE: Reason be damned! I won't... I'm staying!

ADELE [*after a pause, affecting utter resignation*]: If you must... [*Sighing a long sigh.*] What can I say?... I haven't the strength to argue.

[*There is another long pause, during which* BOUBOUROCHE, *still beside her on the chaise longue, takes out his hadkerchief and hides his face in it, sobbing.*]

ADELE [*finally, judging the moment opportune*]: You forgive me, then?

BOUBOUROCHE: What for? [*Blowing his nose between sobs.*] It's all my fault. I'm such a stupid fool!

ADELE: For... For letting you think... For not telling you the secret...

BOUBOUROCHE [*with a gesture of unconcern*]: Pfff!

ADELE: You do, then? You forgive me?

BOUBOUROCHE: Of course...

ADELE: With all your heart?

BOUBOUROCHE: With all my heart.

ADELE: And you'll never, never mention this awful night again?

BOUBOUROCHE: Never!

ADELE: Promise?

BOUBOUROCHE: Yes.

ADELE: You swear?

BOUBOUROCHE [*crossing his heart*]: I swear...

ADELE: There!... [*Like a mother calling down a naughty child.*] The very idea... To think I could ever be unfaithful!... And to you! My Ernest... My dear, sweet Ernest...

BOUBOUROCHE [*properly chastised, thoroughly convinced*]: I know...

ADELE [*taking his hands, gazing into his eyes*]: Look at me, treasure. Look me in the eye. [*He obeys.*] Tell me, yes or no... Do I look like a woman who could lie to you? [*Without waiting for an answer.*] Silly goose!... [*As if to herself.*] All ready to ruin his life, and for what?... For nothing!... Without even telling himself: "It's too stupid! I'm a fool!... Eight years with this woman... Here, for all the world to see..." [*As a contrite* BOUBOUROCHE *is about to reply, stopping him.*] Really, Ernest! Have I ever, once, in all those years, given you the least reason to complain?... [*Stopping him again.*] Haven't I been an absolutely model mistress? The most patient, the most unselfish...

BOUBOUROCHE: Yes...

ADELE: The most faithful...

[BOUBOUROCHE *hangs his head.*]

ADELE: And you would have let all that past fall to pieces?... Our precious past, together... Our love, our caresses... Erased from you memory, rubbed out just... [*Snapping her fingers.*] like that!

BOUBOUROCHE: Adèle...

ADELE: And why? Because you happened to find a man in a... a cupboard!... A man you don't even know... By a foolish trick of fate!... A total stranger... [BOUBOUROCHE *gives a little shrug as* ADELE, *after pausing a moment in her dramatic tirade, continues with a feigned note of disillusion in her voice.*] But I can see that you're not completely convinced...

BOUBOUROCHE: But I am...

ADELE: No. I still see a tinge of doubt in your eyes.

BOUBOUROCHE: No, no... Not at all...

ADELE: Don't say "no"... I can feel it.

BOUBOUROCHE: No, really... I assure you...

ADELE: Well, Ernest... [*As if deciding to make a supreme sacrifice.*] I don't want to leave even the shadow of a doubt between us. Not even the slightest trace of a shadow...

BOUBOUROCHE: But...

ADELE: I know the price I have to pay to convince you, once and for all.

BOUBOUROCHE: But you have—

ADELE [*ignoring his objection, dramatically*]: To ease your mind... [*Sighing.*] It's a high price to pay... A terrible price, but... I'll do anything! Anything! [*Resolutely.*] Yes, I'll... I'll tell you the secret if you insist. The secret that can destroy an innocent life, but... but... Shall I stoop that low, Ernest? Tell me. Just say the word...

BOUBOUROCHE [*offended*]: Please! What kind of cad...? What do you take me for? I'm a gentleman, Adèle... Other people's secrets are no concern of mine!

ADELE [*with a smile of total victory*]: Kiss me, treasure!... I promise I'll never say another word about it. You've suffered enough for your foolishness, now haven't you? [*Leaning toward him, offering her cheek for the kiss of reconciliation.*] Here...

BOUBOUROCHE [*after musing for a moment, suddenly bellowing*]: Ah! Damn swine!

ADELE [*startled, pulling back*]: What?... Me?

BOUBOUROCHE [*quick to explain the misunderstanding*]: Oh là là!... No, no, no... Not you, pussycat!

ADELE ⎫ [*together*]: ⎰ Oh?... Then...?
BOUBOUROCHE ⎭   ⎱ Not in a million years...

BOUBOUROCHE: No, I'm thinking about a certain old imbecile of my acquaintance... In fact, I think I'll go give him a piece of my mind! [*He gets up, takes his hat from the table by the chaise longue, puts it on with an air of determination.*]

ADELE [*getting up surprised*]: What are you... [*As he strides up to the door, upstage.*] Where are you going?

BOUBOUROCHE [*opening the door*]: Don't worry... Just a little score to settle... I won't be long. [*He exits into the vestibule, leaving the double door wide open, so that one*

can see as he opens the front door of the apartment. Just as he does so, THE
GENTLEMAN *from Act One happens by, returning home.*]

ADELE [*standing upstage of the chaise longue, watching, to* BOUBOUROCHE]: But
treasure...

BOUBOUROCHE [*to* THE GENTLEMAN]: Ah! How convenient! Just the one I was
looking for!...

[*He seizes him suddenly and unceremoniously by the collar, and pulls him
bodily into the living room.*]

THE GENTLEMAN [*dumbfounded*]: What?... Monsieur...

ADELE ⎫   ⎧ Ernest...
      ⎬ [*together*]: ⎨
THE GENTLEMAN ⎭   ⎩ What are you...

BOUBOUROCHE [*to* THE GENTLEMAN, *menacingly*]: So! How would you like a
good punch in the nose? Hmm?

THE GENTLEMAN [*terrified,*   ⎫   ⎧ Let me go! Let me... Let me...
    struggling]   ⎬ [*together*]: ⎨ How would you like that?
BOUBOUROCHE [*continuing*]   ⎭   ⎩
ADELE   Ernest... What on earth...

BOUBOUROCHE [*roughing him up*]: My Adèle is a tramp, is she?

ADELE: What?

THE GENTLEMAN [*trying to defend himself*] ⎫   ⎧ Monsieur!... I... I...
      ⎬ [*together*]: ⎨
ADELE ⎭   ⎩ Did he say...

BOUBOUROCHE [*pummeling him*]: Well, take that, you damn fool!... And that,
you meddling old goat!... And that, you... you... You pigeon!...

[THE GENTLEMAN *continues to vociferate with appropriate interjections,
grunts, and groans, while* BOUBOUROCHE, *unrelenting, pursues his assault
before a startled and thoroughly uncomprehending* ADELE, *as the curtain
falls.*]

CURTAIN

THE POOR BEGGAR
AND THE FAIRY GODMOTHER

Adaptation of

Le Pauvre Bougre et le bon génie

by

Alphonse Allais

(1899)

CHARACTERS

THE POOR BEGGAR, a middle-aged vestige of respectability, down at his heels and down on his luck

THE WAITER, an aspiring tenor, good-natured and sympathetic

THE FAIRY GODMOTHER, other-worldly, but not without a good business sense

Paris, turn of the century. The terrace of a middle-class café on a quiet side street. Chairs, tables, etc.

At rise, THE WAITER, *in appropriate garb, is wiping the tables, vocalising like an opera singer, in rising and falling arpeggios.*

THE WAITER: Mu-mu-mu-mu-mu-mu-mu... Ma-ma-ma-ma-ma-ma-ma... Mi-mi-mi-mi-mi-mi-mi... [*He picks up two empty glasses.*] Ah! Talk about being in good voice! Some days... [*Singing.*]

> *Vesti la giubba, e la faccia infarina...*

Listen to that tone!... That vibrato!... That... [*Shrugging.*] And all for what?... [*Looking at the glasses.*] For this!... Beer, beer, beer!... For a bunch of no-goods who don't even know how to tip!... And they call this living!... Living! That's a laugh! [*Singing.*]

> *La gente paga e rider vuole quà...*

Ah! Just think how wild they'd go if they could hear me... The cheers, the applause... [*Daydreaming.*] Tonight... On stage... The Grand Opera of Valence... [*He pauses.*] Valence?... Hmm! The way things are, I wouldn't be choosy!... Still, with a voice like mine... [*With a gesture of resignation.*] Well, no use getting all hot and bothered... [*He exits, singing.*]

> *E se Arlecchin t'invola Colombina,*
> *Ridi Pagliaccio, e ognuno applaudira!*

[*The last few words are sung from the wings. After a few moments,* THE POOR BEGGAR *enters, pathetic relic of a sophisticated gentleman, but still elegant of manner and facile of tongue. He is dressed as neatly as his circumstances allow: shiny frock coat, old silk hat, etc. He lets himself fall in a heap onto one of the chairs.*]

THE POOR BEGGAR: Bah! Let them say what they please... I may have my faults... But damn! When it comes to working up a thirst... [*He shakes his head and smacks his lips.*] Monumental!... A veritable masterpiece of a thirst!... And alas! I should know! I've had them all in my day... Every size and shape... But never one like this! [*He takes a coin from his pocket and raps the table, calling.*] Waiter!... Up and down, up and down... Week after week, all those flights, flights, flights... My feet feel as if I've been scaling the heights! Why... [*He stops and reflects, smiling.*] Ha! Poetry, no less! "...all those flights, flights, flights... I've been scaling the heights..." Not very good, but at least it rhymes! [*He raps and calls again, louder.*] Waiter!

Waiter!... He'd better come soon, or he won't find much left but a dried up bag of bones!

THE WAITER'S VOICE [*offstage*]: Coming, coming...

[*He enters, and approaches* THE POOR BEGGAR*'s table.*]

THE POOR BEGGAR: No offense, but what kept you?

THE WAITER [*recognizing him*]: Ah, monsieur... I didn't know... [*Solicitously.*] And how is monsieur today? [THE POOR BEGGAR *shrugs.*] Still nothing? No job?

THE POOR BEGGAR [*sighing*]: Nothing, my good man... Less than nothing...

THE WAITER: Tsk, tsk!

THE POOR BEGGAR: Wherever I go, it's "sorry, no soap!", as they so quaintly put it.

THE WAITER [*with a silly little chuckle*]: What do they think monsieur is? A laundress?

THE POOR BEGGAR: You find humor in that, do you?

THE WAITER: No, no... But a little laugh now and then, monsieur... Well, what will it be? An absinth, as usual?

THE POOR BEGGAR: Absinth, my friend? For a thirst like mine?... Don't you know it's a sin to drink absinth when you're thirsty? An affront to the Almighty?

THE WAITER: Ah?

THE POOR BEGGAR: Absinth, merely to slake a man's thirst?... Absinth, when a vulgar brew will suffice...

THE WAITER: Monsieur wants a beer?

THE POOR BEGGAR: Please...

THE WAITER: Light or dark?

THE POOR BEGGAR: Light, my good man... [*Suddenly changing his mind.*] No, wait... Make it dark. Today I feel I have a penchant for brunettes...

THE WAITER: Yes, monsieur. One dark beer, coming right up... [*Singing.*]

> *His heart's a hopeless vagabond,*
> *Flitting betwixt brunette and blonde...*

[*He exits.*]

THE POOR BEGGAR: More truth than poetry, his asinine little ditty... Blondes... Brunettes... It's true, my heart never could seem to make up its mind. [*Waxing poetic.*] For some blondes I've known I'd have traded away every last brunette on this earthly sphere... And for some brunettes... Ah, for some brunettes I'd have given up the ghost... Not to mention the lovelies with their auburn hair, and the sweet-breathed young redheads...

[THE WAITER *enters with the glass of beer.*]

THE WAITER: One beer for monsieur!

[THE POOR BEGGAR *grabs it out of his hand and swallows it down in one gulp, as* THE WAITER *looks on in amazement.*]

THE POOR BEGGAR [*with a grimace*]: Ugh! That beer is vile!

THE WAITER: Monsieur?

THE POOR BEGGAR: Unutterably vile!

THE WAITER [*staring at the empty glass*]: But...

THE POOR BEGGAR: Undrinkable, you hear me?

THE WAITER: I never would have guessed...

THE POOR BEGGAR: Not fit to be drunk... Not worth the price...

THE WAITER [with a knowing wink]: Oh?... And what if monsieur liked it? I mean...

THE POOR BEGGAR: I'd have had myself another...

THE WAITER: Aha!... Well, we really don't go in too much for beer, monsieur.

THE POOR BEGGAR: No, I daresay you don't!...

THE WAITER [after a pause, changing the subject, sympathetically]: So, monsieur is still having his troubles, I see?

THE POOR BEGGAR: Alas! All too true! Still solidly entrenched among the ranks of the unemployed... And my meager savings growing slimmer by the day... [He counts out his money.] One franc, my good man, and forty centimes... My worldly wealth... To take me through the year...

THE WAITER: It won't take monsieur very far...

THE POOR BEGGAR: One miserable franc and forty centimes!... A tidy sum for certain corporate endeavors, certain profit-making enterprises better left unnamed... But a piddling nest-egg for one creature, like myself... Ah well! We can hope... And try to forget!... My absinth, young man! I think it's time!... Absinth, absinth! Time to escape on your heavenly wings from the bonds of this earthly prison called life!

THE WAITER [suitably impressed]: Aha!

THE POOR BEGGAR: Sometimes you may see a poor devil in the gutter. And you say: "Look, he's drunk!..." Well, you're wrong... He's no drunkard... He's an escapee, my friend. A wretched escapee...

THE WAITER: And the gendarmes come, and they lock him up, so he won't go try and escape again. Right?

THE POOR BEGGAR: Precisely...

THE WAITER: Straight absinth, monsieur?

THE POOR BEGGAR: Ha!... [Pointing to his money, sadly.] No... With anisette...

THE WAITER: One absinth with anisette, coming right up... [Singing, to the tune of "Alouette."]

> Anisette, gentille Anisette,
> Anisette, you take my cares away...

[He exits.]

THE POOR BEGGAR: Vulgar display of good humor!... Most offensive!... To see the likes of our warbling friend, gainfully employed... Bah! Salt on my wounds!... And employed in such a delightful capacity... Purveyor of oblivion, dispenser of escape...

[THE WAITER returns with the absinth.]

THE WAITER [singing]:

> Absinth hither, absinth yonder,
> Absinth makes the heart grow fonder...

[Speaking.] One absinth with anisette for monsieur.

THE POOR BEGGAR: I must say, you seem in uncommonly high spirits.

THE WAITER: Me, monsieur? Hardly!

THE POOR BEGGAR: One would think, to hear your incessant singing...

THE WAITER: Ah, monsieur shouldn't let my singing fool him.

THE POOR BEGGAR: I shouldn't?

THE WAITER: No, no... I don't sing because I'm happy, monsieur... I sing because... Singing is my life, my profession...

THE POOR BEGGAR [incredulous]: You?

THE WAITER: Absolutely, monsieur! I may look like a waiter, but... [Puffing up his chest.] Actually, I'm a tenor!

THE POOR BEGGAR: Oh? Curious...

THE WAITER: I know, but... Well, it's a very sad story. It's... [Sensing an audience.] Does monsieur have a minute?

THE POOR BEGGAR: A minute? You ask if I have a minute?... I have hundreds... Thousands... That's all I have... Minutes!... Come, come! Tell me your tale...

THE WAITER: If... If monsieur insists... [THE POOR BEGGAR nods.] He'll see he's not the only one... With troubles, I mean...

THE POOR BEGGAR [sententiously]: Life, my friend, is not a bed of roses.

THE WAITER: Well, it all began a few years ago... My first job... I was working as a waiter in a little café, near the Opéra-Comique... The old one, that is... I'm sure monsieur remembers...

THE POOR BEGGAR: Yes. The one that burned down.

THE WAITER: Right... Anyway, one day these two gentlemen come in... Real gentlemen... Reporters... And they hear me singing a few bars of something or other, and they tell me I've got a magnificent voice... Magnificent, they tell me... And everyone says I could wind up at the Opéra. So I drop everything and get myself a teacher, and start taking lessons. Well, in no time at all I'm singing a part... My first part, monsieur... In a little theatre, out in the country...

THE POOR BEGGAR: Success! Congratulations!...

THE WAITER: Ha! Don't I wish... One night, there I am, monsieur... Out on stage... I open my mouth, and all of a sudden... [He opens his mouth and points inside, like a mute.] No voice... Not a sound... I mean nothing... Not a peep!

THE POOR BEGGAR: Ah?

THE WAITER: Talk about luck!... So it's back on with the apron, and back to the café.

THE POOR BEGGAR: As good a profession as any, I daresay.

THE WAITER: Well, maybe monsieur thinks so... It's just not my idea... But there's more. I'm not through... I haven't been waiting on table for a week, and next thing I know, my voice is coming back!... [He pauses, waiting for a reaction that doesn't take place.] I bet monsieur finds that hard to believe.

THE POOR BEGGAR: Oh, I'll believe anything. Nothing would surprise me.

THE WAITER: Anyway, the minute I see I can sing... Well, it's off with the apron and back to the stage... [He pauses.] Monsieur can probably guess the rest.

THE POOR BEGGAR: Don't tell me. You lost your voice again.

THE WAITER: Exactly! And from then on, monsieur, it's the same old story... A magnificent voice when I'm waiting on table, and zero as soon as I get a part to sing.

THE POOR BEGGAR: Droll, to say the least... Of course, you do have a perfect solution.

THE WAITER: I do?

THE POOR BEGGAR: Elementary! You merely go find some cabaret, and ply both your trades... As a singing waiter...

THE WAITER [*musing*]: Hmm! That's not a bad idea, monsieur. I'll have to think it over.

THE POOR BEGGAR: Alas! My own problem isn't quite so simple. I'm neither a singer nor a waiter, I'm afraid. I'm an accountant... An accountant with no accounts... [*Wryly.*] A no-account accountant...

THE WAITER: Now, now... Monsieur shouldn't give up hope. Something is bound to turn up soon. Probably when he least expects it, too...

THE POOR BEGGAR: Thank you, my friend. I welcome the prediction. Frankly, I don't know how much longer I can wait... Upstairs, downstairs... Day after day... One humiliation after another...

THE WAITER: Humiliation is right! How well I know...

THE POOR BEGGAR: Oh, that's the least of my worries, the humiliation... I've had so much practice, I've even learned not to blush... Not the slightest tinge of red...

THE WAITER [*unthinking, ironically*]: No... Monsieur's hat does it for him!

THE POOR BEGGAR [*taking off his silk hat and noticing that, indeed, it has turned dark red*]: Alas, quite so! The old chapeau isn't what it used to be... [*Shaking his head.*] Hmm! Scarlet!... Absolutely scarlet!...

THE WAITER: Not at all like monsieur's coat... Turning all green, I mean... [*Catching himself, trying to soften the remark.*] A very pretty green...

THE POOR BEGGAR: Ah, Nature, Nature! How ineffable her mysteries! Time, that mischievous rogue! Wielding his palette of hues to suit his fancy... Turning old hats red, and old coats green! [*He holds the hat up to the sleeve of his coat.*] Yes, indeed! [*Sarcastically.*] See how nicely the coat sets off the hat!

THE WAITER [*on whom the sarcasm is lost*]: And vice-versa, monsieur.

THE POOR BEGGAR: How much greener the green... How much redder the red...

THE WAITER: It's really not bad, monsieur... The more I look at it... Not bad at all...

THE POOR BEGGAR: Yes, well... Thank you just the same! My own taste runs to less colorful shades of black!... [*Musing.*] Ah! When will I know the joy of buying a new suit? That's all... Nothing fancy, mind you... Even ready to wear...

THE WAITER: That isn't too much to ask, monsieur.

THE POOR BEGGAR: No, my friend... No... I've never been greedy. I've never expected too much out of life. Why, with five francs a day I could be the happiest man alive.

THE WAITER: Five francs, monsieur? That's a drop in the bucket!

THE POOR BEGGAR: Well, I could have made it do... And handsomely, believe me!... Five paltry francs... Ah! Where is the fairy godmother who would grace me with a pittance of five paltry francs a day?

[*All of a sudden the sounds of ethereal music can be heard, and* THE FAIRY GODMOTHER *enters.*]

THE FAIRY GODMOTHER: Hello! Did somebody call for a fairy godmother?

[THE POOR BEGGAR *and* THE WAITER *look on for a long moment in stunned, enraptured silence.*]

THE POOR BEGGAR [*finding his tongue*]: You mean... You... You're... You're really a...

THE FAIRY GODMOTHER: Quite! What's so surprising, if you don't mind my asking?

THE POOR BEGGAR: Nothing... It's just that... [*Recovering his aplomb.*] That is, one hardly expects to meet a real fairy godmother. Not face to face.

THE FAIRY GODMOTHER: I take it, poor beggar, you're the one who called.

THE POOR BEGGAR: Indeed, madame.

THE FAIRY GODMOTHER: And a good thing, too. I'm not one of those fairy godmothers who never bother to answer. I aim to please... Now then, poor beggar, what was it you had in mind?

THE POOR BEGGAR: Well, madame... As I was telling monsieur... [*He points to* THE WAITER.] With five francs a day I could be the happiest man alive...

THE FAIRY GODMOTHER [*laughing*]: Five francs a day?... Ha! No one can accuse you of extravagant tastes! Five francs...

THE POOR BEGGAR: Precisely what I was telling monsieur, madame... I've never been greedy...

THE FAIRY GODMOTHER: I should say! Five francs... And you're sure that would be enough?

THE POOR BEGGAR: Oh, more than enough!

THE FAIRY GODMOTHER: Well, if that's all it takes... So be it, poor beggar! Consider it done!

THE POOR BEGGAR [*ecstatic*]: You mean... You mean, you can actually do it?

THE FAIRY GODMOTHER: Of course I can, silly!... Why, that's child's play for a fairy godmother!

THE POOR BEGGAR: Ah...

THE FAIRY GODMOTHER: Just one problem, poor beggar... Since I've got better things to do with my time than run here every morning with five measly francs...

THE POOR BEGGAR: Of course...

THE FAIRY GODMOTHER: ...otherwise known to you simple mortals as one hundred sous...

THE WAITER: Or five hundred centimes...

THE FAIRY GODMOTHER: Well, if it's all the same to you, I'll just let you have the whole amount in one lump sum...

THE POOR BEGGAR [*unable to believe his ears*]: If it's all the... You'll just... [*Beside himself.*] In one lump sum?... The whole amount? In... In... [*Gesturing toward the table, as if stacking piles of gold.*] In one lump sum?

THE WAITER [*wide-eyed, pointing to the imaginary piles of money*]: See, monsieur? I told monsieur his luck was bound to change!

THE POOR BEGGAR [*to* THE FAIRY GODMOTHER]: And... And when, if I may ask... may I look forward to receiving...

THE FAIRY GODMOTHER: Tsk, tsk, poor beggar! Not so fast, not so fast... I need a few minutes to figure up the total. You wait here. I'll be back...

[*She exits, again to the strains of ethereal music.*]

THE WAITER: Ha! Talk about luck!... Monsieur was looking for a job, and instead he finds a gold mine!

THE POOR BEGGAR [*pursing his lips, as if to minimize the windfall*]: Well... A gold mine... I don't know... After all, five francs a day...

THE WAITER: Too bad monsieur didn't think to ask for more.

THE POOR BEGGAR: More? How did I know? How on earth could I imagine...

THE WAITER: What will monsieur do with all that money?

THE POOR BEGGAR [*sighing*]: First I'm going to buy myself a hat that's not so red, and a coat that's not so green. For a nice little change...

THE WAITER [*with his foolish little chuckle*]: Why not buy a green hat and a red coat, monsieur? For a real big change, I mean...

THE POOR BEGGAR [*as if taking him seriously*]: No, no, my friend. A proper gentleman must always avoid wearing garish attire.

THE WAITER: Ah... [*He pauses.*] I bet monsieur is going to have himself a time!

THE POOR BEGGAR: Oh yes, a fine time! The time of my life! [*Sarcastically.*] Wine, women and song!... On five francs a day? You're out of your mind!

THE WAITER: Oh, I don't know, monsieur... There are women and there are women. I know a few dancers at the Folies-Bergère...

THE POOR BEGGAR: You're right. Damn!... I should have asked for more... Twenty francs, while I was at it... It's all the same to her...

THE WAITER [*struck by an idea*]; In fact, if monsieur wants a good suggestion...

THE POOR BEGGAR: Yes?

THE WAITER: Well, since he's going to get the money in one lump sum... [*He points again to the imaginary piles of money on the table.*] Why not invest it?... An annuity or something... Instead of just eating away at the capital...

THE POOR BEGGAR: Well, I'm not too sure... Morally, that is... She agreed to five francs. She might take a dim view if I turned it into six.

THE WAITER: If monsieur doesn't mind my saying... I'm sure his morals are fine, but I think he's splitting hairs. After all, it's monsieur's money. He can do what he wants.

THE POOR BEGGAR: Perhaps... Perhaps... I'll give it some thought.

THE WAITER: Or even better, he could buy himself a night club... A cabaret, monsieur... That's where the money is! Hand over fist...

THE POOR BEGGAR: Indeed, my good man! I see your point! [*Wryly.*] A cabaret, where, to quote myself, you could ply both your trades... A champagne on your tray and a song on your lips...

THE WAITER: Well... [*Singing.*]

> *Champagne, champagne,*
> *You mischievous wine!*
> *You tickle my brain*
> *With your bubbles divine...*

THE POOR BEGGAR [*cocking his ear*]: Shhh!... Shhh!... [*The ethereal music has begun again.*] I think... [*Looking into the wings.*] Yes, there she is... My guardian angel! My celestial benefactress!... [*Watching as she approaches, offstage.*] But... Hmm! Where are the money-bags?... The sacks overflowing with coin of the realm?... She seems singularly unencumbered!

THE WAITER: She must have brought it all in bills.

THE POOR BEGGAR: I trust... Or in a check...

[THE FAIRY GODMOTHER *enters.*]

THE FAIRY GODMOTHER: Hello again, poor beggar! I hope things weren't too dull while I was gone.

THE POOR BEGGAR: Not at all, madame. I was chatting with monsieur... Discussing plans for the future... How to spend my money...

THE FAIRY GODMOTHER: Oh?

THE POOR BEGGAR: Yes... I haven't been able to make up my mind.

THE FAIRY GODMOTHER: Well, you will in a minute... Here you are, poor beggar...

[*She places a handful of coins on his outstretched palm.*]

THE POOR BEGGAR [*gazing at the coins in disbelief*]: But... But... But...

THE FAIRY GODMOTHER: The full amount... As promised...

THE POOR BEGGAR: But... That's... That's only seven francs and... and fifty centimes! You said I would get it all in one lump sum!

THE FAIRY GODMOTHER: That *is* your lump sum, poor beggar. That's all you've got coming.

THE POOR BEGGAR [*refusing to face the awful truth*]: Seven and a half... You mean... No! Say it isn't so! There's got to be more... You've got to be joking!... Tell me that you're joking...

THE FAIRY GODMOTHER: Poor beggar, I'll thank you to keep in mind, fairy godmothers don't joke!

THE POOR BEGGAR: In other words... If I know my arithmetic... And I am an accountant... In other words, you're telling me I have only a... a day and a half to live?

THE FAIRY GODMOTHER: Unfortunately, poor beggar... Some things even fairy godmothers can't change. I'm afraid my hands are tied. I'm sorry...

THE POOR BEGGAR: *You're* sorry!... A day and a half?

THE FAIRY GODMOTHER: Thirty-six hours, to be exact.

THE WAITER [*shaking his head compassionately*]: That's not a whole lot.

THE FAIRY GODMOTHER: You'll just have to try to make the best of it, poor beggar.

THE POOR BEGGAR: Make the best of it, you say?... [*Defiantly.*] Damn right I'll make the best of it!... And the most of it too!... [*Tossing his hat jauntily in the air.*] "Your father's mustache!..." Or words to that effect...

THE WAITER: Monsieur?

THE POOR BEGGAR: "A short life but a merry one!" That's my motto now... For the rest of my days... [*Correcting himself.*] My day, I mean...

THE FAIRY GODMOTHER: And a half...

THE POOR BEGGAR: And a half... [*To* THE WAITER.] All right... [*Giving a high kick, like a chorus-girl.*] Bring on the girls from the Folies-Bergère...

THE WAITER: Monsieur?

THE POOR BEGGAR: You heard me... Bring on the dancing-girls!

THE FAIRY GODMOTHER [*to* THE WAITER]: You heard him... The dancing-girls!

THE POOR BEGGAR: Tonight I go out in a blaze of glory!... And I'll start with an absinth... A Pernod... The best you've got...

THE WAITER: Yes, monsieur. With anisette?

THE POOR BEGGAR: No! Anisette be damned!... Straight, my friend! Straight!

THE FAIRY GODMOTHER [*to* THE WAITER]: You heard him... Straight!

THE WAITER: One Pernod for monsieur...

THE POOR BEGGAR: Unadulterated, unalloyed, pure, heavenly Pernod!

THE WAITER: Coming right up! [*Singing, to the melody of "Anges purs, anges radieux," from the last scene of Gounod's* Faust.[1]]

> *Pure Pernod, pure heav'n-ly Pernod!*
> *Let his soul fly from here below!*

THE FAIRY GODMOTHER [*joining in the spirit, singing*]:

> *And waft him from the prison infernal,*
> *To life, heavenly life, eternal!*

THE WAITER *and* THE FAIRY GODMOTHER [*majestically, singing together*]:

> *Pure Pernod, pure heav'n-ly Pernod!*
> *Let his soul fly from here below!*

THE POOR BEGGAR: Here, here!
[*All three freeze in a tableau of final apotheosis, as the curtain slowly falls.*]

CURTAIN

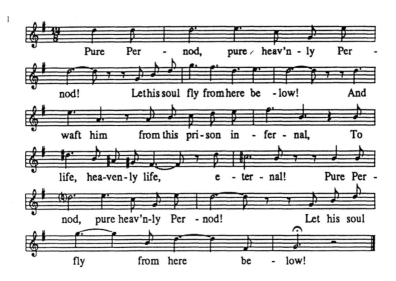

A FITTING CONFUSION

Adaptation of

Tailleur pour dames

by

Georges Feydeau

(1886)

CHARACTERS

MOULINEAUX, a doctor in his thirties, recently married but still with some wild oats to sow

BASSINET, a friend of his, affable but tactless and hapless in the extreme

DARTAGNAN, the husband of Moulineaux's latest conquest, a rake in his own right

ETIENNE, Moulineaux's tender-hearted and outspoken butler

YVONNE, Moulineaux's young wife, suspicious of his fidelity

MADAME AIGREVILLE, his shrew of a mother-in-law, particularly unattractive

SUZANNE, Dartagnan's wife, and Moulineaux's long-time pseudo-patient and would-be inamorata

MIMI, a déclassé friend from Moulineaux's student days, with pretensions to respectability

MADAME D'HERBLAY ⎫
                  ⎬ clients of a certain dressmaker
LILY   ⎭

Act One

The living room in Dr. Moulineaux's apartment. In the rear wall, center, a double door leading to the hall. Near the door, a small table. Down right, the door to Yvonne's bedroom; down left, the door to Moulineaux's. Up right and left, two more doors. Left of center, a desk and armchair. The desk is covered with books, papers, medical instruments, etc. Down right, an end table, flanked by two chairs. On the table, a small bell. Down left, a chaise longue. Other furniture, pictures, medical accessories, etc. ad libitum

At rise, the set is in semi-darkness, indicating that it is still early in the morning. ETIENNE *enters, up left, carrying a feather duster, broom, bucket, etc., and yawning sleepily.*

ETIENNE [*putting down his equipment and partially opening the double door to air out the room*]: There!... [*Rubbing his eyes, yawning.*] Aaah!... Of all times to have to get up! First thing in the morning! Did you ever see...? Just when you finally feel like sleeping... Really, it's all backwards. We do it all wrong. We should wait until we have to get up to go to bed. It would make more sense... [*Yawning.*] Aaah!... Talk about being tired!... [*He gives an even more energetic yawn.*] Aaaaaah!... [*Shaking his head.*] One more like that and I'll never get it shut!... I must be coming down with something... It's the liver, that's what it is... Mine, I mean. Not cook's... [*Yawning.*] I'll have to ask monsieur... That's one good thing about working for a doctor. When you're sick you don't get a bill to make you sicker! And for someone like me... [*Shaking his head.*] Talk about being sick... Really... Monsieur says I've got a bad case of "terminal inertia"... Whatever that is... Something about my *limp* glands... Anyway, I save a bundle. Of course, it was even better before... [*Yawning.*] Six months ago... Before he went and got married... But I shouldn't complain. Madame is very nice... As wives go, that is... And as long as there has to be one... [*Yawning.*] I suppose we could have done a lot worse, monsieur and me!... Well, time to wake him up... [*Moving down left, he stops at the door and shakes his head.*] Did you ever see?... [*Pointing down right, then down left.*] His room... Her room... Why bother to get married? I mean, if you're not even going to... [*With a shrug.*] I guess I'll never understand these society people! [*Knocking on the door, calling.*] Monsieur!... Monsieur!... [*After a pause.*] Hmm! Fast asleep!... I'd better go in... [*He opens the door and stands at the threshold.*] Monsieur!... [*Gaping.*] What? [*He disappears offstage for a few seconds, still speaking.*] Monsieur?... Monsieur?... [*Reappearing.*] And his bed isn't even slept in!... [*With a sudden realization, shocked.*] Oh! Don't tell me... No! I don't believe it!... No, no! Not monsieur!... Someone else, maybe, but... No! Not monsieur!... [*Looking across to the door, down right.*] And his wife... So trusting, poor thing... Did you ever see...?

YVONNE'S VOICE: Etienne?

ETIENNE: Oh my! Speak of the devil...

[YVONNE *enters, down right.*]

YVONNE: Ah, there you are!

ETIENNE [*moving upstage*]: Madame?

YVONNE: Is monsieur out of bed?

ETIENNE: Yes... Yes, he... No! I mean... Yes... That is...

YVONNE: What are you talking about, Etienne? Yes? No?... What on earth is the matter with you?

ETIENNE: The matter, madame?...

YVONNE: Yes! I ask you a perfectly simple question...

[*She crosses toward the door, down left.*]

ETIENNE [*quickly blocking her path*]: No, no! Madame shouldn't...

YVONNE: I what?

ETIENNE: It's monsieur... He's... He's... [*At a loss.*] He's sick!

YVONNE: Sick? My husband?

ETIENNE: Well...

YVONNE: Then I have to... [*Trying to get past him.*] Let me... If he's sick, for goodness' sake...

ETIENNE [*correcting himself*]: Maybe not sick, exactly... Not very, I mean...

YVONNE: But you said...

ETIENNE: And besides, it's... it's... [*Struggling to find an excuse.*] It's full of dust in there!... I've been sweeping... And... And the windows are wide open. Madame will catch cold!

YVONNE: Sweeping, Etienne? When monsieur is sick in bed? Really, what's got into you?

[*She pushes her way past him and into the room, down left.*]

ETIENNE: But madame... [*To himself.*] Oh my! He's done for now!... [*With a shrug.*] Well, he can't say I didn't try...

YVONNE'S VOICE: Oh! That... That...

[*She reappears.*]

YVONNE: That beast! That... That philanderer! [*Crossing right.*] That... That... [*Confronting* ETIENNE, *sarcastically.*] Well, Etienne! Very nice! Congratulations!

ETIENNE [*playing innocent*]: Madame?

YVONNE: "Sick" my foot!

ETIENNE: But I was only—

YVONNE: Monsieur would be proud of you! You're worth every sou he pays you, I'm sure!

ETIENNE: I was only trying to spare madame...

YVONNE: Yes, of course! How can I ever thank you?... [*At the door, down right.*] Oh! Six months, and already he... Oh!

[*She storms out.*]

ETIENNE: Poor thing! I don't blame her. Did you ever see...? It's a shame, that's what it is... Well, he'll never hear the end of it! And it will serve him right if you ask me! [*A knocking is heard offstage.*] Now who on earth...? At eight in the morning... [*More persistent knocking.*] Who's there?

MOULINEAUX'S VOICE [*in a loud whisper*]: Open the door, for heaven's sake! It's me!

ETIENNE [*to himself*]: It's about time!

[*He exits, upstage, ostensibly to open the outer door.*]

ETIENNE'S VOICE: Sorry, monsieur, I—

MOULINEAUX'S VOICE: Yes, yes... Never mind...

[MOULINEAUX *enters, in bedraggled evening clothes, looking very much the worse for wear, with* ETIENNE *at his heels.*]

MOULINEAUX [*softly*]: Just let me get to my room...

ETIENNE [*ingenuously*]: Has monsieur been out all evening?

MOULINEAUX [*at the door, down left*]: Shhh! Not so loud!

ETIENNE: Sorry! [*Repeating, in a whisper.*] Has monsieur been out all evening?

MOULINEAUX: What does it look like?... My wife doesn't know, does she?

ETIENNE: I'm afraid she has a strong suspicion, monsieur. She was here just a moment ago, and...

MOULINEAUX: Damn!

ETIENNE: And none too pleased, I might add... [MOULINEAUX *begins pacing nervously.*] Not that I blame her, if monsieur doesn't mind my saying...

MOULINEAUX: Not that you... What business is it—

ETIENNE: Tsk, tsk, tsk! If monsieur would take a friend's advice... A good friend...

MOULINEAUX: What? Who, damn it?

ETIENNE [*modestly*]: Me, monsieur.

MOULINEAUX: I beg your pardon! I'll thank you to remember your... Oh, never mind!... [*Pacing again.*] Good God, what a night! I should have had my head examined! A place like that!... And then, to have to sleep on that bench!... [*He sneezes.*] I'll be lucky if I don't come down with pneumonia!... The Folies Exotiques indeed!

ETIENNE: Ah? Monsieur spent the night at the Folies Exotiques?

MOULINEAUX: Yes... No!... I mean... Please, Etienne, it's none of your concern.

ETIENNE: One look, and anyone can tell he's been out all night... Doing heaven knows what...

MOULINEAUX: Really, that's quite enough! Go about your business, and leave me to mine!

ETIENNE: Very good, monsieur. I'm going... [*Shaking his head.*] Tsk, tsk, tsk! And at his age... Did you ever see...?

[*He picks up his equipment and exits, up center.*]

MOULINEAUX: Just what I need! A little folk wisdom from... [*Emphasizing.*] my *friend!*... Oh, that place!... Never again, believe me!... [*He sneezes.*] Never!... And it's not as if it was my idea, damn it!... But Madame Dartagnan... Suzanne... That gorgeous creature!... That... That vixen!... That... [*Sighing.*] Ah! I'm putty in her hands!... Those sweet little hands... You'd think I should know better!... "Never have a beautiful woman for a patient!"... That's what they used to tell us... "Especially if she's married... And has a husband... You'll be playing with fire!"... How right they were!... Only they should have added: "And be sure to stay away from the ones who love the Folies Exotiques, and who tell you to meet them there... Under the clock... At two in the morning... And to wait for them..." And wait, and wait, and wait!... She might as well have told me: "Till hell freezes over!"... So there I was, standing under that damn clock, like an idiot. Two... Two fifteen... Two thirty... By three, when I see that I don't see her... that she's nowhere to be seen... Well, you can imagine. I was fit to be tied. Not to mention that I could hardly keep my eyes open... So I came straight back here... "At least I'll get a good night's sleep," I told myself... Just one little problem... I get to the door, and... No key! I left it in my pants... My other ones... Before I got dressed... Dressed up, I mean... [*Sardonically.*] For my big night with Madame Dartagnan... Well, now what? Here I am, locked out of my own apartment... I can't very well ring the bell, or I'll wake Yvonne. I'd pick the lock if I had anything to pick it with... And if I knew how... So the only thing to do is to get some sleep and wait until it's light... On that damn bench downstairs... [*He sits down at his desk.*] Oh! If you never slept on a bench you don't know what you're missing!... I ache all over... [*He sneezes.*] And cold? You can't imagine! [*Picking up a pad and pen from the desk.*] Maybe I should write myself a prescription... [*He pauses.*] On second thought, not if I want to get better! [YVONNE *enters, down right.*]

YVONNE: Well, look who's here!

MOULINEAUX: Yvonne! I—

YVONNE [*interrupting, sarcastically*]: What a nice surprise! Of all people...

MOULINEAUX: You... I... Did you sleep well, my love?... I must say, you're up early.

YVONNE: And so are you, my sweet!

MOULINEAUX [*embarrassed, trying to be natural*]: Me?... Not really... No earlier than usual...

YVONNE: Oh?

MOULINEAUX: Well, maybe a little... Nothing like getting a nice early start... Especially when you have a lot of work to do...

YVONNE [*confronting him, point-blank*]: Where did you spend the night?

MOULINEAUX [*with a start*]: What?

YVONNE: I said: "Where did you spend the night?"

MOULINEAUX: I... I heard you... Where did I spend... You mean... [*With a nervous little laugh.*] You mean, you don't remember?

YVONNE [*curtly*]: Remember what?

MOULINEAUX [*stalling for time*]: What... What I told you... Yesterday, when I left... I... I did tell you, didn't I?... Just before I went out the door... Remember? [*Pointing upstage.*] You were standing there... and I was there... And I told you about... About Bassinet, remember? Poor Bassinet... I said: "I'm going to be with Monsieur Bassinet. He's sick... Terribly sick, and... and..."

YVONNE: And you spent the night with him...

MOULINEAUX: Exactly! I had to... You have no idea how sick he is, poor devil!

YVONNE [*sarcastically*]: Really?

MOULINEAUX: It was my duty, Yvonne! A doctor's first duty is to his patients... Even if it means sitting up with them all night...

YVONNE: Of course!... In evening clothes?

MOULINEAUX [*beginning to babble*]: Yes, in... in... in... No, not always, but... Look, I'll explain... Bassinet is very sick...

YVONNE: Yes, you said that.

MOULINEAUX: He's... He's at death's door. The least little shock could kill him, but... But he has no idea... And, naturally, we want to keep it from him.

So... So a few of us... A few of my colleagues and myself... Well, we decided to have our consultation, but to make believe it was a party... Everything very fancy... Evening clothes and all that... So he wouldn't suspect... A little dancing... You know... A little dancing, a little singing... [*He does a little dance, singing to the tune of* "Sur le Pont d'Avignon."]

> *Cholera, cholera,*
> *If you get it, you'll regret it.*
> *Cholera, cholera,*
> *Sorry friend, but that's the end.*
> *La la la, la la la...*

[*Speaking.*] Really, it worked like a charm. He never suspected a thing...

YVONNE: How clever!

MOULINEAUX: Well, sometimes we doctors have to tell a white lie...

YVONNE: Yes, don't you... Your duty to your patients, after all...

MOULINEAUX: Exactly!

YVONNE: Especially a patient like Bassinet, who's at death's door...

MOULINEAUX [*relieved at having apparently convinced her, with conviction*]: Especially...

[ETIENNE *appears at the double door, up center.*]

ETIENNE [*announcing*]: Monsieur Bassinet.

[BASSINET *enters in hat and coat, as* ETIENNE *exits.*]

BASSINET [*to* MOULINEAUX]: Good morning, monsieur.

MOULINEAUX [*under his breath*]: Good God!

BASSINET [*noticing* YVONNE, *nodding*]: Madame...

MOULINEAUX [*moving quickly to join* BASSINET *in front of the double door, in a whisper*]: Shhh! Don't say a word! You're sick! You're sick!

BASSINET: I'm what?

YVONNE [*with exaggerated affability*]: So nice to see you, Monsieur Bassinet! I hope you're well?

BASSINET [*jovially*]: Thank you, madame! You can see for yourself—

MOULINEAUX [*quickly interrupting*]: How sick he is! You can see how sick... [*To* YVONNE.] Just look... Death's door... [*To* BASSINET, *in a whisper.*] Will you please keep quiet! You're sick, I'm telling you...

BASSINET [*to* MOULINEAUX]: But why...

YVONNE [*to* BASSINET]: I must say, monsieur... You look quite healthy...

BASSINET [*to* YVONNE]: Thank you, madame!

MOULINEAUX [*to* YVONNE]: But he's not!... [*To* BASSINET.] You're not!

BASSINET [*to* MOULINEAUX]: I'm not?

YVONNE: And he says he feels so well!

MOULINEAUX: He says... He says... What does he know? Is he a doctor?... I'm telling you, he's at death's door!

BASSINET [*with a start*]: I am?

MOULINEAUX [*to* BASSINET]: Yes, yes, yes!... [*To* YVONNE.] Just look at him! [*To* BASSINET.] Only we've been trying to keep it from you... The least little shock could kill you! [*Aside.*] Too bad! Better him than me!

[*He moves upstage.*]

BASSINET: My God! What did he say?

YVONNE [*to* BASSINET]: Why yes, monsieur! Tsk tsk tsk! Didn't you know? [*Pointedly.*] That's why my husband spent all night with you...

MOULINEAUX [*aside*]: Ayyy!

BASSINET [*to* YVONNE]: He did?... When?

YVONNE: Why... Just last night... With all those other doctors... The party... The singing, the dancing...

MOULINEAUX [*frantically, to* BASSINET]: Of course! Don't tell me you don't remember! Or... Or... Or maybe you never noticed!... [*To* YVONNE.] Can't you see he's delirious? [*To* BASSINET, *in a whisper, face to face.*] Will you please shut up! All you do is put your foot in your mouth! [*He crosses up right.*]

BASSINET: What? [*Aside.*] If you ask me, he's the sick one! [*Tapping his temple with his forefinger.*] Sick in the head!

YVONNE [*moving toward* BASSINET]: Well now, Monsieur Bassinet... You be sure to take good care of yourself, won't you!... Even if you are the picture of health... [*Glaring at* MOULINEAUX.] For a man at death's door!

BASSINET: But...

YVONNE: Then again, there's no telling... You could linger for days...

BASSINET: But I—

MOULINEAUX [*with a casual wave*]: Oh, weeks!... Months!... Years!...

YVONNE: Yes, I'm sure...

BASSINET: But—

MOULINEAUX: Some people linger all their lives! It's possible...

YVONNE [*to* MOULINEAUX]: At death's door?

BASSINET: But I—

MOULINEAUX [*to* YVONNE]: Yes... It's... It's what we doctors call "chronic"...

YVONNE: And so seldom fatal...

BASSINET: But... But...

MOULINEAUX: Right! Only when they die...

YVONNE [*to* MOULINEAUX]: My! How interesting!

BASSINET [*to* MOULINEAUX]: Monsieur...?

YVONNE [*aside*]: He's not fooling me for one minute! I know what he's up to... [*Crossing up right.*] Just wait until I tell mamma about this! [*She exits.*]

MOULINEAUX [*to* BASSINET, *furious*]: You... You, you... Oh! Have you any idea what you... You and your big mouth! Can't you take a little hint, for heaven's sake?

BASSINET: A little... When you keep telling me I'm dying... What kind of a—

MOULINEAUX: Of course I did! And you... You kept denying it! You wouldn't shut up! Anybody else would have understood... But you...

BASSINET: Understood? Understood what?

MOULINEAUX: What's going on, goddammit!

BASSINET: But I don't have the slightest—

MOULINEAUX: If I tell you you're at death's door, you should stay put! I've got my reasons... But no! You've got to argue...

BASSINET: Please, I—

MOULINEAUX: Besides, who asked you to stick your nose in my business?

BASSINET: I beg your pardon? Stick my—

MOULINEAUX: And at a time like this! Today of all days!... If you had any common sense you wouldn't have come here in the first place...

BASSINET [*beginning to grow indignant*]: Really, monsieur—

MOULINEAUX [*angrily*]: A child would know better than to come to someone's home the morning after a gala at the Folies Exotiques... Especially when they told their wife they were with you the night before... Taking care of you... Because you were so sick...

BASSINET: The Folies... [*Suddenly comprehending.*] Oh!... You mean, you told madame... She thinks that you... That I... Oh! Well, why didn't you say so? I had no idea...

MOULINEAUX: No idea, no idea!... You have to spell everything out for some people!

BASSINET: Well, you can hardly expect me to—

MOULINEAUX: All right, never mind! The damage is done!... [*Brusquely.*] What is it? What do you want? [*Sarcastically.*] To what do I owe the pleasure...?

BASSINET: You mean, why am I here?

MOULINEAUX: So to speak...

BASSINET: Well, I'll tell you... As one friend to another... After all, what's the good of being friends if we can't do a little favor now and then? Don't you agree?

MOULINEAUX: I'm sure...

BASSINET: That's why I'm here...

MOULINEAUX [*aside*]: Now that's more like it! [*To* BASSINET.] Well, I never refuse a favor!

BASSINET: No, monsieur. That's why I came to ask you... I knew you wouldn't say no.

MOULINEAUX: Why *you* came to ask *me*...?

BASSINET: And I'll be terribly grateful, believe me...

MOULINEAUX [*realizing that he has misunderstood*]: Aha... I see... [*Aside.*] I should have known... [*Passing his hand in front of his eyes.*] You'll have to forgive me, monsieur. I'm rather tired this morning. I haven't had a wink of sleep...

BASSINET: Oh, I'm sorry...

MOULINEAUX: I had to spend the night on the bench, downstairs... And if you ever slept on a bench...

BASSINET: Me? Hardly, monsieur...

MOULINEAUX: Well, if you had, you'd know what I mean! I'm really not myself...

[*He sits down on one of the chairs by the end table, down right.*]

BASSINET: Quite all right... I understand...

[*He sits down on the other chair, next to him.*]

MOULINEAUX: Besides, my mother-in-law is coming in from the country this afternoon, for heaven knows how long, and... Well, what more do I have to say?

BASSINET: Indeed... Indeed...

MOULINEAUX [*aside*]: Now to get rid of him... [*He rings the little bell on the end table.*] If you don't mind, monsieur... I'll just be a moment.

BASSINET: Please...

[ETIENNE *appears at the double door.*]

ETIENNE: Monsieur rang?

MOULINEAUX [*getting up*]: Ah, Etienne... [*Joining him at the door, and speaking in a whisper, indicating* BASSINET *with a subtle nod.*] I want that pest out of here in five minutes, understand?

ETIENNE [*whispering*]: Yes, monsieur. The usual?

MOULINEAUX [*whispering*]: The usual... The calling card... Any one you can find... Someone who has to see me immediately... You know...

ETIENNE [*whispering*]: Monsieur can count on me...

MOULINEAUX [*aloud, pretending*]: And be sure everything is ready when madame's mother arrives.

ETIENNE [*aloud*]: Very good, monsieur.
[*He exits.*]

MOULINEAUX [*returning down right, sitting, to* BASSINET]: Now then, you were saying... Something about a favor...

BASSINET: Yes... I don't know if you recall, but last year my uncle died...

MOULINEAUX: Oh, tsk tsk tsk! I'm sorry to hear it...

BASSINET: No need to be, monsieur. I inherited a small fortune.

MOULINEAUX: You did? Congratulations!

BASSINET: Yes... And I used it to buy a house... Around the corner... On Rue de Milan... Number seventy...

MOULINEAUX [*feigning great interest*]: Aha... Aha...

BASSINET: The only trouble is, I'm having a devil of a time renting the apartments...

MOULINEAUX [*nodding sympathetically*]: Well...

BASSINET [*standing up*]: So I thought, if I came to you, maybe you wouldn't mind... Since you see so many patients... Well, I thought maybe you could help me try to rent one or two...
[*He takes a packet of prospectuses from his pocket.*]

MOULINEAUX [*jumping to his feet*]: What?

BASSINET [*handing him a prospectus*]: See? All the information...

MOULINEAUX [*furious*]: Help you try to... You mean to stand there and tell me you had the nerve...

BASSINET: But—

MOULINEAUX: ... to come here...

BASSINET: But monsieur—

MOULINEAUX: ...to burst in on me, first thing in the morning...

BASSINET: Please! Let me—

MOULINEAUX: ...to complicate my life, just for... for... [*He brandishes the prospectus.*] for your apartments?
[*He puts the prospectus into his pocket.*]

BASSINET: But don't you understand? It can help you too!

MOULINEAUX: Of all the...

BASSINET: My apartments are unhealthy! They're... They're cold and damp... They have drafts... They'll do wonders for your practice!

MOULINEAUX: They'll do... You can't be serious!... If you think for one moment I'm going to recommend your damn unhealthy apartments to anyone...
[*He crosses left.*]

BASSINET [*following him*]: Only some of them... Really!... Not all of them are that bad!...

MOULINEAUX: I don't care! Some of them... All of them...

BASSINET: Take One B, for example... It's a beauty! And all furnished!... It's a steal at the price... A dressmaker used to rent it, but she ran off without paying... It's really quite a story if you want a good laugh... You see, she was a dressmaker, I told you, but one day—

MOULINEAUX [*interrupting*]: Excuse me, but I'm not interested! I don't give a damn about your story or your apartment! And I couldn't care less about your dressmaker, understand?

BASSINET: My...? Oh no, not *my* dressmaker, monsieur... [*Chuckling.*] Why would I have—

MOULINEAUX: Whatever!

BASSINET: She was only my tenant...

MOULINEAUX: Yes... Well, what am I supposed to do with her?

BASSINET: You?... Why, nothing... But if you could help me rent her apartment...

MOULINEAUX: Look! That's enough about your apartment! You really picked a fine time... [*Crossing up right.*] As if I didn't have enough to worry about... [*Pointing to the door, up right.*] You saw, just now... My wife... Thanks to you!

BASSINET [*with a note of bitterness*]: Ah, monsieur... Don't complain... At least you have one. Some of us aren't so lucky... [*Sighing.*] Take me... I lost mine...

MOULINEAUX [*absentmindedly, nodding*]: Fine!... Fine!...

BASSINET: "Fine"? What's so fine about it?

MOULINEAUX [*correcting himself*]: Sorry! I meant: "Shame! What a shame!" [*Shaking his head.*] Tsk tsk tsk!

[*He moves down left.*]

BASSINET [*dramatically*]: Yes... Life can be cruel, monsieur! One minute I have a beautiful, lovely wife, and the next minute she's taken from me...

MOULINEAUX: That quick?... By what? Apoplexy?

BASSINET: No... By a soldier... I left them sitting on a park bench one morning... In the Tuileries... To go get a cigar... When I came back they were gone. That's the last I ever saw of her!

MOULINEAUX [*unconvincingly*]: What a shame!... Tsk tsk tsk!

BASSINET [*sighing*]: Oh well...

[*The doorbell rings.*]

MOULINEAUX [*aside*]: Ah, Etienne... Thank heavens!...

[*He moves up toward the double door as* ETIENNE *appears carrying a little tray with a calling card.*]

ETIENNE: Excuse me, monsieur, but there's a gentleman... [*Handing him the card, whispering.*] It was the only one I could find, monsieur. [*Aloud.*] He says he has to see monsieur immediately... Urgent business...

MOULINEAUX: Aha! [*With a broad wink to* ETIENNE, *back turned to* BASSINET.] Of course, Etienne... Of course... [*To* BASSINET.] I'm sorry, Monsieur Bassinet. You'll have to excuse me. [*Holding up the calling card.*] This fellow's a terrible nuisance, but I really have no choice. I'm afraid I'll have to see him...

BASSINET: Certainly... I understand...

MOULINEAUX [*trying to urge him out the double door*]: So please... You will excuse me...

BASSINET [*not budging*]: Believe me, I know the type...
MOULINEAUX: Yes, I imagine...
BASSINET: Some people are born pests... [MOULINEAUX *casts a meaningful glance at* ETIENNE.] You can never get rid of them. [*Sitting down on the chaise longue, down left, to* ETIENNE.] Show him in, young man!
MOULINEAUX: What?
BASSINET [*to* MOULINEAUX]: If he sees that you have a guest, maybe he'll take the hint and leave...
MOULINEAUX [*aside*]: Incredible! [*Aloud.*] But I'm sure it's a personal matter... [*Moving over to the chaise longue, waving the calling card in* BASSINET'S *face.*] I'm sure that Monsieur... Monsieur... [*He tries unsuccessfully to catch a glimpse of the name on the card.*] I mean, I'm sure he wants to speak to me in private!
BASSINET: Oh... Well, if you think so... [*Grabbing the card out of his hand.*] Monsieur Who?, by the way...
MOULINEAUX [*recoiling*]: I beg your—
BASSINET [*reading*]: Chevassus?... Why didn't you say so?... Old Chevassus! He's one of my dearest friends!
MOULINEAUX [*with a start*]: He is?
BASSINET: I'll just say hello, and then I'll be on my way.
MOULINEAUX: But... No! No!... You can't!... [*Grabbing the card back.*] It's... It's not him! It's... It's his father!
BASSINET [*laughing*]: His... Don't be silly! Chevassus? He doesn't have one... He never did!...
MOULINEAUX: But... But...
BASSINET [*reflecting on his last remark*]: That is... I suppose he did, but...
MOULINEAUX: I mean, his uncle!...
BASSINET [*hardly listening*]: ...but long ago, and...
MOULINEAUX: It's his uncle... [*Babbling.*] His brother's father... His... His father's son... His... His uncle...
BASSINET: Oh? His uncle?
MOULINEAUX: Yes!... Yes!... And I'm sure he'd rather not let anyone know he's here...
BASSINET: Aha...
MOULINEAUX: So please... [*He pulls him up bodily from the chaise longue.*] If you don't mind... Etienne will show you out... [*To* ETIENNE.] Etienne, monsieur is leaving...
ETIENNE [*still at the double door*]: Very good, monsieur.
[BASSINET *begins to move toward the door, but once there he stops.*]
BASSINET: Look... [*Moving to the door, up left.*] Why don't I just wait in here until he leaves? That will save me the trouble of coming back tomorrow...
[*He exits.* MOULINEAUX, *hands on hips, agape, watches in disbelief as he shuts the door behind him.*]
ETIENNE: Not meaning to contradict, but I believe monsieur is staying.
MOULINEAUX: Yes... It would seem... [*With a shrug.*] Well, let him! He'll have a good long wait in there...
[BASSINET *opens the door and pokes his head out.*]
BASSINET: I say...
MOULINEAUX: Now what?

BASSINET: I was just thinking... I can help you get rid of him if you like... It's a trick I use sometimes... I'll ring the bell and send in my card. You can tell him there's somebody who wants to see you... Some pest!... See what I mean?

MOULINEAUX: Oh, I do... I do... But it really won't be... [BASSINET *pulls his head back and shuts the door without waiting for* MOULINEAUX'*s answer.*] necessary, thank you!... I said... [*Letting himself fall into the armchair by the desk, shaking his head with a sigh.*] Some days, Etienne! Some days...

ETIENNE: Begging monsieur's pardon, but I should think that, as a doctor... Well... If I had the right to poison people, like monsieur...

MOULINEAUX [*getting up, yawning*]: Good God, what a morning! It never rains but it pours!... I can't keep my eyes open...

ETIENNE: Perhaps monsieur should get some rest... [*Rather ironically.*] After all he's been through...

MOULINEAUX: My sentiments exactly! [*He goes over to the chaise longue.*] What I need is a nap... [*He lies down and stretches out.*] A nice long nap... See that I'm not disturbed.

ETIENNE: Certainly, monsieur... [*He starts to leave, up center, as* MOULINEAUX *already begins to snore, but stops at the door.*] Does monsieur want me to wake him?

MOULINEAUX [*rousing himself*]: Hmm?... What?...

ETIENNE: I asked monsieur if he wants me to come and wake him.

MOULINEAUX: Yes... Tomorrow... Next week... Only not if I'm sleeping...

ETIENNE: Aha... Of course...

[*He exits, as* MOULINEAUX *falls asleep and begins to snore again. After a few moments the doorbell rings, followed by the sounds of general commotion offstage.*]

MADAME AIGREVILLE'S VOICE: I'm here, loves... I'm here!

ETIENNE'S VOICE: But... But...

[MADAME AIGREVILLE *bursts in, up center, closely followed by an anxious* ETIENNE. *She is carrying an overnight bag.*]

MADAME AIGREVILLE [*laying the bag down on the table by the double door*]: Yvonne!... Moulineaux!...

ETIENNE [*trying to quiet her*]: But madame, monsieur is—

MOULINEAUX [*waking with a start*] ⎱
                                    ⎰ [*together*]: ⎰ What in the name of—
MADAME AIGREVILLE   ⎱ I'm here!

ETIENNE [*to* MOULINEAUX]: Monsieur, it's madame...

MOULINEAUX [*jumping up*]: Already?... I mean...

MADAME AIGREVILLE [*to* ETIENNE]: Go call my daughter, young man...

MOULINEAUX [*to* MADAME AIGREVILLE]: Mother!... How nice...

ETIENNE [*at the door, up right, calling*]: Madame... Madame...
    [*He exits.*]

MOULINEAUX [*to* MADAME AIGREVILLE]: How nice to see you!

ETIENNE'S VOICE: It's madame's mother, madame...

MADAME AIGREVILLE: I'm early!

MOULINEAUX: Yes, yes... I see...

[YVONNE *appears at the door, up right, and runs to greet* MADAME AIGREVILLE, *center stage.*]

YVONNE: Mamma!

MADAME AIGREVILLE: Yvonne, precious! I'm here!

YVONNE: Let me look at you, mamma!

[*She gives her a kiss.*]

MOULINEAUX [*aside, rubbing his eyes*]: Damn! It's not a bad dream...

MADAME AIGREVILLE [*going over to the chaise longue, to* MOULINEAUX, *holding out her cheek*]: Moulineaux, you naughty boy! Aren't you going to give mother a nice big kiss too?

MOULINEAUX: Of course I am... As soon as I get over the surprise... the joy...

MADAME AIGREVIILE: Why thank you...

MOULINEAUX: ...the pleasure of waking up suddenly and finding you here... One minute, no mother-in-law... Next minute, there she is... [*Aside.*] Hovering like a harpie!... [*Aloud, to* MADAME AIGREVILLE.] It takes a moment to adjust... to calm the nerves...

MADAME AIGREVILLE: You sweet thing!

MOULINEAUX: Besides, I want to be wide awake. I want to savor the moment to the fullest.

MADAME AIGREVILLE [*on whom the irony is lost, throwing her arms around his neck*]: Moulineaux, you're a gem!

[*She gives him a resounding kiss.*]

YVONNE [*to* MADAME AIGREVILLE, *curtly*]: Yes, isn't he!

MOULINEAUX: I agree... A little tired, but a gem...

MADAME AIGREVILLE [*to* YVONNE]: You're such a lucky girl, Yvonne...

[*While* MADAME AIGREVILLE'*s back is turned,* MOULINEAUX *wipes his mouth surreptitiously on his sleeve.*]

MOULINEAUX [*with mock sincerity*]: Mother!

MADAME AIGREVILLE [*glancing back and forth at them, with a sob in her voice*]: So lucky... So lucky... I'm so happy to be here... And to see you both so... so happy...

YVONNE [*aside*]: Ha!

MADAME AIGREVILLE: So lucky...

MOULINEAUX [*to* MADAME AIGREVILLE]: And we're so happy, mother... to see you so happy... And so lucky that you could come... So lucky...

MADAME AIGREVILLE: Ah! Marriage agrees with you both, I can tell!... [*To* MOULINEAUX.] But tell me, son... Why are you all dressed up? You look as if you're going to a funeral...

MOULINEAUX: Why... It's for you, mother...

MADAME AIGREVILLE: What?

MOULINEAUX: I mean... In your honor...

YVONNE: He means, he's been up all night, mother. That's what he means!

MADAME AIGREVILLE [*to* MOULINEAUX]: You have?

MOULINEAUX: That is...

YVONNE [*pointedly*]: With a very sick patient...

MADAME AIGREVILLE: Tsk tsk tsk! Poor thing...

MOULINEAUX [*misunderstanding*]: Thank you...

MADAME AIGREVILLE: What?... No, no... Your patient...

MOULINEAUX: Oh...

YVONNE: Yes... Very, very sick. For months now he's had only a few days to live...

MADAME AIGREVILLE: Tsk tsk tsk!

YVONNE: And last night monsieur simply had to be at his bedside...

MADAME AIGREVILLE: Of course!... [To MOULINEAUX.] You doctors... So noble... So selfless...

MOULINEAUX [modestly]: Well...

YVONNE [aside, to MOULINEAUX]: So faithful...

MADAME AIGREVILLE: And you have to be out every night, Moulineaux?

MOULINEAUX: Every night?... [Absentmindedly.] No, no... But when there are parties, galas... [Catching himself, and coughing to cover his faux pas.] Sick parties... Patients... So many sick parties to care for... [Coughing.] Galore! Sick parties galore!...

MADAME AIGREVILLE: Do you have a cold, son?

MOULINEAUX [clearing his throat]: Just a little... My throat...

MADAME AIGREVILLE: And your wife isn't making you a nice hot camomile? [To YVONNE.] Really, love, you should!

YVONNE [very dryly, beginning to let her pique show through]: Oh, I wouldn't worry, mamma! I'm sure monsieur can take care of himself!... The way he takes care of all those sick parties!...

MADAME AIGREVILLE: Now, now...

YVONNE: With the very latest treatments!... With singing, and dancing, and...

MADAME AIGREVILLE: My goodness, Yvonne, you sound like an old passcrotch this morning!

YVONNE: I what?

MOULINEAUX [correcting]: Crosspatch... [To YVONNE.] Crosspatch... [To MADAME AIGREVILLE.] Yes, doesn't she! I was just telling her...

MADAME AIGREVILLE [to YVONNE]: What's the trouble, precious? Is something the matter?

YVONNE: The matter? [Pointing to MOULINEAUX.] Ask him!

MADAME AIGREVILLE [to MOULINEAUX]: Is something wrong, son? Are you having a little spat?

MOULINEAUX: Wrong, mother? [Ingenuously.] Why, no... Some people just get up on the wrong side of the bed...

YVONNE: And some people don't get up on any side at all!

MADAME AIGREVILLE: Now, now... Temper, temper... Is that any way for two newlyweds to behave?

MOULINEAUX: But really...

MADAME AIGREVILLE: Well, mother is here now and she's going to patch up our little lovers' quarrel... That's what mothers-in-law are for!

MOULINEAUX [aside]: Talk about the cure being worse than the disease!

[ETIENNE appears at the door, up left, carrying a calling card on a little tray.]

ETIENNE: Monsieur...

MOULINEAUX: Yes, Etienne? What is it?

ETIENNE [joining him, down left, in a whisper]: It's that gentleman, monsieur... He asked me to give monsieur his card...

MOULINEAUX [reading the card, aside]: Bassinet!... Oh, for heaven's sake!... No, not him again! [To ETIENNE, aloud.] Tell him I can't give him an appointment for at least a month.

MADAME AIGREVILLE: What is it, son?

MOULINEAUX: Nothing... No one important... Just one of my patients...

MADAME AIGREVILLE: But if he's sick... If he needs you...

MOULINEAUX: He can wait!

YVONNE [with a wry smile]: So noble... So selfless...

MOULINEAUX [to ETIENNE]: Go tell him, Etienne.

ETIENNE: Very good, monsieur.

[He goes to leave, up left.]

MOULINEAUX [stopping him]: Oh, and while you're there... My dressing-gown... [Pointing down left.] You know where I keep it?

ETIENNE: Certainly, monsieur.

MOULINEAUX: Good. No hurry, but next time you come in here, I'd like you to have it.

ETIENNE: Excuse me... Did I hear...? Monsieur would like me to...

MOULINEAUX: To have it... My dressing-gown...

ETIENNE: Oh, thank you, monsieur! Monsieur is much too kind!

[He exits, down left.]

MOULINEAUX [puzzled, aside]: I am?

[Suddenly BASSINET opens the door, up left, and pokes his head out.]

BASSINET: I say... You haven't forgotten me, I hope!

MOULINEAUX: You...? [Rushing up left and vigorously pushing him out.] Get out of here!...

[He slams the door in BASSINET's face.]

MADAME AIGREVILLE: What on earth...? [To MOULINEAUX.] Who is that person?

MOULINEAUX: Nobody!... A... A patient...

YVONNE: One of those sick, sick parties, mamma!

MADAME AIGREVILLE [to MOULINEAUX]: But... Then why don't you let him in?

MOULINEAUX: Impossible!... He's contagious!

MADAME AIGREVILLE: Him?

MOULINEAUX: And when I say "contagious"... [With a shudder.] Brrr!... Deadly!

YVONNE: Why yes! He's at death's door!

MADAME AIGREVILLE: That man?

MOULINEAUX: That's right!

YVONNE: Couldn't you tell?

MOULINEAUX: At death's door!

MADAME AIGREVILLE: But he looks so... so healthy...

YVONNE [glaring at MOULINEAUX]: Yes, doesn't he!

MOULINEAUX [aside]: Touché!

MADAME AIGREVILLE [aside]: No, there's something going on... If I could talk with Yvonne alone... [To MOULINEAUX.] Excuse me, son, but... Would you mind terribly if my daughter and I had a little chat... In private...

MOULINEAUX: Mind? Not in the slightest... Not when she's in one of her moods! Take your time...

[He exits, down left.]

MADAME AIGREVILLE [leading YVONNE to the chairs, down right]: Now then, precious... You can't fool, mamma... Come, tell me all about it.

[They sit down.]

YVONNE: Oh, mamma... It's... It's... [Breaking out in sobs.] It's a scandal!

MADAME AIGREVILLE: Oh, my! That bad?

YVONNE: Worse! Much worse... He... Moulineaux... He didn't come home...

MADAME AIGREVILLE: He didn't? When?

YVONNE: Last night...

MADAME AIGREVILLE: Last... [*Suddenly understanding.*] Oh, you mean... To sleep...

YVONNE: That's right...

MADAME AIGREVILLE: Last night?

YVONNE [*standing up*]: And who knows how many other nights before that? How would I ever know?

MADAME AIGREVILLE: How?... How, indeed!... I should think it would be obvious! Especially in bed, if you don't mind my saying...

YVONNE [*innocently*]: In bed?

MADAME AIGREVILLE: Really, Yvonne! Some things are too hard for a husband to hide!

YVONNE: But...

MADAME AIGREVILLE [*half in jest*]: You do have a bed, don't you?

YVONNE: Of course, I do...

MADAME AIGREVILLE: You...? And Moulineaux?

YVONNE: Oh yes... He has one too!

MADAME AIGREVILLE: "Too"?... But... Where do you people sleep?

YVONNE: Well... [*Pointing down right.*] There... And... [*Pointing down left.*] And there...

MADAME AIGREVILLE: What? You mean... After only six months...

YVONNE [*sheepishly*]: Oh, it didn't even take that long, mamma.

MADAME AIGREVILLE: Well, precious, there's your problem!

YVONNE [*naively*]: It is?

MADAME AIGREVILLE: I mean, how can a woman know where her man is sleeping, unless they sleep together? It's elementary...

YVONNE: Well, I suppose...

MADAME AIGREVILLE: Married or not... It's only logical, love...

[*Suddenly the door, up left, opens, and* BASSINET *appears, carrying his hat and coat.*]

BASSINET: Oh, pardon me... I thought—

[*He moves downstage.*]

MADAME AIGREVILLE [*jumping up*]: You!... [*To* YVONNE.] It's him! [*Waving him off, as she takes refuge behind the chairs.*] Get away! Get away!

BASSINET [*to* YVONNE]: I wanted to see the doctor...

YVONNE: Yes, I'm sure! To trump up more lies, I suppose!

BASSINET: What?... No... I... [*Taking a few steps, to* MADAME AIGREVILLE.] Madame, is the doctor—

MADAME AIGREVILLE [*recoiling*]: Get away, I told you!... Go to bed! Go to bed!

BASSINET [*moving closer to her*]: But madame, I'm not tired!

MADAME AIGREVILLE [*moving around the chairs, trying desperately to avoid him*]: I don't care! Go to bed!... When you're sick, you go to bed!

BASSINET: Sick? [*Aside.*] What's the matter with these people? [*To* MADAME AIGREVILLE, *trying to approach her.*] Then you'll tell him...? You'll tell the doctor...?

MADAME AIGREVILLE [*waving him off*]: Yes! Anything you say!...

BASSINET [*catching her hand, about to bring it to his lips, with a little bow*]: Thank you, madame... Enchanté, I'm sure...

MADAME AIGREVILLE [*horrified, pulling her hand away, with a shriek*]: Ayyy!... Don't touch me!... Get away! Get away!... Go infect someone else!

[BASSINET *gives a shrug toward the audience as* MADAME AIGREVILLE *frantically wipes her hand on her clothing.*]

BASSINET [to MADAME AIGREVILLE, *bowing*]: Madame... [*To* YVONNE.] Madame... [*Aside.*] They're crazy! Every one of them!

[*He bows his way back to the door, up left, and exits.*]

MADAME AIGREVILLE [*still wiping*]: I wish my son-in-law would leave his patients at home, like every other doctor!... The idea... [*To* YVONNE.] All right now... What's this about your husband? You say he's been gallivanting?

YVONNE: Yes, mamma! I'm sure of it!

[*She begins sobbing again.*]

MADAME AIGREVILLE: Now, now, now... Tell me all about it... First of all, who is she?

YVONNE: "She," mamma? Who?

MADAME AIGREVILLE: Who? Why, the other woman! Who else?... When a man doesn't come home at night, he's not sleeping in the park!

YVONNE [*sighing*]: No, I don't suppose...

MADAME AIGREVILLE: Have you found anything?... You know... A key, an earring...

YVONNE: Well... [*Pulling a lady's glove from her bosom.*] Just this... I found it yesterday in his coat... When I was going through his pockets...

MADAME AIGREVILLE [*taking it from her*]: Hmm! A lady's glove!... That's a start!... And anything in his papers? Any letters...

YVONNE: Oh, mamma! I wouldn't look through his papers!

MADAME AIGREVILLE: You wouldn't...? Come now, precious! How else are you supposed to find out what's in them? Wives do it all the time.

[MOULINEAUX *appears at the door, down left.*]

MOULINEAUX: Well, still having our little chat?

MADAME AIGREVILLE [*to* YVONNE]: I'll take care of this, love. Let me talk to him alone.

YVONNE: Yes, mamma.

[*She stalks off, down right, without giving* MOULINEAUX *a look.*]

MOULINEAUX [*aside*]: I hope the old battle-axe has cooled her off a little!

MADAME AIGREVILLE [*sharply*]: Monsieur!

MOULINEAUX [*aside*]: Oh oh... I guess not... [*To* MADAME AIGREVILLE, *sweetly, joining her center stage.*] Mother?

MADAME AIGREVILLE: I won't beat around the bush! [*Holding up the glove, which she has been holding behind her back.*] Does this look familiar?

MOULINEAUX: That...? Oh, thank you... I've been looking all over—

[*He reaches for the glove.*]

MADAME AIGREVILLE [*slapping his hand with it*]: Not so fast, monsieur! Whose is it?

MOULINEAUX [*ingenuously*]: Whose is what?

MADAME AIGREVILLE: This, monsieur!

MOULINEAUX [*as innocently as possible*]: Why... It's mine... Whose do you
think...

MADAME AIGREVILLE: Yours? A glove this size?

MOULINEAUX: Yes, it's... It's the latest thing for rheumatism... Does wonders
for the circulation... Tightens the nerves... Massages the joints... It's... It's...

MADAME AIGREVILLE [*finishing the sentence*]: It's a lady's glove, monsieur.

MOULINEAUX: A lady's... Oh no!... [*With a little forced laugh.*] It might look
like a lady's, but that's only because it shrank... In the rain... It got all wet...

MADAME AIGREVILLE [*pulling the glove lengthwise*]: And the length,
monsieur?... Have you ever seen a man with fingers this long?
[*Sarcastically.*] Even one whose nerves need tightening... And whose joints
need massaging!

MOULINEAUX: Exactly! It... It shrank in the width and... and got longer in the
length... The rain always does that... The moisture... Something in the
molecules...

MADAME AIGREVILLE [*nodding, ironically*]: I'm sure... Very interesting, thank
you... [*Holding up the glove.*] Especially since it's marked size six and a
half...

MOULINEAUX: Nine!... Nine and a half!... You've got it upside down...

MADAME AIGREVILLE [*losing patience, hands on hips*]: Really, monsieur!
That's enough! What kind of fool do you take me for?

MOULINEAUX [*aside*]: Any kind... I'm not fussy...

MADAME AIGREVILLE: Do you want to know the truth? [*Not waiting for an
answer.*] I'll tell you... You're a cad! An absolute cad! And you don't
deserve a wife like my Yvonne, you... you lecher!

MOULINEAUX: What?

MADAME AIGREVILLE: Yes! I said it and I'm glad! You're a lecher, monsieur!
A depraved, degenerate lecher...

MOULINEAUX: I beg your—

MADAME AIGREVILLE: ...who stays out all night... Heaven only knows where!...
And who comes home with women's gloves in your pocket...

MOULINEAUX [*correcting*]: Glove... One glove...

MADAME AIGREVILLE [*emphasizing*]: *Women's* gloves, monsieur!

MOULINEAUX: But I told you... The moisture...

MADAME AIGREVILLE: Now you just listen to me! If you're cheating on my
daughter... If you dare... I'm warning you! You'll have me to answer to!
And don't you forget it!

MOULINEAUX [*recoiling*]: I... Me? Cheating?

MADAME AIGREVILLE [*pressing her attack*]: I'll thank you to remember you're
a married man, monsieur!... And you've sworn to be faithful...

MOULINEAUX [*beginning to resist*]: To her, damn it! Not to you!

MADAME AIGREVILLE: The law says a wife is supposed to follow her husband.
Well, let me tell you, my friend... We'll follow you! We'll follow you to
the ends of the earth if we have to!

MOULINEAUX: "We"? "We" who?... The law says "the wife"... It doesn't say
anything about her mother, goddammit!

MADAME AIGREVILLE: Well, it should! Whose fault is that?

MOULINEAUX: Of course! I guess they just forgot!

MADAME AIGREVILLE: What kind of a heartless creature are you? To want to
separate a mother from her daughter... From her own flesh and blood...

MOULINEAUX [*at a loss for words*]: "What kind of a..."
MADAME AIGREVILLE: Heartless! Simply heartless!
MOULINEAUX: Oh... [*Exploding.*] Go to blazes!
MADAME AIGREVILLE: What? What did you say?
MOULINEAUX: You heard me! I've had enough of your nagging!
MADAME AIGREVILLE: Monsieur! I never—
MOULINEAUX: I'll do what I please! I don't have to answer to you...
MADAME AIGREVILLE: How dare—
MOULINEAUX: Or to anyone else, thank you! And I don't have to let you stand there and rip me to pieces...
MADAME AIGREVILLE: That's right! Tell me to leave!
MOULINEAUX [*furious*]: You can do what you like!
MADAME AIGREVILLE: I never... [*To herself.*] And then they blame the mother-in-law! [*To* MOULINEAUX, *coldly.*] I'm beginning to feel very unwelcome, monsieur!
[*She moves upstage.*]
MOULINEAUX [*aside*]: Beginning! [*To* MADAME AIGREVILLE, *following her.*] What do you expect? When you keep butting in...
MADAME AIGREVILLE: Go ahead! Tell me to leave, why don't you? [*Dramatically.*] Throw me out of my own daughter's house! Go ahead!
MOULINEAUX: Oh...
MADAME AIGREVILLE: Well, you won't have to tell me twice!
MOULINEAUX [*about to lose his temper*]: You... Good God! Let me out of here before I... [*Resisting the urge to strangle her.*] Oh! That woman!... [*Turning to leave, aside.*] She could give the Lord himself an ulcer!
[*He storms out, down left.*]
MADAME AIGREVILLE [*gradually regaining her composure*]: All the same... Every one of them... Just like my Wenceslas and my poor saint of a mother!... Before he went and died, that is... Well, I know when I'm not wanted! Nothing on earth could keep me here... Not even for one night!... Even if I have to go sleep in the street!
[*The door, up left, opens, and* BASSINET *appears, still carrying his hat and coat.*]
BASSINET [*looking around, aside*]: Where in the name of... How much longer...
MADAME AIGREVILLE [*without noticing him*]: In the meantime, I'd better try to find myself a place to live...
BASSINET [*overhearing*]: What? Did I hear you say you were looking for a place to live, madame?
MADAME AIGREVILLE: I... [*Turning and seeing him.*] Oh! You!
[*She takes refuge behind the desk.*]
BASSINET [*aside*]: Again? What on earth...? [*To* MADAME AIGREVILLE, *chasing her around the desk.*] Listen... Stop...
MADAME AIGREVILLE: Get away! Get away!
BASSINET: Please... I've got just what you're looking for... You can move in right away... And it's furnished, madame... A lovely little apartment...
MADAME AIGREVILLE [*stopping, interested*]: Oh?
BASSINET: Yes... Just a stone's throw... Seventy Rue de Milan... One B...
[*He holds out a prospectus. She pulls back, obviously unwilling to touch him. Finally he hits on the expedient of passing it to her on the crown of his*

hat.]
MADAME AIGREVILLE [*holding it gingerly*]: And... And you say you live there, monsieur?
BASSINET: Me?... [*Laughing.*] No, no, no!... A dressmaker used to, but... It's really quite a story, if you want a good laugh... You see—
MADAME AIGREVILLE [*cutting him off*]: Yes, that's fine... And it's safe? No health problems... No germs, no drafts...?
BASSINET: Safe, madame? To live there, you mean?
MADAME AIGREVILLE: Of course, to live there... What else—
BASSINET: Because sometimes people rent by the night... You know... [*With a broad wink.*] To bring their friends.
MADAME AIGREVILLE [*shocked*]: What?
BASSINET [*realizing his faux pas*]: But I'm sure that's not what you had in mind...
MADAME AIGREVILLE: Indeed!
BASSINET: Well anyway... No germs, no drafts... It's as safe as an apartment can be.
MADAME AIGREVILLE: Aha...
[*During the ensuing exchange, she gradually moves up left, followed at a distance by* BASSINET.]
BASSINET [*aside*]: As long as you don't breathe!... [*To* MADAME AIGREVILLE.] No problems, madame...
MADAME AIGREVILLE: Well...
BASSINET [*with a shrug, aside*]: What do I care? A total stranger!...
MADAME AIGREVILLE: If you're sure...
BASSINET [*aside*]: And besides, it's a favor to Moulineaux... I'll be taking her off his hands... [*To* MADAME AIGREVILLE.] Of course, madame! Of course! [*Aside.*] What are friends for, after all?
MADAME AIGREVILLE [*up left*]: Very well! I'll have a look at it...
BASSINET [*rubbing his hands*]: And you'll love it, believe me!
[*The door, down left, opens, and* MOULINEAUX *enters.*]
MOULINEAUX [*talking to himself*]: Where the devil is that Etienne with my dressing-gown?
MADAME AIGREVILLE [*to* BASSINET]: Excuse me, monsieur... [*Loud enough for* MOULINEAUX *to hear.*] It's getting a little crowded!
BASSINET [*looking around, naively*]: It is?
MADAME AIGREVILLE [*to* BASSINET]: We'll discuss the matter later.
[*She crosses down right, her nose in the air, without deigning to glance at* MOULINEAUX, *and strides out the door into* YVONNE's *room.*]
MOULINEAUX [*watching her leave, to himself*]: No change, I see!
BASSINET [*to* MOULINEAUX]: I say, monsieur... If you want to get the old bag off your hands...
MOULINEAUX: Ah, Bassinet! Just the man I was looking for!
BASSINET [*surprised*]: I am?... But I thought...
MOULINEAUX: You know your apartment... One B... The dressmaker...
BASSINET: Yes...
MOULINEAUX: Well, I've been thinking. I'm going to rent it from you.
BASSINET: You are? [*Aside.*] Drat! Maybe I should auction it off to the highest bidder!

MOULINEAUX: Because... Well, I suppose I can tell you... I'm sure you'll be discreet...

BASSINET: Discretion itself, monsieur...

MOULINEAUX [*confidentially*]: You see... I need a little place to... to...

BASSINET: To bring a friend!

MOULINEAUX: Exactly!... But all very platonic... At least, it is so far. You see, she's a married woman... A patient of mine... I've been treating her for years...

BASSINET: Aha... And what does her husband have to say about all this?

MOULINEAUX [*laughing*]: Her husband?... Who knows? Who cares?... I've never even met him... [*Taking* BASSINET's *prospectus from his pocket.*] Now tell me... How much are you asking?

BASSINET [*pointing to the prospectus*]: Just what it says... Two hundred fifty francs.

MOULINEAUX: A year?... You're right, it's a steal!

BASSINET: Excuse me, monsieur... A month... Of course, if that's too expensive, you can rent it by the hour...

MOULINEAUX: No, no... By the month will be fine! I'll take it!

BASSINET [*unable to believe his ears*]: You will?... When?

MOULINEAUX: Today... Right away... As soon as I can have it...

BASSINET: Today? Well, I don't know... It's not quite ready... I mean, everything is rather helter-skelter and topsy-turvy... All the dressmaker's things... She left in such a hurry!

MOULINEAUX: Yes...

BASSINET: It's really quite a story... You see, she had a—

MOULINEAUX [*cutting him off*]: Yes, yes... Later... You'll tell me tomorrow... Right now all I want is the key.

BASSINET: But I told you, it's not ready...

MOULINEAUX: No problem... I'll make do...

BASSINET: Well, if you're sure...

[ETIENNE *appears at the door, up center, wearing* MOULINEAUX's *dressing-gown.*]

ETIENNE [*announcing*]: Madame Dartagnan, monsieur... For her consultation...

MOULINEAUX: Ah! [*To* BASSINET.] Look... If you don't mind...

BASSINET: Another pest, monsieur? If you want I can ring the bell and send in my—

MOULINEAUX [*pushing him toward the door, up left*]: No, no! That won't be necessary!... You go in here and... and write up the lease... That's it... Write up the lease...

BASSINET: Aha! Good idea!

[MOULINEAUX *pushes him out the door.*]

MOULINEAUX [*to* ETIENNE]: Tell madame... [*Noticing his dressing-gown.*] Etienne! My dressing-gown!... Just what do you think you're—

ETIENNE: But monsieur said... He told me: "I'd like you to have it, Etienne..." And very generous of him!

MOULINEAUX: What?... *With* you, damn it! Not *on* you!

ETIENNE [*sheepishly*]: Oh... I see...

MOULINEAUX: Of all the...

[*The door, up center, opens, and* SUZANNE *enters quickly.*]

SUZANNE [*to* MOULINEAUX]: Monsieur...
MOULINEAUX: Ah... Madame... I was just... [*To* ETIENNE.] You can go now, Etienne.
ETIENNE: Very good, monsieur. [*Aside, shaking his head.*] Did you ever see...? I was sure he told me...
[*He exits, up center.*]
MOULINEAUX [*to* SUZANNE, *as soon as* ETIENNE *has closed the door*]: Suzanne!
SUZANNE: Balthasar!
MOULINEAUX [*cajoling*]: You naughty thing, you!... "Meet me under the clock!"... I could still be waiting!
SUZANNE: I know, dearest! I'm so terribly sorry... Can you ever forgive me?
MOULINEAUX: Well, maybe... [*Suggestively.*] That depends...
SUZANNE: I was sure that my husband would be going off, as usual... And then I would be free... And we... You and I... [*With a passionate sigh.*] Balthasar!
MOULINEAUX: Suzanne!
SUZANNE: But no... He stayed, and stayed, and stayed... He simply didn't budge! The whole night long! I couldn't get rid of him!
MOULINEAUX: I suspected it must be something...
SUZANNE: The man hasn't let me out of his sight for days. He acts that way sometimes. It's almost as if he didn't trust me...
MOULINEAUX: No! You?...
SUZANNE: In fact, he's waiting downstairs at this very moment. He wanted to come up with me, but I told him I didn't think he should... To the doctor's after all...
MOULINEAUX: Of course not! It's not ethical! It just isn't done...
SUZANNE: No... That's what I told him.
MOULINEAUX: And a good thing you did... [*Aside.*] You should never meet the husband. It's bad for the conscience! [*Aloud, gazing romantically into her eyes.*] Ah, Suzanne...
[*He takes her by the hand and leads her down right, to the chairs.*]
SUZANNE: Ah, Balthasar, Balthasar, Balthasar!... What are we doing?... It's madness, I tell you!... I shouldn't be here! I shouldn't...
MOULINEAUX: Yes, you should! Of course you should!
SUZANNE: But... [*Sighing.*] It's too late to turn back... Tell me it's too late...
MOULINEAUX: That's right! It's too late... Come...
[*He holds out one of the chairs for her.*]
SUZANNE: It's just that... This is the first time I've ever... [*Sitting down.*] The very first... Really... Because, I never—
MOULINEAUX [*sitting down next to her*]: I know... I know... And that's why... Ah, Suzanne! I can't tell you the thrill... the bliss... the... [*Waxing lyrical.*] the ecstasy! To know that I'm the first...
SUZANNE: Ah, Balthasar!
MOULINEAUX [*coming back to earth*]: But still, we can't take chances...
SUZANNE: Dearest?
MOULINEAUX: We can't go on meeting like this... Not here... A visit to the doctor is a wonderful excuse, but it can't last forever.
SUZANNE: But...
MOULINEAUX: People will notice. They'll begin to talk...
SUZANNE: Of course... I never thought...

MOULINEAUX: And it won't take them long to discover the truth!... That... That
this is no everyday doctor and patient, but... [*Waxing poetic again.*] but two
passionate hearts... two noble souls yearning to be one, *and to soar off
together to the giddying realm of love!*

SUZANNE: Oh, Balthasar! You're so right! It's all bound to come out...

MOULINEAUX: That is, unless we're careful...

SUZANNE: But how? What can we do?

MOULINEAUX: Well, I was thinking... There's no reason why we can't keep
meeting... As long as it's in some—how shall I say?—some neutral arena...

SUZANNE: Oh no! Not an arena!... I'd much rather a nice little apartment... Like
in the novels.

MOULINEAUX: Exactly! And I've got one!

SUZANNE: You have?

MOULINEAUX: Yes! And it's perfect! Just around the corner... On Rue de
Milan... Number seventy... A cozy little furnished apartment... Just the two
of us... And we can have it any time. Today if you like...

SUZANNE [*having second thoughts*]: Well, I don't know... An apartment... I'm
not sure, Balthasar...

MOULINEAUX: But what's the difference? Here or there? It's just so much
safer... No wagging eyes, no prying tongues...

SUZANNE: Yes... I suppose you're right... [*Resolutely.*] Well, why not!

MOULINEAUX: That's what I say! Why not!

SUZANNE: As long as it's all still *plutonic*, you understand...

MOULINEAUX: "Plu..." [*Hypocritically.*] Certainly! What do you take me for,
Suzanne!

SUZANNE: Because I'd never cheat on my husband, Balthasar!

MOULINEAUX: You'd never... Heaven forbid, my dear lady! The thought never
entered my mind!

SUZANNE: I should hope not...

MOULINEAUX: No, no... Strictly "plutonic"... I give you my word...

SUZANNE [*standing up*]: Then it's settled. In an hour... Seventy Rue de Milan...

MOULINEAUX: One B...

SUZANNE: One B...

MOULINEAUX [*standing up*]: In an hour!

SUZANNE: An hour!... [*Moving upstage.*] Oh, Balthasar! What must you think of
me?... You must think I'm perfectly awful! But really, this is the first time
I've ever... The very first... Really...

MOULINEAUX: I know... I know... [*Aside, as* SUZANNE *reaches the double door.*]
That was easier than I expected!

SUZANNE: Well, I'd better be going. My husband will be wondering...

MOULINEAUX [*joining her, taking her hand*]: If you must, you must. But it's
only au revoir...

[*Just as he is about to bring her hand to his lips, the door opens and*
ETIENNE *appears, still in the dressing-gown.*]

ETIENNE: A gentleman who says he's Monsieur Dartagnan, monsieur...

[*He moves down right.*]

MOULINEAUX [*moving left*] ⎫   ⎧ Who?... But I don't want to see—
                              ⎬ [*together*]: ⎨
SUZANNE [*pulling away*] ⎭   ⎩ My husband? Good heavens!

[DARTAGNAN *enters, up center, coat in hand.*]

DARTAGNAN: Good morning... [*To* SUZANNE.] Ah, Suzanne...

SUZANNE: Anatole!... I was just leaving...

DARTAGNAN [*casually*]: Fine!... I'll join you in a moment. After I've had a quick word or two with the doctor... [*To* MOULINEAUX, *noticing him in his evening clothes and mistaking him for a butler, handing him his coat.*] Thank you, my good man... [MOULINEAUX *stands staring at him blankly for a moment.*] That will be all... [*Waving him off.*] If you don't mind... This is a private conversation... [*To* ETIENNE, *holding out his hand.*] Doctor Moulineaux!... What a pleasure... After all these years...

ETIENNE [*startled, shaking his head*]: Monsieur...

[MOULINEAUX'*s jaw drops in disbelief.*]

SUZANNE [*to* DARTAGNAN]: But... But Anatole...

MOULINEAUX [*in a whisper, to* SUZANNE]: Shhh! Never mind! It's better...

[*He pushes her out the double door, then crosses down left and exits.*]

DARTAGNAN [*to* ETIENNE]: Well, now that we're alone... I thought, since I· was so close... I'm sure it's probably nothing, but it seemed like a good time... You see, I've been getting these nosebleeds recently, and my feet fall asleep.

ETIENNE: Aha... Very interesting... At the same time?

DARTAGNAN: Well, not always...

ETIENNE: Have you tried holding your breath and counting to ten?...

DARTAGNAN: No... No...

ETIENNE: Or putting your head in a sack?...

DARTAGNAN: My head... [*Objecting feebly.*] But... But I thought those were for hiccups...

ETIENNE: Right... Right... I meant, a key...

DARTAGNAN: Monsieur?

ETIENNE: A cold key... You press it against the back of your neck...

DARTAGNAN: Aha...

ETIENNE: A dining-room key...

DARTAGNAN: Does it have to be the dining-room? Won't the front door do as well?

ETIENNE: No, no! The dining-room... Then you pinch your nose shut and stick your head in a basin of water... For an hour and a half...

DARTAGNAN: What?... An hour and a... But... How on earth do I breathe?

ETIENNE: Through your mouth...

DARTAGNAN: Under water?

ETIENNE: It cures nosebleeds, monsieur...

DARTAGNAN: Yes... And anything else!... I... I think I'd rather not...

ETIENNE: It's up to you...

DARTAGNAN: Maybe if you looked at my tongue... Can we sit down?

[*They sit down on the chairs, down right.* DARTAGNAN *sticks his tongue out.*]

ETIENNE: Aha...

DARTAGNAN: How is it?

ETIENNE: Well, for one thing, mine is longer. See?

[*He sticks his tongue out.*]

DARTAGNAN: What?

ETIENNE: And besides, yours is round at the end, but mine is pointed. [*He sticks it out again.*] And I can curl mine up... Like this... [*He illustrates.*] Can you?

DARTAGNAN: I beg your... Really! What kind of doctor are you!

ETIENNE: No kind at all, monsieur.

DARTAGNAN [*jumping up*]: What?

ETIENNE [*standing up*]: But I may as well be. I'm his butler.

DARTAGNAN: His butler!... Then why are you standing here talking to me, for goodness' sake?

ETIENNE: Oh, I don't mind, monsieur. I'll talk to anyone.

DARTAGNAN [*not listening to him, aside*]: Then who the devil did I give my coat to just now?

[*He moves up center, scratching his head. As he reaches the double door,* MOULINEAUX *enters, down left, in his frock coat. At the same moment* BASSINET *enters, up left, still carrying his hat and coat, and with a sheet of paper in his hand.*]

MOULINEAUX [*talking to himself*]: There! All ready...

BASSINET [*to* MOULINEAUX]: Ah, monsieur...

MOULINEAUX: You...

BASSINET [*waving the paper at him*]: The lease, monsieur!

MOULINEAUX [*taking it*]: Yes... Thank you... That's fine...

BASSINET: By the way, I still haven't told you the story... About the dressmaker, I mean... You see, she—

MOULINEAUX [*avoiding him*]: Not now... I'm in a hurry... A date with destiny, my friend!

[*He strides quickly to the door, up center.*]

BASSINET: But it's really very funny... If you want a good laugh...

DARTAGNAN [*stopping* MOULINEAUX *before he reaches the door*]: Ah, doctor! You must excuse me...

MOULINEAUX [*aside*]: Oh my! Him too? [*To* DARTAGNAN.] Doctor?... Who's a doctor?

[*He bolts out.*]

DARTAGNAN [*as* MOULINEAUX *slams the door*]: Oh, pardon me... I thought... [*Aside.*] A patient, I suppose... [*Catching sight of* BASSINET, *who is standing, left, back turned, brushing his hat.*] Ah! Then that must be the doctor... [*To* BASSINET, *joining him.*] Pardon me, monsieur... It was a foolish mistake... I hope you'll excuse me...

BASSINET [*turning around*]: Me, monsieur?

DARTAGNAN: Yes... My coat... Before... Your patient... [*Confused.*] Whoever... I thought... My mistake...

BASSINET [*without the slightest idea what he is talking about*]: Aha... Don't mention it... [*Returning to his idée fixe.*] I say, if you'd like to hear a really funny story...

DARTAGNAN: Monsieur?

BASSINET: It's about my tenant... The dressmaker... That is, she was... My tenant, I mean... Because, one day—

DARTAGNAN [*to* BASSINET, *who has followed him to the door, up center*]: Yes, I'm sure... But if you don't mind... [*Freeing himself.*] Another time... [*With a little bow.*] Monsieur...

[*He exits.*]

BASSINET [*calling after him as he leaves*]: Wait! I haven't finished!... [*As the door closes.*] Hmm! He must be in a hurry... [*Noticing* ETIENNE, *still standing by his chair, who has been watching the proceedings with a smirk.*] Ah! The butler... [*To* ETIENNE.] I say, my good man... I have a terribly funny story...

ETIENNE: Excuse me, monsieur, but they want me in the pantry.

BASSINET [*ignoring his objections, making him sit down next to him, right*]: You see, it's about my tenant... The dressmaker... The one who ran away in the middle of the night... [*Laughing to himself.*] Really, it's just too funny... [*While* BASSINET *is reveling in his story,* ETIENNE *takes advantage of his inattention to get up and slip out the upstage door.*] Anyway, she had this young gigolo who used to... [*Suddenly, noticing that he is all alone, he gets up and looks around the room for* ETIENNE.] Now where did he go, I wonder?... [*To the audience.*] Well, as I was saying... The dressmaker had this gigolo...
[*The orchestra cuts him off, despite his efforts to shout above it. And the curtain falls in his face.*][1]

CURTAIN

---

[1] I reproduce Feydeau's stage direction here, though I assume that present-day directors will find an expedient other than an orchestra to end the act [Translator's note].

Act Two

The apartment on Rue de Milan. In the rear wall, center, a door leading to the hall, opening in. The door is open, and the landing can be glimpsed outside. On each side of the door, a chair. Up right, a dressmaker's wicker mannequin covered with a lady's gown. Up right, a door. Down right and left, a workbench wth appropriate articles strewn in disorder: boxes, swatches of cloth, patterns, scissors, pad and pencil, etc. Near the workbench, right, a chair; left, a canapé. The whole apartment is in obvious disarray.

At rise, the set is empty. After a few moments, MOULINEAUX appears at the door, up center.

MOULINEAUX [talking to himself]: One B... One B... Ah, here we are! [He enters, tries to push the door shut, but finds that it won't close.] Hmm! Broken!... Very nice!... Problems already!... [Tinkering with the doorknob.] I mustn't forget to tell Bassinet... [Turning around quickly, he finds himself face to face with the mannequin and, instinctively, gives a little bow.] Madame... [Realizing his mistake.] Oh... [With a little laugh.] Of course... His famous dressmaker... [Looking around, surveying the disorder.] And all this... Well, it's going to take a little work... But once I put everything in order... [Nodding.] Not bad... Not bad at all... [Continuing his inspection, after a pause.] Ah, Moulineaux... You cad! You bounder!... Her mother is right! You ought to be ashamed! With a nice little wife... It's hard not to feel guilty... [Caressing the back of the canapé.] And I do! I do!... Guilty, guilty, guilty!... I just don't let it bother me, that's all...
[While he is talking, SUZANNE appears at the open door, in hat and coat, carrying a muff.]
SUZANNE [poking her head in, tentatively]: Balthasar...?
MOULINEAUX: Suzanne!
SUZANNE: Am I early?
MOULINEAUX [going to meet her]: Come in! Come in!...
SUZANNE: Well...
[She enters cautiously, lays her muff down on one of the chairs up center, and tries unsuccessfully to shut the door behind her.]
MOULINEAUX: Oh, don't mind that... It's broken. Here, let me... [He takes the other chair and props it against the door.] There!
SUZANNE: Are you sure it's safe, dearest? What if somebody comes in?
MOULINEAUX [taking her by the hand and leading her downstage]: Why should anyone come in? It's as safe as safe can be!
SUZANNE: Because... What we're doing, Balthasar... It's so wrong... So wrong... [Almost as an afterthought.] Especially if anyone saw me...

MOULINEAUX [*aside*]: Especially! [*To* SUZANNE.] Believe me, Suzanne... We couldn't be more alone. [*At the canapé.*] Come... Sit down... [*He takes both her hands in his and sits down.*]

SUZANNE [*resisting*]: But...

MOULINEAUX: Why Suzanne... You're trembling...

SUZANNE [*still standing*]: I know... It's... It's only because this is all so new. My first... adventure!

MOULINEAUX: I know... I know...

SUZANNE: Like a soldier at the front!

MOULINEAUX: Well...

SUZANNE: That's what my husband always says... Even the bravest soldiers are afraid the first time.

MOULINEAUX [*still trying to urge her onto the canapé*]: Yes...

SUZANNE: And he should know. He was in the army... He cooked for a general...

MOULINEAUX: Yes... He speaks from experience... [*Urging.*] Come... Take off your hat...

SUZANNE [*pulling away*]: Oh no! Good heavens!... I can only stay a minute!

MOULINEAUX: What?

SUZANNE: Anatole is downstairs. If he ever came up...

MOULINEAUX [*jumping up*]: Who?

SUZANNE: Anatole... My husband... He insisted on coming with me.

MOULINEAUX [*unable to believe his ears*]: You... You mean, you told him...?

SUZANNE [*hesitating*]: Well... That is... Yes and no.

MOULINEAUX: "Yes and..." But you shouldn't have! No one does... That's... That's not the way it's done...

SUZANNE: But I had to tell him something! You know how he's been acting lately...

MOULINEAUX: I know, but still—

SUZANNE: So I told him... I told him I was going to my tailor's...

MOULINEAUX [*with a relieved little laugh*]: Your what?

SUZANNE: For a fitting... I remembered what you said... About a dressmaker that used to live here...

MOULINEAUX: Quick thinking! [*With a sigh.*] Thank heavens!

SUZANNE: After all, I certainly didn't want him tagging along...

MOULINEAUX: Hardly!

SUZANNE: But I couldn't very well say no, or he'd begin to suspect... Besides, after last night... Making you wait and wait the way I did... Well, I didn't have the heart... I just had to come! [*Naively.*] That was good of me, wasn't it? Aren't you pleased that I did?

MOULINEAUX: Dear, sweet Suzanne!...

SUZANNE [*waiting for an answer*]: Aren't you, Balthasar?

MOULINEAUX [*aside, preoccupied*]: Just knowing he's downstairs... Damn! That spoils everything!

SUZANNE: Balthasar?

MOULINEAUX [*aside*]: I wish she didn't tell me... Talk about putting a damper on things! [*Aloud, mechanically.*] Ah! Dear, sweet Suzanne!...

SUZANNE [*with a smile*]: You said that, dearest.

MOULINEAUX: I did?... Said what?

SUZANNE: What you just said...

MOULINEAUX: Oh... Did I, Suzanne?... Dear, sweet Suzanne...

SUZANNE: Again?... Really, Balthasar... Is something bothering you?

MOULINEAUX [aside]: I don't know what I'm saying!... [Aloud.] Bothering me?

SUZANNE [growing serious]: Oh, I know... Don't pretend. You don't have to tell me. You think I'm perfectly dreadful, don't you!

MOULINEAUX: Me?

SUZANNE: Coming here this way... That's it, isn't it!

MOULINEAUX: No! That's not it at all... Of course not, Suzanne... Dear—

SUZANNE [interrupting]: Sweet Suzanne!... Yes, yes... But really, you shouldn't! Because I never... Believe me... It's the very first time...

MOULINEAUX: I know... I'm sure... [Aside.] Like trying to make love under Damocles' sword! [Aloud.] I know, Suzanne... I know...

SUZANNE: And you don't think I'm just too dreadful for words?

MOULINEAUX: No, no, no...

SUZANNE: And you're pleased that I came?

MOULINEAUX [unconvincingly]: Pleased?... That isn't the word! I'm delighted... Ecstatic!... [Aside.] Two hundred fifty francs a month to stand here and babble!

SUZANNE: But... You seem so cold... I thought, when I came here—

MOULINEAUX: Me? Cold?... How can you say that... when... when all I want... [Trying to sound passionate.] is... is to spend the rest of my life at your feet...

SUZANNE [with a pout]: Oh, that's easy to say...

MOULINEAUX: But I mean it, Suzanne!... I do! I do!... Look!

[He falls to his knees in front of her. At that moment the door, up center, flies open, knocking over the chair, and DARTAGNAN appears.]

DARTAGNAN: Oh my!... Clumsy, clumsy...

[He picks up the chair and replaces it by the door.]

MOULINEAUX [still kneeling, petrified, aside]: My God!... Anatole!... [Aloud, to DARTAGNAN, standing up.] No, no!... You can't come in! It's closed!

DARTAGNAN [entering, looking at the open door]: Closed?

MOULINEAUX [trying not to panic]: I mean... Come in! Please!... Come right in!

DARTAGNAN: Thank you, monsieur... I have...

MOULINEAUX: Please! Make yourself at home!

DARTAGNAN: It's not much fun waiting down there all alone...

MOULINEAUX [trying to sound natural]: Of course! I can imagine...

DARTAGNAN: So I said to myself: "I'm sure they won't mind if I drop in and say hello..."

MOULINEAUX: Not at all! Good idea!

DARTAGNAN: "...as long as I'm not a bother..." [As agreeably as possible.] So please, just go right ahead and make believe I'm not here... After all, you have your work...

MOULINEAUX: Yes... My work...

[He goes over to the workbench, right, and pretends to busy himself with cloths, patterns, etc.]

DARTAGNAN: You were taking madame's measurements. Please don't let me interrupt.

MOULINEAUX: Her measurements?

SUZANNE [*jumping in, to* DARTAGNAN]: That's right... He just finished my
  waist...
MOULINEAUX: Yes, I... Yes, yes... Precisely... Her waist... [*Pretending to write
  some figures on a notepad.*] "Waist... One hundred and four..."

SUZANNE	} [*together*]:	{	What?
DARTAGNAN			How much?

MOULINEAUX: One hundred—
SUZANNE [*scandalized*]: Fifty-two, monsieur! And not one centimeter more!
DARTAGNAN [*laughing*]: I daresay...
MOULINEAUX [*covering his faux pas*]: Centimeter...? Oh, if you want it in
  centimeters... Well... [*Calculating.*] That's right... Fifty-two... Exactly...
  Nowadays the best designers measure in half-centimeters... But if you
  prefer...
DARTAGNAN: Oh? Half...?
MOULINEAUX: Yes... All the great couturiers, monsieur...
DARTAGNAN: Interesting... I didn't know...
MOULINEAUX [*as if it were perfectly logical*]: That way everything comes out
  double.
DARTAGNAN [*chuckling*]: Except the bill, I hope!
MOULINEAUX: No... That's usually triple... That's how you can tell us from
  the—if you'll pardon the expression, monsieur—from the nobodies in the
  field.
DARTAGNAN: Indeed...
MOULINEAUX: And anyway, it was just a rough estimate. It's not easy without a
  tape. Not even for an expert... With an eye like mine... [*Looking around the
  workbench for a tape.*] You don't happen to have one, monsieur?
DARTAGNAN: A tape? [*Laughing.*] No, I can't say I do!... But surely you must
  have one...
MOULINEAUX: One?... I have dozens!... Only not here... They're all in my
  shop... My shops... My huge workshops...
DARTAGNAN: Aha... [*Aside.*] Odd chap, this tailor! [*To* MOULINEAUX.] You
  know, I must say, Monsieur... Monsieur... [*Pausing, trying to recall his
  name.*] Sorry... What was your name again?
SUZANNE [*trying unsuccessfully to save the day*]: It's Monsieur... Monsieur...
MOULINEAUX: Monsieur... You know... You know...
DARTAGNAN: Yuno?... Is that Italian?
MOULINEAUX: Ital... No, no... I mean, yes... That is, sometimes... Si, si!
  Sometimes...
DARTAGNAN: I must say, monsieur... [*Correcting.*] Signor Yuno... You look
  terribly familiar. Have we met?
MOULINEAUX [*turning his back, trying his best to hide his face*]: Met? Us?...
  You and me?... [*Aside.*] Oh my... [*To* DARTAGNAN.] No! Impossible!...
DARTAGNAN: But...
MOULINEAUX: I... I never go out!... Never, monsieur!... Never!
DARTAGNAN [*suddenly remembering*]: I know! The doctor's... Doctor
  Moulineaux... This morning... Madame's doctor...
MOULINEAUX [*with a casual gesture*]: Oh, him...
DARTAGNAN: Do you go to him too?

MOULINEAUX [*as offhand as possible*]: Well, once in a while... I don't make it a habit.

DARTAGNAN: You're smart! They say he's a quack!

MOULINEAUX [*indignantly*]: That's not true!... Not... [*Realizing that he is about to give himself away.*] Not Moulineaux... Not my doctor...

DARTAGNAN: Well, that's what they tell me. [*Nodding to* SUZANNE.] Needless to say, madame doesn't think so! She's been going to him for years...

MOULINEAUX: Oh?

DARTAGNAN: Though I can't imagine why. [SUZANNE *and* MOULINEAUX *exchange glances in spite of themselves.*] At any rate, signore... If that's not where I met you...

MOULINEAUX: No, no... I'm sure!...

DARTAGNAN: Now then... [*He takes the chair near the workbench, right, and places it in front of* MOULINEAUX.] You and my wife... [*Sitting down.*] Tell me, what are you doing?

MOULINEAUX [*agape*]: What... What are we...?

DARTAGNAN: What kind of a gown are you making for her?

MOULINEAUX: What kind of a... [*Recovering.*] Yes, yes... [*Correcting.*] Si, si... Her gown...

DARTAGNAN: Yes... What did you have in mind?

MOULINEAUX: Oh, believe me! A creation!

DARTAGNAN: I'm sure... And what will it look like?

MOULINEAUX: Well... It's going to be a... [*Spouting the first term that comes to mind.*] a dirndl, monsieur... With a lovely pleated bodice... All in Chantilly lace... And a full-flaring skirt... With ruffles, monsieur... Lots and lots of ruffles... And a bustle with ostrich plumes, and a black sable trim...

DARTAGNAN [*impressed*]: Sable?

MOULINEAUX: Only on the legs!

DARTAGNAN: Legs? What legs?

MOULINEAUX: Under the petticoat!... Don't worry, you can't see them...

DARTAGNAN: Good heavens! What a novel combination, I must say!... Ostrich plumes... Black sable...

MOULINEAUX [*perspiring*]: Yes!... Si! It's an inspiration...

DARTAGNAN [*to* SUZANNE]: Not too risqué, my love, I hope... [*To* MOULINEAUX.]: May I have a peek at the model?

MOULINEAUX: The... The model?... Of the gown?

DARTAGNAN: Yes... The design... You have one, don't you?

MOULINEAUX: One?... I have dozens! But they're all in my shops... The designs are in my shops...

DARTAGNAN: Ah... Along with the tapes...

MOULINEAUX [*ignoring his remark*]: Under lock and key!... Competition, you know... It's such a cutthroat business!... My competitors would kill for just one look...

DARTAGNAN: My goodness! You mean we can't choose the one we like?

MOULINEAUX: Yes! Of course! Who's stopping you?... You can choose all you want! You just can't look at them, that's all... [*Aside.*] Good God! Won't he leave?

[LILY *appears at the open door, and knocks.*]

LILY [*entering, without waiting for an answer*]: The door was open... [*Coming*

down left, nodding to each in turn.] Monsieur... Monsieur... Madame...
MOULINEAUX [*aside*]: Oh my! Now what?
[*There is a brief moment of uncomfortable silence while everyone looks quizzically at one another.*]
LILY [*to* MOULINEAUX]: Excuse me, but... Madame Durand...?
MOULINEAUX: What?
LILY: Madame Durand...?
MOULINEAUX: No, Doc... [*Quickly correcting himself.*] Signor Yuno... [*Pointing to* SUZANNE, *still by the canapé.*] Madame Dartagnan... [*Pointing to* DARTAGNAN, *still sitting, right.*] Monsieur...
LILY [*with a little curtsy*]: Delighted!... [*To* MOULINEAUX.] No... I mean, where is she?
MOULINEAUX: Where is who?
LILY: Madame Durand... Isn't she here?
[*There is another brief silence, during which* MOULINEAUX, *at a loss, looks back and forth at* SUZANNE *and* DARTAGNAN.]
MOULINEAUX [*blankly*]: Oh!... Madame Durand... No... No... She's away...
LILY: Too bad! I wanted to see her about my bill.
MOULINEAUX [*nodding, echoing*]: About your bill...
LILY: Yes... For her dress... That is, mine... But she made it...
MOULINEAUX [*suddenly comprehending*]: Oh, you mean Madame Durand! The dressmaker... That Madame Durand!
LILY: That's right...
DARTAGNAN [*to* MOULINEAUX]: Don't you know her, signore?
MOULINEAUX: Know her? Madame Durand?... Certainly I know her! Why shouldn't I know her?... Dear, dear Madame Durand!... She's my partner... [*Aside.*] Bassinet should have warned me she had customers, damn it!
LILY [*to* MOULINEAUX]: Well, as long as you're her partner... I'm Mademoiselle Leluxe... Mademoiselle Lily Leluxe...
MOULINEAUX: Aha... If you say so...
LILY: And I'd like you to do something about my bill, monsieur. It's really much too high.
MOULINEAUX: You're right!... With pleasure! I couldn't agree more...
LILY: Oh?
MOULINEAUX [*writing on the notepad, aside*]: What do I care? As long as it gets rid of her...
LILY [*holding out the bill*]: You see? Three hundred forty francs...
MOULINEAUX: Tsk tsk tsk! Too high! Much too high!... [*With a look toward* DARTAGNAN.] Just what I was saying to Madame Durand...
LILY: Only chintz, after all... Two pieces of chintz...
MOULINEAUX: Yes... Si, si... You were the one with the double chintz... I remember...
LILY: And for chintz... I mean, it's not like satin, or silk...
MOULINEAUX: No, no... You're right... [*To* DARTAGNAN.] She's absolutely right! [*To* SUZANNE.] Three hundred forty francs for chintz! Tsk tsk tsk! [*To* LILY.] Now then, what did you have in mind? How much would you like us to take off, mademoiselle?
LILY [*startled*]: How much would I...
MOULINEAUX: Whatever you say...

LILY: Well... I think three hundred is more than enough, don't you?

MOULINEAUX [*as agreeably as possible*]: Absolutely!... Very fair... [*Figuring on the notepad.*] Three hundred from three hundred and forty... That leaves forty, mademoiselle... Forty francs... [*Changing the bill.*] There! Will that be satisfactory?

LILY [*about to correct him*]: Forty... But monsieur, you... I think there's a mistake...

MOULINEAUX: No, no... That's fine... "The customer is always right!" That's our motto, mademoiselle.

LILY [*not knowing what to say*]: Yes, I... It's... But monsieur, it's really much more... So much more than I—

MOULINEAUX [*interrupting*]: Then let's say thirty-five, for round figures! And because you're such a good customer! [*Changing the bill again.*] Thirty-five!

LILY [*moving upstage*]: Well, that certainly is fair...

DARTAGNAN [*aside, laughing*]: Damn thieves, if you ask me!

LILY [*to* MOULINEAUX]: I must say, it's a pleasure doing business with you, Monsieur... Monsieur...

SUZANNE [*quickly, afraid that* MOULINEAUX *might put his foot in his mouth*]: Yuno!... Signor Yuno!

LILY: Signor Yuno...

MOULINEAUX: Yes... Likewise...

LILY: I'll be on my way...

MOULINEAUX: Si, si... So nice of you to come by...

LILY [*at the door, up center*]: Au revoir, monsieur. I'll be sure to come again... Especially when Madame Durand is away...

[*She nods at the company and exits.*]

DARTAGNAN [*standing up, taking out his watch*]: My my! One thirty!... I'd better be going too... [*Aside.*] My little Mathilde will be furious if I'm not right on time... [*To* MOULINEAUX.] Well, signore... I'm leaving madame in your capable hands.

MOULINEAUX: Si, si...

DARTAGNAN: I'm sure you know how to take care of her needs... [SUZANNE *and* MOULINEAUX *exchange subtle glances.*] Outdo yourself, my friend! No holds barred, as they say... But nothing too vulgar, you understand... Especialy around the hips and... and—if I may say—the bosom...

MOULINEAUX: Yes, especially...

DARTAGNAN [*going over to* SUZANNE]: Remember, my love... Shapely, but not too risqué...

SUZANNE: No... No...

DARTAGNAN [*shaking* MOULINEAUX'S *hand*]: A pleasure meeting you, signore... [*Going to the door, up center.*] How do you say...? Arrivederci!... Bye-bye! [*He exits. As soon as the door closes* MOULINEAUX *makes a dash, stands one of the chairs against it, and falls on it in a heap, obviously worn out by the experience.*]

MOULINEAUX [*heaving a sigh of relief*]: At last! I thought he'd never leave!

SUZANNE [*moving upstage, fanning herself with a handkerchief*]: Oh! Balthasar!... This is terrible!... What now?... Never in all my life...

MOULINEAUX: I know... I know...

SUZANNE: But what are you going to do?

MOULINEAUX: Do? Me?... [*Determined.*] Get out of here, that's what I'm going to do! You can bet this is the last time I ever get caught with... with my gown down!

SUZANNE: No, no! You can't!... You can't leave, Balthasar!... You mustn't...

MOULINEAUX: And why not? You don't expect me to put up with more like—

SUZANNE [*interrupting*]: But Anatole... My husband...

MOULINEAUX: Just give me one good reason...

SUZANNE: He thinks you're my tailor! If he comes back and doesn't find you... He'll suspect... He'll know... He'll know that you and I... that we... Oh, Balthasar! With his temper, he'll kill you!

MOULINEAUX: He will? [*Backing down.*] Hmm... All right, that's a good enough reason... You may have a point... [*Prostrate on the chair.*] Good God! What a lovely mess we've got ourselves into!

SUZANNE [*wringing her hands, up right*]: I knew it!... I just knew it was madness! I just knew!... I never should have come here. Because—

MOULINEAUX: I know... It's the first time...

[*At that moment the door, up center, flies open, knocking over the chair and sending* MOULINEAUX *sprawling on the floor to the canapé, as* BASSINET *appears.*]

SUZANNE [*stifling a little shriek, taking refuge behind the mannequin, up right*]: Oh!

BASSINET [*entering*]: I say... [*He stumbles over the chair.*] Ayyy!

MOULINEAUX [*licking his wounds*]: You!... Can't you even come in like any normal human being?

BASSINET [*limping down left, rubbing his knee*]: Drat it all! Who asked you to sit against the door, monsieur! Really!

MOULINEAUX [*painfully getting to his feet*]: And who asked you to rent me an apartment with a door that doesn't lock! Heaven only knows what else doesn't work! Just look at this place...

BASSINET: But I told you, monsieur... You wanted it right away...

MOULINEAUX: Yes, yes, yes...

BASSINET: I said it would take time to put things in order. After the dressmaker... But you said, "No, no... I'll make do!" You insisted...

MOULINEAUX: But a lock, for goodness' sake!... A door you can shut!... Is that too much to ask? It's like living on the street! Every idiot and his brother can barge right in...

[*He paces up and down.*]

BASSINET: But who would do a thing like that, monsieur?

MOULINEAUX: You, that's who! Who else!... [*Sarcastically.*] Now all we need is your brother!

BASSINET: My brother, monsieur?... But I don't have a—

MOULINEAUX [*down center*]: Never mind! Just get it fixed!

BASSINET [*moving left*]: Certainly, monsieur... As soon as I can find the locksmith. You see, I had to break the lock myself a few days ago... To get in... When the dressmaker left in such a hurry... You remember... [*Laughing.*] When that gigolo of hers went and—

MOULINEAUX [*cutting him off*]: Really, I'm not interested! I just want a door that locks! I don't care about her gigolo!

BASSINET: Oh... Sorry, I thought... Well, the locksmith came to fix it the very same day, monsieur. Only first he said he had to go have lunch, and I haven't seen him since. But I'm sure he'll come back...

MOULINEAUX: Yes... Next month!

BASSINET [*moving up left*]: Anyway, aside from the minor inconveniences... Is everything going... [*With a broad wink.*] according to plan?

MOULINEAUX: Excuse me, Monsieur Bassinet... [*Pointing to* SUZANNE, *still cowering by the mannequin.*] But, as you can see, I'm not alone...

BASSINET [*finally catching sight of* SUZANNE]: Oh... Pardon me... I didn't notice... [*To* SUZANNE, *with a little bow.*] Madame... Please don't go... You're not interrupting... [*With a little laugh.*] Monsieur and I have no secrets!

MOULINEAUX: You're much too kind!

BASSINET [*coming down and settling on the canapé, to* MOULINEAUX]: In fact, I was just going to tell you—

MOULINEAUX: Later! Later! [*Aside.*] Damn leech! That's all I needed!

[*There is a knock at the door, up center, and* MADAME D'HERBLAY *appears.*]

MADAME D'HERBLAY [*entering, looking around, timidly*]: Oh, excuse me... I was looking for Madame Durand.

MOULINEAUX   ⎫   ⎧ Another one?
             ⎬ [*together*]: ⎨
SUZANNE [*hands on hips*] ⎭   ⎩ Oh!

MOULINEAUX: That's the limit!

[*He begins pacing up and down.*]

MADAME D'HERBLAY: I... I came about my dicky...

MOULINEAUX [*gruffly*]: Who?

MADAME D'HERBLAY: My dicky... My blouse... I wanted Madame Durand to—

MOULINEAUX: Yes, but not today! Try next month... Next year...

MADAME D'HERBLAY: But my dicky, monsieur...

MOULINEAUX [*losing patience, upstage*]: Your dicky can go hang!

MADAME D'HERBLAY [*offended, but still timid*]: Well! See if I bother to pay!

MOULINEAUX: Well! See if I bother to give a damn!

MADAME D'HERBLAY [*turning to leave*]: Oh!... It's a wonder they have any customers here at all!... Oh!...

[*She exits, up center.*]

MOULINEAUX: Good riddance!

SUZANNE [*in a whisper, to* MOULINEAUX, *pointing to* BASSINET, *still blithely sitting on the canapé*]: Now what about him?

MOULINEAUX: Just leave him to me! [*He moves down to the canapé.*] Monsieur Bassinet...

BASSINET: Ah! There you are!... As I was saying...

MOULINEAUX [*trying in vain to interrupt*]: Monsieur...

BASSINET: I was just about to tell you... You'll never guess what happened...

MOULINEAUX: Monsieur...

BASSINET: I still haven't got over it... Can you imagine? Of all things, monsieur! I thought I found my wife!

MOULINEAUX: Yes, yes... But monsieur...

BASSINET: After all these years!... You remember, I told you... The Tuileries... The soldier...

MOULINEAUX: Yes...

BASSINET: Well, believe it or not, someone told me about a Madame Bassinet...

On Rue de Seine... So, naturally, I went over...

MOULINEAUX: Excuse me, monsieur, but... [*Pointing to* SUZANNE.] Madame and I...

BASSINET [*naively*]: Oh, she's not bothering me... I don't mind...

MOULINEAUX: You don't...

BASSINET [*continuing*]: Anyway, when I got there and knocked on the door... You'll never guess... She opened it, monsieur... And there she was... A total stranger!

MOULINEAUX: Monsieur...

BASSINET: She wasn't my wife at all!... So, naturally, I excused myself... "Pardon me," I told her... "I expected to find a lady, not you..." Well, it must have been something in the way I said it! Because, really...

MOULINEAUX: I'm sure...

[*All of a sudden* MADAME AIGREVILLE *appears at the door, up center.*]

MADAME AIGREVILLE [*just outside*]: One B... One B... This must be it... [*She enters.*]

BASSINET [*still absorbed in his story, to* MOULINEAUX]: You have no idea...

MOULINEAUX [*turning and catching sight of* MADAME AIGREVILLE, *suppressing a scream*]: Ayyy! [*Aside.*] What's she doing here?

SUZANNE [*furious*]: Another one?

BASSINET [*noticing* MADAME AIGREVILLE, *getting up, turning to her*]: Oh, madame...

SUZANNE [*aside*]: Really, this is simply too much!

MADAME AIGREVILLE [*to* BASSINET]: Ah, you!... I've come to look at your apartment.

MOULINEAUX [*trying to remain inconspicuous, aside*]: What?

BASSINET [*to* MADAME AIGREVILLE]: You... Oh, I'm terribly sorry, madame. It's already rented.

MADAME AIGREVILLE: It is? But you told me... I thought you said... [*Suddenly turning and finding herself face to face with* MOULINEAUX]: Moulineaux! What on earth...

MOULINEAUX [*as casually as possible*]: Hello, mother!

MADAME AIGREVILLE: What are you doing here?

MOULINEAUX: What a nice surprise!

MADAME AIGREVILLE [*sharply*]: I asked you a question! What are you doing here, monsieur?

MOULINEAUX: Me?

MADAME AIGREVILLE: I'm warning you... [*With a look at* SUZANNE, *still up right, pointedly*]: I'm quite prepared to believe the worst!

MOULINEAUX [*innocently*]: Worst what, mother dear?

MADAME AIGREVILLE: I'll ask you once again, monsieur! What are you doing here?

MOULINEAUX [*as naturally as possible*]: Why... Visiting a patient... Why else would I be here?

MADAME AIGREVILLE [*distressed at his logical answer*]: What?

MOULINEAUX [*to* SUZANNE]: Isn't that so, madame? You are my patient, aren't you?

SUZANNE [*picking up the hint*]: Of course, doctor!... And so good of you to come... [*Affecting a little cough.*] In my condition...

MADAME AIGREVILLE [*embarrassed, to* SUZANNE]: Why certainly, madame! I
never doubted for a moment...
SUZANNE: He's so obliging... Such a saint...
MADAME AIGREVILLE: Indeed.
SUZANNE [*very properly, playing her role to the hilt*]: Tell me, madame... To
what do I owe the honor...? Is there something I can do for you?
MADAME AIGREVILLE [*still very embarrassed*]: Do?... Well, that is... I... You
see, I was making the rounds of the neighborhood—
SUZANNE: Of course! For the poor!... How noble, madame! How utterly noble...
MADAME AIGREVILLE [*taken aback*]: What?
SUZANNE: Please! No one can say that I don't support widows and orphans!
[*She takes a coin from her muff, on the chair by the door, and strides down
to* MADAME AIGREVILLE.] Here! Will five francs do?
[*She presses the coin into* MADAME AIGREVILLE'*s palm.*]
MADAME AIGREVILLE [*shocked*]: Five francs, madame? But—
SUZANNE: Unless that's not enough...
MOULINEAUX [*to* MADAME AIGREVILLE, *feigning shock*]: Aren't you ashamed of
yourself! To go begging from door to door...
BASSINET [*shaking his head, scornfully*]: Tsk tsk tsk!
MADAME AIGREVILLE: But I'm not doing anything of the kind!
MOULINEAUX: Tsk tsk tsk!
MADAME AIGREVILLE [*to* SUZANNE]: Here! I don't want your money! [*She gives
it to* MOULINEAUX, *to pass it to* SUZANNE]: I'm not taking a collection! I'm
looking for an apartment!
[MOULINEAUX *mechanically pockets the coin*]
SUZANNE [*to* MADAME AIGREVILLE]: Oh! I do beg your pardon, madame!... No
offense!... [*To* MOULINEAUX, *having caught his maneuver, holding out her
hand.*] If you please...
MOULINEAUX [*giving her the coin*]: Sorry... I wasn't thinking...
SUZANNE [*with affected aplomb, to* MOULINEAUX]: Well, doctor? Aren't you
going to introduce us?
MOULINEAUX [*aghast*]: Intro... [*To* SUZANNE.]: You want me to...? [*She nods.*]
Why certainly! Where are my manners?... [*Introducing, with an acid note
in his voice.*] Madame Aigreville... My mother-in-law... [*Almost
voluptuously.*] Madame Dartagnan... Madame Suzanne Dartagnan...
MADAME AIGREVILLE: Delighted!
SUZANNE: The pleasure is all mine!
MADAME AIGREVILLE [*nodding toward* BASSINET]: And this is Monsieur
Dartagnan, I take it?... [*To* BASSINET.] Not our famous Musketeer,
monsieur...?
[*The others gasp in disbelief.*]
BASSINET: Our what?
MADAME AIGREVILLE [*naively*]: I mean, one wouldn't think to look at you...
SUZANNE [*to* MADAME AIGREVILLE]: Monsieur is just a friend, madame...
MADAME AIGREVILLE: Oh...
MOULINEAUX [*quickly, clearing his throat*]: Pardon the anachronism! [*To*
MADAME AIGREVILLE.] Really, you should know better!
MADAME AIGREVILLE [*not quite comprehending, embarrassed*]: Oh? Did I say
something...? Sorry... [*Changing the subject, to* SUZANNE.] So, you've put

yourself into my son-in-law's hands, I see...

SUZANNE: Yes... Quite... [*Quickly, to avert suspicion.*] My husband, too...

MADAME AIGREVILLE: Aha...

SUZANNE: Especially my husband...

MADAME AIGREVILLE: Oh, is he ill, my dear?

SUZANNE: Well...

MOULINEAUX [*jumping into the breach*]: Yes!... Impetigo!

MADAME AIGREVILLE: Please?

MOULINEAUX: Impetigo! Impetigo!... An eczematose impetigo... With subcutaneous inflammation... and epidermal suppuration...

MADAME AIGREVILLE: Oh, my heavens!

MOULINEAUX: And desquamation!... Lots of desquamation!

MADAME AIGREVILLE: Poor man! What does it come from?

MOULINEAUX [*babbling*]: From... From... From childbirth... Complications...

MADAME AIGREVILLE: What? Him?

MOULINEAUX [*pointing to* SUZANNE]: Her! Her!

SUZANNE: Me?

MADAME AIGREVILLE [to SUZANNE]: Oh, you have a child, my dear?

SUZANNE ⎫   ⎧ No!
          ⎬ [*together*]: ⎨
MOULINEAUX ⎭   ⎩ Yes!

SUZANNE [*realizing she is commiting a faux pas*]: That is...

MOULINEAUX: Almost... She thought... I thought... We thought...

MADAME AIGREVILLE: And Monsieur Dartagnan...?

MOULINEAUX: He... He thought so too! He thought she was going to... But... But then, when she didn't... Well, you know... Nerves! Nerves!... Skin rash... Hives... Eczema... Impetigo!

MADAME AIGREVILLE: Oh my! Poor thing!

MOULINEAUX: The whole business!... Classic case!... Very stubborn!

MADAME AIGREVILLE: How sad...

MOULINEAUX: Yes, very... And now, mother, if you don't mind... I'd like to get on with my consultation.

[SUZANNE, *taking the hint, gives a few little coughs.*]

MADAME AIGREVILLE: Of course... How thoughtless of me... I'll be on my way. [*She goes to leave, up center.*]

MOULINEAUX [*accompanying her, aside*]: Not a minute too soon!

MADAME AIGREVILLE [*aside*]: If Yvonne comes, she just won't find me, that's all.

MOULINEAUX [*holding the door open for her*]: Au revoir, mother dear!

MADAME AIGREVILLE: Don't "mother dear" me, you cad! I'm not forgetting a thing! [*Very proper.*] But I do know how to behave in front of strangers!

MOULINEAUX [*very affable*]: Yes... I'll try to remember to invite some for you...

MADAME AIGREVILLE [*to* SUZANNE]: Madame...

SUZANNE: Madame...

[*Suddenly* MOULINEAUX, *still at the open door, sees* DARTAGNAN *coming up the stairs.*]

MOULINEAUX: Oh, no! Dartagnan!... [*Rushing to join* SUZANNE, *in a whisper.*] Your husband! He's back!

SUZANNE [*petrified*]: What? Good heavens!

[*She grabs her muff and makes a hasty exit, up right.*]

MADAME AIGREVILLE: What?

MOULINEAUX [*trying to push* MADAME AIGREVILLE *out the door, up right*]: You too!... You too!...

MADAME AIGREVILLE [*dumbfounded*]: But... What is it? What are you—

MOULINEAUX: Don't ask questions!... Just get in there!...

[*He succeeds in pushing her out, despite her protestations.*]

BASSINET [*who has been looking on, caught up in the sudden excitement, automatically following* MOULINEAUX *to the door*]: I say... Should I come too, monsieur?

MOULINEAUX [*half out the door*]: You... No, no! You stay!... You tell him... If he asks for a Monsieur Yuno... Signor Yuno... He thinks that's my name...

BASSINET [*puzzled*]: Signor...?

MOULINEAUX: Just tell him I'm busy! Tell him anything you like!... I'm... I'm in conference... With the... the queen of Greenland!... Anything!... But for God's sake, get rid of him!

[*He slams the door in* BASSINET'*s face.*]

BASSINET: Of course, monsieur!... [*Coming down, center.*] Some pest, I suppose... I know the type... [*Hands on hips, puzzled.*] Signor...? [*Tapping his temple with his forefinger.*] I think our friend the doctor needs... a doctor!

[DARTAGNAN *appears at the open door.*]

DARTAGNAN [*entering*]: Hello! It's me again, monsieur... [*Laying his hat on one of the chairs by the door.*] Signore... [*Looking around.*] Oh... Pardon me, I thought... Where's Signor Yuno? Isn't he in?

BASSINET [*facing the audience, back to* DARTAGNAN]: No... That is, yes... But he's busy...

DARTAGNAN [*recognizing him*]: Ah! Our friend the doctor...

BASSINET [*turning around, misunderstanding*]: That's right... Our friend... Oh, you know...? [*Aside.*] Then what's all this "Signor Yuno"...? [*To* DARTAGNAN.] I'm sorry. He's very busy.

DARTAGNAN [*coming down, joining him*]: Our dear friend the doctor...

BASSINET [*echoing, mechanically*]: Yes... Our dear friend the doctor...

DARTAGNAN: What a small world, monsieur! You never know where you're going to meet a familiar face, now do you?

BASSINET [*trying to be agreeable*]: Quite... Quite...

DARTAGNAN: Then again, I don't know why I should be surprised. You and Signor Yuno, after all...

BASSINET: Monsieur?

DARTAGNAN: You do see him, I mean...

BASSINET: Yes...

DARTAGNAN: In fact, he was just telling me, not half an hour ago...

BASSINET: He was?

DARTAGNAN: He's a patient, isn't he?

BASSINET [*misunderstanding*]: Impatient?... Well, as a matter of fact, sometimes... Not always... [*Aside.*] Curious question!

DARTAGNAN [*trying to be funny*]: No... Only when he's sick!

BASSINET: Yes, only... Oh, you noticed... Yes, I daresay...

DARTAGNAN: Tell me, what seems to be his problem exactly?

BASSINET [*unconsciously unbuttoning* DARTAGNAN*'s coat as he talks*]: Well, frankly monsieur... If you ask me, I think... [*Confidentially.*] I think he's got a bat loose in the belfry, as they say...

DARTAGNAN [*rebuttoning his coat*]: I had rather the same impression, myself. Just a layman's opinion... But if you say so too... Well...

BASSINET [*unbuttoning again*]: Yes... Lately he's been behaving rather strangely. Little things, mind you... Nothing serious, but still...

DARTAGNAN [*rebuttoning*]: Yes... And I assume you've suggested that he do something for it?... Hydrotherapy... Cold showers...

BASSINET [*beginning to unbutton again*]: Oh, I don't know that I would want to take the liberty...

DARTAGNAN [*pulling away, rebuttoning*]: Please!... Thank you... It's not necessary...

BASSINET: Though just between you and me... [*Flicking a speck of lint from* DARTAGNAN*'s collar.*] It wouldn't hurt him to take a shower!

DARTAGNAN [*backing away*]: Yes... I'm sure...

BASSINET [*repeating his maneuver*]: But that's his business...

DARTAGNAN [*backing away, deciding to change the subject*]: You know, as long as we're standing here chatting... I wonder if you would mind...

BASSINET [*repeating it again*]: Monsieur?

DARTAGNAN [*stepping to one side*]: It's not that I'm looking for free advice, you understand. It's just that... Well, ordinarily I'm rather hot-blooded by nature...

BASSINET [*grasping* DARTAGNAN*'s lapels and arranging them, hardly listening*]: Yes... Yes, that's nice...

DARTAGNAN [*stepping to the other side*]: But lately I've been having problems... Circulation, monsieur... Nosebleeds, mainly...

BASSINET: Aha...

DARTAGNAN: And my feet keep falling asleep...

BASSINET [*still arranging his lapels*]: Yes... Yes, that's too bad...

DARTAGNAN: In fact... [*In semi-desperation, taking off his coat and draping it over his arm*]: I was mentioning it to your butler...

BASSINET: Oh?... [*At a loss what to do with his hands, finally folding his arms on his chest.*] You know my butler?

DARTAGNAN: Well... That is, we've met...

BASSINET: Which one? Joseph or Baptiste?

DARTAGNAN: I'm afraid I couldn't tell you. All I know is he gave me some rather unusual suggestions...

BASSINET: And massage, monsieur? Did he tell you to try massage? That's what always works for me.

DARTAGNAN: I've tried it, but I'm afraid it hasn't done much good.

BASSINET: Well, maybe you don't know how. You see, the way I do it... First you find yourself a good masseur... Big and strong... The stronger the better... Then you have him take off his clothes and lie down on the table, and you massage him as hard as you can for an hour. If that doesn't get your blood moving, I'll eat my hat!

DARTAGNAN: Aha... You're right, I was doing it all wrong... Thank you, monsieur. I'll try it.

BASSINET: Don't mention it. My pleasure...

[*There is a brief pause as* DARTAGNAN, *remembering the purpose of his*

visit, looks at his watch with an impatient sigh.]
DARTAGNAN: And you say Signor Yuno is too busy to see me?
BASSINET: Oh, much too busy! He's in conference with Her Majesty!
DARTAGNAN: Who?
BASSINET: The green of Queenland!
DARTAGNAN: What?
BASSINET: The green... [*Correcting.*] The queen, I mean... The queen of Greenland, monsieur!
DARTAGNAN: He is?... With a queen?... My my my! A real queen?
BASSINET: Yes, monsieur... Of Greenland...
DARTAGNAN [*with a gesture of admiration*]: Pfff! Talk about high fashion!... You can't get much higher! He must be the best in the business! [*Aside.*] Who would ever think...? A queen...
BASSINET: So if you would like to come back... Maybe another time...
DARTAGNAN: No, no... I don't think so... You see, I wanted to tell him to expect a visit from a... [*Clearing his throat.*] a certain young friend of mine... Madame de Sainte-Vinaigrette...
BASSINET: Aha...
DARTAGNAN: The dear child is simply queen with... [*Correcting.*] simply green with envy. She's dying to know where my wife has her gowns made. A whim... You know...
BASSINET [*nodding*]: Some women...
[*He reaches over and flicks off a speck of lint from* DARTAGNAN's *coat, draped over his arm.*]
DARTAGNAN: So I thought it would be better if I... Well, if I came here first... Just in case... To see if my wife was still here, that is... With Signor Yuno...
BASSINET: Aha...
DARTAGNAN [*confidentially*]: I'm not especially anxious for madame to meet the child. She might not understand, you understand...
BASSINET: I understand...
DARTAGNAN: Some women...
BASSINET: I say, monsieur, you mean... [*Flicking off another speck.*] That lovely lady just now was your wife? The one who was here a few moments ago with... with Signor Yuno?
DARTAGNAN: Why yes...
BASSINET: And you let her go out all alone, monsieur? In Paris?
DARTAGNAN: Oh, heaven forbid! I'd never... I brought her here myself!
BASSINET [*with a sardonic smile*]: Aha... Well, in that case...
DARTAGNAN [*looking at his watch again*]: Tell me, do you think Signor Yuno will be much longer?
BASSINET: Who can say, monsieur? With a queen, after all...
[*He goes to flick off another speck, but* DARTAGNAN *turns aside suddenly at the sound of* MADAME AIGREVILLE's *voice.*]
MADAME AIGREVILLE'S VOICE: No, no, no! I'm telling you, I've got an appointment!
BASSINET [*aside*]: The mother-in-law!
MADAME AIGREVILLE'S VOICE: I'm not staying another minute!
BASSINET [*aside*]: Here's my chance to rent 3 A...
DARTAGNAN: Good heavens...

SUZANNE'S VOICE: But...

BASSINET [*aside*]: I'll go wait for her in the hall...

MOULINEAUX'S VOICE: But...

[BASSINET *exits quickly, up center, unseen by* DARTAGNAN, *who is still looking inquisitively up right.*]

MADAME AIGREVILLE'S VOICE: No, no, no!

DARTAGNAN: My goodness, doctor... What do you suppose...? [*Turning left, finding* BASSINET *gone.*] Doctor?... Now where on earth...? Odd chap, this Doctor Moulineaux, I must say!

[*He moves up center and retrieves his hat from the chair, as* MADAME AIGREVILLE *enters, up right.*]

MADAME AIGREVILLE: The very idea... Trying to keep me here...

DARTAGNAN [*looking up, aside*]: Ah! That must be... [*To* MADAME AIGREVILLE.] Your Queenship...

[*He bows with a little flourish of his hat, then stands at attention with the hat over his heart.*]

MADAME AIGREVILLE: Now who... [*Nodding, politely.*] Monsieur...

DARTAGNAN [*with more flourishes*]: Your Highness!... Your Majesty!...

MADAME AIGREVILLE: My what?

DARTAGNAN [*with a deep bow*]: I bow before your gracious presence!

MADAME AIGREVILLE [*coquettishly*]: Why, thank you, I'm sure! How terribly sweet!... And to whom do I have the honor, monsieur...?

DARTAGNAN [*bowing*]: Monsieur Dartagnan... Monsieur Anatole Dartagnan...

MADAME AIGREVILLE: Oh... Then you must be... I've met your charming wife, monsieur...

DARTAGNAN [*bowing*]: The pleasure is all yours, Your Grace...

MADAME AIGREVILLE [*without transition*]: Tell me, how is your impetigo?

DARTAGNAN: Excuse me?

MADAME AIGREVILLE: Your impetigo, monsieur... You have one, I understand...

DARTAGNAN: I do? [*Aside.*] I didn't know...

MADAME AIGREVILLE: Yes... [*Trying to be sympathetic.*] I imagine when it itches it must drive you crazy!

DARTAGNAN: When it itches?... My...

MADAME AIGREVILLE: You know, monsieur... Your rash... Your eczema...

DARTAGNAN: My... [*As deferentially as possible.*] I beg your pardon! What rash? What eczema?

MADAME AIGREVILLE: Yours, monsieur... [*Aside.*] Oh my! He's sensitive, poor thing! I shouldn't have...

DARTAGNAN: Excuse me, but I don't know what makes you think...

[*He moves left, examining his hands.*]

MADAME AIGREVILLE [*aside*]: Another blunder! [*To* DARTAGNAN.] No, no! My mistake!... Please, pardon the... the... [*Trying to remember the word.*] the anachronism, monsieur...

DARTAGNAN [*aside*]: Anachronism? [*To* MADAME AIGREVILLE, *still very obsequious.*] Not at all... I assure you...

MADAME AIGREVILLE: Thank you! You're too kind...

DARTAGNAN [*aside*]: Hmm! Maybe it means something else in Greenlandish.

MADAME AIGREVILLE [*at the door, up center, ready to leave*]: Well, if you'll

excuse me... It's a pleasure to meet madame's husband, monsieur. Perhaps we'll meet again. [DARTAGNAN *bows with a flourish.*] Monsieur...
[*She exits.*]

DARTAGNAN [*with a gesture of admiration*]: Pfff! Who would ever think...? A queen!... You would never know, to look at her... She seems so... ordinary... [*Catching sight of* MOULINEAUX, *who appears at the door, up right.*] Ah! Signor Yuno... I've been waiting...
[*He comes down right, looking at his watch.*]

MOULINEAUX [*aside*]: Still here, damn it? [*To* SUZANNE, *pushing her back into the room as she appears momentarily at his heels.*] No! Not yet!
[*He pulls the door shut quickly.*]

DARTAGNAN [*turning to look*]: What?

MOULINEAUX [*innocently*]: Hmm?... What's that, monsieur?

DARTAGNAN: Oh... I thought you said something.

MOULINEAUX: Me, monsieur?... No...

DARTAGNAN [*joining him*]: Tell me, signore... My wife... Has she left?

MOULINEAUX: Oh, long ago! Long ago!... She said, if you came back, to tell you she's at the Louvre... In case you want to look for her...

DARTAGNAN [*taking his arm and leading him down center*]: Not at all, my friend... Quite the contrary! This is just fine... You see... [*Confidentially.*] There's a lady... A certain young friend of mine... And I expect she'll be coming here to meet me any moment.

MOULINEAUX: Here, did you say? You told her to meet you here?

DARTAGNAN: So, you can understand... I'd just as soon not have her run into madame...

MOULINEAUX: Aha... I see!... You mean, a little—how shall I say?—affair?

DARTAGNAN [*laughing*]: Oh, little! Very little! Hardly worth mentioning... But still, there's no need for my wife... You understand... You're Italian...

MOULINEAUX: Oh yes!... Si, si! After all, she might... Well, an eye for an eye...

DARTAGNAN: My wife?... No, no! Impossible!

MOULINEAUX [*sardonically*]: Aha... I'm glad to hear it...

DARTAGNAN: Some wives, of course... But mine? No... Never!

MOULINEAUX [*echoing*]: Never!

DARTAGNAN: Believe me, I know what I'm talking about...

MOULINEAUX: I'm sure...

DARTAGNAN: If there's one thing I know, it's married women, my friend. I've had more affairs with them... More than you can count! I know all their tricks! I'm not one of your blind husbands, like so many, monsieur.

MOULINEAUX: Aha...

DARTAGNAN [*laughing*]: I knew one... Would you believe it?... Every time his wife would come to meet me, the old fool would bring her to my place himself!

MOULINEAUX: No!

DARTAGNAN: Yes!... She would tell him she was going to have her fortune told!... Well, guess who was the fortune-teller!

MOULINEAUX [*with affected naiveté*]: You, monsieur?

DARTAGNAN [*laughing*]: Exactly! In the meantime the idiot would be downstairs, waiting.
[*He doubles up with laughter.*]

MOULINEAUX [*joining in*]: No!... [*Slapping him on the back.*] Downstairs?

DARTAGNAN: The stupidity of some people, monsieur!... It's unbelieveable!

MOULINEAUX [*with forced guffaws*]: Yes, isn't it...
[*After a few moments of hilarity, the laughter gradually subsides.*]

DARTAGNAN: Besides, my wife would never... She knows me too well. She knows what I would do the minute I caught her cheating!

MOULINEAUX [*anxiously*]: You mean... A duel, monsieur?

DARTAGNAN: Heavens, no! That's too dangerous... [MOULINEAUX *heaves a sigh of relief.*] I would just kill the man, that's all... No questions asked...

MOULINEAUX: What?

DARTAGNAN: "Bang, bang, bang!"... Between the eyes!...

MOULINEAUX [*aside, with a shudder*]: Good God!

DARTAGNAN: I'd teach him not to trifle with Anatole Dartagnan!

MOULINEAUX: You... Yes, I daresay...

DARTAGNAN [*changing the subject*]: But why are we talking about such things, my friend? That's hardly what I came here to tell you...

MOULINEAUX: Hardly...

DARTAGNAN: I've got good news for you!

MOULINEAUX [*apprehensively*]: For me?

DARTAGNAN: My friend... The young lady... She wants you, Signor Yuno...

MOULINEAUX [*with a start*]: What?

DARTAGNAN: As her tailor...

MOULINEAUX [*recoiling*]: Her tailor? But... What for?

DARTAGNAN: What for? What do you think?... She wants you to make her a gown...

MOULINEAUX: She... [*Aside.*] Oh my! [*To* DARTAGNAN, *sarcastically.*] Now there's a brilliant idea!

DARTAGNAN [*missing his sarcasm*]: Why, thank you...

MOULINEAUX [*forgetting himself*]: No, no! Thank *you* !... You think that's all I've got to do?... Make gowns?... What about my patients, monsieur? My patients...
[*He bites his lip, suddenly realizing his faux pas.*]

DARTAGNAN: But... Take as long as you like, Signor Yuno! She's in no hurry...

MOULINEAUX [*trying to cover it over*]: She... Yes... Quite right...

DARTAGNAN [*rather piqued*]: Really! What kind of a business do you run? Complaining that you have too many customers!... I never...

MOULINEAUX: No, no... I didn't mean—

DARTAGNAN [*more and more worked up*]: Just because crowned heads beat a path to your door!

MOULINEAUX: Crowned—

DARTAGNAN: Either you're a tailor or you're not! Now which is it?

MOULINEAUX [*moving far right*]: But of course I'm a tailor! What else would I be? [*Aside.*] "Bang, bang, bang!"
[*Just then,* MADAME D'HERBLAY *appears, up center.*]

MADAME D'HERBLAY [*at the door, timidly, to* MOULINEAUX]: Ah, monsieur... There you are...

MOULINEAUX [*turning*]: Who...

MADAME D'HERBLAY: I hope you'll excuse me for disturbing you again. I know how busy you must be...

MOULINEAUX: Ah, madame...

[*During their exchange,* DARTAGNAN *goes over to the canapé and sits down.*]

MADAME D'HERBLAY: But I was hoping, perhaps, you might have time for my blouse...

MOULINEAUX [*seizing the occasion to prove himself to* DARTAGNAN]: Yes! Of course!... Your... Your *ducky* ...

MADAME D'HERBLAY: My...?

MOULINEAUX [*as pleasant as he can be*]: Please, come in... Come right in... [*To* DARTAGNAN.] If I'm a tailor, indeed!

MADAME D'HERBLAY [*still apologetic*]: If you're sure I'm not disturbing you...

MOULINEAUX: Disturbing me, madame? A client like you?... The very idea!

MADAME D'HERBLAY [*moving down, reluctantly*]: Why, thank you, monsieur... [*To* DARTAGNAN, *noticing him on the canapé.*] Oh! I hope I'm not interrupting...

DARTAGNAN [*with a wave*]: Please... Please...

MADAME D'HERBLAY: Well, if you're sure... [*Taking off her coat and showing* MOULINEAUX *her blouse.*] You see? It really doesn't fit... See all the tucks and gathers?

MOULINEAUX [*scrutinizing very professionally*]: Yes... Yes... The tucks and gathers...

MADAME D'HERBLAY: It's simply too big, monsieur. You have to cut it on the bias.

MOULINEAUX: Yes... Obviously... [*To* DARTAGNAN.] On the bias...

MADAME D'HERBLAY: I think you're simply going to have to cut it again

MOULINEAUX [*terrified*]: I am?

MADAME D'HERBLAY: And as soon as possible, if it's not asking too much.

MOULINEAUX: Cut it?

MADAME D'HERBLAY: Why yes... Don't you think so?

MOULINEAUX: Certainly, madame! I couldn't agree more... [*Aside, under his breath.*] Cut it, she says... [*He picks up a pair of shears from one of the workbenches.*] Cut it...

[*He returns to* MADAME D'HERBLAY, *brandishing the shears.*]

MADAME D'HERBLAY [*recoiling*]: Good heavens...

MOULINEAUX [*about to cut into the blouse*]: Hold still, will you! How can I—

MADAME D'HERBLAY: Monsieur! What are you—

MOULINEAUX: Well, make up your mind! Do you want me to cut it or don't you?

MADAME D'HERBLAY: Yes! Of course! But not right now... My goodness...

MOULINEAUX: Oh, I thought... [*To* DARTAGNAN.] "As soon as possible," she said...

MADAME D'HERBLAY: As long as you see what has to be done... You can send someone round to pick it up, if you would.

[*She puts on her coat and gets ready to leave.*]

MOULINEAUX [*mechanically opening and closing the shears*]: Yes... Yes...

MADAME D'HERBLAY [*stopping at the door, up center*]: Oh, by the way, monsieur... I've moved.

MOULINEAUX: Aha...

MADAME D'HERBLAY: That is, I'm still at the same address... Only one floor up.

MOULINEAUX [*echoing*]: One floor up...

MADAME D'HERBLAY: You won't forget...

MOULINEAUX: No... No...

MADAME D'HERBLAY: And thank you so much for taking the time...

MOULINEAUX: Oh, don't mention it! My pleasure...

MADAME D'HERBLAY [*nodding*]: Monsieur... [*Nodding to* DARTAGNAN.] Monsieur...

[*She exits.* MOULINEAUX *stands for a moment, staring blankly, still playing absentmindedly with the shears.*]

DARTAGNAN [*watching him, laughing, aside*]: My my! He looks as if he's seen a ghost! Odd chap, I must say!... [*Getting up, to* MOULINEAUX.] You know, maybe a nice cold shower would help...

MOULINEAUX [*rousing himself*]: Maybe what?

DARTAGNAN: A nice cold shower... I think you should take one.

MOULINEAUX [*dumbfounded*]: You think...

DARTAGNAN: It would do you a world of good, you know. And that's not just my opinion.

MOULINEAUX: Oh? Who else, may I ask...

DARTAGNAN: Moulineaux!

MOULINEAUX [*looking at him as if he were out of his mind*]: Moulineaux?

DARTAGNAN: Yes... Doctor Moulineaux... We were chatting just now...

MOULINEAUX: You were...? Just now?

DARTAGNAN: Yes...

MOULINEAUX: My friend, you must be sick!

DARTAGNAN [*laughing*]: Why? Just because I talk to a doctor? Come now!... We happened to meet...

MOULINEAUX: Aha... You and Moulineaux... Balthasar Moulineaux...

DARTAGNAN: Yes...

MOULINEAUX [*moving down right*]: That's the best one yet!

[*While they have been talking,* MIMI *has appeared at the open door.*]

MIMI [*entering, carrying a little dog under her arm, to* DARTAGNAN.] Ah, Anatole...

DARTAGNAN [*rushing to greet her*]: Mathilde, chérie...

MOULINEAUX [*glancing up right, aside*]: Damn! And his wife is still in there!

DARTAGNAN [*leading* MIMI *downstage*]: Come... Let me introduce you... Signor Yuno... Madame de Sainte-Vinaigrette... [*To* MOULINEAUX.] The friend I was telling you about...

MOULINEAUX [*turning*]: Delighted, I'm... [*Thunderstruck, aside.*] No!... Mimi!... Mimi Laflamme!

MIMI [*holding out her hand*]: Monsieur... [*Suddenly recognizing him, pulling her hand away, aside.*] Baba... Baba... It can't be!

MOULINEAUX [*aside*]: I don't believe it! [*Taking her hand back and kissing it.*] Madame...

MIMI [*aside*]: Baba!... Baba le Distingué! Of all people!...

DARTAGNAN [*to* MOULINEAUX]: I'm sure you'll find her worthy of your talents, signore. Madame de Sainte-Vinaigrette is from one of the oldest and finest families of the Boulevard Saint-Germain!

MOULINEAUX: How nice...

MIMI [*aside*]: And he's recognized me! Damnation!... I'd better have a long talk

with him, and in a hurry! [*To* DARTAGNAN, *holding up the dog.*] Look,
Anatole! See how Bijou's little ears are twitching!

DARTAGNAN: Chérie?

MIMI: Mamma's precious wants to go bye-bye... Be an absolute dear and take
him out, won't you? A few times around the block should be enough... Five
or six...

DARTAGNAN [*scandalized*]: Your dog?... Certainly not!

MIMI [*with a frown*]: I beg your pardon? Perhaps you didn't hear me...

DARTAGNAN [*humbled*]: Certainly, Mathilde... Good idea!... Right away...
[*Taking the dog, aside.*] The things I won't do for that woman! It's
humiliating!

[*He exits up center.* MIMI *follows him to the door to watch him leave.*]

MIMI [*when she is sure that he is gone, coming down, joining* MOULINEAUX]:
Baba le Distingué! Is it really you?

MOULINEAUX: Mimi Laflamme!

[*They shake hands warmly.*]

MIMI: What a nice surprise! Small world, isn't it!

MOULINEAUX: I should say!

MIMI: And so far from the Latin Quarter...

MOULINEAUX: Yes... Those wonderful days when we... You and I... All of us...

MIMI: Yes... Those were the days...

MOULINEAUX: Me, studying my medicine... And you... you... [*With a shrug.*]
Whatever...

MIMI: And that famous diploma, Baba? Did you ever get it?

MOULINEAUX [*hands in pockets, trying to appear casual*]: Well, I... Can't you
tell?

MIMI: And so now you're a tailor!

MOULINEAUX [*after a moment of reflection*]: That is... Once you learn to be a
surgeon... [*He snaps his fingers.*] It's so simple!... Besides, it's so much
more chic...

MIMI: Oh?

MOULINEAUX: Yes... Any doctor can be a... a doctor! But to be a tailor too...

MIMI [*laughing*]: Ha! You haven't changed a bit! Same old Baba le Distingué!

MOULINEAUX: Shhh! Please... [*With an anxious glance, up right.*] Not so loud!

MIMI: Oh, I'm sorry... Is someone sick?

MOULINEAUX: No... No... But still... No need to keep screaming "Baba le
Distingué"... Times have changed...

MIMI: But not you!

MOULINEAUX [*fatuously*]: Well... Maybe I'm still "distingué"... I suppose... But
no more "Baba"... It was all right for a student, but I've come a long way...

MIMI: But what else can I call you? That's the only name I ever knew.

MOULINEAUX: It was short for "Balthasar"...

MIMI: No!... Balthasar what?

MOULINEAUX [*without thinking*]: Balthasar Mouli... [*Catching himself just in
time.*] Yuno!

MIMI: Mouliyuno? [*Laughing.*] What a name!

MOULINEAUX: No, no!... Yuno! Just plain Yuno!...

MIMI: Oh, I thought you said...

MOULINEAUX: Balthasar Yuno!

MIMI: Are you Italian?

MOULINEAUX: Just a little...

MIMI [*crossing left in front of him, with a rather affected gait*]: Well, Balthasar... If you're not Baba le Distingué any more, I'm not Mimi Laflamme either!

MOULINEAUX: So I gather...

MIMI: I'm Madame de Sainte-Vinaigrette...

MOULINEAUX: Yes... Mathilde, if I'm not mistaken...

MIMI: That's right...

MOULINEAUX: You mean, you settled down?

MIMI [*sitting on the canapé, seductively*]: Well, let's say "settled in"... First of all, I got married...

MOULINEAUX: You?

MIMI: Yes... An absolute idiot!... Then, once I was a wife, instead of just a... Well, after two days of honeymoon, I left him... For a general...

MOULINEAUX: Damn! Not bad!... A general?... They don't grow on trees! Where the devil did you find him?

MIMI: In the Tuileries... On a park bench... Under a tree...

MOULINEAUX: Oh?

MIMI: One morning, while my dumb bird of a husband went to buy some cigarettes...

MOULINEAUX [*with a quizzical tilt of the head*]: Funny... Someone else told me a story just like that... Only with him it was a cigar...

[*All of a sudden there is a noise of breaking glass from the room, up right.*]

MIMI [*jumping*] ⎫   ⎧ Oh!
                ⎬ [*together*]:   ⎨
MOULINEAUX [*aside*] ⎭   ⎩ Good God!

MOULINEAUX [*looking in the direction of the noise, still aside*]: Suzanne!... I almost forgot... She's losing her temper!

MIMI: What was that?

MOULINEAUX [*innocently*]: What was what?

MIMI: Do you have some kind of an animal in here?

MOULINEAUX: Do I... [*Quickly.*] Yes!... As a matter of fact... A... A... An ostrich...

MIMI: Really?

MOULINEAUX: Yes... I... I need it for the plumes...

MIMI [*getting up*]: Oh, please, Baba... Balthasar... May I see it?

MOULINEAUX: Impossible! It... It's wild!... It bites!... Dumb bird!... [*Trying to change the subject.*] You were saying... Your husband... Have you ever seen him since?

MIMI: Him? Thanks just the same! Talk about dumb... He served his purpose! He made me a lady, if you see what I mean...

MOULINEAUX: Yes...

MIMI: From there it was just a skip and a jump to become a real somebody!

MOULINEAUX [*nodding*]: Madame de...

MIMI: ...de Sainte-Vinaigrette! Exactly!... [*There is another crash.*] Damnation! Are you sure your ostrich is all right?

MOULINEAUX: Fine, thank you! [*Mechanically.*] And you?... [*Realizing the absurdity of his remark.*] I... I mean... Wait here. I'm going to ask her...

MIMI: The ostrich?...

[*The door, up right, flies open, and* SUZANNE *comes storming in.*]

SUZANNE [*furious, coming down right*]: Oh! I never... How much longer...

MOULINEAUX [*jumping at the intrusion*]: Suzanne!

SUZANNE ⎱ [*together*]: ⎰ What do you take me for?

MOULINEAUX ⎰ ⎱ Please... Please...

SUZANNE [*catching sight of* MIMI]: What?... Another woman?... Oh! Now it's all so clear!

MOULINEAUX: Suzanne!...

SUZANNE [*to* MOULINEAUX, *pacing up and down*]: Now I see what you've been up to... Why you've kept me stuck away...

MIMI [*to* MOULINEAUX]: Who is that person?

MOULINEAUX [*to* MIMI]: She... Nobody!... My bookkeeper...

SUZANNE [*still pacing*]: Oh! I never...

MOULINEAUX [*to* MIMI]: Very sick, poor thing!... Nerves!... A mental case... [*To* SUZANNE, *as she passes on her way downstage.*] Please, Suzanne... I can explain...

MIMI: Tsk tsk tsk!

SUZANNE [*still pacing and fuming*]: Of all the cheating, scheming...

MOULINEAUX [*to* SUZANNE, *on her way upstage*]: Please! If you'll only listen...

SUZANNE [*stopping abruptly in her tracks*]: To what? To your lies?

MOULINEAUX: No...

MIMI [*aside*]: Ostrich, indeed!

SUZANNE: Why didn't you just come right out and admit...

MOULINEAUX: But...

SUZANNE: ...that you came here to be with your mistress!

MIMI [*with a start*] ⎱ [*together*]: ⎰ His what?

MOULINEAUX ⎰ ⎱ But Suzanne... Dear, sweet Suzanne...

MIMI [*to* SUZANNE]: I beg your pardon! Nerves or not... Just what do you take me for?...

MOULINEAUX ⎱ [*together*]: ⎰ Please...

SUZANNE ⎰ ⎱ What indeed!

MIMI [*to* SUZANNE, *continuing*]: I came here for a fitting!

[*Both women stand confronting each other, separated only by an increasingly frantic* MOULINEAUX.]

SUZANNE [*to* MIMI]: Oh yes! Tell me... I know that story... [*To* MOULINEAUX.] Don't I, monsieur!

MOULINEAUX ⎱ [*together*]: ⎰ But... But...

MIMI ⎰ ⎱ Yes, I'm sure you do!

MOULINEAUX: Please... Ladies...

SUZANNE [*to* MOULINEAUX]: You have your nerve, monsieur, I must say!

MIMI [*to* MOULINEAUX, *caustically*]: My friend, when a gentleman is his bookkeeper's lover...

MOULINEAUX: His what?

MIMI: ...he owes it to his clients not to let her insult them!

SUZANNE: Bookkeeper? What bookkeeper?

MIMI: Even mental cases!

MOULINEAUX [*exploding*]: Now just one minute! [*To* MIMI.] What do you mean, her lover?

SUZANNE: What is she talking about? Who's a bookkeeper?

MOULINEAUX [*to* SUZANNE]: Nothing, damn it! She's not talking to you!

MIMI: We Sainte-Vinaigrettes... *de* Sainte-Vinaigrettes... aren't accustomed to being insulted!

MOULINEAUX: Please, Mimi... She didn't mean it...

MIMI: If I say I came here for a fitting...

SUZANNE [*to* MOULINEAUX]: Who says I didn't mean it?

MIMI: ...then I came here for a fitting!

MOULINEAUX [*to* SUZANNE]: She did! Really!... That's all...

SUZANNE: Oh, I'm sure.

MIMI [*to* SUZANNE]: And the proof is that I came here with my lover, madame!

MOULINEAUX [*aside*]: Oh my...

SUZANNE [*with a sarcastic little laugh*]: Yes! Of course you did! Your lover!... And where is the gentleman, may I ask?

MIMI: Out walking my dog, if it's any business of yours! He'll be back any moment!

MOULINEAUX [*moving left, aghast*]: Oh my my my! Oh my...

MIMI [*pricking up her ears*]: In fact, I hear him now...

[*She moves up center to the door.*]

SUZANNE: No doubt, madame!

[DARTAGNAN *appears at the door with the dog under his arm.*]

MIMI [*to* DARTAGNAN]: Come in! Come in!... Let everyone see you!... Madame here doesn't believe who you are!

DARTAGNAN [*entering*]: I... Who? I... [*Turning and seeing* SUZANNE, *with a start.*] My wife!

SUZANNE [*with a scream*]: My husband!

MOULINEAUX [*clapping his hands together in despair*]: My God! My God![1]

SUZANNE: You... Oh!

DARTAGNAN: Suzanne!

SUZANNE: You won't get away with this!

DARTAGNAN: Suzanne... Suzanne...

SUZANNE: I'll make you pay, you... you wretch!

[*She stalks out, up center.*]

DARTAGNAN [*following her*]: But Suzanne... [*To* MIMI, *thrusting the dog into her hands.*] Here! Take your damn dog! [*At the door.*] Suzanne...

MIMI: But Anatole...

DARTAGNAN: Go to blazes!

[*He runs out in hot pursuit.*]

MIMI [*holding the dog*]: "Go to..." Oh! The nerve of that man! After all I've... [*Fanning herself.*] Oh... My... Oh... I'm going to faint...

[*She falls in a heap.*]

MOULINEAUX [*frantic, catching her with his right arm and the dog with his left*]: No! Please... Of all times... Mimi, please... Don't... Don't...

---

[1] From here to the end of the act the pace must be frenetic and uninterrupted [Author's note].

[*At that moment* YVONNE *appears outside the open door.*]

YVONNE: One B... [*Entering, calling.*] Mamma?...

MOULINEAUX [*petrified*]: Good God!

YVONNE: Mamma? Are you still here?

MOULINEAUX [*turning, finding himself face to face with* YVONNE]: Yvonne!

YVONNE: You... Here?... And... [*Noticing* MIMI.] Oh! And with a woman in your arms!

MOULINEAUX [*desperately trying to explain*]: Yvonne... Please, it's not—

YVONNE: Well! I've seen quite enough!

MOULINEAUX: But it's not what you—

YVONNE: And I'll thank you never to darken my door again!

[*She strides out, up center.*]

MOULINEAUX [*trying to follow her as best he can*]: But... Wait! Let me explain!... [*Obviously encumbered by his two charges, looking for a way to dispose of them.*] Goddammit! Of all times...

[*Just then* BASSINET *appears at the open door, and pokes his head in.*]

BASSINET: I say...

MOULINEAUX: You... Quick! Come here!

BASSINET [*entering*]: Monsieur, the locksmith—

MOULINEAUX [*shoving* MIMI *and the dog in his face*]: Here! Take these!... [*At the door.*] Yvonne!... Wait! Yvonne!...

[*He runs out.*]

BASSINET [*watching him streak off*]: But monsieur... Who the devil... [*Looking at* MIMI.] What?... [*Stupefied.*] It can't be!... Mimi! You've come back! You've come back!

[*He plants a huge kiss on her cheek.*]

MIMI [*coming to*]: Where... Where am I?... Who... [*Recognizing* BASSINET.] My husband!... Damnation!

[*She gives his face a resounding slap and frees herself.* BASSINET, *agape, collapses onto the canapé, dropping the dog as* MIMI *runs out the open door.*]

BASSINET [*rubbing his cheek, watching her go*]: But it's me, Mimi!... Mimi! Me... Me...

CURTAIN

Act Three

The scene is the same as in Act One.

At rise, the stage is empty. After a few moments, the doorbell rings. There is a brief pause.

ETIENNE'S VOICE [*offstage*]: Never mind, monsieur... It's nothing...

MOULINEAUX [*entering, down left, obviously anxious, muttering*]: I wonder if it's... [*Calling.*] Etienne!... Etienne!...

ETIENNE [*entering, up center*]: Monsieur?

MOULINEAUX: Who was that? Who rang?

ETIENNE: Oh, it's nothing, monsieur... Nothing at all...
   [*He turns to leave.*]

MOULINEAUX: "Nothing"? What do you mean, "nothing"? Someone rang. Who was it?

ETIENNE [*at the double door*]: Only one of monsieur's patients, monsieur... For a treatment... He asked if monsieur was in, and when I said that he was...

MOULINEAUX: You didn't! I thought I told you, Etienne...

ETIENNE: No matter... He said he felt fine all of a sudden, and he left.

MOULINEAUX [*under his breath*]: Idiot!... [*Carping.*] Yes, well... Next time somebody comes, and it's nobody, that's what you tell me: "It's nobody, monsieur..." Not "it's nothing"... Understand?

ETIENNE: I didn't think it made much difference monsieur...

MOULINEAUX: Not to you, but it does to me...

ETIENNE: Yes, monsieur.

MOULINEAUX [*annoyed*]: That's fine... You can go now.
   [*He moves right, obviously out of sorts and deep in thought.* ETIENNE *watches him for a moment.*]

ETIENNE [*shaking his head sympathetically, aside*]: Did you ever see...? Tsk tsk tsk... [*To* MOULINEAUX.] If monsieur doesn't mind my saying...

MOULINEAUX [*looking up*]: Hmm?

ETIENNE: I can understand how monsieur must feel, and how concerned he is... No offense, but if only he had taken my advice...

MOULINEAUX: Etienne...

ETIENNE: About the gala, I mean...

MOULINEAUX: Etienne, I'll thank you—

ETIENNE: I told monsieur no good would come of it!... [MOULINEAUX, *hands on hips, looks at him in disbelief.*] Besides, there are ways of doing things, and there are ways... As long as we're going to do them, at least we should do them right!

MOULINEAUX: Are you quite through?

ETIENNE: Not quite, monsieur...

MOULINEAUX [*sarcastically*]: Oh, please! Don't let me interrupt...

ETIENNE: No... Monsieur should have told me what he intended to do. "Etienne," he should have said, "I'm going to the gala at the Folies Exotiques..." I would have taken the trouble to sleep in monsieur's bed... For appearances' sake...

MOULINEAUX [*unable to contain himself*]: My bed?

ETIENNE: Oh I don't mind... Monsieur is quite clean... [MOULINEAUX *shakes his head.*] And anyway, I would have changed the bedclothes before...

MOULINEAUX: Perhaps even after...

ETIENNE: And madame would never know...

MOULINEAUX [*sighing*]: Ah yes! Madame... Wherever she is...

ETIENNE [*sadly*]: We were wondering the same thing in the pantry, monsieur.

MOULINEAUX: It's almost a whole day since... [*Dramatically.*] since she left my bed and board...

ETIENNE: So to speak! [*Aside.*] Board, yes... [*Gesturing down left and right toward their separate rooms, still aside.*] But bed...? Tsk tsk tsk...

MOULINEAUX: Almost twenty-four hours...

ETIENNE: I know I express the sentiments of all the help, monsieur, when I say that I hope this matter can be resolved...

MOULINEAUX: Thank you, Etienne.

ETIENNE: ...and that monsieur will do his best... If only for me, monsieur...

MOULINEAUX: For you?

ETIENNE [*on the verge of tears*]: It's the first time I've ever gone through something like this, monsieur... The first time...

MOULINEAUX [*aside*]: Where have I heard that before!

ETIENNE: Believe me... The very first time... All my previous employers were faithful to their wives...

MOULINEAUX: Aha...

ETIENNE: To a fault... They never subjected me to such emotions, monsieur... And I'm terribly sensitive... [*Sniffling.*] As I think monsieur can see...
[*The door bell rings.*]

MOULINEAUX [*looking up*]: Etienne?

ETIENNE: Monsieur?

MOULINEAUX: The bell...

ETIENNE: Monsieur will do his best, then? For my sake?

MOULINEAUX: Yes, yes, yes!... Just go see who that is!

ETIENNE: Thank you, monsieur. [*He holds out his hand, but, seeing that* MOULINEAUX *doesn't reciprocate, shakes it in space.*] Thank you... Much obliged...

MOULINEAUX [*crossing left*]: And don't forget this time! I'm not at home for anyone... Except madame, that is...

ETIENNE: Anyone, monsieur?

MOULINEAUX: Anyone, Etienne! I don't care if it's the Pope!
[*He exits, down left.* ETIENNE *exits, up center.*]

ETIENNE'S VOICE: No, I'm sorry, monsieur... I'm sorry... He's not at home...
[DARTAGNAN *enters, up center, with* ETIENNE *at his heels.*]

DARTAGNAN [*at the door*]: But my good man, the concierge distinctly told me that he was.

ETIENNE: And monsieur himself distinctly told me that he wasn't! I should think he would know better than the concierge, monsieur!

DARTAGNAN: Very well... He's not in... Now please go tell him that Monsieur Dartagnan would like to see him. It's urgent!

ETIENNE: Excuse me, but he told me: "I don't care if it's the Pope!" And I'm afraid monsieur isn't even...

DARTAGNAN: No. But I've still got to see him... On account of my wife...

ETIENNE: And he's not seeing anyone, monsieur... On account of his!

DARTAGNAN: Really? Why is that?

ETIENNE [*self-important*]: I'm sorry, but some things are confidential! Family matters... For the master and the help...

DARTAGNAN: Oh?

ETIENNE: Not for outsiders... They can say what they like, but at least I can keep a secret! [*Categorically.*] Wild horses, monsieur!... Wild horses!...

DARTAGNAN: Beg pardon?

ETIENNE: They wouldn't make me talk, monsieur... Not family matters... Monsieur could even try to trick me...

DARTAGNAN: Me? Perish the thought!

ETIENNE: But he'd never worm it out of me!... He could come here and stand right in front of me, and say: "Etienne, my good man... Is it true what I hear?... That things have been all at sixes and sevens?... That Monsieur Moulineaux went to the gala the other night, and didn't come home?..."

DARTAGNAN [*with a chuckle, aside*]: No!

ETIENNE [*continuing*]: "And madame, Etienne... Is it true that no one knows where she is?... That she hasn't been home all night, and that monsieur is worried sick?..."

DARTAGNAN [*aside*]: Of all things...

ETIENNE: Well, I'm sorry, monsieur... But it just wouldn't work! Wild horses...

DARTAGNAN [*nodding*]: Wild horses...

ETIENNE: I'd look monsieur right in the eye, and I'd say: "I don't know what monsieur is talking about! Sorry!"

DARTAGNAN: Admirable... Admirable...

ETIENNE: Much obliged, monsieur. But that's just how I am when it comes to family matters...

DARTAGNAN: Yes, I understand... [*After a pause, offhand.*] Etienne, my good man... Tell me, is it true, what I hear?... That madame hasn't been home all night, and that monsieur is worried sick?

ETIENNE [*surprised*]: What? How did—?

DARTAGNAN: Someone told me...

ETIENNE: The nerve! [*To himself.*] You just can't trust people with a secret! Did you ever see...?

DARTAGNAN: I know what the poor chap is going through, believe me! My wife didn't come home last night either, I'm afraid...

ETIENNE: No! Monsieur's too?

DARTAGNAN: And after what happened yesterday, I'm not surprised! I haven't seen hide nor hair...

ETIENNE: Tsk tsk tsk! It sounds like an epidemic, monsieur!

DARTAGNAN: Not that I really blame her, I suppose... Goodness me, what a scene!... [*Moving down left.*] But I'm sure it won't last. She'll come to her senses...

ETIENNE: Yes, monsieur. I hope so...

DARTAGNAN: Anyway, that's why I have to see the doctor. This is about the time she comes for her daily treatment, so I thought... I thought if I came and waited...

ETIENNE: Maybe so, monsieur... But she won't see him either. Not today... Not even if she's the Pope!... "Nobody!" he said... Orders are orders... At least, until madame comes back home, where she belongs...

DARTAGNAN: Yes, but my good man...

[*The doorbell rings.*]

ETIENNE: Ah!... Excuse me, monsieur... That might just be...

[*He exits, up center.*]

DARTAGNAN [*crossing right*]: No... No two ways about it... I've got to see her and make amends. Even if it means... [*Taking a picture from his pocket.*] giving up Mathilde, forever...

[*He kisses the picture, sighing as* ETIENNE *enters, up center, excitedly.*]

ETIENNE: It is, monsieur! It's the ladies!... I think monsieur had better leave...

DARTAGNAN [*putting the picture back in his pocket*]: What ladies?

ETIENNE: Madame Moulineaux and her mother, monsieur...

DARTAGNAN: His wife?... Lucky devil! I wish I could say the same!

[MADAME AIGREVILLE *storms in, up center, followed by* YVONNE.]

MADAME AIGREVILLE [*to* ETIENNE, *commanding*]: Go tell him I'm here, young man!

DARTAGNAN [*surprised, aside*]: Good heavens!... The queen!

MADAME AIGREVILLE [*to* ETIENNE]: Immediately, understand?

ETIENNE: Very good, Madame Aigreville... Right away...

DARTAGNAN [*still down left, overhearing, aside*]: Madame Who?...

ETIENNE [*turning to leave*]: Ah! I know monsieur will be pleased... Very pleased...

DARTAGNAN [*aside*]: But I thought...

[ETIENNE *exits, down left.*]

MADAME AIGREVILLE [*as he leaves*]: That remains to be seen!

[*She comes down right and takes an authoritative stance.* YVONNE *hangs back, up right.*]

DARTAGNAN [*puzzled, tentatively, approaching* MADAME AIGREVILLE]: Pardon me, madame... But do I understand correctly that you're not...

MADAME AIGREVILLE: Monsieur?

DARTAGNAN: ...that you're not the queen of Greenland?

MADAME AIGREVILLE: The what?... [*With a little laugh.*] Me?... I hardly think so!

DARTAGNAN: But madame, you're the image...

MADAME AIGREVILLE: I am?

DARTAGNAN [*emphasizing*]: Spitting... Spitting...

MADAME AIGREVILLE [*putting her hand to her mouth*]: Oh, I beg—

DARTAGNAN: Two peas in a pod!... You're sure you're not the queen?

MADAME AIGREVILLE: Really, monsieur! I think I would know! [*Aside.*] His eczema must be spreading... To his head!

DARTAGNAN: Sorry, my mistake... [*Trying to make a graceful exit.*] Well, if you'll excuse me, madame... I'm sure you have things to discuss with the doctor...

MADAME AIGREVILLE: To say the least!

DARTAGNAN: So I'll be on my way... [*With a little bow.*]: Your High— [*Correcting.*] Madame...

MADAME AIGREVILLE: Monsieur...

DARTAGNAN [*moving up center, with a bow to* YVONNE]: And Madame Moulineaux... A pleasure, I assure you... [*As* YVONNE *gives a little noncommittal nod, aside.*] Oh! Pretty... Pretty...

[*He exits, leaving the double door ajar.*]

MADAME AIGREVILLE [*to* YVONNE]: Now down to business, precious!

YVONNE: Yes, mamma...

MADAME AIGREVILLE: And you won't forget what I told you... You'll be firm...

YVONNE: Oh, indeed I will, mamma! Indeed I will!

[*The door, down left, opens and* MOULINEAUX *hurries in.*]

MOULINEAUX [*spying* YVONNE, *up right*]: Yvonne!... At last!... [*Rushing to join her, arms outstretched, sighing.*] Ah! You don't know how worried—

MADAME AIGREVILLE [*quickly moving to intercept him, planting herself in front of* YVONNE]: Oh no, monsieur! Back!...

MOULINEAUX [*stopping in his tracks*]: What?

MADAME AIGREVILLE: Not another step, I'm warning you!

MOULINEAUX: But...

MADAME AIGREVILLE: That's not what we're here for!

MOULINEAUX [*trying to talk around her, to* YVONNE]: But Yvonne... I can explain...

MADAME AIGREVILLE: Perhaps you thought you could get away with your seamy little escapade...

MOULINEAUX [*trying to object*]: My seamy... But it wasn't...

MADAME AIGREVILLE: Well, if so, you forgot about me, my good man! You forgot that your wife has a mother!

MOULINEAUX [*aside*]: No such luck!

MADAME AIGREVILLE: And a mother who knows her duty, my friend! [*Very business-like.*] Now then, monsieur... You're my daughter's husband, much though I might regret it... Her spouse in the eyes of the law... [*To* YVONNE.] Alas! [*To* MOULINEAUX.] And I have no choice but to bring her back...

MOULINEAUX [*suddenly softening*]: Oh... At least you're being reasonable...

MADAME AIGREVILLE: ...to live with you under the *conjungle* roof...

MOULINEAUX: The... Well now, that's more like it!

[*He makes a move toward* YVONNE.]

MADAME AIGREVILLE [*menacing*]: Back! Back!... I said: "Not another step!" monsieur!...

MOULINEAUX: But...

MADAME AIGREVILLE: I'm afraid you haven't quite grasped the situation.

MOULINEAUX: You just said...

MADAME AIGREVILLE: We've given it a good deal of thought, my daughter and I... and we've decided that, from now on, you'll be husband and wife in name only.

MOULINEAUX [*to* MADAME AIGREVILLE, *hands on hips*]: Just like that!

MADAME AIGREVILLE: First I thought I would take her back home, monsieur...

With me... That's why we spent last night at the Hotel Royal...

MOULINEAUX [*beginning to pace up and down*]: Yes! While I was worried sick!

MADAME AIGREVILLE [*casually*]: They'll be sending you the bill... But people do talk, monsieur. Tongues wag and fingers point... And I won't have my daughter subjected to hoos and boots...

MOULINEAUX: To what?

MADAME AIGREVILLE: To public ridicule, my friend... To hoos and... [*Correcting.*] Boos... To boos and hoots...

MOULINEAUX: I see... And so?

MADAME AIGREVILLE: And so, we've decided that she will continue to live here...

MOULINEAUX: Yes... Under the "conjungle" roof...

MADAME AIGREVILLE: Exactly!... But only for appearances! I hope that's clear, monsieur!

MOULINEAUX: Yes, thank you! Quite clear! [*Down left, aside.*] We'll work things out ourselves once the old witch goes home! [*To* MADAME AIGREVILLE.] Fine, then... It's settled!... That's that!

MADAME AIGREVILLE: And just to be sure, I'm going to live here with her...

MOULINEAUX: What?

MADAME AIGREVILLE: ...to look after her, and protect her! [*To* YVONNE.] Isn't that right, precious?

YVONNE [*unenthusiastically*]: Yes, mamma...

MOULINEAUX [*furious, aside*]: "Conjungle" is right, damn it! Meddling old gorilla!

MADAME AIGREVILLE [*to* MOULINEAUX]: But don't go getting any ideas, monsieur. We're going to divide the apartment in half...

MOULINEAUX: Oh we are, are we?

MADAME AIGREVILLE [*moving center, pointing left*]: The men's side for you... [*Pointing right.*] The women's side for us...

MOULINEAUX [*almost good-naturedly, with a wave of the hand*]: Aha... And this...?

MADAME AIGREVILLE: No man's land...

MOULINEAUX: Or no woman's, if you'd rather...

MADAME AIGREVILLE [*ignoring the witticism*]: And that, monsieur, is how I intend to bring peace and tranquility to my daughter's unfortunate marriage...

MOULINEAUX: Unfortunate... Un... [*Pacing, trying to control himself, but finally exploding.*] Now let me tell you something! It's crazy!... You're crazy, if you want to know... Divide the apartment... What have I done to deserve this?... [*To* YVONNE.] What, Yvonne? Tell me... [*He continues pacing.*]

YVONNE: Me?

MADAME AIGREVILLE [*by her side, up right*]: Don't answer him, precious! He's trying to trick you!

MOULINEAUX [*down left, sharply*]: Will you let her speak, damn it!

MADAME AIGREVILLE: I'll thank you to keep a civil tongue in your head!

YVONNE [*to* MOULINEAUX, *approaching him*]: Really, monsieur! Do you have the nerve... the gall... to ask me what you've done?

MOULINEAUX: But Yvonne...

MADAME AIGREVILLE [*to* YVONNE]: He does!... He has the gall... He has...

MOULINEAUX [*shouting up right, to* MADAME AIGREVILLE, *furious*]: You... It's my gall, damn it! No one's asking you, you old—

YVONNE: Please, monsieur! Remember that you're talking to my mother!

MOULINEAUX [*trying to calm down*]: Yes... All right, for your sake... [*He takes a deep breath.*] Now, tell me...

YVONNE: I think it's quite obvious... I catch you at the dressmaker's, with your mistress in your arms...

MOULINEAUX [*objecting, quickly*]: But not mine! Not mine!

YVONNE [*with a smirk*]: Not your arms?

MOULINEAUX: Not my mistress!

YVONNE: Oh? Then who was she, monsieur?

MOULINEAUX: Just... Some woman...

YVONNE: Yes... Some woman you just happened to take in your arms...

MOULINEAUX: Yes... No! I mean... I didn't take her! Someone put her there... [*He mimes the action.*] Like that!

YVONNE: Of course! I'm sure they did!... That's why you were hugging her!

MOULINEAUX: But I wasn't...

YVONNE: Please, monsieur! I've got eyes! I can see!... She was fainting and you were hugging her...

MOULINEAUX [*jumping in*]: There! There!... You admit it!... She was sick!... That proves it!

YVONNE: Proves what?... That you chase skirts, monsieur!... Fainting or not!

MADAME AIGREVILLE [*still up right, to* MOULINEAUX]: And you tell me they're your patients!

MOULINEAUX: No, no... [*To* MADAME AIGREVILLE.] That's another one... Please! Don't confuse the issue!... [*Moving toward her.*] The patient you met is Madame Dartagnan... Monsieur Dartagnan's wife!... This one...

MADAME AIGREVILLE [*sharply*]: Yes? Whose is she?

MOULINEAUX [*quickly, without thinking*]: Dartagnan's...

MADAME AIGREVILLE: Oh, I see! He has two!

MOULINEAUX: Yes...

MADAME AIGREVILLE: How nice! He's a bigamist!...

MOULINEAUX: He's... No, no! That's not what I... [*To* YVONNE.] Really, Yvonne, that's not... [*To* MADAME AIGREVILLE.] You keep getting everything all... Can't you mind your own business? It's no concern of yours!

MADAME AIGREVILLE: Indeed! I think my daughter's happiness—

MOULINEAUX: All you can do is meddle! You come here out of a clear blue sky, and all of a sudden...

YVONNE [*to* MOULINEAUX]: Please...

MOULINEAUX: Meddle, meddle, meddle!

MADAME AIGREVILLE: Oh yes! Now it's my fault!... Tell me I'm the unfaithful husband, who sleeps heaven knows where!

YVONNE [*to* MADAME AIGREVILLE]: Mamma, please...

MADAME AIGREVILLE [*pressing her attack, to* MOULINEAUX]: Tell me I'm the philanderer... the... the *adulterator* !... Go ahead, monsieur! Tell me!

MOULINEAUX [*furious*]: Tell you?... No, damn it! I have nothing to tell you! Nothing! Nothing! Not a thing!...

MADAME AIGREVILLE [*simply, as if proving her assertion*]: Aha!
MOULINEAUX [*pointing to* YVONNE]: I'm married to her! She's my wife, not
you! [*He turns aside and crosses himself.*] If I have anything to say, I'm
going to say it to my wife! And in private, thank you!
MADAME AIGREVILLE: Oh no! I suppose you think I'm going to leave you
alone with her?... Let her fall into your clutches?...
MOULINEAUX: My clutches? What clutches?... I'm her husband, remember?... If
I want to have a word with my own wife... alone... I think I have the right!
Don't you?
MADAME AIGREVILLE [*categorically*]: No, monsieur! I don't!
MOULINEAUX [*repressing a cry of rage*]: Oh!...
[*He makes a move toward her as if about to lunge at her throat, but
controls himself, striding nervously up left and then down right.*]
YVONNE [*to* MADAME AIGREVILLE]: I don't mind, mamma... Let him!... I'll listen
to whatever monsieur has to say. [*Very proper.*] After all, I wouldn't want
to give him any reason to criticize...
MADAME AIGREVILLE: But I know you... You're so trusting, so naive. He'll
wrap you around his little finger!... I don't think...
MOULINEAUX [*to* YVONNE, *sarcastically dramatic*]: Yes! You'll fall into my
clutches!
YVONNE [*to* MADAME AIGREVILLE, *pointedly ignoring him*]: Don't worry,
mamma. I'll be careful...
MADAME AIGREVILLE: Well... All right, if you're absolutely sure... [*Turning
toward* MOULINEAUX.] At least some of us try to be reasonable, monsieur!
[*To* YVONNE.] Don't forget, precious... Be firm!
YVONNE: Yes, mamma...
MADAME AIGREVILLE [*aside*]: Lucky for her I'm here! If not they would have
kissed and made up by now... [*Crossing to the door, up right, stopping,
casting a look of disdain over her shoulder at* MOULINEAUX, *still down
right.*] Hmmph!
[*She exits.* YVONNE *moves left, by the chaise longue, turning her back to*
MOULINEAUX, *arms folded, gazing into the distance in an attitude of
indifference. There is a brief moment of uncomfortable silence.*
MOULINEAUX *finally gets up his courage and walks slowly and deliberately
over to her.*]
MOULINEAUX [*very calmly*]: Yvonne...
YVONNE [*without turning to look at him, coldly*]: I'm listening, monsieur...
MOULINEAUX: Please... Try to forget about your mother for a minute. Forget
you even have one!... [*Quickly, realizing that the remark might be
misinterpreted.*] I mean... Not that you have one, but... but some of the
things she says... [*There is another uncomfortable silence.*] You see...
[*Floundering about, hoping for an inspiration.*] That woman, Yvonne...
Dartagnan and his wife... That woman in my arms... The two of them, that
is... Well, that's Dartagnan's business, not mine, Yvonne... [*Waiting for a
reaction.*] Yvonne...?
YVONNE [*still with her back turned*]: Go on, monsieur...
MOULINEAUX: Yes, you see, it's... it's... [*Suddenly inspired.*] It's a scientific
study! Very confidential!... A fascinating case of comparative
physiology!... I was only there as an expert, a specialist...
YVONNE: Oh?

MOULINEAUX: You see, two similar subjects, Yvonne... One perfectly normal... And the other, a rare example of... of... of congenital neuro-endocrinological pathology... With complications!... Lots and lots of fascinating complications! Fainting spells... Amnesia...

YVONNE [*finally turning around*]: And that's all? Really?

MOULINEAUX [*delighted at his apparent success*]: Really! I'd try to explain it if I thought it would help... But... [*With a wave.*] You know... Years and years of school... All terribly scientific... But as long as you can understand what I was doing there, Yvonne... And what I wasn't doing...

YVONNE: Well...

MOULINEAUX: And that it was only an experiment... And that it's over and done with...

YVONNE: Yes! That's what you say...

[MADAME AIGREVILLE *suddenly pokes her head out the door, up right.*]

MADAME AIGREVILLE: Are you finished?

MOULINEAUX: You... No, goddammit! We'll send you a telegram!

MADAME AIGREVILLE [*to* YVONNE]: Don't you believe a word he says, precious!

[*She pulls her head back and slams the door.*]

MOULINEAUX [*furious, aside*]: Old battle-axe!... And just when I was going so strong!... [*Suddenly changing his tone, to* YVONNE, *very gently*]: Don't listen to her... What I'm telling you is true. You know I wouldn't lie... [*Aside.*] Just bend the truth a little!

YVONNE [*weakening*]: Oh... If only I thought I could believe you! But it's hard...

MOULINEAUX [*pressing his advantage*]: Try!... Try, Yvonne!

YVONNE: I would so like to feel that I could trust you again...

MOULINEAUX: You can! You can!...

YVONNE [*sighing*]: No!... I'm afraid I can't!... [*Matter-of-fact.*] You men are all liars...

MOULINEAUX: How can you say that? Who ever told you...

YVONNE: Mamma...

MOULINEAUX [*with a bitter smile*]: Of course! I should have guessed!... [*Fuming.*] Mamma, mamma! Dear, sweet, lovable—

YVONNE [*eager to have an excuse to believe him*]: I suppose if you swore...

MOULINEAUX: Me? Swear?... Damn! I never—

YVONNE: No... I mean, if you swore that what you're telling me is true...

MOULINEAUX: Oh... "Swore"... You mean... [*Holding up his right hand.*] "I swear..."? That kind of "swore"...?

YVONNE: Yes... Just to convince mamma... I'm sure it would...

MOULINEAUX [*sarcastically agreeable*]: Why, certainly! Why not? Anything for mamma!... [*Raising his left hand, and with his right behind his back, crossing his fingers.*] I swear it's the truth, the whole truth... [*Wagging his crossed fingers.*] and nothing but the truth! So help me!

YVONNE: Oh, thank you, Balthasar!... And that woman in your arms...? You swear she was a stranger?

MOULINEAUX [*categorically*]: I swear she was a stranger... [*As if continuing the oath, aside.*] until the first time I met her... [*To* YVONNE.] And if I ever see her again, may everything your mother says about me be true!... There! Now do you forgive me?

YVONNE [*coquettishly*]: Well, almost... Not yet...

MOULINEAUX: But...

YVONNE: When mamma leaves, Balthasar... That's when I'll forgive you...

MOULINEAUX: And can't I even have a little kiss, while I wait?
[*He purses his lips, invitingly. Just then,* DARTAGNAN *appears at the double door, still ajar, unseen by the others.*]

YVONNE [*with a little laugh*]: Oh... I suppose... If you insist...
[*They embrace and kiss.*]

DARTAGNAN [*watching, thunderstruck, aside*]: Good heavens!... Signor Yuno and the doctor's wife!... Lovers?
[*He stands at the threshold in uncomfortable silence, watching and listening.*]

MOULINEAUX: Yvonne!... Angel!...

YVONNE: And you promise me you're going to behave from now on?... Not like the other night, when I didn't know where you were...

MOULINEAUX: I promise!

YVONNE: Instead of coming here and sleeping where you belong, you naughty thing!

DARTAGNAN [*aside*]: Oh my!...

MOULINEAUX: You'll never have any more fault to find, believe me!

YVONNE: Oh... The only fault I find is that... [*With a pout.*] you don't love your wife enough...

MOULINEAUX [*playing along*]: And you don't love your husband enough either! That's your trouble!

DARTAGNAN [*aside*]: Now that's a novel complaint!... [*Clearing his throat, pretending not to notice them.*] Anyone here?... [*Coming down right, without closing the door.*] Anyone at home?... [*To* MOULINEAUX.] Ah, signore...

MOULINEAUX [*aside*]: Dartagnan!... Goddamn! He'll put his foot in it for sure! [*To* DARTAGNAN, *joining him, right.*] Why monsieur, what a surprise!... [*Introducing.*] Monsieur Dartagnan... Madame... Madame Moulineaux...

DARTAGNAN: Yes, yes... I've had the pleasure... Not ten minutes ago... [*Aside, to* MOULINEAUX, *with a little laugh and a nudge.*] Sly devil! Congratulations!

MOULINEAUX: What...?

DARTAGNAN: And everything else is going well too, I hope?

MOULINEAUX [*on edge*]: Fine... Fine...

DARTAGNAN: And our little project?... My wife's gown is progressing?

MOULINEAUX [*trying to be offhand*]: Oh... You know...

DARTAGNAN: Our famous dirndl, with the ruffles, and the ostrich plumes...

MOULINEAUX [*taking him by the arm and almost dragging him up right, abruptly*]: How nice to see you again, monsieur!... Have you seen any good plays lately? [*Without waiting for a reply.*] Neither have I! But nowadays, don't you know... What a shame you can't stay...
[*He tries to escort him to the double door, but* DARTAGNAN *resists.*]

DARTAGNAN [*moving right*]: But signore...

YVONNE [*still down left*]: Balthasar...?

MOULINEAUX [*rushing to her side*]: Yes... Yes, Yvonne dearest?

YVONNE: What does he mean? What gown is he talking about?

MOULINEAUX: Gown...? [*Casually.*] Oh, that... [*Whispering.*] For his wife...
It's... It's for her rheumatism, poor thing!... But please, it's strictly
confidential... She's terribly sensitive...
[*They continue their exchange in whispers.*]
YVONNE: Rheumatism?
MOULINEAUX: Yes... It's... It's like a glove... Only bigger... Tight... Nice and
tight... And electromagnetic! Massages the joints...
YVONNE [*growing suspicious*]: With ruffles?... And ostrich plumes?
MOULINEAUX: Well... In case company comes...
YVONNE: Balthasar...
MOULINEAUX: Now, now, Yvonne... You said you were going to trust me...
[*He gives her a little peck on the lips.*]
DARTAGNAN [*aside*]: My goodness! And with an audience?
MOULINEAUX: And I'm going to hold you to it! [*Aloud.*] You know you're the
only woman I've ever loved...
DARTAGNAN [*aside*]: I never...!
MOULINEAUX: ...and the only one I ever will.
[*He gives her another peck.*]
DARTAGNAN [*aside*]: Have they no shame?
YVONNE [*to* MOULINEAUX]: Well... I'm not sure...
[*While they are thus engaged,* BASSINET *appears at the double door, and
stands for a moment, silently, at the threshold, watching.*]
DARTAGNAN [*up right, catching sight of him, aside*]: Good heavens! Her
husband!... The doctor!
[*He pulls out his handkerchief and waves it frantically at* MOULINEAUX,
trying to get his attention.]
MOULINEAUX [*back turned to him, not noticing, to* YVONNE]: But I love you, I
tell you... I love you! I love you!
DARTAGNAN [*still trying to signal, in a loud whisper*]: Signore!... Signore!...
BASSINET [*at the threshold, smiling*]: That's sweet!
DARTAGNAN: Signor Yuno!...
[*Noticing that* BASSINET *is looking at him quizzically, he pretends to be
fanning himself with the handkerchief, while nodding a greeting to*
BASSINET, *who proceeds to pull out his handkerchief and do likewise. The
two continue to wave and nod during the following exchange.*]
MOULINEAUX [*tenderly*]: I love you, Yvonne!
[*He puts his arms around her and attempts to give her a kiss.*]
YVONNE [*resisting*]: Please! Not in public!
MOULINEAUX: Why? I'm not ashamed... I want everyone to know... Ah,
Yvonne...
[*He locks her in a long, passionate embrace.*]
DARTAGNAN [*aside*]: Really! There's a limit!... Even for an Italian... [*Looking,
not without scorn, at* BASSINET—*who continues smiling, nodding, and
waving his handkerchief, intermittently—aside.*] And that one just stands
there! What kind of man is he?
BASSINET [*clearing his throat*]: Ahem... Ahem...
[*He strides down left, toward* MOULINEAUX, *who is still kissing* YVONNE.]
DARTAGNAN [*aside*]: Well! Finally...
BASSINET [*tapping him on the shoulder*]: I say, monsieur...

DARTAGNAN [*aside*]: Oh my! There's going to be a scene!

BASSINET [*to* MOULINEAUX]: I'm here, you know...

DARTAGNAN [*aside*]: He'll kill him! And who can blame him!

MOULINEAUX [*without turning around, still embracing* YVONNE, *grumbling to* BASSINET]: That's nice... So what?

BASSINET [*good-naturedly*]: Well, I... Aren't you even going to say hello, monsieur?

DARTAGNAN [*aside*]: What...?

MOULINEAUX [*turning around, impatiently*]: Hello!... All right?

BASSINET [*with a little wave*]: Hello there...

MOULINEAUX: Hello!... Hello!... [*Under his breath.*] Damn pest!

DARTAGNAN [*dumbfounded*]: I don't believe it!... [*To* MOULINEAUX.] Signore!... Really, signore! If you don't mind my saying...

YVONNE [*aside*]: "Signore"?... [*To* MOULINEAUX, *puzzled.*] Is he speaking to you, Balthasar?

MOULINEAUX [*on edge*]: Yes, he... [*Aside, to* YVONNE.] He's learning Italian, and... and he likes to use it every chance he gets...

YVONNE: Oh... [*Crossing up right, to a perplexed* DARTAGNAN.] Com'è bella la lingua italiana, non è vero?

MOULINEAUX [*aside*]: Good God!

YVONNE [*continuing*]: Mi piacerebbe molto parlare con Lei, se vuole...

DARTAGNAN [*with a blank look*]: Madame?

MOULINEAUX [*aside*]: If he opens his mouth I'm done for!

YVONNE [*continuing*]: Le piacerebbe, signore?

MOULINEAUX [*pushing* BASSINET *out of his way, rushing up right and grabbing* YVONNE *by the arm*]: Quick!... Didn't you hear your mother calling?

YVONNE [*resisting*]: Mia madre...? [*Correcting.*] My mother...?

MOULINEAUX: Come! You know how she gets when we keep her waiting...

YVONNE: But...

[*He whisks her off and they exit, up right. There is a moment of silence, during which* DARTAGNAN *and* BASSINET *eye each other, back and forth. Finally,* BASSINET *points up right with a little laugh.*]

BASSINET: Now where are they off to in such a hurry?

DARTAGNAN: Where indeed!

BASSINET [*still laughing*]: Our two little lovebirds...

DARTAGNAN [*forcing a laugh*]: Yes... Our two... [*Aside.*] Incredible! He accepts it!... Just like that!

BASSINET: I think they're sweet!

DARTAGNAN: Oh, very... [*Aside.*] My heavens! Is he deaf?... Is he blind?

BASSINET [*still laughing*]: You know, I'm afraid we interrupted them!

DARTAGNAN: I daresay!... And that doesn't bother you, monsieur?

BASSINET: Well... Of course, I hate to spoil their fun... But... C'est la vie!

DARTAGNAN [*echoing, incredulous*]: C'est la vie!... [*Aside.*] What is this world coming to!

BASSINET [*with a touch of exhibitionism*]: Che sarà sarà!

DARTAGNAN: I'm sure... [*Aside.*] No sense of morality... No notion of right and wrong... Simply incredible!... [*Unable to contain himself, to* BASSINET, *approaching him.*] I... Excuse me, my friend, I... I know it's none of my business...

BASSINET [*joining him, center*]: Monsieur?
DARTAGNAN: Heaven knows I'm no prude! But I simply don't understand how... Your wife, monsieur... Your wife...
BASSINET [*taken aback, aside*]: My wife? [*To* DARTAGNAN.] Yes, monsieur? What about her?
DARTAGNAN: That is... How do you let her... I mean, if she were mine... I should think you would be more careful, more... discerning, more... more... more concerned, to say the least!
BASSINET: My wife, monsieur? [*Aside.*] What brought that on, I wonder? [*Aloud.*] My goodness! Give me a chance, drat it all! I've only just found her! I haven't seen her for years!
DARTAGNAN: You haven't?
BASSINET: No... Not until yesterday... We still hardly know each other...
DARTAGNAN [*aside*]: So I see! [*Aloud.*] Oh, I didn't realize...
BASSINET [*aside*]: Why my wife, all of a sudden? [*Aloud.*] Yes... Ever since she ran away, I've been looking—
DARTAGNAN: Ran away? With the tailor?
BASSINET: A sailor...? No, no... With a soldier...
DARTAGNAN: Hmm! Soldiers too! [*Aside.*] Brazen hussy!
BASSINET: It's a fascinatiing story... [*Sensing an audience.*] You see, we were sitting in the Tuileries one morning, and I went—
DARTAGNAN [*cutting him off*]: And you say you just found her again yesterday?
BASSINET: Believe it or not! After all these years! Like a bolt from the blue!... Isn't it always the way? When you least expect it...
DARTAGNAN [*politely*]: Yes... Always the way...
BASSINET: And you'll never guess... When I found her... You'll never guess whose arms was in, monsieur!
DARTAGNAN [*cynically*]: Let me try... Our own Signor Yuno!
BASSINET: Signor Yuno!... [*Surprised.*] How did you know?
DARTAGNAN [*chuckling*]: How did I know?... You know... I know Signor Yuno... [*Aside.*] He takes it all in stride, I must say!
BASSINET: Yes... In fact, when she saw me, she was so overcome that she slapped my face with joy!... I was never so happy...
DARTAGNAN: I'm sure... [*Aside.*] Slaphappy!
BASSINET: After all these years... And now she's back where she belongs!... [*Aside, to himself.*] Won't Moulineaux be surprised when she comes here to meet him!...
[MOULINEAUX *enters, up right.*]
MOULINEAUX [*under his breath*]: There!... A few choice words to mamma... "I swear this... I swear that..." And everything is fine!... [*To* BASSINET.] Ah, my friend... I'm sorry if I was a little abrupt just now...
BASSINET: Not at all!... I understand perfectly...
DARTAGNAN [*to* MOULINEAUX]: Excuse me, signore, but...
MOULINEAUX [*to* DARTAGNAN]: Still here? I thought you left...
DARTAGNAN [*taking him aside, far right, confidentially*]: If you don't mind, I'd like a word with you... It's terribly important...
MOULINEAUX: Oh?
[BASSINET, *naively, moves over to join them, listening.*]
DARTAGNAN [*annoyed, to* BASSINET]: I beg your pardon...

BASSINET [*ingenuously*]: Please! Don't mind me...

DARTAGNAN [*with an embarrassed little laugh*]: It's... It's personal, monsieur...

BASSINET: Aha...

[*He goes over to the desk, left, sits down, and begins thumbing aimlessly through a book during the ensuing dialogue.*]

DARTAGNAN [*to* MOULINEAUX, *softly*]: I can tell you, signore, because I'm sure you'll understand... After all, you know women...

MOULINEAUX [*uneasy*]: Si... Si...

DARTAGNAN: ...and especially my wife!

MOULINEAUX [*objecting*]: Well... Just her measurements...

DARTAGNAN: You see, this is the time she usually comes to see Doctor Moulineaux, and I thought if I waited... Since I haven't seen her since yesterday—

MOULINEAUX: God in heaven!

DARTAGNAN [*misinterpreting his reaction for sympathy*]: I know... That's what I say too! But I'm afraid it doesn't help! The only thing for me to do now is see her and... and make up some story or other... Something that will let me explain away Mathilde...

MOULINEAUX: Oh, by all means... [*Aside.*] But why here, damn it!

DARTAGNAN [*musing*]: Something logical, and not too hard to believe... Something simple, like... like... [*Suddenly inspired.*] I've got it!... Oh! That's a perfect idea!...

MOULINEAUX [*aside*]: Congratulations!

DARTAGNAN: Can I count on you, signore?

MOULINEAUX: Can you...?

DARTAGNAN: To help me?

MOULINEAUX: I suppose...

DARTAGNAN [*delighted*]: Fine!... Then why don't I tell her that Mathilde is your mistress? You have nothing to lose...

MOULINEAUX: Why don't you... [*Horrified.*] No! No, thank you! Thank you just the same!

DARTAGNAN: But...

MOULINEAUX: Not in a million years! [*Aside.*] The icing on the cake!

DARTAGNAN [*pleading*]: But signore... Signor Yuno... Please!... Please! You're my only hope!

MOULINEAUX: No no no, I tell you!... It's insane! I... I can't...

DARTAGNAN: But...

MOULINEAUX [*forgetting himself momentarily*]: Madame Moulineaux would be... [*Clapping his hand to his mouth.*] I mean...

DARTAGNAN: She would...? Why?... [*With a glance toward* BASSINET.] It's not as if you were her husband, after all... Besides, she doesn't have to know!...

MOULINEAUX: No!... No! Absolutely not! Ask someone else!

DARTAGNAN [*desperately*]: But who?

[BASSINET, *still sitting at the desk casually flipping pages, begins to hum a little tune.*]

MOULINEAUX: Anyone!... I don't care!... [*Pointing to* BASSINET.] Him!... Him, for instance!

DARTAGNAN [*with an air of disgusted disbelief*]: Him? [*Aside.*] His mistress's husband?

MOULINEAUX: Why not? He's as good as any!... What difference can it make...?

DARTAGNAN [*shocked*]: Oh, maybe not to him!... And Madame Moulineaux...?

MOULINEAUX [*ingenuously*]: Yes? What about her?

DARTAGNAN: Well, I thought... I just thought... [*Aside.*] Good heavens! These people are utterly depraved! [*To* MOULINEAUX.] If you think it's all right...

MOULINEAUX: Of course it is! Why not?

DARTAGNAN [*resisting*]: I don't know... [*Aside.*] And a doctor, too...

[BASSINET, *still humming, throws the book down on the desk and stands up.*]

BASSINET: I say... Have you two finished?

[*He moves toward them.*]

MOULINEAUX [*to* BASSINET]: Monsieur... My friend has something to ask you.

[*He moves off left, discreetly.*]

BASSINET [*happy to be included in the conversation*]: Oh? Something I can do?

DARTAGNAN: Yes, monsieur... [*Taking him by the arm and leading him down right.*] A favor... A very big favor...

BASSINET: Me?

DARTAGNAN: Immense... Monumental...

BASSINET [*embarrassed*]: I... I'd really like to help, but... It's the end of the month, and... and...

DARTAGNAN: Please! It won't cost you a thing...

BASSINET: Oh... Well, then...

DARTAGNAN: You see... I've had something of a spat with my wife... She caught me with my mistress!

BASSINET [*with a silly little laugh*]: My my! That wasn't very bright!

DARTAGNAN [*forcing a laugh*]: It was stupid!

BASSINET: Well, I didn't want to say...

DARTAGNAN: Yes, and she'll be here any minute... But I don't have to tell you, I'm sure... And what I would like you to do is... It's really very simple... [*Very matter-of-fact.*] I'd appreciate it if you would tell her that Madame de Sainte-Vinaigrette is your mistress.

BASSINET: Aha... That's the favor, monsieur?

DARTAGNAN: Yes...

BASSINET [*noncommittal*]: Very interesting idea...

DARTAGNAN: Then you'll do it?

BASSINET [*turning on his heel*]: But impossible!

DARTAGNAN: But monsieur!... Please!... Please! You're my only hope!

MOULINEAUX [*aside*]: Ha!

BASSINET: Out of the question!

MOULINEAUX [*rushing over to* BASSINET, *down right, in a whisper*]: Say yes! He has a lot of clients who need apartments!

BASSINET [*to* MOULINEAUX]: He does?... [*To* DARTAGNAN, *suddenly.*] I accept!

[MOULINEAUX *retreats, up left.*]

DARTAGNAN [*to* BASSINET]: You mean, you will?

BASSINET: As long as I don't have to get involved, monsieur...

DARTAGNAN: Absolutely!

BASSINET [*jovially*]: And as long as she's pretty...

DARTAGNAN: Oh, very! [*Taking the picture from his pocket.*] Look, here's her picture... [*Holding it out to* BASSINET.] In fact, you can show it to my wife... That will help convince her...

[ETIENNE *appears suddenly at the double door before* BASSINET *has a chance to look.*]

ETIENNE [*announcing*]: Madame Dartagnan!

DARTAGNAN [*excited*]: Ah! Already?... Shhh! Here she is!... [*Stuffing the photo into* BASSINET's *coat pocket.*] Here! Hide this!... Quick! Hide it... [*Aside.*] Not a second too soon!

[SUZANNE *enters and* ETIENNE *exits.*]

MOULINEAUX [*nodding*]: Good morning, madame...

DARTAGNAN [*timidly*]: Hello, Suzanne...

SUZANNE [*to* DARTAGNAN, *scornfully*]: You, monsieur? Here?... [*To* MOULINEAUX.] Excuse me... I'll be going...

DARTAGNAN: Suzanne!... Please! Listen!... I'm innocent!... I can prove it!

SUZANNE [*to* DARTAGNAN]: You'll have your chance, monsieur... In court!

[*She turns to leave, but stops.*]

DARTAGNAN: In court?... Don't say that, Suzanne!... Please! If you'll only listen... It's all a terrible mistake... A misunderstanding...

SUZANNE [*with a withering glance*]: Ha! I understand perfectly!

DARTAGNAN: That woman... I... I don't even know her! I never laid eyes on her...

SUZANNE: Of course!

DARTAGNAN: And if you don't believe me... [*Pointing to* BASSINET.] Ask him! She's his... [*To* BASSINET.] Isn't she, monsieur?

BASSINET [*without much conviction*]: Why yes... Yes, yes...

DARTAGNAN [*to* SUZANNE]: You see?

BASSINET [*continuing*]: Yes...

SUZANNE [*to* DARTAGNAN, *sharply*]: Balderdash, monsieur!

DARTAGNAN: "Balder..." But I'm telling you...

MOULINEAUX [*to* SUZANNE]: Tsk tsk tsk!... Heartless, madame...

DARTAGNAN [*to* SUZANNE]: You're making a mistake... [*Pointing to* BASSINET.] She's his, I tell you!... [*Aside, to* BASSINET.] The picture!... The picture!...

BASSINET [*fishing in his pocket*]: Ah...

[*He moves off, left, as* ETIENNE *appears at the double door.*]

ETIENNE [*announcing*]: Madame...

[*Before he has a chance to give her name,* MIMI *enters.* ETIENNE *shrugs and exits, closing the double door behind him.*]

BASSINET [*looking up, going to meet her*]: Oh, there you are!... Come in! Come in!

SUZANNE [*aside*]: Her!... Anatole's mistress!...

BASSINET [*bringing* MIMI *down right, about to introduce her to* DARTAGNAN]: Monsieur, I'd like you to meet my—

DARTAGNAN [*looking up from his preoccupation*]: Oh no!...

[*He rushes out, crossing down left.*]

BASSINET [*watching, surprised*]: What...? [*Bringing* MIMI *left, to* MOULINEAUX.] Doctor Moulineaux let me introduce my—

MOULINEAUX [*suddenly recognizing her*]: Good God!... Her?... Here?...

[*He rushes out, crossing down right.*]

BASSINET: What's the matter?

MIMI [*annoyed*]: Not very polite, are they!

BASSINET: I say... [*Moving upstage, about to introduce her to* SUZANNE.]

Madame, I'd like you to meet—

SUZANNE [*curtly*]: You needn't bother!

[*She strides out, up left.*]

MIMI: Again?

BASSINET: Maybe something they ate...

[*The door, up right, opens and* YVONNE *enters.*]

BASSINET [*noticing her*]: Ah, madame... [*Bringing* MIMI *up to meet her.*] I'd like to introduce you—

YVONNE [*recognizing* MIMI]: You!... [*To* BASSINET, *sharply.*] Really, monsieur! Enough is enough!

[*She turns on her heel and exits, up right.*]

MIMI: Damnation! Who do they think they are?

BASSINET [*offhand*]: Oh... They do it to me all the time...

MIMI: And you let them?

BASSINET [*half-heartedly*]: Well, no... That is... Just a moment... I'm sure...

[*He goes to the door, up right, and knocks. In the meantime,* MOULINEAUX *has poked his head out the door, down right, and not seeing* BASSINET, *thinks that* MIMI *is alone.*]

MOULINEAUX [*rushing to join her, center*]: Are you out of your mind? Coming here like this...?

MIMI: What...?

MOULINEAUX: To my home, for God's sake!

MIMI: But Baba... I'm with my husband! What's the harm...?

MOULINEAUX: Your what?... Who?... Where?

MIMI [*pointing up right*]: Him!... There!

MOULINEAUX [*shouting*]: Bassinet?

MIMI: Since yesterday... He found me...

BASSINET [*turning around at the sound of his name*]: Ah, monsieur... [*Coming down to join them.*] I'd like to introduce you—

MOULINEAUX [*laughing*]: Him?... That's a good one!

[*He doubles up with laughter as* MIMI *moves down left.*]

BASSINET: What's so funny, monsieur? What's the joke?...

MOULINEAUX: Nothing!... Nothing!... You wouldn't understand!...

[*During the previous exchange,* DARTAGNAN *has peeked out the door, down left. Seeing* MIMI, *he looks around to make sure that* SUZANNE *isn't there, and enters.*]

DARTAGNAN [*to* MIMI, *in a frantic whisper*]: Please, Mathilde! Will you get out of here!... My wife, for heaven's sake... My wife...

MIMI [*losing patience, moving far right*]: Damnation! I've had enough! They can all go hang!

BASSINET [*coming down left, to* DARTAGNAN]: Why all the whispering, monsieur?

[*At that moment,* YVONNE *and* MADAME AIGREVILLE *enter, up right, and* SUZANNE, *up left, simultaneously.*]

YVONNE [*with* MADAME AIGREVILLE *at her side, to* MOULINEAUX]: This is the last straw! You're a cad, monsieur!

MADAME AIGREVILLE [*echoing*]: A cad!

MOULINEAUX [*innocently*]: But... But...

YVONNE: It's not bad enough that you go chasing every skirt in Paris...

MOULINEAUX: But... But...

YVONNE: But to bring them here... Here, to my home, monsieur...

MADAME AIGREVILLE [*echoing*]: Her home!

MOULINEAUX: But who...? Who? Who?

YVONNE: Who? Who?... [*Pointing to* MIMI.] Her, that's who!

MIMI: Me? Me?

MADAME AIGREVILLE [*pointing to* SUZANNE, *still at the door, up left*]: No! Her!

SUZANNE: "Her" who?... Who? Me?

[*She comes downstage, between* MOULINEAUX *and* DARTAGNAN, *resulting in the following disposition, right to left:* MIMI, MADAME AIGREVILLE, YVONNE, SUZANNE, MOULINEAUX, DARTAGNAN, BASSINET.]

MOULINEAUX [*at his wit's end*]: But you don't understand!...

DARTAGNAN [*to* MADAME AIGREVILLE]: I beg your pardon, but... [*With a gesture toward* SUZANNE.] Madame is my wife!

BASSINET [*pointing to* MIMI]: And madame is mine! I'll thank you to remember—

MADAME AIGREVILLE [*looking at* YVONNE] ⎫   ⎧ She is?
YVONNE [*looking at* MOULINEAUX]   ⎬ [*together*]: ⎨ She is?
SUZANNE [*looking at* DARTAGNAN]   ⎪   ⎪ She is?
DARTAGNAN [*looking at* BASSINET]   ⎭   ⎩ She is?

BASSINET: Why yes...

DARTAGNAN [*looking at* YVONNE, *aside*]: Then who on earth...?

MADAME AIGREVILLE [*looking at* MIMI] ⎫   ⎧ His wife?
YVONNE [*looking at* MADAME AIGREVILLE] ⎬ [*together*]: ⎨ His wife?
SUZANNE [*looking at* MOULINEAUX]   ⎭   ⎩ His wife?

BASSINET: I've been trying to introduce you...

DARTAGNAN [*aside*]: Oh my! The picture...

BASSINET: ...only nobody would listen...

DARTAGNAN [*to* SUZANNE, *taking her by the arm and whisking her up left*]: You see? I told you... You didn't believe me... [*Coming back down left, holding out his hand, to* BASSINET, *in a whisper.*] Monsieur... Please the picture...

BASSINET: Oh yes... Of course...

[*He takes it out of his pocket and is about to look at it.*]

DARTAGNAN [*trying to stop him*]: No, no! Don't look! [*He tries to take it from him, but* BASSINET *eludes his grasp.*] No!... Please...

[*There is a moment of give and take before* BASSINET *finally succeeds in looking at the picture.*]

BASSINET [*surprised*]: I say!...

DARTAGNAN [*between his teeth, aside*]: That does it!

BASSINET: If I didn't know better... [*To* DARTAGNAN, *showing him the picture.*] It's the image of my wife, monsieur... Don't you think?

DARTAGNAN [*pretending to scrutinize it, offhand*]: Your... No... No... [*Touching his nose.*] Too big... [*Touching his chin.*] Too big...

BASSINET: But... [*To* MOULINEAUX.] Monsieur... [*Showing it to him.*] Don't you think this looks just like my wife?

MOULINEAUX: Like your... No... No... [*Touching his chin.*] Too small... [*Touching his nose.*] Too small...

BASSINET [*to* MIMI, *showing her the picture*]: I say... Don't you think... Look...

MIMI [*pretending to be offended*]: That?... Really, Perceval!... Is that what you think I look like?

BASSINET [*studying the picture*]: Well, now that you mention it... No... I guess not...

SUZANNE [*coming down to* DARTAGNAN, *pointing to* MIMI]: You mean, that woman... She really is his wife?

DARTAGNAN: Of course! I've been trying to tell you...

SUZANNE: Oh! Anatole, dearest!... I... What can I say?

DARTAGNAN [*with a noble gesture*]: Please!... Please!... I forgive you...

YVONNE [*swallowing her pride, to* MOULINEAUX]: And can you forgive me?

DARTAGNAN [*puzzled, aside*]: For what? Being his mistress?

MOULINEAUX [*to* YVONNE]: Do you have to ask, Yvonne?

MADAME AIGREVILLE [*aside*]: Lucky for them I was here to make peace!

YVONNE: Oh, Balthasar! What a dear, faithful, wonderful husband you are!

MOULINEAUX: Ayyy!

DARTAGNAN [*with a start*]: Husband...?

MOULINEAUX: That is...

DARTAGNAN: But... Doctor Moulineaux...? [*To* BASSINET.] Doctor...?

BASSINET: Not me, monsieur... [*Pointing to* MOULINEAUX.] Him!

MOULINEAUX [*aside*]: Swine!

BASSINET: He's the doctor...

DARTAGNAN: He is...? But... Signor Yuno...?

YVONNE: Yuno?

MADAME AIGREVILLE: Yuno?

MIMI: Yuno?

DARTAGNAN [*to* MOULINEAUX]: But I thought you were a tailor...

MOULINEAUX [*covering up, before* YVONNE *and* MADAME AIGREVILLE *grow suspicious, speaking as fast as he can*]: Italian, monsieur?... You thought I was Italian? Me, Italian?... Well, I did have an aunt once who married an Italian, and... It's really a funny story, if you'd like a good laugh! You see, she had a young gigolo, this aunt of mine...

BASSINET: She did?

MOULINEAUX: And one day he went out and he bought her a parrot... And...

[*The others shout him down with appropriate cries: "Never mind!", "We're not interested!", "Who cares!", etc., as the curtain falls.*]

CURTAIN

A FLEA IN HER REAR
or, Ants in Her Pants

Adaptation of

La Puce à l'oreille

by

Georges Feydeau

(1907)

CHARACTERS

CHANDEBISE, fortyish, a very respectable bourgeois

LOCHE, the Hotel Paramour's lumpish and woebegone porter, Chandebise's double

EDOUARD, Chandebise's inarticulate nephew, naive and very worldly-unwise

TOURNEL, a colleague of Chandebise, madly in love with the latter's wife

FINACHE, a doctor friend of Chandebise

HOMENIDES DE HISTANGUA, an irascible Spaniard with only a rudimentary knowledge of English

MOUSQUETARD, an ex-army man, now manager of the Hotel Paramour

ETIENNE, the Chandebises' butler

POPOFF, a lubricious Russian gentleman, guest at the Hotel Paramour

BLAISE, Mousquetard's aged uncle, employed at the hotel

GISELE, Chandebise's attractive wife, in her mid-thirties or younger

LUCIENNE, her girlhood friend, married to Homenides de Histangua

NANA, a former entertainer, now Mousquetard's buxom and neurotic wife

ANTOINETTE, the Chandebises' cook, Edouard's instructress in matters amatory

BABETTE, the maid at the Hotel Paramour

Several unnamed clients of the Hotel Paramour, ad libitum

Act One

The elegant English-style drawing room of Monsieur and Madame Chandebise, in Paris, furnished in mahogany. In the oblique-cornered wall, up left, a fireplace, appropriately decorated, with a mirror above it. In the center of the rear wall, a shallow bay, luxuriously draped, with a double door opening outward and revealing a vestibule with a bench; above the bench, in a niche, a telephone. (To the right of the bench, unseen, is assumed to be the front door, opening onto a staircase.) Also in the rear wall, on both sides of the bay, up left and up right, a door opening outward. Between the bay and the stage left door, a high chiffonier, doubling as a filing-cabinet, with several drawers; between the bay and the stage right door, a low table. In the wall, down right, a high double window, draped in the same material as the bay, with a butler's cord hanging on the upstage side. Upstage right, against the side wall, a three-drawer cabinet. In front of the window, a backless bench; leaning against it, a collapsible writing-desk, folded up at rise—the kind that opens out into an X-shaped stand—with paper and writing materials inside. Midstage right, close to the bench and somewhat upstage of it, a canapé with its ornate mahogany see-through back toward the footlights, but at an angle, with two cushions. Facing it, a small casual table, covered with several magazines, with a chair on each side. In the wall, down left, a door opening inward, with a key in the keyhole. Down left, a large oblong table, perpendicular to the footlights, also with a chair on each side. On the walls, English-style engravings. Lamps, rugs, other furnishings and appropriate bric-a-brac, ad libitum.

At rise, EDOUARD, *back toward the bay, is leaning against the chiffonier, several drawers of which are open, perusing a document that he has, ostensibly, just taken from one of them. After a few moments the door, up right, opens slowly and* ANTOINETTE, *in cook's uniform, pokes her head out, glancing furtively about the room. Catching sight of* EDOUARD, *she enters, tiptoes over to him, and, covering his eyes with her hands from behind, gives him a resounding kiss on the back of the neck.*

EDOUARD [*surprised, with a grunt*]: Ouf! [*Turning to her, trying to regain his aplomb, holding up an admonishing forefinger.*] Uh-uh!

ANTOINETTE ⎫ ⎧ Don't worry! They're out.
EDOUARD [*shaking his head* ⎬ [*together*]: ⎨
 and wagging his finger] ⎭ ⎩ Tsk tsk tsk!

ANTOINETTE [*leaning toward him*]: Come on... [*She purses her lips invitingly and closes her eyes.*] Just a peck...

[EDOUARD *looks at her for a moment, half-smiling, half-annoyed, not sure whether to laugh or get angry. Then, in a sudden burst of passion, he takes her in his arms and plants a long, voracious kiss on her lips. At that moment, the double door opens and* FINACHE *and* ETIENNE *appear in the vestibule, the former in street clothes, coat and hat in hand, the latter wearing a long butler's apron.*]

ETIENNE [*stepping aside and showing* FINACHE *in*]: If monsieur would like to wait—

ANTOINETTE *and* EDOUARD [*together, with a start*]: Oh!

[*They quickly push each other away and* EDOUARD *makes a dash for the door, up left, and runs out. Meanwhile, as* ANTOINETTE, *obviously embarrassed, moves off to the right and stands by the door,* FINACHE *comes down left by the oblong table, lays down his hat and coat, and tries to look inconspicuous.*]

ETIENNE [*still in the bay, hands on hips*]: Of all the... [*To* ANTOINETTE.] You!... What are you doing in here?

ANTOINETTE   } [*together*]: {   Me?... I...

FINACHE [*aside*]   I would have thought it was obvious!

ANTOINETTE [*babbling*]: I... I came to see what they wanted for dinner tonight.

ETIENNE: "Dinner" my foot!... You know perfectly well that monsieur and madame are out! [*To* FINACHE.] "Dinner" she says!

[FINACHE *gives a noncommittal shrug and sits down on the stage right side of the table.*]

ANTOINETTE: But Etienne—

ETIENNE [*approaching her, right*]: Don't "But Etienne" me!... Out!... Back to your pots and pans, woman!... A cook's place is down in the kitchen, not up here.

ANTOINETTE: But—

ETIENNE: "Out," I said! [*Pointing to the door, up right, and waving her off.*] Out!

ANTOINETTE [*grumbling*]: I'm going...

[*She exits, right, as* ETIENNE *brushes his hands together, cymbal-style, as if to say: "That's that!"*]

FINACHE [*to* ETIENNE]: My goodness, Etienne! I must say you're one husband who knows how to lay the law down!

ETIENNE [*coming downstage*]: Well, you have to. If we don't show them who's boss... [*Crossing to* FINACHE.] No thank you!

FINACHE [*with mock applause and a chuckle*]: A husband after my own heart!

ETIENNE [*pointing to the door, up right*]: She's as faithful as a puppy dog, that one... But jealous? Like a tiger...

FINACHE: Oh?

ETIENNE: Always spying on me, trying to catch me... [*Leaning over to him, confidentially.*] And with the chambermaid, no less... She thinks that... Imagine! Me and a... a chambermaid!

FINACHE [*affecting disbelief*]: No!

ETIENNE: Yes... Believe me, when I say "jealous"...

FINACHE [*with a look toward the chiffonier, obviously recalling the recent scene*]: Yes, I'm sure...

ETIENNE: Like a tiger!

[*He moves about the bay, adjusting the drapes, etc.*]

FINACHE [*getting up*]: Well, my friend... Since monsieur isn't here...

[*He picks up his hat and coat and moves as if to leave.*]

ETIENNE [*coming downstage to head him off, hands in his apron pockets, good-naturedly*]: Oh, please... Monsieur doesn't have to leave. I'll be happy to keep him company.

[*He takes the hat and coat from* FINACHE *and puts them back on the oblong table.*]

FINACHE: You'll... That's terribly kind of you... And terribly tempting...

ETIENNE [*with an offhand wave*]: Pfff!

FINACHE: But I really couldn't take advantage...

ETIENNE: Not at all!... I have all the time in the world... Please...

[*He holds out the same chair for him.*]

FINACHE: Aha... [*He sits down again, reluctantly.*] Indeed... [*Nodding, with a tinge of sarcasm.*] How fortunate...

ETIENNE [*going around the table and sitting down across from a rather surprised* FINACHE]: There!

[*There is a long moment of silence, more uncomfortabe for* FINACHE, *trying to find an excuse to leave, than for* ETIENNE, *smiling good-naturedly, quite willing to settle in.*]

FINACHE [*finally breaking the silence*]: And when did you say monsieur would be back?

ETIENNE: When...? [*Reflecting.*] I don't think I did, monsieur. [*Scratching his head.*] Did I?

FINACHE [*with a wave of the hand*]: No matter... But you do know when you expect him, don't you?

ETIENNE [*consulting his pocket watch*]: Oh... It might be a quarter of an hour, monsieur... Or maybe a half...

FINACHE: Aha... Yes... Well, in that case, my friend... [*Getting up.*] As much as I would love to sit and chat with you... I'm afraid I'd really better be going. I have a patient just around the corner. Very sick... Very...

ETIENNE: Tsk tsk tsk!

FINACHE: Yes... He's on his way to the grave, and I don't want to keep him waiting.

ETIENNE: Monsieur?

FINACHE [*taking his coat and moving up, toward the bay*]: I won't be long... I can get rid of him in fifteen minutes.

ETIENNE [*following him, rather shocked*]: Oh! "Get rid"...? Is monsieur going to—

FINACHE [*interrupting him with a laugh, realizing his naive misunderstanding*]: No, no!... Not "get rid of *him*..." I mean, get rid of the visit...

ETIENNE [*with a sigh of relief*]: Ah... I didn't think monsieur would... At least not on purpose...

FINACHE: Hardly... Well... I'll be on my way...

[*As he is about to leave,* ETIENNE *notices that his hat is still on the oblong table.*]

ETIENNE: Ah!... Monsieur was forgetting...

[*He comes down, takes the hat, and holds it out to* FINACHE.]

FINACHE [*joining him, center stage*]: Thank you, Etienne.

ETIENNE: My pleasure, monsieur. [*Putting the hat on* FINACHE*'s head himself.*] There!

FINACHE: I beg... [*Shaking his head in resigned disbelief and going back toward the bay.*] You needn't bother to see me out. [*Stopping at the double door, with an afterthought, and coming back down, to* ETIENNE.] Oh... And if monsieur gets back before I do, please tell him that I've examined the client he sent me, and that he's in perfect health... [*Taking a paper from his pocket, showing it to him.*] And that I've brought the certificate... He can feel free to insure him... No problem at all...
[*He puts the paper back in his pocket.*]

ETIENNE [*mechanically*]: "No problem at all..."

FINACHE [*with a smile*]: I can see you're terribly interested!

ETIENNE [*with a casual wave of the hand*]: Oh... Pfff!

FINACHE: Well, frankly, neither am I... But the president of monsieur's company is, I assure you!

ETIENNE: Yes... The head cheese!

FINACHE: "The head..." [*With a chuckle.*] If you insist!

ETIENNE: I mean, that's what monsieur always calls him.

FINACHE [*still laughing*]: Yes... Well, you can bet the head cheese isn't about to insure him for a hundred thousand and have him croak the next day!

ETIENNE: A whole hundred thousand?... Whew! That would make him a millionaire!... It would almost be worth dying...

FINACHE: Somehow I don't think monsieur's client would agree!... [*Still chuckling.*] Anyway, please tell him that his Señor Homenides should be able to live forever... You have that?... What are you going to tell him?

ETIENNE: That his "señor" should be able to live forever... [*Groping for the name.*] Señor...

FINACHE: Homenides...

ETIENNE [*misunderstanding*]: How many?... How should I know how many days? Forever is forever, monsieur. I never counted—

FINACHE: No, no... Homenides... That's his name. Don Carlos Homenides de Histangua... He's Spanish.

ETIENNE: Histangua?... Why didn't monsieur say so in the first place?... We know him.

FINACHE: "We"...?

ETIENNE: Monsieur and Madame Chandebise and me... In fact, his wife is here this minute. In the sitting-room... Waiting for madame... They were even here for dinner night before last... Both of them...

FINACHE: Really! [*Turning upstage as if to leave, muttering.*] Small world...

ETIENNE [*calling to stop him*]: Ah! Monsieur...
[FINACHE *stops in his tracks as* ETIENNE *sits down at the table on the same chair as before.*]

FINACHE [*returning to the table, aside*]: Again?

ETIENNE [*making himself comfortable*]: As long as monsieur is here... I was wondering... I was wondering if I could ask him... When someone has a little pain in the stomach... Like a little ache... [*Gesturing toward the other chair.*] Please... Monsieur doesn't have to stand.

FINACHE [*sitting down, still holding his coat*]: Too kind...

ETIENNE: Actually, two little pains... [*Poking each side of his belly several times.*] All the time...

FINACHE: Tsk tsk tsk!

ETIENNE: Does monsieur know what that is?

FINACHE [*pretending to be serious, looking him in the eye*]: Of course, Etienne! It's the ovaries.

ETIENNE: Well, that's what I've got... [*Poking.*] Here... And here...

FINACHE [*trying not to laugh*]: Well, if I were you, I would have them removed. And the sooner the better.

[*He gets up.*]

ETIENNE: My ovaries? Never, monsieur! [*Crossing up toward the bay.*] They're mine and I'm going to keep them...

[*The door, up right, opens and* LUCIENNE, *in street clothes, appears.* FINACHE *respectfully takes off his hat.*]

LUCIENNE [*noticing* ETIENNE]: Ah! You... [*Catching sight of* FINACHE, *still by the oblong table.*] Oh... Excuse me, monsieur. I hope I'm not intruding...

FINACHE [*dismissing the idea with a wave of the hand and a little bow*]: Madame...

[*He puts his hat on the table, still holding his coat.*]

LUCIENNE [*coming down by the little table facing the canapé, to* ETIENNE]: I hope you haven't forgotten me. You did say that Madame Chandebise would be right along?

ETIENNE: I did indeed, madame.

LUCIENNE: Aha... Because...

ETIENNE: And I told madame that madame told me that if Madame... [*Groping for her name.*] Madame...

LUCIENNE: Homenides de Histangua...

ETIENNE: Right!... It was on the tip of my tongue... [*Continuing.*] That if madame showed her face this afternoon... I should be sure not to let her leave until she got back... That's what madame told me. "Be sure not to let her leave, Etienne. I absolutely have to see her."

LUCIENNE: Yes, well... That's what she said in her note. Though frankly I can't imagine what could possibly be so important.

ETIENNE: Neither can I, madame.

LUCIENNE [*ignoring his remark*]: Well, I suppose I can wait a little longer.

[*She moves up right, as if to go out and return to the sitting-room, but stops as* ETIENNE *continues.*]

ETIENNE [*pointing to* FINACHE]: It's like I was just telling monsieur, madame... We were having a little chat...

FINACHE: Quite...

ETIENNE [*introducing*]: Doctor Finache... [FINACHE *and* LUCIENNE *nod politely to each other.*] Chief medical examiner for monsieur's company, madame... Requiem Life...

LUCIENNE [*coming back down to the little table, right center*]: Aha...

ETIENNE [*coming down left, toward* FINACHE]: In fact, monsieur was just telling me that he examined madame's husband this morning.

FINACHE [*to* ETIENNE, *as if to cut short his indiscreet revelation*]: Etienne...

| ETIENNE [*ignoring him*] ⎫ | | ⎧ Small world, like they say... |
| LUCIENNE ⎬ [*together*]: ⎨ Examined him? [*To* FINACHE.] |
| ⎭ | | ⎩ Don Carlos? |

FINACHE [*crossing toward her*]: Yes, madame. I had the pleasure...

LUCIENNE: But what on earth for?

FINACHE: Oh, no need to worry... Just one of those little formalities insurance companies insist on...

LUCIENNE: Ah...

FINACHE: And I'm happy to tell you that he's in excellent health. As strong as an ox...

LUCIENNE: I think you mean a bull, doctor, all things considered! And twice as energetic... [*With an obvious implication.*] If you know what I mean!...

FINACHE [*with a little laugh*]: Indeed!

LUCIENNE [*with a sigh, letting herself fall onto one of the chairs, right center, sotto voce*]: Really, doctor... The man wears me out!... These Spaniards!...

FINACHE: Congratulations, madame! Not every wife can say that!

LUCIENNE: No, but sometimes I wish...

[*She sighs and gives a meaningful gesture, shaking her head.*]

ETIENNE [*who has been eavesdropping, still standing by the oblong table, to* LUCIENNE, *with a sigh*]: Ah... Madame Plouchette used to complain like that too, madame.

FINACHE [*to* ETIENNE, *in a reprimanding tone*] ⎱ [*together*]: ⎰ Etienne! Really...
LUCIENNE [*to* ETIENNE] ⎰ ⎱ Who, monsieur?

ETIENNE: My wife... My Antoinette... She used to complain like that all the time. [LUCIENNE *and* FINACHE *exchange rather amused glances.*] No more, though... Not now... Not with my ovaries...

LUCIENNE [*not sure she has heard correctly, to* ETIENNE]: Please?

ETIENNE [*to* LUCIENNE, *continuing his thought*]: I'm not the man I used to be.

LUCIENNE: No... I imagine...

ETIENNE [*coming down center, to* LUCIENNE]: Maybe what she needs is a man like... like Monsieur... Monsieur... [*Groping for the name again.*] Like madame's husband, madame.

FINACHE [*between the two of them, very tongue-in-cheek*]: Well, Etienne... If madame doesn't object... And if Monsieur... [*Correcting himself.*] Señor Homenides de Histangua is willing... Perhaps something could be arranged.

ETIENNE [*shocked, to* FINACHE] ⎱ [*together*]: ⎰ Monsieur! Never!...
LUCIENNE [*getting up, to* FINACHE, *jovially*] ⎰ ⎱ Really, doctor! I hardly think so!

FINACHE [*crossing left, with a laugh, behind* ETIENNE, *taking his hat from the table*]: Well, I'd better be on my way if I want to get back in fifteen minutes. [*With a little bow, to* LUCIENNE.] Delighted, madame...

LUCIENNE [*still standing by the chair*]: Monsieur...

[FINACHE *turns and moves up toward the bay.*]

ETIENNE [*following him*]: But monsieur... About my ovaries...

FINACHE [*reaching the double door*]: It's nothing a good purge won't take care of, Etienne. [*As he exits into the vestibule.*] Take two enemas...

ETIENNE: Ah...?

FINACHE [*putting on his hat*]: And call me in the morning.

[ETIENNE *follows him out.*]

LUCIENNE [*watching them leave, then looking at her watch*]: Seven past one already!... Is this what she means by "I can't wait to see you!"?

[*She sits down again on the same chair by the small table, takes a magazine and flips through it with evident lack of interest. After a few moments the door, up left, opens and* EDOUARD *enters, still examining the document he had taken from the chiffonier. He goes to the chiffonier as if to return it to its proper drawer; but before he has a chance to do so, he looks up and notices* LUCIENNE.]

EDOUARD [*addressing her in the unintelligible speech of someone with a severe cleft palate*]: Oh! Ah-uh ee, ah-ah! ["Oh! Pardon me, madame!"]

LUCIENNE [*looking up, quizzically*]: Hmm?

EDOUARD: Ah oo ai-i oo ee uh i-eh-uh" ["Are you waiting to see the director?"]

LUCIENNE [*nonplussed, but trying to be polite*]: Monsieur?

EDOUARD: I eh: "Ah oo ai-i oo ee uh i-eh-uh?" ["I said: 'Are you waiting to see the director?'"] [*Specifying.*] Uh i-eh-uh o ee ai-uh-ee... ["The director of the agency..."]

LUCIENNE [*with an uncomfortable little smile*]: Excuse me, monsieur... I didn't quite catch what you were saying.

EDOUARD [*approaching her, center stage, and speaking very slowly and deliberately*]: O... I aw o-ee a-i i oo er ai-i oo ee uh— ["No... I was only asking if you were waiting to see the—"]

LUCIENNE [*cutting him off with a wave, as if to excuse her own lack of comprehension*]: No, no, monsieur... [*Pointing to herself.*] French... Me French... Française... Französisch...   ·

[*She gets up.*]

EDOUARD [*nodding, pointing to himself*]: Ee oo! Ee oo! ["Me too! Me too!"]

LUCIENNE: Perhaps if you spoke to the butler, monsieur... I don't live here. I'm only waiting for Madame Chandebise. She's expecting me... [*Looking at her watch, muttering to herself.*] At least I thought she was...

EDOUARD: O... I eh ou ah-uh, ah-ah... ["Oh... I beg your pardon, madame..."] [*Bowing his way backwards, up left, toward the chiffonier.*] I aw o-ee a-i, ee-aw, i oo aw-eh oo ee uh i-eh-uh... ["I was only asking, because, if you wanted to see the director..."]

LUCIENNE [*not understanding a word but still trying to be polite*]: Yes, monsieur... I'm sure...

[EDOUARD *arrives at the chiffonier and replaces the document.*]

EDOUARD [*closing the drawer, with a little nod*]: I eh ou ah-uh, ah-ah... Ee eh-oo ee... ["I beg your pardon, madame... Please excuse me..."] [*Bowing out the door, up left.*] Ah-ah... ["Madame..."]

[*He leaves, as* LUCIENNE, *wide-eyed, watches him go.*]

LUCIENNE [*after a moment, crossing left, toward the oblong table, shaking her head*]: Who in the name of heaven... What kind of a...

[*At that moment the double door opens and* ETIENNE *appears.*]

ETIENNE [*entering*]   }   { Ah! Madame is still
                                    } [*together*]: waiting, I see.
LUCIENNE [*back to him, pondering* }
         her recent encounter]   }   { I never...

ETIENNE: I hope she's not losing patience.

LUCIENNE [*turning and noticing him, ignoring his question and gesturing*]: You, there... Young man...

ETIENNE: Etienne, madame... Madame may call me by my first name. I don't mind.

LUCIENNE: Yes... Etienne... You wouldn't happen to know... Just now... There was a man in here... A very strange one... He talked some sort of... some

sort of Apache gibberish or other... [*Imitating.*] "Ah oo ee ah oo oo ah ee..."
Like that...

ETIENNE [*coming down center, laughing*]: Ah! Madame... That was no man...
That was just Monsieur Edouard.

LUCIENNE: Oh? Some kind of foreigner, is he?

ETIENNE: Him? Don't be... [*Catching himself.*] Madame can't be serious... He's
monsieur's nephew.

LUCIENNE: No!

ETIENNE: He is, madame... A full-blooded nephew... Monsieur's late brother's
son...

LUCIENNE: A full-blooded idiot, you mean... I couldn't understand one blessed
word he said.

ETIENNE: Oh no, madame... That's because he's got a clipped pellet...

LUCIENNE: A what?

ETIENNE: A clipped pellet... [*He opens his mouth and points inside.*] That's
what monsieur and madame call it anyway.

LUCIENNE: Ah! A cleft—

ETIENNE: Something about his bowels... And the way they come out when he
opens his mouth... All "ah ee ah oo oo ee ah..." Like madame was saying...
It's a nuisance when someone's not used to it.

LUCIENNE [*sitting down on the chair on the stage right side of the oblong
table*]: Yes... I'm sure...
[*She gives an impatient glance at her watch.*]

ETIENNE: That's why monsieur took him on as his secretary. He knew he could
never get a job...

LUCIENNE: What with his bowels!

ETIENNE: Exactly!... Of course, when he writes there's no problem. He puts in
all the continents... But no one can write all the time, madame.

LUCIENNE: No...

ETIENNE: Sooner or later he'd have to open his mouth, and out would come all
those bowels... [*Moving around the oblong table.*] Tsk tsk tsk!... Such a
nice young man too... No bad habits... Why, he doesn't even have a
mistress, if madame can imagine!... At least, not that I know of...

LUCIENNE [*getting up*]: And you would know if anyone would, Etienne!

ETIENNE: Madame is too kind...
[*Just then the double door opens and* GISELE *appears, in hat and coat, and
carrying a large handbag.*]

ETIENNE [*pointing, to* LUCIENNE]: Ah! It's madame, madame.

LUCIENNE [*to* GISELE, *who comes rushing in*]: There you are! [*Going to meet
her.*] I'd almost given up!

GISELE [*meeting her, center stage*]: Oh, you poor, poor dear!... I'm so
dreadfully sorry, precious...
[*They kiss each other on both cheeks.*]

ETIENNE [*to* GISELE]: It's not like madame to be late...

GISELE [*going to the oblong table, left, and putting down her handbag, to
* ETIENNE, *with a withering look*]: Thank you, Etienne!... You may go now.
[*She takes off her coat and lays it over the back of the chair on the stage
right side of the table.*]

ETIENNE [*to* LUCIENNE, *with a bow*]: If madame will excuse me... [LUCIENNE,

*moving right, toward the canapé, gives a little wave, as if to say: "If,
indeed!", as* ETIENNE *continues, nodding.*] It's been a pleasure chatting with
her.

[*He leaves, up center.*]

GISELE [*pulling out her hatpins and taking off her hat, to* LUCIENNE]: I've kept
you waiting...

LUCIENNE [*at the stage left end of the canapé, with a touch of wry humor*]: Oh?
I hadn't noticed.

GISELE: But really, I can explain. I've only been running all over the map!... It's
frightful... Simply frightful...

[*She goes up right to the low table to the right of the bay and lays down her
hat, but keeps one of the hatpins in hand.*]

LUCIENNE: What is it, love?

GISELE: If I asked you to come, it's... it's because... [*Hesitating.*] It's Victor,
Lucienne... [*Coming down right and joining her at the canapé, point
blank.*] He's cheating on me!

LUCIENNE: Chandebise?... Victor-Emmanuel?

GISELE: How many Victors am I married to? Of course!

LUCIENNE [*shocked*]: Well, I must say—

GISELE [*cutting her off*]: That swine!... That... That... [*Plunging the hatpin into
the canapé cushion nearest her with each of the following words.*] utter...
unprincipled... unspeakable swine!

LUCIENNE: Gisèle...

GISELE: But I'll catch him!... Oh, yes! You'll see!

[*She stalks up right to the low table and replaces the hatpin.*]

LUCIENNE [*as* GISELE *comes down to the stage right end of the canapé*]: "Catch
him..."? You mean you have no proof?

GISELE: Not yet... But I will have! I'll have all the proof I need, believe me!

LUCIENNE [*going over and standing by her*]: How, love?

GISELE [*gradually calming down*]: I don't know. That's why you're here...

LUCIENNE: Me?

GISELE: I'm sure you'll think of something.

[*She sits down.*]

LUCIENNE: You're sure I—

GISELE: Of course you will, Lucienne. You can't say no. You mustn't...

LUCIENNE: But—

GISELE: Not you... Not my best and dearest friend...

LUCIENNE: I know, but—

GISELE: And my oldest... [*Emphasizing.*] My very, very oldest...

LUCIENNE: But—

GISELE: Oh, I know it's been years since we've seen each other. Ten, at least...
But now that we've found each other again... Well, just because little
Lucienne Vicard has turned into Lucienne Homenides de... de... [*Fishing
for the name.*] de...

LUCIENNE: Histangua...

[*She sits down on the canapé, facing* GISELE *in profile.*]

GISELE: Well, your name may be longer, precious, but your heart hasn't
changed. You're still the same sweet little Lucienne... My truest, and best,
and dearest friend...

LUCIENNE: Yes... And oldest...

GISELE: And I simply couldn't dream of asking anyone else to help me.

LUCIENNE [*without much conviction*]: I'm flattered.

GISELE: So... What do we do to catch him red-handed?

LUCIENNE: Really, Gisèle, I'm hardly the one to ask.

GISELE: But you must have an idea. Surely in the last ten years...

LUCIENNE: Besides, how do you know that you even have to? I mean, he may be absolutely the most faithful husband on the face of the earth.

GISELE: That swine?

LUCIENNE: You yourself just admitted that you have no proof.

GISELE: Please! I know what I know!... I'm not that simple little schoolgirl, fresh from the convent, who let everyone pull the wool over her eyes.

LUCIENNE: Then you must have a reason. Something...

GISELE [*preparing to reveal her proof*]: Tell me, Lucienne... What would *you* say if your husband... A husband who had been a... a husband for years... In every sense of the word, I mean... Every night of the week, every week of the year... If all of a sudden, one fine day... Poof!... No more...

LUCIENNE: "Poof"?

GISELE: Nothing... Finito, as you say in Spanish...

LUCIENNE: That's Italian, love... But I know what you mean... All of a sudden... "Poof," as you put it...

GISELE: Yes... What would you say?

LUCIENNE [*with a little laugh, relishing the prospect*]: Frankly?... [*Sighing.*] "Ahhh!..." That's what I'd say! I'd heave a long sigh, Gisèle, then turn over and get some sleep for a change!

GISELE: Oh yes! That's easy to say, before... Before it actually happens! I was beginning to feel that way too. All that love, love, love... Day after day...

LUCIENNE: And night after night!

GISELE: Just one long, dull honeymoon... I know... I even began to wish something would happen. Anything... Nothing serious, mind you... Just something different, to break the monotony...

LUCIENNE: How well I know...

GISELE [*very matter-of-fact*]: Why, I even thought about getting myself a lover.

LUCIENNE: A lover? You?

GISELE: In fact, I had one all picked out.

LUCIENNE: "Nothing serious," indeed!

GISELE: And you'll never guess who, so don't try to get it out of me!... But he's the image of Monsieur Tournel, Lucienne... The gentleman you met at dinner, night before last...

LUCIENNE: Aha...

GISELE: I'm surprised you didn't notice... Under the table, I mean... His knee, his foot...

LUCIENNE: Really, I wasn't looking...

GISELE: No, but woman's intuition, precious... I'm surprised I have to tell you how close I came.

LUCIENNE: Oh?

GISELE [*holding out her thumb and forefinger, barely apart*]: That close!... And he himself kept saying that he's Victor-Emmanuel's oldest and dearest friend... And "who else would make a better lover, after all?..." And that he "would be an absolutely perfect choice, madame..."

LUCIENNE: Indeed!

GISELE [*getting up*]: Well, no thank you!... Not now... Why bother to be unfaithful, Lucienne?... Now that he's gone and done it for me, that lowlife!

LUCIENNE [*getting up*]: Your logic escapes me, love... [*Moving left.*] But I do know one thing... If you ask me, you're absolutely mad about your husband.

GISELE: Me?... That...

LUCIENNE: If not, why should you care if he cheats? What difference—

GISELE: But he has no right... He simply has no right!

LUCIENNE: But you do have a right to cheat on him, if I understand...

GISELE [*a little petulantly*]: Yes!... And I still would, believe me... [LUCIENNE *gives a little shrug.*] Why? Is there something wrong with that?

LUCIENNE: Well, Gisèle... [*Going to the oblong table and finally taking off her hat and coat.*] I suppose... [*Placing her hat on the table and her coat over the back of the chair opposite* GISELE's.] Only, you still haven't convinced me that you have the slightest reason...

GISELE [*joining her at the table*]: But I just told you! For years the man was a... a torrent... a flood... a...

LUCIENNE: Yes, you said—

GISELE: ...a raging river!... [*As if to cap her comparisons.*] Niagara Falls, Lucienne!... And then, all of a sudden...

LUCIENNE: Poof!... I know...

GISELE: That's right! Not a trickle...

LUCIENNE: Well... [*Sitting down on the chair where she has just placed her coat.*] Some rivers are like that, love. But that doesn't mean that they leave their beds, now does it?

GISELE: Oh?

LUCIENNE: It's like those people you see at the casinos... They sit night after night, betting huge amounts of money... Then, all of a sudden, next time you see them, there they are betting a single measly franc.

GISELE: Fine!... Then let him bet his single measly franc! But let him bet something, for heaven's sake! Anything!... [*Storming up right to the low table, gesticulating as she goes.*] But no! All he does is... is... is stare at the table!

LUCIENNE: So? What does that prove? Only that he has no more money to bet... Not that he's betting it somewhere else... Really, Gisèle...

GISELE: Oh? Well... [*Coming back down left, to the oblong table, echoing, a little sarcastically.*] Really, Lucienne... [*Rummaging in her handbag.*] If that doesn't convince you, then perhaps this will! [*She pulls out a pair of man's suspenders, brandishing them as she speaks.*] Or should I say "these"?

LUCIENNE [*unable to distinguish the objects in question as* GISELE *shakes them in front of her face*]: Those what? What are they?

GISELE [*holding them still for her to see, categorically*]: Suspenders! And do you know whose they are, these suspenders?

LUCIENNE: Your husband's, I imagine...

GISELE: Aha! You're not so quick to take his side now, are you!

[*She puts the suspenders back into the handbag.*]

LUCIENNE: His side?... What do you mean, "take his side"? [*As* GISELE *goes up right and lays the bag on the low table, next to her hat.*] I only assume, Gisèle, that if you're holding a pair of gentleman's suspenders, the gentleman in question is your husband and not some stranger.

GISELE [*returning center stage*]: Precisely! [*About to offer the definitive proof.*] Then perhaps you can explain to me how the gentleman in question... my husband, Lucienne... how he happened to receive them in the mail this morning?

LUCIENNE: In the mail?

GISELE: Yes... In a neat little package. I opened it by mistake... While I was going through his letters.

LUCIENNE [*with a little laugh*]: Oh?

GISELE: And even you have to admit... If someone had to send him back his suspenders, obviously he must have left them somewhere. Right?

LUCIENNE [*getting up and moving right, toward the canapé*]: I suppose...

GISELE: You suppose, indeed!... And would you like me to tell you where that "somewhere" is? The Hotel Paramour, precious!

LUCIENNE: The what?

GISELE: Not exactly some cozy little family boarding-house!

LUCIENNE: The Hotel Paramour?

GISELE [*crossing right, to the cabinet against the up right wall*]: That's what I said... [*She opens one of the drawers, takes out a little box, and comes down right, joining* LUCIENNE *by the canapé.*] See? Here's the box they came in... [*Holding it up.*] No... [*Putting the box down on the small table facing the canapé, shaking her head.*] It's all simply too clear...

LUCIENNE: Tsk tsk tsk... [*Becoming convinced.*] Who would have thought...

GISELE [*pacing up right, between the canapé and the cabinet*]: At first I told myself: "No, there's got to be a reason..." I couldn't believe that... that...

LUCIENNE: That Niagara Falls could dry up over night!

GISELE [*at the canapé, with a sigh*]: Oh!... I tried to make excuses. Maybe this, maybe that... Who knows what? [*Taking the box from the table.*] But then this!... No, no, no! I'm sorry!... There's only one explanation!

[*She goes over to the cabinet and replaces the box in its drawer.*]

LUCIENNE [*sighing, convinced*]: Yes, I'm afraid...

GISELE [*coming back down and joining her at the canapé*]: And if you ever saw it, Lucienne! That Hotel Paramour!... Really! Simply the gaudiest, most vulgar... Oh!

LUCIENNE: If I...? You mean, you know the place, Gisèle?

GISELE: Of course! That's why I'm so late. I wanted to find out once and for all... I said to myself: "There's only one thing to do. I'll go talk to the owner... Or the manager, or someone... I'll ask him point blank..."

LUCIENNE: Aha...

GISELE: Well, I did... But if you think it's easy talking to such people... It's frightful!... Simply frightful!... Can you guess what he told me?... "I'm sorry, but if I gave out the names of our clients I'm afraid madame would never want to be one of them."

LUCIENNE: Oh!

GISELE: Imagine! Saying a thing like that to me!... As if I would dream of setting foot in that... that...

LUCIENNE: Tsk tsk tsk!

GISELE: And then not another single, solitary word!... So we can just forget about any help...

LUCIENNE: "We"...?

GISELE: Now then, precious, you're better at this than I am. And you know all the facts. Tell me, what should I do?

LUCIENNE: Just like that, love?...

GISELE: Please... Try!... Try to get an inspiration...

LUCIENNE: I don't know... Perhaps... I suppose you can just come right out and ask him...

GISELE [*with a sarcastic laugh*]: Ha!... Is that your inspiration? You know perfectly well he would lie through his teeth!... No, there must be something! Think, Lucienne! Think...

LUCIENNE [*hitting on an idea, half-jokingly*]: Well, there's always the famous perfumed letter. That just might work...

GISELE: The what?

LUCIENNE: At least, it always seems to in the theater. It's not terribly clever... But then, with men, don't you know...

GISELE: But what is it? Tell me...

LUCIENNE: Well, the wife writes a letter to the husband. A mad, passionate letter... Reeking with perfume... But as if it were from some other woman, of course... Then, at the end, she tells him where to meet her... [*In mock-dramatic tone.*] For a tryst!

GISELE: A twist?

LUCIENNE: A tryst, love... A rendezvous... And naturally she keeps it. If he does too... Well, that proves something, doesn't it?

GISELE: You're right. It's not terribly clever... But... [*Moving right, toward the window, and taking the folded writing-desk from in front of the bench.*] It's worth a try. [*Taking the desk to the canapé, opening it, and sitting down in front of it.*] I'll do it!... [*Preparing to write, as* LUCIENNE *comes round and stands close by.*] Now then... [*Stopping suddenly.*] Oh no! Wait... I can't... He'll recognize my writing! [*Getting up.*] But not yours!... He certainly won't know yours. [*Taking* LUCIENNE'*s hand and pulling her toward her as if to make her sit in her place.*] Here... You write it...

LUCIENNE [*resisting*]: Me?... Heavens, no! Not a letter...

GISELE [*pulling*]: Please, Lucienne! You've got to!... There's no one else, precious!

LUCIENNE: But...

GISELE [*with a petulant pout*]: Are you my oldest and dearest friend, or aren't you?

LUCIENNE: Well... I suppose... [*Resigned, sitting at the desk as* GISELE *moves over.*] All right... Give me some stationery.

GISELE [*reaching into a compartment and taking out a sheet*]: Here...

LUCIENNE: Not yours, silly! He'll recognize it.

GISELE: Of course! What was I thinking... [*She gets up and goes to the cabinet against the up right wall.*] I think I may have just the thing... [*She opens a drawer and takes out a few sheets, garishly trimmed with lace and decorated with flowers.*] I bought it for my sister's children... [*Brandishing them at* LUCIENNE.] For their little "thank you" notes...

LUCIENNE: My goodness, no!... He'll think your taste is all in your tongue, Gisèle... He'll never come to a... [*Emphasizing.*] a tryst with someone who writes on that! Don't you have something a little more... discreet? Simple but suggestive...

GISELE [*going back to the cabinet and taking out a box*]: Well, there's always this... [*Giving it to her.*] It's simple enough... But it's not too suggestive...

LUCIENNE: No... But it's going to have to do. I think with enough perfume...

GISELE: Oh, that's no problem! I have just the perfect *eau de toilette*. It's utterly vile... [*Going over to the window and giving the butler's cord two tugs.*] I was going to give it to my sister...

[*She moves up toward the cabinet, up right. At that moment the door, up left, opens and* EDOUARD *appears, a dossier in hand, and looks about the room inquisitively.*]

EDOUARD [*still speaking throughout the scene, without benefit of consonants, and barely intelligible*]: Oh, I beg your pardon!...

GISELE: Yes, Edouard...?

EDOUARD: I was looking to see if my uncle had come back...

GISELE [*apparently understanding him perfectly*]: No, he hasn't... Not yet... Why?

[*Throughout their conversation,* LUCIENNE *looks on with increasing amazement, staring back and forth at each one in turn.*]

EDOUARD: Because I have a stack of correspondence to have him sign... And a number of questions about a contract I'm preparing... I'm not quite sure about a few of the details. I was hoping—

GISELE [*interrupting*]: Yes, well... He won't be long.

EDOUARD: Then I'll just have to wait. [*With a little laugh in* LUCIENNE'*s direction.*] Some things can't be hurried, can they!

[LUCIENNE, *quite nonplussed, gives a polite shrug.*]

GISELE: No, they can't... [*As* LUCIENNE *sits gaping at her in wonderment.*] What is it, precious? What's the matter?

LUCIENNE: Nothing... Nothing...

EDOUARD [*coming center, to* LUCIENNE, *good-naturedly*]: You see? Everything comes to him who waits, as they say! [*With a chuckle.*] Or to her, madame... [LUCIENNE *gives a noncommittal nod.*] I hope my aunt didn't keep you waiting too long.

LUCIENNE [*responding as if she understands*]: Yes, monsieur... Of course... We chatted a few moments ago, you and I...

GISELE [*with a sly little smile, as* EDOUARD *looks on, approving*]: No, no, Lucienne... He was saying that he hopes I didn't keep you waiting too long. And that everything comes to him who waits...

EDOUARD [*adding, emphatically*]: Or to her!

GISELE: Or to her...

LUCIENNE [*rather taken aback, but trying to be agreeable*]: Yes... Quite so...

GISELE [*introducing*]: Monsieur Edouard Chandebise, our nephew... Madame Homenides de Histangua...

[*She comes down right.*]

LUCIENNE [*getting up, with a nod, to* EDOUARD]: Charmed, monsieur, I'm sure... You must excuse me if I didn't catch everything you said. I'm a little hard of hearing.

EDOUARD: Oh, it's good of you to say so, madame. But really, it's not you. Nobody understands me.

LUCIENNE [*nodding, but not understanding a word*]: Aha... Aha...

EDOUARD: On account of my speech problem...
LUCIENNE: Aha... [*Turning to* GISELE.] What?
GISELE: He says nobody understands him, because he has a speech problem.
LUCIENNE [*pretending not to have noticed, to* EDOUARD]: Oh? Really?... I
 hadn't... Well, perhaps a mild one... Now that you mention it...
EDOUARD [*bowing and scraping, to* LUCIENNE]: Thank you, madame. You're
 much too kind.
 [*During the preceding exchange the double door opens and* ANTOINETTE
 enters.]
ANTOINETTE [*moving down between* LUCIENNE, *still standing at the canapé, and*
 EDOUARD, *center, to* GISELE]: Madame rang?
GISELE [*still down right, as* LUCIENNE *sits back down on the canapé*]: Ah?...
 Yes, I did, Antoinette... But for Adèle, not for you... Two rings... Didn't
 you hear?
ANTOINETTE: Yes, madame. But Adèle is upstairs, taking her nap. So I came
 instead.
GISELE [*moving toward the canapé*]: She is?... Well, you'll do.
ANTOINETTE [*with a little curtsy*]: Thank you, madame.
GISELE [*gesturing toward the double door*]: In my dressing-room, Antoinette...
 You'll find some toilet water...
ANTOINETTE: I will? [*Aside.*] Is there a leak?
GISELE: It's in a little round flask... In the right-hand drawer of my vanity... It
 says "Ecstatique"...
ANTOINETTE: If madame doesn't mind my asking, why would she want to keep
 something like that? [*Aside.*] And in her vanity!
GISELE: You're right, Antoinette. It's absolutely vile... [*Without transition.*]
 You may use some if you like...
ANTOINETTE [*with a grimace*]: Oh, thanks just the same, madame, but I can't
 think what for...
GISELE: Why, to sprinkle behind your ears, silly!
 [*She waves her off.*]
ANTOINETTE [*aside*]: My God!
GISELE [*in a whisper, to* LUCIENNE]: Really! Sometimes that child can be simply
 too stupid! "What for" indeed! [*Laughing.*] Did you ever...
 [*During her observations,* ANTOINETTE *turns to leave; but instead of
 returning directly to the double door she moves in a semi-circle about a
 very flustered* EDOUARD, *still standing center, pursing her lips and miming
 a kiss. Then, back to audience, she gives him a healthy pinch on the left
 buttock with her left hand and calmly moves up toward the bay.*]
EDOUARD [*jumping, as* ANTOINETTE, *perfectly prim and proper, exits, up
 center*]: Ayyy!
LUCIENNE } [*together, with a start*]: { Good heavens!
GISELE } { What?
EDOUARD: Nothing... It's nothing... [*Pointing.*] My hip... It hurts sometimes...
 [*Rubbing his backside as he bows his way backwards, up left.*]
 Rheumatism... [*At the door.*] Now, if you'll excuse me... I'll go wait for my
 uncle.
GISELE: Yes, do... He'll be along shortly.
EDOUARD [*with a little bow, to* LUCIENNE]: Madame...

LUCIENNE: Monsieur...

EDOUARD [to LUCIENNE]: It's been a pleasure, I assure you...
[He leaves. The two women watch him go out, look at each other, and, after a moment, burst out laughing.]

LUCIENNE: How in the name of... Gisèle, love... How do you understand a word that person says?

GISELE: Just practice... [Going over to the little table facing the canapé.] But you, precious... I simply loved the way you pretended not to notice!

LUCIENNE: Well really... I didn't want to hurt the poor child's feelings.
[As they continue laughing the door, up right, opens and ANTOINETTE enters, coming down right, toward GISELE.]

ANTOINETTE [holding out the flask at arm's length, with a grimace, to GISELE]: Is this what madame wanted?

GISELE [taking it from her]: Yes, Antoinette. Thank you... That will be all.

ANTOINETTE: Very good, madame. [Aside.] I hope so.
[She leaves, up center.]

GISELE: Well, now for our letter... Shall we? [She sits on one of the chairs at the small table, facing LUCIENNE, who is still sitting on the canapé.] I think we have time before my husband comes back.

LUCIENNE: I suppose... [Preparing to write, with a little sigh.] Now then, how do we begin this famous billet doux?

GISELE: Well...

LUCIENNE: First of all... Where did it happen? Where did our mysterious stranger first see this irresistible lothario?

GISELE [correcting]: No... Victor-Emmanuel...

LUCIENNE: Victor... Yes, I know... Where did she see him?... Have you two been to the theater recently?

GISELE: Why... Last Wednesday, in fact... Yes... The Palais-Royal... With Monsieur Tournel... The one I almost took as a lover... I just told you...

LUCIENNE: Aha! Very good! [Reading aloud as she writes.] "Monsieur... I saw you the other evening at the Palais-Royal... We were watching a play..."
[Noting GISELE, who is making a little pout.] What's the matter?

GISELE: Really... Isn't that a little drab? For love at first sight, I mean...

LUCIENNE: Drab?

GISELE: It's good, but it... It almost sounds like one of his insurance contracts. It seems to me we should come right out with it... Something more passionate... Perhaps, like... [Ruminating.] like... "I am the stranger who sat yearning in her box at the Palais-Royal last Wednesday evening, drinking in your manly beauty..."

LUCIENNE [rather startled]: Aha...

GISELE: And no "Monsieur"... Just straight to the point!

LUCIENNE: Yes... Well... [Leaving the rejected sheet on the writing-desk, she takes a fresh one and begins to write again, reading as she goes.] "I am the stranger who sat..."

GISELE [dictating]: "...who sat yearning in her box at the Palais-Royal..."

LUCIENNE: "...yearning in her box at the Palais-Royal... last Wednesday evening..."

GISELE: "...last Wednesday evening..."

LUCIENNE: Yes, I've got that.

GISELE [*from the beginning, summarizing, half in a whisper*]: "...the stranger... yearning in her box... Palais-Royal... Wednesday evening..." [*Continuing.*] "...drinking in your manly beauty..."

LUCIENNE [*after writing the last phrase*]: Indeed!

GISELE: Yes... That's passionate, don't you think? And it doesn't mince words! [LUCIENNE *gives an appropriate tilt of the head in reply.*] All right... Let's continue...

LUCIENNE: Yes, let's... [*Reading as she writes.*] "You were sitting in your box with your wife and another gentleman..."

GISELE: Monsieur Tournel...

LUCIENNE: Yes, but it wouldn't be her place to say so.

GISELE: No...

LUCIENNE [*continuing*]: "Somebody next to me mentioned your name..."

GISELE [*repeating with a nod*]: "...mentioned your name..."

LUCIENNE: "...and I learned who you are..."

GISELE: Excellent! Just like that!...

LUCIENNE [*still writing*]: "Ever since that night..."

GISELE [*correcting*]: "Fateful..." [LUCIENNE *gives a questioning look.*] "That fateful night..."

LUCIENNE: If you insist... "Ever since that fateful night, I dream only of you..."

GISELE: Fine! But... You don't think it's a trifle exaggerated, do you?

LUCIENNE: Of course it is! But it's supposed to be... To us, not to him...

GISELE: Well, if you're sure...

LUCIENNE [*continuing*]: "I am ready to sacrifice my virtue to my love, utter folly though it be..."

GISELE: Oh, I like that!... Then say: "I pray that you will commit the supreme sacrifice with me."

LUCIENNE [*putting down the pen*]: Really, Gisèle, I don't think so... That sounds as if you wanted to kill each other, love. Say something like: "Please come and let us sacrifice it together..."

GISELE: Yes... That's good! Put that down.

LUCIENNE [*writing*]: "...sacrifice it together. I shall await you this evening, at five o'clock, at the Hotel Paramour..."

GISELE: Oh, should we...? The same hotel, I mean... Won't that make him suspicious?

LUCIENNE: Not a bit... It will get him excited!

GISELE: Well... If you think...

LUCIENNE: Now the address...

GISELE [*thinking*]: The address... The... Ah! [*She gets up and goes over to the cabinet, up right, where she has replaced the box the suspenders came in, opens the drawer, takes it out, and reads from the label.*] "Thirteen, Rue Cherchez-La-Femme, Saint-Cloud."

LUCIENNE [*writing, as* GISELE *replaces the box in the drawer and returns to the little table, sitting down again*]: "...Cherchez-La-Femme, Saint Cloud."

GISELE: Yes, in an utterly unspeakable section!... If only you could have seen it, precious...

LUCIENNE: I can imagine... [*Still concentrating on the letter.*] Now one last detail... "Our room will be reserved in your name."

GISELE: No, no... Put "lovenest"... "Our lovenest will be reserved..."

LUCIENNE [*writing*]: If you insist... And signed: "A woman who loves you."

GISELE: "Madly... Who loves you madly!"

LUCIENNE: You're learning, love. [*She finishes writing and puts down the pen.*] There!... "Finito," as they say... [*Emphasizing.*] in Italian!... Now for the perfume...

GISELE [*who has been opening the flask during the preceding, handing it to her*]: Here... [*Accidentally hitting* LUCIENNE'*s hand and spilling some of the perfume on the rejected sheet of stationery on the writing desk*]: Oh!

LUCIENNE [*taking the flask*]: Careful!

GISELE: That one doesn't matter...

LUCIENNE [*sprinkling the perfume rather generously over the letter and waving it to dry*]: That should be enough.

GISELE [*getting up and looking at it, rather taken aback*]: Enough, indeed!... My goodness! Look what you've done... It's getting all smudged...

LUCIENNE [*getting up*]: Darn!

[*She goes over to the cabinet, up right, and lays down the flask.*]

GISELE: It looks frightful! You'll have to do it over.

LUCIENNE [*coming back to the canapé, reflecting for a moment*]: No... This is going to do just fine. [*Holding it out.*] You can still read it.

GISELE: But—

LUCIENNE: You'll see, love... Listen... [*Sitting down, reading as she writes.*] "P. S. Please forgive my flood of girlish tears, but how can I keep them from flowing at the merest thought of you! I beg you to let them be tears of joy and not of despair." [*Spoken.*] There! [*With a touch of sarcasm.*] Not too much like an insurance contract now, I hope!

GISELE: Hardly... But... About the perfume... Won't he think there are too many tears for just one woman? I mean, it looks as if you ran it under a tap or something.

LUCIENNE: Don't worry, love. It looks perfectly fine. You'll see... Now his address... [*Taking an envelope and writing.*] "Monsieur Victor-Emmanuel Chandebise, 95, Boulevard Malesherbes." There!... [*Putting the letter in the envelope and sealing it.*] "Ecstatique," go do your best!

[*She gets up and begins to move center.*]

GISELE [*with a sigh*]: Yes... [*She goes to the writing-desk, about to fold it up.*] Or your worst...

LUCIENNE [*stopping her, returning to the desk*]: Ah! [*Putting the envelope down.*] One final touch... [*Writing.*] "Personal."

GISELE: Perfect!

[*She folds up the desk and returns it to its original position, down right, against the bench by the window.*]

LUCIENNE [*holding up the letter, moving center*]: Now all we need is a messenger to send it... [*With a laugh.*] To bring it, that is!

GISELE [*joining her*]: Yes...

LUCIENNE: You do have someone to go look for one, I hope...

GISELE: Why... I rather thought... I thought you could, Lucienne.

LUCIENNE: Me?... You mean, I write the letter and find a messenger too?

GISELE: Well really, Lucienne... I can't very well have Etienne go find a messenger, and then have the messenger come here and give him back his letter!

LUCIENNE: Yes, but—

GISELE: And I certainly can't go out and look for one myself. Why, if my husband ever asked him to describe her... The mystery lady... [LUCIENNE *is about to object, weakly, but* GISELE *cuts her off.*] But with you... Well, there's no problem.

LUCIENNE: Yes... First the letter, now the messenger... You're sure there's nothing else?

GISELE: Please, precious!... You can't say no...

LUCIENNE [*with a sigh, relenting*]: No... I don't suppose...

GISELE [*throwing her arms around her neck*]: Oh, thank you! Thank you! [*The doorbell rings.*]

LUCIENNE: But really, there's a limit.

GISELE [*quickly disengaging*]: Ah! That must be Victor-Emmanuel... [*She hurries up right, to the cabinet, at the same time gesturing toward the door, up right, as* LUCIENNE *snatches up her hat and coat from the table and chair, down left.*] Quick! That way... Down the hall... Then out through the sitting-room...
[*She places the perfume flask in one of the cabinet drawers.*]

LUCIENNE [*crossing right, to the door*]: I know... I know... [*Blowing her a kiss.*] Bye-bye, love...

GISELE [*reciprocating*]: Bye-bye... And thank you, precious...
[*As* LUCIENNE *leaves, the double door opens and reveals* CHANDEBISE *and* ETIENNE, *the former carrying his hat and coat, with* TOURNEL *behind them, hat in hand, wearing his coat and carrying a briefcase.*]

CHANDEBISE [*to* ETIENNE]: And you're sure the doctor is coming right back?

ETIENNE: That's what he said, monsieur.

CHANDEBISE: Thank you. [*Handing him his hat and coat.*] Here... [*Motioning toward the door, down left.*] In there... [*To* TOURNEL, *as* ETIENNE *leaves, down left.*] Please... After you... [*Coming center, as* TOURNEL, *preceding him, comes down left to the stage left side of the oblong table, neither noticing* GISELE, *still up right.*] I'll just be a moment... A few letters to sign...

GISELE: Yes... And poor Edouard...

CHANDEBISE [*to* GISELE, *surprised to see her*]: Ah! Gisèle...

GISELE: He's been on pins and needles.

CHANDEBISE: I didn't know you were here...
[ETIENNE *reenters, down left, and unobtrusively crosses up to the bay and exits.*]

TOURNEL [*to* GISELE, *with a polite little nod*]: Madame...

GISELE [*to* TOURNEL, *returning his greeting*]: Monsieur...

CHANDEBISE: Monsieur and I met on the stairs...

GISELE [*indifferent*]: Aha...

TOURNEL: Yes... [*Putting his hat and briefcase down on the table, taking some papers from the latter, and laying them down also, to* CHANDEBISE.] Several lucky new clients for Requiem Life, my friend...

CHANDEBISE [*moving toward the table, to* TOURNEL]: Excellent! The more the merrier!... I'll have a look in a minute.
[*While speaking he has been tugging at his pants as if they are too loose.*]

GISELE [*to* CHANDEBISE, *noticing his discomfort, wryly*]: Why, whatever is the matter, treasure? [*With an air of affected innocence.*] Is something wrong with your suspenders?

CHANDEBISE: My... No... That is...

GISELE: Not the ones I bought you?

CHANDEBISE: The ones you... Yes...

GISELE: But they were just fine before.

CHANDEBISE: Yes, but... I... I pulled them a little loose.

GISELE: Well, that's no problem. [*With mock solicitude, moving as if about to join him.*] Here... Let me fix them.

CHANDEBISE [*instinctively pulling back*]: No, no... Quite all right... [*Waving her away, going toward the door, up left, to* TOURNEL.] If you don't mind waiting... Those letters...

TOURNEL: Please... Don't stand on ceremony.

[CHANDEBISE *opens the door.*]

EDOUARD'S VOICE [*with a tone of impatience, as if to say: "It's about time!"*]: Ah!

CHANDEBISE [*at the threshold, to the unseen* EDOUARD, *sharply*]: Yes, yes!... I know!... [*As he exits.*] I was busy!...

[*The moment the door is closed,* TOURNEL, *watching him go, excitedly crosses to* GISELE, *who has moved up right and is standing by the low table near the door.*]

TOURNEL [*passionately*]: Ah, Gisèle!... Gisèle!... I dreamt of you last night. I dreamt...

GISELE [*holding out her hands to ward him off*]: Monsieur...

TOURNEL ⎫   ⎧ All night... I dreamt...
          ⎬ [*together*]: ⎨
GISELE [*eluding him*] ⎭   ⎩ Please...

[*She crosses down left to the oblong table and picks up her coat from the chair.*]

TOURNEL [*following her*]: I dreamt that you and I... That... Ah! You know what I dreamt, Gisèle!

GISELE [*returning up right with* TOURNEL *at her heels*]: Really, monsieur!... I'm sorry, but that's all over!

TOURNEL: Over?... But... But how?... It's only just beginning!

GISELE [*at the low table*]: Thank you just the same! [*Picking up her handbag and hat.*] There's simply no need to cheat on him, now that he's cheating on me, now is there?

TOURNEL [*surprised*]: He...? But—

GISELE: It makes no sense... No sense at all...

TOURNEL: But—

GISELE: That sort of thing is fine when there's nothing else on your mind...

TOURNEL: But Gisèle... Gisèle... Yesterday you said... You led me on... You let me believe...

GISELE: Yes, but that was yesterday... Before the suspenders...

TOURNEL: The what?

GISELE: Today, with the suspenders... Well, it's all changed. Understand? [*She goes to the door, up right.*]

TOURNEL: No, I... [*As* GISELE *opens the door.*] Wait... Wait... [*Running to the door as she exits and closes it in his face.*] Gisèle... [*Crossing down left, to the oblong table, at a loss.*] "Suspenders"...? What is that supposed to mean?

[*The door, up left, opens and* EDOUARD *appears at the threshold.*]

EDOUARD [*jovially, still in his inarticulate speech*]: Monsieur... My uncle says he can see you now.

TOURNEL [*gruffly*]: What?

EDOUARD [*entering, trying unsuccessfully to make himself understood*]: My uncle says he can see you now, monsieur.

TOURNEL: Yes, well... When you decide what you have to tell me...

EDOUARD [*taking a pencil and pad of paper from his pocket*]: Here!... [*Articulating as clearly as he can while he writes.*] My un-... cle... says... he... can... see... you... now...

[*He rips off the sheet, comes down to* TOURNEL, *and gives it to him.*]

TOURNEL [*reading*]: "My uncle says he can see you now..." [*Sarcastically.*] Thank you! Why didn't you say so!

[*Still grumbling, he picks up his papers from the oblong table, leaving his briefcase and hat, and exits through the door, up left.*]

EDOUARD [*at the oblong table, once* TOURNEL *has left*]: Old fart! [*He illustrates the exclamation by encircling his mouth with thumb and forefinger, and vibrating his lips in the direction of* TOURNEL'*s exit.*] Did you ever... [*Coming down left as he talks to himself.*] I take the trouble to come in here and get him, and all he does is complain...

[*As he continues his diatribe the double door opens and* ETIENNE *shows in* FINACHE, *who is carrying his hat and coat.*]

ETIENNE [*at the threshold*]: Yes, monsieur. He's back.

FINACHE ⎱
         ⎰ [*together*]: ⎰ Ah! Good...
EDOUARD [*down left, unaware of them*] ⎰   ⎱ Some people!

ETIENNE [*to* FINACHE]: I'll go let him know that monsieur is here.

FINACHE [*to* ETIENNE]: Yes... Please... [*As* ETIENNE *turns to go, as an afterthought.*] And if you don't mind...

[*He hands him his hat and coat.* ETIENNE *gives a little bow and leaves.*]

EDOUARD [*as* FINACHE, *coming down left to the downstage end of the oblong table, contemplates him from behind*]: No manners... I tell him as nicely as you please: "My uncle can see you now, monsieur." I even write it down. And all he can say is: "Why didn't you say so!"... Old fart!

[*He turns toward the door, up left, and repeats his sound effect, almost in* FINACHE'*s face.*]

FINACHE: What?

EDOUARD [*recoiling*]: Oh! Doctor... I... I didn't know...

FINACHE [*not really understanding*]: Quite all right, Edouard... [*With a little laugh.*] So... Talking to ourselves now, are we?

EDOUARD: Talking...? Oh no, doctor... I was thinking out loud... Something that happened... Someone... [*Pointing to the door, up left.*] Just now...

FINACHE [*with a wave of the hand*]: Yes, yes... No need to explain... [*He turns aside and gives an uncomprehending shrug.*] Really... [*Approaching him, changing his tone.*] Now then, young man... On more important matters... [*Confidentially.*] Anything new to report?... [*With a meaningful wink.*] Like our love life, perhaps?

EDOUARD: Shhh!

FINACHE: Are we having ourselves that little... [*With a friendly nudge, emphasizing.*] fling I prescribed?

EDOUARD: Shhh! Monsieur... Please...

FINACHE [*moving aside, jovially*]: Ah, yes! I forgot... We mustn't sully that reputation!... Monsieur Innocence-in-the-Flesh!

EDOUARD: No... Please...

FINACHE: Though, of course, between a young man and his doctor... Well, there comes a time—

EDOUARD: Yes, but—

FINACHE: ...when his doctor is more like his confessor... And he has to get down to the naked truth... [*Chuckling at the afterthought.*] If you'll pardon the expression!... No matter what the rest of the family thinks! Right?

EDOUARD [*with a nervous little laugh*]: Yes...

FINACHE: So, tell me... Did you do what I suggested? Did you go there?

EDOUARD: Where?

FINACHE: You know... The Hotel Paramour... Did you—

EDOUARD: Shhh! Please...

FINACHE: Come, come... We're alone...

EDOUARD: I know, but...

FINACHE: Well, did you?

EDOUARD [*after a long hesitation, glancing left and right, then, in a whisper*]: Yes...

FINACHE [*with mock admiration, applauding*]: Bravo, young man!... And...?

EDOUARD [*with an ecstatic glance heavenward, sighing*]: Ahhh...

FINACHE: Aha! Aha!... See? Doctor knows best!... I told you... Whenever I want to have myself a... a time... that's the only place I go. [*He gives him another round of mock applause.*] Not a bad cure, wouldn't you say?

EDOUARD: Yes... But still... Shhh!... Please...

FINACHE: Don't worry! Mum's the word! Cross my heart... [*As he crosses his heart he feels at his breast pocket, suddenly remembering something.*] Ah! I almost forgot... Talking about cures... [*Taking a small case from his pocket.*] My friend, you're going to be absolutely delighted... It just arrived from the laboratory...

EDOUARD: What...?

FINACHE [*opening the case and holding it out to him*]: See? The first working model of the Finache Prosthetic Palate!

EDOUARD: Ah...

FINACHE: Feast your eyes, young man!... No, better: feast your tongue!... Because, thanks to this simple-looking device... Thanks to this little silver beauty... and my years of research... you'll be able to speak just like everyone else!

EDOUARD: I will?

FINACHE [*very professorial*]: After all, the cause of your problem is a congenital malocclusion of the palatal arch...

EDOUARD: Aha...

FINACHE: An incomplete closure while still *in utero*...

EDOUARD [*on whom the Latin is lost*]: I oo-eh-o?

FINACHE: In the womb, that is...

EDOUARD: Ah...

FINACHE: Yes... [*Jovially.*] No doubt you were a trifle impatient to come out... Not that anyone would blame you... The result is that your speech sounds, instead of being projected outward, are diverted upward and absorbed into your mask...

EDOUARD: My... [*Pointing to his face, shaking his head.*] I never wear one...

FINACHE [*with a quizzical tilt of the head, then suddenly understanding*]: You never... [*Laughing.*] No, no... Your mask... Your sinus cavities... [*Continuing.*] Producing a marked degree of verbal unintelligibility...

EDOUARD: You mean, nobody understands me.

FINACHE: Beg pardon?

EDOUARD: You mean, nobody understands me.

FINACHE [*still not understanding, with a shrug*]: Quite... Now, with the Finache Prosthetic Palate we can correct all that. [*He removes the device from the case and holds it up.*] And in sterling silver, no less!

EDOUARD [*admiringly*]: Ah...

FINACHE: Not too... unpalatable, wouldn't you say?

[*He chuckles at his bon mot.*]

EDOUARD [*enthusiastically*]: And you're sure I'll be able to talk?

FINACHE: Sorry?

EDOUARD: You're sure I'll be able to... Oh! [*Frustrated, he takes the device from him and is about to insert it into his mouth.*] Just a minute...

FINACHE [*seizing his wrist*]: No, no! Not yet... First you have to soak it in boric acid... To disinfect it... Heaven only knows who's handled it!

EDOUARD: Of course... Right away... [*He moves quickly upstage, as if to leave; then, stopping short, he returns to* FINACHE.] I was only asking if... [*Taking the case and replacing the device.*] if you're sure... [*Holding it up, speaking as slowly and clearly as he can.*] if you're sure I'll be able to talk...

FINACHE: Aha... Talk?... Indeed I'm sure! Why, if you had any talent you could even be an actor!

EDOUARD [*growing more and more excited*]: Ah! Monsieur... Thank you! Thank you!...

[*He flings his arms around* FINACHE's *neck.*]

FINACHE [*defending himself with a laugh, sharing in his pleasure*]: Yes... Yes... Now just go soak it... You can thank me later!

EDOUARD [*going up toward the double door, holding high the little case like a trophy*]: Ha!

FINACHE [*still down left, calling after him*]: One packet of powder in a large glass of warm water...

EDOUARD [*stopping in the bay, facing him, theatrically*]: To soak or not to soak...

CHANDEBISE'S VOICE [*offstage*]: Edouard!

EDOUARD: That is the question!

CHANDEBISE'S VOICE: Come in here!

[EDOUARD *turns to leave.*]

FINACHE: Wait!... They're calling you in there...

EDOUARD: Too bad!... Later... Later...

[*He leaves excitedly, still brandishing the case. At about the same moment,* CHANDEBISE *enters, up left.*]

CHANDEBISE: Edouard...

FINACHE [*moving up to join him*]: He'll be right back... [*Pointing toward the double door.*] He had something important...

CHANDEBISE: Ah, Finache...

FINACHE: Chandebise...

[*They shake hands, up left.*]

CHANDEBISE: Good to see you... You're just the person I wanted to talk to.

FINACHE: Oh? I came by a little while ago. Didn't Etienne tell you?

CHANDEBISE: Yes... With Señor Histangua's certificate...

FINACHE [*taking it from his pocket and handing it to him*]: Right...

CHANDEBISE: Thank you... [*Continuing.*] And something about his living forever...

FINACHE [*laughing*]: If not longer!...

CHANDEBISE [*hemming and hawing, obviously uncomfortable*]: Yes... Well... Since you're here... [*Indicating the chair on the stage right side of the oblong table.*] Please... [*Putting the certificate in his pocket.*] I... I was hoping I might discuss something with you...

FINACHE [*sitting down, aside*]: His ovaries, too?

CHANDEBISE [*sitting down across from him*]: Something rather... Well... Rather delicate...

FINACHE: Of course... Feel free...

CHANDEBISE: You see... I... I'm having a problem...

FINACHE: Cramps, my friend?...

CHANDEBISE: Not that simple, I'm afraid... [*Reluctantly.*] You know my wife, Finache... [FINACHE *nods.*] You know what a delightful creature she is...

FINACHE: Quite!

CHANDEBISE: ...and that I've never been one of your footloose husbands...

FINACHE: Oh?

CHANDEBISE: What do you mean, "Oh?"

FINACHE: No, my friend, I only meant—

CHANDEBISE: Never!... Why should I be, with a woman like that?... Wife and lover rolled into one... Like me... The perfect husband... Always ready to satisfy her every desire... And willing, Finache!... And able!... [*Emphasizing.*] Her every desire...

FINACHE: Oh?

CHANDEBISE: What do you mean, "Oh?" Believe me...

FINACHE: I do... I... It's just that I don't quite see why you feel you have to tell me.

CHANDEBISE [*getting up, nervously, and sitting on the upstage right corner of the table, beside* FINACHE, *point blank*]: Were you ever in the army, Finache?

FINACHE: What?

CHANDEBISE: The army...

FINACHE: Yes... In the Quartermasters... [*Laughing.*] When they found out I was a doctor... But why—

CHANDEBISE [*cutting him off*]: But you did learn to shoot a rifle...

FINACHE: Well... Yes, more or less... Not too well, but—

CHANDEBISE: But you did... And you were able to load it, and aim it, and... and when the sergeant yelled "Fire!", you were able to pull the trigger.

FINACHE: Yes... [*Laughing.*] I never hit the target, but I was able to pull the trigger! And I never killed any of my comrades either, so I guess I... [*Stopping short.*] Why do you ask?

CHANDEBISE: Well, I learned to shoot too. And very well, Finache!... I could show you my medals...

FINACHE: No need...

CHANDEBISE: Yes... Until one day, when I had an awful dream... A nightmare... [*Correcting himself.*] One night, that is... I dreamt that I had a magnificent rifle, and that I was waiting to shoot at the target... Then along came the sergeant, with a sneer on his face... And I thought: "Good God, he looks just like my father!" And he said to me: "All right, son! Let's see how you shoot with a real man's rifle!" So there I was, with my finger on the trigger... The rifle at my cheek, taking aim... Taking aim... And all of a sudden I heard him yell "Fire!"

FINACHE: Ah...

CHANDEBISE: But when I tried to pull the trigger, the rifle seemed to melt... [*Getting up and moving center.*] That magnificent rifle... No bang, no bullets... Nothing!

FINACHE [*turning round on his chair to face him*]: Fascinating, my friend... Though I really fail to see—

CHANDEBISE [*taking one of the chairs from the small table, left, and straddling the seat*]: That dream ruined me, Finache. Every time I went to shoot, from that moment on, that damnable sergeant would be there, before my eyes, sneering... And my finger would freeze... I couldn't shoot again to save my life!

FINACHE: No more medals...

CHANDEBISE: Hardly!

FINACHE [*getting up, as if to cut short the conversation*]: Ah, yes... The mysterious power of dreams... As the poet says: "To sleep, perchance to dream... Aye, there's the rub..." A classic case of auto-suggestion...

CHANDEBISE: But it didn't end there!

FINACHE: Oh...

CHANDEBISE: No... That's what I have to talk to you about.

FINACHE [*as if to say: "Finally!"*]: Aha...
[*He turns his chair to face* CHANDEBISE *and sits back down.*]

CHANDEBISE: Yes... You see, I have the same problem now with my wife.

FINACHE: She looks like your father?

CHANDEBISE: No, no... She... I... [*Not certain how to approach the delicate subject.*] Last month, one night, I was with her... [*He gets up and replaces the chair by the small table, right.*] As usual, believe me... At my passionate best, if I do say so myself... [FINACHE *nods understandingly.*] When all of a sudden, I don't know why, but... but—

FINACHE [*attempting a touch of levity*]: The sergeant came in!

CHANDEBISE [*still standing by the small table, mechanically*]: Yes... What? No... Not the... No, but he might as well have... All of a sudden I felt strange all over. Uncomfortable... Almost as if... [*Little by little he crouches down, as if growing smaller, and affects an angelic little voice.*] As if I were a child... A tiny little child...

FINACHE: Yes... A classic case of auto-suggestion... That's not hard to explain. Not hard at all...

CHANDEBISE: No... Not hard at all... [*With a meaningful pout and a shake of the head.*] Exactly... [*Changing his tone.*] At first I thought: "Pfff!... It's nothing... Just a temporary setback... After all, I've won my laurels! Defeat, today... Tomorrow, victory..."

FINACHE: "In love and war," Chandebise...

CHANDEBISE: Yes, but the next day... [*Correcting himself.*] The next night... There I was, don't you know?... Wondering... Will I? Won't I?... Yes? No?... Stupid, wasn't it!

FINACHE: Quite... Auto-suggestion...

CHANDEBISE: Well, I don't have to tell you... Nothing... Zero...

FINACHE: Zero?

CHANDEBISE: Nothing!

FINACHE: Poor Chandebise!

CHANDEBISE: "Poor Chandebise" is right! Every night for a month... Same story... Will I? Won't I?... Now I don't even dare ask. I know that I won't... And each night, it never fails...

FINACHE [*with a wry little laugh*]: Well... I wouldn't say that exactly...

CHANDEBISE [*coming center*]: Please! It's no joking matter!

FINACHE [*getting up*]: Certainly not... [*Turning the chair around to its original position.*] But it's no tragedy either. [*Joining him, center.*] We hear that every day. Auto-suggestion, plain and simple... Will-power my friend! That's the cure! You know what they say: "Where there's a will..."

CHANDEBISE: Yes... But in my case, where there's a will, there's a "won't!"

FINACHE: Bah! See?... That's your problem... You defeat yourself before you begin. The fear of failure... Instead of all that worry, you should stand up tall, throw your shoulders back, hold your head high...

CHANDEBISE: In bed?

FINACHE: In... Figuratively speaking...

CHANDEBISE: Ah...

FINACHE: Puff up your chest... Take yourself in hand...

CHANDEBISE: Figuratively...

FINACHE: ...and tell yourself: "I am the master of my fate, I am the captain of my soul..."

CHANDEBISE: Well...

FINACHE: Besides, everything you've been saying... It's your wife you should have been telling, not your doctor. Just the two of you... Quietly, calmly... Instead of all your "Will I?"s and "Won't I?"s...

CHANDEBISE: Maybe...

FINACHE: No "maybes" about it!... She would have made light of it. You both would have had a friendly little laugh, and that would have been that! No more "Yes? No?"... Only "Let's..."

CHANDEBISE: Yes, you're probably right...

FINACHE: I know I am!... Backbone, my friend!... Backbone... Not to mention more physical exercise...

CHANDEBISE [*with a little wave, dismissing the idea*]: Ha!

FINACHE: The outdoor kind, I mean... Less work, more play... Just look at you! You've got the weight of the world on your shoulders!... [*Going behind him, pulling back his drooping shoulders.*] Stand up tall... Shoulders back... Head high...

CHANDEBISE: Figuratively?

FINACHE: Literally!... [*Continuing his maneuver, and adding to it a knee in the small of* CHANDEBISE's *back.*] Backbone!... [*He moves around him, right.*]

And those new therapeutic suspenders I prescribed?... The American ones?... Do you wear them?

CHANDEBISE [*lifting his vest to show them*]: These?... Of course!

FINACHE: Oh?... Because so far they don't seem to have... Well, keep wearing them. It takes time...

CHANDEBISE: In fact, just to force myself, I've given away all my old ones. To my nephew, Edouard... I only wish these weren't so blasted ugly!

FINACHE: Bah! No one sees them...

CHANDEBISE: Not true! A moment ago my wife came within an inch...

FINACHE: Pfff!... So?

CHANDEBISE [*moving left*]: No thank you! These ugly things? That's all I need! Along with everything else...

FINACHE: Vanity... Vanity...

CHANDEBISE: Besides, if she knew I've given away the ones she bought me...

FINACHE [*changing his tone*]: Come... Take off your jacket and let me listen to your chest.

[*Just as* CHANDEBISE *rejoins him, about to comply, the double door opens and* LUCIENNE *appears, in hat and coat, with* ETIENNE *right behind her.*]

LUCIENNE [*entering, to* ETIENNE]: Yes, please...

CHANDEBISE [*quickly readjusting his jacket, already half removed*]: Oh...

LUCIENNE [*to* ETIENNE, *continuing*]: Tell madame...

CHANDEBISE [*to* FINACHE, *waving him away*]: Later...

ETIENNE [*to* LUCIENNE]: Very good, madame.

[*He leaves.*]

CHANDEBISE [*to* LUCIENNE, *moving toward her*]: Ah! What a pleasant surprise...

LUCIENNE: Monsieur...

CHANDEBISE: You've come to see my wife, I imagine...

LUCIENNE [*as* FINACHE *comes down right, behind the canapé, to be out of the way*]: Yes... That is, I've come back. I was here before, but I had a little errand. I've already seen her... [*With a nod toward* FINACHE.] And monsieur as well...

FINACHE [*with a polite bow*]: Once again, madame...

CHANDEBISE [*to* LUCIENNE]: Ah... Then I needn't introduce you...

[*Just then the door, up right, opens and* GISELE *appears.*]

GISELE [*entering, catching sight of* LUCIENNE, *and gesturing*]: Ah...

LUCIENNE [*moving right, to join her*]: Gisèle, love...

CHANDEBISE [*up center, trying to attract* GISELE'*s attention*]: Hello! I'm back...

GISELE [*ignoring him, to* LUCIENNE, *whispering*]: Well?

LUCIENNE [*whispering*]: It's all done. The messenger is right behind me...

GISELE [*whispering*]: Good!

[*The double door opens and* ETIENNE *appears, carrying a letter on a small tray.*]

ETIENNE [*at the door, to* CHANDEBISE, *who is still trying unsuccessfully to attract* GISELE'*s attention*]: Monsieur...

CHANDEBISE [*turning*]: Hmm?

ETIENNE: It's a letter for monsieur... Marked "Personal"...

LUCIENNE [*to* GISELE, *whispering*]: There!

CHANDEBISE: For me?... [*Taking the letter and waving off* ETIENNE, *who leaves.*] I wonder who... [*To the two women.*] If you don't mind...

[*He takes a pince-nez from his pocket, plants it firmly on the tip of his nose, and comes down center, reading to himself as the two women observe with interest.*]

GISELE [*to* LUCIENNE, *whispering*]: See?

CHANDEBISE [*startled, his jaw dropping, unable to hold back an exclamation*]: Good God in... Did you ever...

GISELE [*with feigned innocence*]: What is it, treasure? Not bad news, I hope?

CHANDEBISE: No... No, just... Just business... Insurance business... Nothing important...

GISELE: I'm so glad! [*To* LUCIENNE, *whispering.*] Indeed!... Come, I've seen enough!

[*She takes* LUCIENNE *by the hand and they both exit, up right.*]

CHANDEBISE [*as soon as he sees them leave, going to the canapé, taking* FINACHE *by the arm and coming down with him, far right, with a sigh*]: Ah! Finache, Finache, Finache!... You'll never guess...

FINACHE: Hmm?

CHANDEBISE: Never in a million years!... [*Fanning his brow with the letter.*] Women... Can you figure them out?

FINACHE [*pointing toward the door, up right*]: Those two?

CHANDEBISE: No!... [*Shaking the letter under his nose.*] This one!

FINACHE: Who?

[*During their exchange, the door, up left, opens and* TOURNEL *appears, without his coat, still holding his papers.*]

TOURNEL [*entering, to* CHANDEBISE]: Excuse me, but... [*With good-humored sarcasm.*] I'm still here, you know!

CHANDEBISE [*to* TOURNEL]: Ah, Tournel... Come in here...

TOURNEL [*coming down left to the oblong table and putting his papers down on his briefcase*]: What is it? [*To* FINACHE, *nodding.*] Doctor...

[*He crosses right.*]

FINACHE [*shaking hands with him*]: Monsieur...

CHANDEBISE: My friends, hold on to your hats...

TOURNEL: Ah... Just a minute...

[*He crosses left, to the oblong table, about to pick up his hat.*]

CHANDEBISE [*to* TOURNEL]: No, no, Tournel... I mean figuratively...

TOURNEL [*stopping in his tracks, embarrassed*]: Oh... [*Crossing back right and rejoining them.*] I thought...

CHANDEBISE: It seems... It seems I've made... How shall I put it?... A conquest!

FINACHE ⎱ [*together*]: ⎰ You?
TOURNEL ⎰   ⎱ No!

CHANDEBISE [*to* TOURNEL]: Yes! [*To* FINACHE.] Me!... Gives you a turn, what?... Well, listen to this! [*Reading.*] "I am the stranger who sat yearning in her box at the Palais-Royal last Wednesday evening..."

FINACHE: Who on earth...?

CHANDEBISE: Wait! Listen... [*Emphasizing every word.*] "drinking in your manly beauty..."

FINACHE ⎱ [*together*]: ⎰ No!
TOURNEL ⎰   ⎱ You?

CHANDEBISE: That's what she says... [*Reading.*] "your manly beauty..."

TOURNEL: Now I've heard everything!

CHANDEBISE [*shaking his hand, wryly*]: Thank you!

TOURNEL [*taking the letter, deciphering it with difficulty and reading aloud*]: "You were sitting... in your box..." [*To* FINACHE.] It's a little hard to read... It looks as if she was sitting in the bathtub... [*Continuing.*] "with your wife... and another gentleman..."

CHANDEBISE: Yes, Tournel... Notice: "another gentleman..." [*Getting back at him.*] In other words, just some "Monsieur X..." Nobody special... Hardly worth mentioning...

TOURNEL: Oh?

CHANDEBISE [*taking back the letter, crossing up left as he reads, with* FINACHE *and* TOURNEL *at his heels*]: "Somebody next to me mentioned your name and I learned who you are..."

[*By now the trio are standing center stage.*]

CHANDEBISE [*continuing*]: "Ever since that fateful night..." [*To* FINACHE.] "Fateful..." [*Continuing.*] "Ever since that fateful night, I dream only of you..."

FINACHE *and* TOURNEL [*together, to* CHANDEBISE]: You?... [*Looking at each other, shaking their heads in doubt.*] No!...

CHANDEBISE: She dreams about me... [*With a little poke to* TOURNEL'*s ribs.*] Only me!...

TOURNEL: Does it say that?

CHANDEBISE: Of course it does!

FINACHE [*looking over* CHANDEBISE'*s shoulder, to* TOURNEL]: You're right... It is hard to read... But yes... That's what it says.

TOURNEL: Good grief! That's hard to believe... [*To* FINACHE.] Don't you think?

FINACHE [*trying to remain noncommittal*]: Pfff! There's no explaining dreams...

TOURNEL: Obviously!... Or accounting for tastes!... It must be something she ate. [*To* FINACHE.] Stomach trouble?

FINACHE: Liver, more likely...

CHANDEBISE: Listen, you two...

TOURNEL [*laughing, to* CHANDEBISE]: Don't mind me...

FINACHE [*likewise*]: Or me... Just joking...

CHANDEBISE: Yes, well... [*Holding up the letter.*] This one isn't joking! Just listen to the rest... [*Moving left as he reads.*] "I am ready to sacrifice my virtue to my love..."

FINACHE [*following him*]: Oh...

CHANDEBISE [*at the oblong table, continuing*]: "...utter folly though it be..."

TOURNEL [*still center, to* FINACHE]: That much I agree with!

CHANDEBISE [*ignoring his jest, continuing*]: "Please come and let us sacrifice it together..." Ha! She's picked the right one! [*To* FINACHE.] Hasn't she, Finache! After what I just told you...

FINACHE: Bah!

[*He sits down on the stage left side of the oblong table.*]

CHANDEBISE [*reading*]: "I shall await you this evening, at five o'clock, at the Hotel Paramour..."

FINACHE [*with a start*]: The Hotel... Did you say the Hotel Paramour?

CHANDEBISE [*standing on the stage right side of the table, scrutinizing the address*]: Yes... "Thirteen, Rue Cherchez-La-Femme, Saint Cloud..."

FINACHE [*apostrophizing*]: Ah! Bravo, madame—

TOURNEL [*interrupting*]: Or mademoiselle—

FINACHE [*ignoring his interjection, still apostrophizing*]: You know how to pick your hotels!

TOURNEL [*continuing his reflection*]: She doesn't say which she is, does she?

CHANDEBISE [*ignoring him, to* FINACHE, *sitting down across from him*]: Why? Do you know it?

FINACHE [*to* CHANDEBISE]: Know it? I hope to say I do, Chandebise! It's the only one I ever use when I... Well, you know... Now and then... Whenever...

CHANDEBISE: I never knew... I mean, I know so little about such things...

FINACHE: Yes... The Hotel Paramour... I'm sure Monsieur Tournel here must know it...

TOURNEL [*moving left, standing at the upstage end of the table, between them, as* CHANDEBISE *peruses the rest of the letter*]: Me?... No... I think I've heard the name, but—

CHANDEBISE [*suddenly interrupting*]: Ah! [*Holding out the letter, to* FINACHE.] Look!... [*To* TOURNEL.] Look!... She cried, poor thing... That's why... Her tears...

FINACHE *and* TOURNEL [*together*]: No!

CHANDEBISE: Yes!... Listen... [*Reading.*] "P. S. Please forgive my flood of girlish tears, but how can I keep them from flowing at the merest thought of you! I beg you to let them be tears of joy and not despair..." She must have cried her eyes out, by the look of it.

[*He waves the letter under* TOURNEL'*s nose.*]

TOURNEL [*sniffing, with a grimace*]: Ah... Phew!... Good grief!

CHANDEBISE ⎱
       [*together*]:
FINACHE ⎰

    ⎰ What is it?

    ⎱ Hmm?

TOURNEL: What the devil did she eat to make her tears smell so bad! [*Coming down center, holding his nose, to* FINACHE.] I told you it was her stomach, doctor!

FINACHE [*with mock seriousness*]: Please! A woman's tears are sacred!

CHANDEBISE [*getting up*]: That's right, you two! Joke all you like... But I have the last laugh. [*To* TOURNEL.] See, Tournel?... You're not the only heartbreaker... Who would have thought...? There we were, at the Palais-Royal, calmly watching... What play was it?

TOURNEL: Who knows? They're all alike... When you've seen one...

CHANDEBISE: And all that time, who would have dreamt...? There she was... [*Emphasizing.*] drinking in our manly beauty!

TOURNEL [*pointing, to* CHANDEBISE]: Well, yours, at least!

CHANDEBISE [*to* TOURNEL]: You didn't notice, did you? You didn't see some ravishing stranger staring in our direction?

TOURNEL: Well, actually... I thought I did for a moment...

CHANDEBISE: Ah?

TOURNEL: But frankly, Chandebise, I thought it was me she was staring at...

CHANDEBISE: You thought... You... [*After a moment, his jaw drops as if he is hit by a sudden realization, and he slaps his forehead with the heel of his palm.*] Of course! Of course!... Damnation!

TOURNEL: What?

CHANDEBISE [*jumping up*]: It was!... Why didn't I think...

FINACHE [*getting up*] ⎫   ⎧ It was what?
                 ⎬ [*together*]: ⎨
TOURNEL   ⎭   ⎩ What's the matter?

CHANDEBISE: It's so obvious!... [*To* TOURNEL.] Of course it was you! [*To* FINACHE.] It was him! Don't you see?

FINACHE   ⎫   ⎧ Him?
                ⎬ [*together*]: ⎨
TOURNEL   ⎭   ⎩ Me?

CHANDEBISE: Of course! Who else?... [*To* TOURNEL.] It was you she was staring at! And when somebody mentioned my name, and said it was my box... Don't you see? She assumed you were me...

TOURNEL: Oh? You think so?

CHANDEBISE: Damn! I know so!

TOURNEL [*with a shrug, to* FINACHE]: Possibly, I suppose... [*To* CHANDEBISE, *smugly, becoming convinced.*] Yes, probably...

CHANDEBISE [*to* TOURNEL]: I mean, look at me... [*To* FINACHE.] Look at me... [*Moving up left, looking at himself in the mirror.*] I have no illusions!... What mysterious stranger would... [*Recalling the letter.*] would drink in my manly beauty!... Come now! Really!...

TOURNEL [*objecting* pro forma]: Well...

CHANDEBISE [*continuing, to* TOURNEL]: But you, Tournel... Look at you! Handsome, dashing... You've turned more than one woman's head in your day!... [*To* FINACHE.] He has, believe me!

FINACHE: Oh, I do...

TOURNEL [*fatuously*]: I admit I do have a certain charm...

CHANDEBISE [*coming down left, joining* FINACHE]: Listen to him! "A certain charm..."

TOURNEL: But handsome?... I don't think...

CHANDEBISE: No "buts", my friend... Why, women have tried to kill themselves over you... [*To* FINACHE.] They have, you know...

FINACHE: Ah?

TOURNEL: Well... Only one...

CHANDEBISE [*to* FINACHE]: You see? [*To* TOURNEL.] Still...

TOURNEL: Besides, she failed...

CHANDEBISE: I don't care... She tried, didn't she?

TOURNEL: Well, perhaps... I was never really sure. It may have been only a case of bad oyster stew.

CHANDEBISE and FINACHE [*together*]: Oyster stew?

TOURNEL: Yes... At dinner one night... I'd just left her in a huff. "Forever!" I told her... She told everyone she ate it on purpose, to end it all.

CHANDEBISE [*to* FINACHE]: You see?

TOURNEL: But I have my doubts. I mean, when you want to kill yourself there are certainly better ways than bad oyster stew.

CHANDEBISE: Never mind! [*Crossing right, joining him downstage.*] It's obvious... [*Holding up the letter.*] This was meant for you! It has my name and address, but you're the one she wrote it to.

TOURNEL [*hesitating, to* FINACHE]: Do you think so, monsieur?

FINACHE: Oh... [*Not wanting to become involved.*] Pfff!

CHANDEBISE [*to* TOURNEL]: Of course he does!... And since you're the one she wants, you're the one she's going to get!

TOURNEL [*protesting feebly*]: I don't know...

CHANDEBISE: This evening... Five o'clock, Tournel!...

TOURNEL: I really don't think—

CHANDEBISE: And anyway, I'm not free. We're having a banquet tonight for our American director. Besides, I would never...

FINACHE [*coming down left, casually, to* CHANDEBISE]: No oyster stew, I hope...

TOURNEL [*to* CHANDEBISE]: Really, I don't know...

CHANDEBISE [*to* TOURNEL]: Come, come... You're dying to go and you know it!

TOURNEL: I am?

CHANDEBISE: It's as plain as the nose on your face! [*Scrutinizing him with his pince-nez.*] Look! It's twitching!

TOURNEL: It is? [*Crossing his eyes, trying unsuccessfully to see, then going up left, to the mirror and looking.*] My heavens, you're right!... [*Laughing.*] That settles it! I accept!

[*He rejoins* CHANDEBISE *and shakes his hand vigorously.*]

CHANDEBISE: Sly dog, you!

[*He gives him a friendly poke in the ribs and moves upstage a few steps, taking off his pince-nez and pocketing it.*]

TOURNEL [*moving left, to* FINACHE, *almost confidentially*]: I must say, it comes at an opportune moment...

FINACHE: Oh?

TOURNEL: Yes... I thought I had an affair in the making, but it seems to have been postponed for the moment.

CHANDEBISE [*overhearing, quickly returning and poking his head between them*]: Oh? And who's the lucky lady?

TOURNEL: Who?... Really, Chandebise... It wouldn't be cricket to tell you...

[*He moves right.*]

CHANDEBISE [*mimicking, to* FINACHE]: "It wouldn't be cricket..." [*To* TOURNEL.] Sly dog!

TOURNEL [*to* CHANDEBISE]: Your mysterious stranger will help me fill the gap... [*Reaching for the letter.*] All right, give it here...

CHANDEBISE [*pulling it away*]: Not on your life, Tournel! I don't get letters like this very often! At least I'd like my grandchildren to think... [*To* FINACHE.] If I have any, that is... [*To* TOURNEL.] I'd like them to find it in my papers, and think: "My goodness, but grandpapa must have been a handsome devil, to get letters like this!"

TOURNEL: But I—

CHANDEBISE: Besides, what do you need it for? Just go to the Hotel... Whatever it's called... And ask for the room reserved in my name.

TOURNEL: Well...

CHANDEBISE [*to* FINACHE, *taking him by the arm*]: Come, Finache... You were going to listen to my chest.

[*He and* FINACHE *move toward the door, down left.*]

TOURNEL [*running after them, waving his papers*]: Wait!... What about the papers...?

CHANDEBISE [*at the door*]: Two minutes, and I'm all yours... [*To* FINACHE.]

Come... We won't be disturbed in here...

FINACHE: After you...

[*They exit as* CHANDEBISE *folds up the letter and places it in his breast pocket.*]

TOURNEL [*at the door, as they leave, grumbling*]: Two minutes!... After that it will be something else! [*After a moment, pondering his upcoming adventure with not a little relish.*] Ah... Hotel Paramour, indeed!... [*The door, up right, opens and* GISELE *appears, wearing her hat and coat.*] Ah, madame...

[*He moves center, as if to greet her.*]

GISELE [*entering, looking around*]: Isn't he here?

TOURNEL: Who?

GISELE: My husband...

TOURNEL [*pointing down left*]: Oh... He's in there, with the doctor. I'll go get him...

GISELE: No, no... Don't disturb him... Just be good enough to tell him that Madame de Histangua and I have gone out...

TOURNEL: Madame de Histangua...

GISELE: And that I may be home quite late... He needn't be concerned.

TOURNEL: Ah... Well, he's coming home late tonight too, if I'm not—

GISELE [*quickly, trying to make him give himself away*]: Really? Why?

TOURNEL: Something about his American director... A banquet for him, I think he said...

GISELE: Oh, he told you that, did he? Well, isn't that nice to know!... Except that it's a lie, Monsieur Tournel!

TOURNEL: Oh?

GISELE: The banquet is tomorrow. I saw the invitation.

TOURNEL: Ah... Then he's made a mistake. I'd better go tell him...

[*He makes a move toward the door, down left.*]

GISELE [*coming down by the canapé, stopping him with a gesture*]: No need, monsieur!... He knows... It's no mistake...

TOURNEL: But—

GISELE: He wants an excuse to stay out, that's all... [*Imitating.*] "I could have sworn the banquet was tonight, Gisèle!..." Oh yes, I know what he's up to!

TOURNEL [*approaching her, trying to repair his gaffe*]: No, really, madame... He told me... I'm sure he really thinks it's tonight... I mean, why should he lie to me? He has no reason—

GISELE: No! No reason to lie to *you*... But he does have, to lie to *me!* Is that what you're saying?

TOURNEL: He... No! Not at all!... You're putting words in my mouth...

GISELE: Oh! I can see through your little game too, monsieur!

TOURNEL: "Game"...?

GISELE: Now that he's having an affair... Now that you know I don't want one with you... [*Coming downstage.*] and that you can stop chasing me...

TOURNEL [*following her*]: But... What connection—

GISELE: ...you think you may as well paint him as the world's most faithful husband!

TOURNEL: But—

GISELE: Well, it won't work!

TOURNEL: But—
GISELE: No! It's simply too obvious, Monsieur Tournel!
TOURNEL: But I'm telling you...
GISELE: Good-bye!
[*She moves back up right.*]
TOURNEL [*following her*]: Gisèle!... Please...
GISELE [*at the door*]: Oh!... Go... [*In utter frustration.*] Go fry an egg!
[*She exits and slams the door in his face.*]
TOURNEL [*jumping back*]: Oh!
[*At that moment the double door opens and* EDOUARD *appears. He is holding a glass of water and a small packet.*]
EDOUARD [*entering, noticing* TOURNEL *and addressing him, still unintelligibly*]: Ah! Monsieur Tournel... In a better mood, I hope...
TOURNEL [*crossing left, in front of him*]: You?... Go fry an egg!
[*He exits, up left, and slams the door.*]
EDOUARD [*watching him leave, shaking his head*]: No... [*He repeats his previous sound effect in* TOURNEL'*s direction, gives a shrug, and comes down left to the upstage end of the oblong table, as if ready to get down to serious business.*] Now... [*Putting down the glass.*] Water... [*Opening the packet.*] Boric acid... [*He pours the powder, takes the prosthetic device from his pocket, and holds it between thumb and forefinger above the glass, like a wafer above a chalice, reverently.*] Ah!... [*Dropping the device into the glass, he takes the latter over to the fireplace and places it lovingly on the mantelpiece.*] There!
[*He traces a small, almost imperceptible sign of the cross in front of the glass, just as the double door opens and* ETIENNE *appears.*]
ETIENNE [*announcing*]: Monsieur Señor Histangua de Homenides...
HOMENIDES [*at the threshold, correcting him*]: Homenides de Histangua, boy!... Don Carlos Homenides de Histangua!
ETIENNE: Beg pardon! [*Aside, with a shrug.*] Whatever...
[*He leaves.*]
HOMENIDES [*coming straight in, declaiming his greeting without looking left or right, arriving center stage, and speaking with a thick Spanish accent*]: Good-days, mis amigos!...
EDOUARD: Ah! Monsieur...
HOMENIDES: You... You... Ees no here, Mossié Chandépisse?
EDOUARD [*barely intelligible*]: Why yes... I'm sure he'll only be a moment...
HOMENIDES [*scratching his head*]: Por favor?... You inglés, mossié?... You Eengleesh?
EDOUARD: No, no...
HOMENIDES: Qué idioma...? What language you speak?... Ee ee ah ah...
EDOUARD: I said... [*Just as he is about to make another attempt, the door, down left, opens and* FINACHE *appears.*] Never mind! There he is...
FINACHE [*entering, followed by* CHANDEBISE]: So... As I say, just do as I told you...
[*He begins to move upstage, as if to leave.*]
CHANDEBISE: Well, I'll try...
HOMENIDES [*to* CHANDEBISE]: Holá, Chandépisse!...
CHANDEBISE: Ah! My friend...

[*They meet down left and shake hands.*]

HOMENIDES: I have cone for to see you.

CHANDEBISE: Yes... And how goes it?

HOMENIDES: Eet goes... Eet goes...

FINACHE [*at the bay, overhearing, to* CHANDEBISE]: Me too, Chandebise... I'll be going...

HOMENIDES: Ah! El médico... [*To* FINACHE.] Mossié... How goes, eh? [*He moves up to him and shakes his hand.*]

FINACHE: Fine, thank you. And you?

HOMENIDES: Ees pleasure... We meet again...

FINACHE: Yes, but not for long, I'm afraid... I hope you'll excuse me.

HOMENIDES: Esscuse? For why?... What you do, mi amigo?

FINACHE: No... I mean... I was just leaving.

HOMENIDES: Ah, sí! Sí!... [*With a wave of the hand.*] You go!... You go!...

FINACHE [*with a touch of sarcasm*]: Thank you, mi amigo... [*With a nod, to* EDOUARD, *up left.*] Young man... [*At the double door, to* CHANDEBISE, *still down left.*] I'll see myself out, Chandebise...

[*He gives* CHANDEBISE *a quasi-military salute and turns to leave.*]

CHANDEBISE [*returning the salute*] ⎱   ⎰ Finache...
EDOUARD [*with a nod*]   ⎭ [*together*]: ⎱ Bye-bye...
HOMENIDES [*with a wave*]   ⎰   ⎭ Adios... Adios...

FINACHE [*stopping at the threshold, with an afterthought, to* EDOUARD]: Oh... [*Giving him a sly chuckle.*] Next time, give my best to the Para—

EDOUARD [*cutting him off, appalled*]: Shhh!

FINACHE [*covering his indiscretion*]: ...to the parents... My best to them...

[*He goes out.* EDOUARD, *flustered, turns on his heels and exits quickly, up left, as* HOMENIDES *comes down and rejoins* CHANDEBISE.]

CHANDEBISE: Parents?... [*To* HOMENIDES, *puzzled.*] His parents are dead...

HOMENIDES: Tsk tsk tsk!

CHANDEBISE: Finache should know... They were his patients!

HOMENIDES: Sí, sí... Tsk tsk tsk! [*With no transition.*] So, mi esposa, mossié...? My wife... He ees here, no?

CHANDEBISE [*aside*]: He...? [*Correcting him.*] She... She...

HOMENIDES: No, no... No "she, she..." [*Correcting him in turn.*] "Sí, sí, mossié..." "Sí, sí..." So, ees here my wife, no?

CHANDEBISE [*not wanting to argue the point*]: Yes, monsieur... [*Emphasizing.*] She... is here with Madame Chandebise...

HOMENIDES: Ah, sí... I know he cone here... He tell to me I cone here too, after her behind.

CHANDEBISE: After her behind?

HOMENIDES: Sí, sí... He cone first... Before me...

CHANDEBISE: Aha... Yes... Well, she's here, monsieur. Shall I tell her you've arrived?

HOMENIDES: No, no... You no have to do thees theeng... [*Moving up toward the canapé.*] Always he make me wet...

CHANDEBISE [*again attempting to correct him*]: She... She...

HOMENIDES: Please... "Sí, sí..." Ees no so deefeecolt... You try...

CHANDEBISE [*giving up*]: Sí, sí...

HOMENIDES: Bueno! See?... [*Picking up his train of thought.*] So, I say...

Always he make me wet, my wife... Thees tine ees my turn... I make her wet!

CHANDEBISE: Yes... Well...

HOMENIDES [*moving up center, pointing to the double door*]: So... She ees frien of you, mossié?

CHANDEBISE [*quite confused*]: Who?...

HOMENIDES [*pointing*]: Thees one... El médico...

CHANDEBISE [*about to correct him*]: "He..." [*Thinking better of it, with a gesture of resignation.*] Yes... Sí, sí...

HOMENIDES: Good, mi amigo! Bueno... Becose I see heen thees morneeng... Een you offeece...

CHANDEBISE: Yes... So he tells me...

HOMENIDES: Sí... She make me for to peess...

CHANDEBISE [*joining him, center stage*]: Monsieur?...

HOMENIDES: Sí, sí... She tell to me: "You feell me op, por favor..."

CHANDEBISE: "Feel..."?

HOMENIDES: She geeve to me leettle cop. She tell to me: "Please you feell me op, mossié..."

CHANDEBISE: Ah... Yes, of course... A specimen...

HOMENIDES: Bot for why she do thees theeng? For why, eh?

CHANDEBISE [*gently mocking*]: For why?... For because it was part of the examination...

HOMENIDES: Bot for why, I say... Ees for mi esposa I buy eensurance. My wife... Ees no for me...

CHANDEBISE: Oh?... My goodness, why didn't you say so before?

HOMENIDES: Bot you no ask, Mossié Chandépisse. I tell to you: "Mossié, I cone for to buy eensurance..." You no ask to me for who ees I buy...

CHANDEBISE: No... Now that you mention it... I guess I never did...

HOMENIDES: No... You no ask...

CHANDEBISE [*moving up left toward the chiffonier, jovially*]: Well, that's no problem... [*At the chiffonier, about to open one of the drawers.*] Madame de Histangua can simply come to the office and—

HOMENIDES [*cutting him off, peremptorily*]: An?... An?... El médico, she make her for to do thees theeng too? She tell to my wife: "Here, por favor! You feell me op...?

CHANDEBISE: Why, yes... I'm sure—

HOMENIDES: No, no! He no do thees theeng, mi esposa!

CHANDEBISE: But—

HOMENIDES: No, no! No for estranyher...

CHANDEBISE [*coming down, joining him center stage*]: But monsieur... A doctor is no stranger... Even one you don't know...

HOMENIDES: No, no, no, mossié!... Nevair!... [*Growing more volatile, crossing left in front of him.*] Nunca!... Jamás!... [*Stamping his foot with each syllable.*] No no no...!

CHANDEBISE [*following behind*]: But she has to... It's the rule...

HOMENIDES [*at the downstage end of the oblong table, turning suddenly, face to face with CHANDEBISE, violently*]: Ees no for me, thees rule! I break!... I peess thees morneeng! I peess for her... Ees plenty enough!

CHANDEBISE: I beg your pardon, monsieur, but that really isn't done...

HOMENIDES [*crossing right, in front of him*]: Ah? Bueno!... So, I no buy you eensurance!

CHANDEBISE [*following him, as conciliatory as possible*]: Come now, my friend! I've heard of jealous husbands... But really, don't you think—

HOMENIDES [*stopping down center*]: Celoso?... No celoso... I no be yhealous! Ees only for becose I theenk of her... her... [*Searching for the right word, finding it only in Spanish.*] dignidad! You onderstan?

CHANDEBISE: Of course... Her dignity... But—

HOMENIDES: I no be yhealous hosban...

CHANDEBISE [*trying to be agreeable*]: And you certainly needn't be, monsieur. Madame de Histangua is a model wife, I'm sure.

HOMENIDES [*with a casual wave of the hand*]: No, no...

CHANDEBISE: No?

HOMENIDES: No... No, no... Ees no why... Ees no why I no be yhealous... Ees I no be celoso, porque mi esposa sabe... I no be yhealous, for becose my wife, he know what I do eef... [*Wagging his forefinger, his features contorted in an expression of rage.*] eef...

CHANDEBISE: Oh?

HOMENIDES: Sí, sí! He know... He know... [*Taking a revolver from his pocket and pointing the barrel at him.*] You see thees, eh?

CHANDEBISE [*instinctively putting up his hand, and moving sidewise around* HOMENIDES *in one complete revolution, as the latter continues to point the gun*]: Eh... Psss! Careful!... Please, monsieur... That's not a toy...

HOMENIDES: Ees no danyher... I no load...

CHANDEBISE: Ah...

HOMENIDES [*as an afterthought*]: I theenk...

[*He squints and looks into the barrel.*]

CHANDEBISE [*carefully pushing it aside*]: Please...

HOMENIDES [*returning to his idée fixe*]: Ah, sí! My wife, he know what I do eef I fine her weeth other man, together!... Sí, sí! He know... [*Going over to the canapé and aiming the gun, teeth clenched.*] "Bam!"... Heen, her... Los dos... One boulett, mossié!...

CHANDEBISE: One?... You mean... [*Moving center stage.*] Two birds with one stone?...

[*He puts both hands together in a gesture that evokes two individuals face to face.*]

HOMENIDES: Estone?... No estone!... One boulett, mi amigo!... [*Aiming again at the canapé.*] "Bam!"

[*He blows imaginary smoke from the barrel, coming down right, as the door, up left, opens and* TOURNEL *appears on the threshold.*]

TOURNEL [*as* HOMENIDES *puts the gun in his back pocket*]: I say, Chandebise...

CHANDEBISE: Yes, yes... Just a moment...

TOURNEL: Please!... You know, I do have another engagement!

CHANDEBISE [*with a knowing smile*]: Yes, I know!... Get the papers ready and I'll be right with you...

TOURNEL [*with a sigh*]: Of course... [*Aside.*] Ready? They've been ready for hours!

[*He leaves, closing the door silently behind him.*]

HOMENIDES [*to* CHANDEBISE]: Who she ees, thees man?

CHANDEBISE [*pointing up left, while still facing* HOMENIDES]: Him?... Monsieur Tournel...

HOMENIDES: Toenail?

CHANDEBISE: One of my dearest friends... And one of Requiem Life's finest agents, monsieur...

HOMENIDES: Eh?

CHANDEBISE [*thinking that* TOURNEL *is still there, about to introduce him*]: A charming fellow... [*Turning.*] Monsieur Tournel, Monsieur Homeni... Ah! Now where did he... Well, you'll have to take my word! Charming, what?... Something of a Don Juan, if you know what I mean, but aside from that...

HOMENIDES: Ha ha! Eef I know!... Ha ha!... Sí! I know what ees...

CHANDEBISE: That's why he's in such a hurry. He has a—how shall I say?—a rendezvous this evening!

HOMENIDES [*laughing*]: Aha!

CHANDEBISE: Yes... A mysterious stranger is waiting to meet him... That is, when I say "to meet *him*..." It could be that it's me, because... [*Pulling the letter half-way out of his breast pocket, caressing it as he speaks.*] Because actually she wrote the letter to me...

HOMENIDES: Oh?

CHANDEBISE: And when I say a letter... [*He touches the letter with his middle finger, like something hot, and shakes his fingers from the wrist.*] Hot, my friend!... Burning!... Passionate!

HOMENIDES: Ees true?... [*Curious.*] An who he ees, thees woman?

CHANDEBISE: I haven't the slightest idea. She didn't sign it. [*He takes the letter completely out and holds it gingerly between thumb and forefinger, as if pretending to be afraid to burn himself.*] Obviously some society lady... Married, I'm sure...

HOMENIDES: Oh? For why you theenk? You have raisin een head...?

CHANDEBISE: Monsieur?

HOMENIDES: You have raisin een head for to theenk thees theeng, mossié?

CHANDEBISE: Yes... [*Gently mocking him.*] And a very good "raisin" to think so, too. First of all, the style... The tone... It has society written all over it.

HOMENIDES: Oh? [*Approaching him.*] I look... I look...

CHANDEBISE: The... The... How shall I put it?... The other kind are much less romantic... Much more direct...

HOMENIDES [*joining him*]: You show, eh?

CHANDEBISE: Here, my friend... See for yourself...
[*He hands him the letter.*]

HOMENIDES [*taking it and unfolding it, pretending to find it very hot*]: Ees hot bidet, no?

CHANDEBISE: Monsieur?

HOMENIDES: Hot bidet... "Bidet doux"... No es la palabra?... Ees no how you say...?
[*He begins looking over the letter, crossing down left as he reads.*]

CHANDEBISE [*repressing a laugh*]: Almost... Not quite...

HOMENIDES [*sniffing*]: An have beeg esmell, thees bidet! No?

CHANDEBISE: Yes... It's perfumed...

HOMENIDES [*reading*]: Ha ha ha!... Ees fonny... I like... I like...

CHANDEBISE: Oh? I'm not sure it's funny, exactly... [*As* HOMENIDES, *far left, suddenly scrutinizes the letter with added concern.*] Although I suppose—

HOMENIDES [*suddenly interrupting with a loud cry*]: Ayyy!

CHANDEBISE: What...?

HOMENIDES [*crossing far right, with giant strides, brandishing the letter, furiously apostrophizing his wife in a flood of Spanish oaths*]: Caramba!... Maldita la perra que te parió, mujer!... Ayyy! Beetch!...

CHANDEBISE [*coming down center*]: Please... What—

HOMENIDES: La puta!... La ramera!... La... La... [*At a loss to find a strong enough epithet, to* CHANDEBISE, *raging.*] Ees her writeeng! Mi esposa... Ees my wife, he write thees bidet! My wife! [*Approaching him.*] My wife!

CHANDEBISE [*thunderstruck*]: What?

HOMENIDES: Ayyy, carajo!... [*Leaping, backing him sharply against the oblong table.*] You! [*Flinging the letter on the table.*] Hijo de puta!... Feelthy eswine!

CHANDEBISE [*trying to break free*]: Monsieur... For heaven's—

HOMENIDES [*with one hand holding him by the throat, and with the other feeling his pockets for his gun*]: My arm... My arm... Where eet ees, my arm?

CHANDEBISE [*pointing, not without difficulty, to his offending arm*]: Here, damn it! Where do you think...

HOMENIDES: No thees arm!... [*Taking the revolver from his back pocket.*] Thees one!... Thees!

[*He points it at a terrified* CHANDEBISE.]

CHANDEBISE: For God's sake, monsieur...

HOMENIDES [*holding him against the table with a knee in the stomach, loading the gun*]: So! He write to you, my wife!... Ees to you he write thees bidet of love!

CHANDEBISE [*managing to free himself, escaping down far left*]: No, no!... That's not true! It can't be your wife, my friend... Mi amigo...

HOMENIDES: Sí, sí! Ees! Ees!

CHANDEBISE: Really, women all write the same these days...

HOMENIDES: No, no, no! Ees my wife! Ees my wife!

CHANDEBISE: And besides, I'm not the one who's going... It's Tournel... Monsieur Tournel...

HOMENIDES: Who she, Toenail?... You good frien?... [*Pointing to the door, up left.*] You Don Juan?...

CHANDEBISE: Yes... That one...

HOMENIDES: Bueno! I keell heen, thees Toenail!

CHANDEBISE: Kill... But you can't! You mustn't!... He... He hasn't done anything yet! [*Moving up along the stage left side of the table, trying to reach the door, up left.*] I'll go tell him... You'll see! No problem!...

HOMENIDES [*making a parallel beeline in the same direction and heading him off, barring his exit*]: Sí, sí! Ees problen... Beeg problen... For heen! For her! Los dos!...

CHANDEBISE: But—

HOMENIDES: No! You no tell to heen! I no want for you tell to heen!... I want for thees Toenail, she do what she do!

CHANDEBISE: With your wife?

HOMENIDES: Sí, sí! Then I have proof! An then I keell!

CHANDEBISE [*trying to calm him down*]: But monsieur... Señor...

HOMENIDES: Heen! Her!... An you!

CHANDEBISE: Me?... Why me? I told you—

HOMENIDES: One boulett only!... "Bam!"... [*Holding up three fingers.*] Los tres!...

CHANDEBISE: Three?

[*Just then the voices of* LUCIENNE *and* GISELE *are heard offstage.*]

HOMENIDES: Ah! Mi esposa!... Ees voice... [*Pushing him, under threat of the gun, toward the door, down left.*] You go!... You go!...

CHANDEBISE: But Histangua, my friend!... Mi amigo...

HOMENIDES: Sí, sí! I you frien!... Bot I keell you!

CHANDEBISE: But—

HOMENIDES: Like dog I keell you! [*Pointing threateningly toward the door with the gun, as* CHANDEBISE *tries unsuccessfully to protest.*] You go!... Or "Bam!"... I shoot...

CHANDEBISE [*with his hands raised, as conciliatory as possible*]: No, no... I'm going...

[*He disappears out the door, down left, and* HOMENIDES *turns the key in the lock.*]

HOMENIDES [*in a sweat, sighing*]: Ha!

[*He takes a handkerchief from his pocket and mops his brow as* LUCIENNE *enters, up right, followed by* GISELE, *each in hat and coat, apparently about to leave.*]

LUCIENNE [*to* HOMENIDES]: Ah, querido mío... You're here...

HOMENIDES [*trying to appear calm, but obviously distracted*]: Sí, sí... I arrive...

GISELE [*crossing down left, holding out her hand to* HOMENIDES]: Monsieur de Histangua... What a pleasure...

HOMENIDES [*leaving her hand dangling*]: Sí, sí... Ees for me pleasure also, madame... How goes, eh?

GISELE [*gradually withdrawing her hand*]: Fine... Fine, thank you...

HOMENIDES: An you hosban, madame...? Goes fine also?

GISELE: Yes, thank you...

HOMENIDES: An you chiles, madame?

GISELE: My... Why, I have none, monsieur...

HOMENIDES: Tsk tsk tsk! Ees too bad!... Sone other tine, maybe...

GISELE [*laughing*]: Well...

[*She retreats toward the bay, ready to leave.*]

LUCIENNE [*who has been observing her husband's behavior, after a brief silence, coming center stage, to* HOMENIDES, *still down left*]: Is something wrong?

HOMENIDES [*repressing his rage*]: Wrong?... For why you theenk? For why you ask ees sonetheeng wrong?... Ees fine!... Everytheeng...

LUCIENNE [*unconvinced*]: Well... Madame Chandebise and I were just on our way...

HOMENIDES: Sí, sí! You go...

LUCIENNE: We'll be dining out this evening. Don't expect me home too early.

HOMENIDES: Sí, sí... I know... I know...

LUCIENNE: You know?... Did I tell you?

HOMENIDES: No, no... I no say: "I know, I know..." I say: "No, no..." I no esspect... You go...

LUCIENNE [*still disturbed by his behavior*]: Yes, well... [*About to turn and leave, but thinking better of it.*] Really, are you sure there's nothing wrong?

HOMENIDES [*angrily*]: Notheeng!... I tell to you, notheeng! [*Waving her off.*] You go...

LUCIENNE: Well... Bye-bye, then...

[*She moves up toward* GISELE, *at the bay.*]

GISELE [*to* HOMENIDES]: Bye-bye, monsieur...

HOMENIDES: Sí, sí! Good-bye!... [*Crossing down right, to* LUCIENNE, *furiously.*] Good-bye! Good-bye! Good-bye!... Have good tine weeth... [*Pointedly, looking at* GISELE, *but obviously with someone else in mind.*] weeth you frien!

LUCIENNE [*coming back center, hands on hips*]: Qué tienes, querido mío? Qué te pasa? Porqué me pones una cara así...?

HOMENIDES [*growing angrier the more he tries to be calm*]: Te aseguro que no tengo nada... [*Wringing his handkerchief with each exclamation.*] Nada! Nada! Nada!

LUCIENNE: Ah... Dios! Qué carácter tan insoportable tienes! [*To* GISELE, *rejoining her at the double door.*] Come, love...

GISELE [*with a little flutter of the fingers in* HOMENIDES'*s direction*]: Bye-bye... [*They leave. A moment later there is a knocking on the door, down left.*]

HOMENIDES [*ignoring it, pacing right and left, downstage, in a rage, sputtering and fuming*]: Ayyy! La puta sin vergüenza!... La perra!... La... La... La mujerzuela!... La... La... Eslot!... Feelthy eslot!... Qué mujer más... más... [*He arrives down left to the sound of more insistent knocking as the door is repeatedly shaken from behind.*]

CHANDEBISE'S VOICE: Monsieur de Histangua... Please, my friend... Señor...

HOMENIDES [*banging on the door with his fist*]: You!... Basta!... Silencio, me entiende?... Enough, you! Or I shoot!

[*The knocking stops suddenly.* HOMENIDES, *still seething, moves up and arrives near the door, up left, just as it opens to reveal* TOURNEL *on the threshold, wearing his coat.*]

TOURNEL [*stepping in, looking around quickly*]: Ah...

HOMENIDES [*aside, clenching his teeth, mopping his brow*]: Ha! Heen!...

TOURNEL [*coming down left, to* HOMENIDES]: Monsieur Chandebise isn't here, I see?

HOMENIDES [*following him, with an affected smile, obviously disguising his thirst for blood*]: No, mossié... No... She no ees here...

TOURNEL [*without noticing his state*]: "She"...? No, no... "Monsieur," I said... Not "Madame"...

HOMENIDES [*mopping his brow*]: Sí, sí! Mossié Chandépisse, she no ees here!

TOURNEL [*moving center stage, with a shrug*]: Aha... Well, if you don't mind... If you see her... [*Correcting.*] him... please tell him that I've left everything on his desk. It's all quite self-explanatory.

HOMENIDES [*joining him, looking him in the eye, tucking his handkerchief into his breast pocket*]: Sí... Sí...

TOURNEL: Because I really can't wait any longer. I have other fish to fry, as they say.

HOMENIDES: Sí... Sí... [*Letting himself lose his aplomb, angrily.*] Go fry you feesh, mossié!... You go!... You go!... I want you for to fry beeg feesh!

TOURNEL [*dismayed by his sudden outburst*]: Please?

HOMENIDES: My feesh!... Sí, sí! You fry!... [*Curling his fingers in front of* TOURNEL*'s neck, as if about to strangle him.*] You go!

TOURNEL: Monsieur?

HOMENIDES: You go, or else...

TOURNEL: Or else...?

HOMENIDES [*suddenly regaining his composure*]: Notheeng, mossié... Notheeng! [*Very amiably, with a pleasant little wave toward the bay.*] Sí... You go, eh?

TOURNEL [*coming up to the oblong table and picking up his hat, but not his briefcase*]: I say... [*Moving upstage, aside.*] Curious chap!... [*At the double door, with a nod, to* HOMENIDES.] Monsieur... [*He exits.*]

HOMENIDES [*venting his frustration, with a sigh*]: Ahhh! [*Taking out the handkerchief again and mopping his brow.*] Carajo!... Qué día! Qué día!... [*He puts away the handkerchief and fans himself with his hand.*] Ay! Qué calor!... [*Panting from his ordeal, he notices the glass on the mantelpiece, that* EDOUARD *has left there.*] Ah... Agua... Bueno! I dreenk... [*He rushes up left and takes a healthy swallow.*] Ah... [*Suddenly noticing the taste.*] Pfffui! [*After coughing, gagging, spitting, and making appropriate grimaces of disgust.*] Ayyyy! What ees?... El médico, she no leave fron thees morneeng, I hope!

[*As he puts the glass down on the oblong table and comes down, far left,* EDOUARD *enters, up left, coming center stage and looking around.*]

EDOUARD: Uncle...? [*Noticing* HOMENIDES.] Ah! Monsieur Homenides... Is my uncle—

HOMENIDES [*rushing toward him*]: You!... [*Calming down.*] Ees good you here... I go!

EDOUARD: Oh?

HOMENIDES: Sí... So soon I go... [*Pointing to the door, down left.*] Thees door... You open!... I permeet...

EDOUARD: What?

HOMENIDES [*taking him under the armpits and turning him bodily toward the door*]: Sí, sí... You open, eh?... I permeet she escape...

EDOUARD: "She"?... She who?

HOMENIDES: Ee oo! Ee oo!... [*Striding furiously up to the double door.*] Ayyy!... Mi mujer, con un amante... Ayyy! La puta!... Eslot! Feelthy eslot! [*He exits, swearing and fuming, and slams the double door.*]

EDOUARD [*watching him go, still stunned by the encounter, mocking his Spanish invective*]: Ah oo ee ah!... Oo ah, oo eh!... [*Flicking his joined fingers outward from his chin, in a gesture of scorn.*] Ayayay! Ayayay! [*Coming to the door, down left, pondering out loud.*] "She"...? "She"...? [*He unlocks the door, opens it, and jumps back in surprise as a disheveled* CHANDEBISE *appears on the threshold.*] You...?

CHANDEBISE [*not daring to come out*]: Has... Has he left?

EDOUARD: Who?

CHANDEBISE [*stammering*]: Ho... Ho...

EDOUARD: "Hoho?..." Hoho who?

CHANDEBISE: "Hoho who"?... Ho... Ho... Homenides!

EDOUARD: Gone!

CHANDEBISE: And his wife?

EDOUARD: Gone too... With Gisèle...

CHANDEBISE: Oh my!... And Tournel?

EDOUARD: Gone!... Everyone... Gone...

CHANDEBISE [*taking a few steps into the room*]: Good God!... That means... There's not a moment to lose!... [*Panicking.*] Who can I send there to warn them?... [*After a brief reflection.*] Ah! Etienne!...

EDOUARD: "There"?... Where?

CHANDEBISE: To the... the... Never mind... Just "there"... [*Shaking him by the lapels.*] Listen!... We're sitting on a keg of dynamite! You can't imagine... He's going to kill someone... Two people... God knows how many people!...

EDOUARD: "He"?... Who?

CHANDEBISE: Ee oo! Ee oo!... I can't stop to explain... I have just enough time before the banquet to go find Tournel and warn him. You wait here... [*Looking around.*] My hat, damn it! Where...? [*Realizing that it is in the room, down left.*] Ah... [*Moving to go get it, but stopping at the door.*] Oh!... And if he comes back—

EDOUARD: Who?... If who—

CHANDEBISE: Tournel! If Tournel comes back, tell him that, whatever he does, he absolutely, positively musn't go to... to... That he mustn't go "there" tonight... To his meeting... He'll understand... It's a matter of life and death!

[*He exits quickly, down left, as* EDOUARD *stands gaping, shaking his head. A few seconds later* CHANDEBISE *comes running back in, grabs up the letter from the oblong table, and makes another hasty exit.*]

EDOUARD [*moving right, in a state*]: "Life and death..." What on earth...

[*The double door opens suddenly and* TOURNEL *appears.*]

TOURNEL [*entering, to* EDOUARD]: Ah, you...

EDOUARD: Monsieur Tournel!

TOURNEL: I think I must have left my briefcase... [*Spotting it on the oblong table.*] Ah...

EDOUARD [*bounding across the stage, confronting him, and babbling incomprehensibly*]: For heaven's sake! Don't go to your meeting tonight!... There!... You know where!... Don't go! It's a matter of life and death!

TOURNEL [*turning him around and pushing him away*]: Quiet, you!... I haven't the slightest idea what you're saying!

[*He turns to leave.*]

EDOUARD [*regaining his balance and running after him*]: Monsieur!... Monsieur Tournel!...

TOURNEL [*avoiding his grasp*]: Enough is enough!

[*He dashes out the double door.*]

EDOUARD [*suddenly hitting on an expedient*]: Ah... [*Opening his mouth and pointing inside, then looking over toward the mantelpiece and realizing that the glass with the prosthesis is no longer there.*] Oh my!... Where... [*Hurrying over to the mantelpiece, looking around, and spying the glass on the oblong table.*] Ah... [*He quickly puts the device into his mouth, makes a few grimaces as he adjusts it with his thumbs, and runs toward the bay, shouting.*] Monsieur!... Monsieur Tournel!

[*As he arrives at the double door,* CHANDEBISE *enters, down left, in hat and coat.*]

CHANDEBISE [*to* EDOUARD]: What...? Who on earth are you screaming at?

EDOUARD [*halfway out the door, letting flow a rapid torrent of perfectly articulate and intelligible speech*]: Tournel, of course! Who else?... Just now, I told him what you told me to tell him... But he wouldn't even listen! He just went running out...

CHANDEBISE [*agape, letting himself fall onto a chair*]: He can talk! Good God! He... He... He can talk!

EDOUARD [*running out and calling, as the curtain falls*]: Monsieur!... Monsieur Tournel!... Monsieur Tournel!...

CURTAIN

Act Two

The second floor of the Hotel Paramour, very garish and gaudy, as its name and function suggest. The set is divided into two parts by a wall that extends down close to the footlights. Stage right, occupying about three-fifths of the set, a large central hall, its walls appropriately papered and decorated. In the center of the hall's upstage wall, a staircase coming up from the ground floor and leading to the upper floors. Against the down right wall, a console; next to it, a coatrack with a porter's livery jacket and cap hanging on one of its branches. In the up right corner, a corridor leading off right, ostensibly to a number of rooms, the door to the first of which is plainly visible in the upstage wall, right. Between that door and the staircase, mounted up on the wall, an electric bell-panel that lights up and rings to summon various employees. In the stage right wall, between the console and the corridor, a bedroom door opening outward from the hall into the room. Against the dividing wall, downstage, a bench. The remaining two-fifths of the set, stage left, represents two contiguous bedrooms, only one of whose interiors—the one closer to the footlights—is visible, and whose door, at about the middle of the dividing wall, also opens outward from the hall into the room, as does the corresponding door to the other, unseen, bedroom, further upstage in the dividing wall. In this visible bedroom, against its upstage wall, a fancily canopied and curtained bed, foot toward the door. In its up left wall, a window opening onto a garden. Down left, a door leading to a bathroom. To the right of the bed, between it and the door to the hall, a chair. Downstage, against the dividing wall, a small table. Left, between the window and the bathroom door, another chair. In the rear wall, on each side of the bed at eye level, an electric button decorated like a bull's-eye, large enough to be clearly seen by the audience. When pressed, these buttons cause the bed and its entire wall-panel to pivot on a revolving platform, thereby substituting another identical bed from the unseen room next door in its place. [1]

At rise, BABETTE, *in maid's attire, has almost finished tidying up the visible bedroom. Her mop and pail are by the bathroom door, down left. The condition of the room would indicate that she has not done too thorough a job. After she has dusted here and there with a feather duster for a moment or two,* MOUSQUETARD *appears in the corridor, up right.*

MOUSQUETARD [*entering, looking around*]: Babette... Babette... [*Crossing left, to the open bedroom door, to* BABETTE]: Well?
BABETTE [*unruffled*]: Monsieur?

---

[1] Feydeau, typically, takes great care to explain in detail the mechanical working of this bed and the construction of the buttons. Given the technical sophistication of today's theater, these details need not be reproduced here [Translator's note].

MOUSQUETARD [*at the threshold*]: What are you doing?

BABETTE: Making up the room, monsieur... [*Giving a few last touches.*] There! All done...

MOUSQUETARD [*going into the room, critically*]: All done?... You call this room made up?... Look at the bed! Looks as if it was just slept in, goddammit!

BABETTE: Oh? And what did monsieur expect?

[*She comes down left to retrieve her mop and pail.*]

MOUSQUETARD: Funny!... Thank you, mademoiselle! We can do without your humor. Next thing you'll be telling me that I'm running a bordello!

BABETTE: Well...

MOUSQUETARD: "Well" nothing! This is a luxury hotel... First-class... Married couples only...

BABETTE: Yes, monsieur... Only not married to each other!

MOUSQUETARD [*approaching*]: So? Each one is married to someone, aren't they? They're twice as married... That's even better.

BABETTE: Well...

MOUSQUETARD: And who asked you? None of your business!... Now make up this bed... [*He stalks over to the bed and gives the sheets a vigorous tug.*] And be quick about it! [*Exiting into the hall, as* NANA *arrives at the head of the stairs, to* BABETTE, *sharply.*] You hear?

BABETTE: Yes, monsieur...

[*She makes an obscene gesture at him behind his back and begins to make up the bed. As* MOUSQUETARD *crosses up right he is intercepted by* NANA, *carrying a pile of linen. She is over fifty and overfed, still clinging to a fast fading beauty: too made up, wearing too many jewels, and too tightly corseted.*]

NANA [*to* MOUSQUETARD]: Problems, Mousquetard?

[*She comes down left and lays the linen on the console.*]

MOUSQUETARD: Just that stupid new one... Couldn't make up a bed if her life depended on it!... Believe me, if I had her in my regiment...

[*He mimes squashing a bug in his palm with his thumb.*]

NANA: Well, at least she's trying. That's more than the last—

MOUSQUETARD: Trying?... "Trying" is right! Too damn trying!

NANA: But—

MOUSQUETARD: Any more trying, and she's out of here... Out on her...

[*He gives his backslide a slap.*]

NANA: But...

MOUSQUETARD [*misunderstanding*]: Exactly! I've had it up to... [*Catching sight of* BLAISE, *dragging himself up to the landing, obviously the worse for wear.*] Ah! Another one! [*To* BLAISE.] You!

NANA [*to* BLAISE]: You're late again, Blaise.

BLAISE [*to* NANA]: Sorry, Madame Nana... I—

MOUSQUETARD [*grabbing him by the collar*]: Where in hell...? You know what time it is? [*As* BLAISE *opens his mouth to offer a reply.*] I'll tell you! Five o'clock!... You should be in bed by now! Not swilling it down at the corner pub!

BLAISE: Me?

MOUSQUETARD: You want this job or don't you?

BLAISE [*timidly*]: Yes...

MOUSQUETARD: Then act like it!... Now go get to bed, goddammit! [BLAISE *begins lumbering left, toward the door to the unseen bedroom, but stops as* MOUSQUETARD *continues.*] Very nice!... [*Grumbling.*] Useless old... Damn lucky he has his rheumatism!... [*To* NANA.] And that I have a heart! If he wasn't my uncle... [*He draws his thumb across his neck in a significant gesture.*] Damn lucky!

BLAISE [*at the door*]: But—

MOUSQUETARD: Some gratitude! Instead of thanking me for a good job, good wages... Just drink, drink, drink!... [*Approaching* BLAISE.] They should shut all those places down! A blot on public morals, that's all they are!

BLAISE: But—

MOUSQUETARD [*to* BLAISE]: And what if we needed the sick old man? Hmm?... What if we needed him, and you weren't here? Then what? Who would I get to be him? Not me, I'm sure... [*Pointing to* NANA.] Not her...

NANA [*with a little laugh*]: Me?

BLAISE: But... But—

MOUSQUETARD: A nice kettle of fish if we had a raid!

BLAISE: But I thought...

MOUSQUETARD: Thought? You?... I'm not paying you to think! I'm paying you to go to bed! [*Pointing up left.*] Now get out of here and get to work!

BLAISE [*about to protest feebly, but resigned, sighing*]: Haaa...

[*He exits to the unseen room. By this time* BABETTE *has finished with the bed and disappears into the bathroom, down left, with mop and pail, leaving the duster behind.*]

MOUSQUETARD [*watching* BLAISE *leave*]: Family, damn it! Typical!... All take, no give!...

[*At the same moment the door, midstage right, opens and* POPOFF, *in Cossack garb, comes rushing out.*]

POPOFF [*striding up to* MOUSQUETARD, *behind his back*]: Nu?

MOUSQUETARD [*turning, with a start*]: Hmm?

POPOFF [*to* NANA]: Nu, nu?... Nu, nu?

NANA [*to* POPOFF, *casually*]: "Nana," monsieur...

POPOFF [*to* MOUSQUETARD] ⎫ [*together*]: ⎧ Nu?

NANA [*almost to herself*] ⎭   ⎩ Not "Nounou"...

POPOFF [*ignoring her, to* MOUSQUETARD, *in Russian, anxiously*]: Któ-to preeshlá?... Któ-to?... Da?... Da, da?

MOUSQUETARD [*to* POPOFF] ⎫ [*together*]: ⎧ Monsieur...?

NANA [*aside*] ⎭   ⎩ "Dada?"

POPOFF [*to* MOUSQUETARD, *impatiently*]: Ya skazál... Któ-to preeshlá?... Któ-to?... [*Giving up on him, turning to* NANA, *in his broken English.*] For me, gaspazhá...? Come someone, da?

NANA [*shaking her head*]: No, monsieur... Not yet...

POPOFF [*frustrated*]: Yet no? Ach!... [*To* NANA.] Spaseébah... [*To* MOUSQUETARD.] Spaseébah... [*Storming back right, to his room, under his breath.*] Kagdá?... Kagdá?...

[*He exits and slams the door.* NANA *and* MOUSQUETARD *look at each other with questioning shrugs.*]

MOUSQUETARD: What did he say?

NANA: I think he was asking if anyone's come for him.

MOUSQUETARD: Then why in hell can't he just ask? Instead of all that "Toto toto, da da" business!

NANA: Well, at least he's trying... [MOUSQUETARD *gives her a look as if to say:* "*That again?*"] Poor thing! It's the third time he's come here and the third time he's been stood up.

MOUSQUETARD: I'm not surprised. [*Imitating.*] "Nu nu, da, da..." [*To* NANA.] What woman in her right mind...

NANA [*with a laugh*]: Or even her wrong one!... [*She goes over to the console, about to retrieve the pile of linen.*] Anyway, I've got to take these upstairs... [BABETTE *enters from the bathroom, down left, with mop and pail, takes the duster and begins giving a few more finishing touches.*]

MOUSQUETARD [*to* NANA]: You? [*Crossing down right, stopping her.*] Don't you dare! [*Calling left.*] Babette!... Babette!... [*To* NANA.] That's what I pay *her* for! Not you, damn it!

BABETTE [*at the threshold of the door to the hall*]: Monsieur?

MOUSQUETARD [*pointing to the linen*]: Those!... Upstairs!... And be quick about it!

BABETTE: Me, monsieur?

MOUSQUETARD [*sarcastically, hands on hips*]: No, me! [*Going left, to the bedroom door, looking in, to* BABETTE, *as she crosses right, toward the corridor, with her paraphernalia.*] You're sure this room is made up now?

BABETTE [*laying it all down*]: Yes, monsieur. [*Coming down to the console to get the linen.*] For all the good it does... Made up now, unmade up tonight...

MOUSQUETARD: Thank you! You can spare us your wisdom! [*He waves her off toward the staircase, sits down on the bench downstage, and lights up a cigarette.*]

NANA [*to* MOUSQUETARD, *as* BABETTE *moves back upstage with the linen*]: Oh, before I forget, Mousquetard... [BABETTE *stops at the staircase to listen.*] Be sure not to rent it tonight. It's taken...

MOUSQUETARD [*pointing over his shoulder*]: This one? Tonight?... Who...?

NANA: Monsieur Chandebise... [*To* BABETTE.] You won't forget, Babette...

BABETTE: No, madame... The one... [*Mimicking* EDOUARD's *inarticulate speech.*] oo aw y i ["who talks like this"]...

MOUSQUETARD [*puffing*]: And he's coming tonight?

NANA [*pulling a paper from her ample bosom*]: That's what his wire says. [*She moves toward him to show it, stopping as she notices* BABETTE *following behind inquisitively, turning to her, sarcastically.*] Was there something I can do for you, Babette?

BABETTE [*missing her intent*]: No, madame. But thank you for asking.

NANA: Yes, well... You can go now.

BABETTE: If I think of anything...

NANA [*waving her off*]: Yes...

MOUSQUETARD [*who has been following the exchange, shaking his head, aside*]: Stupid...
[BABETTE *moves toward the staircase.*]

NANA [*stopping her*]: No, not that way... [*Pointing up right, to the corridor.*] The back stairs... The guests will be arriving. [*Attempting a bon mot.*] No need to air our clean linen in public...

BABETTE: No, madame.

[*She exits into the corridor as* NANA *approaches* MOUSQUETARD, *holding out the wire.*]

NANA: See?... [*Reading.*] "Arriving afternoon five o'clock... Reserve room... Same last week... Chandebise." [*Pointing left.*] That's this one...

MOUSQUETARD [*getting up*]: Good! Let's give it the once-over. [*He goes into the bedroom, followed by* NANA, *looking around.*] Well, it's better. At least she's trying...

NANA [*giving him a look*]: Oh?... [*Moving down left.*] And the bathroom? Let me just make sure...

[*She exits into the bathroom.*]

MOUSQUETARD [*upstage*]: Better check the bed too... [*He presses the large bull's-eye button on the stage right side of the bed.*] See if my idiot uncle is ready... [*The entire panel of the wall pivots counterclockwise, causing the identical bed from the room next door to come into position, with* BLAISE *lying in it, wearing a nightshirt and a kerchief knotted at the forehead.*] Ah...

BLAISE [*groaning*]: Oh! My back!... My aching—

MOUSQUETARD [*cutting him off*]: Don't waste your breath! It's only me. Just checking...

BLAISE [*sitting up*]: See? I'm ready...

MOUSQUETARD: Damn well better be!... All right, back in your box!... [*He presses the button again and the wall-panel pivots clockwise, bringing the first bed back to its original position.*] There! [*As* NANA *enters from the bathroom.*] Ready for action!...

NANA: Everything's fine in there...

MOUSQUETARD: Good!... [*Moving right, toward the door.*] In here too... [*Exiting into the hall, with* NANA *close behind.*] By the way, where's Loche?

NANA: Loche?... In the cellar... Piling the wood...

MOUSQUETARD [*far right*]: The cellar...? With all that wine...? Are you out of your mind, woman? Sending that drunkard to the cellar...

NANA: Don't worry, my love. It's all locked up.

MOUSQUETARD: That's like sending a fox to guard the whorehouse!

NANA [*correcting*]: The "henhouse..."

MOUSQUETARD: Same thing...

NANA [*joining him, right*]: Besides, he's reformed...

MOUSQUETARD: Him?... I know him, believe me! Three years in the regiment... Doing my laundry, shining my shoes... When he was sober, that is!... All week... [*Imitating.*] "I swear! Never another drop!..." Ha!... Then come Sunday, and "Boom!"... I'd have to smack him around, one end of the barracks to the other, just to sober him up. [*Pounding his fist into his palm.*] But good...

NANA [*giving him a hug*]: I'm sure... There's no one like my Brutus when he puts his back into it!

MOUSQUETARD: Then a couple of kicks, to Kingdom Come!... Kept him all week... Till Sunday... [*Relishing the recollection.*] Loved it... [*After a brief pause.*] So did he! Used to tell me... Said he was proud as Punch to get beaten by a lieutenant!

NANA: But if he still drinks...

MOUSQUETARD: Well... Six days out of seven's not bad. And he's still a damn good worker. Too dumb to be dishonest... And not like your servants today, who scream bloody murder if you lay a finger on them!...

NANA [*moving left*]: Or a foot!

MOUSQUETARD: No, not Loche... Always comes back for more... When I saw him a couple of weeks ago, out of a job... Well, "Why not?" I said to myself... Guess I'm just soft-hearted... [*After a few mimed punches.*] As long as he doesn't wear me out!

[*Just then* LOCHE *appears, trudging up the stairs, carrying a hod of logs on his shoulders. He is in workclothes, covered by a long, full-body apron, and wearing cloth scuffs on his feet. Despite his uncombed hair and disheveled appearance, he is the very image of* CHANDEBISE, *social difference notwithstanding.*]

NANA: Ah! Speak of the devil...

MOUSQUETARD [*to* LOCHE, *who has arrived at the landing*]: Yes, Loche? What is it?

LOCHE [*holding out a piece of paper and, at the same time, managing a vague little salute, to* MOUSQUETARD, *in a less-than-elegant drawl*]: A dispatch, colonel...

MOUSQUETARD [*moving left, approaching him, mocking*]: "A dispatch..." [*To* LOCHE.] Give it here... [*Taking the paper from his hand in passing, crossing left, toward* NANA.] "A dispatch..." [*Unfolding it, as* LOCHE *takes a few steps downstage and stands looking at him, agape, in beatific admiration, giving feeble little semi-salutes.*] Damn! What an ugly sonofabitch! Ever see...? [*To* LOCHE, *who is still standing with a simple-minded smile.*] Well? You just going to stand there staring at me, idiot?

NANA [*to* MOUSQUETARD, *pointing to the paper*]: What is it?

MOUSQUETARD [*scanning the text and reading the signature*]: Ha! That Chandebise again...

NANA: Again?

MOUSQUETARD [*reading, as* BABETTE *appears coming slowly down the stairs*]: "Reserve room my name..."

NANA: Not taking any chances, is he!

MOUSQUETARD: "Party will identify self... Every courtesy appreciated..." [*To* BABETTE, *who has arrived at the landing, and to* LOCHE.] Hear that, you two? [*Mimicking* EDOUARD's *speech.*] "Eh-ee ur-uh-ee uh-ee-ee-ai-eh!" [*Continuing.*] If someone asks for Monsieur Chandebise's room... [*Pointing right.*] You put them in there... [*He puts the wire in his pocket.*]

BABETTE [*as* LOCHE *gives a little silent salute*]: Yes, monsieur.

MOUSQUETARD: Good! You can go now... [*With a mock salute to* LOCHE, *waving them both off.*] Out!... [*To* LOCHE, *who stands gazing at* MOUSQUETARD *in rapt admiration as* BABETTE *exits into the corridor.*] Well?... You deaf too, nitwit? [*Taking him by the arm, pointing him toward the stairs.*] "Out!" I said... [*He gives him a swift kick in the rear.*] Out!

LOCHE: Ahhh...

MOUSQUETARD [*as* LOCHE, *never taking his eyes off him, works his way up the stairs, one by one, to* NANA]: See? He worships me... Can't get enough... [*To* LOCHE, *gruffly, at the foot of the stairs.*] And be quick about it, damn it!

[LOCHE *hurries to obey, almost stumbling over the top steps.*]

NANA [*coming down left as he exits out of sight*]: Poor thing... He means well...

[*Just then the door, midstage right, opens and* POPOFF *comes rushing out, as before, striding up to* MOUSQUETARD, *who is standing, back turned, looking up the stairs, watching* LOCHE *leave.*]

POPOFF: Nu? Nu?

MOUSQUETARD [*turning round abruptly*]: Wha...? You!

POPOFF [*peremptorily*]: Yest któ-to, pazhálysta? Da?... Któ-to? Da? Da?

MOUSQUETARD [*with a vigorous shake of the head*]: No Toto, no Toto!... No Dada either... Sorry!

POPOFF [*dejected*]: Ach! [*Going back to his room.*] Spaseébah!... Spaseébah!... [*As he exits, to himself.*] Ya nyeh panyeemáyu... Ya nyeh...

[*He slams the door.*]

MOUSQUETARD [*coming downstage*]: Damn jack-in-the-box! [*As* FINACHE *appears, coming up the stairs.*] I wish to hell he would—

FINACHE [*arriving at the landing, catching sight of him*]: Ah! Colonel!... My friend... [*To* NANA, *who is standing down left.*] Madame...

NANA \
        } [*together*]: {   What a pleasant surprise...
MOUSQUETARD /
                          Ah!... Doctor Finache...

FINACHE [*coming downstage, between them, to* MOUSQUETARD, *shaking hands*]: I hope you have a room for me. I didn't think to wire.

NANA [*replying, as* MOUSQUETARD *opens his mouth to answer*]: For you? Always!

FINACHE [*to* NANA]: No one has asked for me yet, I take it?

MOUSQUETARD [*beating* NANA *to the punch, good-naturedly, replying*]: Not yet... No one... [*Jokingly.*] No Toto... No Toto...

NANA [*laughing*]: No Dada either...

FINACHE [*looking at them in turn*]: Toto?... Dada?...

MOUSQUETARD: Just a little joke between madame and myself... [*Continuing.*] Everything going well, I hope?

FINACHE: Oh, very...

NANA: Still the same little... affair, if you don't mind my asking?

FINACHE: Why, yes...

NANA: Because it's been a good month since... I mean, we never see you...

FINACHE: Oh, I flit here and there...

MOUSQUETARD: Tsk tsk tsk! [*Wagging a finger.*] Unfaithful! Tsk tsk tsk!

FINACHE: Not at all! The same woman all month... Really!

MOUSQUETARD: Not to her! To us!... Unfaithful to us, monsieur!

FINACHE: Oh... Well...

MOUSQUETARD: Because if every lover was faithful to every woman... I might as well close up shop!

FINACHE [*with a laugh, to* MOUSQUETARD]: Quite... [*To* NANA.] Quite... [*Moving upstage a little, pointing downstairs, with a change of tone.*] By the way... Just now... There wasn't a soul at the desk. I could have walked off with all the silverware! Where is he?

NANA: You mean Loche?

FINACHE [*coming back down*]: Who?... No... That handsome devil... Maurice...

MOUSQUETARD: Ah! That's right... You wouldn't know... [*A little pointedly.*] A whole month, after all... [*Drawing his thumb across his throat.*] Fired him...

FINACHE: Fired?... Why? He did so much for the scenery!

MOUSQUETARD [*nodding*]: Too much! Too damn pretty...

NANA [*to* FINACHE]: All the ladies fell head over heels, monsieur!
[*She moves upstage a little.*]

FINACHE [*crossing left, in front of her*]: Now that's a good one!

MOUSQUETARD [*following him*]: Couldn't have that, you know... If a client can't bring his ladyfriend here and not have to worry that the help is going to steal her... Well... Trust, monsieur... This is an establishment built on trust.

FINACHE [*coming downstage, sitting on the bench*]: I should hope...

MOUSQUETARD: And discipline! Believe me, I wasn't an officer for nothing!

FINACHE: Oh! You mean "colonel" isn't just a nickname?

NANA [*coming downstage, to* FINACHE, *almost offended*]: A nickname?... [*To* MOUSQUETARD.] Tell him, Mousquetard!

MOUSQUETARD [*saluting*]: "Lieutenant Brutus Mousquetard, twenty-ninth infantry regiment, reporting..."

FINACHE: "Lieutenant"...? But...

MOUSQUETARD: What's a couple of ranks, more or less? After all...

FINACHE: Especially once you're a civilian...

MOUSQUETARD: And you?... What were you?

FINACHE: Me? Just a lowly private, I'm afraid...

MOUSQUETARD: Ah... Well... [*Returning to the matter at hand, to* NANA.] We can put the doctor in number ten if it's ready.

NANA: I'll go see.
[*She goes to the staircase and begins walking up during the ensuing exchange.*]

MOUSQUETARD [*to* FINACHE]: Will that do, sergeant?

FINACHE [*getting up, moving toward the center of the hall while watching* NANA *leave, not realizing that he is talking to him*]: Hmm?... Me?... Oh... [*With a laugh.*] Well, yes... I suppose... [*Pointing to the wall, down left.*] If this one isn't free... I would have preferred...

MOUSQUETARD: Same thing... Very same... Only one flight up...

FINACHE   No problem...
                    } [*together*]: {
NANA [*almost at the top of the stairs*]   I'll just be a minute.

MOUSQUETARD [*to* NANA]: Very good, pumpkin...

FINACHE [*to* MOUSQUETARD, *as* NANA *disappears from view*]: Quite a woman, that one!

MOUSQUETARD: And very efficient...

FINACHE: It's funny, but... I keep thinking I used to know her...

MOUSQUETARD: Probably did... Everyone knew Nana Nuñez... Years ago... The dancer...

FINACHE [*coming left, joining him, searching his memory*]: Nana...

MOUSQUETARD: The one they used to say: "Dances on her right leg... Dances on her left leg... And between the two, makes a damn good living!"

FINACHE: Nana...

MOUSQUETARD: Or Fifi La Flèche... Alias "Pussy-In-Boots"... Called herself those when she was the baron's mistress... Baron de Cocovin...

FINACHE: Fifi La Flèche... [*Suddenly remembering.*] Ah! Of course!... The one
they served up one night in the giant birthday cake...
MOUSQUETARD: That's the one!... On a big silver platter... Without a stitch...
FINACHE: Yes...
MOUSQUETARD: Just a little whipped cream...
FINACHE: Yes...
MOUSQUETARD: I married her!
FINACHE: Married...?
MOUSQUETARD: Loved my uniform... Fell for me, hook, line, and sinker...
[*Laughing.*] Me and everyone else in the regiment...
FINACHE [*with a nostalgic little nod*]: Pussy-In-Boots...
[*He laughs.*]
MOUSQUETARD [*still laughing*]: That's her!... [*Suddenly serious, almost
confidential.*] Even wanted to keep me, she did!
FINACHE: Oh?
MOUSQUETARD: "Not a chance," I told her. None of that gigolo stuff for me!...
With her money, her reputation... And her... [*He mimes a busty physique.*]
Well, a catch like that... "Marriage or nothing," I told her... "Take it or
leave it!"
FINACHE: And she took it, I see! [*Sitting down on the bench.*] Congratulations!
MOUSQUETARD [*coming down, standing by him*]: But first I laid the law down...
Got my principles, after all... Told her: "From now on, no more funny
business... No more lovers..."
FINACHE: No more birthday cakes...
MOUSQUETARD [*continuing*]: Because... [*Leaning over to him.*] I don't know if
you're like me, sergeant, but I always figure that whenever you get
married, your wife should get rid of her lovers.
FINACHE: At the very least...
MOUSQUETARD: I'm for decency and respectability... Don't want any fingers
pointing at me!... So we opened this place... [*He moves off a little to the
right, as* FINACHE *gets up.*] Live a nice quiet life, plain and simple... Work
hard... Put aside a little something for our old age... You know...
FINACHE: Indeed... Very wise...
MOUSQUETARD: In fact... What we were talking about before... Remember?
About that life insurance...?
FINACHE: Last month... Yes...
MOUSQUETARD: Well, I think it's time, doctor... I'm forty-four now... And
Nana... Fifi... [*Correcting.*] Madame Mousquetard is... [*Clearing his
throat.*] is fifty...
FINACHE [*dubious*]: Ah?
MOUSQUETARD [*with an approximate wiggle of his downturned palm*]: ...ish...
ish...
FINACHE [*trying to remain professionally serious*]: Good! That's a good
spread... Five or six years younger...
MOUSQUETARD: Yes... Might be better if it was the wife, but... Anyway, about
the insurance... If I can get her insured so that when she dies...
FINACHE: Your wife?... At fifty...
MOUSQUETARD: Ish... ish...
FINACHE: Yes... But for you it would be less expensive, you understand...

MOUSQUETARD: Oh? That's fine... Long as, when she dies...

FINACHE: No, no... It doesn't work that way!... *You* would have to die...

MOUSQUETARD: Me?... But... That's not what I had in mind...

FINACHE: Well... Maybe we can work out a joint arrangement... Come see us... Any weekday, ten to twelve... Requiem Life... 95, Boulevard Malesherbes...

MOUSQUETARD [*writing on his cuff*]: Aha... Boulevard Malesherbes... And I ask for...?

FINACHE: The director... I'll let him know.

MOUSQUETARD: Excellent!... Because you understand... If I had to die myself...

FINACHE: Of course...

MOUSQUETARD: Much obliged!

FINACHE: Think nothing of it, colonel!

[NANA *appears at the top of the stairs.*]

NANA [*calling down*]: If the sergeant would like to come up and see the room...

FINACHE [*chuckling to himself*]: "The sergeant..." [*Going up to the staircase, to* NANA.] If, indeed!... [*He goes briskly up the stairs, stopping at the top with an afterthought, to* MOUSQUETARD, *who is at the bottom watching him leave.*] Oh... If anyone asks for me, let me know right away!

[*As he exits out of sight, followed by* NANA, *the door, midstage right, opens and* POPOFF *storms out again. The following monosyllabic exchange is delivered at a rapid pace and in a regular rhythm.*]

POPOFF [*behind* MOUSQUETARD's *back*]: Nu?

MOUSQUETARD [*quickly turning around*]: Who...?

POPOFF: Nu? Nu?

MOUSQUETARD: Oh, you!

POPOFF: Nu?

MOUSQUETARD: No!

POPOFF: Yet no?

MOUSQUETARD: No!

POPOFF: Nyet?

[*As he turns to go back to his room,* GISELE *appears, coming up the stairs, wearing hat and coat, and with her face heavily veiled.*]

MOUSQUETARD [*impatiently, continuing the same pace and rhythm*]: No! No!

POPOFF: Ach! [*At the threshold, suddenly noticing* GISELE, *admiringly.*] Oh...

MOUSQUETARD [*to* GISELE]: Madame?

POPOFF: For me? She?... She?...

GISELE [*at the landing, to* MOUSQUETARD]: The room reserved for Monsieur Chandebise, please...

MOUSQUETARD: Of course... [*Moving left.*] Right this way...

[GISELE, *ignoring his invitation, and obviously ill at ease, comes tentatively down center.*]

POPOFF [*approaching her inquisitively, and circling several times, staring at her veiled face and bursting into song*]:

> Ochi chórniyeh, óchi strástniyeh,
> Ochi zhgúchiyeh ee prekrásniyeh...

GISELE: Monsieur...?

POPOFF [*still singing*]:

> Kák lyublyú ya vas,
> Kák bayús ya vas...

[*Suddenly realizing she is not the one he is expecting, disappointed, speaking.*] Ach! Nyet!... No she... No she... [*Crossing right, singing.*]

> Znát, uvídyel vas
> Yá nyeh v'dóbryi chas...

[*He exits into his room and slams the door.*]

GISELE [*to* MOUSQUETARD]: Who on earth...?

MOUSQUETARD [*joining her, down center*]: Don't mind him, madame... [*Tapping his forehead.*] He's a foreign gentleman.

GISELE [*taking a few steps down right*]: Foreign or not!... [*Lifting her veil a little.*] Has anyone else come asking for the room, monsieur?

MOUSQUETARD: Not yet... [*Moving toward her.*] But I'm sure... [*Squinting for a moment, then suddenly recognizing her.*] Why... It's madame!

GISELE [*with a start, putting her hand to her face*]: Monsieur...?

MOUSQUETARD: The lady from this morning!

GISELE: I...

MOUSQUETARD: Well now, I'm flattered! I knew once madame saw how discreet we are... I knew we'd have the pleasure...

GISELE: I—

MOUSQUETARD: Only I didn't think so soon...

GISELE: Really, monsieur! I'm not—

MOUSQUETARD [*interrupting, with a little bow*]: And it is a pleasure... [*Moving left, to the door of the visible bedroom.*] If madame will step this way... [*He arrives at the door and steps back to let her pass.*]

GISELE [*striding in front of him*]: Indeed!

[*She pauses briefly at the door, looks down her nose at him, then enters the room and stands nervously by the window, far left.*]

MOUSQUETARD [*following her in*]: She can see... All very comfortable... [*Pumping the bed with his fist.*] The bed—

GISELE [*cutting him off, haughtily*]: The bed is no concern of mine, monsieur!

[*Nose in the air, she crosses right, in front of him.*]

MOUSQUETARD [*surprised*]: Aha... [*Under his breath, moving down left, toward the bathroom.*] Must be one of those weird ones! [*Aloud, to* GISELE.] And the bathroom, madame... [*Opening the door, pointing inside.*] Hot and cold running water... Bathtub, shower... Toilet...

GISELE: Really, I have no intention of using them, thank you!

MOUSQUETARD: Ah... [*Closing the door, turning aside with a grimace of disgust.*] Well... One other important detail... [*Going up to the bed.*] In case there's ever a raid, we have these buttons...

[*He points to each side of the bed.*]

GISELE [*crossing back left, losing patience*]: Please, monsieur! I'm really not interested in your... equipment! Now would you kindly leave!

MOUSQUETARD: If... [*At the door to the hall.*] If madame is sure there's nothing—

GISELE: Not a thing, monsieur!... I'm quite sure! Nothing!... [*Waving him out.*] Now please...

[MOUSQUETARD, *agape and speechless, exits into the hall.*]

MOUSQUETARD [*closing the door behind him, under his breath*]: Nasty bitch!

GISELE [*under her breath*]: Tactless boor!

[*During the following scene, still in hat and coat, she busies herself inspecting the room, opens the window to air it out, etc.*]

MOUSQUETARD [*coming center, noticing* LOCHE *plodding down the stairs carrying his empty hod, to him*]: Well? [LOCHE, *with his usual look of rapturous admiration, gives him his quasi-salute, which* MOUSQUETARD *more or less returns.*] Finished?

LOCHE: One more load, colonel...

[*He salutes again.*]

MOUSQUETARD: Well, hop to it! [*Half-heartedly saluting.*] It's getting late... And while you're at it, put your uniform on. The guests are arriving... [*Pointing down right, to the jacket and cap hanging on the coatrack.*] That's no place to leave it, damn it!... [LOCHE *salutes and is about to comply, when the electric bell-panel on the wall by the corridor rings, lighting one of its lights.*] Hold on, Loche!... [LOCHE *stops in his tracks, turns, and gives* MOUSQUETARD *his look as the latter moves up right and consults the panel.*] Our crazy damn Cossack!... [*Coming back down center and pointing right, to* POPOFF'*s room.*] Go see what he wants...

[LOCHE *puts his hod down against the staircase railing, gives his usual salute, and, without turning his tender gaze from* MOUSQUETARD, *knocks on the door.*]

POPOFF'S VOICE: Da, da!... Da, da!

[LOCHE *exits into the room, head still turned in* MOUSQUETARD'*s direction, just as* GISELE, *who has been engaged in her inspection, exits into the bathroom. At the same time,* TOURNEL, *who has been coming up the last few stairs, arrives at the landing, hat and coat in hand.*]

TOURNEL [*entering, to* MOUSQUETARD]: I say... You... Monsieur Chandebise's room, please...

MOUSQUETARD [*without taking a good look at him*]: Ah! Good evening Monsieur Chande... [*Looking at him, stopping.*] But... Excuse me, but you're not...

TOURNEL: No... I... [*Coming down center, very officially.*] I'm his representative.

MOUSQUETARD: Oh... [*Shrugging.*] I guess... [*Taking the wire from his pocket, scanning it, reading to himself.*] "Every courtesy appreciated..." [*To* TOURNEL.] Yes... I guess... [*Pointing left.*] That one, monsieur... Number five... [TOURNEL *nods a thank you.*] Monsieur's... [*Emphasizing.*] friend is here already.

TOURNEL: Oh? [*Confidentially.*] And, is she... Is she... [*He puts his joined fingertips to his lips and gives them a kiss.*] Hmm?

MOUSQUETARD: Monsieur?... I'm not sure my opinion... I mean, as long as monsieur thinks so...

TOURNEL: But I don't even know her.

MOUSQUETARD: Oh?

TOURNEL: So I thought... Before jumping in on all fours, if you know what I mean... While I can still turn back... After all, she could be an old bag!

MOUSQUETARD: No, no... Don't worry... Not the nicest disposition, but she's pretty enough.

TOURNEL: Good... It's not her disposition I'm here for, now is it!

MOUSQUETARD [*with an approving laugh*]: No, monsieur! [*Crossing left, in front of him.*] I don't suppose...

[*He goes over to the door, with* TOURNEL *at his heels, and raps discreetly. Getting no answer, he looks at* TOURNEL *with a shrug, and opens the door. They both go in, a little surprised to see the room empty. While* TOURNEL *lays his hat and coat on the little table, downstage, against the dividing wall,* MOUSQUETARD *goes over and shuts the window. In the meantime,* LOCHE *has come out of* POPOFF's *room, standing at the open door and addressing* POPOFF, *who is in the doorway.*]

LOCHE: Very good, general... [*He salutes.*] I'll try to find him.

POPOFF: Da, da! Da, da!

[*He goes inside and shuts the door.*]

MOUSQUETARD [*pointing to the bathroom door, to* TOURNEL]: Must be in there...

LOCHE [*grumbling to himself*]: "Dada, Dada..." How should I know where his father is? [*Turning upstage.*] "Dada..." [*Going to the staircase, muttering.*] A drink... I'll get him a drink... That'll keep him quiet...

[*He retrieves his empty hod and goes down the stairs. At the same time* MOUSQUETARD *goes over to the bathroom door and raps.*]

GISELE'S VOICE [*muffled, but sharply*]: Yes?

MOUSQUETARD [*his ear against the door*]: Madame's gentleman is here...

GISELE'S VOICE: Thank you!

MOUSQUETARD [*to* TOURNEL, *bowing his way right, in a respectful semi-circle in front of him*]: She is...

TOURNEL: Yes... Much obliged...

MOUSQUETARD [*at the door to the hall, clasping his hands in front of him in a gesture of anticipated victory*]: Good luck, monsieur!

[*He exits into the hall and leaves up the stairs as* TOURNEL *closes the door.*]

TOURNEL [*examining the room, musing*]: Hmm... Not bad at all... Nicely furnished... [*Noticing the two buttons by the bed.*] Electric bells and everything... [*Inspecting them.*] Big enough, I must say!... Good for target practice if you ever get bored!... [*He mimes shooting a pistol at one of them.*] Not that I plan to, I hope... [*Chuckling.*] Now then... [*Looking around, as if for a hiding-place.*] Something clever... [*At the bed, hitting on an idea.*] Ah! This should get a laugh... [*He sits on the side of the bed and pulls the canopy curtains around him, hiding himself completely, except for his head.*] Just to break the ice...

[*He pulls his head behind the curtains just as* GISELE, *still in hat and coat, comes bolting out of the bathroom expecting to find her husband.*]

GISELE [*obviously ready for the confrontation*]: So! There you... [*She stops short, surprised not to find anyone.*] What...? Where did he—

TOURNEL [*from behind the curtains*]: Peek-a-boo!

GISELE [*looking toward the bed*]: Ah!... [*Aside.*] I'll "peek-a-boo" him!

TOURNEL [*parting the curtains ever so slightly*]: Peek-a-beek-a-boo!

GISELE [*striding up to the bed, violently pulling aside the stage left curtain with her right hand and giving* TOURNEL *a swift slap across the face with the back of her left, shouting]:* Peek-a-boo!

TOURNEL: Oh!

[He jumps off the bed.]

GISELE *[jumping back, speechless]*

TOURNEL *[at the chair near the hall door]*

[together]:

Oh!... It's not... It's...It's... *[Stammering.]* Monsieur... Monsieur Tournel... Gisèle!... You! *[Rubbing his cheek.]* I... I had no idea, madame... I mean...

GISELE: But—

TOURNEL: What a pleasant surprise! I—

GISELE: But... What are you doing here?

TOURNEL: Me?... I... *[With as much panache as he can muster.]* What difference...? After all... *[Quickly, trying to find a suitable excuse.]* A fling, madame... Just an innocent escapade... Nothing, really...

GISELE: But—

TOURNEL: Some woman... No one special... I don't even know her... She saw me at the theater... Love at first sight...

GISELE: But—

TOURNEL *[eager to get on to other matters]:* You know the sort of thing. She wrote to me... Asked me to meet her... I... I didn't want to hurt her feelings, so—

GISELE: No, no, no! I can't believe—

TOURNEL *[misinterpreting her protests]:* Please, Gisèle, believe me! Whoever she is... She means nothing to me! Nothing!

GISELE: Monsieur...

TOURNEL: But you... A dream come true!... Here... Now... Standing in front of me...

GISELE: Monsieur...

TOURNEL: The love of my life... Mine! All mine!... *[Trying to embrace her.]* It's fate, don't you see?

GISELE: Please! *[Moving right.]* Let me go!

TOURNEL: But Gisèle...

GISELE *[at the little table, taking a stand]:* She didn't write to you! She wrote to my husband! Victor-Emmanuel...

TOURNEL: No! She didn't! She couldn't have!... He's ugly!... You know he's ugly!... But we were in the box... Together... Remember?... She thought that he—

GISELE *[trying to interrupt]:* No, no, no...

TOURNEL: She thought that I—

GISELE: Monsieur—

TOURNEL: She... She—

GISELE: Monsieur! I wrote that letter!

TOURNEL: You?

GISELE: Yes!... To my husband...

TOURNEL: You... You...

GISELE: I... *[Heaving a sigh, preliminary to a difficult explanation.]* I wanted to see if he...

TOURNEL: If he...?

GISELE: If he would come... If he would cheat on me... That's all...

TOURNEL: Aha!... And he didn't, did he! [*Before she has a chance to answer.*] See? You see?... You said it was over between us... You and me... Because you thought he was cheating... But you see? He wasn't!... He didn't come, did he! He sent me in his place... [GISELE *keeps trying, unsuccessfully, to get a word in edgewise.*] He knew it made more sense... I mean... [*A little fatuously.*] Me, after all...

GISELE [*becoming convinced*]: My goodness, you're right...

TOURNEL [*pressing his advantage*]: And do you know what he said when he got that letter? Your letter...? He said: "What the devil can she want with me? Doesn't she know I'd never cheat on my wife?..."

GISELE: He did?

TOURNEL: Yes!... Word for word...

GISELE: Oh, monsieur... I... I'm... [*Throwing her arms around his neck.*] I'm so happy! So... [*She plants several kisses on both cheeks.*] And to think...

TOURNEL: Ah, madame!... Gisèle!... Gisèle!... [*Embracing her around the waist with his right arm, and, with his left, punctuating his overblown oratory.*] How deeply you must regret... How repentant you must be... To have doubted such a man! [*He plants a voracious kiss on her lips with passionate growls.*] Harrrgh! Harrrgh!... A prince!... A saint!... [*Likewise.*] Harrrgh! Harrrgh!... You realize now... [*Likewise.*] Harrrgh! Harrrgh!... that he's above reproach... that... that... [*Likewise.*] Harrrgh! Harrrgh!... that you have no need to be faithful anymore... No reason... [*Kissing her repeatedly.*] Harrrgh! Harrrgh! Harrrgh!... No right, Gisèle!... No right!...

GISELE [*embracing him in turn*]: Oh! Yes, yes!... [*Kissing him with equal fervor but less noise.*] How wrong I was! How utterly... [*Kissing.*] unspeakably... [*Kissing.*] shamefully wrong I was, ever to suspect him!... [*Continuing to punctuate her comments with kisses.*] Poor, dear Chandebise!... Dear, sweet Victor-Emmanuel!... So lovable, so faithful... [*Apostrophising.*] Oh, can you ever forgive me, treasure!

TOURNEL [*lyrically*]: He can, Gisèle!... He will... [*Kissing her.*] Harrrgh! Harrrgh! Harrrgh!... I will!... I do!... Just say you'll be mine... That's all that matters!

GISELE: Oh yes!... That will teach me...

TOURNEL: Gisèle! Gisèle! Gisèle!

GISELE: And to think... I thought...

TOURNEL: To think... You thought...

GISELE: I thought it was my husband going "peek-a-boo" on the bed!

TOURNEL: No matter... [*Gesturing her toward the bed.*] Come... We'll go "peek-a-boo" together!... You and I... Just for him...

GISELE [*suddenly realizing the extent of his expectations*]: What?

TOURNEL: Peek-a-boo! [*Pressing her passionately to his bosom.*] Ah! Gisèle!... Gisèle!...

GISELE [*resisting*]   } [*together*]: { Monsieur!... Monsieur Tournel!...

TOURNEL   My Gisèle!

GISELE: Please!... What's got into you? [*She breaks free and moves left, to the window, fanning herself with her hand.*] Let me catch my—

TOURNEL [*following her, insistent*]: No, no! Let's strike... While the iron's hot... [*He embraces her.*]

GISELE: But monsieur—
TOURNEL [*babbling*]: While my... While your... Whatever...
GISELE: Please—

TOURNEL ⎫   ⎧ Come... Come...
        ⎬ [*together*]: ⎨
GISELE ⎭   ⎩ Monsieur—

TOURNEL [*pulling her bodily toward the bed, as if pronouncing the decisive argument*]: Peek-a-boo, Gisèle!... Peek-a-boo! Peek-a-boo!
GISELE [*struggling*]: Monsieur Tournel—
TOURNEL: Not "Monsieur Tournel"... Please, call me Adonis... [*Redoubling his efforts.*] Come...
GISELE [*panicking*]: What are you... Where are you... Where are you taking me?
TOURNEL [*with one knee on the bed, persisting*]: Where? [*Lyrically.*] To Paradise, Gisèle!... To ecstasy... To bliss...
GISELE [*managing to catch him off balance, pushing him away, onto the bed*]: Are you out of your mind, monsieur? [*Coming downstage.*] What do you take me for?

TOURNEL   ⎫   ⎧ What?... What do I...
                     ⎬ [*together*]: ⎨
GISELE [*hands on hips*] ⎭   ⎩ Really!

TOURNEL: But I... But you... But I thought you said... I thought you wanted to—
GISELE: To be your lover... Yes!... But to go to bed with you? Really! Do you think I'm a... a... One of those, Monsieur Tournel?
TOURNEL [*on the edge of the bed, confused*]: But... But what, then? If not...
GISELE [*drawing herself up to her full height*]: What?... Romance, what else? Affection... Emotion...
TOURNEL [*echoing, blandly, with an open-mouthed nod*]: Affection...
GISELE [*continuing*]: My hand in yours... Your gaze in mine...
TOURNEL: Aha...
GISELE: I wanted to give you the best of myself... The best part of me...
TOURNEL: Oh?... [*Slowly raising his eyes, in a look charged with meaning.*] Which one?
GISELE: My heart, monsieur... My soul...
TOURNEL: Pfff!... Not quite the part I had in mind...
GISELE [*eyeing him up and down, still rather haughty*]: Just what did you expect?
TOURNEL [*standing up*]: Expect?... What any man would expect... Any man with blood in his veins... Any man in love, Gisèle! [*Approaching her, getting carried away again.*] With the woman of his dreams!... The woman he was meant for...
GISELE [*eluding him, moving right*]: Monsieur...
TOURNEL [*following her*]: ...and who was meant for him!... The woman whose husband practically threw her into his arms!
GISELE: Please...
[*During the following exchange they continue their cat-and-mouse chase around the room.*]
TOURNEL: Because he did! He's the one... He sent me... He told me...
GISELE: Stay away!
TOURNEL: And now you're the one who tells me... Who doesn't want... Who

won't... Who...

GISELE			Monsieur...
	} [together]:	{	
TOURNEL			Ah! Did you ever...!

[*He tries to corner her against the bathroom door and embrace her.*]

GISELE [*eluding him and crossing right, taking refuge between the little table and the wall*]: Monsieur Tournel! Control yourself!... Please!

TOURNEL: And you think I'll be satisfied with your little romance?... Your hand in mine, and that sort of thing?...

GISELE: Monsieur...

TOURNEL: Half a loaf, Gisèle!... And not the best half, by a long shot!... Your heart? Your soul?... Ha! Heart, soul... My foot!

GISELE: But—

TOURNEL [*pacing back and forth, sarcastically*]: Thank you, madame! I appreciate your offer!... [*Dramatically.*] Days of desire... Nights of frustration... And if I'm good, the pleasure... [*Emphasizing.*] the privilege of running madame's errands... Of walking madame's dog when he has to take a... a walk! [*Stalking back to* GISELE, *who is cowering behind the little table.*] Oh no, madame! [*Pounding the table with his fist.*] No! No! No!

GISELE: Monsieur... Please!

TOURNEL [*right in her face*]: No!... [*Almost threatening.*] And since you're so naive... So ignorant of the basic rules of love... I... I'll teach you, madame! I'll teach you!

GISELE [*terrified*]: Monsieur...

TOURNEL: What? You think I'll just leave the way I came in? Be a laughing-stock?... Even to myself?

GISELE: Monsieur Tournel...

TOURNEL: No, no! You're mine! [*Grasping her around the waist.*] You're mine, Gisèle! [*Pulling her over to the bed.*] I want you! I... I... I want you and...

GISELE [*struggling*]			Monsieur...
	} [together]:	{	
TOURNEL			...and I'm going to have you!

GISELE: Adonis...

TOURNEL [*wildly insistent*]: You're mine! All mine!... [GISELE, *with a supreme effort and a well-directed knee, manages to push him away.*] Ayyyy!

GISELE [*jumping up on the bed, crouching on both knees, with her finger on the electric button on the stage right side*]: One step closer, and I'll ring!

TOURNEL: Ring!... Ring to your heart's content! Ring your head off!... They won't get in!

[*He limps over to the hall door and bolts it shut.* GISELE, *in a panic, presses the button. The wall panel immediately pivots on its axis, producing the other bed, in which* BLAISE *is lying, ready for work.*]

GISELE [*disappearing into the other room*]: My God!... Help! Help!

TOURNEL [*at the door, his back still turned, misinterpreting her cries*]: Yes!... [*Mimicking.*] "Help! Help! Help!"... [*Returning to the bed.*] Too late for help now!... [*Triumphantly, aside.*] I've got her! She's mine!... [*Mad with passion, he leaps onto the bed, lunging blindly at* BLAISE, *hugging and kissing him.*] Ah! Gisèle!... Harrrgh! Harrrgh! Gisèle...

BLAISE [*groaning*]: Oh! My back!...

TOURNEL [*recoiling in horror*] ⎫   ⎧ Aaaah!... Who...?
                                       ⎬ [*together*]: ⎨
BLAISE   ⎭   ⎩ My aching back!...

TOURNEL [*frantically wiping his mouth*]: What in the name of... [*To* BLAISE.] Where did you—

BLAISE [*sitting up*]: Hmm?

TOURNEL: Where on earth... [*Running to the hall door, unbolting it and opening it, calling.*] Gisèle! Gisèle!... [*He looks outside briefly, and, seeing no one, comes back inside, leaving the door open, then runs down left to the bathroom door, knocking and calling.*] Gisèle!... Gisèle!...
[*He exits precipitously into the bathroom just as* GISELE *dashes madly out the door of the unseen bedroom, into the hall. In the meantime,* BLAISE, *unconcerned, has put on his pince-nez and begun reading a newspaper.*]

GISELE [*frantically looking around*]: My God!... Where... How did I... [*Calling.*] Tournel!... Monsieur Tournel!... [*To herself.*] Oh! Enough of this place! I'm leaving!
[*She hurries upstage and rushes down the stairs. No sooner is she out of sight, than* POPOFF *comes dashing out of his room.*]

POPOFF [*calling*]: Chelovyék... Boy!... Garçonne!... [*Stopping, looking around, seeing no one there.*] Ach! Nee-któ!... Nu? Gdyéh...? [*Going over to the staircase, leaning over and calling down.*] Garçonne!... Garçonne!...
[*Just then* GISELE *comes leaping up the stairs as fast as her legs will carry her.*]

GISELE: My God! Down there... Victor-Emmanuel!... Coming up...
[*Noticing* POPOFF'*s door open, she runs inside as* POPOFF, *still by the staircase, looks on in surprise. After a brief moment his surprise turns to lubricious delight, and he stalks after her.*]

POPOFF [*leering in anticipation*]: Da, da! Da, da!
[*He exits into his room and closes the door behind him just as* LOCHE, *coming up the stairs, arrives at the landing.*]

LOCHE [*mumbling to himself*]: No whisky anywhere!... [*Struck by a thought.*] Ah! Maybe Blaise... [*Going left, to the door of the unseen bedroom, and opening it, calling.*] Monsieur Blaise...

BLAISE [*still sitting up in bed with his paper*]: In here!...

LOCHE [*coming down to the bedroom door, to himself*]: Already? [*At the threshold, to* BLAISE, *with a little salute*]: Excuse me, corporal... A little drink... You wouldn't happen to have...? Just a little...

BLAISE [*pointing in the direction of the unseen bedroom*]: In there, Loche... A bottle of gin... Behind the cupboard... But... [*Putting his forefinger to his lips.*] Shhh!

LOCHE: Ah...
[*He moves back upstage and exits into the unseen bedroom just as* TOURNEL *enters from the bathroom.*]

TOURNEL [*looking around frantically: crossing right, looking under the little table, under his hat and coat, etc.*]: Where the devil...
[*He goes out into the hall, moving upstage toward the staircase. At the same time* GISELE *comes flying out the door, right, followed by a*

clinging POPOFF, *attempting to defend herself against his advances.*]

POPOFF [*pawing at her*]

GISELE [*pushing him away*]

[*together*]:

Nyet!... Ochi chórniyeh!...
Go no! Go no!...
Don't touch me, you...
Let me go! Let me...

POPOFF: Ya vas lyublyú!...

TOURNEL: Ah! Gisèle... [*Coming downstage to join her.*] There you... [GISELE *unleashes a violent slap aimed at* POPOFF's *cheek, but* TOURNEL *arrives between them just in time to receive it.*] Aaaah!

GISELE

TOURNEL [*rubbing his cheek, to* GISELE]

[*together*]:

Oh!

Again?

POPOFF [*to* TOURNEL]: Spaseébah! [*Shaking his hand.*] Spaseébah!

[*He exits into his room, mumbling, as* GISELE, *obviously in a state, runs left, into the visible bedroom, followed by* TOURNEL.]

TOURNEL [*closing the door behind him*]: Ah! Gisèle!... Gisèle!...

GISELE [*alternately fanning herself with her hand and clutching her bosom*]: Ah! Monsieur Tournel!...

TOURNEL: Please... "Adonis"...

GISELE: It's too much... [*Almost panting.*] My heart... My... My husband, monsieur...

TOURNEL: Please... Not "monsieur"...

GISELE: But... But my husband...

TOURNEL: Of course, my love...

GISELE: No! You don't understand! He's... He's here! My husband!

TOURNEL [*mechanically*]: Of course... Of... [*Suddenly understanding, with a start.*] Here?... Chandebise?

GISELE: Yes! Victor-Emmanuel!... Disguised as an employee!

TOURNEL: As an—

GISELE: How?... Why?... God only knows!... To catch us, obviously!

TOURNEL: But... But that's impossible! He can't be...

[*Just then* BLAISE, *of whose continued presence they were unaware, groans one of his pro forma complaints.*]

BLAISE: Oh! My back!... My aching—

GISELE [*screaming*]

TOURNEL [*jumping back*]

[*together*]:

Aaaah!

What...?

GISELE [*horrified, pointing to* BLAISE]: That!... Who...?

TOURNEL [*pointing to him*]: That?... Who knows? He came from nowhere!... One minute you were there, next minute he was! [*To* BLAISE.] You!... What are you doing here?

BLAISE [*putting down his paper*]: Me, monsieur?... You called me in...

GISELE

TOURNEL

[*together*]:

What?

Me?

GISELE [*going up to the bed, to* TOURNEL]: You need spectators too?

TOURNEL [*following her*]: But—

GISELE [*waxing hysterical*]: Get him out of here!

TOURNEL: I don't have the slightest idea—

GISELE: I don't care!

BLAISE [*mumbling, with a shrug*]   Must be some mistake...

} [*together*]:

GISELE   Get him out!

[BLAISE *reaches over and pushes the stage-left button himself, as* GISELE *and* TOURNEL *continue their exchange.*]

TOURNEL: But Gisèle... Gisèle...

[*As the wall-panel pivots, without their noticing,* BLAISE *goes disappearing into the other room.*]

GISELE   Out! Out! Out!

} [*together*]:

TOURNEL   ·   I assure you...

[*By now the pivoting operation is completed and the beds are once again exchanged, this time with* LOCHE *sitting on the original one, an open gin bottle in his right hand.*]

LOCHE [*elbow raised, obviously caught in the act*]: Ah... Oh my... I was just—
[*He gives a little salute with the bottle.*]

TOURNEL [*bolting off, far right*]   Chandebise! [*Aside.*] Good God!

} [*together*]:

GISELE [*bolting off, far left*]   God in heaven! [*Aside.*] I'm done for!

TOURNEL [*returning quickly to the bed, palms prayerfully joined, to* LOCHE]: My friend!...

GISELE [*likewise*]: Please! Please!...

LOCHE: Huh?

[*The following exclamations are delivered rapid-fire, almost on top of each other, as* LOCHE *looks back and forth between them, with a stupid, open-mouthed expression.*]

TOURNEL [*to* LOCHE]: I know what you're thinking, but—

GISELE [*to* LOCHE]: Let me explain—

TOURNEL: We're innocent!

GISELE: I know how it looks, but—

TOURNEL: Innocent, believe me!...

GISELE: Really...

TOURNEL: No matter what you think—

GISELE: Believe him! Believe him!

TOURNEL: I had no idea—

GISELE: He had no idea... I had no—

TOURNEL: She had no idea... We—

GISELE: We had no idea—

TOURNEL [*beginning to regain his composure, still haranguing the uncomprehending* LOCHE]: It's all on account of that letter!

GISELE: Yes! That letter... It's... It's all my fault!

TOURNEL: It is! It is!

GISELE: I... I wrote it, treasure! [*Kneeling by the bed.*] Please!... Can you ever forgive me? I... I thought you were unfaithful... Cheating on me... I... I thought...

LOCHE   Me?

} [*together*]:

GISELE   I thought—

TOURNEL: She thought—

GISELE [*still pleading with* LOCHE]: Please! Tell me you believe me! Tell me—

LOCHE [*puzzled, but trying to be agreeable*]: I do! I do!...
[*He turns aside with a shrug and bursts out in a long, imbecilic laugh.*]

GISELE [*jumping to her feet, recoiling*]: Please! Don't!... I can't stand it when you laugh like that!

LOCHE [*cutting short his laughter*]: You can't?

GISELE [*approaching the bed again*]: See? You don't believe me! I can tell...

TOURNEL [*to* LOCHE] ⎫
⎬ [*together*]: ⎧ But it's true...
GISELE [*wringing her hands*] ⎭   ⎩ Ah! Good God!

TOURNEL [*to* LOCHE]: It's so obvious—

GISELE [*to* LOCHE]: How can I convince you? How—
[LOCHE *suddenly stands down from the bed.*]

LOCHE: Listen, you two... [*Coming down between them.*] Excuse me, but... I've got to bring a gin to number four. [*Pointing vaguely right.*] "Nu nu"... The general...
[*He gives a couple of his typical salutes and moves right, toward the hall door, with* GISELE *and* TOURNEL *at his heels.*]

GISELE [*grabbing him by the left arm and turning him to face her*]: Please! What's got into you?

LOCHE: Me?

TOURNEL [*at the door, to head him off, grabbing him by the other arm and turning him back around, face to face*]: For heaven's sake, my friend! Is this any time to talk about gin?

LOCHE [*shaking free*]: But I've got to! [*Pointing right.*] He's waiting... Number four... If I can't find his Dada I can at least bring him a drink... [*Holding up the bottle.*] See?

GISELE [*losing control*]: No, no, no! I can't stand it!... [*To* LOCHE.] Enough of this charade!... Please!... Curse me! Hit me! Beat me!... Anything!...
[*She falls to her knees.*]

LOCHE: Huh?

GISELE: Anything is better than this... this cold, cynical calm of yours!

TOURNEL [*falling to his knees also, almost pathetically*]: Me too!... Beat me! Beat me, my friend!
[LOCHE, *standing between them—*GISELE *to his left,* TOURNEL *to his right— looks back and forth at each one, jaws agape, scratching his head.*]

LOCHE [*to* GISELE]: But madame...

GISELE [*to* LOCHE, *groaning*]: Ah! You see?... "Madame"... You called me... [*To* TOURNEL.] He called me "madame"...

LOCHE: So?

GISELE [*seizing his left hand in hers, pleading*]: Please!... Call me "Gisèle"...

TOURNEL [*on his other side, seizing his right hand, along with the bottle*]: Please! Call her "Gisèle"...
[*Plainly uncomfortable,* LOCHE *kneels down between them to be on their level.*]

LOCHE [*mumbling to himself*]: Why not?... [*To* GISELE.] But Madame Gisèle...

TOURNEL [*to* LOCHE]: No, no! No "madame"... You sound like a peasant!... "Gisèle"... Just plain "Gisèle"...

LOCHE: Aha... [*To* GISELE.] But plain Gisèle...

GISELE: Please!... Say that you believe me... Tell me...

LOCHE [*without much conviction*]: I believe you.

TOURNEL: Thank heaven!

GISELE [*carried away, to* LOCHE]: Then kiss me!

LOCHE: Huh?

GISELE: Kiss me! Kiss me!... Or I'll think you're still angry...

[LOCHE *gives a shrug, as if to say: "Why not!", then faces her squarely, wipes his mouth on his sleeve and, without letting go of the bottle, throws his arms around her neck and gives her a noisy kiss on both cheeks.*]

TOURNEL [*encouraging him*]: Go on!... That's it!...

GISELE [*beaming, to* LOCHE, *kissing his hands*]: Ah! Thank you! Thank you, treasure!...

LOCHE [*licking his lips, aside, as* GISELE *stands up*]: Mmmm!

TOURNEL [*standing up also, and stepping back, holding out his arms, to* LOCHE]: And me...

LOCHE [*standing up, to* TOURNEL]: You too? [*Aside.*] Pfff!

TOURNEL: Yes... To prove that you believe me...

LOCHE: Well...

[*He gives him an unenthusiastic peck on the cheek.*]

TOURNEL [*with a sigh of relief and satisfaction*]: Good... Good... Very good...

LOCHE [*misunderstanding*]: Yes... [*Pointing to* GISELE.] But madame was better...

GISELE [*to* LOCHE]: "Madame"...?

LOCHE [*about to move right, toward the hall door*] ⎫
                                                      ⎬ [*together*]: ⎰ And now...
GISELE [*disillusioned, to* TOURNEL] ⎭   ⎱ You hear?

LOCHE [*with a couple of his little salutes*]: I've got to get this gin to number four.

GISELE: Again?

TOURNEL [*to* LOCHE, *stopping him and pulling him back*]: What kind of joke...

GISELE [to LOCHE, *pulling him by the arm*]: Please! Are you my husband or aren't you?

LOCHE: Me? [*With his imbecilic laugh.*] I just work here...

GISELE [*recoiling, startled, holding
                    him by one arm*] ⎫
                                      ⎬ [*together*]: ⎰ You...
TOURNEL [*likewise, holding him
                    by the other*] ⎭   ⎱ What?

GISELE: My God! [*To* TOURNEL, *panicking.*] His mind... It's gone! [*To* LOCHE.] Victor... Victor-Emmanuel!...

LOCHE: Who?

GISELE: It's me!... I'm... I'm me!

LOCHE [*breaking free*]: And I'm me, madame!... [*With a salute.*] Loche!

GISELE [*to* LOCHE]: Loche? [*To* TOURNEL.] Loche?

TOURNEL [*to* GISELE]: Loche? [*To* LOCHE.] Loche?

LOCHE: Loche!... [*Retreating left, to the bed, standing by the head.*] Ask Blaise if you don't believe me!

GISELE [*to* LOCHE, *following him, stopping at the foot of the bed*]: Blaise? [*To*

TOURNEL.] Blaise?

TOURNEL [*following, stopping between them, to* GISELE]: Blaise? [*To* LOCHE.] Blaise?

LOCHE: Blaise!... Our sick old man... The one who... [*He presses one of the buttons.*] Here... You'll see...

[*The wall pivots before the gaping gaze of* GISELE *and* TOURNEL, *bringing back the other bed.*]

TOURNEL ⎫		⎧ What in the name...?
	[*together*]:	
GISELE ⎭		⎩ Who...? What...?

BLAISE: Oh! My aching back!... My—

GISELE: Did you ever...?

LOCHE [*to* BLAISE]: Never mind! Not now!... Just tell us who I am...

TOURNEL ⎫		⎧ I never...
	[*together*]:	
BLAISE [*sitting up, to* LOCHE] ⎭		⎩ Too much gin?

LOCHE: Not me... [*Pointing at the others.*] Tell them...

GISELE [*recovering her aplomb, to* BLAISE]: Yes!... Who is he?

BLAISE: Him?... That's Loche...

GISELE *and* **TOURNEL** [*stepping back in amazement, to* BLAISE, *together*]: Loche? [*To each other, dumbfounded.*] Loche?

BLAISE: Loche... The porter...

[MOUSQUETARD *appears, coming down the stairs.*]

GISELE *and* **TOURNEL** [*looking first at each other, then at* LOCHE, *then at* BLAISE]: But... But... But...

MOUSQUETARD [*at the landing, looking around*]: Loche?...

TOURNEL ⎫		⎧ It's impossible!
	[*together*]:	
GISELE ⎭		⎩ It can't be...

TOURNEL: Two peas in a pod!... It's... [*To* GISELE.] It's got to be a trick!

MOUSQUETARD [*calling*]: Loche!... Loche!...

LOCHE [*moving right, toward the hall door, shouting*]: In here, colonel!... [*To the others.*] The boss... I've got to go...

GISELE [*grabbing him by the arm as he passes in front of her*]: Yes... Well... [*She pulls him aside, turning him round, and strides toward the door.*] We'll just see about this!...

[*She opens the door and exits into the hall.*]

TOURNEL [*to* LOCHE, *grabbing him by the other arm and turning him in the other direction*]: Out of the way, you!

[*He follows her out, but not before managing a quick, sardonic salute to the befuddled* LOCHE, *who stands at the door, saluting weakly.*]

GISELE [*to* MOUSQUETARD]: Monsieur!

MOUSQUETARD: Madame?

GISELE: Be good enough to tell us who... [*Pointing to* LOCHE.] that gentleman is!

TOURNEL [*to* MOUSQUETARD]: If you please!

MOUSQUETARD [*turning to look, angrily, to* LOCHE]: You!

[GISELE *and* TOURNEL *follow* LOCHE *with their eyes as he passes right, in front of them, coming center.*]

LOCHE [*to* MOUSQUETARD]: Colonel?

MOUSQUETARD [*joining him, center*]: What are you... And with a bottle, damn it!

LOCHE: But I'm not—

MOUSQUETARD [*grabbing him by the arm and punctuating his reprimand with a number of kicks in the rear*]: I thought I told you... if I ever caught you drinking... Damn drunkard!... [*As* LOCHE *reacts to each of the kicks with a jump in the air and an ambivalent "Ah!",* GISELE *and* TOURNEL, *cowering against each other close to the door, echo each exclamation with an "Oh!" and a little start, as if receiving the blow themselves.*] Damn lush!

GISELE and **TOURNEL** [*together, to each other*]: Lush? [*Together, to* MOUSQUETARD.] Lush?

LOCHE [*to* GISELE *and* TOURNEL, *as* MOUSQUETARD *lets go*]: See? I told you—

MOUSQUETARD [*grabbing the bottle from him, as they turn to each other and silently mouth the word "lush"*]: Give me that!

LOCHE [*to* MOUSQUETARD]: But... It's for number four...

MOUSQUETARD: I'll "number four" you, goddammit! [*He gives him another series of kicks, as before, with the same reaction from* GISELE *and* TOURNEL.] One!... Two!... Three!... And four!...

LOCHE: But...

MOUSQUETARD [*pointing to the staircase*]: Now get your ass out of here! And be quick about it, you hear?

LOCHE: Yes, colonel... [*Loping off, saluting with one hand and rubbing his behind with the other, to* GISELE *and* TOURNEL.] See? I told you...
[*He disappears down the stairs as* TOURNEL, *shrugging his shoulders and shaking his head in disbelief, crosses down right.*]

MOUSQUETARD [*to* GISELE *and* TOURNEL]: Forgive me, monsieur... madame... Our porter likes his liquor!
[*He turns and exits up the stairs, leaving them utterly thunderstruck and gaping for a long moment.*]

GISELE [*finally*]: The porter!... Can you believe—

TOURNEL [*standing against the console, suddenly*]: Gisèle!

GISELE: What?

TOURNEL: We kissed the porter!

GISELE: I know! I just said...

TOURNEL [*shaking his head*]: Sorry... I didn't hear... I... I... [*He begins pacing up and down.*] Two peas in a pod! It's... It's not possible!...

GISELE: No, but... What other explanation...? [*Pointing center, to the scene of the recent action.*] If I hadn't seen him kicking him that way, I might suspect... But... No, no... Chandebise would never let...

TOURNEL [*stopping, shaking his head*]: Never!
[*He begins pacing again.*]

GISELE: Not even to try to make me believe... He would never let anyone kick him in the... the...

TOURNEL [*stopping*]: Thighs!

GISELE: Never!

TOURNEL: No!

GISELE [*dragging herself downstage and falling in a heap onto the bench, as* TOURNEL, *down right, continues pacing*]: Oh! It's simply too much!... [*Fanning herself with her hand.*] Please... A glass of water... Could you...?

TOURNEL [*stopping, unthinkingly feeling his pockets*]: Water? [*Looking around.*] Where? [GISELE *stands up and points silently to the door of the visible bedroom.*] Of course... [*He hurriedly crosses left, goes into the room, stops, and approaches* BLAISE, *who is still in bed reading his paper.*] You... I say... Is there any water...?

BLAISE [*looking up, pointing down left, as* GISELE *follows* TOURNEL *into the room*]: In there... Where else...?

TOURNEL: Ah!... Of course... Of course...
  [*He crosses left and exits into the bathroom.*]

GISELE [*crossing left, to* BLAISE, *without waiting for a reaction*]: The porter, God in heaven!... Can you imagine...?

BLAISE [*nodding, in an attempt at profundity*]: Life... Life...
  [*He returns to his paper with a philosophical nod as* GISELE *goes over to the window, opens it a little, and takes a few deep breaths.* LOCHE, *meantime, has come up the staircase from downstairs, carrying another hod full of logs. As he arrives at the landing* BABETTE *appears coming down from upstairs. At the same time,* GISELE, *in the bedroom, closes the window.*]

GISELE [*looking toward the bathroom, as* LOCHE *takes a few steps up the stairs*]: Really! How long... A simple glass of water... [*Exiting into the bathroom, to the unseen* TOURNEL.] Well?
  [*Just as she closes the door,* EDOUARD *comes dashing up the stairs, in obvious high spirits, pulling* ANTOINETTE *by the hand. He is hatless but wearing a coat; she is wearing both.*]

EDOUARD [*coming down center, to* ANTOINETTE, *on his right, speaking without a trace of his impediment, and with humorously exaggerated gallantry*]: Come, Poodles!... Come, my little turtledove... Love of my life!... Off to our room! [*Dramatically, reciting.*]

  The fateful hour draws nigh; the hour
  When love must bud, and bloom, and flower...

ANTOINETTE: Pretty!

BABETTE [*with a nod, to* EDOUARD]: Monsieur Chandebise... [*Aside, to herself, surprised at his ability to speak.*] Ah oo ee ah ah!...
  [*She exits into the corridor, up right.*]

LOCHE [*approaching* EDOUARD *and* ANTOINETTE, *standing between them, to* EDOUARD]: Can I help you, monsieur?

EDOUARD: I should say you—

ANTOINETTE		
	[*together, with a start, thinking they recognize* CHANDEBISE]:	Monsieur!
EDOUARD		Aaaah!

EDOUARD [*turning on his heel*]: Victor-Emmanuel!
  [*He bounds off, left, into the unseen bedroom at the same time as* ANTOINETTE, *no less shocked, bounds right, taking refuge in* POPOFF's *room, both slamming their respective doors simultaneously behind them. At the same time,* BLAISE, *still in bed, puts aside his paper and resumes his official supine position.*]

LOCHE [*scratching his head, moving up toward the stairs*]: Another one with his "Victor-Emmanuel"!

[*As he slowly disappears up the staircase* GISELE *enters from the bathroom, with* TOURNEL *close behind.*]

TOURNEL: Feeling better?

GISELE: A little... No, not really... I... I think I'm going to faint...

TOURNEL [*rushing over to her*]: No, no!... Don't!... Please!...

GISELE: Really! If you think I want to...

TOURNEL: Here... Come... [*Guiding her very gingerly, backing her toward the bed.*] Lie down a moment... Come...

GISELE: Perhaps I'd better... [*She collapses onto the bed, apparently forgetting about the presence of* BLAISE, *then springs up with a scream.*] Ahhhh!

BLAISE [*as* GISELE *dashes left*] ⎱ [*together*]: ⎰ Please, madame!
TOURNEL ⎰ ⎱ What...?

BLAISE [*sitting up*]: That's not what he pays me for...

TOURNEL [*to* BLAISE]: You again?... Are you still—

BLAISE: But you called me in, monsieur... Or somebody...

GISELE [*coming back toward the bed*]: No! This is too much! [*Shaking* TOURNEL *by the shoulders, shouting hysterically.*] Get him out of here! [*Right by the bed, without realizing that she is standing on the rotating platform.*] Get him out!

TOURNEL ⎱ [*together*]: ⎰ Of course...
GISELE [*stamping her foot*] ⎰ ⎱ Now!... This minute!

TOURNEL [*to* BLAISE]: You!... Back where you came from!

[*He presses the stage right button.*]

GISELE [*to* BLAISE, *furious*]: Sneaking into people's bedrooms that way!... You must be... [*Suddenly feeling herself moving as the wall begins to pivot.*] Ah! What...?

TOURNEL [*grabbing her as she comes by*]: Oh là là!

GISELE [*clinging to him*]: My God!

TOURNEL ⎱ [*facing the audience, together*]: ⎰ There, there...
GISELE ⎰ ⎱ My God! I never...

[*The other bed turns into view, bringing with it a crouching* EDOUARD, *still in his coat, startled and stammering.*]

EDOUARD: Wh... Wh... What...? Who...? [*As the bed comes to a stop.*] H... H... How...? [*Looking up and recognizing the others with a scream.*] Aaaah!

GISELE and TOURNEL [*together, turning and recognizing him, jumping back in a single bound*]: Edouard!

[*They look at each other for a moment in consternation, then make a mad dash for the hall door, but not before* TOURNEL *scurries to whisk up his coat from the little table, though forgetting his hat.*]

EDOUARD [*shouting after them*]: Ex... Excuse me! It's the bed... [*As they exit.*] It... It moved!

GISELE [*running across the hall*] ⎱ [*together*]: ⎰ It... It can't be him!... He talks!
TOURNEL [*on her heels*] ⎰ ⎱ He talks! He talks! It can't be him!

EDOUARD [*jumping down from the bed, flabbergasted*]: It... It...

GISELE [*up right, stopping*] ⎫   ⎧ I've had enough!
　　　　　　　　　　　　　 ⎬ [*together*]:   ⎨
EDOUARD　　　　　　　　 ⎭   ⎩ It turned around!

GISELE [*running to the staircase*]: I'm leaving!

TOURNEL: I should say!

[*They both disappear down the stairs.*]

EDOUARD [*moving right*]: And those two... Here?... Gisèle and... [*Exiting into the hall.*] If they saw me... How can I ever... Darn! That's a pretty pickle! [*He closes the door behind him, looking around.*] And Antoinette...? [*Looking right, at the door to* POPOFF's *room, remembering where she ran.*] Ah! In there... What's she doing?... [*Striding purposefully to the door and pushing it open, at the threshold.*] Antoinette?...

ANTOINETTE'S VOICE [*as he enters*]: Oh!

EDOUARD'S VOICE: Poodles! What are you—

[*Suddenly one can hear, from the direction of* POPOFF's *room, the sounds of a violent brouhaha, as physical as it is vociferous—breaking glass, furniture thrown over, etc.—peppered with appropriate cries, oaths and exclamations, shouted by* EDOUARD, ANTOINETTE, *and* POPOFF, *among them a number in Russian. The noise continues as* GISELE *appears, running frantically up the stairs, followed by* TOURNEL.]

TOURNEL ⎫   ⎧ Your butler, Gisèle...
　　　　 ⎬ [*together*]:   ⎨
GISELE　 ⎭   ⎩ My God! Now Etienne!

TOURNEL: What's your butler doing down there?

GISELE: How should I—

TOURNEL: Good God!

[*They both make a dash for the corridor, and run off. In the meantime the noise offstage has grown louder and more violent. All of a sudden the door to* POPOFF's *room flies open and* EDOUARD *comes hurtling onstage, as if catapulted out, with an evidently angry* POPOFF *on his tail.*]

POPOFF [*shouting*]: Out! Out!... You out, ya skazál!... You out!

EDOUARD [*recovering his equilibrium*]: But monsieur—

POPOFF: Ach! Vwí nyeh panyeemáyetyeh?... Chórt poberí!

[*He gives him a sharp slap in the face.*]

EDOUARD: Oh! [POPOFF *slaps him again, this time causing* EDOUARD *to spit his prosthetic palate onto the floor.*] Ptu!... [*Speaking in the same inarticulate manner as before.*] My palate!... I've dropped my palate!

[*He tries to bend down to pick it up.*]

POPOFF [*lifting him up bodily and hauling him off, up left, toward the unseen bedroom*]: Nyet! Nyet!... You go!

EDOUARD [*ineffectually trying to resist*]: My palate!

POPOFF [*opening the door and hurling him out*]: You go!

EDOUARD [*as he disappears into the room*]: I want my palate!

POPOFF: Da, da!... Éta vsyó, moy dro'og! [*Crossing right, back to his room, mumbling angrily, as* ETIENNE *is seen coming up the stairs.*] Shto do'omayet, étut... étut... [*Opening the door, victoriously, addressing the unseen* ANTOINETTE.] Ha! Now you, now me, dyévooshka!

[*He exits into the room. Scarcely has he shut the door behind him, than* ETIENNE, *in hat and coat, arrives at the landing and comes down center, looking around, obviously for someone in authority.*]

ETIENNE: Where is everybody? What kind of hotel... [*He suddenly notices the silver prosthesis on the floor and gives it a little push with his foot just as* BABETTE *enters from the corridor, up right.*] Ooh!... [*Bending down and picking it up.*] Silver!... [*Screwing up his face.*] Ugh! All wet...

BABETTE: Monsieur? Was there something—

ETIENNE: Ah! Mademoiselle... [*She comes down center, joining him.*] See what I just found?

BABETTE		Ooh!
	[*together*]:	
ETIENNE		Here on the floor...

BABETTE: Fancy...

ETIENNE: Silver... Whatever it is...

[*He hands it to her. At the same time* EDOUARD, *still in his coat, comes out of the room, back bowed and head down, eyes on the floor, looking for his prosthesis.*]

BABETTE: Like some kind of old jewelry... See?

[*She holds it up to her bosom like a brooch, posing for an admiring* ETIENNE.]

EDOUARD [*to himself*]: It must be here somewhere...

[*Looking here and there, still bent over, he arrives, unnoticed, almost beside* ETIENNE, *whose back is turned to him.*]

ETIENNE [*to* BABETTE]: Very pretty!

[EDOUARD *looks up suddenly and recognizes him. Appalled, he turns on his heel without straightening up and, knees bent, occupying as little space as possible, takes a couple of giant steps back to the room he just left.*]

EDOUARD [*as he disappears inside, to himself*]: No! Etienne too?

BABETTE [*to* ETIENNE, *neither of whom have noticed the preceding*]: One of the lady guests must have dropped it. I'll leave it in the office.

[*She begins to move up toward the stairs, stopping as* ETIENNE *calls to her.*]

ETIENNE: Wait...

BABETTE: Monsieur?

ETIENNE: A lady didn't come for Monsieur Chandebise's room, by any chance?

BABETTE: Yes, as a matter of fact... [*Aside.*] Monsieur Ah-oo-ee-ah-ah!

ETIENNE: Ah! Where is she?

BABETTE: Oh, monsieur!... I'm not allowed—

ETIENNE: Come, come! I've got to warn her! It's life or death! Her husband is after her...

BABETTE: Oh!

ETIENNE: And he wants to kill her!

BABETTE: My God!... I... Well... [*Pointing right, to* POPOFF's *room.*] I saw her go in there...

ETIENNE [*crossing in front of her and going to the door*]: Good!

[*He knocks. At the same time* BABETTE *moves back up toward the stairs.*]

POPOFF'S VOICE: Da? Da?... In, pazhálysta!... In!

ETIENNE [*exiting into the room*]: Excuse me, monsieur, but—

POPOFF'S VOICE		Nu?
	[*together*]:	
ANTOINETTE'S VOICE [*screaming*]		Etienne!

ETIENNE'S VOICE: Antoinette!

POPOFF'S VOICE: Shto?

[*Suddenly, as before, one can hear offstage the sounds of another set-to, no less vocal or violent than the first. The noise brings* BABETTE *back downstage just as* ANTOINETTE—*hat in hand, hair tousled, and without the blouse that she has apparently not had time to put on—comes dashing out, almost bumping into her.*]

ANTOINETTE [*streaking to the staircase*]: Help! Help!...

[*She runs downstairs, two steps at a time. A second later* ETIENNE *comes flying out in hot pursuit, with* POPOFF *right on his tail, adjusting his clothes.*]

ETIENNE: Stop!... [*To* BABETTE.] Stop her!

POPOFF [*seizing him by the arm, and turning him violently around and up against the stage right wall*]: I kill! I kill!

[*He pounds* ETIENNE *against the wall several times, each time repeating his "I kill!", and each time with a groan from* ETIENNE *as well as a grimace and twinge from the startled* BABETTE, *still by the staircase.*]

ETIENNE [*struggling*]: Let me—

POPOFF [*pounding*]: I kill! I kill!

ETIENNE: She's my wife, I tell you!

POPOFF [*with one final shove*]: Da!... Pfui! [*Letting go.*] Now you go!

[*He brushes his hands together, up and down, and exits into his room.*]

ETIENNE: Damn! [*Dusting himself off, trying to recover his aplomb.*] Of all the... [*To* BABETTE.] She cheats on *me*, and I'm the one who... [*Rubbing his bruises.*] Oh!...

BABETTE [*approaching him*]: You didn't tell me *you* were the husband!

ETIENNE: If you think I knew!...

[*In the meantime,* LOCHE *has come down from upstairs, lugging his empty hod.*]

BABETTE [*moving back toward the staircase*]: Oh well...

ETIENNE: On me... A butler!... The little witch! [*As* BABETTE *and* LOCHE *stop by the stairs to exchange a pleasantry.*] Well, cheat on me, will she? [*He strides up to the staircase, about to go down, but stops short at the sight of* LOCHE, *astonished, taking him for* CHANDEBISE.] Oh! Monsieur... What are you...

LOCHE [*with a salute*]: Hmm?

ETIENNE: I mean... What is monsieur doing...? [*Pointing to the hod.*] And with that?...

LOCHE: This?... So? How else...

ETIENNE: But I thought monsieur wanted me to... [*Forgetting his shock, and looking for sympathy.*] Ah! Monsieur... Monsieur... My wife is cheating on me, monsieur!

LOCHE [*with a stupid little laugh*]: Oh?

ETIENNE: Yes!... [*Pointing to* POPOFF'*s room.*] And with some foreigner!

LOCHE: Ah... The general...

ETIENNE: Whoever... [*Returning to his concern.*] But since monsieur is here himself... I mean, since he doesn't need me... I'd like to go catch her and teach her a lesson. If monsieur doesn't mind...

LOCHE: Why not?

[*He dismisses him with his little salute.*]

ETIENNE: Thank you, monsieur!... [*Dashing downstairs, in pursuit.*] Cheat on a butler, will she!

[*He disappears down the stairs.*]

LOCHE [*to* BABETTE, *tapping his temple*]: They're all cuckoo today!

ETIENNE'S VOICE [*coming from downstairs*] ⎱ [*together*]: ⎰ Sorry!... Sorry!

LUCIENNE'S VOICE [*likewise*] ⎰   ⎱ Please! Watch your step!

LOCHE [*to* BABETTE, *as the bell panel in the corridor lights up and rings*]: You think they've been drinking?

BABETTE [*moving toward the corridor, looking up and pointing at the panel, to* LOCHE]: They want you in there...

LOCHE: Ah... [*Crossing right.*] I'm coming... I'm coming...

[*He lumbers off into the corridor, giving his reflexive little salutes, as* LUCIENNE *comes up the stairs, looking back over her shoulder.*]

LUCIENNE [*surprised, to herself*]: Why... That was Gisèle's butler... I'm sure it was...

BABETTE [*up right, to* LUCIENNE]: Was madame looking for someone?

LUCIENNE [*noticing her, approaching right*]: Ah, mademoiselle... That... That person, just now... The one who almost knocked me over... Wasn't that Monsieur Chandebise's butler?

BABETTE: Could be, madame... That's the name he asked for... All I know is, it's a crazy story! He comes in here and says he has to warn some lady... Says her husband is after her... That he wants to kill her!... And then, when he sees her... "Bam!" Turns out that she's the wife and he's the husband! Go figure it out!

LUCIENNE: Yes, well... Some people... [*Changing the subject.*] Tell me... Where is the room reserved for Monsieur Chandebise?

BABETTE: Monsieur Chande... [*Hesitating.*] Madame is someone, isn't she?

LUCIENNE: I beg your pardon?

BABETTE: I mean, he said: "If someone comes and asks for Monsieur Chandebise's room..." [*Pointing left, to the visible bedroom.*] "put them in there..." [*With a shrug.*] Number five, madame...

[*She turns and goes up the stairs.*]

LUCIENNE: Fine... Thank you... [*Going over to the door indicated and knocking discreetly a couple of times; then, with her left ear to the door, in a whisper*]: Gisèle... Gisèle...

[*At that moment* EDOUARD *enters quietly from the unseen bedroom, back bowed and eyes on the ground, as before, apparently looking for his prosthesis.*]

EDOUARD [*to himself, still inarticulate*]: It's got to be here somewhere...

[*He looks here and there in an arc, coming round behind* LUCIENNE, *as unaware of her presence as she is of his.*]

LUCIENNE [*getting no response, to herself*]: That's strange...

[*As she knocks again,* EDOUARD *looks up, still without her noticing him. He recognizes her and stands thunderstruck for an instant, silently mouthing "Madame de Histangua," then turns and makes for the stairs as* LUCIENNE *opens the door and goes into the room.*]

EDOUARD [*dashing downstairs in muted panic*]: Let me out of here!

LUCIENNE: Gisèle?... [*Looking around, surprised.*] I'm sure... [*Noticing* TOURNEL's *hat on the little table, nodding.*] Hmm! [*Looking at her watch.*] I'm sure she said: "I'll catch him between five and five fifteen... You come at five thirty and that will be that!" [*Going left, to the bathroom, looking inside.*] Gisèle?...

[*As she continues looking around, with appropriate muttered expressions of surprise,* EDOUARD *comes bolting back up the stairs, reaching all the way to the footlights in panic.*]

EDOUARD [*without stopping*]: My uncle!... Again!

[*He continues in his trajectory, turning upstage and exiting, terrified, back into the unseen bedroom, up left.*]

LUCIENNE [*coming out into the hall, downstage*]: Strange!... Well, I'm certainly not going to wait...

[*As she turns to go back toward the staircase,* CHANDEBISE *comes hurrying up the stairs, dressed as in the first act, and wearing a hat and coat.*]

CHANDEBISE [*stopping at the landing, looking around, and noticing* LUCIENNE]: Ah! There you are!

LUCIENNE: Monsieur Chandebise!

CHANDEBISE [*grasping her by the hand and coming down center*]: Thank heaven I'm not too late!

LUCIENNE: What is it? What's the—

CHANDEBISE [*cutting her off*]: Did Etienne find you? My butler... Did you see him?

LUCIENNE: Yes... [*About to explain.*] That is... Why?

CHANDEBISE: To warn you... I sent him... I... I couldn't come myself... [*Almost babbling.*] On account of the banquet... But... But the banquet is tomorrow, not tonight... So... I got here as fast as I could!

LUCIENNE [*hardly understanding a word*]: To warn me? About what?

CHANDEBISE [*changing his tone*]: Ah! Poor child!... Why didn't you tell me?

LUCIENNE: Tell you...?

CHANDEBISE: That you loved me!

LUCIENNE [*stepping back, with a start*]: What?

CHANDEBISE [*with a gesture, as if to say: "No use denying it!"*]: I know! I know!... But why bother with a letter? You could have just told me...

LUCIENNE: A letter?

CHANDEBISE: And then, not even to sign it...

LUCIENNE [*suddenly understanding, slapping the heel of her palm to her forehead*]: Oh, good heavens! [*To* CHANDEBISE.] But... But what makes you think that I... that I—

CHANDEBISE [*interrupting*]: Because I accidentally showed it to your husband!

LUCIENNE [*jumping back*]: You what?

CHANDEBISE: And he recognized your writing...

LUCIENNE: He... He...

CHANDEBISE: And he's going to kill you!

LUCIENNE: Ay, Dios!... Where is he?

CHANDEBISE: Right behind me...

LUCIENNE: Right be... [*Terrified.*] And you just stand there? [*Taking to her heels.*] Good Lord!

[*She makes a beeline for the staircase and bolts downstairs, with* CHANDEBISE *right behind.*]

CHANDEBISE: Wait! Not that way!...

[*As they disappear down the stairs,* NANA *enters from the corridor, up right.*]

NANA [*at the staircase, calling*]: Babette!... Babette!... [*Standing on the landing in such a way as to obstruct passage up or down the stairs.*] Where is that stupid...

[*Suddenly* CHANDEBISE *appears running back up the stairs, in obvious panic, with* LUCIENNE *only a step behind, no less so.*]

CHANDEBISE ⎫
⎬ [*together*]:
LUCIENNE ⎭

⎰ I told you! Not that way!...
⎱ My husband! Dios mío!

CHANDEBISE: Every man for himself!

NANA: What on—

CHANDEBISE [*bumping into her and pivoting her around*]: Out of my way!

NANA [*bumping into* LUCIENNE]: Who—

LUCIENNE [*trying to get by her, pivoting her around in the other direction*]: Please!

[*She dashes left into the visible bedroom, taking refuge in the bathroom. Meanwhile,* CHANDEBISE *bolts off right, into* POPOFF'*s room.*]

NANA [*agog, not knowing where to look first*]: Madame... Monsieur...

[*At the same moment,* GISELE, *her face veiled, still in coat and hat, enters quickly from the corridor, up right, with* TOURNEL *right behind, hatless but wearing his coat, both making for the stairs with the obvious intention of leaving.*]

GISELE [*to* TOURNEL, *continuing a remark begun offstage*]: ...and the sooner the better, my friend! [*To* NANA, *almost bumping into her.*] Let me by!

[*She pushes her out of the way, pivoting her around as* CHANDEBISE *had done a moment before.*]

NANA: Ah!

TOURNEL [*to* GISELE]: Not another minute! [*To a disoriented* NANA, *pivoting her in the other direction*]: Move, damn it!

[*They both rush headlong down the stairs.*]

NANA [*staggering*]: What...? Who...?

[*Just as* GISELE *and* TOURNEL *disappear from view,* HOMENIDES *can be heard shouting offstage, apparently downstairs.*]

HOMENIDES'S VOICE: So! Where he ees, thees eslot?... Where? Where?... An thees lover!

GISELE'S VOICE ⎫
⎬ [*together*]:
TOURNEL'S VOICE ⎭

⎰ Ayyy!
⎱ Good God!

HOMENIDES'S VOICE [*as he obviously catches sight of them*]: Ho! You!... I keell!...

NANA [*peering down the stairs as* GISELE *and* TOURNEL *come streaking back up*]: What...?

HOMENIDES'S VOICE: I shoot!... I estrangle!...

GISELE: Him!... Histangua!... [*Bumping into* NANA, *pivoting as before.*] Get away! Get—

TOURNEL [*on her heels, to* NANA, *turning her in the other direction*]: You again?

[*They both bolt right, disappearing into the corridor. As* NANA, *panting, staggers dizzily by the staircase,* HOMENIDES *comes erupting up the stairs*

like a madman, brandishing his revolver.]
HOMENIDES: Toenail!... Toenail!... Weeth señora who hide face...
NANA [*terrified*]: Ayyy!
HOMENIDES [*at the landing*]: Ees wife! [*About to make for the corridor.*]
Feelthy eslot!
NANA [*trying to head him off*]: Monsieur! Where do you think you're—
HOMENIDES [*pivoting her around even more violently than the others*]: Ho ho! I
keell! I keell then dead!... [*As he runs right, into the corridor.*] Heen!
Her!... Los dos!
NANA [*reeling*]: Ah... [*Shouting.*] Mousquetard!... Help! Help!... Brutus!...
[MOUSQUETARD *comes running down the stairs, followed by* BABETTE.]
MOUSQUETARD [*to* NANA, *on her left*]: What is it? What's the—
NANA [*panting*]: Ah... He's crazy... Mad!... He... He wants to kill everyone...
MOUSQUETARD [*with a start*]: He?... Who?
NANA [*pointing weakly toward the corridor*]: Him... [*She collapses in a heap, as*
BABETTE, *on her right, rushes to catch her.*] Ah... Ah...
BABETTE [*about to buckle under her weight, calling to* MOUSQUETARD]:
Monsieur!
MOUSQUETARD: Hold on! Don't let her... [*Grabbing her himself and propping
her up.*] There!... That's it! [*To* BABETTE, *pointing up right to the one visible
door in the corridor.*] Here... Bring her in there... [*Tugging* NANA *up right.*]
And get her some smelling salts!...
BABETTE [*as the sounds of a quarrel, offstage, begin to issue forth, ostensibly
from* POPOFF'*s room*]: Yes, monsieur.
[MOUSQUETARD *drags* NANA *in, accompanied by* BABETTE, *leaving the stage
empty for a few seconds. A moment later he comes back out and shuts the
door behind him. All the while, the noise from* POPOFF'*s room grows in
volume and intensity, with* POPOFF *shouting a variety of English and
Russian expletives, and* CHANDEBISE *countering appropriately.*]
POPOFF'S VOICE: Who you? Who you?... Why you here?... Pachemú?... Out!
Out!
CHANDEBISE'S VOICE [*above* POPOFF'*s din*]: But I can't, I tell you! There's a
lunatic out there!
MOUSQUETARD [*coming downstage at the noise, looking right*]: Now what?
[*The door to* POPOFF'*s room opens suddenly and both he and* CHANDEBISE
*come hurtling out, the latter clinging desperately to the door jamb as the
former, clutching him around the waist from behind, tries to pull him
away.*]

POPOFF [*tugging*] ⎫   ⎧ Shto vwí? Shto!... You away! You away!
              ⎬ [*together*]: ⎨
CHANDEBISE [*resisting*] ⎭   ⎩ Let me... Let me go! Let me...

MOUSQUETARD [*approaching*]: Eh! You two!
[*At that moment* POPOFF *succeeds in wrenching* CHANDEBISE *free and hurls
him pirouetting to his left, where he bumps bodily into* MOUSQUETARD. *The
latter, grabbing him, continues his trajectory and flings him, reeling,
against the bench, downstage, where he comes to an abrupt and
involuntary stop.*]
CHANDEBISE [*falling in a heap onto the bench, to* MOUSQUETARD, *as* POPOFF,
grumbling to himself, exits into his room]: What do you think you're—
MOUSQUETARD [*center, jumping back, surprised and angry, as he thinks he*

recognizes him]: Loche! You!...

CHANDEBISE [*getting up, going over and planting himself in front of him, ready for a confrontation*]: I beg your pardon! Just what do you think—

MOUSQUETARD [*grabbing his left arm with his left hand and giving him a swift kick in the backside with each of the following invectives, gradually turning him counterclockwise*]: Damn fool!

CHANDEBISE [*with a little jump at each kick*]: What?

MOUSQUETARD [*kicking*]: Pig!

CHANDEBISE: But...

MOUSQUETARD: Swine!

CHANDEBISE: But... But...

MOUSQUETARD: Damn horse's ass!

[*By now, as a result of the kicks,* CHANDEBISE *has circled around him and is back in his original spot.*]

CHANDEBISE [*breaking free*]: Listen, you!... Just what do you think—

MOUSQUETARD [*assuming a threatening stance*]: Oh?

CHANDEBISE [*edging right*]: I'm Victor-Emmanuel Chandebise, damn it!... Of the Requiem Life Insurance Company!

MOUSQUETARD [*far right*]: Oh yes! Of course you are!... And I'm Napoleon! Damn drunkard! [*To himself.*] Drunk out of his bloody mind! Damn Loche!

CHANDEBISE [*striding up to him, giving him a slap across the face*]: Monsieur!

MOUSQUETARD: Oh!

CHANDEBISE [*with all the dignity and aplomb he can muster*]: My seconds will visit you in the morning, my friend!

[*He gives him a crisp military salute, very different from the kind* LOCHE *has been offering throughout.*]

MOUSQUETARD [*furious, grabbing him by the left arm as before*]: Well now!... [*Kicking him again with each exclamation, pivoting him counterclockwise.*] Take that for your bloody seconds!...

CHANDEBISE [*jumping, as before*]: Oh!

MOUSQUETARD: And that for your bloody salute!

CHANDEBISE [*likewise*]: Oh!

MOUSQUETARD: And that for your bloody Chandebise!

CHANDEBISE [*likewise*]: Oh!

MOUSQUETARD: And that!... And that!... And that!...

[CHANDEBISE, *finally arrives again back at his original position.*]

CHANDEBISE [*pulling away*]: Damnation! [*Confronting* MOUSQUETARD, *nose to nose, with as much authority as possible under the circumstances*]: Will you please tell me—

MOUSQUETARD [*grabbing him by the collar of his outercoat*]: And what's all this? Not bad enough he's drunk!...

[*He tries to pull the coat off.*]

CHANDEBISE [*resisting*] ⎫ [*together*]: ⎧ What? What are you—

MOUSQUETARD [*pulling*] ⎭ ⎩ What kind of joke...

[*He succeeds in pulling it off his back.*]

CHANDEBISE: But—

MOUSQUETARD [*pulling off* CHANDEBISE'*s hat*]: And this too, damn it!

[*He comes down right and hangs the hat and coat on the coatrack by the console, removing the cap and livery jacket hanging on it.*]

CHANDEBISE: Good God! The man is a lunatic!

MOUSQUETARD [*returning to* CHANDEBISE *with the servant's garb, flinging the cap in his face*]: Now put this on!

CHANDEBISE: But—

[*As he tries to resist,* MOUSQUETARD *forces the cap onto his head.*]

MOUSQUETARD: Put it on, I said!... [*Pulling it down above his ears, giving him a distinctly moronic appearance; then, slapping him on the crown.*] There, damn it!

CHANDEBISE: Ayyy!

MOUSQUETARD [*thrusting the jacket at him, sharply*]: Now this!

CHANDEBISE [*trying to resist*]: No!... I... [*With a trace of a whimper.*] I don't want to... I don't—

MOUSQUETARD [*taking his arms and forcing them into the sleeves*]: You what?... Don't you tell *me* you don't want to, my friend!

CHANDEBISE [*frightened, hunching his shoulders in submission*]: I do... I want to...

MOUSQUETARD: Now get out of here! [*Pointing to the staircase.*] Up to your room and sleep it off! You hear me?

CHANDEBISE [*rushing to comply*]: I'm going... I'm... [*At the stairs, under his breath, as* MOUSQUETARD *gives him an obviously sarcastic salute*]: Damn lunatic!

MOUSQUETARD: What? Did I hear you... [*Bolting up to the staircase, as if to chase him.*] Haven't had enough?... Want more, maybe?

CHANDEBISE [*running up the stairs*]: No, no!... I'm going!

MOUSQUETARD [*following him up the first few steps, shaking his fist*]: Get your drunken ass out of here! And no backtalk, understand?

[CHANDEBISE *stumbles in his haste, catches himself, and disappears up the rest of the stairs.*][1]

MOUSQUETARD [*coming down to the landing*]: Goddamn gin! [*Coming center.*] No more for that lush, goddammit!

[*Suddenly* BABETTE *comes running out of the room in the corridor, up right, leaving the door open.* NANA *can be heard offstage uttering spasmodic little sighs and groans—"Haaa... Hooo...", or the like—which continue during the following exchange until the door is closed.*]

BABETTE [*running down to* MOUSQUETARD]: Monsieur! Monsieur!...

MOUSQUETARD: Hmm?

BABETTE [*pointing up left*]: It's madame's nerves, monsieur!... She's having an attack!

MOUSQUETARD [*impatient*]: That's nice! [*To* BABETTE.] Listen... Go upstairs to number ten and get the sergeant...

BABETTE: Who?

MOUSQUETARD: The doctor... Finache... Ask him to come down and have a look.

BABETTE: Yes, monsieur...

[*She runs up the stairs.*]

---

[1] As with the instructions for the working of the revolving bed, Feydeau goes to great lengths to describe in detail how the actor who plays the dual role must effect his quick change, thanks to a specially constructed costume and aided by backstage acolytes; details which, as before, need not be reproduced [Translator's note].

MOUSQUETARD: Of all damn times!... [*Going upstage to the door.*] Always something... [*Going into the room, addressing the unseen* NANA *with a sudden change of tone.*] What's the matter, pumpkin? Not feeling well...? [*He shuts the door behind him. A moment later* LOCHE *enters from the corridor, up right, carrying a rather cumbersome package, untying his long apron and managing to remove it without putting down the package as he comes down center.*]

LOCHE: There!... Now to bring this to the station... [*Coming down right, to the coatrack, hanging up the apron and expecting to find his cap and livery jacket.*] Ha!... That's funny... [*Looking around on the floor.*] Who do you suppose...? Some nerve!... [*Taking* CHANDEBISE's *hat and coat with his free hand.*] Well, at least they left me theirs, whoever... [*Putting on the hat.*] Perfect!... [*Struggling to put on the coat over his vest, without thinking to put down the package.*] Why not?... I'll give them back theirs when they give me back mine! [*As he moves upstage to leave, the bell panel rings and lights up.*] Ah... What do they want now?

[*As he exits into the corridor,* BABETTE *appears coming down the stairs followed by* FINACHE.]

BABETTE: This way...

FINACHE [*adjusting his clothes, which he has obviously just put on in haste, grumbling*]: If they think I come here to see patients... [*To* BABETTE.] What's her trouble?

BABETTE: Just a little spill, monsieur...

FINACHE: Oh? Where did she fall? Not on her head, I hope...

BABETTE [*as they reach the landing*]: Fall?... Who said she fell? She had a spill, I said... One of her nervous spills... She gets them all the time.

FINACHE: Aha... [*Under his breath.*] Spill... Spell... [*To* BABETTE.] And that's what you called me down here for? A case of nerves?

BABETTE: Well, as long as monsieur took the trouble to get dressed...

[*They cross to the room up right and she opens the door, amid* NANA's *offstage groans. No sooner have they exited than* CHANDEBISE *appears at the top of the stairs, still in* LOCHE's *cap and jacket, cautiously peering about to see if* MOUSQUETARD *is anywhere around.*]

CHANDEBISE [*muttering to himself*]: Is he gone, I hope?... Damn maniac!... [*Risking a few steps down the stairs.*] Good God! Did you ever...? [*Risking a few more.*] If that's how they treat all their guests... [*Coming down to the landing.*] It's a wonder they're still in business! [*Still circumspect, he makes his way down right, over to the coatrack, looking for his own hat and coat.*] What?... Now that's a good one! [*Looking around on the floor.*] Where in blazes...?

[*As he continues, bent over, looking on the floor, behind the console, etc.* GISELE *comes bolting down the stairs with* TOURNEL *close behind, both clearly the worse for having been chased upstairs, throughout the upper stories, hither and yon.*]

GISELE: I... I think... I think we've managed to shake him.

TOURNEL: Not for long!

GISELE: Quick! Outside... A cab...

TOURNEL [*noticing* CHANDEBISE, *back turned, still bent over searching*]: Ah... The porter... Maybe he can—

GISELE: I hope... [*Rushing down right, to* CHANDEBISE.] Loche!... A cab! And hurry!

CHANDEBISE [*still bent over, but turning his head in her direction*]: What?

TOURNEL [*hurrying over, to* CHANDEBISE]: A cab!

CHANDEBISE [*recognizing* GISELE, *straightening up with a start*]: My... Gisèle! What—

[*The two following "What?"s come in rapid-fire succession.*]

TOURNEL: What?

GISELE: What?... [*She stands petrified for a brief moment, agape, then screams.*] My God! It *was* him!... It was! [*Running upstage to the staircase.*] It was!

[*She disappears down the stairs in a flash.*]

CHANDEBISE: And Tournel!... With my wife!

TOURNEL [*shaking like a leaf*]: It *was* him! [*To* CHANDEBISE.] It *was* you!

CHANDEBISE [*lunging at him, his hands about his throat, shaking him*]: What are you... [*Shaking.*] What are you doing here... [*Shaking.*] with my wife?

[*He gives him a sharp thrust counterclockwise, sending him reeling, down left.*]

TOURNEL [*half-strangled*] ⎱ [*together*]: ⎰ But... But Chandebise...

CHANDEBISE ⎰   ⎱ What? What?

TOURNEL: We just told you! [*Pointing to the door to the visible bedroom.*] In there!

CHANDEBISE [*furious, crossing to him, at the top of his lungs*]: Told me? [*Pushing him against the bench.*] Told me what?

TOURNEL [*quaking*]: But—

CHANDEBISE: Where? [*Shaking him.*] Answer me!

TOURNEL: But... But...

CHANDEBISE: Answer me, damn you!

[*The fracas brings* MOUSQUETARD *storming out of the room, up right. He sees the altercation and strides purposefully down left to put an end to it.*]

MOUSQUETARD: Listen, you two... [*Grabbing* CHANDEBISE, *whose back is still turned, by the right arm and flinging him aside.*] How long do you... [*Suddenly recognizing him, as* TOURNEL, *taking advantage of the confusion, charges off down the stairs.*] Goddammit, Loche! Again?

CHANDEBISE: God! Him!... The maniac!

MOUSQUETARD: You... You idiot!

[*As before, he gives him a series of sharp little kicks in the behind, accompanying each with an insult, and each one sending* CHANDEBISE *a foot off the ground.*]

CHANDEBISE: Oh!

MOUSQUETARD: You swine!

CHANDEBISE: Oooh!

MOUSQUETARD: You swill!

CHANDEBISE: Ayyy!

MOUSQUETARD: You scum!

CHANDEBISE: Please!...

MOUSQUETARD: Enough?

CHANDEBISE [*weakly*]: Yes...

MOUSQUETARD [*still punctuating each exclamation with a kick*]: Want more?...

More?... More?...

CHANDEBISE [*managing to pull away*]: No, no!... Please!... [*Making a dash, as best he can, for the staircase.*] Help! Help!... He's... He's crazy!

MOUSQUETARD [*chasing him up the stairs*]: Crazy? I'll show you who's crazy, you drunken bastard!... When I get through with you, you'll wish you never heard the word "gin"!

[*His last few words are heard from offstage, as he gallops after CHANDEBISE, who, falling on all fours, clambers desperately up the last few steps. Just as they disappear, POPOFF, attracted by the din and obviously out of patience, comes storming out of his room, leaving the door open.*]

POPOFF [*gesticulating*]: Bózheh moy!... Bózheh!... Pachemú...? [*Going to the staircase, looking up the stairs.*] Shto...? Shto éta?... [*Hands on hips.*] Hoo ha!... [*Making a quick decision.*] Da!... I go complain!... Such big nose! Why all day such big nose!

[*He disappears down the stairs, muttering as he goes. The moment he is out of sight, both the door to the unseen bedroom and the bathroom door in the visible bedroom open. EDOUARD pokes his head cautiously out of the former at the same moment that LUCIENNE comes out of the latter, crossing right, to the hall door, and pressing her ear against it, listening.*]

EDOUARD ⎫ [*together*]: ⎰ Ah...
LUCIENNE ⎭   ⎱ He must be gone...

EDOUARD: The coast is clear... [*Coming out into the hall.*] Now or never... [*Remembering his lost prosthesis, he decides to take one last look on the floor, coming round to his left in an arc just as LUCIENNE exits circumspectly into the hall, leaving the door open.*] It must be here somewhere... [*Bumping into her.*] Ah! [*Recognizing her, covering his face with his hands, aside.*] Her too?

[*He turns and is about to run off.*]

LUCIENNE [*recognizing him despite his efforts*]: Monsieur!... [*Grasping him by the arm, frantically.*] Don't go!

EDOUARD [*babbling self-defensively*]: Who... Who...

LUCIENNE: Please, Monsieur Edouard! Don't leave me!

EDOUARD [*realizing that all pretense is useless*] ⎫ [*together*]: ⎰ Ah...
LUCIENNE ⎭   ⎱ Please!... I beg you!

EDOUARD: Madame...?

LUCIENNE: Don Carlos... My husband, monsieur... He's after me... With a gun!...

EDOUARD: What?

LUCIENNE: He wants to kill me!... He wants to kill everyone!

EDOUARD: My goodness!

LUCIENNE: Please! Don't leave me!

EDOUARD [*with panache*]: Certainly not!

HOMENIDES'S VOICE [*coming from upstairs*]: So! Where they are?

LUCIENNE [*clutching EDOUARD's arm, casting a horrified glance toward the upper floor*]: It's him!

HOMENIDES'S VOICE: I look all over...

EDOUARD: Him? [*Losing his gallant resolve.*] Come on!...

[*He pulls her upstage, intent on running down the stairs, but they bump into* POPOFF, *who is just coming up.* *Terrified, they beat a retreat;* EDOUARD, *dashing into the visible bedroom, slamming the door and leaning against it with his shoulder;* LUCIENNE, *rushing into* POPOFF's *room.* POPOFF, *meanwhile, standing at the landing, has watched their flight. Suddenly, seeing* LUCIENNE *run into his room, his attitude changes.*]

POPOFF [*jubilant*]: Nu?

HOMENIDES'S VOICE: Up, down... Arriba, abajo...

POPOFF [*with a lubricious leer*]: Prekrásnaya dyévooshka... Prekrásnaya!... [*Striding down right, rubbing his hands.*] Da!

[*He exits into his room just as* HOMENIDES *comes hurtling down the stairs.*]

HOMENIDES [*bounding onto the landing, at the top of his lungs*]: So! Where they are, eh?... For to keell! Heen! Her!... [*Coming center.*] For to slowtair! Sí, sí!... [*Seeing nobody.*] Caramba! Where eet ees, thees roon of Mossié Chandépisse?... Dónde?... Where? Where?

[*He dashes back upstage and continues down the stairs just as* LOCHE *comes loping in, up right, still carrying the package.*]

LOCHE [*coming down right*]: What's all the noise?

[*The door to* POPOFF's *room flies open and* LUCIENNE, *locked in the former's embrace, struggles out of the room.*]

LUCIENNE [*to* POPOFF]: Take your hands... Take them off of me, I said! [*Wrenching free.*] How dare you! You... You lecher!

[*She gives him a healthy slap across the face.*]

POPOFF: Shto?... Ach! [*Cursing angrily.*] Frantsóoskaya sóoka! Frantsóoskaya sóoka!

[*He turns in highest dudgeon and exits to his room, slamming the door.*]

LOCHE [*with his imbecilic little laugh, to* LUCIENNE]: Touché, madame!

LUCIENNE [*noticing him*]: Ah! [*Running down right to join him.*] Monsieur Chandebise! Thank heaven you're here!

LOCHE: Hmm?... You too?

LUCIENNE [*throwing her arms around him for protection*]: You're a godsend!

LOCHE: Me?

LUCIENNE [*almost collapsing into his arms*]: Please! Save me!... Hide me!...

LOCHE: But I'm not—

LUCIENNE: My husband... He's going to kill me! [LOCHE *gives a start.*] Please! Hide me!... Don't let him find me!

LOCHE [*holding her up, not without difficulty, considering her weight and his package, and virtually dragging her with one arm around her waist, with little tugs, up to the staircase*]: This way, madame... Come... Down the stairs and out the door...

[*When they reach the stairs they make their way awkwardly down the first few steps, with* LOCHE *still trying to hold her up and guide her. No sooner do their heads disappear from view, than* HOMENIDES, *apparently spying* LUCIENNE *from downstairs, can be heard vociferating.*]

HOMENIDES'S VOICE: Ho ho! Ees her!... Ay, carajo!... You!... Woman!...

[LUCIENNE *comes charging madly back up the stairs, followed closely by a lumbering* LOCHE, *still toting his package.* HOMENIDES's *invectives continue throughout the following, growing closer.*]

LUCIENNE [*hysterical*]: It's him!... Good Lord!

[*She runs down left, to the door of the visible bedroom, and tries desperately to open it.*]

LOCHE [*joining her*]: Hurry, madame...

EDOUARD [*still leaning against the door from inside, with all his might, terrified*]: Go away! Go away!

LOCHE [*gesturing right*]: In there! In there!

LUCIENNE [*about to seek refuge in* POPOFF'*s room, suddenly remembering*]: That pervert?... Never! [*Looking around frantically, making a dash for the door of the other bedroom.*] In there!

LOCHE: But Blaise... Madame...

[*She rushes in, with* LOCHE *behind her, and slams the door a moment before* HOMENIDES'*s head comes into view.*]

HOMENIDES [*storming up the stairs and onto the landing, brandishing his gun*]: Ees no escape, woman!... I keell!... You! Heen!... Los dos!... I slowtair!

[BABETTE, *attracted by the noise, steps out of the room, up right.*]

BABETTE [*at the corridor*]: Monsieur?... Was there something—

HOMENIDES: Sí, sí! Sonetheeng!... Where she ees, Mossié Chandépisse? Where she ees weeth woman?

BABETTE: Monsieur Chandebise? [*Impatiently, pointing to the visible bedroom.*] In there... Number five...

[*She gives a shrug and exits into the corridor as* HOMENIDES *strides up to the door.*]

HOMENIDES [*pounding*]: Open!... You open! I cone for to keell!

EDOUARD [*shouting*]: There's no one in here!

HOMENIDES [*ramming the door with his shoulder*]: You open! You open!... I count... [*Ramming it with each number.*] Uno... Dos... Tres... [*With the final blow he pushes the door open, sending* EDOUARD *sprawling backwards and almost falling as* HOMENIDES *lunges for his throat, backing him against the wall, down left.*] Mi esposa!... Where he ees, my woman?... I keell! Sí, sí... I slowtair!... Where he ees?

EDOUARD [*babbling in terror*]: I... I don't know!... I don't have her!... Look! Search me!...

[*He turns his trouser pockets inside out, as if to prove the point.*]

HOMENIDES [*pushing him away and striding around the room, cursing, as* EDOUARD *comes down left*]: Ay!... La puta!... La perra!... Beetch! Feelthy eslot!... I fine you... I keell!... You! Heen!... Los dos!... Sí, sí! [*Standing by the bed.*] Like so, I keell... One boulett only! Los dos! Los dos!... [*Taking aim at the electric button on the stage left side.*] Like so!

[*On the word "so!" he fires at the bull's-eye button. The bed pivots around, revealing* LUCIENNE *and* LOCHE *sitting huddled and quaking on the other bed.*]

LUCIENNE [*screaming*]: Ahhh!

HOMENIDES: Ees you! Ees you!

[LUCIENNE *leaps up and bolts into the hall, followed by* LOCHE, *who, still lugging his package, managing a little salute as he leaves, pulls the door shut behind him.* HOMENIDES *takes off after them, firing several shots in the air and running into the door just as* LOCHE *pulls it shut. As* LUCIENNE *and* LOCHE *go scampering down the stairs, the door, sticking, resists* HOMENIDES'*s furious tugs just long enough for a crowd, drawn by the shots, to pour onstage:* BABETTE *and* BLAISE, *from the corridor;* MOUSQUETARD, *from upstairs;* FINACHE, *from the room, up right, with* NANA, *in an obvious state of nervous prostration, clinging to the door jamb;* POPOFF, *from his room; as well as a number of previously unseen guests in varying states of undress. As* HOMENIDES *finally gets the door open and makes for the stairs,* MOUSQUETARD *grabs his arm and holds it in the air. But* HOMENIDES *continues shooting and cursing, amid appropriate screams and shouts from the company, as the curtain falls.*]

CURTAIN

Act Three

The scene is the same as in Act One.

At rise the set is empty and all the doors are closed. After a few moments ANTOINETTE *comes rushing in, up center, cook's apron and bonnet in hand, quickly pulling the door shut behind her.[1] It is obvious that she has just been donning her uniform in great haste.*

ANTOINETTE: My God... Etienne... Right behind me... [*Clumsily buttoning the last few buttons of her dress.*] Damnation!
ETIENNE'S VOICE [*offstage right*]: Antoinette!... Antoinette!...
[*She runs over to the double door and bolts it.*]
ETIENNE'S VOICE [*closer*]: Antoinette!...
ANTOINETTE [*quickly putting on the apron and bonnet*]: God!
ETIENNE'S VOICE [*from behind the double door*]: You hear me?... [*As he shakes the panels from behind, trying to pull the door open.*] Open up!... Antoinette!... [*To himself.*] Locked herself in, the little witch!... [*Shouting.*] Antoinette!... [*Grumbling, as his voice moves off to the right.*] Well, we'll see about that!
ANTOINETTE [*quickly unbolting the door*]: There!...
[*She crosses on tiptoes, as fast as she can, to the door, down left, exiting just as* ETIENNE *comes storming in, up right, dressed as he was in Act Two.*]
ETIENNE: Antoi... [*Stopping short and looking around.*] Now where in the name of... [*Shouting.*] Antoinette!...
ANTOINETTE [*appearing at the door, down left, very calmly*]: Please, Etienne! I heard you! You don't have to scream!
ETIENNE: Well, woman? [*Coming downstage.*] What's the meaning of this?
ANTOINETTE [*feigning utter innocence*]: "This?"... This what?
ETIENNE [*pointing up center*]: That! That's what!... Locking yourself in...
ANTOINETTE: Me? Locking myself... Who says?
ETIENNE: I do!
ANTOINETTE: But I didn't... Whatever makes you think—
ETIENNE [*furious at her calm, interrupting*]: Oh? Well... [*Striding up to the double door.*] Then who... [*Turning the knob.*] Tell me... [*He pulls the door open, dumbfounded.*] Hmm!
ANTOINETTE [*leaning up against the oblong table, arms crossed, with a sneer*

---

[1] Feydeau specifies in a note that, throughout the act, only one panel of the double door in the bay, up center, should be open at any time, except where otherwise expressly indicated [Translator's note].

in her voice]: Don't blame me if you can't open a simple door!

ETIENNE: If I... Bah! Never mind! [*Approaching her.*] Never mind the damn
door! Just tell me what you were doing at the Hotel Paramour!... [*Almost on
top of her.*] Hmm? Hmm?...

ANTOINETTE: The what?

ETIENNE: The Hotel Paramour... In Saint-Cloud...

ANTOINETTE: What on earth is that?

ETIENNE: Don't give me "What on earth..." You know perfectly well, woman! I
suppose you'll tell me I didn't catch you there! Less than an hour ago!

ANTOINETTE: "Catch" me?... At... At some hotel?... Have you been drinking?

ETIENNE: Not "some" hotel... *That* hotel!

ANTOINETTE: Me?

ETIENNE: Yes, you!

ANTOINETTE: How? [*Hands on hips, very calmly.*] I haven't set foot outside all
day.

ETIENNE: You haven't... Damn! That's a good one!... [*As if to himself.*] She
hasn't set foot... [*To* ANTOINETTE.] I knew you'd come up with all kinds of
excuses... But to tell me you weren't even there!... I saw you, damn it! With
my own two eyes!

ANTOINETTE: So?

ETIENNE: "So"?...

ANTOINETTE: So you saw me... What does that prove?

ETIENNE: "What does that..." Oh!... Half naked?... In the arms of some... some
goddamn Cossack?

ANTOINETTE: Me?

ETIENNE [*almost nose to nose*]: Yes, you! [*Feeling his chin.*] I can still feel
where he punched me!

ANTOINETTE: In his arms?... Me? Half naked?...

ETIENNE: At least half!... Maybe more!

ANTOINETTE [*with incontrovertible logic*]: But I don't talk a word of Cossack!
How could I be—

ETIENNE [*interrupting, with a cynical little laugh*]: Ha ha ha! You don't talk...
For *that* who has to talk! I'm sure he used his hands!... And a few other
things!

ANTOINETTE: I wouldn't know. I told you... I haven't set foot outside all day.

ETIENNE: Oh!... Goddamn!... [*Crossing right, seething, under his breath.*] Can
you believe... [*Turning, to* ANTOINETTE.] Well, we'll see about that!

[*He moves up, toward the double door.*]

ANTOINETTE [*taking a step toward him*]: What are you going to do?

ETIENNE [*approaching her*]: Ask Ploumard... That's what I'm going to do!

ANTOINETTE: Ploumard? The concierge?

ETIENNE: Believe me, he'll know who's "set foot outside" and who hasn't!

[*As he turns to move back up toward the bay,* ANTOINETTE *grabs him by the
arm. During their following rapid exchange, each time he frees himself she
grabs him again, attempting to pull him back.*]

ANTOINETTE ⎫
                ⎬ [*together*]:
ETIENNE   ⎭

⎧ Etienne! Are you crazy?... You're not going
⎪ to drag the concierge into this?... He'll think
⎪ you're out of your mind!
⎨ See?... Didn't think of that, did you?... You
⎪ thought you could get away with it, but now
⎩ you know I've got you! See?

ANTOINETTE [*grabbing him*]: Please, Etienne!

ETIENNE [*pushing her away*]: Don't "Please, Etienne" me, woman!

ANTOINETTE [*coming down left to the oblong table, defiantly*]: Fine! Ask him! See if I care!

[*She takes a resolute stand, arms crossed, facing the audience with her back to the table, as* ETIENNE *rushes offstage into the vestibule, leaving both panels of the double door open, making a dash for the telephone in the niche in the wall.*]

ETIENNE [*cranking the handle and lifting the receiver as the phone rings, after a brief moment, shouting into the mouthpiece*]: Hello... Is that you, Monsieur Ploumard?... This is Etienne, upstairs... Yes... Antoinette's husband... [ANTOINETTE, *still facing the audience, grimaces.*] Fine, thank you... [*Trying to interrupt.*] I was wondering, monsieur... Yes... [*Having difficulty getting his word in edgewise.*] I was wondering if you can tell me... Yes, monsieur, she certainly is... I was wondering... Yes, I certainly am... [*With a withering look in* ANTOINETTE'*s direction, sarcastically.*] Very lucky... Look, I was wondering if you can tell me... Yes... I was wondering if you can tell me what time she left this afternoon... [*There is a pause, during which* ANTOINETTE *clenches her teeth and winces, obviously expecting the worst.*] No, not you!... Her!... My wife... What time did she go out? [*There is another pause as* ANTOINETTE'*s grimace intensifies.*] What?... What do you mean, "She didn't go out all day"...?

ANTOINETTE [*her face suddenly brightening, aside*]: Aaaah!

ETIENNE [*still shouting into the phone*]: Of course she did! You must have seen her pass by your booth!... She... [*There is another long pause.*] She what?... Came downstairs and chewed the fat with you...?

ANTOINETTE [*with a sly smile, aside*] ⎫
                                          ⎬ [*together*]: ⎰ Ah!
ETIENNE [*continuing*]   ⎭   ⎱ But...

ANTOINETTE [*aside, jubilant*]: Good old Ploumard!

ETIENNE [*continuing*]: But that's impossible!

ANTOINETTE [*aside*]: You can bet he'll make me pay, the old lecher!

ETIENNE [*unable to believe
   his ears, continuing*]   ⎫
                                   ⎬ [*together*]: ⎰ She... I know she...
ANTOINETTE [*aside, with an   ⎭   ⎱ Oh well...
   offhand shrug*]

ETIENNE [*continuing*]: Oh!... Never mind! I'm sorry to bother you!

[*He slams down the receiver and comes back downstairs, furious, closing both panels of the double door behind him.*]

ANTOINETTE: See?

ETIENNE: Shut your mouth, woman! [*Moving down right, to himself.*] "Didn't go out..." Ha!

ANTOINETTE [*crossing upstage, toward the door, up right*]: See how stupid it is to be so jealous?

ETIENNE [*moving back up left*]: Yes... Well... [*Pointing up right.*] Back to your kitchen! We'll talk about this later!

ANTOINETTE: Oh! Any time you like...

[*She shrugs her shoulders and exits, up right. A moment later the front doorbell rings.*]

ETIENNE [*shaking his head, grumbling*]: "Didn't go out..." Went down and "chewed the fat"... [*The bell rings again.*] Yes, yes! I'm coming... [*At the double door, to himself.*] Either she's the world's biggest liar... And Ploumard, too!... Or I'd better get my head examined! [*The bell rings again, more insistently.*] Yes, yes, yes! Hold your horses!...

[*He exits, leaving the door open. For a few moments the stage is empty, but one can hear the front door open and close.*]

GISELE'S VOICE: Well, it took you long enough!

ETIENNE'S VOICE: I'm sorry, madame...

[GISELE *enters, followed by* TOURNEL *and* ETIENNE. *She and* TOURNEL *are dressed as they were at the end of Act Two.*]

GISELE [*striding down right, to the canapé, as* TOURNEL *hangs back in the bay, to* ETIENNE]: Didn't you hear the bell?

ETIENNE [*stopping center, obviously preoccupied*]: Yes, madame... I... Sorry, I—

GISELE [*agitated, interrupting*]: Has Monsieur Chandebise returned yet, Etienne?... Has he come back... [*Aside, sarcastically.*] from his banquet!

ETIENNE: Monsieur, madame?... I hardly think so.

GISELE: Yes, well... [*Waving him off.*] That will be all...

ETIENNE: Very good, madame... [*He turns to leave, upstage, still preoccupied by his encounter with* ANTOINETTE, *and mumbling to himself as he passes* TOURNEL, *absentmindedly looking through him.*] Little swine!

TOURNEL [*mistaking the intent of his exclamation*]: I beg your pardon? What did you—

ETIENNE [*stopping, realizing his gaffe, to* TOURNEL]: No, no... Not monsieur... I meant someone else! Another little swine... [*Mumbling to himself.*] "Didn't go out all day..."

[*Shaking his head, he exits and closes the double door behind him. As soon as he is gone,* TOURNEL, *eager to put his recent nightmare behind him, takes a few tentative steps toward the same door.*]

TOURNEL [*clearing his throat, to* GISELE, *uncomfortably and with noticeably less animal passion than before*]: Well, my love... Now that you're safely home, I'll be on my way.

GISELE: What?... You're not going to leave me now, I hope!

[*She takes off her hat, coat, and gloves, and lays them on the cabinet, up right.*]

TOURNEL: Oh? You want me to—

GISELE: Of all times!... [*Nervously moving back and forth.*] God only knows what he'll be like when he gets back!... You saw him at that hotel! The second time he caught us... Really! I thought he was going to strangle you on the spot!... I mean... Maybe he will! Maybe this time he really will!

TOURNEL [*very calmly*]: Aha... Then you think I'd better stay...

GISELE: Well, I certainly don't want to be all alone if he tries to kill you!

TOURNEL [*a little confused by her logic*]: Aha... No...

[*He comes downstage.*]

GISELE: I must say, you don't seem too eager...

TOURNEL [*very unenthusiastically*]: Oh... If I had a choice...

GISELE: Of course! [*To herself.*] They're all the same!... Heroes before and cowards after... When they have to pay the piper...

TOURNEL [*overhearing*]: "After"? After what?... We didn't do anything to pay the piper for!

GISELE [*going up to him*]: Oh? Well, that's not your fault! You certainly tried your best!

TOURNEL: Well...

GISELE: And anyway, he doesn't know if we did or we didn't! Just finding us there, he's bound to think... what he's bound to think.

TOURNEL: Can you blame him?

GISELE: And you saw how he flew off the handle! God in heaven!...

TOURNEL: I guess I did!... Only, I can't understand why he waited till the second time...

GISELE: I know...

TOURNEL: Because the first... When he just appeared all of a sudden on the bed... And with a bottle...

GISELE [*recalling*]: Oh!

TOURNEL: I mean, he certainly didn't seem too terribly upset to see us. He even seemed a little... I don't know... a little pleased, didn't you think?

GISELE: I should say! He even kissed us!

TOURNEL: Right!... And then, one two three! There he is, a few minutes later, dressed up like a... a domestic, for heaven's sake!... And lunging at us... With fire in his eyes...

GISELE: Ready to kill you...

TOURNEL: I say... What surprises me is that it took him that long! I mean, with things like that it either hits you all at once or it doesn't. You don't usually stop and think!

GISELE: Exactly! [*Moving left, in front of him, toward the oblong table.*] That's what makes it so puzzling!

[*The doorbell rings.*]

TOURNEL ⎱ [*together*]: ⎰ Ah!...
GISELE ⎰   ⎱ Oh my! That could be him!

TOURNEL [*retreating down right, behind the canapé, anxiously*]: So soon?

[*One can hear the sound of the front door, offstage up right, opening.*]

ETIENNE'S VOICE [*coming from the same direction*]: Ah... Madame...

LUCIENNE'S VOICE [*likewise, excitedly*]: Has Madame Chandebise returned?

[*One hears the door closing.*]

ETIENNE'S VOICE: Yes, madame. She has.

LUCIENNE'S VOICE: Good!

GISELE [*moving up, toward the bay, to* TOURNEL, *in passing, with a sigh of relief*]: Ah... Thank heaven! It's only Lucienne... [*She opens the double door.*] Come in... Come in...

[LUCIENNE *enters, in a flurry of agitation, dressed as she was at the end of Act Two.*]

LUCIENNE [*crossing in front of* GISELE, *down left, toward the oblong table*]:

Ah! Gisèle! Gisèle! Gisèle!... What an absolute disaster!...

GISELE [*following her, raising her eyes heavenward*]: Ha! You're telling me!

LUCIENNE: Look! I'm still trembling!

[*She stands by the table and illustrates.*]

GISELE ⎫   ⎧ Oh!
       ⎬ [*together, sympathetically*]:   ⎨
TOURNEL ⎭   ⎩ Tsk tsk tsk!

LUCIENNE [*collapsing onto the chair, on the stage right side of the table*]: I can't go home... I simply can't face Don Carlos!

GISELE ⎫   ⎧ What's the matter?
       ⎬ [*together*]:   ⎨
TOURNEL ⎭   ⎩ Tsk tsk tsk!

LUCIENNE [*to TOURNEL, apparently noticing him for the first time*]: Ah, Monsieur Tournel... Please, you must excuse me...

TOURNEL [*to LUCIENNE*]: Not at all... We were just—

LUCIENNE [*not listening to him, pursuing her train of thought*]: I'll go anywhere... I'll live on the streets... I'll... I'll sleep under the bridges...

GISELE [*approaching her*]: There, there, now, precious... Tell me—

LUCIENNE: Anywhere, as long as I don't have to face him! The man is an animal... A... a beast... A...

TOURNEL: A Spaniard...

LUCIENNE: ...a maniac!... I'd be too afraid...

GISELE [*to LUCIENNE*]: I don't blame you one bit! [*Crossing right, toward TOURNEL.*] Why, when he saw us at that hotel... Monsieur Tournel and me... I don't know what got into him! He came running after us like a madman... And with a gun, Lucienne! He chased us all over the hotel with a gun! As if he wanted to kill us!

TOURNEL [*to LUCIENNE*]: That's right!

LUCIENNE [*to TOURNEL*]: Who, you?... [*Getting up, to GISELE.*] You too? You two too?... [*To TOURNEL.*] You two too?

TOURNEL [*not quite comprehending*]: Please?

LUCIENNE [*to TOURNEL*]: He went chasing you two too?

TOURNEL: Chasing?... Good grief, I'll say...!

GISELE [*to LUCIENNE*]: Upstairs... Downstairs...

TOURNEL: All over the place!... The man was out of control!

LUCIENNE [*steadying herself against the oblong table, fanning her face with her hand, sighing*]: Oh!... My heart still hasn't stopped beating...

TOURNEL [*about to comment on her observation*]: Oh?...

LUCIENNE [*ignoring him, to GISELE*]: Why, if not for your husband, love, I don't know what I would have done!

GISELE: My... Victor-Emmanuel?

LUCIENNE: Yes... I probably would have collapsed on the spot if he hadn't caught me and dragged me out. Heaven only knows what would have happened then!

GISELE [*approaching her*]: You mean, it was my husband who—

LUCIENNE [*interrupting*]: Yes! And believe me, Gisèle, he almost frightened me as much! He just wasn't himself. Something... [*Shaking her head, with a shrug.*] I don't know...

GISELE: You noticed...? [*To TOURNEL, who is still at the canapé.*] She noticed it too!

LUCIENNE: I should say I did!... When I saw him before... Mind you, not ten minutes before... He was perfectly normal, perfectly coherent. He warned me about Don Carlos and pleaded with me to leave.

GISELE: Ah...

LUCIENNE: Then, "Boom!" That... That scene... That... That monstrous nightmare... And next thing I knew we were both stumbling down the stairs. And when we got to the bottom he gave me the oddest look, all out of breath, and he said: "Who is that barbarian anyway, madame? Someone you know?"

GISELE: "Know"?

TOURNEL   ⎤
           ⎬ [*together*]:   { "Know"?
GISELE   ⎦   { No!

TOURNEL: No!

LUCIENNE: Yes!... Well, you can just imagine!... "What," I said. "Someone I know?... Of course I do! He's my husband! You know him too... As well as you know me!" [*Imitating.*] "You?... You?... You who?"

GISELE: "You who?"

TOURNEL: "You who?"

LUCIENNE: Yes! That's what he said. [*Imitating.*] "But I don't know you, madame... I'm afraid we've never met..."

GISELE: What?

LUCIENNE: And he stood there giving me stupid little salutes... [*She illustrates.*] And grinning...

TOURNEL: Tsk tsk tsk!

LUCIENNE: All I could think was: "Good Lord! Victor-Emmanuel has lost his mind!... Poor Gisèle!"

GISELE: Oh!

LUCIENNE: Then suddenly he began babbling... All kinds of nonsense... I couldn't make heads or tails...

GISELE [*to* TOURNEL]: Just like us!

TOURNEL [*to* LUCIENNE]: Just like us!

LUCIENNE: Things like... I don't know... Like, he was the porter, and... and something about carrying up the wood... And about someone taking his uniform... Really, all kinds of foolishness!

GISELE: It doesn't make any sense!

TOURNEL [*shaking his head*]: No sense at all!...

LUCIENNE: Then next thing I knew, out of a clear blue sky, he was tugging at my sleeve and telling me we had to go buy a bottle of wine!... Me! Did you ever...?

GISELE [*shocked*]   ⎤
                               ⎬ [*together*]:   { Oh!... It's simply too—
TOURNEL [*still shaking his head*] ⎦   { None at all!... None at all!...

LUCIENNE: Well, you can just imagine!... I was beside myself!

TOURNEL: Tsk tsk tsk!

LUCIENNE: "Please, Monsieur Chandebise!" I begged him... "Monsieur Chandebise!... Monsieur..." But he just stood there, saluting and grinning, and... and muttering something like "Loche... Loche... Loche..."

GISELE [*nodding, to* TOURNEL, *approaching him, right*]: Just like us...

TOURNEL [*nodding, to* LUCIENNE]: Just like us...

[*He goes to the little table near the canapé and sits down on the stage left chair.*]

LUCIENNE [*continuing*]: "Really!... Victor-Emmanuel!... [*Imitating* LOCHE'*s voice.*] "No, damn it!..."

GISELE [*putting her hand to her mouth*]: Lucienne!

LUCIENNE [*ignoring her implied reprimand, continuing to imitate his voice*]: "No!..." [*Mimicking his salutes.*] "Aristotle!... Aristotle!..."

GISELE *and* TOURNEL [*looking at each other*]: Oh!

LUCIENNE: Well, I just threw up my hands! That was the last straw!

TOURNEL [*nodding, knowingly*]: The one that brought the camels back...

LUCIENNE [*to* TOURNEL, *quizzically*]: Camels?...

GISELE [*to* TOURNEL, *no less so*] ⎫   ⎧ Back?
                                   ⎬ [*together*]: ⎨
LUCIENNE [*continuing*] ⎭   ⎩ What camels?

GISELE [*continuing*]: Back from where?

TOURNEL [*looking at each of them in turn*]: No, no... It's an expression. "The straw that brought the camels back..."

LUCIENNE [*to* TOURNEL]: "Broke," monsieur...

TOURNEL: Hmm?

GISELE [*to* TOURNEL]: "...that *broke* the camel's back..."

TOURNEL [*rather abashed*]: Oh... I say... [*With a shrug.*] Whatever...

LUCIENNE: Anyway, it was!... [*To* GISELE, *approaching her, right.*] I just turned around and left him standing there... And I got back here as fast as I could!

TOURNEL: Tsk tsk tsk!

LUCIENNE: Oh!... Just let me sit down before I... [*Sighing.*] before I absolutely die of exhaustion!

[*She goes over and stands by* TOURNEL'*s chair, waiting for him to get up and offer it.*]

TOURNEL [*remaining seated*]: By all means, madame... [*Gesturing toward the other chair, to the right of the table.*] Please... By all means...

[GISELE *gives him a disapproving look, then takes* LUCIENNE *by the arm and helps her to the chair.*]

LUCIENNE [*sitting down, fanning her face and sighing, to* GISELE]: Thank you, love...

GISELE [*moving left, shaking her head*]: I don't understand it! I... [*Pausing at the oblong table.*] Either he's gone utterly mad... Or else it's a trick. [*Returning center.*] Some kind of sick little game he's playing...

TOURNEL: Tsk tsk tsk! [*After a brief pause, during which* GISELE *and* LUCIENNE *sigh their bewilderment, profoundly.*] As Marie-Antoinette said when she lost her head on the guillotine... [LUCIENNE *and* GISELE *look at him, expecting a quote.*] "It's been quite a day!"

GISELE [*after another brief pause, to* TOURNEL]: That's it? That's all?

TOURNEL: No, no... She said: "Let them eat cake" too... But that was before...

GISELE: I imagine...

LUCIENNE [*impatient, getting back to the problem at hand*]: Please, you two!... Really! What are we going to do? Between my husband, who wants to blow my brains out...

GISELE: And mine, whose brains have utterly turned to mush...

[*The three of them heave a weighty sigh, shaking their heads. Just then the doorbell rings. Reflexively,* LUCIENNE *and* TOURNEL *jump to their feet and huddle by* GISELE, *center stage. The ensuing exchange is pronounced in a rapid, almost frantic whisper.*]

LUCIENNE [*stammering*]: Some... Someone rang!

GISELE: Oh!

TOURNEL: It... It could be Chandebise.

GISELE [*to* TOURNEL]: Why? He has his key.

TOURNEL [*to* GISELE]: But maybe he forgot it.

GISELE: Maybe...

TOURNEL: It happens sometimes.

GISELE: I suppose...

TOURNEL [*facing* LUCIENNE *and* GISELE, *back to audience*]: I know from experience. One winter a few years ago... It was a dark and stormy night, and the snow was coming down—

GISELE [*sharply*]: Please, monsieur! Not now! This is no time for stories!

TOURNEL [*abashed*]: Oh... I say... [*He goes back to the chair he just vacated, and sits down, mumbling.*] I thought...

[*There is a tense pause as they all wait expectantly.*]

LUCIENNE: What's taking so long?

GISELE [*to* LUCIENNE]: That *was* the doorbell, wasn't it?

LUCIENNE: Of course...

GISELE: I mean, if somebody rang...

TOURNEL [*chiming in*]: Then... Then somebody must be at the door. It stands to reason...

[LUCIENNE *and* GISELE *turn and give him a look, as if to say: "Thank you for the profound observation." At the same moment the outer door can be heard to open and then close.*]

GISELE *and* LUCIENNE [*hearing it, looking anxiously at each other, together*]: Oh!

[*They stand rooted to the spot, not knowing what to expect. A moment later,* ETIENNE *comes running in, up center, and stands in the bay, obviously upset.*]

ETIENNE [*to* GISELE]: Madame!... Oh, madame!...

GISELE: Yes? What is it, Etienne?

ETIENNE: It's... It's... It's...

GISELE [*taking a few steps toward him*]: Well?

ETIENNE: It's monsieur, madame!

TOURNEL *and* LUCIENNE [*looking at each other, together, as the former jumps to his feet*]: Oh!

ETIENNE: But... But...

GISELE: "But... But..." But what?

ETIENNE: But I don't know what's wrong with him, madame. I... I opened the door, and... and he came in... Like this... [*He imitates* LOCHE's *gait and his little salutes.*] And... And he asked me: "Is this where Monsieur Chandebise lives, private?"

GISELE, LUCIENNE, *and* TOURNEL [*looking at one another, together*]: What?

ETIENNE [*to* GISELE, *approaching*]: That's right, madame! At first I thought he was just playing a joke. So I went along with it, and I laughed: "Ha ha! Ha ha!... Of course this is where he lives," I told him. "Where else would Monsieur Chandebise live but in the Chandebise residence!... Ha ha! Ha ha!... And by the way, if monsieur doesn't mind, I'm a corporal!... Ha ha ha!.." But he wasn't joking, madame!

GISELE, LUCIENNE, and TOURNEL [looking at one another, together]: Oh!

ETIENNE [to GISELE, shaking his head]: No, madame! [To LUCIENNE, likewise.] Madame... [To TOURNEL, likewise.] Monsieur...

GISELE: Oh! No, no, no!... [To TOURNEL.] He's not going to start that little game again!... [To ETIENNE.] Where is monsieur now, Etienne?

ETIENNE: In the vestibule, madame... Waiting...

LUCIENNE and TOURNEL [together]: What?

GISELE [to ETIENNE]: Waiting?

LUCIENNE and TOURNEL [together]: In the vestibule?

ETIENNE [to GISELE]: For Monsieur Chandebise!

GISELE: Oh!... Did you ever...!

[She strides up to the bay, followed by the others, and pushes both panels of the door open. LUCIENNE and TOURNEL are on the stage right side of the door; GISELE and ETIENNE, on the left, with the latter a respectful distance behind. As the door opens one sees LOCHE, dressed as at the end of Act Two, in CHANDEBISE's coat and hat, sitting rather timidly on the edge of the bench against the wall, hat on head, waiting patiently. When he sees the others his serious expression changes to his imbecilic smile.]

GISELE, LUCIENNE, and TOURNEL [stunned, jumping back]: Oh!

ETIENNE [to GISELE, in a whisper]: Madame can see for herself...

GISELE [to LOCHE]: What... What are you doing here?

LOCHE [half standing up, with an open-mouthed moronic expression]: Huh?

GISELE: Since when do you sit there like... like some ordinary, vulgar peddlar! Really!...

LOCHE [taking off his hat]: Madame?

GISELE, LUCIENNE, and TOURNEL [looking at one another, together]: "Madame"?...

GISELE: "Madame" indeed! [To LOCHE.] Come in, for heaven's sake!

[She steps back down a few paces, evidently on edge.]

LOCHE [coming to the threshold]: But... I'm waiting for Monsieur Chandebise, madame.

GISELE [to LOCHE]		You're...
LUCIENNE [to TOURNEL]	[together]:	What?
TOURNEL [to LUCIENNE]		I say...

GISELE [to LOCHE]: What are you talking about?

ETIENNE [to GISELE, softly]: I told madame...

LOCHE [suddenly recognizing ETIENNE]: Oh, you!... I thought I recognized you! [He comes down and gives him a good-natured slap in the stomach with the crown of his hat.] You're the one who was at the hotel... The Paramour... I remember... The one whose wife was doing it with the general—

ETIENNE [interrupting him, with repressed anger]	[together]:	Please monsieur! It's not necessary...
GISELE [to ETIENNE]		What?... What is he saying?

LOCHE [turning to GISELE, recognizing her]: Oh! And madame too... The one who made me kiss her... [With a little salute.] Madame...

[*He purses his lips and begins to approach her, apparently ready to repeat.*]

GISELE: God in heaven! [*Taking refuge, right, behind* TOURNEL, *to ward him off.*] Tournel! What's the matter with him?

TOURNEL [*to* LOCHE]: Really, my friend...

LOCHE [*recognizing him*]: Ah! And monsieur too... Madame's gigolo!

LUCIENNE ⎫   ⎧ What?
        ⎬ [*together*]: ⎨
GISELE ⎭   ⎩ My...

LOCHE [*continuing, to* TOURNEL, *good-naturedly*]: Of all people... [*Reaching out to him.*] Monsieur!

[*He goes to embrace him.*]

TOURNEL [*fending him off*]: For heaven's sake! Enough is enough! Please, Victor-Emmanuel...

[*He comes down, right center, with* GISELE *still clinging behind him, as* LUCIENNE *moves away from the bay, toward the low table, up right.*]

LOCHE [*correcting*]: No, no... "Loche... Loche..."

LUCIENNE [*at the table*]: See?... "Loche! Loche! Loche!" [*To* GISELE *and* TOURNEL.] What did I tell you?

LOCHE [*suddenly noticing* LUCIENNE, *recognizing her*]: Oh! And madame... [*With a leer.*] The one I went running to get away from that crazy cannibal with!... [*Approaching her at the table, arms outstretched.*] Son of a... What do you know!... All of you! My lucky day!...

LUCIENNE [*backed up against the wall behind the table, rather gingerly*]: Yes... [*Edging her way, right.*] Isn't it...

[*Once out from behind the table, she comes quickly down, right center, to join* GISELE *and* TOURNEL.]

LOCHE [*holding his sides, chortling*]: Tee hee! Tee hee!... What a small world!... You mean, all of you live together?... Tee hee! Tee hee!

GISELE ⎫   ⎧ God!
TOURNEL ⎬ [*together*]: ⎨ Tsk tsk tsk!
LUCIENNE ⎭   ⎩ Oh!

LOCHE [*lumbering down left, toward the oblong table, muttering to himself*]: A nice family... But a little...

[*He taps his temple with his forefinger. Looking at the trio, still huddling right, and realizing that they have no doubt caught his pejorative gesture, he changes it to a couple of little salutes and stands grinning at them.*]

GISELE: What is it? What's the matter with him?

LUCIENNE [*to* GISELE, *in a whisper*]: Really, love! You've got to have him examined!

ETIENNE [*who throughout the preceding has remained up left, by the bay, now coming down toward the trio, to* GISELE, *sotto voce*]: Would madame want me to telephone the doctor?

GISELE [*at her wit's end, to* ETIENNE]: No... Yes... Oh! I... Do what you like!

ETIENNE: Very good, madame.

[*He goes back up toward the double door.*]

LOCHE [*approaching him, gesturing for his attention*]: Private...

GISELE ⎫   ⎧ "Private..."
TOURNEL ⎬ [*looking at one another, together*]: ⎨ Tsk tsk tsk!
LUCIENNE ⎭   ⎩ What?

ETIENNE [*at the double door*]: Monsieur?

LOCHE [*following him to the door*]: You won't forget to tell Monsieur Chandebise...?

ETIENNE [*to* LOCHE, *as the others look at one another and shake their heads*]: No, monsieur. I'll be sure to tell him.

[*He exits, shaking his head as well, and shuts the door behind him.*]

GISELE [*to* LUCIENNE, sotto voce]: But why?... [*To* TOURNEL.] Why is he doing this?

TOURNEL: Tsk tsk tsk!

GISELE [*to* TOURNEL, *likewise*]: It's a trap!... It's got to be... [*To* LUCIENNE.] There's no other explanation.

LOCHE [*coming down right toward the others*]: It's about my uniform, you know. That's what I came to tell him.

LUCIENNE ⎫
⎬ [*quick to agree, together*]: ⎰ Of course...
TOURNEL ⎭ ⎱ Your uniform...

LOCHE: First it was hanging there, and then it wasn't.

LUCIENNE ⎫
⎬ [*likewise, together*]: ⎰ Of course... Of course...
TOURNEL ⎭ ⎱ Yes... Yes...

GISELE [*beside herself, crossing in front of* TOURNEL *and confronting* LOCHE, *once and for all*]: No, no, no! I'm sorry! That's quite enough! Understand?

LOCHE: Huh?

GISELE [*as authoritatively as possible*]: If you're ill, monsieur, please say so! We'll have you treated!... [LOCHE *is about to object, feebly, but* GISELE *cuts him off.*] But if, on the other hand, this is just some little act... Well, I'm sorry to tell you, but it's stupid! You hear me?

LOCHE: Huh?

GISELE: Monsieur Tournel and I explained to you exactly what happened. We proved, as plain as day, that there is nothing... nothing whatever between us.

LOCHE [*scratching his head*]: Huh?

GISELE: And there never has been!... [*Pointing to* LUCIENNE.] Madame Homenides can vouch for us!

LUCIENNE: Absolutely!

GISELE: Now, if that's not enough for you... If you insist on being stubborn and believing that... that... Well, that's up to you, monsieur! I suggest... [*While speaking she seizes* TOURNEL *by the sleeve as he stands exchanging observations with* LUCIENNE.] that you take the matter up with Monsieur Tournel!

[*So saying, she pulls the unsuspecting* TOURNEL *aside and flings him around in an arc and into* LOCHE's *stomach.*]

TOURNEL [*caught off balance*]: Me?... I say...

LOCHE [*continuing the movement and sending* TOURNEL *off to his left, toward the oblong table*]: Huh?

GISELE [*to* LOCHE]: Yes, yes, yes! Believe us or not! It's up to you!... But I do think the least you can do is stop acting like an idiot, and conduct yourself with the... the dignity that the situation demands!

LOCHE: Me?

GISELE: One minute you believe us... You're hugging and kissing us... Then ten minutes later you're trying to... [*Pointing to* TOURNEL.] to strangle Monsieur Tournel! Really!...

LOCHE: I... [*Turning to* TOURNEL.] Did I do that?

TOURNEL [*feeling his throat*]: I daresay...

LOCHE: But—

GISELE [*to* LOCHE]: It's just too absurd!... Now tell me once and for all... Do you believe me or don't you?

LOCHE [*very confused*]: Of course I do...

[*He turns aside and gives a bewildered shrug.*]

GISELE: Then prove it! Come give me a kiss and let's forget about all this nonsense!

LOCHE: A kiss?... [*Wiping his lips on his sleeve.*] All you want!

LUCIENNE ⎫   ⎧ Finally!
              ⎬ [*sighing, much relieved, together*]:   ⎨
TOURNEL ⎭   ⎩ At last!

LOCHE [*to* GISELE, *drawing close to her*]: You tell me when to stop!

[*He purses his lips and is about to plant a kiss on her mouth. At the same moment* TOURNEL *approaches them.*]

GISELE [*pushing* LOCHE *away and turning her head aside in disgust*]: Oh!

TOURNEL [*as* LOCHE *lands heavily on his toe*]: Ayyy!... [*Holding his shoe and hopping about in pain.*] Good grief!...

LUCIENNE [*ignoring* TOURNEL, *to* GISELE]: What is it, love?

GISELE [*likewise, to* LUCIENNE]: He... [*To* LOCHE.] Oh! You've been drinking!

LOCHE   ⎫   ⎧ Me?
             ⎬ [*together*]:   ⎨
GISELE ⎭   ⎩ You...

GISELE: You utterly reek!

LOCHE [*as* TOURNEL, *limping, draws closer*]: I do?

GISELE [*grabbing his chin and forcibly turning his head in* TOURNEL's *direction, his mouth about an inch from the latter's nose, to* TOURNEL]: Oh! Just smell that, my friend!

TOURNEL [*gagging*]: Aaaah!

GISELE [*to* TOURNEL]: You see? [*Striding down right, to* LOCHE, *hands on hips, reproachfully, as* TOURNEL *stands fanning his nose.*] So! Monsieur drinks now, does he?

LOCHE [*dismissing the accusation*]: Pfff!... You call that drinking? Half a dozen lousy little slugs...

LUCIENNE *and* TOURNEL [*together*]: Oh!

LOCHE: ...to keep body and soul together!... [*To* GISELE.] You would've too, madame...

GISELE [*crossing up left*]: I knew it! [*Pointing an accusing finger at him.*] He's drunk!... Completely drunk!

LOCHE   ⎫   ⎧ Me?
                                    ⎬ [*together*]: ⎨
LUCIENNE *and* TOURNEL ⎭   ⎩ Oh!

LOCHE [*to* GISELE, *coming left, behind her*]: But I'm not... I...

[*He goes to give her his promised kiss.*]

GISELE [*waving him off*]: Please, monsieur! Go sleep off your drunken debauch somewhere else!

LOCHE: But... But...

TOURNEL [*approaching him*]: Really, Victor-Emmanuel... You, of all people...

LOCHE [*losing patience, but still deferentially, to* TOURNEL]: No, no... "Loche," please!... [*Articulating carefully.*] "Loche!"... "Loche!"... [*With each exclamation he exhales squarely in* TOURNEL'*s face, forcing him to back up toward* LUCIENNE.]

TOURNEL: Ah...

LOCHE: "Loche!"...

TOURNEL: Fine... [*Shielding his face, nodding.*] Loche... Loche... Whatever you say...

LUCIENNE [*coming quickly around to escape the line of fire, and crossing over to join* GISELE, *left*]: Oh!

LOCHE [*to* TOURNEL]: Loche!... That's what I say... [*Backing him up, as if spelling the name.*] L... oche... Loche!... [*Mumbling.*] Not Victor whoever...

GISELE: Disgusting!

LUCIENNE: Absolutely!

[*The door, upstage, flies open and* ETIENNE *steps quickly inside, as* TOURNEL *crosses left, joining* LUCIENNE *and* GISELE.]

ETIENNE [*to* GISELE]: The doctor, madame...

LUCIENNE, GISELE, *and* TOURNEL [*together*]: Ah...

FINACHE [*entering upstage in a hurry, wearing his overcoat, to* GISELE]: Now what's all this...? Etienne tells me he was just trying to telephone me... [*Noticing* LOCHE, *left, with a friendly little wave.*] Ah, Chandebise...

LOCHE [*turning to see whom he is addressing*]: Chandebise?... Where?... [FINACHE *gives his supposed witticism a polite little chuckle.*]

FINACHE [*to* GISELE, *as* LOCHE *comes down right, looking about for* CHANDEBISE]: What's the trouble?

LOCHE [*to himself*]: Damned if I see him...

GISELE [*to* FINACHE, *pointing to* LOCHE, *who is now behind the canapé*]: The trouble is... that monsieur is dead drunk!

FINACHE [*to* GISELE, *pointing*] ⎱
⎰ [*together*]: ⎱ Him?... Come now!
ETIENNE [*still upstage*] ⎰ ⎰ Monsieur?... Drunk?

LUCIENNE ⎱
⎰ [*together, to* FINACHE, *agreeing*]: ⎱ Very... Very...
TOURNEL ⎰ ⎰ I say... He really is...

LOCHE: Me?

GISELE [*to* FINACHE]: Just smell his breath if you don't believe me! [TOURNEL *gives a disgusted grimace as* FINACHE *approaches* LOCHE, *down right.*]

FINACHE [*to* LOCHE]: You, my friend?... Tipsy?

GISELE [*to* FINACHE]: Not "tipsy"!... Drunk!

LOCHE [*shrugging his shoulders, exhaling in* FINACHE'*s face*]: Pfff!

FINACHE [*recoiling*]: Oh!... Oh my!... [*To* GISELE.] I see what you mean!

ETIENNE [*coming down right, toward the little table near the canapé, shocked, to* LOCHE]: Oh, no... Not monsieur...

LOCHE [*quite at sea*]: Huh?

FINACHE [*to* LOCHE, *but keeping his distance*]: My poor, dear friend... What on earth did they pour down your gullet to get you so... so...

GISELE [*quick to supply the word, to* FINACHE]: So drunk, monsieur! [*Pointedly, looking at* LOCHE, *as if spelling.*] D... r... unk... Drunk!

LOCHE [*to* FINACHE]: What? You too?... [*Losing patience.*] Listen, you joker...

FINACHE [*stepping back*]: "Joker"?... [*To* GISELE.] Did he say...

LOCHE [*holding his downturned palm to his chin*]: I've had it up to here with... with...

GISELE [*duplicating his gesture, but at eye level*] ⎫
TOURNEL [*looking at* LUCIENNE] ⎬ [*together*]: ⎰ Up to here, he means!
LUCIENNE [*looking at* TOURNEL] ⎭ ⎱ Tsk tsk tsk!
Oh, my!

LOCHE [*continuing, to* FINACHE, *becoming almost aggressive*]: ...with your "drunk"... [*To the others.*] With all your "drunk, drunk, drunk!" All of you!... [*To* FINACHE.] If I'm drunk I'll be a... a... an onkey's muncle!

FINACHE [*trying to calm him down*]: Yes... You're right, my friend..

[*He moves around behind the canapé.*]

LOCHE [*to* FINACHE]: You're right, I'm right!... [*He crosses left and goes to address* GISELE, LUCIENNE, *and* TOURNEL *in quick succession, each of whom, at his approach, will give him an anxious look and scamper right, crossing to join* FINACHE.] Damn right!... [*To* GISELE.] Don't think that, just because I'm only a private, you can walk all over me... [*To* LUCIENNE, *as* GISELE *crosses right and takes refuge next to* FINACHE.] Like you've all been doing since I got here!... [*To* TOURNEL, *as* LUCIENNE *does likewise.*] Whoever you all are!

GISELE, FINACHE *and* LUCIENNE [*looking at one another and muttering, as* TOURNEL *hurriedly joins them, together*]: "Whoever..."!

LOCHE: I came here to see Monsieur Chandebise! And I want to see him! That's all there is to it!

[*He gives them a series of his little salutes, more out of habit than respect, plants his hat firmly back on his head, and begins pacing angrily up and down. Meanwhile the group–lined up against the back of the canapé as follows:* FINACHE, GISELE, LUCIENNE, *and* TOURNEL, *right to left, with* ETIENNE *still by the little table–continue to gaze at him in open-mouthed bewilderment.*]

FINACHE [*unable to believe his ears*] ⎫ ⎰ Oh là là...
⎬ [*together*]: ⎱
GISELE [*to* FINACHE] ⎭ You see?

LUCIENNE [*to* FINACHE]: His mind seems clear for a moment or two, then... Psssh! Nothing!...

TOURNEL [*to* FINACHE]: Since this afternoon, doctor...

FINACHE: My, my, my!

[*They all keep watching, shaking their heads in silence, as* LOCHE *continues pacing beside the oblong table, grumbling. Suddenly he stops as he notices them staring at him.*]

LOCHE: Well?

[*He sits down testily on the chair on the stage right side of the table as the group behind the canapé continue their observations, sotto voce, without taking their eyes off him.*]

TOURNEL ⎫ [together]: ⎧ I say!

LUCIENNE ⎭   ⎩ Oh!

FINACHE [to GISELE]: And you're sure he's never acted like this before?

GISELE: Never! [To ETIENNE.] Has he, Etienne?

ETIENNE [still at a respectful distance]: Certainly not, madame!

FINACHE: Because the fact is... [Waxing professional.] We never see such symptoms of complete hallucinatory amnesia...

TOURNEL [nodding, knowingly]: Indeed...

FINACHE: ...with such total alienation of the very concept of personal individuation...

TOURNEL [nodding]: Indeed...

FINACHE: ...except in the case of confirmed, inveterate alcoholics.

GISELE ⎫   ⎧ Victor-Emmanuel?

LUCIENNE ⎪   ⎪ No!
          ⎬ [together]: ⎨
TOURNEL ⎪   ⎪ Tsk tsk tsk!

ETIENNE ⎭   ⎩ Oh! Not monsieur!

FINACHE: The next stage, I'm afraid, is delirium tremens... [The others' jaws drop.] And, after that... [With a gesture of despair and a shake of the head.] Pfff!...

GISELE, LUCIENNE, TOURNEL, and ETIENNE [with piteous looks at LOCHE, gasping, together]: Ah...

LOCHE [annoyed at their attention, taking off his hat and slamming it on the table]: Well?

GISELE [to FINACHE]: But... But that's impossible! The most he ever drinks is a... [Holding up her thumb and little finger tip.] a thimbleful after meals.

TOURNEL [to FINACHE]: And more often than not he leaves half of that!

ETIENNE [to FINACHE]: That's right, monsieur! I've got to finish it myself so as not to let it go to waste...

LUCIENNE [to FINACHE]: You don't mean to say that one little glass after meals—

FINACHE [to LUCIENNE]: Ah, but I do, madame! [TOURNEL begins nodding in agreement.] For some people that's quite enough!... Alcoholism isn't a matter of quantity, but of... of one's... [Searching for a high-sounding term.] individual metabolic complexion.

GISELE: What?

LUCIENNE: Meta...?

FINACHE: ...bolic complexion...

ETIENNE [following the conversation with interest] ⎫   ⎧ Oh!
                                                    ⎬ [together]: ⎨
GISELE [aside, to LUCIENNE]   ⎭   ⎩ Complexion...?

TOURNEL [self-importantly]: Indeed... [To FINACHE.] They wouldn't understand, doctor. [To LUCIENNE and GISELE.] The effect on the body of what we eat and drink...

FINACHE: Quite...

TOURNEL: Like chocolate, for example. It can give you pimples...

[ETIENNE self-consciously feels his face.]

FINACHE [unthinkingly]: Yes... [Realizing TOURNEL's gaffe, brusquely.] No!...

That is... Not that kind of complexion...

TOURNEL [*embarrassed*]: Oh... I thought...

FINACHE: The... The make-up... The metabolic make-up...

GISELE [*aside, to* LUCIENNE]: Make-up...?

LUCIENNE [*naively, to* FINACHE]: You mean, to cover the pimples...

FINACHE: No, no... [*To* GISELE *and* LUCIENNE.] You don't... All I'm saying is that it's a very individual matter. One person can drink a whole bottle of pure alcohol a day and it will never affect him.

ETIENNE [*nodding, trying to understand, to himself*]: It won't give him pimples...

FINACHE: Another one can drink a... [*To* GISELE.] a thimbleful, and he becomes an alcoholic.

GISELE   ⎫   ⎧ God in heaven!
LUCIENNE   ⎬ [*together*]:   ⎨ Oh my!
TOURNEL [*nodding*] ⎭   ⎩ Indeed... Indeed...

LOCHE [*who, during the preceding, has been sitting impatiently, drumming on the table, turns and gives a sudden little lurch in their direction, noisily clearing his throat to call attention to his continued presence*]: Ahem! Ahem!...

GISELE, LUCIENNE, *and* TOURNEL [*instinctively pulling back, together*]: Oh!

FINACHE [*continuing his explanation*]: And those are the ones who really have to worry. Precisely because they never suspect it... [*To* LUCIENNE, *echoing her previous comment.*] "One little glass, after meals..." First one... Then another... Until one fine day, "Bam!" And... [*Pointing to* LOCHE.] And there's your result!

GISELE, LUCIENNE, *and* TOURNEL [*huddling together, sighing, with more piteous glances in* LOCHE's *direction, pointing at him*]: Ah...

LOCHE [*staring at them for a moment*]: Listen, you jokers!... [*The three of them look at one another, agape, as* FINACHE *gives a knowing little shrug and nod, as if to say: "We've heard that before!"*] How long are you going to stand there like a damn picket fence?

GISELE   ⎫   ⎧ What?
LUCIENNE   ⎬ [*together*]:   ⎨ Monsieur?
TOURNEL   ⎪   ⎪ Please?
FINACHE   ⎭   ⎩ Sorry?

LOCHE [*putting on his hat, out of patience, and standing up*]: With all your blah-blah-blah! [*Pointing his finger, imitating them.*] And "ha!"... And "ho!"... I hope you're having fun!

GISELE   ⎫   ⎧ But... But...
LUCIENNE   ⎬ [*together*]:   ⎨ Fun, monsieur?
TOURNEL   ⎪   ⎪ My dear friend...
FINACHE   ⎭   ⎩ Come now...

LOCHE: You know what I mean!

GISELE [*to* LOCHE]: But really, Victor—

LOCHE [*to* GISELE, *almost violently*]: Loche!... How many times—

GISELE [*quickly acquiescing*]: Loche... Loche...

LOCHE [*to the group*]: And it better stop, that's all! It better stop, before you make me mad!

FINACHE [*approaching him*]: Come, come... What's the trouble?...

LOCHE: I'm nobody's fool, goddammit!

FINACHE: Of course you're not... [*To the others, whispering.*] Irritability... One of the symptoms...

LOCHE [*overhearing, coming toward him*]: What?

FINACHE: Nothing, my friend... Here, hold out your hand...

LOCHE: My hand?

FINACHE [*illustrating, holding out his arm, palm down and fingers spread*]: Like this...

LOCHE [*complying mechanically*]: What for?

[*His hand quivers noticeably.*]

GISELE [*moving toward* FINACHE *and* LOCHE, *to* LUCIENNE *and* TOURNEL]: Look how it's shaking!

LUCIENNE }   { Oh my!
TOURNEL } [*together*]: { Tsk tsk tsk!
ETIENNE [*still apart from the others*] } { Oh, monsieur!

FINACHE [*holding* LOCHE'*s forearm, to the others*]: You see? The typical alcoholic tremor... Another one...

LOCHE [*furious, pulling his arm away*]: No, no, no, no, no! [*The others recoil a step or two, aghast, as he snorts his anger and lumbers menacingly right, between* FINACHE *and* GISELE.] That's enough, I said! [*Stamping his feet.*] Enough! Enough! Enough!

GISELE }   { Victor...
LUCIENNE } { Oh!
TOURNEL } [*pulling back even further, together*]: { I say...
ETIENNE } { Monsieur!

FINACHE [*approaching*]: Now, now... Now, now...

GISELE [*to* LOCHE, *at the end of her rope*]: For heaven's sake, Victor-Emmanuel...

LOCHE [*exploding at her*]: Loche!

GISELE [*quickly*]: Loche!

[LUCIENNE, TOURNEL, *and* FINACHE, *trying to appease him, echo her in rapid succession.*]

LUCIENNE: Loche!

TOURNEL: Loche!

FINACHE: Loche!

LOCHE [*with as much of a crescendo as his nasal twang can muster, saluting each of them in turn, with each outburst, to* TOURNEL]: Loche! [*To* LUCIENNE.] Loche!

FINACHE: My friend...

LOCHE [*continuing, to* FINACHE]: Loche! [*To* GISELE.] Loche!

GISELE [*to* LOCHE]: Please!... Control yourself... Try—

LOCHE [*furious, to* GISELE, *right in her face*]: Oh... Go shit in your hat, lady!

[*There is a long moment of utterly stunned silence as everyone stands transfixed.*]

GISELE [*finally*]: What did... [*To* FINACHE.] What did he—

FINACHE [*quickly taking her by the arm*]: Nothing!... Nothing, madame!...

GISELE: I... I never...

FINACHE [*leading her up, center stage, as* LUCIENNE *and* TOURNEL *move up right, leaving* ETIENNE *in place, still gaping in disbelief at* LOCHE, *who has begun pacing nervously back and forth downstage*]: Don't pay any attention... Come... When they're in that condition they don't know what they're saying. You'll just make him angry...

GISELE: Him?... I'll make *him* angry...?

FINACHE: Please...

GISELE: I don't care! Alcoholic or not!... He's not going to tell me to go sh—

FINACHE [*cutting her off*]: Shhh! Shhh!

LUCIENNE [*echoing, quickly*]: Shhh!

TOURNEL [*likewise*]: Shhh!

GISELE [*to* FINACHE, *scandalized, pointing at* LOCHE]: You heard him!

FINACHE [*coaxing her toward the door, up right, and motioning* LUCIENNE *and* TOURNEL *in the same direction*]: Please... He's not responsible... [*As* GISELE *reaches the door.*] Come... Let me take care of it... Etienne and I will put him to bed.

GISELE: Yes! Do, by all means!

[*She retrieves her coat, hat, and gloves from the cabinet, up right, and exits archly.*]

FINACHE [*as she leaves*]: At least we'll try... [*Nodding to* TOURNEL, *who, with* LUCIENNE, *has reached the door.*] Monsieur... [*To* LUCIENNE.] My apologies, madame...

LUCIENNE [*to* FINACHE]: Yes... Well... [*To* TOURNEL.] And at his age... Really!

TOURNEL [*to* LUCIENNE]: Oh, you never know... I saw a twelve-year old alcoholic once. I remember... It was a lovely spring morning, and I had just—

LUCIENNE [*to* TOURNEL]: No, no, monsieur!... Later!... Please! Later...

[*They exit, up right, as* ETIENNE, *shaking his head, goes up toward the bay.*]

FINACHE [*coming back down, to* LOCHE, *who is still pacing*]: Well now, my friend...

[ETIENNE *stops at the double door to observe the encounter.*]

LOCHE [*stopping, down center*]: Damn! [*To* FINACHE, *with a little salute.*] Lucky you smelled trouble and got 'em out of here in time!... [*Menacingly.*] One more minute...

FINACHE: Of course... I could tell...

LOCHE [*calming down*]: What's the matter with 'em anyway? A little soft in the head, maybe?

FINACHE [*nodding in feigned agreement*]: Soft in the... Yes, a... a little...

[ETIENNE *comes down center toward them, though keeping a discreet distance.*]

LOCHE [*to* FINACHE]: Bloody batty, if you ask me!... Every one of 'em...

FINACHE [*still humoring him*]: Yes... Batty... Soft in the head...

LOCHE [*to* ETIENNE, *who is a few steps up left of him*]: See? I knew it...

ETIENNE [*taking his cue from* FINACHE, *echoing*]: Batty... Soft in the head...

LOCHE: You two should've let me know... [*Pointing to the canapé where the trio had been standing.*] A little wink or something... Or you could've just whispered, "They're batty!", real soft... [FINACHE *has taken advantage of his outstretched arm to take hold of his wrist subtly, with his left hand, and feel his pulse.*] What's the matter? [*To* FINACHE.] What are you doing?

FINACHE [*surreptitiously taking out his watch with his right hand and counting, replying as casually as possible*]: Oh? Just being friendly...

LOCHE: Ah... [*Continuing his thought.*] If you told me I wouldn't 've lost my temper. I would've played along...

FINACHE [*pocketing his watch and dropping* LOCHE'*s hand*]: Of course...

LOCHE [*laughing*]: I know how it is with crackpots like that... [*To* ETIENNE.] You've got to agree with everything they say!

FINACHE [*sticking out his tongue and wagging it in* LOCHE'*s face*]: Aaaah!

LOCHE: Huh?

FINACHE: Do this...
[*He repeats the gesture.*]

LOCHE: Why? [*To* ETIENNE.] What for?

ETIENNE: He's just being friendly, monsieur...

FINACHE: Aaaah!

LOCHE [*with a shrug, complying*]: Aaaah!

FINACHE [*scrutinizing, mumbling to himself*]: Hmm... Interesting... All coated... [*To* ETIENNE, *in a whisper, motioning him to come over.*] Is it always like this?

ETIENNE [sotto voce]: I couldn't say, monsieur. I've never looked.

FINACHE [*just loud enough for* LOCHE *to overhear*]: Yes... His tongue has quite a coat...

LOCHE [*good-humored, with a laugh, taking off his hat, to* FINACHE]: And a nice hat too, monsieur! [*He jokingly hangs his hat on his outstretched tongue, crossing left with a self-satisfied belly-laugh.*] Ho ho!... Ho ho ho!

FINACHE [*forcing a laugh*]: Ha ha!... That's a good one!... Very funny, monsieur... Very... [*Aside, to* ETIENNE, *giving him a nudge.*] Laugh! Laugh, for goodness' sake!

ETIENNE: Me?... Oh... [*Giving a couple of dry, unconvincing little laughs.*] Ha!... Ha!...

LOCHE [*by the oblong table, replacing his hat on his head, pointing to* ETIENNE, *with a little salute in his direction*]: Even he thinks so... The flunky...

ETIENNE [*to himself, as* FINACHE *moves left, between him and* LOCHE]: Flunky...?

FINACHE [*to* LOCHE, *forcing another laugh*]: Yes... Very... Ha ha ha!... [*Becoming suddenly serious.*] Now then... We've had a good laugh... And now we're going to be serious and listen to reason, aren't we?

LOCHE: Huh?

FINACHE: Look... I'm your friend...

LOCHE: You?... Says who?... [*Approaching him, squinting, to examine him more closely.*] I never saw you before in my life...

FINACHE: Aha... Aha, well... You see, I'm the doctor...

LOCHE: Oh?

FINACHE: The nice man who comes and takes care of you... [*As if talking to a child.*] Your booboos... Your sniffles... You know... Pills, medicine, diets...

LOCHE: Sure... [*Aside.*] I know what a doctor is!

FINACHE: Camomile...

LOCHE [*aside*]: Does he think I'm batty too?

FINACHE [*trying to jog his memory*]: Exercise... Suspenders...

LOCHE: Huh?

FINACHE [*emphasizing*]: American suspenders...

LOCHE: Oh?... [*Shrugging.*] If you say so... You're the doctor.

FINACHE: Yes. And I can tell just by looking at you that you're tired... Very tired...

LOCHE [*impressed*]: You can?

FINACHE: Very... [*To* ETIENNE.] Isn't he, Etienne?

ETIENNE: Oh yes, monsieur! Very tired!

LOCHE: And why not, mother of God!... Up at five... Get the hotel swept by six... The floors waxed by seven... And all day, bringing up the wood... Up and down... Up and down...

FINACHE: Of course... [*Exchanging troubled glances with* ETIENNE, *then continuing, to* LOCHE.] Well now... That's why, you know what you're going to do? You're going to get undressed and get into bed.

LOCHE: What? [*Resisting.*] Damned if I am! [*To himself, mumbling.*] Bed?...

FINACHE: Ah... Well then... At least you're going to make yourself nice and comfortable... You're going to take off that coat, and... and Etienne is going to bring you a robe.

LOCHE: But... What about my uniform?

FINACHE: Your... [*Quick to agree.*] Of course... Later... This is just for now. [*To* ETIENNE, *motioning him toward the door, down left.*] Etienne...

ETIENNE [*softly*]: Yes, monsieur...

[*He crosses left, behind the oblong table, and exits, still shaking his head.*]

FINACHE: There! [*Pushing* LOCHE *gently left, with a series of little thrusts toward the same door.*] And now, we're going to lie down on the big soft bed in there and go nighty-night...

LOCHE [*turning around*]: We are?

FINACHE: Yes, we... [*Correcting himself.*] You are...

[*In front of the oblong table, he tries to coax him toward the door.*]

LOCHE   ⎫   ⎧ But I don't...
               ⎬ [*together*]:   ⎨
FINACHE   ⎭   ⎩ Now, now...

LOCHE: But what about Monsieur Chandebise?

FINACHE: Monsieur... [*Aside.*] My, my! [*To* LOCHE.] Don't you worry about him... If he says anything, you just let me know...

LOCHE: Ah...

[ETIENNE *enters, down left, with a dressing-gown.*]

ETIENNE [*to* FINACHE, *giving it to him*]: The robe, monsieur...

FINACHE: Fine... [*To* LOCHE.] Now, off with that nasty old coat... Come...

LOCHE [*relenting, as* FINACHE *and* ETIENNE *gently but forcibly remove his coat and hat*]: Well...

FINACHE: There!... [*As he and* ETIENNE *help him on with the robe.*] What do you think of that!

LOCHE [*tying the cords around his waist, admiring himself*]: Oooh!... I bet even Colonel Mousquetard hasn't got one like this! [*As* ETIENNE *goes over and lays* LOCHE's *hat on the table and his coat on the chair on the stage left side of it.*] It sure is nicer than my uniform!

FINACHE: Your... [*With a sigh.*] Yes, I'm sure... Now, you know what? A little bird tells me you must be thirsty!

LOCHE [*good-humored*]: Ha! Damn smart little bird!

FINACHE [*laughing along with him, condescendingly*]: Isn't it!... Well, that's why I've got a special drink for you...

LOCHE: A drink?

FINACHE [*as* ETIENNE *rejoins him*]: It may not taste too good, but you're going to show us if you can get it all down in one swallow... Like a good soldier!

LOCHE [*with a little salute*]: Yes, monsieur!... A real stiff one, huh?

FINACHE: Yes... Very... [*To* ETIENNE, *emphasizing.*] Very...

LOCHE: Don't worry! I can handle it!

FINACHE [*aside, to* ETIENNE, *on his right,* sotto voce]: Is there any ammonia in the house?

LOCHE [*to* FINACHE'*s left, continuing his thought*]: They haven't invented a drink this Loche can't handle!

ETIENNE [*to* FINACHE, *replying in a whisper*]: Yes, monsieur.

[LOCHE *goes up and sits down on the chair on the stage right side of the table, smacking his lips in anticipation.*]

FINACHE [*to* ETIENNE, *still softly*]: Good!... We're going to give him ten drops in a large glass of water. Then, once his head is a little clearer, you'll give him... Here, let me write it down for you... [*Still down left, looking around.*] Is there something to write on?

ETIENNE [*pointing down right to the folded writing-desk*]: Over there, monsieur...

FINACHE: Ah... [*Crossing right.*] While I write the prescription you see if you can get him into bed.

ETIENNE [*following him part way*]: I'll do my best, monsieur. [*Returning left, to* LOCHE.] Come... [*Holding out his arm.*] If monsieur would like me to give him a hand...

[*During the following exchange,* FINACHE *takes the writing-desk and unfolds it in front of the canapé.*]

LOCHE [*getting up, rather touched, and taking* ETIENNE'*s arm*]: Oh... Thank you... That's nice of you... Real nice...

ETIENNE: Monsieur is too kind.

LOCHE [*giving a couple of little salutes with his free hand as they move left, toward the door*]: So... You say you were a corporal?

ETIENNE: A... [*With a little sigh and a shake of the head.*] No... Not really...

LOCHE [*somewhat disillusioned*]: Oh... Well, anyway... [*Stopping as they reach the door.*] By the way, I'm sorry about your wife.

ETIENNE: Monsieur?

LOCHE: About you catching her doing it in the hotel, I mean... With the general... And making you a... [*Giving him the cuckold sign behind his head, laughing moronically.*] a you-know-what! Like you told me...

ETIENNE: Yes, well... She didn't, monsieur... And I'm not... [*Opening the door and stepping back to let* LOCHE *pass.*] She was with the concierge. They were chewing the fat.

LOCHE [*still chuckling as he exits*]: Is that what they call it now?

[ETIENNE *follows him out.*][1]

FINACHE [*behind the writing-desk, facing the audience, sniffing*]: Damn! What smells so bad? [*He picks up the sheet of stationery on which* LUCIENNE, *in*

---

[1] Feydeau, concerned as ever with practical technicalities, specifies here in a note that, once offstage, the actor playing LOCHE and CHANDEBISE must, at this point, change back into the former's costume—except, that is, for the cap—concealed under the dressing-gown, since he will not have time to do so after LOCHE's next scene [Translator's note].

Act One, had begun to write the letter, and on which she had spilled some of the toilet water.] This? [*He sniffs it, holding it up in such a way that the audience can see the writing on the under side and recognize it, then turns his head with a grimace.*] Pffu!... My goodness, that's strong!... [*He replaces it on the pile of similar sheets, comes around the writing-table and sits down on the canapé, back to the audience, ready to write his prescription, just as one hears the front door slam.*] Ah! Who can that— [*The door, up center, flies open and* EDOUARD *comes rushing in, quite out of breath.*]

EDOUARD [*noticing* FINACHE, *still seated, and letting loose a volley of speech as inarticulate as at first*]: Ah! Monsieur!... Doctor!... That hotel of yours...

FINACHE: Edouard!

EDOUARD: Never in my life... Believe me, never...

FINACHE [*not understanding a word*]: What?

EDOUARD: The things I went through...

FINACHE ⎫ ⎧ Please! Not so fast... Not so...
         ⎬ [*together*]: ⎨
EDOUARD ⎭ ⎩ Oh! The things... You have no idea...

FINACHE: Please! Put in your palate! What did I invent it for if you're not going to use it?

EDOUARD: I can't! I lost it...

FINACHE: You what?

EDOUARD: Some crazy foreigner knocked it out of my mouth... [*Miming punching himself in the mouth.*] He punched me in the jaw.

FINACHE [*barely managing to understand*]: Punched you in the jaw, you say?

EDOUARD: Yes!

FINACHE: A farmer?... Why on earth—

EDOUARD: No, no!... A foreigner!... [*Trying to articulate.*] A foreigner!

FINACHE [*finally comprehending*]: Aha... But why—

EDOUARD [*excitedly, as he moves down left toward the oblong table*]: And if you think that's all!... It was a nightmare, I'm telling you!... All those people I kept running into!... Tournel... Gisèle... And Chandebise! My uncle...

FINACHE [*trying to slow him down*]: Please...

EDOUARD [*continuing, unabated*]: My uncle! With a load of logs on his back, of all things!... And Madame Homenides... And her husband... Running all over the place with a gun! [*Miming appropriately.*] "Bang bang! Bang bang!"... I'm telling you...

FINACHE: Yes... Please...

EDOUARD: You can't imagine!... A nightmare! A God-awful nightmare!

[*As he lets himself fall in a heap onto the chair on the stage right side of the table,* ANTOINETTE *enters, up right.*]

ANTOINETTE [*to* FINACHE]: Monsieur... Madame asked me to ask monsieur how monsieur is doing.

FINACHE [*momentarily confused*]: Monsieur?... Ah! Better... Tell her he's doing better... [*Getting up.*] No... On second thought I'll go tell her myself.

EDOUARD [*to* FINACHE]: What is it? What's the matter?

FINACHE [*moving upstage toward the door, up right, as* ETIENNE *enters, down left*]: Nothing... Chandebise is... He's not quite himself.

EDOUARD [nodding] ⎱
                   ⎰ [together]: ⎰ Aha... Aha...
ETIENNE [to FINACHE] ⎰   ⎱ Monsieur is in bed, monsieur.

FINACHE [as ETIENNE retrieves LOCHE's hat from the table and moves upstage]: Ah! Good!...

ETIENNE [to EDOUARD, in passing]: Good evening, monsieur.

EDOUARD: Good evening, Etienne.

FINACHE [up right, by ANTOINETTE, to ETIENNE]: You go get the ammonia, Etienne, while I talk to madame.

ETIENNE [to FINACHE]: Very good, monsieur...

[ETIENNE leaves through the double door, leaving both panels open, at the same time as FINACHE and ANTOINETTE exit, up right, leaving EDOUARD alone, still seated.]

EDOUARD [heaving a long sigh]: My goodness!... What a hotel!... [Getting up.] Like all hell breaking loose!... [Dramatically.] The sound... The fury... [Coming down center.] And me in the middle, like a candle in the wind!... [Declaiming.] "Out, out brief candle!..." [There is a knock at the door, down left.] "Life's but a walking shadow... A tale..." [There is another knock, to which he replies without changing tone.] Come in!... [Continuing.] "A tale told by an idiot..."

LOCHE [entering, down left, precisely on the word "idiot," still bundled up in the robe with a foulard around his neck]: Monsieur...

EDOUARD [jumping back in surprise]: Victor-Emmanuel!

LOCHE [affecting a tone of good-natured severity]: Oooh! The young man I saw today at the Hotel Paramour!...

[He gives him one of his little salutes.]

EDOUARD [aside, assuming a reprimand] ⎱
                                      ⎰ [together]: ⎰ Oh my! He recognized me.
LOCHE [with his imbecilic laugh]   ⎰   ⎱ Another one! What do you know!

EDOUARD [to LOCHE, approaching him, to justify himself, in an inarticulate outburst]: But... But... I was there for a reason... I assure you... I... I heard there was someone who... who...

LOCHE [bewildered] ⎱
                   ⎰ [together]: ⎰ Hoo hoo? Hoo hoo?
EDOUARD   ⎰   ⎱ ...someone who...

LOCHE [crouching down and squinting up into EDOUARD's mouth to see what he has in his throat, to himself]: What's he got in there?

EDOUARD: ...who... who...

LOCHE: Spit!... Spit out!...

EDOUARD: ...who wanted to buy insurance... A policy... A new client... Someone who—

LOCHE [abandoning his inspection, cutting him off]: Who gives a damn!

EDOUARD: What?

LOCHE: Hoo hoo! Hoo ha! Hoo hee!... Excuse me... That's nice. But I just want to know where's that drink he promised me?

EDOUARD: "Drink"?... "He" who? "He" who?

LOCHE [aside]: Again? [To EDOUARD.] Hee hoo hoo ha!... He promised me a drink just now, and I'm thirsty as a sonofabitch!...

EDOUARD [*articulating slowly*]: Yes... Who, "he"?... Who? Who?

LOCHE [*suddenly understanding*]: Oh... Who?... [*Pointing down right.*] The doctor, that's who.

EDOUARD [*happy to see the subject change*]: Ah! I see... He must have forgotten... [*Accompanying his assurance with appropriate gestures.*] I'll go see... Right away...

LOCHE [*half understanding*]: Thank you... Because I'm dry as a bone, tell him... Ready to croak...

EDOUARD: Of course... Right away...

LOCHE [*giving him a little salute; then, turning to leave, aside*]: Hoo ha... Ha hoo...

[*He exits into the room, down left, and closes the door behind him.*]

EDOUARD [*still in front of the oblong table*]: Hmm! I thought for sure he was going to give me a talking-to!... [*Imitating.*] "Shame on you, Edouard! You... In a place like that!... What would your poor parents think if they knew!..." I must say, he didn't seem to give it a second thought.[1]

[*One can hear the front door open and close. The next instant* CHANDEBISE *appears in livery jacket and cap, visible through the open double doorway of the bay, entering from the right side of the vestibule and placing a bunch of keys in his pocket.*]

EDOUARD [*catching sight of him at the threshold, with a shriek of disbelief*]: Aaaah!

CHANDEBISE [*entering, coming center stage, startled at the reaction*]: What's the trouble, Edouard?

EDOUARD: My God!... [*Stammering.*] H... H... How... [*Pointing alternately to the door, down left, and to* CHANDEBISE.] Th... Th... There!... And there!...

CHANDEBISE [*upstage of the oblong table*]: What?... What is it?

EDOUARD [*in a panic, bumping into the table and the chairs*]: My God! I've... I've lost my mind!

CHANDEBISE [*taking a step or two toward him*]		Edouard... What in the name of...
EDOUARD [*raising his forearms in a cross, backing around the table and edging upstage*]	[*together*]:	No, no!... Back!...Back!

CHANDEBISE: What's the—

EDOUARD: Vade retro, Satanas!... Back!... Back!... [*Turning to flee out the door, up left.*] I've lost my mind! I've lost...

[*He exits, still babbling.*]

CHANDEBISE [*watching him go, at a loss*]: Pfff! "Lost his mind" is right!... [*To himself.*] Like everyone else today!... Is it something in the air?... And that hotel!... What a... [*Noticing his coat on the chair on the stage left side of the oblong table.*] Ah!... Now who do you suppose...? Well, whoever... It's not a minute too soon! [*Removing his livery jacket and cap as he talks, placing them on the table.*] I've had enough of this blasted outfit! [*Coming around the table and putting on his coat.*] Even the concierge didn't know me!... Tried to make me use the back stairs, of all things...

---

[1] Feydeau suggests in a stage direction that EDOUARD's monologue can be shortened or lengthened accordingly, intended, as it is, only to give the actor playing the dual role time to arrange his costume appropriately and come quickly around behind the set in order to make his imminent entrance as CHANDEBISE [Translator's note].

[*Just as* CHANDEBISE *finishes his last few words,* EDOUARD *is seen bolting through the vestibule, from left to right, as* ETIENNE *appears in his path.*]

EDOUARD [*grabbing* ETIENNE *and shaking him*]: I... I've lost my mind!... I... I... I...

[*He lets him go and dashes off, right, continuing his exclamation offstage as a puzzled* ETIENNE *watches him disappear.*]

ETIENNE [*calling after him in the wings*] ⎫
                         ⎬ [*together*]: ⎧ Monsieur!...
CHANDEBISE [*noticing their encounter*] ⎭   ⎩ Again?

ETIENNE [*coming down center, to himself*]: Now what's got into him, I wonder?

CHANDEBISE [*assuming the question to be meant for him, to* ETIENNE]: You and me both, Etienne!

ETIENNE [*pleasantly surprised to hear his name, to* CHANDEBISE]: Ah... Monsieur knows who I am?

CHANDEBISE [*coming back right, around the table, toward* ETIENNE]: Knows who you... Of course I know who you are! What kind of a stupid question—

ETIENNE: No kind, monsieur!... I only meant... I meant...

[*At that moment he is saved from an explanation by the sudden return of* EDOUARD, *bursting in, up right, followed by* GISELE, TOURNEL, FINACHE, *and* LUCIENNE, *all now coatless and hatless.* ETIENNE *backs off, a discreet distance upstage.*]

EDOUARD [*as inarticulately as usual, but trying to explain with gestures*]: But there are two of him, I tell you!... Two! Two! Two!... [*Pointing to* CHANDEBISE.] There!... [*Pointing to the door, down left.*] And there!

GISELE ⎫   ⎧ Two?... [*Looking at* TOURNEL.]
                                   ⎪ Two what?
TOURNEL ⎪   ⎪ Two?... [*Looking at* GISELE.]
          ⎬ [*to* EDOUARD, *together*]: ⎨ Two what?
FINACHE ⎪   ⎪ What?... [*Looking at* LUCIENNE.]
                                     ⎪ What does he mean?
LUCIENNE ⎭   ⎩ What?... [*Looking at* FINACHE.]
                                      What does he mean?

EDOUARD [*dashing back to the bay and out the double door, leaving both panels still open*]: My God!... My God!...

TOURNEL [*to* GISELE] ⎫   ⎧ I can't imagine!
GISELE [*to* TOURNEL] ⎪   ⎪ I can't imagine!
                      ⎬ [*replying together*]: ⎨
LUCIENNE [*to* FINACHE] ⎪   ⎪ Who knows?
FINACHE [*to* LUCIENNE] ⎭   ⎩ Who knows?

[EDOUARD *disappears through the vestibule, off left, still vociferating appropriately. At the same time* GISELE *comes center, toward* CHANDEBISE, *as* TOURNEL *comes down right, by the canapé.*]

GISELE [*to* CHANDEBISE]: We'd like to speak with you, Victor—

CHANDEBISE [*noticing her for the first time, sharply*]: You?... You, here?... [*Catching sight of* TOURNEL, *as well, and pointing.*] And with him?... With that... that...

GISELE ⎱ [together]: ⎰ What?
TOURNEL ⎰   ⎱ My friend...

CHANDEBISE [leaping right, to TOURNEL, and lunging angrily for his throat]: So! [Shaking him bodily, then pivoting him around, as he speaks, and pushing him left, toward the downstage end of the oblong table, as FINACHE and LUCIENNE, following the action, tentatively approach GISELE, center stage.] Maybe now you'd like to tell me what you two were doing when I caught you in that... that bordello!

LUCIENNE [looking at FINACHE, quickly, as if echoing CHANDEBISE's last word]: Oh!

FINACHE [looking at LUCIENNE, likewise]: Oh!

TOURNEL ⎱ [together]: ⎰ But... But...
GISELE ⎰   ⎱ What, again?

TOURNEL [to CHANDEBISE, still in his grip, as FINACHE, LUCIENNE, and GISELE, still engrossed in the action, come to the stage right side of the table]: But my friend, we've told you a dozen times!

CHANDEBISE [pushing him around the table and up the stage left side]: Told me?... Told me what?... How long do you think I'll let you make a fool of me?... [Pointing upstage.] Out, damn you!

GISELE [to CHANDEBISE]: Victor! Please...

CHANDEBISE [releasing TOURNEL and storming toward the others]: All of you!... Out!... Out!

LUCIENNE: Really, Monsieur Chandebise... I—

CHANDEBISE [noticing her for the first time]: Ah, madame... Not you... Sorry... [To the others.] The rest of you... [Pointing up right.] Out!... I can't stand the sight of you!
[He begins pacing nervously about.]

FINACHE [quietly, urging GISELE and LUCIENNE toward the door, up right]: Come... You mustn't upset him... He's in the midst of an attack.

LUCIENNE [to FINACHE] ⎱ [together]: ⎰ Me too?
GISELE   ⎰   ⎱ Oh!

FINACHE [to LUCIENNE, nodding] ⎱ [together]: ⎰ Yes, I think you'd better...Come... Attacks, attacks! I'm getting sick of his attacks!
GISELE   ⎰

FINACHE [seeing them out]: You'll come back later... [As LUCIENNE and GISELE exit, up right, to TOURNEL, still far left, recovering from his experience.] You too, Tournel... Please...

TOURNEL [crossing right and following the others]: It's absurd! He can't remember from one minute to the next!
[He exits.]

ETIENNE [who has been looking on throughout, shaking his head]: Tsk tsk tsk! [He exits, up center, closing both panels of the double door behind him.]

FINACHE [coming down left to CHANDEBISE, who is at the downstage end of the oblong table, addressing him gently]: Now then, Chandebise... What seems to be the trouble?

CHANDEBISE: Ah, Finache!... I'm sorry if I lost my temper just now, but—

FINACHE [*exaggeratedly sympathetic*]: Please! No need... It helps to get things off your chest. When something is bothering you...

CHANDEBISE: Oh!... I wish I could get over it, but—

FINACHE: No "buts," my friend! You will! Of course you will!... Why, you're already doing better... You're beginning to recognize people... To know who you are...

CHANDEBISE [*looking at him, aghast*]: What?

FINACHE: Much better...

CHANDEBISE [*angrily*]: "Recognize people..."? Know who I am...? What? You too?

FINACHE: Please...

CHANDEBISE: What is this? Some kind of joke?... Since when don't I recognize people, or know who I am?

FINACHE: No... I... I didn't mean that...

CHANDEBISE: Maybe I lost my temper, but I haven't lost my mind!

FINACHE: Of course you haven't... Of course... I didn't mean—

CHANDEBISE [*calming down, with a gesture, as if to say: "Let's not talk about it."*]: Pfff!

FINACHE: Still, if I were you... Really, I would have stayed in bed.

CHANDEBISE: What?

FINACHE: I mean... Why did you have to get dressed?... [*Pointing to his coat.*] With all that...

CHANDEBISE: Why?... That's a good one! [*Coming around to the stage left side of the table and moving up alongside it as he speaks.*] Because I was damn sick and tired of running around like... [*Pointing to* LOCHE's *uniform and cap on the oblong table.*] like one of the help! That's why!

FINACHE: Like... [*Raising his eyes heavenward in a look of resigned despair.*] Oh...

CHANDEBISE [*circling the table and coming down the other side*]: Me! [*Pointing to the livery.*] In that! Can you imagine?... In that!

FINACHE [*aside*]: Again with his obsession... Just when I thought...

CHANDEBISE: And believe me, that's not all! That Hotel Paramour of yours is quite the place, I must say!

FINACHE: Aha... You've been there?

CHANDEBISE: Have I!

FINACHE: You never told me...

CHANDEBISE: Well I have!... And good God, what goings-on!... Some lunatic who runs the place...

FINACHE [*pretending to believe him*]: Aha... Aha...

CHANDEBISE: Has to kick me every damn time he sees me... God only knows why!... Then that... [*Pointing.*] that damnable uniform!... Makes me wear it... Forces it on me...

FINACHE: Aha... Aha...

CHANDEBISE: And next thing I know I'm locked in a room... Almost break my neck climbing up over the goddamn roof!

FINACHE: Tsk tsk tsk!

CHANDEBISE: And to top it all off, Homenides!... Would you believe it?

FINACHE: Aha... Yes, of course...

CHANDEBISE [*emphasizing*]: Ho-me-ni-des! Of all people!... [*Raising his downturned palm to his chin.*] Up to here, believe me!

FINACHE: Oh, I do... I do... [*Aside.*] My God! He's even sicker than I thought!

CHANDEBISE: No! That's one hotel I'll never forget!

[*As he moves far left, muttering appropriately, the double door opens and* ETIENNE *appears carrying a little tray with a glass of water and the bottle of ammonia.*]

ETIENNE [*to* FINACHE]: Ah... Monsieur...

CHANDEBISE [*assuming that it is he being addressed*]: Yes, Etienne? What is it?

ETIENNE [*pleased that* CHANDEBISE *knows him*]: Ah?... [*To* CHANDEBISE.] Me?... Nothing, monsieur... [*Coming downstage, toward* FINACHE.] The doctor... He asked me...

FINACHE [*to* CHANDEBISE, *quickly*]: Yes, yes... I asked him...

CHANDEBISE: Ah...

[*He shrugs and moves up left as* ETIENNE *holds out the tray to* FINACHE.]

FINACHE [*to* ETIENNE, *in a whisper*]: Thank you...

[*He takes the bottle and glass, leaving the tray in* ETIENNE'*s hands, and, during the following exchange, squeezes the ammonia, drop by drop, into the water.*]

ETIENNE [*to* FINACHE, *in a whisper*]: I should think monsieur... [*Turning his head away from the bottle, almost gagging from the fumes.*] must be very pleased...

FINACHE [*counting out the drops, as he too keeps his nose a discreet distance from the bottle*]: Three... Four... [*To* ETIENNE.] Pleased?

ETIENNE [*in a whisper, using the tray to shield his nose*]: Monsieur Chandebise seems so much better.

FINACHE [*continuing his count*]: Hardly! He's worse, if anything... Six... Seven...

ETIENNE: Oh? But...

FINACHE [*holding the bottle even farther from his nose, still whispering*]: He's delirious, I'm afraid!... Nine... And ten... There!

CHANDEBISE [*curious, coming down toward the oblong table, to* FINACHE, *as* ETIENNE *takes the bottle from him and moves right, to the canapé, shaking his head*]: Is something wrong, Finache? Not feeling well?...

FINACHE: Me?... No... Fine... [*Approaching him, swishing the mixture around in the glass, but still turning his head aside.*] Fine... [*Holding it out to him.*] Here...

CHANDEBISE: Hmm?

FINACHE: Drink this...

CHANDEBISE: Me?... Why?

FINACHE: After all you've been through... It... It will pick you up...

CHANDEBISE: Ah?

FINACHE: Or calm you down... [*Aside.*] One or the other...

CHANDEBISE: Well, if you say so... I'm sure I can use it.

[*He takes the glass.*]

FINACHE [*holding his hand over the glass as* CHANDEBISE *is about to drink, to keep the fumes from escaping*]: All at once... It's a little strong...

CHANDEBISE [*with a gesture and a shrug*]: Pfff...

[*Casually, he takes a healthy mouthful; but no sooner is the liquid in his mouth than his face freezes in a grimace of disgust, and, sputtering and gagging, he slams the half-empty glass down on the table and dashes toward the window, down right.*]

FINACHE [*following on his heels, as* CHANDEBISE *flings the window open*]: No... I told you... Swallow it... Swallow it...

CHANDEBISE [*spitting out the window*]: Aaaach!... Ptui!... Ptui!... Good God!...

ETIENNE *and* FINACHE [*together*]: Oh!

CHANDEBISE [*almost choking*]: Yeccchhh!... [*Furious, to* FINACHE.] What kind of a stupid... [*Pointing to the door, up right, through which the others had exited a moment before.*] Are you crazy too? [ETIENNE *turns aside and gives an irony-charged look.*] If that's your idea of a practical joke, it's pretty tasteless!

FINACHE: Really, Chandebise, I—

CHANDEBISE: Or not tasteless enough, damn it! Of all the damn... [*Pushing* FINACHE *aside and crossing in front of him, angrily.*] Out of my way!... [*While speaking he strides up left, leaving the window open.*]

FINACHE [*following him*]: Where are you going?

CHANDEBISE: To rinse my mouth out, thank you!

FINACHE: But really, my friend, you have to—

[CHANDEBISE *exits, up left, still grimacing and noisily clearing his throat. As he slams the door, behind him the doorbell rings.*]

ETIENNE [*turning and exiting, up center, with the tray under his arm and the bottle in hand, leaving the double door ajar*]: Now who can that be?

MOUSQUETARD'S VOICE [*offstage, up right*]: Monsieur Chandebise, please?

ETIENNE'S VOICE [*from the same direction*]: Yes, monsieur...

MOUSQUETARD'S VOICE: What do you mean, "yes"? You're not him...

ETIENNE'S VOICE   ⎱   ⎰ No, monsieur...
FINACHE [*going to the*   ⎰ [*together*]:   ⎱
half-open door, looking out*] ⎰   ⎰ Mousquetard?

ETIENNE'S VOICE: I only meant that monsieur has the right place, monsieur.

FINACHE [*to himself*]: What's he doing here? [*Addressing the unseen* MOUSQUETARD *in the vestibule.*] Mousquetard!

MOUSQUETARD'S VOICE: Ah! Doctor Finache! What a nice surprise!

FINACHE: Come in! Come in!... [*He crosses down right to the canapé as* MOUSQUETARD *enters, in coat and hat, followed by* ETIENNE.] It's about your insurance, right?

[*He sits down on the canapé.*]

MOUSQUETARD: Oh no, monsieur! I wouldn't take the liberty at night... I'll come by some morning for that...

FINACHE: Ah... Then... To what do we owe—

MOUSQUETARD: No... I came by to bring back something we found at the hotel... Belongs to Monsieur Edouard Chandebise, it says...

FINACHE: Edouard?

MOUSQUETARD [*taking the prosthesis from his vest pocket and holding it out*]: Looks kind of valuable, so I thought maybe I'd better...

ETIENNE [*standing inquisitively by* MOUSQUETARD, *recognizing it*]: Oh... That silver thing!... I'm the one who found it...

MOUSQUETARD [*to* ETIENNE]: You?

ETIENNE: Yes, monsieur. On the floor...

FINACHE [*trying to get a good look at the half-hidden object in* MOUSQUETARD'S *hand*]: Here... Let me... [MOUSQUETARD *comes down and hands it to him.*] Ah! Of course... His palate... He told me... [*To* MOUSQUETARD.] The Finache Prosthetic Palate, my friend...

MOUSQUETARD: The what?

FINACHE: A minor medical miracle, Mousquetard... The first of its kind... A prosthesis... An artificial one...

MOUSQUETARD [*impressed, shaking his fingers up and down from the wrist*]: Phew!... Maybe I could use a fake one too... They tell me mine's enlarged... My pros... Whatever...

FINACHE: Enlarged? Your pros... [*Realizing the misunderstanding.*] Ah!... No... No... That's something else... This one goes in the mouth.

MOUSQUETARD: Oh...

FINACHE [*getting back to the subject at hand*]: But tell me, how did you know whose it was?

MOUSQUETARD: The name and address, monsieur... They're engraved...

FINACHE: They are? [*Examining the underside of the prosthesis.*] My goodness, so they are!... [*Reading.*] "Edouard Chandebise, 95, Boulevard Malesherbes..." Clever of the laboratory to take that precaution... [*Musing to himself.*] I'll have to remember...

ETIENNE [*following the conversation with interest*]: And terribly convenient if you forget your address!...

[*He laughs.*]

FINACHE [*to* MOUSQUETARD, *ignoring* ETIENNE'S *witticism as the latter shrugs and moves up to the bay*]: Well, he'll certainly be pleased! [*Getting up.*] Let me go tell him...

[*As he moves to leave,* ANTOINETTE *comes rushing in, up center, past a surprised* ETIENNE.]

ANTOINETTE [*to* FINACHE]: Monsieur!... Doctor... It's Monsieur Edouard... I don't know what's got into him, but... but I just found him in the bathroom... Stark naked, monsieur... Taking a cold shower!...

FINACHE   } [*together*]: { Good heavens! What now?

MOUSQUETARD [*to himself*] }   { A shower?

FINACHE: More madness!... [*Moving upstage, to* ANTOINETTE, *with* MOUSQUETARD *following behind.*] Where...? Show me...

ANTOINETTE [*pointing to the stage left side of the vestibule*]: This way, monsieur...

FINACHE [*approaching the bay*]: They're all crazy today!

[*He exits in the indicated direction, with* ANTOINETTE *close behind, leaving the door open.*]

MOUSQUETARD [*on the stage right side of the bay, watching them leave, to himself*]: Ever hear...? [*Coming down left, toward the oblong table.*] A shower, this time of day?... [*Suddenly he notices the livery jacket and cap left on the table by* CHANDEBISE.] What the... Is that...? [*Going over to the table.*] Loche's uniform?... Here?... What in hell is it doing... [*He examines it.*] How in the name of... [*To* ETIENNE.] You... Butler... Was my porter here today?

ETIENNE: Monsieur's porter?... I hardly think so. I'm sure I can't imagine why—

[*Before he has a chance to complete his sentence, the door, up left, opens and* CHANDEBISE *comes in, still grimacing and sputtering.*]

CHANDEBISE [*striding down, far left*]: God, what a foul concoction!

MOUSQUETARD [*looking up, with a start*]: What?... Loche!...

CHANDEBISE [*terrified*]: Ayyy!

MOUSQUETARD [*leaping in
    his direction*]
                    [*together*]:
CHANDEBISE [*avoiding him*]

    You? Here?...
    What are you...
    The lunatic from the hotel!...
    In my house!...

[*The two, on opposite sides of the table, move back and forth, here and there, up and down, in a frantic around-the-table chase for a long moment, peppered with appropriate exclamations and interjections.*]

MOUSQUETARD [*finally succeeding in intercepting him, on the stage left side of the table, and grabbing him by the throat*]: What are you doing here, you drunken swine? [*Shaking him.*] Answer me! [*As* ETIENNE *looks around anxiously, unable to decide whether to intervene or summon help.*] Answer me, damn you! [*Slowly and deliberately, punctuating each shake.*] What... are... you... doing...

CHANDEBISE [*struggling to reply*]: Me?... What am *I*...

MOUSQUETARD: And dragging my expensive uniform all over town, to boot!

CHANDEBISE: But I... I...

ETIENNE [*finally deciding, coming downstage, to* MOUSQUETARD, *trying heroically to pull him off*]: Monsieur!... Please!... [*Still attempting to observe proper decorum.*] Does monsieur know what he's doing?

MOUSQUETARD [*still pummeling* CHANDEBISE, *to* ETIENNE]: Listen, you! Kiss my—

CHANDEBISE [*covering* MOUSQUETARD's *obvious last word with his own interjection, as he manages, thanks to* ETIENNE's *intervention, to break free*]: Aaaah! [*To* ETIENNE.] Hold onto him, Etienne!... [*Making his way upstage to the double door, much the worse for the encounter.*] Hold onto him!

MOUSQUETARD
             [*together*]:
CHANDEBISE

    Damn!
    Don't let him go!...

[CHANDEBISE *exits, in a panic, slamming one panel and leaving the other open.*]

ETIENNE [*still struggling with* MOUSQUETARD]: But monsieur... That's Monsieur Chandebise! My employer, monsieur... My boss...

[*An especially loud slam is heard offstage, up right, from the supposed direction of the front door.*]

MOUSQUETARD [*pushing him away*]: Your boss, my ass! He's my porter, goddammit!

[*He grabs up the livery jacket and cap.*]

ETIENNE: But I know my boss!

MOUSQUETARD [*running upstage, to the double door*]: And I know my ass!... [*As he exits.*] I mean...

ETIENNE [*following him*]: Wait, monsieur!... Please!...

[*He exits on* MOUSQUETARD's *heels, slamming the open panel, and leaving the stage empty. After a few moments of uncharacteristic calm, the door, up right, is pulled ajar and* CHANDEBISE *very gingerly pokes his head in.*]

CHANDEBISE [*nervously, looking about*]: Is he... [*Seeing that he is gone, and coming down right, almost to the footlights, mumbling to himself.*] Thank heaven I thought to slam the front door and make him think I was running downstairs!... Let him chase me to his heart's content! [*With a deep breath and a sigh.*] All the way back to that hotel, I hope!

[*Just then one can hear, offstage, the indistinct sound of voices from the sitting-room, quickly coming closer.*]

ETIENNE'S VOICE: Yes, monsieur! I'll announce you...

HOMENIDES'S VOICE: No, no! No, no!

CHANDEBISE: What?... Now who...

HOMENIDES'S VOICE: No announce! No announce!... [CHANDEBISE'*s jaw drops as he apparently recognizes the voice.*] Ees no need for to announce!

ETIENNE'S VOICE [*coming closer*]: But monsieur—

HOMENIDES'S VOICE [*behind the double door*]: I go een!

[*Both panels of the double door fly open suddenly and* HOMENIDES *appears at the threshold, in resolute pose, with a large, oblong, wooden case tucked under one arm.*]

CHANDEBISE [*still down far right*] ⎫   ⎧ Oh!
                                     ⎬ [*together*]: ⎨
HOMENIDES [*catching sight of him*] ⎭   ⎩ Ah! Heen...

ETIENNE [*visible in the vestibule*]: Well... [*To* HOMENIDES.] If monsieur insists... [*He shuts the door.*]

CHANDEBISE [*as amiably as his panic will permit, to* HOMENIDES]: Ah! Señor... [*Aside.*] Oh my!

[*He makes a move to cross upstage toward the door, up left, seeing it as an escape route.*]

HOMENIDES [*stalking toward him, center stage, and barring his exit, in the most peremptory of tones*]: You stay!

CHANDEBISE: My friend...

HOMENIDES [*with a withering glance*]: Ees no more frien! Ees feeneesh weeth frien!

CHANDEBISE: But...

HOMENIDES [*moving right, to the little table facing the canapé, and sharply depositing the wooden case on it*]: Aha!... So!... You escape fron me today, mi amigo! Bot no for long! Now I here, now you here... [*With undeniable logic.*] Now we here!

CHANDEBISE [*weakly*] ⎫   ⎧ Yes... Yes...
                       ⎬ [*together*]: ⎨
HOMENIDES   ⎭   ⎩ Me... You... Los dos!

CHANDEBISE: Mi amigo...

HOMENIDES: Ha! Before, you locky!... Before, I go for to keell you, eh? Weeth reevolvair! [*Pointing an imaginary gun.*] "Bam bam!"

CHANDEBISE: But—

HOMENIDES: Bot policía, she cone... She take me to estación... To yhendarmé... Sí, sí... An yhendarmé, she take reevolvair, an she say: "Señor, I let you for to go... Bot first I put you on payroll, señor...

CHANDEBISE: On...?

HOMENIDES: Payroll... [*Quoting.*] "You make promeese... You make promeese you no more use reevolvair again! Bueno?"

CHANDEBISE ⎫   ⎧ Bueno, bueno!...
           ⎬ [*together*]:   ⎨
HOMENIDES ⎭   ⎩ An so I make promeese!

CHANDEBISE [*aside, with a sigh of relief*]: God bless that "yhendarmé"!

HOMENIDES: Sí, sí... [*After a brief pause, opening the wooden case.*] So now no reevolvair... Now I breeng peesstool... [*He holds it up and shows a pair of dueling pistols inside.*]

CHANDEBISE: You what?

HOMENIDES : Sí... [*With a reassuring gesture.*] Bot no ees need for to worry you head, Chandépisse! I no want for to keell youself now...

CHANDEBISE: How considerate!

HOMENIDES: No, no... Before, eef I do, ees fine... [*With a flourish of the hand.*] No problen... I catch you weeth señora...

CHANDEBISE: But—

HOMENIDES: Catch you weeth red ham, how you say... Red ham en mi esposa... [*Very matter-of-fact.*] An so, eef I keell, no ees problen before...

CHANDEBISE: But I wasn't—

HOMENIDES: Bot now eef I do, no ees sane theeng! Now you no weeth mi esposa... No weeth red ham... You onderstan... Eef I keell now, señor, ees cole blod. I no can do...

CHANDEBISE: No... I should hope...

HOMENIDES [*with no transition*]: An so, we fight duelo!

CHANDEBISE [*recoiling*]: We what?

HOMENIDES: Sí, sí...

CHANDEBISE [*with a nervous little laugh*]: You can't be serious monsieur... Mi amigo...

HOMENIDES [*ignoring his objection*]: Weeth peesstool... Bot sane way like en mi país... Een my contry... [*Taking the pistol-case and holding it up.*] One peesstool, he have boulett... One peesstool, he no have... You peeck!

CHANDEBISE: I... Not on your life! You're mad if you think—

HOMENIDES [*cutting him off with a sudden blood-curdling roar that reduces him to silence and sets him back on his heels*]: Grrraaahhhrrr!
[*Immediately resuming his matter-of-fact manner, he lays the open case down on the canapé, takes a piece of chalk from his pocket, and quickly outlines a circle on the left side of a bewildered* CHANDEBISE's *chest.*]

CHANDEBISE [*timidly*]: What are you—

HOMENIDES: Bueno! [*Outlining a similar circle on his own chest.*] An now I do me... [*Putting the chalk away.*] So! Ees done!... [*Pointing first to* CHANDEBISE's *circle, then to his own.*] Cow's-eye for me... Cow's-eye for you... [*Miming.*] "Bam bam! Bam bam!"

CHANDEBISE: But... You just said... One gun isn't even loaded...

HOMENIDES: Sí, sí... Ees how we fight duelo en mi país...

CHANDEBISE [*summoning up enough courage to object*]: Yes, well... This is my "país," thank you!

HOMENIDES [*ignoring his remark, he takes the pistols from the case, holding them both in one hand by the butts and offering them, very amiably*]: So! You peeck, yes?

CHANDEBISE [*cringing out of the potential line of fire*]: No! I... Who ever heard—

HOMENIDES: Sí, sí! You peeck! You peeck!

CHANDEBISE [*trying desperately to make light of the situation, gently mimicking*]: No! I no pick!... I no pick anything! Ever! [*With a nervous chuckle, attempting to defuse the crisis, trying to skirt around* HOMENIDES *and head upstage.*] Not even my nose!

HOMENIDES [*barring his flight, with another tremendous roar, cutting short his little laugh*]: Grrraaahhhrrr!... So! You no peeck?... [*Snarling.*] Ha ha!... Bueno! So *I* peeck!... Sí! An I keell!

CHANDEBISE: Good God, he's serious!... [*Managing to elude* HOMENIDES's *grasp and dashing like a frightened jackrabbit up to the double door.*] He means it!... Help!... Help!...

[*He flings both panels open and runs out, still shouting.*]

HOMENIDES [*streaking after him*]: Chandépisse!... [*Not a little ingenuously.*] For why you go? Ees how we do een my contry. Ees how...

[*The last few words are heard from offstage as he exits, still carrying the two pistols, and leaving the double door open.*]

CHANDEBISE'S VOICE [*from the right of the vestibule*] ⎫
HOMENIDES'S VOICE [*following in the same direction*] ⎬ [*together*]: ⎧ Help! Help!...
God in heaven!...
Chandépisse!...
You no go, Chandépisse!...

[*The door, up right, opens and* CHANDEBISE *bursts in.*]

CHANDEBISE [*frantic*]: Help!... [*He makes a beeline for the door, down left, pulling it open and leaping inside to supposed safety.*] Ah!... [*No sooner has he disappeared into the room than he is heard screaming.*] Ayyy! [*Reappearing at the threshold, hysterical.*] Me! Me!... In there! In my bed!... Me!... I... It's haunted!... It's... It's...

HOMENIDES'S VOICE [*behind the door, up right*]: Where she ees, thees Chandépisse?

CHANDEBISE [*at the sound of his voice*]: Good God! [*Looking around desperately, he streaks up to the double door and rushes out, shouting.*] Help! Help!...[1]

HOMENIDES [*storming in, up right, just as* CHANDEBISE *slams the double door behind him*]: Ah!... [*Noticing his exit.*] You no go! [*Lunging at the double door, trying in vain to open it.*] You no go!

PSEUDO-CHANDEBISE'S VOICE [*moving backstage toward the door, up left*]: Help!... Help!...

HOMENIDES [*running left, following the sound of the voice, trying unsuccessfully to open the door*]: You open, Chandépisse!... You open!

PSEUDO-CHANDEBISE'S VOICE [*moving backstage toward the door, up right*]: Help!... Help!...

HOMENIDES [*running right, trying even more vigorously to open that door*]: You open!... Ay, carajo!... You open, Chandépisse!

---

[1] Feydeau indicates that, at this point, CHANDEBISE's backstage shouts of "Help!" are to be taken over and continued throughout by the stage manager (though anyone able to mimic his voice would do). The substitute also parries each of HOMENIDES's (and, later, LOCHE's) successive attempts to open the doors—up center, left, and right—by holding them shut from behind. These expedients allow the actor playing the dual role to put on the dressing-gown and foulard, and prepare for his momentary appearance as LOCHE, while the audience still assumes CHANDEBISE to be behind the door, up right [Translator's note].

[*As* HOMENIDES *is in the midst of his unsuccessful efforts, the door, down left, opens, and* LOCHE, *in dressing-gown and foulard, appears, hair tousled and bleary-eyed.*]

LOCHE [*half-asleep*]: Damn! How's anybody supposed to sleep in this—

HOMENIDES [*suddenly spying him, with a shout*]: Ha! Heen! [*He immediately forgets about the door and, still carrying the pistols, strides down left.*] Bueno! [*Brandishing one of the pistols in one hand.*] I peeck for me!

LOCHE: Huh?

HOMENIDES [*offering the other pistol, in his other hand, to* LOCHE]: You peeck for you!

LOCHE [*recognizing him*]: My God! The maniac!...

HOMENIDES [*coming down, far left*]: An now, I keell!

LOCHE: What? [*Beating a bewildered retreat upstage, as fast as his lumbering gait will allow, trying to open the door, up left, to no avail.*] Ayyy!

HOMENIDES [*hot on his heels, ready to pounce, snarling*]: Ha ha! Now you no go!... Ees no escape!... Ees feeneesh!

LOCHE [*eluding him, trying unsuccessfully to open the double door*]: Ayayay! [*Loping right, two steps ahead of* HOMENIDES, *and trying the door, up right, likewise with no luck.*] Ayayayay!

[*Panicking, he turns downstage and, realizing that his only means of escape is the window, left open by* CHANDEBISE, *reaches it just before the panting* HOMENIDES *catches up with him. Desperate, he clambers up onto the sill and jumps out, but not before managing a little salute to* HOMENIDES, *who ineffectually lunges at him.*]

HOMENIDES [*at the window, unable to repress a gesture of shocked concern*]: Oh!... Pobrecito!... She go break neck!... Tsk tsk tsk!... [*Leaning out and looking down, to check.*] Ah! No... Ees fine... She no break notheeng... She steell leeve... [*Without transition, in the same tone of voice.*] So! I keell!... [*Moving off left, to the canapé.*] Sí, sí! I keell!... [*He replaces the pistols in the case, leaving it open; then, opening his collar and fanning his face with one hand, heaving a sigh.*] Haaa!... Qué tengo sed!... [*Tongue drooping, he looks around the room for something to drink.*] No hay nada que beber en esta casa?... No ees for to dreenk, notheeng?... [*Suddenly his glance lights on the half-empty glass left by* CHANDEBISE *on the oblong table.*] Aha!... Ees! Ees!... [*Going over and picking it up.*] Bueno! Ees sonetheeng!... [*No sooner does he take a gulp than, slamming the glass back down, he contorts his face in a grimace of unspeakable disgust, and, seeing nowhere to get rid of the mouthful, rushes over to the open window and noisily spits it out, with no concern for delicacy or decorum.*] Pfffuuu!... Yeccchhh! Pfffuuu!...

[*As he stands there sputtering, wiping his mouth with the back of his hand,* LOCHE *is heard to react, apparently hit by the shower.*]

LOCHE'S VOICE: Hey!

HOMENIDES [*leaning out the window, looking down, very offhand*]: Esscuse, por favor!... [*Returning to his own concerns, still grimacing.*] Aaaaaccchhh!... [*Recalling his similar experience toward the end of Act One.*] Ees no first tine I dreenk soch theeng in thees house!... Ay! Caramba! Qué malditas cosas beben en esta casa! [*As he takes several deep, energetic breaths in an attempt to regain his composure, standing now by the writing-desk, left open in front of the canapé by* FINACHE, *a smell suddenly*

attracts his attention and he looks about sniffing the air inquisitively.]
Holá! Qué es eso?... Ees esmell... Ees parfoum... [*Sniffing suspiciously.*]
Ees sane parfoum I esmell thees morneeng!... [*Sniffing around the desk, hit
by a realization.*] Een bidet!... Een bidet doux fron Luciana... Sí! Esa
carta!... Esa carta maldita!... [*Spying the pile of stationery still on the desk.*]
Ay! Ees papél!... Sane papél!... [*He picks up the offending sheet of paper,
still lying on top where* FINACHE *had left it, and takes a long whiff.*] Sí, sí!...
[*Examining it and noticing the writing on it.*] Oh! Ees escrito,
sonetheeng!... [*After a moment his jaw drops as he notices his wife's
handwriting.*] Ay! La escritura de Luciana!... What ees? What ees?... Mi
esposa, he write thees theeng!... [*Reading.*] "I sow you the other eveneeng
at the Palaisse-Royal... We were watcheeng a play..." [*Enraged.*] Hijo de
puta! Ees sane!... Sane theeng like hot bidet he write to Chandépisse!...
[*Taking the other letter from his pocket.*] Sane theeng like thees one!
[*Comparing them.*] For why?... Porqué está con los papeles de Señora
Chandépisse?... For why here?... Oh! I fine out!... Sí, sí! I go fine out for
sure! [*He storms upstage to the door, up right, and pounds vigorously and
repeatedly.*] Ábrame la puerta!... Ábrame, carajo!... You open!... You
open!...
[*The door opens and* TOURNEL *appears.*]

TOURNEL [*impatiently*]: What is it?

HOMENIDES   ⎫   ⎧ Ah! Toenail!... [*Lunging at his throat.*] Ees you, eh?
              ⎬ [*together*]:   ⎨
TOURNEL   ⎭   ⎩ What the devil do you... Good grief! Him!...

HOMENIDES [*pulling him in and pivoting him violently around*]: You tell me...
[*Waving both sheets in his face with one hand, clutching him with the
other.*] Thees lettair...

TOURNEL [*struggling*] ⎫   ⎧ Let me go, you... you...
                        ⎬ [*together*]:   ⎨
HOMENIDES   ⎭   ⎩ Thees lettair...

[GISELE *appears at the open door, up right.*]

GISELE [*entering and coming a few steps down right*]: What in the name—

HOMENIDES [*pushing away* TOURNEL *and advancing determinedly right, to
GISELE, *as* TOURNEL *staggers down to the little table near the canapé and
stands propped against it, catching his breath*]: Ha! You!... You tell to me,
por favor!... [*Waving in her face the sheet of paper he has just found.*]
Thees! Thees!... For why I fine thees theeng en su escritorio de usted?
[*Pointing to the writing-desk.*] Een you desque, señora...
[*He pronounces "deskay."*]

GISELE [*recognizing the paper, with a start*]: What? [*Indignantly, taking the
offensive.*] How dare you go rummaging through my papers, monsieur!

HOMENIDES: I no go, how you say... I fine for becose I esmell... Sí, sí... [*He
sniffs, to illustrate.*] I esmell...

GISELE: Still...

HOMENIDES: Bot ees notheeng... No mattair... [*Struggling to contain his rage.*]
Ees mattair one theeng only. For why ees mi esposa, he write?

GISELE: Aha... Well, actually...

HOMENIDES [*brandishing the other sheet, the one containing the full text of the
letter*]: An for why ees mi Luciana, he feell op bidet...

TOURNEL [*aside, doubting his ears*]: Fills up the...?

HOMENIDES [*waving the same letter, to* GISELE, *continuing*]: ...thees bidet doux, señora... [*As* TOURNEL *gives a little nod of comprehension.*] weeth soch deesgosteeng theeng!

GISELE [*to* HOMENIDES]: The fact is...

TOURNEL [*to* GISELE, sotto voce]: Tell him!... Tell him, for heaven's sake!

HOMENIDES: An to meet een hotel!... Ha! [*Pointing.*] Ees here, een you house, he make op soch theeng?

GISELE [*taking the bull by the horns*]: Yes, monsieur! It is!... And if you weren't so stubborn you would realize that... that... that that just proves how innocent she is!

HOMENIDES [*suddenly interested*]: How ees so?... How?... How?

GISELE: How?... Because if there were anything at all between your wife and my husband, she wouldn't be so careless as to leave that...

[*She points to the sheet of stationery that he found on the desk.*]

TOURNEL [*continuing* GISELE'*s thought, pointing to* GISELE]: ...in *her* desque!

[*He pronounces "deskay," à la* HOMENIDES.]

GISELE [*to* HOMENIDES]: Now would she!

HOMENIDES [*accepting the logic, but still confused*]: So?... So? So? [*Taking both sheets in one hand, waving them, to* TOURNEL.] So how?... [*Likewise, to* GISELE.] So how?

GISELE [*looking upstage and catching sight of* LUCIENNE, *approaching, through the open doorway, up right*]: How?... [*Pointing up right, at the end of her rope.*] Here she is, monsieur. You can ask her "how" yourself!

[*She comes down and stands by the writing-desk, as* HOMENIDES *rushes up to meet* LUCIENNE.]

HOMENIDES [*to* LUCIENNE]: Ay! Luciana...

LUCIENNE [*instinctively pulling back*]: Oh!... Don Carlos...

[*She turns to leave.*]

HOMENIDES [*seizing her by the wrist with his free hand*]: No, no! You no go, señora!... [*Pulling her down toward the others, right center.*] You tell to me... Por favor!... One word...

LUCIENNE: Please...

HOMENIDES [*to* LUCIENNE, *on his right*]: One word only... [*Pleading.*] For to confort me... For to make me no for to reck my brain... For to pain my boosoom...

LUCIENNE: But—

HOMENIDES [*waving the two letters in her face*]: Thees lettair... For why you write? You tell to me... One word...

LUCIENNE [*looking back and forth, between him and* GISELE]: But... But... I can't...

GISELE [*to* LUCIENNE]: Yes you can, precious! I give you permission...

LUCIENNE [*to* GISELE]: You... Are you sure, love?

HOMENIDES [*pleading, to* LUCIENNE]			Oh! Sí!... Sí...
TOURNEL [*still at the little table, to* LUCIENNE]	}	[*together*]: {	Tell him!... Tell him!...

LUCIENNE [*to* GISELE, *surprised*]: You don't mind?

HOMENIDES [*continuing, to* LUCIENNE]: Sí, sí! Por favor!...

GISELE [*to* LUCIENNE]: Go on... We don't want him to "wreck" his brain, now do we?

HOMENIDES [*to* LUCIENNE, *continuing*]: Sí, sí!... [*To* GISELE, *reacting to her observation.*] No, no!... [To LUCIENNE.] Sí! [*To* GISELE.] No!...

LUCIENNE [*cutting short his confusion*]: Well... [*To* HOMENIDES, *with a little good-natured sarcasm.*] I must say, Don Othello—

HOMENIDES [*suddenly suspicious again*]: Don quién?... Don qué?... Don who?... [*Pointing to himself.*] Don Carlos, yo!... [*Menacingly.*] Who she ees, thees Don Othello?

LUCIENNE [*calming him, with a laugh*]: No, no... In Shakespeare, silly!... El teatro!... El esposo el más celoso del mundo!... [*Pointing to* HOMENIDES, *addressing* GISELE.] Qué tonto! Qué tonto!

[*The following "sí" are pronounced in a regular rhythm.*]

HOMENIDES [*agreeing, with a smile*]: Sí... Sí...

GISELE [*nodding, in uncomprehending agreement*]: Sí...

TOURNEL *and* **GISELE** [*together*]: Sí...

LUCIENNE *and* **TOURNEL** [*together*]: Sí...

LUCIENNE: Sí... [*To* HOMENIDES, *explaining*]: Pues, mi querido... Es que Gisela creía tener motivo de dudar de la fidelidad de su marido...

HOMENIDES: Cómo?

LUCIENNE: Y entonces, para probarlo, decidió darle una cita galante... a la cual también asistiría, ella.

HOMENIDES [*impatient*]: Pero, la carta! La carta!... El bidet doux, eh?

LUCIENNE [*beginning to lose patience as well*]: Eh! La carta!... Espera, hombre!... [*Calming down, explaining the fine points.*] Sí ella hubiese escrito la carta a su marido, éste hubiera reconocido su escritura.

HOMENIDES [*his eyes lighting up as he begins to understand*]: Después?... Después?...

LUCIENNE: Entonces, ella me encargó de escribirla en su lugar.

HOMENIDES: No! Es verdad? [*To a thoroughly uncomprehending* GISELE.] Es verdad, señora? [*Pointing to* LUCIENNE, *still addressing* GISELE.] Es verdad lo que dice?... Ees true thees theeng he say?

GISELE [*assuming that* LUCIENNE *has accurately related the events, to* HOMENIDES]: Oh! Sí, sí!... [*Aside.*] I suppose!

HOMENIDES [*to* GISELE]: Ah! Señora! Señora!... Quando pienso que me he metido tantas ideas en la cabeza!

GISELE [*with a little bow*]: Please... Don't mention it... [*Aside.*] Really...

HOMENIDES [*to* GISELE]: When I theenk thees theeng I theenk! Thees theeng I theenk!... [*To* LUCIENNE, *hitting his forehead with the heel of his palm.*] Ay! Qué estúpido!... Qué estúpido soy! [*Turning to* TOURNEL, *who is still by the little table, and beating his breast with each exclamation, as if pronouncing a "mea culpa."*] Ah! No soy más que un bruto! Un bruto! Un bruto! Un bruto!

TOURNEL [*to* HOMENIDES, *gently mocking*]: Careful, monsieur, for to not pain your bosom!

HOMENIDES [*ignoring him, to* LUCIENNE]: Ah! Querida! Perdóname mis estupideces!... Esscuse... Esscuse...

LUCIENNE [*coyly*]: Well... I forgive you... If you promise never to do it again!

HOMENIDES [*embracing her and leading her over to the canapé*]: Ah! Querida mía! Yo te quiero!... My darleeng!

[*He covers her with passionate Latin kisses.*]

GISELE [*to* TOURNEL, *joining him*]: It doesn't take long to make up in Spanish!

TOURNEL: No... But really, that was more than one word...

[*As* HOMENIDES *and* LUCIENNE, *still embracing, go to sit down on the* canapé, LUCIENNE *inadvertently sits on the open pistol-case.*]

LUCIENNE [*jumping up*]: What... [*Noticing the pistols.*] Oh! Don Carlos!...

HOMENIDES [*taking the pistols in hand, good-naturedly showing them*]: Ha ha! No es nada!... Notheeng!... I no need no more! No need...

[LUCIENNE *sits back down and* HOMENIDES *returns to his embrace, pistols in hand notwithstanding. At that moment the door, up center, opens and* FINACHE, EDOUARD, *and* CHANDEBISE *make a hasty entrance, leaving both panels open.*]

FINACHE [*coming down center, with* EDOUARD *close behind*]: But I'm telling you! You're not making any sense, you two!

TOURNEL [*turning to greet them*]: I say...

[*They ignore him.*]

EDOUARD [*naked to the waist, wrapped in a bath towel, prosthesis in hand, to* FINACHE, *inarticulately*]: And I'm telling you! I saw him—

FINACHE [*interrupting, pointing to the prosthesis*]: Please!... Put it in!

EDOUARD [*grumblingly complying, adjusting it with his thumbs, then repeating with perfect diction*]: I'm telling you! I saw him in two places at once! [*Pointing first toward the vestibule, then toward the door, down left.*] There!... And there!

CHANDEBISE [*coming straight down left, to* FINACHE]: He's right! I saw me too!... Him... Me... Face to face... [*Pointing to the same door.*] In there! In my bed!

FINACHE [*continuing downstage, followed by a protesting* EDOUARD]: Bah!

EDOUARD [*to* FINACHE] } [*together*]: { But I'm telling you...

GISELE [*crossing left, joining* CHANDEBISE] } [*together*]: { Really, Victor-Emmanuel...

HOMENIDES [*still on the* canapé, *with pistols waving, to* FINACHE]: Qué?... Qué hay?

CHANDEBISE [*suddenly noticing* HOMENIDES, *until then concealed by* LUCIENNE]: Him?... Still here?...

[*He turns to flee at the sight of the pistols.*]

HOMENIDES [*standing, gesturing him to stay*]: No, no! You no go!... You no go, Chandépisse!... I no go for to keell you no more!

CHANDEBISE: You—

HOMENIDES: No ees need!... [*Pointing to* LUCIENNE.] He essplain to me everytheeng!...

CHANDEBISE: He... [*Correcting himself.*] She...! She...!

HOMENIDES: Sí, sí!... [*Replacing the pistols in the case.*] An now I know... Thees woman who write lettair... Thees estranyher who seet een Palaisse-Royal, an who have... How you say?... Who have ants een her pants... He no ees my wife...

CHANDEBISE: Oh?

HOMENIDES: He ees *you* wife, mossié!

CHANDEBISE [*startled, to* GISELE]: What?

GISELE [*to* CHANDEBISE]: How many times do we have to tell you?

[*She moves up left and stands by the chiffonier, drumming her fingers.*]

CHANDEBISE: Me?

GISELE [to CHANDEBISE]: You!

TOURNEL [crossing toward CHANDEBISE]: Good grief! A dozen times, my friend... And each time we kiss and make up! [Pointing to CHANDEBISE, himself, and GISELE, in turn.] You... Me... Her... [He moves up left, joining GISELE, with whom he stands exchanging appropriate gestures.]

CHANDEBISE: We what?...

HOMENIDES: An to theenk... [Pointing left.] Ees for thees I make you for to jomp out fron weendow!

CHANDEBISE [utterly flabbergasted]: Me?

LUCIENNE [standing up], FINACHE, EDOUARD, TOURNEL, and GISELE [together]: Out the window?

HOMENIDES [beating his breast]: Qué bruto!... Ay!

CHANDEBISE [to HOMENIDES]: Me?... You made me jump out the window?

HOMENIDES: Por supuesto!... Why? You no remembair? You cone fron here... [He points to the door, down left.] An nesst theeng... Hop! [Miming a swan dive.] Out fron weendow you jomp!

CHANDEBISE [moving far left with great strides]: That does it! [To FINACHE.] You see? Him too!... It's... It's some kind of... I don't know... Some mass hallucination!

FINACHE [to CHANDEBISE]: But my dear friend...

CHANDEBISE [continuing, to HOMENIDES]: What you saw jump out the window... And what you thought was me... [To FINACHE.] That's what I saw in my bed!

EDOUARD: And what I saw... [Pointing to each place in turn.] There... And there!

CHANDEBISE: Exactly! And the proof is that I know I didn't jump out any window!

TOURNEL: I say...

HOMENIDES [to CHANDEBISE]: What you say?

TOURNEL [thinking the question is meant for him]: I said: "I say..."

HOMENIDES [to TOURNEL]: No you... No you...

GISELE [continuing, not without a touch of sarcasm regarding his sanity, to CHANDEBISE]: Are you sure, Victor-Emmanuel? After all...

CHANDEBISE [to GISELE]: Of course I'm sure!... Don't you think I'd know...?

GISELE: Well...

HOMENIDES [to CHANDEBISE]: Bot eef no ees you who jomp out fron weendow...

FINACHE [taking his head in his hands]: Oh là là!... Is everyone crazy, or is it just me?

[Just then ETIENNE and MOUSQUETARD appear at the door, up center.]

ETIENNE [announcing]: Monsieur Mousquetard!

MOUSQUETARD [entering, with the dressing-gown under his arm]: Begging your pardon... [Coming center, looking around, correcting himself.] Your pardons... All of you...

[As all the others draw closer to MOUSQUETARD, a panicking CHANDEBISE, still far left, opening his mouth in a silent shriek, crawls down on all fours and, unseen by the rest, hides under the oblong table.]

FINACHE ⎱ [*together*]: ⎰ Mousquetard!

EDOUARD ⎰   ⎱ Monsieur!

GISELE: The owner of that... that...

TOURNEL [*supplying an acceptable word*]: Establishment!...

MOUSQUETARD [*continuing his story*]: But just now, while I'm passing by outside... [*Pointing down right.*] my porter jumps out that window... Don't ask me why!... And damn near lands on my goddamn head! [*Putting his hand to his mouth to excuse his vulgarity, to the two women.*] Oh...

HOMENIDES ⎱ Cómo?

MOUSQUETARD ⎰ Sorry!

FINACHE ⎱ [*together*]: ⎰ What?

EDOUARD ⎰   ⎱ Who?

TOURNEL ⎱ When?

LUCIENNE ⎰ Why?

GISELE [*echoing* TOURNEL, *with a look in his direction*]: I say!

MOUSQUETARD [*continuing*]: All wet... [*Holding up the dressing-gown.*] And then tries to run off with this...

GISELE: But... That's my husband's! How did your porter... [*Turning to where* CHANDEBISE *had been standing.*] Your robe, treasure... Your... [*Looking around.*] Now where did he... [*Calling.*] Victor!... Victor-Emmanuel!... [*She moves quickly upstage and opens the door, up left, looking for him outside.*] Victor-Emmanuel!...

HOMENIDES, FINACHE, EDOUARD, TOURNEL, *and* LUCIENNE [*looking around, echoing, together*]: Victor-Emmanuel!

[ETIENNE *and* TOURNEL, *simultaneously, go quickly to the doors, up right and down left, respectively, open them, and look outside, while, at the same time,* HOMENIDES *goes up center and peers out the open double door. Just as they are all doing so,* MOUSQUETARD *suddenly notices* CHANDEBISE *on all fours under the table.*]

MOUSQUETARD [*pointing with a yell*]: You!

HOMENIDES, FINACHE, EDOUARD, LUCIENNE, GISELE, TOURNEL, *and* ETIENNE [*together*]: What?

MOUSQUETARD: Loche!... Again, that damnable Loche!

[*During the following, he goes about the table in an attempt to collar* CHANDEBISE.]

GISELE *and* TOURNEL [*approaching each other, left, together*]: Loche?

FINACHE *and* EDOUARD [*looking at each other, together*]: Loche?

LUCIENNE *and* HOMENIDES [*likewise*]: Loche?

ETIENNE [*still at the door, up right, to himself*]: Loche?

CHANDEBISE [*as* MOUSQUETARD *drags him out, resisting*]: No, no!... I... I...

MOUSQUETARD [*pivoting him around, as before, with repeated kicks to the backside, as the others look on in consternation*]: Animal!... Pig!... Swine!...

LUCIENNE, HOMENIDES, EDOUARD, *and* FINACHE [*lined up, at an angle, with* LUCIENNE *farthest down right and* FINACHE *farthest up left, all gawking in disbelief, together*]: Oh!

GISELE [*to* MOUSQUETARD, *trying to come between him and* CHANDEBISE]: But monsieur!... What are you doing? That's my husband!

MOUSQUETARD [*to* GISELE]: Your what?

CHANDEBISE [*trying to recover his aplomb, to anyone who will listen*]: He... I'm telling you... It's an obsession!... Every time he sees me he's got to kick me in the—

MOUSQUETARD [*to* GISELE]: Your husband?... Him?

GISELE: Of course! Monsieur Chandebise...

MOUSQUETARD: But... But he can't be!... He... He's the spit and image of Loche, my porter... The bloody spit—

[*The following exclamations, the first of which cuts off* MOUSQUETARD *in mid-sentence, are delivered rapid-fire, until* TOURNEL'*s reply.*]

GISELE: Loche?

LUCIENNE: Really?

HOMENIDES: Es verdad?

EDOUARD: Is it possible?

FINACHE: Can you believe it?

TOURNEL [*still left, to* MOUSQUETARD]: Loche, you say?...

MOUSQUETARD: Yes... The one who just jumped out the window...

[TOURNEL *moves up toward the fireplace, shaking his head.*]

CHANDEBISE [*as the others voice their amazement with a long, simultaneous "Aaaah!"*]: But that explains everything!... The one I saw in my bed just now... The one I thought was me... That was Loche!

LUCIENNE, HOMENIDES, EDOUARD, *and* FINACHE [*together*]: It was Loche!

GISELE [*to* TOURNEL]: And the one we saw at the hotel... With the bottle of whisky...

TOURNEL: The one we kissed!...

GISELE, HOMENIDES, EDOUARD, FINACHE, *and* CHANDEBISE [*together*]: It was Loche!

LUCIENNE: And the one who tried to drag me off to buy some wine!...

EDOUARD: And who went around lugging a load of wood on his back!...

GISELE, HOMENIDES, FINACHE, *and* CHANDEBISE [*together*]: It was Loche!

MOUSQUETARD: Right! [*Leaving* CHANDEBISE *and* GISELE, *moving right, toward* LUCIENNE, *addressing the group of four, still in line.*] That damn lush Loche!

CHANDEBISE [*as* MOUSQUETARD *once again puts his hand to his mouth*]: Well, I'll be... Blast! I'm sorry he ran off. I'd have liked to see my double face to face!

MOUSQUETARD [*to* CHANDEBISE]: Well, just come to the Hotel Paramour any day!

ETIENNE [*who, still up right, has been observing all the preceding in bewildered silence, to himself*]: Or any night!

CHANDEBISE [*to* MOUSQUETARD]: Me, monsieur?... Never again! I've had my fill!

GISELE [*a little snidely, to* CHANDEBISE]: Not even for a twist with the beautiful stranger of the Palais-Royal?

LUCIENNE [*to* GISELE, *laughing*]: "Tryst," love... "Tryst"...

HOMENIDES [*laughing*]: Sí, sí!... [*Looking at* LUCIENNE.] The beauteefool estranyher...

CHANDEBISE [*with a note of mock reproach, to* GISELE]: That's right... Make fun... You and that silly little trap of yours!... That letter... That perfume...

GISELE [*to* CHANDEBISE]: I'm sorry, treasure. But what else could I do? I couldn't help thinking you were being... well, unfaithful...

CHANDEBISE: Me?... Unfaithful?... But why, good God? Why?

GISELE: Well, frankly... [*Embarrassed.*] Because...

[*She whispers in his ear for a moment as* FINACHE *draws close, straining to listen. In the meantime,* TOURNEL, *pleased to see the couple reunited, and probably envisioning future personal advantage, looks on approvingly.*]

CHANDEBISE [*surprised at* GISELE'*s revelation*]: What?... For so little?

GISELE: Little?... Nothing, you mean!

CHANDEBISE: But such a small thing?

GISELE: Yes! [*With a sly wink full of innuendo.*] A very small thing!...

[FINACHE, *eavesdropping, represses a guffaw.*]

CHANDEBISE [*catching her implication*]: Oh... I...

GISELE: But sometimes it's the smallest things that make us the most suspicious. It's not hard...

FINACHE [*aside, chuckling*]: No!

CHANDEBISE: Well! [*Confidently.*] We'll see about that... small thing... [*Whispering to her.*] Tonight!... And make it bigger...

GISELE: You, treasure?

FINACHE [*still listening in, with a nudge, aside to* CHANDEBISE]: And harder!

CHANDEBISE [*to* GISELE]: At least, I'll try...

[*They embrace.*]

TOURNEL [*coming back down center, toward the others, calling for their attention*]: I say... I knew a lady once who suspected her lover... And one beautiful summer day, just when he least expected, she—

[LUCIENNE, HOMENIDES, EDOUARD, FINACHE, *and* ETIENNE—*the last named coming down center—drown him out with a variety of exclamations, such as "Please!", "Later!", "No, no! Not now!", "Por favor, Toenail!", and the like, while* CHANDEBISE *and* GISELE *continue their embrace as the curtain falls.*]

CURTAIN

GOING TO POT

Adaptation of

On purge Bébé

by

Georges Feydeau

(1910)

CHARACTERS

FOLLAVOINE, a porcelain manufacturer in his mid- or late thirties, and a long-suffering husband

CHOUILLOUX, a very distinguished government official

TRUCHET, the rather effete paramour of Chouilloux's wife

JULIE, Follavoine's wife, probably somewhat younger, and with little respect for logic or decorum

MADAME CHOUILLOUX, Chouilloux's philandering wife, a matron clinging to what is left of her youth

ROSE, the Follavoines' maid, not overly bright

BABY, the Follavoines' seven-year-old brat of a son, Alexander, alias Toto

Follavoine's study. Down right, a door leading to Follavoine's bedroom. Up right, the door to his wife's room. Up center, a double door leading to the hall. On each side of this door, a cabinet, the front of which is formed by two glassed panels, covered on the inside by an opaque material concealing the interior. Stage left, running almost the entire length of the wall, a large window appropriately curtained in the style of the period. Near this window, a large desk, facing the audience and covered with various articles: a dictionary, miscellaneous books, folders, loose papers scattered here and there, a box of rubber bands, etc. Under the desk, a wastepaper basket. Behind it, a chair. In front of it, to the left, an armchair. Up right, not far from the doors, a sofa placed slightly diagonally. To the right of this sofa, an end table; to the left, a small chair.

At rise, FOLLAVOINE *is seen bent over his desk, busily consulting his dictionary.*

FOLLAVOINE: Let's see now, Aleutian Islands... Aleutian Islands... Aleutian...
  [*A knock is heard at the door.* FOLLAVOINE *answers angrily without looking up from his dictionary.*] Come in! Come in! [*To* ROSE, *entering, up center.*] What is it?
ROSE: It's madame. She wishes to see monsieur.
FOLLAVOINE: Good! Let her come and see me. She knows where I am.
ROSE: Madame is in the bathroom. She says she's too busy to be disturbed.
FOLLAVOINE: Oh really? Well, you can tell her I'm busy too. I'm sorry, but I'm working.
ROSE [*indifferently*]: Yes, monsieur.
FOLLAVOINE: What does she want anyway?
ROSE: I couldn't say, monsieur.
FOLLAVOINE: Well, go find out.
ROSE: Yes, monsieur.
FOLLAVOINE [*under his breath*]: Too busy... [*Calling to* ROSE *as she reaches the door, up right.*] Wait a minute! While you're here...
ROSE: Monsieur?
FOLLAVOINE: You wouldn't know, off hand... where the Aleutians are?
ROSE: Monsieur?
FOLLAVOINE: The Aleutians... You wouldn't happen to know where they are, would you?
ROSE: Oh no! No, monsieur. I don't put things away around here. Madame is the one who—
FOLLAVOINE [*standing up straight*]: What? "Put things away..."! What are you talking about? The Aleutians! The Aleutians! They're islands, idiot! Islands! Earth surrounded by water. You know what that is?
ROSE [*opening her eyes wide*]: Earth surrounded by water?

FOLLAVOINE: Yes. Earth surrounded by water. What do you call it?

ROSE: Mud?

FOLLAVOINE: Mud? No, no... Not mud! It's mud when there's just a little earth and a little water. When there's a lot of earth and a lot of water it's called an island.

ROSE [*amazed*]: Oh?

FOLLAVOINE: That's what the Aleutians are. Islands. You understand? They aren't in the apartment.

ROSE [*trying her best to understand*]: Oh yes, monsieur. They're outside the apartment.

FOLLAVOINE: Of course they're outside the apartment!

ROSE: Yes, monsieur, I understand. But I haven't seen them.

FOLLAVOINE: That's fine! Thank you!

ROSE [*trying to justify herself*]: I haven't been in Paris very long.

FOLLAVOINE: Yes, yes. That's fine.

ROSE: And I get out so little!

FOLLAVOINE: Yes... That's right, that's right... [*He pushes her gently toward the door, up center, and she leaves.*] Ha! It's incredible! That girl doesn't know a thing. Absolutely nothing. What did she learn in school, I wonder? [*He crosses to his desk, leaning against it once again to consult the dictionary.*] Now let's see. Eleutians... Eleutians... That's funny. "Elephant, Eleusis, elevate..." But no Eleutians! It should be right here between "Eleusis" and "elevate." Bah! This dictionary is worthless!

[JULIE *storms in. She is dressed in a dirty bathrobe, with curlers in her hair and her stockings down around her ankles. A covered wash-bucket, full of water, is hanging from her arm.*]

JULIE: Well! Very nice! Too busy to speak to me!

FOLLAVOINE [*jumping at the sudden intrusion*]: Julie! For God's sake, don't burst in here like that!

JULIE [*sarcastically*]: Oh, I beg your pardon! [*Affectedly polite.*] Are you really too busy to speak to me... darling?

FOLLAVOINE [*angrily*]: You're a fine one to talk! Why must *I* always come running? Why—

JULIE [*with an acid smile*]: Of course. You're absolutely right. We're only married, after all!

FOLLAVOINE: So? What difference—

JULIE: Oh! If I were someone else's wife, I'm sure you could find the time—

FOLLAVOINE: All right!... That's enough! I'm busy!

JULIE [*putting down her bucket where she stands, center stage, and moving right*]: Busy! He's busy! Isn't that fine!

FOLLAVOINE: Yes, that's what I said. Busy! [*Suddenly noticing* JULIE'*s bucket.*] What's that doing here?

JULIE: What?

FOLLAVOINE: Are you crazy, bringing your wash-bucket in here?

JULIE: Where? What wash-bucket?

FOLLAVOINE [*pointing to it*]: That!

JULIE: Oh, that's nothing. [*As ingenuously as possible.*] It's just my dirty water.

FOLLAVOINE: And what am I supposed to do with it?

JULIE: It's not for you, silly. I'm going to empty it out.

FOLLAVOINE: In here?

JULIE: Of course not! What kind of a question... Do I usually empty my dirty water in your study? Really, I do have a little sense, you know.

FOLLAVOINE: Then why bring it in here in the first place?

JULIE: Because I just happened to have the bucket in my hand when Rose brought me your answer... Your charming answer... [*Sarcastically.*] I didn't dare keep you waiting!

FOLLAVOINE: And you couldn't leave it outside the door?

JULIE [*becoming annoyed at* FOLLAVOINE'*s criticism*]: Oh, for heaven's sake! If it bothers you so much it's your own fault. You shouldn't have said you were too busy to talk with me. Busy! I can just imagine! With what?

FOLLAVOINE [*grumbling*]: With certain things—

JULIE: What things?

FOLLAVOINE: Certain things, I said... I was looking up the Aleutian Islands in the dictionary. There! Now you know.

JULIE: The Aleutian Islands? The Aleutian... Are you insane? You're going there I suppose?

FOLLAVOINE: No, I'm not going there!

JULIE [*sitting down on the sofa*]: Then what difference could it possibly make where they are? Why does a porcelain manufacturer have to know about the Aleutian Islands, of all things?

FOLLAVOINE [*still grumbling*]: If you think I give a damn! Believe me, if it was just for myself... But it's for Baby. He comes up with such questions! Children think their parents know everything. [*Imitating his son.*] "Daddy, where's the Aleutian Islands?" [*In his own voice.*] "Ha?" [BABY'*s voice.*] "The Aleutians, daddy, the Aleutians?" Believe me, I heard him the first time. The Aleutians... How should I know where they are? You, do you know?

JULIE: Yes, I think... They're... I've seen them somewhere, on a map... but I don't remember exactly—

FOLLAVOINE: Ah! Just like me. But I couldn't tell Baby that I didn't remember exactly! What would he think of his father? So I tried to use my ingenuity. "Shame on you," I told him. "You shouldn't ask such questions. The Aleutians! That's not for children!"

JULIE: Ha ha! That's your ingenuity? What a stupid answer!

FOLLAVOINE: Unfortunately, it happens to be one of the questions in his geography lesson.

JULIE: Naturally!

FOLLAVOINE: Why do they have to keep teaching children geography nowadays! With railroads and boats that take you anywhere you want to go... And with timetables that tell you everything—

JULIE: What? What has that got to do with it?

FOLLAVOINE: Just what I said. When you're looking for a city, who has to go running to a geography book? Just look at a timetable!

JULIE: And that's how you help your son? A lot of good that does him.

FOLLAVOINE: Well, damn it! What do you want from me? I did my best. I tried to look as if I really knew the answer but just didn't want to talk about it. So I said to him: "Look, if I tell you the answer, what good will it do you? It's better if you try to find it out for yourself. Later on, if you still want to know, I'll tell you." So I close the door and make a beeline for the dictionary to look it up. What do I find? Zero.

JULIE: Zero?

FOLLAVOINE: Nothing. Absolutely nothing.

JULIE [*skeptical*]: In the dictionary? Let me have a look.

FOLLAVOINE: Sure, sure! Look to your heart's content! [JULIE *begins scanning the page.*] Really, you should have a talk with Baby's teacher. Tell her not to fill his head with things even grown-ups don't know... and that aren't in the dictionary.

JULIE [*suddenly looking up from the dictionary, with a sarcastic laugh*]: Oh no! Ha ha ha!... Of all the stupid... Ha ha ha!

FOLLAVOINE: What's so funny?

JULIE: You've been looking under the E's!

FOLLAVOINE [*not quite understanding*]: Well? Isn't it in the E's?

JULIE [*very condescending*]: In the E's? The Aleutians? No wonder you couldn't find it!

FOLLAVOINE: All right then, if it's not in the E's, where is it?

JULIE [*turning to another page*]: You'll see, you'll see... "Illegible, illegitimate, ill-fated, ill-favored..." Hmm! [*Surprised.*] Now how did that happen?

FOLLAVOINE: What?

JULIE: It isn't there.

FOLLAVOINE [*triumphantly*]: Aha! I told you, know-it-all!

JULIE [*embarrassed*]: I don't understand. It should be between "illegitimate" and "ill-fated."

FOLLAVOINE: Maybe now you'll believe me when I tell you that dictionary is useless. You can look for a word under any letter you please, it's all the same. You'll never find the one you're looking for.

JULIE [*still staring at the open page*]: I just don't understand—

FOLLAVOINE: That should teach you!

JULIE: Well at least I looked under the I's. That's a lot more logical than the E's.

FOLLAVOINE: Sure! "More logical than the E's." Ha ha! Why not the A's while you're at it?

JULIE: "The A's... The A's..." What are you talking about, "the A's"! [*She gradually changes her tone.*] The A's... As a matter of fact, maybe... Aleutians, Aleutians... It seems to me... A... A... A...

FOLLAVOINE [*imitating*]: Ayayayayay!

JULIE [*scanning the columns quickly*]: "Aleph, Aleppo, alert, Aleut..." [*Triumphant.*] Aha! I've found it! "Aleutian Islands"!

FOLLAVOINE [*rushing to her side*]: You've found it? You've found... [*In his haste he accidently kicks* JULIE's *bucket, which has been sitting on the floor since her entrance.*] Damn! [FOLLAVOINE *picks up the bucket and, not knowing where to put it, places it on a corner of his desk.*]

JULIE: There, large as life: "Aleutian Islands, a chain of islands extending southward from Alaska, belonging to the United States."

FOLLAVOINE [*with a pleased expression, as if he had found it himself*]: Fine, fine!

JULIE: And it even gives the area and the population: "1,461 square miles, 1,300 inhabitants."

FOLLAVOINE: Isn't that always the way! A minute ago we didn't know the first thing about them, and now we know more than we need. That's life!

JULIE: And to think we were looking under the E's and the I's.

FOLLAVOINE: We could have looked till doomsday.

JULIE [*picking up her bucket*]: And all the time it was right there, in the A's.

FOLLAVOINE: Just like I said.

JULIE: You? Oh, now, just a moment! You said it... Yes, you said it, but you didn't mean it.

FOLLAVOINE [*moving toward* JULIE]: What are you talking about, I didn't mean it?

JULIE: Absolutely not! You were making fun of me. "Sure, why not the A's while you're at it?"

FOLLAVOINE: Now wait a minute—

JULIE: It was at that very moment that I got a sudden vision of the word.

FOLLAVOINE: "Vision"! That's wonderful! She got a vision of the word! I tell her why not look in the A's, and suddenly she gets a vision! Just like a woman!

JULIE: Oh! That's too much! Really! Who took the dictionary and looked it up? Who, I ask you?

FOLLAVOINE: Sure, under the I's. Ha!

JULIE: Like you, looking in the E's! But who found it in the A's? Answer me that! Who?

FOLLAVOINE [*sitting down at his desk and raising his eyes to the ceiling in an offhand manner*]: Very clever! After I tell you to look in the A's.

JULIE [*shaking the bucket furiously as she speaks*]: Oh! You know perfectly well I found it! I found it! I—

FOLLAVOINE [*rushing to take the bucket from her*]: All right! You found it! You found it! There, are you happy?

[*He looks on all sides for a place to put it.*]

JULIE: What are you looking for?

FOLLAVOINE: Nothing! Just some place to put this... this damned...

JULIE: Well, put it on the floor!

FOLLAVOINE [*placing it on the floor, angrily*]: There!

JULIE: The nerve! To say that you found it when you know perfectly well that I—

FOLLAVOINE [*out of patience*]: You're right! I admit it. You found it! You, you, you! All alone!

JULIE: Absolutely! And don't think you're doing me any favors either. Trying to tell me I didn't have a vision—

FOLLAVOINE: All right, all right! That's enough! Now, for God's sake, go get dressed. It's about time. Already eleven o'clock and you're still running around in that filthy bathrobe...

JULIE: Of course! Change the subject!

FOLLAVOINE: Just look at yourself! Charming! Curlers in your hair, stockings down around your ankles...

JULIE [*pulling up her stockings*]: And whose ankles should they be around? Yours?... There, I've fixed them. Are you happy?

FOLLAVOINE: Ha! If you think they'll stay up for more than half a minute the way you fixed them! It wouldn't kill you to wear garters, you know.

JULIE: And how am I supposed to attach then? I'm not wearing a corset.

FOLLAVOINE: Then go put one on, for God's sake! Who's stopping you?

JULIE: Why not? Maybe you'd like me to put on a hoop-skirt just to clean the bathroom!

[*While speaking she has picked up the bucket and moved toward her room.*]

FOLLAVOINE: Well who the devil tells you to clean the bathroom in the first place? You have a maid, don't you? What on earth is she for?

JULIE [*returning in a huff and depositing the bucket at* FOLLAVOINE's *feet*]: I should let my maid clean the bathroom?

FOLLAVOINE [*moving off, stage right, to avoid another discussion*]: Bah!

JULIE: Thank you just the same! Let her scratch and break everything? My mirrors, my bottles... Oh no! I'd rather do it myself.

[*She sits in the armchair near the desk, casually resting one leg on the bucket, as if it were a footstool.*]

FOLLAVOINE: Then why, may I ask, do you have a maid if you won't let her do anything?

JULIE: She... She helps me.

FOLLAVOINE: Sure! Sure she does! You do her work, and she helps you! How?

JULIE [*embarrassed*]: She... Well... She watches me.

FOLLAVOINE: Isn't that nice! She watches you. I pay the girl a salary like that just to stand and watch you. Lovely!

JULIE: Oh please! Don't talk about money all the time. It's so... so middle class!

FOLLAVOINE: Middle class! Middle... Listen! I think when I give her such a salary I'm entitled to—

JULIE [*getting up and approaching* FOLLAVOINE]: And besides, what are you complaining about? Do *I* get a salary? No. So, if it doesn't cost you any more, what's the difference who does the housework?

FOLLAVOINE: The difference... The difference is that I'm paying a maid to do the housework for my wife. I'm not paying a wife to do the housework for my maid. If that's how it is, we could do without the maid.

JULIE: Aha! I knew that's what you were geting at! I knew it! You begrudge me a maid!

FOLLAVOINE: Wait a minute! What are you talking about... "begrudge you a maid"?

JULIE: Just what I said.

FOLLAVOINE [*out of replies, in desperation*]: For God's sake, pull up your stockings!

JULIE [*angrily complying*]: Oh!... Such a fuss just because I like to clean the bathroom myself. [*She moves toward* FOLLAVOINE's *desk, talking as she goes.*] I'm sure you're the first husband to criticize his wife for being a good housekeeper.

FOLLAVOINE: Now just a moment! There's a difference between being a good housekeeper and—

JULIE [*nervously arranging the papers spread over the desk*]: I suppose you'd rather see me do like other women we know. Go out every day... Spend all my time at the hairdresser's...

FOLLAVOINE [*seeing how she is disturbing his papers*]: What are you doing?

[*He rushes to the desk.*]

JULIE: ...at the dressmaker's

FOLLAVOINE [*defending his papers as best he can*]: Please!

JULIE: ...at the races...

FOLLAVOINE: Please! For heaven's sake!

JULIE: ...out in the morning, out at night, always running around, running around, spending your money... *Your* money!

FOLLAVOINE: Will you please—

JULIE: A wonderful life you'd like me to lead.

FOLLAVOINE: ...leave those papers alone! Leave them alone!

[*He pulls her away, stage left.*]

JULIE: Now what's the matter?

FOLLAVOINE [*trying to put his papers back in order*]: My papers, damn it! That's what's the matter! Who asked you to touch them?

JULIE: I can't stand seeing such a mess.

FOLLAVOINE: Then look the other way. Just leave my papers alone!

JULIE: Your papers, your papers! If you think I care about your papers...

[*She moves to leave, picking up her bucket as she passes.*]

FOLLAVOINE: Fine! Then prove it. Go putter around in your own room!

[*Grumbling under his breath.*] Always fussing with something... Always—

[*While speaking he sits down at his desk.*]

JULIE [*returning to the desk*]: So that's how you'd like me to be, I suppose?

FOLLAVOINE [*exasperated, almost shouting*]: How I'd like you to be?... How I'd like you to be what? What on earth are you talking about?

JULIE: Like those other women. That's what I'm talking about.

FOLLAVOINE [*thoroughly exasperated*]: I don't care! Just leave my papers alone! That's all I'm asking!

JULIE [*moving stage right with long, sultry movements, simulating the walk of a socialite, and still carrying the bucket, dangling precariously from her arm*]: A high brow? Maybe that's what you'd like me to be? [*Changing her tone.*] Sorry! I wasn't cut out for that sort of thing. My family—

FOLLAVOINE: All right! All right! That's fine!

JULIE [*moving to his desk and placing the bucket on some of his papers just as he is about to pick them up*]: My family—

FOLLAVOINE [*watching incredulously*]: Oh! For God's sake!

JULIE [*louder than the preceding times*]: My family didn't bring me up—

FOLLAVOINE: Oh!

JULIE: ...to be a gadabout or a socialite. They taught me how to be a good housekeeper.

FOLLAVOINE: Look, that's lovely... Very interesting... But it's already after eleven and—

JULIE: That's how I was brought up... Just to be a good housekeeper, and never depend on someone else to do my work. Because in life, you can never tell when some day you're going to have to take care of yourself.

[*She moves stage right with a self-righteous air.*]

FOLLAVOINE [*out of arguments*]: Fix your stockings!

JULIE: Oh! [*Without troubling to sit down, she fixes first one stocking, then the other.*] That's how my family brought me up, ever since I can remember. Now it's second nature. [*She sits down in the armchair near the desk.*] Whether it's right or wrong, that's how I am. I take after my mother.

FOLLAVOINE [*busily looking through his papers, answering half-unconsciously*]: Ah yes! Mother-in-law...

JULIE: No! My mother!

FOLLAVOINE: That's what I said, didn't I?

JULIE: No, you didn't! When I say "my mother," it sounds tender and affectionate. It's polite. When you say "mother-in-law" it sounds sarcastic and mean.

FOLLAVOINE: Sure, sure!... You're absolutely right.

JULIE: If I say "my mother" I mean "my mother." You don't have to remind me that she's your mother-in-law.

FOLLAVOINE: Look... I assure you, if I said "mother-in-law" it's only because as far as *I'm* concerned your mother—

JULIE [*jumping up as if on fire and holding on to the edges of the desk while lunging toward* FOLLAVOINE]: What? What? My mother is what? Has she ever done anything to you? Has she ever—

FOLLAVOINE [*recoiling*]: No! No! No! I didn't say that. All I said was that as far as I'm concerned your mother is my—

JULIE: That's enough! That's enough! Leave my mother alone!

FOLLAVOINE [*speechless*]: What?

JULIE: I don't know why you're always picking on my poor mother. Always making fun of her. It just isn't right!

FOLLAVOINE: Me? What did I—

JULIE: And why? Just because I committed the... the crime of bringing my wash-bucket into your study.

FOLAVOINE: Now listen—

JULIE: All that fuss over a wash-bucket! [*She picks it up from the desk.*] See! I'm taking it out. Now you won't have anything to argue about.
[*She moves toward the door.*]

FOLLAVOINE [*mumbling, trying to look absorbed in his papers*]: Fine!... Fine!

JULIE: You'd think I was a criminal! [*As she arrives at the door of her room and stops, a thought goes through her mind; she turns around, returns to the desk, and places the bucket in the same spot as before.*] And don't you forget it, either. Next time you want to find fault with me—

FOLLAVOINE: Now just a minute! Not that damned bucket again?

JULIE [*ignoring his remark*]: The next time you want to find fault with me, be man enough to come right out with it... without dragging my poor mother into it!

FOLLAVOINE: But for God Almighty's sake! What did I say? What did I say, damn it?

JULIE: Oh, nothing at all! Of course not! Now go and deny it, hypocrite!

FOLLAVOINE [*with no strength left to argue*]: Oh!
[*He gets up and moves down right.*]

JULIE [*going over to his desk and once again meddling with his papers*]: I know perfectly well what you were going to say.

FOLLAVOINE [*turning toward her*]: But I wasn't going to... [*Suddenly he notices her arranging his papers.*] Oh no! No! Not again? [*He rushes to stop her.*] Once and for all, will you please leave those papers alone!... What's this mania all of a sudden to play with my papers?

JULIE: I like to see things in their place.

FOLLAVOINE: Ha! You like to see things in their place. That's a good one! How about this? This... This...

JULIE [*taking the bucket*]: So? What about it?

FOLLAVOINE [*grumbling*]: Like to see things in their place! My foot! If you're so neat why don't you go get dressed? A minute ago you were almost out the door... You and that damnable bucket! Why didn't you just keep going? Why—

JULIE: I have to speak to you.

FOLLAVOINE [*gently pushing her toward her room*]: Later!

JULIE: This can't wait until later. It's important.

FOLLAVOINE: Look! Whatever it is, it'll have to wait. It's already after eleven. Chouilloux and his wife are coming to lunch and you aren't even dressed yet. Look at you!

JULIE: "Chouilloux and his wife"!... I wouldn't give two cents for either one of them!

FOLLAVOINE: Maybe not. Just don't forget that Chouilloux is an important man to have on my side. He's the one who—

JULIE: I don't care who he is. He'll wait. Who's more important, Chouilloux or Baby?

FOLLAVOINE [*realizing that another argument is imminent*]: Baby? Baby? What are you talking about?

JULIE [*crossing in front of him, toward stage left*]: Go ahead! Tell me Chouilloux is more important!

[*She sits down in the chair by the desk, holding the bucket on her lap.*]

FOLLAVOINE [*almost shrieking*]: What are you talking about? What?... "Chouilloux... Baby... Baby... Chouilloux"! Of course Baby's more important! I don't see... Just because I'm going out of my way to be nice to Chouilloux... What on earth does that have to do with Baby? [*He tries to calm down.*] Now look, be reasonable. Chouilloux will be here any minute now. He's coming before lunch so we can talk about some very important business.

JULIE: Talk all you want. I'm not stopping you.

FOLLAVOINE: But I'm telling you, he'll be here any minute. You aren't going to let him see you like that, I hope! That filthy bathrobe, that... that bucket on your lap, and those damned stockings down around your ankles again!

JULIE [*putting down the bucket angrily in front of her*]: Oh! That's all you can talk about! My stockings! [*She stands up, puts one foot on the bucket, and adjusts the stocking.*] I suppose Chouilloux never saw stockings fall down before. When his wife gets up in the morning I suppose she puts on an evening gown!

FOLLAVOINE [*while* JULIE *nervously adjusts the other stocking*]: Believe me, I don't know what she wears when she gets up. All I know is that nobody... nobody wears what you're wearing when they invite people they don't know to lunch.

JULIE [*running through* FOLLAVOINE's *papers, apparently looking for something*]: Never mind! You make up for me. You're overdressed!

FOLLAVOINE: I happen to be dressed just right. When people come to lunch... [*He notices what* JULIE *is doing.*] What are you looking for? Just what are you looking for?

JULIE [*taking some elastic bands from a box*]: Your elastic bands.

FOLLAVOINE: My... What on earth for?

JULIE: Maybe then you'll stop hounding me about my stockings.

[*She puts an elastic around each leg to hold up the stockings.*]

FOLLAVOINE: Just a minute! I need those for my reports. They aren't garters.

JULIE: They aren't garters, because no one uses them for garters. But if I'm using them for garters, then they *are* garters. See?

FOLLAVOINE: God! What a mess!

JULIE: You make me laugh. You're dressed "just right"! "Just right"!... I've never seen anything more ridiculous. Eleven in the morning and you look as if you're going to a wedding or something. And for Chouilloux! That fool! Letting his wife two-time him the way she does!

FOLLAVOINE [*looking at her with an air of amazement*]: His wife? Two-time him? What do you know about all that?

JULIE [*happy to have a ready answer*]: All I know is what you told me.

FOLLAVOINE: Me?

JULIE: I don't even know the man. I wouldn't make up a story about someone I don't even know.

FOLLAVOINE: What a terrible thing to say! His wife... two-timing him!

JULIE: It must be true. You told me.

FOLLAVOINE: All right, all right! I told you. But when I told you I didn't know Chouilloux would turn out to be so important to me. Now I realize—

JULIE [*interrupting, giving him tit for tat*]: So now his wife doesn't two-time him any more?

FOLLAVOINE: No... Yes... I mean, what's the difference? It's none of our business! That's not why we're inviting him to lunch!

JULIE: Fine!

FOLLAVOINE: The fact is, Chouilloux is an important man. He can do a lot for me.

JULIE: Like what?

FOLLAVOINE: Like a big business deal I'm working on. I don't have time to go into it.

JULIE: That's all you think about. Business deals.

FOLLAVOINE: Look. Does it bother you so much that his wife is two-timing him? What difference does it make—

JULIE: Bother me? Ha ha ha! Not at all! She could do the same thing with a dozen men and it wouldn't bother me. The only thing that bothers me is that you have to go and invite her here for lunch. That woman... Here, in my house!

FOLLAVOINE: What could I do? I couldn't very well invite him and not invite her.

JULIE: And her boyfriend, Horace Truchet? You had to invite him too?

FOLLAVOINE: Of course I did. The three of them go everywhere together. If I didn't invite Truchet it would have looked bad. Even Chouilloux would have wondered why.

JULIE [*crossing her arms indignantly*]: Lovely! We get all three of them! The whole triangle! Just lovely! [*She picks up her bucket and moves stage right.*] Nice friends to bring home to your wife! And a fine example for Baby!

FOLLAVOINE: Baby? What does Baby know? He's only seven.

JULIE: He won't be seven forever.

FOLLAVOINE: No. But meanwhile that's all he is.

JULIE: Very nice! Your own child, and you don't care how he grows up. You don't care about anything... If he's healthy, if he's sick...

FOLLAVOINE: Now just what is that supposed to mean? What have I done now?

JULIE [*placing the bucket on the floor, center stage, then moving to join* FOLLAVOINE, *who has just sat down at the desk*]: If you'd only listen! For an hour I've been trying to tell you that Baby isn't feeling well. But can I get a word in edgewise? Ha! Every time I open my mouth and say "Baby," you say "Chouilloux"! That's all you're interested in: "Chouilloux! Chouilloux"! All the time: "Chouilloux"!

FOLLAVOINE [*losing his patience*]: What is it? What do you have to tell me?

JULIE: I have to speak to you.

FOLLAVOINE: Go ahead! Speak! I'm listening!

JULIE: Hmm! It's about time!

[*She moves center stage and sits down on the bucket, as if it were a stool.*]

FOLLAVOINE: Oh no! No!

JULIE: What?

FOLLAVOINE: You can't find any other place to sit? You think that's what a wash-bucket is for?

JULIE: What difference does it make? I'm perfectly comfortable.

FOLLAVOINE: I'm not asking you if you're comfortable! A wash-bucket isn't something to sit on. Will you please sit on a chair like every other human being!

JULIE: My, my! Aren't we proper! [*She looks at him scornfully for a moment, then gets up.*] Such affectation.

FOLLAVOINE: "Affectation" my... You could slip and knock that thing over. If you think I want your dirty water all over my rug...

JULIE: So what? It could stand a washing.

FOLLAVOINE: Thanks just the same! If you don't mind, I'd rather not!... Now what's all this talk about Baby? What do you have to tell me?

JULIE [*sarcastically*]: Oh, is it all right? Are you sure I may?

FOLLAVOINE: Yes... you *may!*

JULIE [*bringing the small chair to the desk and sitting next to* FOLLAVOINE]: Well, I'll tell you. I'm worried.

FOLLAVOINE: Oh?

JULIE: It's about Toto.

FOLLAVOINE: I know, you've said that!... Why? What's the matter?

JULIE: He hasn't gone this morning.

FOLLAVOINE [*repeating like an echo, without understanding*]: He hasn't gone this morning.

JULIE: No.

FOLLAVOINE: Where?

JULIE: Where? Where?... Nowhere! "He hasn't gone"... period. That's all. Do I have to spell it out for you?

FOLLAVOINE [*suddenly understanding*]: Ah!... Oh, oh!... He hasn't gone...

JULIE: That's right. We've tried all morning. Four different times. No luck. Absolutely nothing. Once I thought... maybe... almost... But no. No luck.

FOLLAVOINE: So? He's a little constipated. So what?

JULIE [*annoyed*]: "A little constipated... So what?"

FOLLAVOINE: Yes. What do you want me to do about it?

JULIE [*horrified*]: Oh! What do I want you... Oh!

FOLLAVOINE: For God's sake! I can't go *for* him, I don't suppose!

JULIE [*getting up*]: Oh! Very clever! You're a comedian. Of course you can't go *for* him!

FOLLAVOINE: So?

JULIE: No one's asking you to go *for* him! Still, just because you can't go *for* someone, that's no reason to let them burst! Really, how can you be so heartless?

FOLLAVOINE [*getting up and moving toward* JULIE, *replying almost good-humoredly*]: Heartless? Now look... You don't expect me to start crying just because Baby's a little constipated?

JULIE: I think you should take it seriously. Constipation is no joke.

FOLLAVOINE [*incredulous*]: Oh?

JULIE: I remember reading in a book... a history book... that an illegitimate son of Louis the Fifteenth almost died of a stubborn case of constipation. And he was only seven.

FOLLAVOINE: All right. But it was a stubborn case, and he was illegitimate. There's no connection.

JULIE: But Baby is seven, and he's constipated, just like him.

FOLLAVOINE: So? Give him some medicine. That's all you have to do.

JULIE: I know, I know.

FOLLAVOINE: Well then, what's the trouble? Go give it to him.

JULIE: Thank you! Thank you very much! I didn't need you to tell me that. The problem is what I should give him. There are so many different kinds.

FOLLAVOINE: Give him a little castor oil. It's as good as anything else.

JULIE [*grimacing at the thought*]: Ugh! Castor oil? Oh no! No, I can't stomach it. It makes me sick!

FOLLAVOINE: You? Who's talking about you? It's for your son, not for you.

JULIE: That doesn't matter. Just looking at it... Just talking about it makes me... No, no! Definitely not! And besides, I don't see why you're making such a fuss. We have a full bottle of mineral oil. There's no reason why I shouldn't use that just because you insist on castor oil.

FOLLAVOINE: Me! Just because I—

JULIE [*categorically*]: Mineral oil! That's what I'll give him! Mineral oil...

FOLLAVOINE: Fine, fine! Give him mineral oil. I don't know why you bothered to ask me in the first place.

JULIE: To find out what I should do.

FOLLAVOINE: Sure, I believe you!

[*He sits at the desk and begins to busy himself.*]

JULIE: If you think it's going to be fun trying to make him take it...

FOLLAVOINE [*engrossed in his papers*]: What?

JULIE: His mineral oil.

FOLLAVOINE: Oh...

[*He becomes increasingly absorbed in his papers.*]

JULIE: It's always the way. Every time I let his grandmother take him out.

FOLLAVOINE [*mechanically, still wrapped up in his work*]: What grandmother?

JULIE [*sarcastic*]: What? How many does he have? Your mother lives in Düsseldorf. Who do you suppose I'm talking about? My mother, of course!

FOLLAVOINE: Of course, your mother...

JULIE: Yes! [*Imitating him.*] "*Your* mother! *Your* mother!" I know she's my mother! That's all you can ever say: "Your mother!" As if you were blaming me for it!

FOLLAVOINE: Me?... What?

JULIE: I don't understand. Every time she takes Baby out, it never fails. She fills him so full of junk—

FOLLAVOINE [*still absorbed in his work*]: All grandmothers are like that.

JULIE: I don't care, she shouldn't do it. I told her especially—

FOLLAVOINE: Look. I'm sure she didn't think that—

JULIE [*becoming angry*]: You're right! That's just the trouble. She didn't think.

FOLLAVOINE [*indulgent*]: Well, after all...

JULIE [*furious*]: Never mind! Don't tell me, "Well, after all." I'll never understand it, the way you always stand up for my mother, always taking her side against me. I say she shouldn't do it!

FOLLAVOINE [*to end the discussion*]: Fine, fine! You're right!

JULIE: What happens? Baby doesn't go, and now we have to give him something for it. Lovely!

FOLLAVOINE: So? Why all the fuss? I admit it's a nuisance, but for heaven's sake, it isn't going to kill him.

JULIE: Oh! "It isn't going to kill him"! Well I should hope not!... What a thing to say about your own child! Your own child!... He *is* yours, you know!

FOLLAVOINE: I should hope so!

JULIE: I'm not like Madame Chouilloux, I assure you! I don't go around letting my "cousin"... my *"cousin"*... do my husband's work for him! I assure you—

FOLLAVOINE: All right, all right! That's enough! Enough!

JULIE: When I have a child, I have it with my own husband! I assure you—

FOLLAVOINE: Well whoever said you didn't? Who?... Who?

JULIE [*sitting in the chair near the desk*]: A wonderful father you are! It would serve you right if he wasn't your child! Believe me—

FOLLAVOINE: Oh?

JULIE: It would serve you right if... if he was someone else's. If I had him with... with... [*Picking the first name that comes to her.*] with Louis the Fifteenth.

FOLLAVOINE [*amused, despite his anger*]: Louis the Fifteenth?

JULIE: Yes!

FOLLAVOINE: Ha ha! Good God! That would be something!

JULIE: That's right, laugh! Go ahead, laugh!

FOLLAVOINE [*exasperated*]: Now listen. That's enough! Everything is settled. It's over... Finished... We've decided Baby needs some medicine. All right, go give it to him.

JULIE: It's so easy to say. But if you think it won't be a struggle—

FOLLAVOINE: So it's going to be a struggle. Too bad! That's that! Now for God's sake go get dressed, and let me have a little quiet. Chouilloux will be here, and I don't even know what I'm going to say to him.

[*He gets up and moves over toward one of the cabinets.*]

JULIE [*getting up, moving toward her room and mumbling to herself*]: When I think of making him take that awful stuff! The poor little thing! It makes me sick just thinking about it.

FOLLAVOINE [*turning around from the cabinets and noticing the bucket, which she has left in the middle of the floor*]: Julie! Julie!

JULIE: What?

FOLLAVOINE [*pointing to it*]: Will you please get that thing out of here! Believe me, I've seen enough of it!

JULIE [*furious, moving toward the bucket*]: Oh! That's all I hear. "The bucket, the bucket"! If it isn't "Chouilloux" it's "the bucket"! Oh!...

FOLLAVOINE: Well, for God's sake! My study is hardly the place to flaunt a damned wash-bucket around!

[*While speaking he takes a chamber pot from the cabinet, displaying it during his last few words.*]

JULIE: That's a good one! That really is! I suppose your study is the place to "flaunt" a chamber pot!

FOLLAVOINE: A chamber pot?

JULIE: That's what I said. Unless that thing in your hands is a new idea for a hat!

FOLLAVOINE: How can you compare your wash-bucket to... to this? A wash-bucket is nothing but a... a wash-bucket. A common, ordinary everyday thing... A thing you try to keep out of sight. But this... This is—

JULIE: A chamber pot! A common, ordinary everyday thing you try to keep out of sight!

FOLLAVOINE [*lyrically*]: Maybe that's all it is for you, for someone who doesn't know any better. But for me... For me it's a thing of beauty, the fruit of my labors. It's the result of my intellect. It's my product, my... my bread and butter.

JULIE [*with a sarcastic little curtsy*]: Then eat it, why don't you!

FOLLAVOINE [*placing the chamber pot on the end table by the sofa*]: Ha ha! Very funny! But you won't joke about it when it begins making a small fortune for us!

JULIE: A fortune? From chamber pots?

FOLLAVOINE: That's what I said. You might not think so, but with the help of God... and Chouilloux... we can be rich overnight.

JULIE: What? What kind of nonsense—

FOLLAVOINE: It's no nonsense. I didn't mention it before because I wanted it to be a surprise, if everything works out all right. It's all a part of the government's plan to improve conditions in the army. They're trying to make the soldiers as comfortable as they can. Why, they've even given them house slippers.

JULIE: House slippers? For soldiers? My, how very military!

FOLLAVOINE: And that's not all. They've just come up with a way to keep them from catching cold.

JULIE: Oh?

FOLLAVOINE: Instead of making them go out at night, in all kinds of weather, every time... Well, instead, they're going to give each soldier his own chamber pot.

JULIE [*appalled*]: No!

FOLLAVOINE: Personal, with his own number on it.

JULIE: That should be lovely!

FOLLAVOINE: Soon they'll be taking bids to see what this new equipment should be made of, and who's going to manufacture it. Naturally, I decided to make a bid for my porcelain. That's where Chouilloux comes in. He's the chairman of the committee that's examining all the different models before the government decides to award the contract. Now you can see why I have to play up to him, can't you? Since I have the patent for unbreakable porcelain, if I can only make an impression on him, I'll be sure to get it.

JULIE: And then what?

FOLLAVOINE: "Then what?" What do you mean, "Then what?" If everything goes right we'll make a fortune. I'll be the army's exclusive supplier.

JULIE: The army's exclusive supplier of chamber pots?

FOLLAVOINE [proudly]: Of every single chamber pot in the army.

JULIE: And... And everyone will know?

FOLLAVOINE: Of course! Everyone will know!

JULIE: Oh no! No, no, no, no, no, no! I don't want to be known as the wife of the man who sells chamber pots! Oh no!

FOLLAVOINE: What? What are you talking about? We'll make a fortune, I tell you.

JULIE: I don't care! It's revolting!

FOLLAVOINE: But for goodness' sake, how different is it from what I'm doing now? I sell chamber pots every day of the week. Not so many, maybe, but I sell them.

JULIE [moving to the desk]: Oh! You sell them, you sell them! Of course you sell them. But you sell other things too. It's only natural for a porcelain manufacturer to sell things made of porcelain. All kinds of things. But to specialize! To become all of a sudden the man who sells nothing but chamber pots... No! No, not even for the government!

FOLLAVOINE: You don't know what you're saying! Just think—

JULIE: I have thought! Oh no! Thank you just the same! I refuse to go through life crowned with a chamber pot! I can just hear people now, wherever I go: "Who is that lady... Oh, she's the wife of the man who makes the chamber pots." No, no! Thank you just the same!

FOLLAVOINE [becoming more and more disconcerted by her objections]: Listen, for heaven's sake! Whatever you do, don't talk like that when Chouilloux is here. That's all I need!

JULIE: Oh! Don't worry! I have nothing to say to your Chouilloux!

FOLLAVOINE: Maybe there's a way we can work things out... With a middleman or something. But please, just one thing... Don't ruin this for me. I'm begging you. When Chouilloux gets here, for God's sake, be nice to him. Be polite—

JULIE: Well, really! I don't think I'm exactly in the habit of being impolite. I do know how to act in society.

FOLLAVOINE: Of course you do...

JULIE: My father once had the President to dinner, you know...

FOLLAVOINE: Sure, before you were born!

JULIE: Never mind! He still had him to dinner. And—

FOLLAVOINE: That's right, that's right... Now please... [He pushes her gently up right, toward her room.] Go give Baby his medicine, and get dressed. And take your bucket while you're at it.

JULIE [moving off toward her room, accompanied by FOLLAVOINE]: I've got my bucket. I've got it. Really, I don't need you to tell me what to do all the time.

[The doorbell rings.]

FOLLAVOINE: Ah! That must be Chouilloux. Now please... Please hurry up and finish dressing. If he came in here now—

JULIE [*on the threshold*]: So he'd see me. Who cares?

FOLLAVOINE [*gently pushing her out*]: If it's all the same with you, I'd rather he didn't! [*He closes the door and comes down right.*] Oh! Women, women, women! [*He picks up the chamber pot, walks back and forth a little while waiting to receive his guest.*] What on earth is that girl waiting for? Why doesn't she show him in? [*He goes to the door, up center, opening it slightly to peek out, then opens it all the way, surprised not to see anyone.*] Nobody? [*Calling offstage.*] Rose!... Rose! [*He returns to the desk, without closing the door.*]

ROSE [*on the threshold*]: Monsieur?

FOLLAVOINE [*standing at his desk, with the chamber pot in his left hand*]: Who was that? Who just rang?

ROSE: It was a lady. She wanted monsieur to pull one of her teeth. I told her the dentist lives upstairs.

FOLLAVOINE: What a nuisance! Always the same mistake... Day in, day out...

ROSE [*staring at the chamber pot*]: Oh! Monsieur!

FOLLAVOINE: What?

ROSE: Excuse me, but... Did monsieur know... Did monsieur know...

FOLLAVOINE [*impatiently*]: Did I know what?

ROSE: ...that... that he has his... his chamber pot in his hand?

FOLLAVOINE: Yes, yes. I know.

ROSE: Oh! I thought maybe it was a mistake. Excuse me, monsieur.

FOLLAVOINE: And besides, it isn't just a chamber pot. It's a piece of military equipment.

[*He places the pot on a stack of his papers on his desk.*]

ROSE: Oh my! It's funny how much it looks like a chamber pot, monsieur!

FOLLAVOINE: Yes!... You can leave now. [ROSE *exits, up center, as* FOLLAVOINE *sits at his desk and begins to make various calculations.*] Now let me see. If we figure that in peace time there are about... hmm... three hundred thousand men in the army. That means three hundred thousand chamber pots. And if each pot costs—

JULIE [*still dressed as in the preceding scene, appearing suddenly in the doorway, up right*]: Maximilien, would you come here a minute.

FOLLAVOINE [*absorbed in his calculations*]: Shhh! Can't you see I'm busy?

JULIE [*moving downstage, still carrying the bucket*]: I'm asking you to come here a minute! Baby won't take his medicine.

FOLLAVOINE: Well then, make him take it! Show him who's boss! [*Suddenly noticing the bucket.*] Oh no!

JULIE: What?

FOLLAVOINE [*standing up*]: Are you bringing that thing in here again?

JULIE: Well, I didn't have time to empty it yet. Now please, come and help me with—

FOLLAVOINE [*in a rage*]: No, no, no! I've seen enough of that damned thing! Now get it out of here! Get it out of here!

JULIE: But I'm telling you that Baby—

FOLLAVOINE: I said get it out of here!

JULIE: But Baby—

FOLLAVOINE: I don't care! Get that thing out of here!

JULIE: But—

FOLLAVOINE: Out! Out! Out!

JULIE [*haughtily placing the bucket in the middle of the floor*]: Now just you wait a minute! I'm sick and tired of hearing about my bucket!

FOLLAVOINE: What?

JULIE: That's all you can say: "Get it out of here! Get it out of here!" I'm not your maid, you know!

FOLLAVOINE [*unable to believe his ears*]: I beg your pardon!

JULIE: You'd think I was supposed to do everything around here! If my bucket bothers you so much, you can get rid of it yourself!

FOLLAVOINE: Me?

JULIE: I brought it in. You can take it out.

FOLLAVOINE: But for God's sake! It's your dirty water, not mine!

JULIE: Well then, I give it to you. There! It's yours!

[*She moves off toward her room.*]

FOLLAVOINE [*following her and trying to catch her by the hem of her robe*]: Julie! Are you out of your mind?... Julie!

JULIE: It's yours, I said! All yours!

[*She runs into her room.*]

FOLLAVOINE: Julie! Get this thing out of here! Julie!

ROSE [*entering suddenly from the hall and presenting* CHOUILLOUX, *a very well-dressed and distinguished gentleman*]: Monsieur Chouilloux.

FOLLAVOINE: Get this thing—

CHOUILLOUX: Good afternoon, my friend.

FOLLAVOINE [*still at* JULIE's *door, without turning around*]: Oh shut up! [*He turns around suddenly, as* ROSE *leaves, and recognizes* CHOUILLOUX.] Monsieur Chouilloux! Oh! Monsieur Chouilloux, I didn't realize... I... Oh! Please excuse me!

CHOUILLOUX: Am I a little early?

FOLLAVOINE: No, no... Not at all. I... I was just speaking to my wife. I... I didn't hear you ring.

CHOUILLOUX: Oh, but I did ring. And the young lady let me in. [*Trying to be funny.*] I don't walk through walls, you know!

FOLLAVOINE [*obsequiously*]: Ha ha ha! Very good! Very good!

CHOUILLOUX [*modestly*]: Well—

FOLLAVOINE [*hurrying to take his hat*]: Here... I'll take that.

CHOUILLOUX: Much obliged. [*He moves downstage and stops short, amazed at the sight of the bucket.*] My word!

FOLLAVOINE [*putting the hat on one of the cabinets, then dashing downstage to place himself between* CHOUILLOUX *and the bucket*]: Oh, I beg your pardon! I... This... My... My wife was here a moment ago and... and this... She must have forgotten this... this... [*Calling.*] Rose! Rose!

ROSE'S VOICE: Yes, monsieur.

FOLLAVOINE: Come in here! [*To* CHOUILLOUX.] Really, I don't know what to say. Especially at a time when I have the honor... the great honor...

CHOUILLOUX [*bowing quickly several times*]: Oh, please! Please—

FOLLAVOINE [*bowing in emulation*]: Oh, but it is! It is an honor, Monsieur Chouilloux! A great honor!

CHOUILLOUX: Too kind! Much too kind!

ROSE [*appearing at the door*]: Monsieur called?

FOLLAVOINE: Yes. Take madame's bucket out of here, will you?

ROSE [*surprised*]: Oh! Whatever is it doing in here?

FOLLAVOINE: She... She left it. By mistake.

ROSE: Oh my! She must be looking high and low for it.
[*She picks it up.*]

FOLLAVOINE: Yes!... Now go take it to her. And while you're there, tell her Monsieur Chouilloux is here.

ROSE: Yes, monsieur.
[*She exits, up right.*]

CHOUILLOUX: Please don't trouble her on my account.

FOLLAVOINE: It's no trouble at all. If I don't hurry her a little... You know how women are. Never ready!

CHOUILLOUX: Ah! Believe me, I can hardly say the same for Madame Chouilloux. Every morning she gets up at the crack of dawn, always the first one up. She does a lot of hiking, you know. It's splendid exercise for her. Of course, at my age... I'm afraid that sort of thing is a little strenuous. She does have her cousin, though. She takes her exercise with him.

FOLLAVOINE [*trying to be agreeable*]: Yes, yes! So I've been told.

CHOUILLOUX: Of course, that suits me fine.

FOLLAVOINE: Yes... It keeps it all in the family.

CHOUILLOUX: That's right. All in the family... And then too, it doesn't tire me out. [*They laugh; then, turning to move upstage,* CHOUILLOUX *catches sight of the chamber pot.*] Ah! I see you've been working on our little venture.

FOLLAVOINE [*following him*]: Yes, yes...

CHOUILLOUX [*with conviction*]: That's the chamber pot.

FOLLAVOINE: That's the... Yes, yes! You recognized it?

CHOUILLOUX [*modestly*]: Well... [*Observing it carefully.*] You know, it doesn't look bad. Not bad at all... And you say it's made of unbreakable porcelain?

FOLLAVOINE: That's right. Absolutely unbreakable.

CHOUILLOUX: Fine! Of course, you understand this is the feature that especially attracts the undersecretary and myself.

FOLLAVOINE: Yes, yes...

CHOUILLOUX: Because if it were just ordinary porcelain, you know, we really wouldn't be interested.

FOLLAVOINE: Oh no! I agree with you!

CHOUILLOUX: You just look at it and it breaks.

FOLLAVOINE: In no time at all.

CHOUILLOUX: And it would be a waste of the government's money.

FOLLAVOINE: Absolutely! Whereas this one... Just look! It's solid. It will never wear out. Here, take it, feel it. You're an expert.

CHOUILLOUX: Oh, not really!

FOLLAVOINE: Yes, you are! Here, feel how light it is.

CHOUILLOUX [*taking the pot and weighing it in his hand*]: Why yes, you're right. Strange, it scarcely seems to weigh anything at all.

FOLLAVOINE: And feel how nice it is to touch. See? You could almost say it would be a pleasure to... Well, you understand... [*Changing his tone.*] Now of course, we can make it in white or in color. If you want, for the army... Maybe with stripes. Blue, white and red.

CHOUILLOUX: Oh, I don't think so. That would be rather pretentious.

FOLLAVOINE: Yes, you're absolutely right. And it would be a needless expense.

CHOUILLOUX: At any rate, we have time to think about all that. [*Placing the pot on the table and approaching* FOLLAVOINE.] You know, we've had a look at some enamel samples too. They aren't bad either.

FOLLAVOINE: Oh! Monsieur Chouilloux! No, you don't mean that! You wouldn't consider enamel!

CHOUILLOUX: Why not?

FOLLAVOINE: Well really! It's not for my own personal interest. I leave that out of it entirely. But Monsieur Chouilloux... Enamel?... It has such an unpleasant smell. And besides, it isn't nearly as clean as porcelain. Really, there's no comparison.

CHOUILLOUX: Of course, there are two sides to the—

FOLLAVOINE: Not to mention the question of health. Certainly you must know that most cases of appendicitis come from using enamel utensils.

CHOUILLOUX [*half laughing, half serious*]: Well, as far as that goes, I don't think... Considering the use they're going to be put to...

FOLLAVOINE: Ah, but you never know! The youth today are so thoughtless! Just picture a few soldiers. They want to try out their new equipment... They mix up a big punch, piping hot. The heat cracks the enamel... A few chips fall into the punch... They drink, they swallow... Well, you can imagine what I mean, can't you?

CHOUILLOUX [*still amused*]: Not really! I assure you I never had the experience of drinking punch from a—

FOLLAVOINE: No! But you *were* in the army.

CHOUILLOUX: I'm afraid not. When I went for my physical examination they made me undress, and then someone said to me: "Your eyes are no good." That settled my military career then and there. I've been in the War Ministry ever since.

FOLLAVOINE: Oh? Well, anyway, Monsieur Chouilloux, take my word for it. No enamel! Take vulcanized rubber, if you must, or even celluloid. Of course, in the long run nothing is as good as porcelain. The only trouble is that it's generally too fragile. But once that's taken care of... Look, let me show you. [*He takes the pot from the table.*] You'll see how solid it is. [*He raises the pot in the air as if to throw it to the floor, then changes his mind.*] No! Here, with the rug, it wouldn't prove anything. But in there, in the hall, on the bare floor... Just watch! [*While talking he goes to open the door, up center, then returns center stage beside* CHOUILLOUX, *still holding the pot.*] Over there, Monsieur Chouilloux, over there! [CHOUILLOUX *takes a few steps in that direction;* FOLLAVOINE *holds him back.*] No, no. Stay right here but look over there! [FOLLAVOINE *prepares to hurl the pot.*] Watch closely now! [*He winds up to throw.*] One! Two! Three! [*He throws it through the doorway.*] There!

[*At the very moment he says "There!" the pot hits the floor and breaks into a thousand pieces. For a moment the two characters stand gazing in astonishmment.*[1]]

---

[1] Should the pot fail to break as it hits the floor—as has occasionally happened—the actor playing the role of Follavoine may simply say: "You see! Unbreakable! And you know, you can throw it as many times as you like. Just to prove it to you, watch: One! Two! Three!... There!" etc. [Author's note].

CHOUILLOUX: It broke!

FOLLAVOINE: Hmm!

CHOUILLOUX: It broke!

FOLLAVOINE: Yes... it... it broke.

CHOUILLOUX [*walking over to the door*]: No... No doubt about it. It's not an optical illusion.

FOLLAVOINE [*joining him*]: No... No... It broke all right. Funny, I don't understand it. That's the first time... Believe me, it's the first time that ever happened.

CHOUILLOUX [*moving downstage*]: Perhaps it hit a flaw.

FOLLAVOINE [*joining him*]: Perhaps. That must be it. Of course! Anyway, it really doesn't matter. It just proves that... that... Well, like they always say: "The exception proves the rule." Because I assure you, it never breaks. Never.

CHOUILLOUX: Never?

FOLLAVOINE: Never!... Well, all right, maybe one in a thousand...

CHOUILLOUX: Ah! One in a thousand...

FOLLAVOINE: Yes, and... and even then... Look, I'll prove it to you. [*He goes to the same cabinet and takes out another pot.*] Here's another one. You'll see. We'll be able to throw it all over the place. Forget about the first one. It wasn't baked right.

CHOUILLOUX: I see. It was half-baked.

FOLLAVOINE [*placing himself in the center of the stage, next to* CHOUILLOUX]: There. Now watch. One! Two!... [*Suddenly changing his mind.*] No, wait. Here... You throw this one yourself.

[*He hands the pot to* CHOUILLOUX.]

CHOUILLOUX: Me?

FOLLAVOINE: Certainly! That way you'll get a better idea.

CHOUILLOUX: Oh?

[FOLLAVOINE *moves off a little, to the left.* CHOUILLOUX *takes his place.*]

FOLLAVOINE: Go ahead!

CHOUILLOUX: All right. [*Swinging the pot.*] One! Two!...

[*He stops, obviously nervous.*]

FOLLAVOINE: Go on, go on! What's the matter?

CHOUILLOUX: Nothing... It's just... It's the first time I've ever bowled with a... with a... I feel silly.

FOLLAVOINE: Go ahead! Don't be afraid. I assure you, one in a thousand...

CHOUILLOUX: One ! Two! And three!

[*He flings the pot.*]

FOLLAVOINE: There!

[*Once again the pot breaks as it hits the floor. The two characters stand motionless, thunderstruck.*]

CHOUILLOUX [*walking up to the door after a little while, to survey the damage*]: It broke!

FOLLAVOINE [*joining him*]: It broke!... It... I... It...

CHOUILLOUX: Two in a thousand!

FOLLAVOINE: All right! Two in a thousand!... Look, I just don't understand it. There must be something... It must be the way we throw them. I know when my foreman throws them... Never! Absolutely never!

CHOUILLOUX: Never?

FOLLAVOINE: Never!

CHOUILLOUX [*sitting down on the sofa while* FOLLAVOINE *shuts the door, up center*]: That's very interesting.

FOLLAVOINE [*sensing* CHOUILLOUX'*s doubt*]: But... Certainly you must be able to appreciate the difference between ordinary breakable porcelain and—

CHOUILLOUX: And unbreakable porcelain.

FOLLAVOINE: Yes! [*Sheepishly.*] Still, I can tell I haven't exactly convinced you.

CHOUILLOUX: Oh, but you have... You have! I understand perfectly. They're the very same pots. Only, instead of breaking, they don't break.

FOLLAVOINE: Exactly!

CHOUILLOUX: Very interesting...

JULIE [*entering suddenly from her room in the same state of undress, but this time without the bucket*]: Maximilien, will you please come here a minute? This child will drive me insane! I can't do a thing with him!

FOLLAVOINE [*leaping toward* JULIE *and speaking to her in angry, muffled tones*]: What? Are you crazy? Coming in here like that! Just look at yourself! [*Pointing to* CHOUILLOUX, *who has risen at* JULIE'*s entrance.*] Monsieur Chouilloux is here!

JULIE: Monsieur Chouilloux can go hang!

CHOUILLOUX: What?

FOLLAVOINE [*in a near frenzy*]: No! No! [*To* JULIE.] What are you saying? Please, for God's sake! [*Awkwardly making introductions.*] Monsieur Chouilloux... My wife...

CHOUILLOUX: Madame...

JULIE [*very quickly*]: Yes, yes! How do you do. You'll excuse me for coming in like this, won't you?

CHOUILLOUX [*very gallant*]: Please, Madame, think nothing of it. A beautiful woman looks good no matter what she wears!

JULIE [*hardly listening to the compliment*]: Thank you. [*To* FOLLAVOINE.] Now look, Baby is being very difficult. I can't even mention the word "laxative."

FOLLAVOINE: Well that's just too bad! I'm sorry for you! But I'm discussing serious business with Monsieur Chouilloux. I've got more important things on my mind than giving your son a laxative!

JULIE [*scandalized, to* CHOUILLOUX]: Oh! That's a father for you, Monsieur Chouilloux! That's a father!

CHOUILLOUX [*not knowing what to answer*]: Well...

FOLLAVOINE [*to* JULIE]: Will you please go get dressed! I'm absolutely ashamed that you should let anyone see you like that! I should think you would have a little dignity, a little—

JULIE: Oh, please! If you think I care how I look at a time like this—

CHOUILLOUX [*trying to appear interested*]: Is your child ill, Madame?

JULIE: Yes, he is.

FOLLAVOINE: But it's nothing, Monsieur Chouilloux. Nothing at all.

JULIE [*as if to prove her assertion*]: He hasn't gone all morning!

CHOUILLOUX: Oh?

FOLLAVOINE: All right. So... So his bowels are taking a little rest.

JULIE [*to* CHOUILLOUX]: And he... he says it's nothing! What does he care?

FOLLAVOINE: Well, why all the fuss? All he needs is a laxative.

JULIE: I know, I know! But just try giving it to him if you're so smart! That's why I asked you to come in. Ha! I should have known better! All the nice jobs are for me!

FOLLAVOINE: For heaven's sake, you'd think it was something serious.

CHOUILLOUX [shaking his head, with conviction]: No, no... Of course it's not serious. But still, you should never take something like that too lightly.

JULIE: Aha! [To FOLLAVOINE.] You hear that? And he knows what he's talking about!

FOLLAVOINE [obsequiously]: Oh? Really, Monsieur Chouilloux?

CHOUILLOUX: Of course! [To JULIE.] Is the child usually subject to... if I may ask... to constipation?

JULIE: Well... yes, as a matter of fact. A little.

CHOUILLOUX: He is? Well, you should watch that. Some fine day, if it ever develops into enteritis, he'll have a devil of a time getting rid of it.

JULIE [to FOLLAVOINE]: You see?

CHOUILLOUX: I know all about it. I had a case that lasted five years!

JULIE [instinctively turning her head towards her son's room, up right]: Oh! [Turning her head back toward CHOUILLOUX.] Poor dear!

CHOUILLOUX [nodding]: Thank you.

JULIE: What?

CHOUILLOUX: Oh, I thought you were talking to me.

JULIE: No, no...

CHOUILLOUX [contnuing his story]: Yes indeed! Five long years! I caught it in the war.

JULIE: 1870?

CHOUILLOUX: No... 1888.

JULIE [looking at him quizzically]: 1888? But... there was no war in 1888.

CHOUILLOUX: No, Madame. You misunderstand. When I say "in the war" I mean the War Ministry. I'm an official there.

JULIE: Oh, I see.

FOLLAVOINE: Yes, Monsieur Chouilloux is—

JULIE: Yes, I know!

CHOUILLOUX: I used to get terribly thirsty. I didn't care what water I drank. Any water at all... I thought I was smart. Why listen to all that talk about germs... microbes? Water from the faucet? Bah! Why not? Well! I can tell you, I wasn't so smart! Before long I had a good case of enteritis. For three years I almost lived in the clinic at Plombières trying to get rid of it.

JULIE [jumping to conclusions]: Oh! Then you think we should take Baby to Plombières?

CHOUILLOUX: No, no! His case sounds more like the... the constipated form of enteritis. For him the clinic at Chatel-Guyon would be better. You see, my case was different. I had rather a... [Sensing an audience.] Shall we sit down?

FOLLAVOINE [while CHOUILLOUX and JULIE sit down on the sofa]: By all means, Monsieur Chouilloux. Please go on!

CHOUILLOUX: I had rather a... if you don't mind... a... relaxed enteritis.

JULIE: Oh?

FOLLAVOINE [affecting great interest]: You don't say!

CHOUILLOUX: Yes. So in my case Plombières was recommended. Oh! What a treatment!

JULIE [*thinking only of her son*]: And what's the treatment at Chatel-Guyon?

CHOUILLOUX: At Chatel... Why, I wouldn't know. I was never there. But at Plombières! Every morning, an internal rinse: a quart, maybe a quart and a half—

JULIE: Yes, that's fine, Monsieur Chouilloux. But at Chatel-Guyon do they—

CHOUILLOUX: Really, I wouldn't know. I was never there. [*Continuing.*] Then, after the rinse, I would have a bath. For a whole hour. Then a massage...

JULIE [*impatient*]: Yes, but—

CHOUILLOUX: And then lunch. Nothing but bland foods: broths, noodles, macaroni, rice puddings—

JULIE: But what about Chatel-Guyon?

FOLLAVOINE [*angrily*]: Monsieur Chouilloux keeps telling you he was never there!

CHOUILLOUX: I'm sorry, but I really don't know—

FOLLAVOINE: He can only tell you about his diet at Plombières.

JULIE [*ingenuously*]: But I don't care about his diet at Plombières.

CHOUILLOUX: Oh? Excuse me! I thought—

JULIE: Why should I care about his diet at Plombières when Baby needs the diet at Chatel-Guyon? [*Getting up.*] Monsieur Chouilloux, you're an intelligent person. You know what I mean.

CHOUILLOUX: Of course! Of course!

JULIE: He might as well be telling me how they go fishing off the Grand Banks of Newfoundland! It would be very interesting, but it wouldn't have anything to do with Baby's health.

CHOUILLOUX [*trying to be agreeable*]: That's right.

JULIE: I'm not here to listen to stories. I have to give Baby his medicine.

FOLLAVOINE [*who has had all he can take*]: Fine! Then go... go give Baby his medicine! Go—

JULIE [*very politely*]: You will excuse me, Monsieur Chouilloux?

CHOUILLOUX [*rising*]: Please...

JULIE [*to* FOLLAVOINE, *dryly*]: And you won't come with me?

FOLLAVOINE: No! No! No!

JULIE: Oh! What a father! What a father!

FOLLAVOINE: Sure, sure! You're right!... Now go get dressed!

JULIE: What a father!

[*She exits, up right.*]

FOLLAVOINE [*watching her leave*]: The idea! Coming in here dressed like that! Really, Monsieur Chouilloux, I don't know...

CHOUILLOUX: Your wife is a most charming person, I must say.

FOLLAVOINE: Yes! Charming... Absolutely charming! At times she's a little... But outside of that... Charming! I'm sorry you haven't seen her at her best. Believe me, when she dresses up—

CHOUILLOUX: Yes, I can just imagine.

FOLLAVOINE: Without her curlers and all that... She really has such beautiful hair, you know... A nice natural curl...

CHOUILLOUX: Oh?

FOLLAVOINE: Of course, when you see her like this... And especially now, when she's worried about her Baby...

CHOUILLOUX [*sitting in the chair near the desk*]: Oh, I'm sure there's no need to be concerned.

FOLLAVOINE [*following him*]: None at all! But just try to tell her that! You saw what happened when you mentioned the clinic at Chatel-Guyon? Now that's all she'll be able to think about: Chatel-Guyon!

CHOUILLOUX: I hope I haven't said anything to—

FOLLAVOINE: No, no! Not at all! I just couldn't help laughing to myself when you began talking about your diet at Plombières.
[*He laughs.*]

CHOUILLOUX [*joining in*]: That didn't interest her in the slightest.

FOLLAVOINE [*still laughing*]: Not a bit.

CHOUILLOUX: Ha ha! And all the time I thought... Ha ha!
[*While* CHOUILLOUX *and* FOLLAVOINE *are laughing heartily, the door to* JULIE's *room opens suddenly.* JULIE *appears, dragging* BABY *with one hand, and with the other holding a glass. Against her chest she is pressing a bottle of mineral oil.*]

JULIE [*to* BABY]: All right! Now you just wait and see what your father has to say! He's absolutely furious with you! [*To* FOLLAVOINE.] Go ahead, tell him. [*Seeing that* FOLLAVOINE *and* CHOUILLOUX *are still laughing, she gives her husband a quick kick in the shins, addressing him in a low but frantic voice, so that* BABY *cannot hear.*] Will you please listen to me!

FOLLAVOINE [*jumping*]: Owww!... What on earth—

JULIE: I'm telling Baby you're furious with him. If he sees you both splitting your sides—

FOLLAVOINE: What? What? Now what's the matter?

JULIE [*sending* BABY *to him*]: The matter is that I'm asking you to make your son obey! Will you please give him his medicine!

FOLLAVOINE: Me?

JULIE: Yes, you! [*She places the bottle and glass on the end table near the sofa.*] There! There's the bottle and the glass. I give up!

FOLLAVOINE: But why me all of a sudden?

JULIE: If you don't mind! You *are* his father, you know! If you don't show a little authority once in a while...

FOLLAVOINE [*looking at the ceiling, then at* CHOUILLOUX, *with a sigh of resignation*]: Excuse me for a moment Monsieur Chouilloux.

CHOUILLOUX: Please!

FOLLAVOINE [*severely, to* BABY]: Now then, young man... What's the meaning of this? I'm very angry with you, do you understand?

BABY [*stamping his foot*]: I don't care! I don't wanna waxative!

FOLLAVOINE: What?

JULIE: There! You see? That's what I've been putting up with for the last half hour.

CHOUILLOUX [*putting his hand on* BABY's *shoulder*]: Come now! Is that any way for a big boy to talk?
[BABY *pulls himself away, petulantly.*]

FOLLAVOINE [*who has seen his son's gesture, to* BABY]: Where are your manners? Now say hello to the gentleman.

BABY [*stamping his foot*]: I don't care! I don't wanna waxative!

FOLLAVOINE [*shaking* BABY *by the shoulders*]: Well you just listen to me! No one's asking you what you want! Little brat! What makes you think—

JULIE [*jumping to* BABY's *defense, pulling* FOLLAVOINE *away*]: Oh! You brute! Leave him alone!

FOLLAVOINE: Oh!

[*He stifles a curse and angrily stalks over to his desk, but without sitting down.*]

JULIE [*to* CHOUILLOUX]: Really, we'll have to think of some way to make him take it. His tongue is all coated. [*To* BABY.] Show your tongue to the gentleman.

CHOUILLOUX [*trying to be agreeable*]: Wait just a moment. [*He goes down on one knee to see* BABY *more easily, then takes a reading glass from his pocket to inspect his tongue.*] Now, then, let's see!

JULIE [*to* BABY]: Go on, darling, show him your tongue.

[BABY *sticks out his tongue.*]

CHOUILLOUX: It looks all right to me.

JULIE: Still, you can tell by his breath. [*To* BABY.] Go ahead... Say "aaah" in the nice man's face.

CHOUILLOUX [*instinctively protecting himself*]: Oh, thank you just the same.

JULIE: What? You don't mean to say you're afraid of a baby's breath?

CHOUILLOUX: Not at all! It's just—

JULIE: Well then? [*To* BABY, *pushing his head toward* CHOUILLOUX's *face.*] Go on, darling... Say "aaah" in his face.

CHOUILLOUX: No! Really, I assure you, it isn't necessary! I can tell perfectly well... [*He sits down and addresses* BABY *as agreeably as he can.*] Now then young man, what's the trouble? Is that any way for a big boy to act? [*No reply from* BABY.] What's your name? [BABY *sulks but doesn't answer.*]

FOLLAVOINE [*to* BABY]: Go ahead, tell the gentleman your name!

BABY: I don't wanna waxative.

FOLLAVOINE [*champing at the bit*]: Oh! [*To* CHOUILLOUX.] His name is Toto.

CHOUILLOUX: Ah?

FOLLAVOINE: It's short for Alexander.

CHOUILLOUX: Oh? How unusual... [*To* BABY.] And how old are you? Six?

JULIE [*offended*]: He's seven, if you please!

CHOUILLOUX: Well now! You're seven years old and your name is Toto. And when a young man's name is Toto, and he's seven years old, should he make such a fuss about taking a little medicine?

BABY: I don't care! I don't wanna waxative!

CHOUILLOUX: That's not very nice. What will you say when you grow up and have to go to war?

JULIE [*drawing* BABY *to her, as if to protect him, and rapping the desk to ward off a curse*]: What are you saying!

BABY [*hiding in his mother's skirts*]: I don't care! I don't wanna go to war!

CHOUILLOUX: No, you don't want to. But if there's a war, you'll have to go.

BABY: I don't care! I'll wun away... to Switzerwand!

CHOUILLOUX: What?

JULIE [*covering* BABY *with kisses*]: Ah! Mamma's little angel! Isn't he smart!

CHOUILLOUX [*to* FOLLAVOINE]: Congratulations, monsieur! I suppose he has you to thank for such ideas!

FOLLAVOINE [*defending himself*]: No! Of course not! [*To* BABY.] You should never say things like that! You understand... Alexander?

JULIE [*taking* BABY *to the sofa*]: For goodness' sake, leave the poor child alone! You don't have to make him think about such things at his age. He's Mamma's little darling! Now he's going to be a big brave man and take his medicine. There!

[*While speaking she has filled the glass on the end table.*]

BABY: I don't wanna waxative!

JULIE: But I tell you, you have to—

FOLLAVOINE [*coming over to the sofa*]: Now look, Toto. If you took it right away it would all be over by now. You'd be finished.

BABY: I don't care! I don't wanna!

FOLLAVOINE: Listen here! You're going to obey, you understand?

BABY [*running stage left*]: I don't wanna!

CHOUILLOUX [*standing up, to* BABY]: When I was your age... When I was very small... If my parents told me something... Well, believe me—

BABY [*right in* CHOUILLOUX'*s face*]: Aw shuddup!

[JULIE *and* FOLLAVOINE *exchange shocked glances.*]

CHOUILLOUX: What did he say?

FOLLAVOINE [*grabbing* BABY *and quickly placing him behind his back*]: Nothing! Nothing!

CHOUILLOUX [*letting it pass, sitting down in the armchair*]: Oh...

FOLLAVOINE [*furious, shaking* BABY]: Now look, I've had enough of this nonsense! You're going to do what you're told, and be quick about it! You're not going to get away with—

JULIE [*pulling* BABY *from his grasp*]: Really! Are you insane? Do you have to beat the poor child?

FOLLAVOINE [*softly, to* JULIE]: You... You heard what he said! He said "shut up!" He—

JULIE: All right, so he said "shut up!" It's not a dirty word!

FOLLAVOINE [*trying not to swear*]: Oh!

JULIE [*to* BABY, *caressing him*]: Mamma's little baby!

[*She takes him to the sofa and sits down.*]

FOLLAVOINE [*sitting down at the desk and finally giving vent to his rage*]: Damn!... Oh! Goddamn!

JULIE [*to* BABY, *kissing him as she speaks*]: Never you mind! Your father is just a nasty man. But don't you be afraid. Mamma's right here.

FOLLAVOINE [*furious*]: That's lovely! Just lovely! Start putting ideas like that in his head!

JULIE [*taking the full glass of mineral oil from the table*]: And why not? When you begin bullying the poor little thing! And especially now, when he's not well!

FOLLAVOINE [*turning his chair, back to* JULIE, *as if to ignore her completely*]: All right, then. From now on leave me out of it!

JULIE: With pleasure! [*To* BABY, *as sweetly as possible, and putting the glass to his lips.*] There! Now be a dear and take your medicine.

BABY [*pursing his lips and moving his head away*]: No! I don't wanna!

JULIE [*casting a look of rage at* FOLLAVOINE; *then, controlling herself, in a cajoling voice, to* BABY]: Please! Just for me?

BABY: No! I don't wanna!

JULIE [*repeating her glance to* FOLLAVOINE; *then, again to* BABY]: Please angel, be a dear!

BABY: No!

JULIE [*gritting her teeth*]: Oh! [*Casting a vicious look at* FOLLAVOINE.] You see what happens when you interfere!

FOLLAVOINE [*stupefied*]: When I—

JULIE: Yes, you! [*To* BABY.] Now listen, Toto! If you take your medicine like a good boy, Mamma's going to give you a peppermint.

BABY: Gimme a peppermint first!

JULIE: No, afterwards!

BABY: Now! Now!

JULIE: Well, I'll let you have it now, but only if you promise to take your medicine.

BABY [*nodding*]: Uh-huh.

JULIE: You promise?

BABY: Uh-huh.

JULIE: Your word of honor?

BABY [*in a long drawl*]: Uh-huh...

JULIE: All right, I believe you. [*To* FOLLAVOINE, *who is still facing the other direction, his eyes toward the ceiling in an attitude of resignation.*] Father! [FOLLAVOINE, *absorbed in thought, doesn't answer.*] Maximilien!

CHOUILLOUX [*mechanically*]: Maximilien!

FOLLAVOINE [*as if waking from a dream*]: Hmm?... Ha?... What?

JULIE [*curtly*]: The box of peppermints!

CHOUILLOUX: The box of peppermints!

FOLLAVOINE [*opening his desk drawer with the sigh of a martyr and taking out the box*]: The box of peppermints! [*He gets up, at the same time addressing* CHOUILLOUX.] Please forgive me, Monsieur Chouilloux. I didn't mean to subject you to a family crisis.

CHOUILLOUX: Not at all! This is very interesting... for someone who never had children...

FOLLAVOINE [*giving the box to* JULIE]: Here!

JULIE [*taking out a peppermint*]: Thank you. [*To* BABY.] Now open wide, angel... [*Putting it in his mouth.*] There!

FOLLAVOINE [*to* CHOUILLOUX]: Still, this is hardly why I invited you to lunch!

CHOUILLOUX: Oh, well...

JULIE [*to* BABY]: Good?

BABY: Yup!

JULIE [*holding the glass out to him*]: That's fine! Now be an angel and take your medicine.

BABY [*running off*]: No! I don't wanna waxative!

JULIE [*taken aback, placing the glass on the end table*]: What?

FOLLAVOINE: There! Goddammit! There!

JULIE: But Toto, you promised! I gave you a peppermint!

BABY: I don't care! I don't wanna waxative!

FOLLAVOINE [*hardly able to contain himself*]: Oh, that child! That child!

JULIE [*furious, addressing* FOLLAVOINE *while chasing* BABY *around the room*]: Is that all you can say? "That child! That child!" Instead of helping me!

You can see I have my hands full!

[*She lifts* BABY *bodily and carries him over to the sofa.*]

FOLLAVOINE [*livid with rage*]: What? For God's sake! Just a minute ago you told me—

JULIE: Oh! Forget it! I should have known—

[*While speaking she walks toward her room.*]

FOLLAVOINE: All right... What do you want? What? What? What are you going to do?

JULIE: What do you think? I'm going to try something else. That's what I'm going to do! [*Once at the threshold she turns and looks directly at* CHOUILLOUX.] Oh! He has to pick a time like this to invite people to lunch! [*She slams the door as she leaves.*]

FOLLAVOINE [*jumping up, absolutely mortified*]: Oh!

CHOUILLOUX [*rising*]: What did she say?

FOLLAVOINE [*innocently*]: Who?... Who?

CHOUILLOUX: Your wife... What did she say?

FOLLAVOINE: My wife?... Nothing!... Nothing!... She said: "I... I don't know what time... we can have a bite of lunch!"

CHOUILLOUX [*sitting down*]: Oh well, it really doesn't matter.

FOLLAVOINE [*going over to* BABY, *who is still on the sofa, and taking his hand to make him get up*]: Shame on you, Toto! Breaking your word like that! You should be ashamed of yourself! Shouldn't he, Monsieur Chouilloux?

CHOUILLOUX [*most circumspect*]: Oh, really... I... I'd rather stay out of it. Really...

FOLLAVOINE [*bending over to* BABY's *height, and speaking to him as rationally as possible*]: Now look, Toto! You're seven years old. That means you're a young man. You shouldn't be acting like a baby any more. Now if you behave and take your medicine, like a big boy, I have a surprise for you. [*He straightens up.*]

BABY: What?

FOLLAVOINE: Well... I'll tell you where the Aleutian Islands are. How about that!

BABY: Oh! I don't care! I don't wanna know!

FOLLAVOINE: That's not very nice. Especially after all the trouble we had finding them!... I'll tell you. They're near Alaska.

BABY [*indifferent*]: Oh...

FOLLAVOINE: And besides, they have an area of... of... They have a population of... Oh! Forget it! [*He lets go of* BABY *and starts moving stage left.*]

BABY [*catching him by his coat*]: And Wake Michigan?

FOLLAVOINE: What?

BABY: Where's Wake Michigan, daddy?

FOLLAVOINE [*mechanically repeating the question*]: "Where's Lake Michigan?"

BABY: Yes! Wake Michigan!

FOLLAVOINE: All right! I heard you! [*Aside.*] Him and his damned questions! [*To* CHOUILLOUX.] Lake Michigan, Monsieur Chouilloux?... You wouldn't remember offhand where it is?

CHOUILLOUX: Lake Michigan?... Why certainly. It's in America... The United

States...

FOLLAVOINE: Of course! What was I thinking...?

CHOUILLOUX: In the state of Michigan.

FOLLAVOINE: Of course! Michigan! I couldn't remember the name of the state, that's all.

CHOUILLOUX: Lake Michigan!... [*Reminiscing*.] Why, in '77 I went swimming in it.

FOLLAVOINE: No! You? [*To* BABY, *bending over and pointing to* CHOUILLOUX.] You see, Toto! You were looking for Lake Michigan. Well, what do you know! Here's a man... You wouldn't think anything just to look at him... But you know what? He's gone swimming in it!... Now I hope after that you'll be a good boy and take your medicine!

BABY [*returning to the sofa*]: No! I don't wanna!

FOLLAVOINE [*raising his eyes to heaven, in despair*]: Oh!

CHOUILLOUX: He has a mind of his own, your son!

FOLLAVOINE: You can say that again!

JULIE [*returning with a second glass just like the first and approaching the sofa*]: All right! Here's another glass! [*She fills it with mineral oil*.] And just to show Baby how easy it is... You know what? Daddy's going to drink a big glass too!

FOLLAVOINE: What?

JULIE [*putting the glass under his nose*]: Aren't you!

FOLLAVOINE [*taking refuge behind his desk*]: Me? Not on your life! Thank you just the same!

JULIE [*curtly, in a low voice*]: For heaven's sake! You're not going to say no!

FOLLAVOINE: Oh yes I am! Wild horses wouldn't get me to drink that stuff! You can drink it! You, not me!

JULIE: Oh! You won't even do a little thing like that for your own son!

FOLLAVOINE [*pushing away the glass that* JULIE *obstinately keeps putting to his lips*]: My own son! My own... He's your son too, you know!

JULIE [*setting the glass on the desk*]: I see! I should do all the dirty work, I suppose! Of course! All the dirty work! Maybe you don't think I've done enough for him since he was born? And even before? Maybe you think it was easy carrying him for nine months! [*Waxing poetic*.] Nine long months, in the depths of my womb!

FOLLAVOINE: Ha! In the depths of your womb! Where did you dig that one up? The depths of your womb!

BABY: Mamma!

JULIE: What is it, angel?

BABY: Why... Why d'you cawwy me nine mumphs? [*Pointing to* FOLLAVOINE.] Why din't he?

JULIE [*lifting* BABY *and placing him on the sofa, where she sits down*]: Ha! Why? Because your father... If you had to wait for him to do it... He knew that was one job I had to do myself!

FOLLAVOINE [*to* CHOUILLOUX]: Really, I ask you... Is that something to tell a baby?

BABY: You shoulda asked anuvver man.

FOLLAVOINE [*furious*]: There! How do you like that! "You should have asked another man"! Very nice!

JULIE [*to* BABY, *sarcastically*]: Oh, you know! They're all alike!

BABY: Oh no! I won't be wike dat!

JULIE [*caressing him*]: That's my little angel. At least you have a heart.

FOLLAVOINE [*to* CHOUILLOUX]: Really, Monsieur Chouilloux, I don't know what to say. Subjecting you to... It's incredible... Absolutely incredible!

CHOUILLOUX [*getting up*]: Not at all! It's charming! Children say such clever things. Out of the mouths of babes, you know!

JULIE [*to* BABY]: You see the difference between a father and a mother! Your father won't even take a laxative for you!

BABY: I don't care! I don't want him to take a waxative!

FOLLAVOINE [*moving to the sofa, to* JULIE]: Ha ha! You see? He's more reasonable than you are!

CHOUILLOUX [*joining* FOLLAVOINE]: He doesn't want his father to drink it.

BABY [*pointing to* CHOUILLOUX]: I want *him* to dwink it!

FOLLAVOINE   Ayyy!
                                      } [*together*]: {
CHOUILLOUX [*instinctively withdrawing*]   What?

JULIE [*happy to be able to please her son*]: You want him to drink it? All right! He'll drink it!

[*She takes the glass from the end table and, with* BABY *clinging to her skirts, moves toward* CHOUILLOUX.]

FOLLAVOINE [*stopping her*]: For God's sake! You aren't serious!

JULIE [*brushing him aside*]: Shhh! Don't butt in! [*To* CHOUILLOUX.] Here, Monsieur Chouilloux, be a dear.

CHOUILLOUX [*fuming*]: Really! That child is impossible!... Oh— [JULIE *has placed the glass forcibly to his lips just as he says his last words, with the result that, while sighing his "oh" he accidentally takes a mouthful.*] Aaaaah! Pfaw! Pfuiii!

JULIE [*still accompanied by* BABY, *continuing to hold the glass out to* CHOUILLOUX]: Be an angel, Monsieur Chouilloux. Drink a little just to make him happy.

[*She presses the glass to his lips once again.*]

CHOUILLOUX [*spitting*]: Ah!... Ptui! Ptui!... No, no! My dear woman! No! No thank you!

FOLLAVOINE [*beside himself*]: Julie!

JULIE [*to* CHOUILLOUX]: Just a little. Just half a glass.

[*She approaches him again.*]

CHOUILLOUX [*defending himself*]: No, no! Really, I'd love to help, but—

FOLLAVOINE: Julie! You can't be serious! Monsieur Chouilloux isn't here to... to take that!

JULIE: My goodness! How can a grown man make so much fuss over a little mineral oil?

CHOUILLOUX [*backed up against the chair, stage left*]: That's all well and good, but—

JULIE [*to* CHOUILLOUX]: A child I can understand. But a man of your age? [*Wheedling.*] Now be a dear, Monsieur Chouilloux.

[*She puts the glass under his nose.*]

FOLLAVOINE: Julie! For heaven's sake!

CHOUILLOUX: No, no! I'm terribly sorry! Not a laxative! With my intestines... Absolutely not!

FOLLAVOINE: Of course not!

JULIE: Come now! What can half a glass of mineral oil do to your intestines?

FOLLAVOINE: Julie!

JULIE: And besides, if I have to choose between Baby's health and your intestines, there's no question—

FOLLAVOINE: Julie! Please!

CHOUILLOUX: Look here, my dear woman! I don't even know if your child needs a laxative!

JULIE [drawing BABY aside]: Oh for goodness' sake! Not in front of Baby! That's all I need!

FOLLAVOINE: Julie!

CHOUILLOUX [to JULIE]: I beg your pardon if I've said something—

JULIE [to CHOUILLOUX]: After all my trouble! After all my begging and coaxing—

FOLLAVOINE: Julie! Julie!

JULIE: And now you go tell him he shouldn't take his medicine!

CHOUILLOUX: Not at all! Only, I thought—

JULIE [ready to chew his head off]: You thought! You thought!

FOLLAVOINE: Julie!

JULIE [continuing, to CHOUILLOUX]: What do you know about it? Where did you find out? At Plombières?... You couldn't have! The diet is just the opposite at Plombières! You said so yourself! Just the opposite!

CHOUILLOUX   ⎱   ⎰ All right! I take it back! I—
            ⎰ [together]: ⎱
FOLLAVOINE   ⎰   ⎱ Julie! Please! That's enough!

JULIE [moving stage right with BABY, her rage unabated]: And what business is it of his anyway? He should mind his own business! Do I butt in when I see his wife making him a laughingstock? Two-timing him with her cousin! [She places the glass on the end table.]

CHOUILLOUX [to JULIE, electrified]: What did you say?

FOLLAVOINE [not knowing where to turn or what to say]: God in heaven! [Without thinking any more of CHOUILLOUX, JULIE has lifted BABY onto the sofa and sits down next to him.]

CHOUILLOUX: My wife?... Her cousin?...

FOLLAVOINE: No, Monsieur Chouilloux! It isn't true!

CHOUILLOUX [pushing FOLLAVOINE aside]: Leave me alone! Leave me... I... I... Aaaah! [He clutches his throat as if choking with rage.] Water! Water! [He notices the other glass that JULIE had set on the desk and rushes over to it, forgetting what it contains, emptying it with a healthy swallow.]

FOLLAVOINE: Oh!

BABY [delighted]: Mamma! Mamma! Wook! [He jumps up and down, pointing gleefully at CHOUILLOUX, and finally climbs playfully onto his father's chair.]

FOLLAVOINE [out of his mind]: Monsieur Chouilloux! For heaven's sake! [Suddenly CHOUILLOUX's face becomes contorted, his eyes glazed; he begins to cast frantic glances all around the room. Then, apparently remembering where FOLLAVOINE keeps his chamber pots, he rushes madly toward the cabinet.]

FOLLAVOINE [realizing what he is looking for, running after him]: No! No! Not that way!... There aren't any more! [*He pushes him toward the door, down right.*] That way! In there! [CHOUILLOUX *rushes precipitously from the room;* FOLLAVOINE *closes the door behind him, then turns angrily to* JULIE.] Congratulations! Isn't that lovely! Just lovely! Now you've done it! [*He paces nervously.*]

JULIE: Well! He should have minded his own business!

FOLLAVOINE: Telling him he's a laughingstock!... That his wife is two-timing him!

JULIE: So? Isn't it true?

FOLLAVOINE: That's no reason to tell it to him, to his face!

BABY: Mamma!

JULIE: What is it, angel? Do you want your medicine?

BABY: No!... What's a waffingstock?

JULIE [*with a sarcastic smile*]: Ha! [*Pointing to the door through which* CHOUILLOUX *has just made his hurried exit.*] You just saw one, darling. That man who just ran out... He's a laughingstock, because his wife is two-timing him!

FOLLAVOINE [*suddenly stops pacing and turns around*]: Is that something to tell a child? I ask you, is that—

JULIE: If he drank it right away, when I asked him—

FOLLAVOINE: Sure! A laxative! That's all, just a laxative!... You're incredible! Absolutely incredible!

[*He begins pacing again.*]

JULIE: Well! When someone invites you to their house you take what they give you! He has no manners, that's his trouble! Of all things! He comes here for the first time and what does he talk about?... His intestines! Really! Where was he brought up?

FOLLAVOINE: Oh! You're a fine one to talk! You... You ask him to... to purge himself, for God's sake!

JULIE [*rising to join* FOLLAVOINE]: What? Since when did I ask him to "purge" himself? What business is it of mine if he "purges" himself? I asked him to drink a little mineral oil, that's all! I didn't ask him to "purge" himself!

FOLLAVOINE [*imitating*]: "I asked him to drink a little mineral oil, that's all!" Sure, that's all! It's not your fault if he just happens to purge himself in the bargain!

JULIE [*sitting in the armchair, with* BABY *by her side*]: Anyway, that's his business. What do I care!

[*The doorbell rings.*]

FOLLAVOINE: And what about me? Now I'll never get the contract!

JULIE: Oh! That's all you care about!

FOLLAVOINE: It's all down the drain now!

ROSE [*appearing at the door, up center*]: Madame Chouilloux and Monsieur Truchet.

[*She leaves.*]

FOLLAVOINE: Oh no! No! [*To* JULIE.] You talk to them! After all this... No! I couldn't!

[*He walks toward the door, down right.*]

JULIE [*getting up*]: What? But Maximilien, I don't even know them!

FOLLAVOINE: Too bad! You'll think of something!

[*He exits.*]

MADAME CHOUILLOUX [*entering, up center, in great haste, followed by* TRUCHET]: Ah! Madame Follavoine, I presume?

JULIE [*bewildered*]: What?... No!... I mean yes! Yes!

[*She is backed up against the desk, with* BABY *hiding behind her skirts.*]

MADAME CHOUILLOUX: I am so delighted, my dear! I was afraid we might be late. [*Noticing* JULIE's *attire.*] But I'm so happy to see I was mistaken.

JULIE: Yes... Well... You must excuse me! I... I haven't dressed yet. You see... I...

MADAME CHOUILLOUX: Please, my dear! You really mustn't stand on ceremony for us! [*Introducing.*] Monsieur Truchet, my cousin... It was so good of you, my dear, to insist—

TRUCHET: I do hope you haven't put yourself out...

JULIE: No, no! Not at all!

MADAME CHOUILLOUX [*catching sight of* BABY's *head as he peeks from behind* JULIE's *robe*]: Oh, my dear! Is that your adorable little girl?

JULIE [*presenting* BABY]: No!... Yes!... That is, he's a little boy!

MADAME CHOUILLOUX: Oh? Well, at that age, don't you know? It's so hard to tell the difference.

JULIE [*trying to be agreeable*]: Of course!

TRUCHET: And your husband?... He will be joining us, I hope?

JULIE [*pointing to the door, down right*]: Yes!... Yes!... He's in there.

BABY [*ingenuously*]: Wiv a waffingstock! And... And his wife is a two-timer!

JULIE [*to* BABY, *quickly pulling him behind her*]: Shhh!

MADAME CHOUILLOUX [*wondering if she has heard correctly*]: What was that?

JULIE: Nothing! Nothing! He's... He's one of my husband's employees... A German fellow, you know... Laffingschtock... Helmut Laffingschtock!

MADAME CHOUILLOUX: And his wife...

JULIE: ...is a Tüteheimer! One of the Düsseldorf Tüteheimers!

MADAME CHOUILLOUX: Oh, my dear... What delightful names!

JULIE [*with a forced laugh*]: Yes, aren't they!

MADAME CHOUILLOUX: Laffingschtock! And his wife, a Tüteheimer!... Oh, that reminds me. My husband should be arriving any moment.

JULIE: He's here! He's here!

MADAME CHOUILLOUX: Oh? With them?

JULIE: "Them"?... Who?

MADAME CHOUILLOUX: Why, with your husband, and... Herr Laffingschtock.

JULIE: Oh!... Yes!... Yes, of course! [*At a loss for something to say.*] Please, won't you sit down?

[MADAME CHOUILLOUX *sits down on the sofa while* TRUCHET *moves upstage in search of another chair. Just at that moment the door, down right, opens and* CHOUILLOUX *comes storming through, followed by* FOLLAVOINE.]

FOLLAVOINE } [*together*]: { But Monsieur Chouilloux! I assure you—

CHOUILLOUX } [*together*]: { Leave me alone! Leave me—

MADAME CHOUILLOUX [*going to her husband*]: Ah! Abélard!

CHOUILLOUX: You!... You wretch!

MADAME CHOUILLOUX *and* TRUCHET [*stupefied, together*]: What?

FOLLAVOINE [*standing by the sofa*]: God in heaven!

CHOUILLOUX [*pointing to his wife*]: There she is! Look at her! The adultress!

MADAME CHOUILLOUX: Me?

CHOUILLOUX [*going to* TRUCHET, *and pointing to him*]: There he is! The faithless friend!

TRUCHET: But—

CHOUILLOUX [*pointing to himself*]: And here he is! Look at him! Here he is, the trusting husband!... The blind fool!...

FOLLAVOINE [*who has joined* CHOUILLOUX, *center*]: God in heaven!

CHOUILLOUX: The laughingstock!

FOLLAVOINE [*to* CHOUILLOUX]: But Monsieur—

MADAME CHOUILLOUX [*to* CHOUILLOUX]: This is absurd, my dear! Utterly absurd!

TRUCHET [*likewise*]: Whoever told you such things?

CHOUILLOUX: Who told me? Who? Who? [*Pointing to* FOLLAVOINE.] There! Ask him who told me! [*Pointing to* JULIE.] Ask her!

FOLLAVOINE ⎫   ⎧ It isn't true, Monsieur
          ⎬ [*together*]:   ⎨ Chouilloux! It isn't—
MADAME CHOUILLOUX ⎪   ⎩
[*going to* CHOUILLOUX] ⎭   My dear—

CHOUILLOUX [*waving his wife aside with a broad gesture*]: Out of my sight, woman! I've seen the last of you! [*Moving towards* TRUCHET.] And as for you, Monsieur Truchet, I shall meet you on the field of honor! [*He goes to pick up his hat.*]

MADAME CHOUILLOUX [*running after him*]: Abélard! For goodness' sake, listen to me!

TRUCHET [*following him also*]: Chouilloux, my friend—

MADAME CHOUILLOUX: It isn't—

CHOUILLOUX: Enough! [*He leaves, up center, followed by his wife.*]

TRUCHET [*returning, and going directly to* FOLLAVOINE]: Did you tell him all those things?

FOLLAVOINE: No! No! It's all a misunderstanding... A terrible misunderstanding!

TRUCHET: I see! Well, you'll pay for it, my friend! [*He slaps him across the face.*]

FOLLAVOINE: Aaaah!

TRUCHET: Monsieur, you may choose your weapon! Good day!

FOLLAVOINE [*rubbing his cheek*]: Oh! That... That... Damn!

JULIE [*after a while, hands on her hips, looking* FOLLAVOINE *up and down with a contemptuous little smile*]: Well! I hope you're happy now! What a fine mess you've got us into!

FOLLAVOINE: What?... Me?... Are you going to stand there and tell me it's all my fault?

JULIE [*shrugging her shoulders*]: Of course it is! Who told you to go and invite all those people for lunch?

FOLLAVOINE: Me?... Me?...

JULIE: Oh! Leave me alone! You'll never change! [*She exits, furious, up right.*]

FOLLAVOINE: My fault! It's all my fault! I have a duel on my hands on account of her, and it's my fault! [*He collapses onto the sofa.*] Oh no! No! That woman! She's going to drive me out of my mind! She... I...

[*Choking with indignation, he notices the other glass of mineral oil on the end table, and, forgetting its contents, grabs it up and swallows it in one gulp.*]

BABY [*who has been watching the scene*]: Oh!

FOLLAVOINE: Aaaaah! Pfaw! Pfuiii!

[*He makes a beeline for his room, down right.*]

BABY [*as soon as* FOLLAVOINE *is gone, clapping his hands together in glee*]: Goody! Goody! [*He goes to the table near the sofa, takes the empty glass, turns it upside down to make sure it really is quite empty, then once again begins clapping.*] Goody! Goody! [*Running up right to* JULIE's *room, glass in hand, he opens the door and calls.*] Mamma! Mamma!

JULIE'S VOICE: What? What is it?

BABY: Mamma! C'm here!

JULIE [*entering and joining him*]: What is it, Mamma's little angel?

BABY [*without batting an eyelash*]: Wook! I dwank it.

[*He holds out the empty glass.*]

JULIE: What?

BABY [*turning the glass upside down to prove it is empty*]: I dwank my waxative.

JULIE [*kneeling beside him*]: You drank it? Oh! You little angel! What a good boy! Now you see, it wasn't so terrible after all!

BABY [*with a malicious smile*]: Oh no!

FOLLAVOINE [*bursting into the room wearing his hat and coat*]: No! I won't stay here another minute! I've had enough!

[*He goes to his desk and takes a few papers, which he nervously arranges in his briefcase before leaving.*]

JULIE [*without even noticing* FOLLAVOINE's *actions*]: Maximilien! Baby took his medicine!

FOLLAVOINE: I don't give a good goddamn!

[*He storms out, up center.*]

JULIE [*shocked*]: Oh!... Did you hear that? Did you hear... He doesn't give a... [*To* BABY.] See, that's your father for you! He doesn't give... Well! It's a lucky thing you have your mother, precious! And you'll always love her, angel, won't you!

[*She covers him with kisses.*]

CURTAIN

THE AUTHORS

Alphonse Allais (1854-1905)

A founder of the celebrated Montmartre cabaret *Le Chat Noir,* and one of the most prolific and original of the humorists of the nineties, Allais was the author of light verse, monologues and, especially, of brief prose sketches contributed to various humor periodicals. His prodigious wordplay, his whimsical irreverence toward the bourgeoisie in general and its technology in particular—despite his own scientific leanings—his taste for the exaggeratedly bizarre, and his off-beat, often macabre wit, have particularly endeared him to more recent generations. One of only a pair of bona fide stage pieces, both in one act, *Le Pauvre Bougre et le bon génie* was dramatized by him from one of those sketches and was first performed at the Théâtre des Mathurins on May 24, 1899.

Georges Courteline (pseud. Georges-Victor Moinaux) (1860-1929)

After a brief military service and an almost-as-brief career in government administration, for each of which he proved eminently unsuited, Courteline, son of noted humorist Jules Moinaux, turned his lively, often caustic wit and his stylistic and linguistic sensitivity to popular journalism in 1883, drawing largely on his own experiences in both bureaucracies for his sketches, short stories and, most of all, his much appreciated comic theater. A regular contributor to the daily *L'Echo de Paris* from 1890 and for many years thereafter, he virtually stopped writing professionally in 1912, leaving a voluminous output for which he was—and is—generally considered one of the leading French humorists of the period. That high opinion eventually won out over political infighting, and he was elected to the Académie Française in 1926, two years before being similarly honored by the Académie Goncourt. *Boubouroche,* thought by many to be his most impressive comedy, was adapted by him from his short story on the same subject, itself based on a real-life incident involving his colleague author Catulle Mendès and the latter's unfaithful mistress. The comedy was first performed at Antoine's Théâtre Libre on April 27, 1893, and subsequently entered the repertory of the Comédie Française on February 21, 1910.

Georges Feydeau (1863-1921)

Recognized as the most important and remarkable practitioner of French farce since Molière, Feydeau early exploited his comic theatrical gifts, developing his technique through a determined study of Labiche, Meilhac, and lesser-known predecessor Alfred Hennequin. From his beginnings as a youthful writer of salon monologues and one-act trifles, he blossomed into one of the most widely performed comic playwrights of his own and succeeding generations, enlivening his intricately crafted situational comedy, in some three dozen works, with not a little observation of societal and individual foibles, linguistic drollery, and a delightful lunacy that offers a generous foretaste of the latterday absurd. Of the trio of plays translated here, the highly successful *Tailleur pour dames* was the first of his three-acts, forerunner to the wild, exorbitant extravagances of *La Puce à l'oreille,* one of his last, in which he pushed the genre to almost excruciating excess before turning his talents to the less ambitious but no-less-disquieting complexities and confusions of a half-dozen tableaux of marital bedlam—represented here by *On purge Bébé*—that were to end his career in an artistic reflection of his personal reality. The three plays premiered, respectively, on December 17, 1886, March 2, 1907, and April 12, 1910; the first, at the Théâtre de la Renaissance and the latter two at the Théâtre des Nouveautés.

Ludovic Halévy (1834-1908)

Best known for a twenty-odd-year collaboration with playwright Henri Meilhac that peppered the Paris stage of the Second Empire's waning years not only with light-hearted comedies but also with operettic and operatic libretti as diverse as Offenbachian froth (*La Belle Hélène, Orphée aux enfers,* et al.) and Bizet's *Carmen,* Halévy was later to become a successful novelist. It was as much the sentimental realism of his popular novels, if not more than his comedies and libretti, that earned him election to the Académie Française in 1884. His and Meilhac's *Tout pour les dames!* and *La Mi-carême,* typical of their one-act collaborative efforts, were first performed, respectively, on September 8, 1867, at the Théâtre des Variétés, and April 2, 1874, at the Théâtre du Palais-Royal.

Eugène Labiche (1815-1888)

When, some ten years before his death, Labiche had penned his last theater piece and devoted himself to the publication of the fifty-seven comedies of his so-called *Théâtre complet,* prefaced by playwright Emile Augier (Paris, 1878-79). his reading public would be denied more than a hundred of the works that his Parisian theatergoing public had attended with delight over the years since 1838. (Happily, a more recent collection of his *Œuvres complètes,* dating from 1966, lives up to its title, including even several of his previously unpublished comedies.) Unusually prolific, owing both to his own comic inventiveness and to his battery of collaborators—only some seven of his hundred-seventy-plus works were, in fact, signed without at least one—Labiche rarely knew a Paris theatrical season with fewer than a pair of his plays on the boards; and, during his heyday, between 1845 and 1865, it was not uncommon for him to have six, seven, eight, or even nine productions in a single year. Many if not most of these were *vaudevilles* in the French sense of the term—farce interspersed with song—while several, even more musically ambitious, were full-fledged comic opera libretti with scores by the likes of Delibes and other lesser-known composers of the day. A master at depicting the concerns, pretensions and affectations of the bourgeoisie in wittily appropriate dialogue, with plots replete with farcical entanglements that his disciple Feydeau would manipulate to perfection, Labiche was honored with election to the Académie Française in 1880. *Les Suites d'un premier lit,* written with his most frequent collaborator, Marc-Michel, premiered at the Théâtre du Vaudeville on May 8, 1852.

Marc-(Antoine-Amédée) Michel (1812-1868)

A native of Marseille transplanted to Paris in his early twenties, Marc-Michel became one of the more appreciated wits of the Latin Quarter, thanks both to his comedies and to his sardonic reports and descriptions of Parisian hoodlumdom appearing in the court proceedings of the *Journal des tribunaux* and the legal review *Le Droit,* verbal caricatures worthy of a Daumier in prose. One of Labiche's favorite co-authors (see above), he contributed, between 1838 and 1862, to over forty of his comedies—on occasion with a third—and was author in his own right of another fifty or so, most with a variety of less prominent collaborators.

Henri Meilhac (1831-1897)

Besides his many comedies and Offenbach libretti co-authored with Halévy, in which he is generally credited with most of the plot construction and farcical imbroglio, Meilhac wrote more than a score of comedies and libretti on his own or with other collaborators. He was, for example, co-author, with Philippe Gilles, of the libretto to Massenet's opera *Manon.* In 1889, after the death of Labiche, Meilhac was elected to fill his seat in the Académie Française, joining collaborator Halévy, elected five years before. Not the least of his claims to theatrical remembrance and gratitude is his well-documented influence on the technique of the young Feydeau, especially evident here in *La Mi-carême.*

Mélesville (pseud. Anne-Honoré-Joseph Duveyrier) (1787-1865)

Bosom friend of Scribe and collaborator with him for thirty-odd years, Mélesville early abandoned a career in law in favor of the theater. The earliest of his plays—he wrote or co-authored some three hundred in all, testimony to the evanescence of theatrical celebrity—were popular melodramas in the style of the opening years of the nineteenth century. It was his acquaintance with Scribe, however, that turned him to comedy, and that collaboration produced some five dozen works. Like Scribe, he was also author of several opera libretti, best-known (or least little-known) among them being Hérold's *Zampa,* whose overture, at least, has remained in the symphonic repertory. Mélesville had several other collaborators, notably his brother, Charles Duveyrier, civil-servant-cum-playwright. None, however, was as celebrated as Scribe, with the exception of Labiche, with whom he collaborated on a pair of early *vaudevilles.* Scribe's and his one-act, *Le Soprano,* premiered at the Théâtre du Gymnase Dramatique on November 30, 1831.

Victorien Sardou (1831-1908)

One of the best-known Parisian playwrights spanning the Second Empire and Third Republic, thanks almost as much to his personal and political contacts as to his solid, workmanlike dramatic skills, Sardou enjoyed great popularity in a variety of theatrical genres: farce and *vaudeville,* comedy of manners, social and political satire, and, especially, historical drama in the most grand and grandiose style, vehicles for the likes of Sarah Bernhardt. An avowed disciple of Scribe and a champion of his "well-made play" (see below), Sardou is said to have refined his craftsmanship in plot development by studying the first acts of certain of his model's plays and, from the givens, working them out to his own logical conclusions. If he lacked his master's prodigious productivitiy, and if his sixty-some plays (including two first produced in the United States) and several opera libretti—a respectable enough figure by any standards—fall far short of the voluminous Scribean repertoire, at least part of the reason may lie in his unwillingness, except in a few instances, to follow the then common theatrical practice of working with collaborators in order to grind out scripts by the ream. (On the other hand, he was more than once faced with accusations of plagiarism, charges that he successfully refuted.) Elected to the Académie Française in 1877, Sardou is remembered today for Puccini's operatic setting of his *La Tosca* rather than for any of the other works that had earned him that honor. His little-known *L'Ecureuil,* one of his earliest comedies—a *vaudeville* in his original, here freely adapted— was first produced on February 9, 1861 at the Théâtre du Vaudeville. It is one of a number curiously omitted from the fifteen volumes of his misnamed *Théâtre complet* (Paris, 1934-61).

(Augustin)-Eugène Scribe (1791-1861)

With a name known to almost all theatrical professionals and a vast repertory known to almost none, Scribe today has the debatable distinction of being one of the French playwrights frequently alluded to but seldom read, and even less performed. Such was not the case, however, during his reign as virtual "King of the Boulevard." Making Labiche's later creativity almost pale in comparison, Scribe was to write at least three hundred forty scripts, and possibly even more—his so-called *Œuvres complètes* (Paris, 1874-75) numbered seventy-six volumes—most with a variety of collaborators far more celebrated in their own day than in ours. Between 1820, year of his first success after almost forty fruitless attempts, and 1845, when his productivity began to wane, very relatively speaking, not a theater season passed in Paris without seeing at least a half-dozen of his plays produced. Indeed, a dozen or more per year was not an uncommon figure, and the 1823 season alone counted the phenomenal number of twenty-two. Not limited to a single genre or to the theaters of the Boulevard, and eventually welcomed even at the Comédie Française with interpreters like the tragedienne Rachel and the legendary Sarah Bernhardt, Scribe was equally comfortable—and prolific—in *vaudevilles,* less frivolous comedies of manners, historical plays, and opera libretti, both comic and serious. Far better known today for some of the latter than for practically any of the former, he provided texts for a dozen of Auber's operas, among them *Fra Diavolo;* for several of Meyerbeer's, including *Les Huguenots* and *Le Prophète;* for *La Juive,* by Fromental Halévy (uncle of Meilhac's dramatist collaborator); and for others by Donizetti, Gounod, Rossini, Adam, and Boieldieu. His incredible production resulted not only in a sizable personal fortune but also, only halfway through his career, in 1834, in election to the Académie Française. Scribe's legacy, especially to his comic successors, and the one for which his name continues to be evoked by theater historians (whether or not they have read him), is the famous *pièce bien faite,* the "well-made play," in which rigorous plot construction and the development of minor cause into major effect, with a goodly dose of suspense before the inevitable dénouement, were of greater importance than character study or subtlety of language. *Le Soprano,* here generously adapted, was one of his legion of plays written in collaboration with Mélesville (see above).

Brief bibliography of general, biographical, and critical readings in English

Arvin, Neil Cole. *Eugène Scribe and the French Theatre, 1815-1860.* Cambridge: Harvard University Press, 1924; reprint ed., New York: Benjamin Blom, 1967.

_____. "The Technique of Scribe's *comédies-vaudevilles.*" *Modern Philology* 16 (July 1918): 47-63.

Baker, Stuart Eddy. *Georges Feydeau and the Aesthetics of Farce.* Ann Arbor: UMI Research Press, 1981.

Bentley, Eric. *The Life of the Drama.* New York: Applause, 1991.

_____. "The Psychology of Farce." In *"Let's Get a Divorce!" and Other Plays.* Edited by Eric Bentley. New York: Hill and Wang, 1958.

Bermel, Albert. *Farce: A History from Aristophanes to Woody Allen.* New York: Simon and Schuster, 1982.

_____. Introduction to *The Plays of Georges Courteline.* Translated by Albert Bermel and Jacques Barzun. London: Heinemann, 1961. Pp. vii-xix.

Blistein, Elmer. *Comedy in Action.* Durham, N.C.: Duke University Press, 1964.

Daniels, May. *The French Drama of the Unspoken.* Edinburgh: Edinburgh University Press, 1953.

Davis, Jessica Milner. *Farce.* London: Methuen, 1978.

Esteban, Manuel A. *Georges Feydeau.* Boston: Twayne, 1983.

Feibleman, James Kern. *In Praise of Comedy: A Study of Its Theory and Practice.* New York: Russell and Russell, 1962.

Hansen, Eric C. *Ludovic Halévy: A Study of Frivolity and Fatalism in Nineteenth Century France.* Lanham, Maryland: University Press of America, 1987.

Hart, Jerome Alfred. *Sardou and the Sardou Plays.* Philadelphia: Lippincott, 1913.

Kington, Miles. Introduction to *The World of Alphonse Allais.* Translated by Miles Kington. London: Chatto and Windus, 1976. Pp. 7-15.

Koon, Helene and Richard Switzer. *Eugène Scribe.* Boston: Twayne, 1980.

Lauter, Paul, ed. *Theories of Comedy.* Garden City, N.Y.: Doubleday and Co., 1964.

Matthews, Brander. *French Dramatists of the Nineteenth Century.* 3rd ed. New York: Charles Scribner's Sons, 1901; reprint ed., New York: Benjamin Blom, 1968. (Contains essays on Labiche, Meilhac and Halévy, Sardou, and Scribe.)

Olson, Elder. *The Theory of Comedy.* Bloomington: Indiana University Press, 1968.

Pendle, Karin. *Eugène Scribe and French Opera of the Nineteenth Century.* Ann Arbor: UMI Research Press, 1979.

Pronko, Leonard Cabell. *Eugène Labiche and Georges Feydeau.* London: Macmillan, 1982.

_____. *Georges Feydeau.* New York: Ungar, 1975.

Shapiro, Norman R. Introduction to *Feydeau, First to Last: Eight One-Act Comedies.* Translated by Norman R. Shapiro. Ithaca: Cornell University Press, 1982. Pp. 9-36.

_____. Introduction to *Four Farces of Georges Feydeau.* Translated by Norman R. Shapiro. Chicago: University of Chicago Press, 1970. Pp. xiii-liv.

Taylor, John Russell. *The Rise and Fall of the Well-Made Play.* New York: Hill and Wang, 1969.

Wimsatt, W. K. *The Idea of Comedy.* Englewood Cliffs, N. J.: Prentice-Hall, 1969.

Witt, Donald E. *Eugène Scribe and Nineteenth Century Theater: From Vaudeville to Grand Opera.* Ann Arbor: University Microfilms International, 1986.

Edited and Adapted by

Norman R. Shapiro:

THE PREGNANT PAUSE OR LOVE'S LABOR LOST
by Georges Feydeau

Hector Ennepèque, first-time father-to-be, is in extended labor and protracted comic convulsions over his wife Léonie's imminent delivery. Before the baby's arrival, this hilarious farce gives birth to multiple comic harangues all aimed at the helpless henpecked husband. When Hector tries to rebound from the recriminations of his aristorcratic in-laws, he is swatted aside by an Amazon midwife who takes charge of everything.

$6.95 paper/vol. 1/ISBN: 0-936839-58-9

A SLAP IN THE FARCE & A MATTER OF WIFE AND DEATH
by Eugène Labiche

An accidental grope on a dimly-lit bus, earns for the painter, Antoine, a slap whose force resounds around Labiche's wildly comic labyrinth, from which there is no escape, except, alas for (what else?) romance and marriage. In *A Matter of Wife and Death*, an eccentric millionaire, Tim Van Lust is perpetually frustrated in his super-passionate proposals of marriage. Van Lust's despair, an attempt at comical self-destruction, is short-lived, however, as fate and an unexpected telegram from (where else?) America ties one knot while unravelling another.

$7.95 paper/vol. 2/ISBN: 0-936839-82-1

THE BRAZILIAN
by Henri Meilhac & Ludovic Halévy

Two amorous actresses are out to capture the affections of a wealthy Paris producer. The wily Micheline spreads the rumor that Rafaella is being courted by a murderously jealous Brazilian. But her plot backfires when instead of cooling his passions down, the producer's interest heats up. Micheline is non-plussed when the tempestuous Brazilian suitor actually shows up at Rafaella's house. The mad improvisation which follows is a romp in the best tradition of door-slamming French bedroom farce.

$6.95 paper/vol. 3/ISBN: 0-936839-59-7

Breinigsville, PA USA
18 April 2010
236376BV00004B/7/P